FOREVER IN THE PATH

FOREVER IN THE PATH

The Black Experience at Michigan State University

Pero G. Dagbovie

MICHIGAN STATE UNIVERSITY PRESS | *East Lansing*

Michigan State University Press
East Lansing, Michigan 48823-5245

Library of Congress Cataloging-in-Publication Data

Names: Dagbovie, Pero Gaglo, author.
Title: Forever in the path : the Black experience at Michigan State University / Pero G. Dagbovie.
Description: East Lansing : Michigan State University Press, [2025] | Includes bibliographical references.
Identifiers: LCCN 2023050128 | ISBN 9781611864946 (cloth) | ISBN 9781609177638 (PDF) | ISBN 9781628955248 (ePub)
Subjects: LCSH: Michigan State University—History. | African American college students—Michigan—East Lansing—History.
Classification: LCC LD3248.M5 D35 2024 | DDC 378.774/26—dc23/eng/20240402
LC record available at https://lccn.loc.gov/2023050128

Book design by Anastasia Wraight
Cover design by Erin Kirk

Visit Michigan State University Press at *www.msupress.org*

Could these old sentinels speak,
They could tell of wonderful changes
That have taken place in their time.
—*William James Beal*

When from these scenes we wander
And twilight shadows fade,
Our memory still will linger
Where light and shadows played;
In the evening oft we'll gather
And pledge our faith anew,
Sing our love for Alma Mater
And thy praises, MSU.
—*"MSU Shadows"*

How many days of sadness must I
Spend to get one day of gladness
And tell me how much sorrow must I
Spend to get one bright tomorrow
—*Dionne Warwick*

Many a time I sit and wonder why
This race so, so very hard to run
Then I say to my soul, take courage
Battle to be won
Like a ship that's tossed and driven
Battered by the angry sea, yeah
Say the tide of time was ragin'
Don't let the fury fall on me, no no
—*Bob Marley*

It is the centrality of the Afro-American
experience that makes its past so significant,
a past that has a sobering but redemptive
quality for our nation, not as an escapist
journey to some gossamer glory of bygone
days but possibly as a vehicle for present
enlightenment, guidance, and enrichment.
—*Benjamin Quarles*

Contents

Preface

While giving me a firm handshake that defied his age, Donald Seymour Vest Sr. said proudly, "I was the first Black cheerleader at MSU!" His energy and enthusiasm were contagious.

With unbridled curiosity, I asked, "When did you graduate?"

"In 1952," he responded.

"What was it like for you at Michigan State back in the day?" I eagerly asked, secretly hoping this seventy-two-year-old Spartan historymaker would regale me with some captivating tales of his experiences in East Lansing.

Vest began by recounting that whenever he saw another Black student on campus, he shouted out a greeting. This ritual made sense. During the 1940s the total student population averaged about nineteen thousand per year, and Black students accounted for less than 1 percent of the Spartan student body. Former MSU director of athletics Clarence Underwood and a small cohort of other first-year African American students arrived on campus in the fall of 1955, and in the years since Vest graduated, the situation hadn't changed much. During the mid-1950s, there were approximately one hundred Blacks enrolled in Michigan State. While Vest may have at times felt isolated and come across racial prejudice, it seemed that he enjoyed his time in East Lansing. Like Black alumni before him, he appreciated his Spartan experience, found a sense of belonging and community, and took great pride in his special accomplishments.

The brief, impromptu exchange I had with Vest took place after I delivered my first major talk about this book during the 2002 homecoming weekend for the MSU Black Alumni

Association's Gospel Brunch Address. At the time, about six months after the first African American Celebratory, I didn't totally appreciate the historical significance of this event. It was part of a deeper tradition than I realized. Two decades earlier, during the festive homecoming weekend, a group then self-identified as the Black Alumni Committee hosted a series of events on and near campus, including a Sunday brunch in the MSU Union Building Ballroom. More than five hundred Black alumni showed up for this memorable gathering.

Seven months after lobbying for the continuation of the College of Urban Development, in October 1981, the Michigan State University Black Alumni Inc. (MSUBA), formerly the Black Alumni Committee and now an affiliate club of the MSU Alumni Association, held its first general membership meeting. Under the leadership of Veda Dove Washington (president), Terry Young (vice-president), Wanda Dean Lipscomb (secretary), and Lural Baltimore (treasurer), along with the elected twelve-member board of directors, the organization began its efforts by recruiting members and creating a scholarship program for African American undergraduate students. In a short piece for the Black Alumni Committee's 1980 program, "Black Students at MSU: A Thumbnail History," alumna Sharon Peters, who would go on to hold public office in Michigan and dedicate herself to child welfare, emphasized that Black alumni needed to do what they could to help Black students. In their promotional materials a decade later, MSUBA leadership reiterated that the overarching purpose of the organization was to support and promote the welfare and interests of the university's Black alumni, students, faculty and staff.

To this day, I regret not only my then inability to wholistically contextualize the 2002 MSUBA gathering but also not having the foresight to have followed up with Vest. As I later learned, he lived an eventful life. Born in 1930 in Ypsilanti, Michigan, Vest, like many Black Aggies and Spartans before him, enrolled in Michigan State with the intention of studying agriculture. His grandfather, a great influence in his life, was a farmer. Vest ultimately decided to pursue a degree in the social sciences. He was studious, devoting much of his time to his academic endeavors and Reserve Officers' Training Corps (ROTC) training. With his fellow Armor cadets engaged in tank training, he spent a lot of time in Demonstration Hall and further honed his tactical skills while attending summer camp at Fort Knox, Kentucky. A classmate of All-American offensive tackle Don E. Coleman who didn't start playing football until his senior year of high school, Dick Lord (one of the first Blacks to play collegiate hockey), and the first African American to play varsity basketball at Michigan State, Rickey Ayala, Vest was a stand-out member of the varsity men's gymnastics team. In 1950, he became the first African American cheerleader at the university and perhaps the first in the Big Ten Conference. Vest was an indispensable member of a young but talented gymnastics squad that officially began competing in the late 1940s. A member of Kappa Alpha Psi nearly five years before the Delta Pi chapter was founded at Michigan State, Vest was among the small handful of Black students to appear in the MSU *Wolverine* yearbooks from 1950 until 1952.

MSC cheerleaders in the pyramid formation. Donald Vest, Michigan State's first African American cheerleader, is at the top. Courtesy of Michigan State University Archives and Historical Collections.

After graduating from Michigan State, Vest served in the U.S. Army during the Korean War and then settled in Detroit with his wife, Hilda, whom he met on campus during his senior year. On August 8, 1953, in an announcement published in the widely read *Michigan Chronicle*, "Young Bride Relays Sentimental Details of Westward Journey," Hilda spoke of the Black love that Michigan State helped cultivate, recalling, "Our marriage climaxed a romance which began while we were attending Michigan State college." In the early 1960s, Don secured a position in central placement services for Ford Motor Company and in 1974 was named supervisor of this division for the expansive metro Detroit area. He was particularly committed to helping Black college graduates secure employment. During the mid- to late 1970s, he regularly published advertisements and announcements in leading Black newspapers such as the *Michigan Chronicle* and the *New York Amsterdam News*, calling upon young African Americans to seize hold of potential professional development and career opportunities.

Vest's presence at the 2002 MSU Black Alumni Association's Gospel Brunch was, in retrospect, unsurprising. He had long been invested in creating meaningful networks for Black

Spartans. In the late 1950s, he was a founding member of the Big Ten Club of Detroit, a group of African American Big Ten alumni who sponsored social events in the Motor City. In 1964, a decade and a half before the official founding of the MSUBA, he became the president of a new Michigan State Alumni group, a Detroit-based organization that sought to maintain partnerships between African American alums and the university. He remained connected to MSU long after graduating. In August 1990, he returned with Hilda to East Lansing to participate on a panel in commemoration of the twenty-fifth anniversary of Detroit's legendary Broadside Press. Exemplifying his alma mater's historic tradition of outreach and engagement, Vest committed much of his life to service in his adopted city. "As a husband, father of three creative young adults, and an involved resident of Detroit," Kenneth Ingraham reflected in a tribute article titled "Donald Vest Involved in Community's Life" in the *Michigan Chronicle* (March 26, 1977), "Vest is equally concerned with helping to make his community a harmonious and satisfying place to live. Vest directs his concerns for the community by involving himself in a variety of undertakings which he believes contribute to improving the quality of life in the city."

Vest was a recognized leader in Detroit's Russell Woods neighborhood. Beginning in the late 1960s, he served as the chairperson of the community's popular annual arts festival and was the driving force behind community enrichment and beautification programs for years to come. Involved in countless other civic endeavors throughout his life, he was active in many organizations in Detroit, including the Friends of the Detroit Public Library, the Arts League of Michigan/Carr Center, the Brazeal Dennard Chorale, and the Museum of African American History, where he served as president in the 1980s. An amateur historian in his own right and an avid supporter of Detroit's thriving Black Arts Movement, he and Hilda acquired Broadside Press in the mid-1980s, created the Broadside Poet's Theatre, contributed to a major oral history project on Black Detroit, and in 2005 established the African American Literature Special Collections of the Purdy-Kresge Library at Wayne State University.

Vest also became a passionate Civil War reenactor in the 102nd Regiment Infantry U.S. Colored Troops Black History Group, performing throughout the nation during the 1990s and 2000s, including at a special program in Washington, D.C. He conducted research on African American Civil War soldiers, wholeheartedly believing these unrecognized freedom fighters deserved a place in American history. Black history shaped his world view. He understood his experiences were part of the broader Black experience in the United States that was shaped by oppression and resistance. He was a proud Black cultural nationalist and community activist, symbolized by the simple dashiki he rocked underneath his fall jacket when I met him. Following his death in January 2015, Vest was remembered for being a man of action who embraced many causes with great vigor and commitment. When I met Donald Seymour Vest Sr., I was unaware of all he'd accomplished during his remarkable life. He embodied what historian and longtime executive editor of *Ebony* magazine Lerone Bennett Jr. considered "living history." Vest, his classmates, and the many other Black Spartans hailing from multiple generations who enjoyed themselves at the informal 2002 reunion in Lansing had many stories and memories they could have shared with me, accounts that don't exist in documents in the Michigan State University Archives and Historical Collections.

To date, very little has been written and published on the experiences of Black students (as well as faculty and staff) before, during, and after Vest's time on campus. Unsurprisingly, in their institutional histories published in 1915 and 1955 respectively, longtime Michigan State professors William James Beal and Madison Kuhn totally ignored the Black presence at the college. The first major exploration of Black student life at MSU is Spartan football legend and longtime MSU administrator Don Coleman's 1971 unpublished PhD dissertation, "The Status of the Black Student Aide Program and the Black Student Movement at Michigan State University." Focusing on Black students' experiences during the late 1960s and the Black Student Aide Program, Coleman's study sheds light on consequential racial incidents on campus, highlighting the responses and activities of Black organizations like the Black Students' Alliance (BSA), the Black Liberation Front, International (BLFI), the Pan-African Students Organization in the Americas (PASOA), and the Black United Front (BUF). In his extensive appendices, he also included rare documents related to Black student activism during the late 1960s. Shortly after Coleman earned his doctorate, Katherine Elizabeth White completed a dissertation, "Student Activism at Michigan State University during the Decade of the 1960's," that canvasses civil rights activities and instances of Black student-activism on campus informed by *State News* coverage.

Coleman was not alone in documenting the more contemporary history of Black student life at MSU. During the late 1960s and early 1970s, Ruth Simms Hamilton, the university's first Black woman professor hired in 1968, painstakingly archived Black students' experiences. She clipped and preserved countless *State News* articles, collected Black student organizations' publications, and interviewed numerous Black students. She also taught Black students how to meticulously document their exposure to on-campus racial incidents. During the Black Campus Movement, Black student-activists recognized the value of knowing and preserving their history, often recounting how their predecessors paved the way for them. In the early 1970s, several of Hamilton's mentees were among the first systemic chroniclers of Black students' experiences in East Lansing. Billye Suttles, who attended MSU during the Black Power era and served as a secretary for the BSA, wrote a penetrative ethnographic essay for a course taught by Hamilton—"Prelude to Protest: The University and the Black Student" (1970)—in which she candidly explored everyday aspects of Black student life. Several years later, students Curtis Williams and Ahmed Karega, with the help of Coleman and about seven other Black student-activists, proudly announced they had begun working on a comprehensive pictorial history of African Americans on campus. However, it never came to fruition. In June 1973, Sharon Peters, one of Hamilton's research assistants who was working on a master's degree at the time, completed a robust study on the history of Black students at MSU. Peters's insightful unpublished manuscript drew largely from in-depth interviews with twenty-five faculty members, administrators, and students who attended the university from the mid-1940s through the 1960s.

On September 18, 1973, the first MSU Black student newspaper, the *Grapevine Journal*, published W. Kim Heron's brief essay on the history of Black students at MSU, unambiguously titled essay, "Black Students at MSU." Inspired by those Black students who came before him, Heron announced his plans for organizing a multipart account of this rich yet underappreciated saga. Though he never completed the larger study he alluded to, in his straightforward piece, Heron touched upon the experiences of several generations of Black students beginning with Myrtle Bessie Craig (later Myrtle Craig Mowbray, class of '07), the first Black woman to graduate from the State Agricultural College, at the time also referred to as Michigan Agricultural College and M.A.C. Heron approached his role as a chronicler of MSU's underacknowledged Black history with great care. He collaborated with Ruth Simms Hamilton and conducted interviews with Mowbray, Coleman, Herschel Irons, Jason Lovette, Charles Thorton, Richard Thomas, and other MSU graduates, staff, and faculty. Amid claims that on-campus Black student activism was on the decline during the early 1970s, Heron summoned Black students to revisit their collective past for inspiration.

Three decades later, like Heron, undergraduate student Terrance Wilbert believed Black students of his generation could be motivated by an awareness of their predecessors' contributions to changing Michigan State's culture. I served as Wilbert's mentor in the Ronald E. McNair Postbaccalaureate Achievement Program and the Summer Research Opportunity Program, and he completed a well-researched project focusing on the history of the Black student occupation of the Hannah Administration Building in May 1989. His final paper, "Black Student Activism at Michigan State University: A Historical Analysis," represents the first significant exploration of this major event in the history of African Americans at MSU. Keith R. Widder's *Michigan Agricultural College: The Evolution of a Land-Grant Philosophy, 1855–1925* (2005) includes an informative chapter on African American students at M.A.C. and MSC from the days of William Ora Thompson, the first known African American to graduate from the college in 1904, to Clarice A. Pretlow who graduated in 1930. In 2006, MSU alumnus Johnny Smith wrote an excellent MA thesis on Black football players at MSU from the post–World War II era through the early 1970s. A year later, his expansive essay "'Breaking the Plane': Integration and Black Protest in Michigan State Football during the 1960s" was published in the *Michigan Historical Review*.

In the late 1990s, MSU archivist Dorothy Frye curated a no-frills, yet informative online exhibit for the MSU Archives and Historical Collections that piqued my interest, "The African American Presence at MSU: Pioneers, Groundbreakers, and Leaders, 1900–1970." Subdivided into three brief sections (1900–1929, 1930–1950s, and "Historic Firsts"), this retrospective serves as a very basic starting point for those interested in MSU's Black past. In 2012, the exhibit was expanded by Eve Avdoulos, and five years later its findings were included in the first volume of *Taken from the Archives*, edited by Ed Busch, Hillary Gatlin, Megan Bagley Maline, Sarah O'Brien, and Jennie Rankin. In her PhD dissertation, "A History of Black Women Faculty at Michigan State University, 1968–2009" (2012), Marshanda Smith identifies more than ninety Black women faculty at MSU. Her interviews with more than a few of these Black women pathbreakers are revealing. The famed 1965–1966 football team coached by Duffy Daugherty has garnered notable attention. In 2014, sportswriter Tom Shanahan released *Raye of Light: Jimmy Raye, Duffy Daugherty, the Integration of College Football, and the 1965–66 Michigan State Spartans*. In 2022, Maya Washington published *Through the Banks of the Red Cedar: My Father and the Team That Changed the Game*, a companion volume to her illuminating documentary that was previewed on campus in 2015. Washington offers readers moving snapshots into Gene Washington's inspiring life, how this track and football star contributed to President Hannah and Duffy Daugherty's deliberate integration experiment, and the place of MSU football in the context of the broader Black Freedom Struggle during the mid- to late 1960s.

Building upon a tradition established by James B. Hamilton's *What a Time to Live: The Autobiography of James B. Hamilton* (1995), several insightful memoirs on Black life at MSU were published in the twenty-first century by MSU faculty and administrators, namely Clarence Underwood's *Greener Pastures: A Pioneer Athletics Administrator Climbs from Spartan Beginnings to the Top at Michigan State* (2005), Robert L. Green's *At the Crossroads of Fear and Freedom: The Fight for Social and Educational Justice* (2015), former MSU president Clifton R. Wharton Jr.'s *Privilege and Prejudice: The Life of a Black Pioneer* (2015), and Maya Washington's 2022 autobiography-biography.

Forever in the Path offers the first wide-ranging, straightforward, and sequential history of African Americans at Michigan State University from the late nineteenth century through the late twentieth century. I do not claim this book to be definitive. I've attempted to be as comprehensive as possible, making some practical and difficult decisions about what to include and focus on. I'm sure some readers, especially those who attended MSU from *Brown v. Board of Education of Topeka* (1954) through the 1970s, will be quick to point out what or who I didn't include or discuss in enough detail. I accept such criticism as an affirmation of the complexity and vastness of the Black historical experience at MSU. Without question, much more can be written about this riveting history, especially from the late 1960s until the late 1980s. A favorable outcome for me would be that this book serves as a spark for someone to do more research on this broad-ranging subject. The countless documents in the University Archives and Historical Collections, specifically since John A. Hannah's long presidency, have many more stories to tell. This book is one historian's snapshot of a fascinating saga. My research compelled me to revisit *The Teachings of Ptah Hotep*. This vizier instructs us to consider multiple perspectives, "for the limits of are not reached." In Ptah Hotep's view, artists do not possess that perfection to which they should aspire. I hope what I explore in the pages that follow add texture and complexity to interpretations of MSU's rich and fascinating history.

Introduction

Early in the fall of 1902, nineteen-and-a-half-year-old Myrtle Bessie Craig arrived at Michigan Agricultural College (M.A.C.).[1] She was one of the 328 new students whose names appear in an early October issue of the *M.A.C. Record*. "The present year promises much to friends of M.A.C.," the college's leadership announced. In September 1902, the campus was especially beautiful, "the excessive summer rains having made all vegetation appear at its best." Myrtle had recently graduated from George R. Smith College, a historically Black college opened in Sedalia, Missouri, in 1894. Because this school was not on M.A.C.'s accredited list of colleges for standard admission into the four-year courses, Myrtle was admitted into the newly established five-year courses for agricultural students and for women. She was thrilled to have passed the basic entrance examinations in arithmetic, geography, grammar, spelling, penmanship, and U.S. history. Committed to self-improvement, she understood it would take her five instead of four years to graduate from M.A.C.[2]

Setting foot on campus in 1902 was a sort of homecoming for Myrtle. She was born in 1883 in Adrian, Michigan, a small town located in the southeast corner of the state about seventy-six miles from Lansing. During the antebellum era, Adrian, the country seat of Lenawee County, was a hotbed of vigorous abolitionist activism. The small rural city had an intricate Underground Railroad network. In the early twentieth century, her father, Stephen, worked as a barber in downtown Lansing, and while living in Sedalia, Myrtle occasionally visited him on weekends. She strolled about campus and was aware of M.A.C.'s growing reputation under Jonathan L. Snyder's innovative presidency. She read the school's enticing advertisements: "Fifteen minutes from Lansing by electric car line. For pleasant and healthful surroundings, completeness of equipment and ability of teaching force it is unsurpassed in the country"; the delightful description of M.A.C. continued, "the *religious*, *moral* and *social environments* are of the highest type." Myrtle was excited about embarking on a new chapter in her life, eager to take advantage of the "*broad*, *thorough* and *practical*" education at "a cost as low as the lowest" that M.A.C. promised. "When I first entered, I thought the school to be a wonderful place," she recalled in 1972.[3]

Craig's return to her home state obliged her to make significant adjustments. Life for African Americans in Ingham County and in Sedalia was strikingly different. In 1900, Sedalia was home to a thriving Black community of fifteen thousand strong who had their own flourishing cultural institutions, including a newspaper, *The Sedalia Times*. Required to provide a testimony of good character for admission at George R. Smith College, Myrtle's former classmates were African Americans. She didn't stand out, nor was she noticeably exceptional. She was surrounded by Black excellence. She was engulfed in a Black Girl Magic movement in days of yore. In central Michigan, Craig was atypical. By virtue of her African heritage, she stood out in a crowd. Though tight-knit, Lansing's Black community was miniscule. In the dawning of the twentieth century, there were 323 African Americans out of a total population of about 16,500 in the state capital. Of the 854 students enrolled in M.A.C. in 1902 (711 men and 143 women), Craig was one of a handful of Black students.

Craig's decision to attend M.A.C. was somewhat prearranged. A proud Lansing resident, her protective father made it clear to his beloved only child that she had little choice in the matter. "When it came time for me to go to college," Myrtle recalled, "he said it was either Michigan Agricultural College or none at all, he couldn't afford anything else." During the early twentieth century, its accessibility, welcoming environment, and fine reputation lured Craig and other Black students to M.A.C. Though she was initially a bit skeptical about what she "could do at an agricultural school," she soon discovered the opportunities for women that existed at M.A.C.[4] Thanks in part to the persistence of Michigan native Mary Mayo, an outspoken champion of higher education for women, the college established a women's program in 1896. Myrtle was well prepared for M.A.C.'s rigorous and efficient domestic science curriculum. While a student in Sedalia, she gained vital hands-on experience in home economics, working as a live-in domestic servant for a middle-class White couple.

Through the dawning of the twenty-first century, it was widely accepted that Craig (later Myrtle Craig Mowbray) was the first African American to graduate from M.A.C. This proud Black woman believed this. "I wasn't the first Black to attend, mind you," Mowbray told a staff writer for the *Grapevine Journal* in the early 1970s, "but as far as I know, I was the first to graduate."[5] During her visit back to campus in 1972, she herself "almost casually" announced to those in the Alumni Association's offices her claim to fame. "I wanted them to put out the red carpet for me when I came back," a proud eighty-nine-year-old Mowbray remarked, "and they sure did!"[6] Since the late 1990s, she has been occasionally evoked during on-campus Black History Month commemorations and spotlighted on university websites. A large stately photo of her was once on display in the first-floor lounge of MSU's Union Building, and the university's Mowbray Scholars Program honors her legacy. Her story was featured in *Women at MSU: 150 Groundbreaking Years*, an exhibit displayed in the Special Collections Gallery in the MSU Main Library in 2021 and 2022.

Craig was never explicitly identified in any of the college's records by her race and didn't earn the title of being the first Black graduate until the early 1970s. During her first two years on campus, she lived a somewhat sheltered life in what was then called Collegeville.[7] She boarded in the homes of Addison M. Brown, former member of the Michigan Senate and secretary of the college's Board of Agriculture, and Chace Newman, an instructor in mechanical drawing. As she did while attending school in Sedalia, Craig toiled for several years as a live-in domestic worker to support her education. The college's longtime librarian and champion of student success, Linda Eoline Landon, mentored her, and Craig took classes from some of the college's most influential professors, including Maude Gilchrist, the dean of home economics, and botanist and fellow Adrian native William J. Beal. In 1907, President Snyder knew Craig well enough to compose several glowing recommendations for her. It goes without saying that her professors and classmates knew she was a Black woman who took pride in her racial heritage. She wasn't associated with schooling or known for her erudition outside of the M.A.C. community. Most Whites who casually interacted with her in the Lansing area instinctively assumed she was a struggling domestic worker like many of the city's Black women. At the time, there were very few Black women professionals in the city like proud Lansing homeowner Daisy L. Godfrey, who served as the matron of the Lansing Police Department from the late 1890s through 1918. Godfrey was known in the Black community as a "Policeman Woman." Carefully navigating her position, Godfrey developed a stellar reputation among Lansing's power brokers. "She was regarded as absolutely trustworthy and was held in high esteem by her superiors."[8]

Just as Godfrey was a recognizable figure around Lansing's first City Hall that housed the Lansing Police Department, those visiting campus for the special 1907 commencement must have noticed Myrtle Bessie Craig, at least momentarily. President Theodore Roosevelt spoke at the 1907 semicentennial. Along with her ninety-five classmates, Craig received her diploma from the twenty-sixth president of the United States. She could boast that she had met the president, participated in 'Roosevelt Day,' and had been among the countless people to receive his firm handshake. Some of the estimated twenty to twenty-five thousand exuberant onlookers in the large all-White crowd witnessed a dignified Black woman walk across the custom-built raised stage not too far east of President Snyder's house. One can only imagine how President Roosevelt and those seated on or very close to the podium reacted. A headshot of Craig appears in the college's 1907 yearbook, the *Wolverine*. A striking class photo also exists of her with her White classmates in the women's course. Positioned standing on the right end in the second row, her expression exudes seriousness, confidence, pride, and humility. She wore spectacles, and, like several of her classmates, her hair was done up in a popular, Paris-inspired Edwardian cottage loaf–style pompadour. She looks as if she followed the advice of philanthropist, civil rights activist, Black economic nationalist, and self-made millionaire and hair culturalist Madam C. J. Walker, who had just burst onto the Black cultural scene with her haircare manufacturing company. With a little tweaking, Craig could have easily converted her coiffure to resemble the Gibson Girl style that vaudeville performer and 'Queen of the Cakewalk' Aida Overton Walker often sported.

In 2005, we learned that another African American earned the first known Black MSU graduate designation. Twenty-eight-year-old, Kentucky-born William Ora Thompson, who enrolled in M.A.C. in 1899 after attending high school in Indiana, graduated in 1904. A headshot of him never appeared in the *Wolverine*. One of the few existing photos of Thompson is one his son shared with local Lansing historian Jesse Lasorda that appeared in the *Lansing State Journal* in 2005. Suited up and rocking a one-inch sandy brown, wavy Afro, a smiling Thompson looks as if he is in a moment of deep contemplation. Was this photo perhaps snapped on the day that he, the son of former enslaved African Americans, made history at M.A.C. in 1904?

In a 1973 interview with *Grapevine Journal* editor W. Kim Heron, Myrtle Craig Mowbray recalled there were "as many as four Black students on campus in all most of the time while she was at M.A.C.—all four were women incidentally." The historical record indicates that at least one other Black man attended the college for a significant amount of time before Thompson and Craig, and that a few other African Americans were on campus for a couple years in the early to mid-1890s. Charles Augustus Warren was enrolled in M.A.C. from 1896 until 1899. Like Craig, Warren was a Michigander. He was born in Saginaw in 1871 or 1872 and grew up in Grand Rapids. Warren is in a rare photo from the late 1890s with his classmates, and a handsome photo of him appears in the *Michigan Manual of Freedmen's Progress* (1915), an exhaustive study launched and subsidized by Governor Woodbridge Nathan Ferris and compiled by Charles's brother and secretary of the Freedmen's Progress Commission, Francis H. Warren. Gazing off to his left, a middle-aged Charles A. Warren looks sharp, flaunting a crisp, white, high-on-the-neck, starched-collar dress shirt with an immaculately knotted tie. There is a noticeable stickpin affixed to his black, wool lounge suit blazer. His thick, black mustache noticeably contrasts with his salt-and-pepper hair, which is meticulously parted to the side. Warren was clearly well aware of the rules of men's Edwardian fashion culture. A contemporary of W. E. B. Du Bois, he looks like a consummate Black professional, as if he was an official in the National Association for the Advancement of Colored People (NAACP) or Marcus Mosiah Garvey's Universal Negro Improvement Association.

Warren, Thompson, and Craig came of age during what historian Rayford W. Logan aptly called "the nadir" of American race relations, a time when African Americans faced unimaginable obstacles. The three Black Aggies exuded dignity, confidence, and respectability. They were at M.A.C. during the presidency of Jonathan L. Snyder, who was more progressive than his

Myrtle Bessie Craig, '07, in the *Jubilee Wolverine* (1907). Courtesy of Michigan State University Archives and Historical Collections (*Jubilee Wolverine*, 1907).

William Ora Thompson. Courtesy of Michigan State University Archives and Historical Collections.

Charles Augustus Warren, circa 1915.
*Michigan Manual of Freedmen's
Progress* (1915).

predecessors toward African Americans. It's plausible that other African Americans graduated from the college before Thompson. As was the case at Whites-only colleges and universities throughout the nation, a handful of Black students conceivably passed as White at The State Agricultural College between the Reconstruction era and the early twentieth century. Others could have simply disappeared from the public historical record. A few African American men attended the college before Warren enrolled in 1896, either as full-time students for a brief period or as participants in the variety of available short courses. There appears to possibly be an unidentified African American man in the "Class of '98" photo in the 1896 *Wolverine*. In the early 1900s, a photo of an unidentified African American man taking part in the popular butter making short course also appears in an issue of the *M.A.C. Record*.[9]

In late April 1893, Booker T. Washington, the adept president of Tuskegee Normal and Industrial Institute "for the training of colored young men and women," wrote the first of several letters to presidents of The State Agricultural College. He asked President Oscar Clute if he knew of any Black male students or alumni who could teach "mechanical or agricultural work" at Tuskegee. "There have been very few colored students at this institution. There has not been one for several years," Clute promptly responded. "None of those whom we have had have graduated." A year later, Washington followed up with President Lewis G. Gorton. "Please be kind enough to let me know whether or not you have, in any of the departments in your institution, a colored man who is competent to teach any of the branches that are taught in your institution." Gorton informed the resourceful Washington that there was at least one African American male student at M.A.C. in 1894.[10] The "few" Black students mentioned by Clute and Gorton remain

Short course M.A.C. students participate in a "Class in Butter Making" in the early 1900s. Courtesy of Michigan State University Archives and Historical Collections.

a mystery, and the exact identity of the student whose name Gorton passed along to Booker T. is unclear. Evidence strongly suggests Gorton may have referred to John Wesley Hoffman. Born between 1869 and 1871 in Charleston, South Carolina, Hoffman briefly attended M.A.C. between the early 1890s and 1894 to study dairy. In 1902, one amateur Black historian dubbed him "the leading Negro scientist of the world" who introduced "the science of dairying and the latest scientific butter making among his people in the South."[11]

Hoffman repeatedly boasted of many accomplishments, including belonging to numerous scientific associations and studying at Harvard University, Cornell University, the Agassiz Scientific Institute, and the Agricultural College of Guelph in Ontario, Canada. In biographical sketches released during the early twentieth century, Hoffman publicized he "pursued his studies" in dairy science and agricultural chemistry at M.A.C. This was deliberate. He knew M.A.C. had a first-rate reputation as an agricultural school, and associating himself with its dairy program served as a feather in his cap. He cleverly employed the M.A.C. name to his advantage. After momentarily studying at M.A.C. in the early 1890s, for several years he taught horticulture, bacteriology, dairy, and agricultural chemistry at Tuskegee for approximately forty-eight dollars per month including board.[12] Sometime in 1896, Hoffman left Tuskegee for the State Agricultural and Mechanical College in Orangeburg, South Carolina, where he remained for about four years. During the early twentieth century, he worked at an assortment of other Black colleges, including George R. Smith College, Myrtle Bessie Craig's alma mater, and Florida State Industrial College. In the spring of 1905, Hoffman applied for a job at the Institute of Colored Youth in Pennsylvania and claimed to have graduated from M.A.C. The principal wrote to President Snyder, asking about Hoffman's academic record. Snyder responded that there was no record of Hoffman graduating from M.A.C. "We know nothing whatever of his teaching ability as a teacher," Snyder responded, "We do not have a record of his work since leaving this college."[13]

There was another young African American male student who may have crossed paths on campus with Hoffman. Between 1894 and 1896, William Francis Cheek, later known as Frank W. Cheek, was enrolled in M.A.C.'s agricultural course. He was noticeably younger than Hoffman and many of his classmates. Born in Detroit sometime in about 1878, he attended the college as a teenager. In late June 1894, the Detroit Public High School held its forty-seventh annual commencement exercises at the Detroit Opera House, and Detroit's *Evening News* listed a "Frank Cheek" among the hundreds of students who had been recommended for promotion to high school. A member of his family's church choir, he must have been an exceptional student to have breezed through high school to enter M.A.C., perhaps as what the college identified as a "special" student or a sub-freshman. He probably benefited from family connections. His father, George, was a successful barber and, by 1899, had for a long time served James McMillan, an influential businessman and Michigan Republican senator in office from 1889 until 1902, serving as chairman of the Michigan Republican Party. Known by the college's board and leadership, McMillan may have helped George get his only son into M.A.C. According to the *Detroit Tribune*, Frank's family was "well-known in Detroit's cultural and business circles of two generations." Frank must have been a mature, courageous, and independent teen to have moved to the Lansing area away from his family and Detroit's established Black community.[14]

Why he left M.A.C. in 1896 after two years of study is unknown. Frank returned to Detroit and worked as a clerk for the American Car and Foundry Company. He then served in the Michigan National Guard, as a soldier in the Thirty-Second Michigan Volunteers during the Philippine-American War, and as a corporal in the "old Company K." In September 1899, "through the influence of Senator McMillan," he was appointed first lieutenant in the Forty-Eighth Infantry in the Philippine-American War. The "handsome, well-built young fellow," opined a writer for the *Detroit Free Press*, was "the only young colored man in Detroit who is eligible to the position." Before embarking for the Philippines, Lieutenant Cheek rustled up a dozen Black recruits from Detroit, Bay City, and Saginaw and headed for Fort Thomas in Newport, Kentucky. The Forty-Eighth U.S. regiment was composed of 1,200 Black men, the vast majority of whom hailed from Georgia. It was an impressive group. "It was not only a splendid appearing, but perfectly drilled body of men, and a crowd of 10,000 white people gathered to witness their dress parade." In mid-November 1899, a patriotic Frank wrote to a friend, William Winkler, sharing his homespun impressions of Filipino culture and valorous deeds on the battlefields. Frank's regiment, in his words, "made some very important captures" and covered much terrain in the mountains. After about twenty months of service, in July 1901 Frank returned to Detroit, and a large reception was held at his father's home in his honor. "It wasn't very hard work," Frank boasted to the *Detroit Free Press*. "Our boys stood the work in fine shape." The prideful veteran added, "in service, we only lost one man killed and fifty-four wounded. Comparing this with the record of the best white regiment that saw the same service we did, our superiority in standing the climate and the work can easily be seen."[15]

Within a year after returning home, Frank moved to Washington, D.C., and quickly joined the ranks of what the *Colored American* called the city's Black "social elite." He married educator Charlotte E. Onley. They purchased a home in the city's burgeoning Black community, and Frank secured a highly respected job. Out of a Black population "of about ninety thousand people," there were only a small handful of Black clerks in the national capital's local government. Cheek was one of these race representatives. Called "one of the most efficient clerks in the assessor's office" by the *Washington Bee*, in December 1913, he was dealt a harsh blow. Without warning, he was "handed a slip of paper 8 by 4" and let go, making "room for some white woman." Upon hearing this news, one of Cheek's close friends lamented, "It is doubtful if any colored American is safe in the local government. You see, the anti-Taft Republicans wanted change in the administration." By mid-January 1914, Cheek became very ill. At the young age of thirty-six, he died in his home on North Street Northwest. He was buried in Arlington National Cemetery. Five months after his death, a group of Black Veterans of Foreign Wars of the United States met in Detroit at the Hotel Tuller and created the Frank Cheek Post, later known as the Lt. Frank W. Cheek Post No. 53. It was officially chartered in 1927, and the leadership urged "all Negro ex-service men who have seen overseas service" to join. The camp was active in Detroit as late as the 1940s.[16]

Discovering Frank W. Cheek's and John Wesley Hoffman's presence at M.A.C. raises an important question. Were there other African Americans, full- or part-time, at the college during the nineteenth century? Likely, there were a handful. Between 1904 and the end of World War II, at least thirty-three African Americans earned bachelor's degrees from the college. In the summers of 1949 and 1950, at least twenty African Americans graduated, and in 1950 there were twenty-five Black Lansingites enrolled in Michigan State. Though the Black student population at the college during its first century was small, throughout the first half of the twentieth century, many African American Michiganders benefitted from Michigan State's commitment to outreach and extension, services that were regularly publicized by the local and national Black press. In the mid-1930s, a group of Black caseworkers from Detroit took a special summer course at the college in social work. A decade later, Detroiter Lonnie Saunders, civil rights advocate and "Michigan's first Negro milk inspector," participated in a state-of-the-art dairy conference at Michigan State. Young African Americans like eighteen-year-old Carleton Dungey were also able to benefit from opportunities at MSC. In 1949, this multitalented Cassopolis, Michigan, young farmer, who managed his mother's thirty-two-acre farm, helped his high school Future Farmers of America (FFA) parliamentary procedure team win a state championship held at America's first agricultural college. His award-winning project on fire protection earned him a partial scholarship to attend the college and the highest award granted by the FFA. In line with the scientific farming embraced at MSC, Dungey remarked, "The guy that tries the new methods is going to make the money and have better crops."[17]

The first registered on-campus Black student organization, the Gamma Tau chapter of Alpha Phi Alpha fraternity, was founded in 1948. In 1954, a group of African American women founded the Delta Zeta chapter of Alpha Kappa Alpha Sorority, Inc., and ten Black Spartans played on the Rose Bowl–winning varsity football team. About four years later, Black student-activists founded a chapter of the NAACP on campus. In 1960, there were probably no more than 125 Black students at Michigan State University of Agriculture and Applied Science.[18] Six years later, the Black presence on Duffy Daugherty's football team was remarkable. There were eighteen Blacks on the 1966 team. It was an unprecedented squad that started eight Black players on defense and featured defensive end Charles "Bubba" Smith, quarterback Jimmy Raye, two Black running backs, and wide receiver Gene Washington. The team was skippered by Black co-captains, seniors defensive back George Webster and running back and star hurdler Clinton Jones who in 1965 was named "Mr. MSU" at the university's popular, annual Spinster Spin dance sponsored by the Spartan Women's League and Associated Women Students. Four history-making Spartans were selected in the first round of the 1967 NFL/AFL draft: Smith (1), Jones (2), Webster (5), and Washington (8). The Blacks on this historic team weren't representative of the pint-sized Black student population in the mid-1960s. Following a short-lived recruitment program called Project Ethyl, in 1967 MSU began Project Detroit, also called the Detroit Project, in hopes of increasing the number of Black students. Although this initiative wasn't the catalyst for the colossal rise in the Black student population, it was the first deliberate Black student recruiting effort in the university's history as well as one of the first initiatives of its kind in the state. In the fall 1967 semester, there were approximately seven hundred Black students on campus, accounting for about 2 percent of the total student population. The 156 Black incoming undergraduate students represented less than 2 percent of the 1967 Spartan first-year class. Several months following the assassination of Martin Luther King Jr. that mobilized Black student-activists at MSU and across the nation, in the fall of 1968, the incoming Black student body doubled, and there were about one thousand total Black students on campus. In 1968, the university's School for Advanced Graduate Studies, lead by the innovative and generous dean Milton Muelder, began moderately recruiting Black graduate students.[19]

By 1969, during an apex of the nationwide Black student movement, there were at least 1,500 African American students enrolled at MSU (approximately 15 percent of whom were graduate students) and about a half dozen on-campus Black student organizations existed. In 1970, during the first year of Clifton R. Wharton Jr.'s historic presidency, and when the university submitted its first official affirmative action plan to the U.S. Department of Health, Education and Welfare, there were nearly 2,000 Black students enrolled in MSU. A year later, there were 2,573 African American Spartans. In 1972, there were 2,678 Black students enrolled, but by the end of the decade this population of learners decreased by 12 percent. Between 1971 and 1981, the Black student population averaged roughly 2,400 per year. Black students were by far the largest traditionally underrepresented student group, making up at least 80 percent of the "minority student enrollment" during the early 1970s.[20] In 1973, the university held the first Latino Visitation Day, and Chicano aides were added to the Minority Aide Program, formerly known as the Black Student Aide Program. According to the Chicano Students for Progressive Action, Chicano students—the second largest underrepresented group—numbered about two hundred in the early 1970s.[21] In a mere decade, during the Civil Rights Movement and the Black Power era, the Black student population swiftly and astronomically increased. As was the case at countless other predominantly White institutions (PWIs) in higher education,[22] between the mid-1960s and the early 1970s, a bona fide Black student–centered integration strategy emerged at MSU. A recognizable and clearly visible number of Black students suddenly populated the campus, and they made their presence known. During the 1980s, the MSU Black student population averaged about 2,500 per year, and by 1994, the Black student population rose to 3,000 for the first time. The total Black student enrollment in the fall of 2002 remains a record breaker at 3,675. According to the university's enrollment reports, since 2011 the total Black student enrollment has fluctuated between approximately 3,100 and 3,500.[23]

Historians tend to write about topics they are passionate about and to which they can relate. How else can we explain why they dedicate so much time to researching and telling stories about bygone days and their protagonists? I am one of these sleuths. I primarily wrote this book because I'm fascinated by the history of African Americans at Michigan State University. For three decades, I have lived in East Lansing, a stone's throw away from MSU's beautiful campus. I can hear the bells from Beaumont Tower's carillon, the MSU Marching Band practicing, and the cheers from Spartan Stadium on football Saturdays. Nearly every day, I walk in my subjects' footsteps. A Spartan alum, I feel a deep and inexpressible connection with them. I often contemplate the obstacles Black students, faculty, and staff faced before, during, and after the modern Civil Rights Movement. I'm inspired by what they accomplished during times I can only imagine. If only the towering trees and old buildings on campus could speak.

In the fall of 2021 when I wrote significant parts of this book, there were 3,438 Black students at all levels enrolled in MSU and ninety-five tenure-system Black faculty members employed by MSU, accounting for 4.8 percent of the university's tenure-system faculty. In 1994, there were also ninety-five tenure-system faculty. There weren't any Black faculty at Michigan State until approximately one hundred years after its founding. The first Black faculty member, World War II veteran David W. D. Dickson (PhD, Harvard, English literature), was hired in 1948. Four decades later, in 1988, there were seventy-one tenure-system Black faculty out of a total of more than 2,000. Between 2006 and 2016, the number of Black tenure-system faculty decreased from 105 to 86. In the mid-1960s, there were less than a dozen Black faculty, and during the 1970s, less than 2.5 percent of the faculty at MSU were Black. By April 1973, the number of tenure-system Black faculty reached fifty. Considering contemporary discussions about the challenges faced by African American faculty at PWIs like MSU, several questions arise when contemplating the experiences of early Black faculty at MSC and MSU. How did African American faculty get by during the Hannah and Wharton years? How did they cope with the social and cultural isolation, the various subtle and overt microaggressions, and the campus climate? The well-documented struggles faced by African American faculty at PWIs today were magnified fifty to sixty years ago.

"Since historians always write from points of view that are shaped by their personal histories and social contexts," Lynn Hunt observes, "their accounts cannot claim to be entirely objective."[24] Despite this inevitable truth and my intimate connection with my subjects, I strive for fair-mindedness in my approach and to represent things said, thought, felt, and done in the past as accurately as possible. To borrow from Sara Maza's excellent *Thinking about History*, I set out "to explain the unfolding of change in the past, and to make the people and places of the time come alive for their readers."[25] At times while reconstructing people's lives and thought based upon limited sources, I employ what Sarah Haley aptly calls "speculative accounting." In her excellent book *No Mercy Here: Gender, Punishment, and the Making of Jim Crow Modernity*—a study on Black women in jails, prisons, convict camps, and chain gangs in Georgia during the Jim Crow era—she meticulously and creatively analyzes the archives that "circumscribed the knowledge" she pursued. She judiciously imagines her subjects' "social and interior lives and intellectual contributions."[26] This method is fundamental to the historian's craft and my approach. Edward Hallett Carr perhaps put it best in his classic *What Is History?* "The belief in a hard core of historical facts existing objectively and independently of the interpretation of the historian is a preposterous fallacy." Historians are compelled to demonstrate "imaginative understanding for the minds of the people" they study, "for the thought behind their acts."[27]

This book provides a sweeping and engaging overview of the African American experience at what we now call Michigan State University from the late nineteenth century through the late twentieth century. Probing many personalities and important events, incidents, and turning points, this book is a blend of intellectual history, social history, educational history, and institutional history. More than anything else, this book is part of the African American biographical tradition. At its core, it's a collection of biographies. Arnold Rampersad's musings on the biographer's craft guided my approach. "Biography is an art precisely to the extent that we recognize that what a biographer does to recapture is impossible to recapture absolutely—that is, the spirit and the truth of his or her subject's life." Rampersad continues, "Biographers can only work hard and honestly, and hope to come reasonably close to the original. A facsimile or a precise definition of a life is impossible."[28]

I haven't tried to tell the complete and definitive story. This is unachievable. Generations of African Americans, primarily students, are deliberately at the center of my book. Black people didn't exist within a vacuum at the college and later university. How Whites viewed, portrayed, and treated African American culture and people, especially students, is a part of the story that shouldn't be ignored but doesn't preponderantly shape this narrative. The African descendants who joined and integrated the campus community were inevitably impacted by the local and national racial climates of their times. I therefore touch upon national happenings and the Black image in White M.A.C., MSC, and MSU minds, from time-to-time unpacking examples of on-campus racial prejudice and anti-Black racism. This book isn't a traditional, top-down history of the college and university. Except for the presidencies of Jonathan L. Snyder, John A. Hannah, and Clifton R. Wharton Jr. within the context of African Americans' experiences and notions of race, I don't detail the evolution of the institution under the leadership of the eleven presidents from the late 1890s until the late 1980s.[29]

In part because a critical mass of Black faculty was not hired until the post–civil rights era, much of this book zooms in on individual and groups of Black students, particularly those who integrated the institution from *Plessy v. Ferguson* (1896) until the landmark Supreme Court decision *Brown v. Board of Education of Topeka* (1954). The modern, classical Civil Rights Movement spanned from the mid-1950s until the passage of the Voting Rights Act (1965), coinciding with Hannah's long and transformative presidency. During and following this period, the Black experience at MSU becomes much more complex and multidimensional. The more recent or contemporary history of African Americans at MSU deserves its own book. The post–*Brown v. Board of Education* African American presence at MSU isn't totally absent from this book. The second half contains snapshots of key personalities, noteworthy events, dramatic reforms at the university, and Black student organizing and protest during the second half of the twentieth century. Often supported by Black faculty, staff, and administrators, during the late 1960s and early 1970s, Black students helped transform MSU in extraordinary ways. In the late 1980s, a new generation of Black student-activists rekindled the spirit of their radical predecessors, a legacy that has continued to reverberate in Black student life "on the banks of the Red Cedar" into the twenty-first century.

Several books have recently been released on the Black experience at PWIs, and many excellent historical studies have been published on how African American students transformed higher education and college and university campus culture throughout the nation during the turbulent 1960s and 1970s.[30] As historian Stefan M. Bradley convincingly argues, during this spirited period, African American students embraced the "power to control space and place," striving to change PWIs and make them distinctly their own.[31] Accounts such as Bradley's help us better understand the present status of Black students and contemporary debates in higher education about the commonly talked about trinity: diversity, equity, and inclusion. The endeavors of those students who came of age during the Civil Rights–Black Power Movement belong to a longer tradition. This history dates to their earliest predecessors who faced a similar yet distinctly different set of circumstances and obstacles. At MSU, this history began in the late nineteenth century. The lives of the trailblazers and pathfinders from the Progressive Era—or "the nadir" of U.S. race relations—until the era of World War II have been noticeably overlooked and underappreciated. These bold Black students chartered new terrain and broke down barriers. Without the benefit of Black faculty to mentor them or Black student organizations to foster their collective sense of belonging, they paved the way for future generations of African American students and change at the university.

My archaeological approach was tedious and laborious, but quite simple and straightforward. In search of African American students who were often rendered voiceless by the archives, I scoured through college yearbooks (mainly the *Wolverine*) and student directories, the *M.A.C. Record* (later the *Michigan State Record*), the *Holcad*, the *Lansing State Journal* and numerous local and national newspapers, M.A.C. and MSC commencement programs, minutes from meetings of the State Board of Agriculture and Board of Trustees, census records, and countless documents in the MSU Archives and Historical Collections. Some students were harder to locate than others, and coverage of my protagonists varied in newspapers and archival sources. When seeking to track down African Americans in MSU's early history until the middle of the Hannah years, researchers soon realize that the archives are incomplete. Many documents related to the early Black presence at the college weren't preserved; they weren't included in the college's newspapers, records, or presidents' voluminous papers. I provide as much information as possible about my many subjects' family histories, experiences at the college, and future lives and explore and imagine how these historical figures' upbringings and educational and social experiences at the college informed their futures. These frontrunners' personal histories deserve to be included in the broader history of MSU. Often defying the odds, they helped diversify the campus and laid the foundations for the unparalleled integration of, and Black student activism at, MSU in the late 1960s and early 1970s and beyond. The people whose stories are recounted in this book can teach us much, making sure their and "our memory still will linger."

Abbreviations

AAAS	African American and African Studies
ABPsi	Association of Black Psychologists
ACHR	American Council on Human Rights
AME	African Methodist Episcopal
AMS	American Mathematical Society
ANWC	Association for Non-White Concerns in Personnel and Guidance
APGA	American Personnel and Guidance Association
ATL	American Thought and Language
ASMSU	Associated Students of Michigan State University
BAC	Black Arts Company
BFAA	Black Faculty and Administrators Association
BLFI	Black Liberation Front, International
BPA	Black Parents Association
BSA	Black Students' Alliance
BSE	Black Students of Engineering
BUF	Black United Front
BWEA	Black Women's Employees Association of Michigan State University

CAC	Connecticut Agricultural College
CIAA	Central Intercollegiate Athletic Association
COMGA	Commission on Geography and Afro-America
CORE	Congress of Racial Equality
CRC	Civil Rights Commission
DGEI	Detroit Geographic Expedition and Institute
EEOP	Engineering Equal Opportunity Program
GLCO	Greater Lansing Community Organization
HBCUs	historically Black colleges and universities
IAUP	International Association of University Presidents
IFC	interfraternity council
JBHE	*Journal of Blacks in Higher Education*
LAWC	Lansing Association of Women's Clubs
LSJ	*Lansing State Journal*
LYPM	Lansing Young Peoples Movement
M.A.C.	Michigan Agricultural College
MDPH	Michigan Department of Public Health
MIAA	Michigan Intercollegiate Athletic Association
MSC	Michigan State College
MSU	Michigan State University
MSUIC-MP	MSU's Inner City Mathematics Project
NAACP	National Association for the Advancement of Colored People
NAM	National Association of Mathematicians
NMSU	New Mexico State University
OBA	Office of Black Affairs
PASOA	Pan-African Students Organization in the Americas
PEC	Prince Edward County
PUSH	People United to Save Humanity
PWIs	predominantly White institutions
ROTC	Reserve Officers' Training Corps
SCLC	Southern Christian Leadership Conference
SDS	Students for a Democratic Society
SHS	Students for Human Survival
SMAB	Student Media Appropriations Board
SNCC	Student Nonviolent Coordinating Committee
SSC	Student Strike Committee
STEP	Student Tutorial Education Project

TIAA	Teachers Insurance and Annuity Association of America
UAHC	Michigan State University Archives and Historical Collections
UAP	Urban Affairs Program
U of M	University of Michigan

Chapter 1

Recognizably Absent

I n August 1970, an interesting article appeared on the front page of the widely circulated *State News*. In "Black Educator Influenced Founding of MSU," the paper's first Black associate campus editor, Jeanne Saddler, wrote that the Woodstock Manual Labor Institute, founded in Lenawee County in 1844 by formerly enslaved Underground Railroad conductor Prior Foster, "was the major influence that led to the establishment of Michigan Agricultural College in 1855." Drawing upon the research of local historian Blanche Coggan, Saddler suggested that Woodstock, a school for "colored people and others" officially chartered by the Michigan Legislature in 1848, philosophically laid the foundations for the creation of the Agricultural College of the State of Michigan. While the history of Woodstock is compelling, no evidence exists to suggest that Prior's school, whose main building burned down in 1855, inspired the establishment of America's first agricultural college.[1]

"The legislature shall encourage the promotion of intellectual, scientific and agricultural improvement; and shall, as soon as practical, provide for the establishment of an agricultural school." This pronouncement in the 1850 Constitution of Michigan (article 13, section 2) represents the first major reference in the public historical record to what, more than one century later, would become Michigan State University. The Michigan Legislature unambiguously envisioned this innovational agricultural school as providing "instruction in agriculture and the natural sciences connected therewith." This consequential piece of legislation was introduced in same year as the contentious Fugitive Slave Act was passed by Congress as part of the Compromise of 1850.

As Michigan legislators contemplated the creation of a new state-funded agricultural school, pro-slavery and abolitionist camps fiercely battled each other. In 1850, the nation's economic prosperity depended upon the coerced and unpaid labor of approximately 3,204,000 African American women, men, and children. These enslaved people comprised roughly 14 percent of the slavery-dependent country's total population.

Established by a bill that Governor Kinsley S. Bingham signed on February 12, 1855, what we now call MSU was founded as the Agricultural College of the State of Michigan on 677 acres of mainly undomesticated land several miles east of the then small town of Lansing, the state capital. Fourteen years after the Territory of Michigan was established, this large tract of land was part of the more than four million acres of land the United States government coercively acquired from Native people through the 1819 Treaty of Saginaw. As highlighted by the MSU Native American Institute, when the college officially opened, the Anishinaabe sustained an "Indian Encampment" south of the Red Cedar River. The inception of the college was an ambitious experiment in agricultural education. "We have no guides, no precedents," remarked the college's inaugural president in 1857. "Established on no precedent, it is like a pioneer in the march of men and the march of mind."[2] Before the passage of the consequential Morrill or Land-Grant College Act of 1862, which depended upon a state-sponsored system of Native American dispossession, the initial purpose of the college was idealistically envisioned as being liberal and practical, relevant to the industrial classes, enterprising, reformist, and democratic in nature. With civilizationist ideals, the college was created primarily to educate, enlighten, acculturate, and rehabilitate the agricultural masses of White Michigan men from humble and farming backgrounds. It wasn't founded as an egalitarian institution. White women wouldn't join the college's student body until 1870. Given the minute African American population in Michigan in 1855, who accounted for less than 1 percent of the state's total population, Black Michiganders were neither implicitly nor explicitly considered among the agricultural masses to be afforded the opportunity to receive this type of novel education. From its formative years, the college was among the many "historically white colleges and universities."[3]

On May 13, 1857, at the new institution's dedication, the college's first president and Director of the Farm Joseph R. Williams recounted episodes from the "terrific history of our race." His notion of "our race" didn't encompass African Americans. The college's founders didn't imagine African Americans would be among their pupils. The college's burgeoning mission and aspirations were debated, adjusted, and inevitably molded by unpredictable times and changes in leadership. Under the portfolio of the State Board of Education, it was unmistakable that the college was charged with upgrading and teaching the science and practice of agriculture. Established about three decades after the first and short-lived vocational secondary school for farmers and agriculturalists, Maine's Gardiner Lyceum, the Agricultural College of the State of Michigan became the nation's first agricultural college. Two decades after Michigan became the twenty-sixth state of the Union and banned slavery in its constitution, the college officially opened its doors to sixty-five admitted students. The curriculum suggests these eager learners were offered a relatively balanced experience; a basic liberal arts education rooted in hands-on rudimentary scientific agricultural instruction. The library possessed 1,200 volumes, but manual labor and the farm were essential elements of the college's educational outlook.

The first graduating class was comprised of seven White men. They took their classes in College Hall (built in 1856 where Beaumont Tower now stands) from less than ten faculty members, performed three hours of farm work per day, and were required to live on campus and pay about ten dollars for room and board and matriculation fees, including ten dollars at the beginning of each term for the sensible purpose of settling accounts at the end of the term. These hard-working students were awarded their degrees in November 1861, seven months after the outbreak of the Civil War. As advertised, they received an education of "thorough and practical instruction in those sciences and arts which bear directly upon agriculture and kindred industrial pursuits." They were, claimed the college's leadership, "farmers thus made possessors of both science and practice."[4] Serving behind Union lines, none of these mavericks from Michigan participated in the college's inaugural commencement ceremony.

Whatever motivated the seven graduates' military enlistment and whatever their perceptions of Black culture or race entailed, we will never exactly know. In a bare-bones sense, they fought to end slavery. As historian Eric Foner underscores, slavery was the "fundamental cause" of this devastating armed conflict and "resulted in perhaps the most radical social and political transformation in American history—the destruction of slavery, the central institution of southern life and the greatest concentration of economic wealth and political power in the entire country."[5] In segregated units that didn't see as much combat as their White counterparts and were most often commanded by White officers, two hundred thousand freedom-seeking African Americans served in the Union army and navy, proving to be central to the Civil War's monumental outcome. A member of the State Agricultural College's class of 1861, Henry D. Benham, was one of the many commissioned officers who assisted a company captain of an African American regiment. He served as first lieutenant, Company B, First Michigan Colored Infantry. Commonly known as the 102nd U.S. Colored Troops Infantry, this regiment was the first and only Black regiment from Michigan to see battle during the Civil War. Born in about 1840, Benham came of age in a family of farmers in Eaton Rapids, Michigan. It's doubtful Benham knew any Black farmers. Fifty years after he graduated, there were very few Black-owned farms in Eaton County. Joining at least 360,000 other Union soldiers, this Aggie alumnus died of smallpox or dysentery in Beaufort, South Carolina, on July 3, 1864.

In his diary, 102nd U.S. Colored Troop Infantry hospital steward James Benjamin Franklin Curtis recalled that Lieutenant Benham ordered "his colored boy" to perform various tasks for him and that he was "a very fine young man and was greatly beloved by all who know him." One wonders what Benham's perceptions of and disposition toward African Americans entailed. Did he treat "his colored boy" as if he was enslaved? How did he interact with the

African-descended men in his company composed mainly of Blacks from Canada and Detroit who were dubbed the "Corps D'Afrique" by the *Detroit Free Press*? Did he engage with them intellectually, given that many of these Black men were educated? How did he fraternize with those in his company who were once enslaved? What were his thoughts about the Fugitive Slave Act of 1850 and John Brown's raid nine years later? Like Curtis and many other White men serving behind Union lines, was Benham ambivalent toward African Americans? Did he, like Curtis, use racial slurs to refer to the Black men in the First Michigan Colored Infantry while also admiring their service? Did he share Curtis's sentiments that "slavery caused this war and now for *God's sake* crush it"?[6]

One thing remains quite certain: Benham's service in the First Michigan Colored Infantry exposed him for the first time to a diverse group of self-sacrificing African American men who vehemently despised slavery. Fighting side by side with these proud Black men and bound by a life-changing shared experience for months on end, Benham witnessed and unknowingly took part in a Black culture entirely absent from his experiences at the State Agricultural College. He was likely the college's first graduate to socialize and rub shoulders with African Americans in this capacity. Eight decades later, another Spartan alumnus, Lt. Col. Lawrence A. Strobel, '30, served "with one of the first combat units composed of Negro troops to reach the Southwest Pacific."[7]

It is unremarkable that no known African Americans graduated from Benham's alma mater during its formative years from "Mr. Lincoln's War" through the Gilded Age. Considering the college's ideals and objectives, African Americans who aspired to acquire a practical education centered on agriculture would have found much to gain from attending the Agricultural College of the State of Michigan or State Agricultural College. In 1853, twenty-one-year-old African American Samuel C. Watson, who reportedly passed for a White man, was admitted to the University of Michigan. From the early 1820s until the outbreak of the Civil War, about a dozen African Americans earned degrees from colleges and universities in the United States. In the first decade of the State Agricultural College's existence, the Black population in Mid-Michigan and the rest of the state was small, despite the fact they were, overall, more educated than their counterparts in other northern states. The vast majority of African Americans in the polarized country were enslaved in the southern states.

In the decade before the abolition of slavery in 1865, many African-descended enslaved people, "cultivators of the soil," could have taught a thing or two to those attending the college about the subtleties of strenuous day-to-day farm work and the dignity of manual labor. From "sunup to sundown," they tilled the soil, planted, and harvested a variety of crops, and intimately connected with nature. Agricultural work was the central feature of their lives. As President Williams defined the role of college in 1857, their lives were devoted "exclusively to the cultivation of the earth." Without recognizing the irony, Williams's reflections at the college's opening ceremony in 1857, with a few minor modifications, applied to Black people and their struggles for education, justice, and human rights: "By reason of traditional neglect and prejudice, seven-eighths of the race, on whose toil all subsist, have been deemed unworthy of mental cultivation, while the smaller fraction, who live, some by most honorable toil and devotion to human interests, and some on the miseries, credulity, ignorance, and even crimes of mankind, have been deemed worthy of the highest advantages of education." Williams the civilizationist continued, "the parasite, insinuating itself among the bark, has been carefully nurtured, while the parent tree, grappling with its strong roots in the earth, has been neglected." Williams and his colleagues agreed with the undertone of Governor Kinsley S. Bingham's long-winded speech at the college's 1857 grand opening. The governor opined that "African slaves" in "the Southern States of our own country" were held "in the most profound ignorance," preventing their "dark minds" from acquiring knowledge.[8]

African Americans certainly could have been among the "agricultural masses" identified by the State Agricultural College's architects. The act passed by the Michigan Legislature to establish the college didn't explicitly prohibit African Americans from enrolling. The institution's early leaders often emphasized that their beloved school was "free" and open to Michigan's male citizens who passed "a good examination in the branches embraced in a Common School Education." Those seeking admission had to demonstrate proficiency in "Arithmetic, Geography, Grammar, Reading, Spelling, and Penmanship." Did Canadian-born and African-descended inventor Elijah McCoy, whose family relocated to Ypsilanti, Michigan, in the late 1850s, ever consider attending the State Agricultural College instead of going to school in Edinburgh, Scotland? While the parents of the first known African American to graduate from State Agricultural College, William Ora Thompson, '04, were once enslaved, no known formerly enslaved African Americans attended the college.

In 1860, nearly 90 percent of the 4,441,730 African Americans in the country were enslaved in the South. There were only about five hundred Blacks in Detroit, and the Black population of Lansing and Ingham County was twenty-seven and thirty-seven, respectively. The Black population in the state capital grew slowly until 1900. In 1870, there were 77 Blacks in the city, 208 in 1880, 341 in 1890, and 323 in 1900. In Michigan in 1860, there were 6,799 Blacks out of a total population of 749,113, and by 1900, there were 15,816 Blacks in the state out of a total population of 2,810,173. In 1860, nearly 50 percent of all Black Michiganders "between age six and twenty were in school."[9] As noted by the authors of *Michigan Manual of Freedmen's Progress* (1915), in 1880 there were "only two professional [Afro-American] men in the State." Three decades later, there were approximately one hundred Black "professional persons" in the state who owned real estate. There were approximately thirty-two enslaved Blacks in the territory in 1820, and racism and discrimination certainly existed in Michigan during the college's formative years. The state's 1835 and 1850 Constitutions prohibited slavery, and the college was, theoretically, open to African Americans (only men until 1870) who were eligible to attend and able to pass the faculty's basic entrance examination.

In *The Dawn of Detroit: A Chronicle of Slavery and Freedom in the City* (2017), Tiya Miles painstakingly unearths the underacknowledged importance of slavery, and the subjugation of Blacks accompanying this wicked system, to the growth of Detroit from the eighteenth century through the immediate post–War of 1812 era.[10] Between 1833 and the Civil War, more than a few anti-Black race riots took place in Detroit, and African Americans were, for the most part, not allowed to vote or serve on juries in Michigan until following the Civil War. The state also mimicked Ohio's Black code, a restrictive set of humiliating policies rendering free Blacks to a quasi free status. Many of Michigan's schools weren't integrated during the 1830s. About a decade after the Agricultural College of the State of Michigan opened its doors to students, in 1866, an eighteen-year-old, Kentucky-born African American Civil War veteran, John Taylor, was accused of attacking and murdering his boss's relatives. While he was under the custody of the local sheriff, a "well organized" White mob "of at least two hundred" broke into the county jailhouse in Mason, Michigan, apprehended Taylor, lynched him, and "riddled" his body with bullets. Urged by the sheriff, Governor Blair attempted to track down "the ring leaders," but the case was soon dropped. Reminiscing in detail on "Ingham's Only Hanging" fifty years later, a writer for the *Lansing State Journal* interviewed a few men who participated in the atrocity and condemned the lynching of Taylor at "Hog's Back." In 1916, Taylor's skull was supposedly "still in possession of an Ingham County doctor."[11]

African Americans undoubtedly faced various forms of oppression in Michigan. As fervently argued by legal historian Paul Finkelman, the state's history of treatment of Blacks from its founding through the early twentieth century is "enormously complicated and full of surprises." In many ways, it was a "Beacon of Liberty for fugitive slaves and free Blacks seeking a better life" during the antebellum era. During M.A.C.'s formative years, the state was, comparatively speaking, relatively progressive in terms of race relations. The antislavery movement in Michigan, especially its intricate and nationally recognized Underground Railroad system, is well known today. Yet there's much more to the state's thought-provoking early, racial, pre–Progressive Era reformist culture. The state's inherited Black Codes were rarely enforced. African Americans often voted in local school board elections and lived in nearly every county in the Lower and Upper Peninsulas in the mid-1850s. Many early White settlers preached racial equality, and the state's White residents often defied the Fugitive Slave Law of 1850. "At no time did Michigan law require [de jure] segregation" and the state got rid of "racial terminology" in its constitution by the mid-1870s. In response to the U.S. Supreme Court's striking down of the Civil Rights Act of 1875 in 1883, the Michigan Legislature passed a bold Civil Rights Act of 1885 protecting, at least rhetorically, "all citizens in their civil rights." By the dawning of the twentieth century, writes Finkelman, "Michigan had some of the strongest civil rights laws in the nation and a supreme court committed to enforcing them."[12] White animosities toward Black people in Michigan, primarily in the Detroit metropolitan area, increased significantly beginning during the era of World War I. Black–White race relations worsened, and anti-Black behavior became normalized in Michigan's more urban areas. This was par for the course given the unprecedented increase in the state's Black population, especially in Detroit. Between 1910 and 1930, the Black population in the city increased by an incredible 1,900 percent. Between 1930 and 1970, it grew by 450 percent.[13]

Given the fact that nearly 50 percent of Michigan's African American youth were in school on the eve of the Civil War when nearly all their brethren and sistren in the South were enslaved, it isn't a stretch of the imagination to conjecture that some African Americans set their sights on attending the State Agricultural College during the era of Reconstruction and the early years of the Progressive Era. The first known full-time Black student enrolled in the college several years after the Panic of 1893 had subsided. It's possible a handful of other African Americans enrolled in the college or took advantage of its various outreach programs, such as the farmers' institutes established in 1876 amid one of the nation's controversial presidential elections signaling the end of Reconstruction. What were the college leadership's views of African Americans and race, especially prior to the impactful presidency of Jonathan L. Snyder from 1896 until 1915? Apart from native Michigander Lewis G. Gorton (1893–1895), the first six presidents were born in the Northeastern United States where, by 1804, slavery had been abolished or gradual abolition had been introduced. Several of the pre-Snyder presidents were active in Republican politics, including the first president of the college, Joseph R. Williams (1857–1859), and Edwin Willits (1885–1889). Except for Theophilus Caper Abbot (1863–1885), none of the college's early presidents served more than four years in office or encouraged African American students to come to campus.

Of the faculty at the college during its first fifty years, New York–born longtime chemistry professor Robert C. Kedzie attended Oberlin College in the 1840s. About five years before he arrived in Lorain County, Ohio, the college, a hub of antislavery activism, admitted its first Black student. In the second half of the 1840s, at least four African Americans graduated from Oberlin. Kedzie was influenced by this abolitionist ethos. In the early 1850s, he read Harriet Beecher Stowe's popular *Uncle Tom's Cabin* (1852) and commented to a friend: "food and earthly cares had little hold on us till wife and I, in tears and choking sobs, had read that wonderful book."[14] A year before he began teaching at the State Agricultural College, Kedzie served behind Union lines as a surgeon in the Civil War. The racial politics of William James Beal, known as the Grand Old Man of M.A.C. who was at the college from 1871 until 1910, are harder to pinpoint. His upbringing suggests he was socialized to recognize African Americans' humanity. He was born to Quaker parents in 1833 in Adrian, Michigan, "a hot spot of abolitionist awareness and political activism." His parents were contemporaries of radical abolitionist Laura Smith Haviland, founder of the Logan Female Anti-Slavery Society (1832) and the Raisin Institute (1837), "a safe space for African American fugitives from slavery."[15] While attending the University of Michigan in the late 1850s and early 1860s, Beal lived in Ann Arbor, home of the Michigan State Anti-Slavery Society and the abolitionist newspaper *Signal of Liberty*. Charles A. Warren, Thompson, and Myrtle Bessie Craig took classes from Beal. He probably treated them with impartiality in the classroom, while simultaneously embracing aspects of the scientific racism espoused by his mentor, biologist and geologist Jean Louis Rodolphe Agassiz.

The college's founders, early presidents, and movers and shakers were not abolitionists or allies in the Black Freedom Struggle. Like the college's founding president Williams, when they spoke about "our race," "human progress," and Michigan's citizens, they implicitly alluded to White people. They didn't appear to actively espouse anti-Black racism, support slavery, or endorse Jim Crow segregation. Throughout the nineteenth century and well into the twentieth century, the college's leadership also didn't publicly critique American racism, support the struggle for Black social justice, create programs with Black clientele in mind, or recruit African American students or faculty. In his shrewd and calculated ways, President John A. Hannah, who served from 1941 until 1969, challenged this complacent tradition. The lack of Black presence, physically and ideologically, at America's first agricultural college during its first four decades is nothing unexpected when viewed within the context of U.S. educational history.

Yet, when compared with other colleges and universities in Michigan, M.A.C. appears to have been moving at a snail-like pace, dawdling without concerns about enrolling Black students, beyond a few here and there. African Americans attended Hillsdale College, Kalamazoo College, Wayne State University, Olivet College, the Detroit College of Law, and the University of Michigan, the oldest postsecondary school in the state, well before they enrolled in M.A.C. The first Black student to graduate from Albion College, James A. Welton, '04, did so in the same year that William O. Thompson graduated from M.A.C. When Myrtle Bessie Craig graduated from M.A.C. in 1907, another Black woman, Emma Norman Todd, became the first Black graduate from Central Michigan Normal in Mt. Pleasant, Michigan (now known as Central Michigan University).

The University of Michigan's first Black varsity football player in the twentieth century, Willis Ward, joined the squad in 1932 and was benched in 1934 when the Wolverines played Georgia Tech in the Big House. But the early Black presence at the University of Michigan is noteworthy. Between 1853 and the early twentieth century, a significant number of African Americans matriculated through U of M. The section "Afro-Americans Engaged in Professional Pursuits" in the *Michigan Manual of Freedmen's Progress* introduces readers to at least a dozen African Americans who attended the university during the late nineteenth and early twentieth centuries. Twenty-three years after the first African American man was admitted to U of M, in 1876, Mary Henrietta Graham became the first African American woman to enroll in the university. Ann Arbor High School graduate and class valedictorian George Jewett played on the varsity football team during the 1890–1891 and 1892–1893 seasons. Proficient in German, Italian, and French, Jewett excelled in the classroom and on the gridiron. The extraordinary halfback and skilled kicker faced much racism while donning the Maize and Blue. In a game against Albion in late October 1890, Jewett was targeted and verbally assaulted, and a riot almost broke out. Two years later, he was knocked unconscious in a contest against Purdue. Boilermaker fans reportedly hurled racist epithets at him during the game, chanting "kill the coon." He left Michigan in 1893 and transferred to Northwestern, becoming the first African American to play on their varsity football squad. According to Rashid Faisal, after completing his medical degree at Northwestern University, Jewett supposedly coached at M.A.C., Ypsilanti Normal College, and Olivet College.[16] About a decade after Jewett left Ann Arbor, a Black student organization, the Colored Students Club, was founded at U of M. In 1909, a chapter of Alpha Phi Alpha was established on campus, and in 1925, the Negro-Caucasian Club, a unique interracial student civil rights organization, was founded.

How do we explain M.A.C.'s early, miniscule Black student enrollment compared to U of M's? One viable explanation is that the Black students who attended U of M were exceptional students whose genius, despite their race, earned them entrance into the state's oldest university. By the early 1850s, U of M modeled itself as a research university. Between 1841 and 1906, the university created nine colleges and schools, including literature and the arts, medicine, engineering, law, dentistry, pharmacy, music, theatre and dance, and architecture and urban planning. Talented African Americans who wanted to study in such fields found U of M an ideal destination. Celebrated in the *Michigan Manual of Freedmen's Progress* compiled by Francis H. Warren in 1915, Detroit native Eugene J. Marshall must have been exceptionally gifted. In 1915, he was considered one of the most highly-educated Blacks in the state. He graduated from U of M's law department and was the class orator of the University of Michigan in 1903. Taking a cue from European universities, the entrance exam for U of M tested students in math, geography, Greek, and Latin. Very few African Americans knew Greek or Latin during the nineteenth century. Most African American students who enrolled in M.A.C. from the 1890s through the early twentieth century, like their White counterparts, didn't have to be schooled in classical education or Greek or Latin to gain admission into the college and graduate. A basic common school education was required. They had to be willing to work hard, especially in the agricultural course. Unlike their counterparts at U of M, the vast majority of African Americans who attended M.A.C. during the Progressive Era came to East Lansing to learn scientific agriculture, acquire industrial training, perhaps dabble in engineering, become teachers, and, in the case of women like Craig, to study home economics.

For a variety of reasons, the vast majority of college-aged African Americans in Michigan through as late as the early twentieth century could not afford to attend school beyond their teenage years. By 1910, the authors of the *Michigan Manual of Freedmen's Progress* observed, "the greatest number of successes among Negro businessmen must be credited to farmers." They continued, "Michigan Negroes have demonstrated their ability to control the forces of nature. With 640 farms operated by them in the state, the 1,385 persons engaged in agricultural pursuits . . . are distributed over the state." In Cass County, there were 171 Black-owned farms valued at more than $660,000.00.[17] Like some of their skeptical White counterparts, those college-eligible African Americans from farming backgrounds may have questioned the college's scientific work and habitual dismissal of old-school farmers' so-called backwards ways. They possibly questioned how they could be enlightened about their life's work. Most African American Michiganders also likely viewed the college as being well beyond their communities' reach. It was declared in 1855 that the Agricultural College's tuition "shall be free forever to pupils from this state," and several years later, Governor Kinsley S. Bingham even called the institution a "Free Agricultural College." Yet, there were still significant costs and sacrifices associated with attending college.

In their exhaustive *The College-Bred Negro American* (1910), W. E. B. Du Bois, "the father of the Black intelligentsia," and sociologist Augustus Granville Dill documented that by 1860, about thirty African Americans had graduated from an American college. While the first seven White men graduated from the Agricultural College of the State of Michigan in 1861, several Black men also earned their bachelor's degrees in the United States. In the decade of the 1860s, about forty-four African Americans graduated; in the 1870s, 313; during the 1880s, 738; and during the 1890s 1,126 joined the exclusive ranks of their predecessors. All told, between 1857 and 1900, about 2,315 African Americans, disproportionately men, graduated from colleges and universities in the United States.[18] From the era of Reconstruction through the era of Jim Crow segregation, the overwhelming majority of African American college-goers attended one of the more than one hundred historically Black colleges and universities (HBCUs), about a fifth of which were supported by the Second Morrill Act of 1890. Signed into law by President Benjamin Harrison, "The Second Morrill Act required states to establish separate Land-grant Institutions for Black students or demonstrate that admission to the 1862 Land-grant was not restricted by race. The act granted money, instead of land, and resulted in the designation of a set of Historically Black Colleges and Universities (HBCUs) as Land-grant Universities to begin receiving federal funds to support teaching, research and Extension intended to serve underserved communities."[19] During the State Agricultural College's first fifty years, education for African Americans was largely a privilege. The absence of a Black student presence in Collegeville (what we now call East Lansing) through the late nineteenth century, despite Black firsts at other predominantly White institutions, should not be considered alarming or suspect.

African Americans born between the establishment of the state of Michigan in 1837 and the end of Reconstruction in 1877 shared the sentiments of the first Black woman to graduate from M.A.C. When reflecting on her life at age eighty-nine, Myrtle Craig Mowbray maintained she was "born too soon."[20] Hindsight is indisputably 20/20, and the course of one's life is unforeseeable. But Mowbray's point was clear. She knew her educational pursuits, employment prospects, dreams and aspirations, and overall quality of life would have been different, in her mind less arduous, if she had been born during the immediate aftermath of World War II and attended MSU during the groundbreaking presidency of Clifton R. Wharton Jr.

While a handful of African American students attended the college before the landmark *Plessy v. Ferguson* (1896) Supreme Court decision, existing evidence strongly suggests that the first known full-time Black student, Charles Augustus Warren, enrolled in the college in the fall of 1896, and eight years later, William Ora Thompson became the first known African American to graduate from Michigan Agricultural College. As the only African American students on campus during their times, Warren, Thompson, and Craig willingly bore the burdens of representing their race. They were among the only Black people whom their professors and classmates informally knew or interacted with on intellectual and scholarly terms. Intellectually equal to their classmates, Warren and Thompson were members of what W. E. B. Du Bois popularized as the Talented Tenth. They were considered exceptional, college-educated Black men of high moral standards who would uplift, redeem, educate, and rescue the "masses" of their people beyond "the banks of the Red Cedar." Similarly, like the countless Black women reformers active in everyday rehabilitation and liberation efforts through organizations like the National Association of Colored Women, Craig embraced the mantra "Lifting as We Climb." An experienced, professional domestic worker, she was undoubtedly more skilled than many of her classmates in the women's course, known later as home economics.

The lives of Warren, Thompson, and Craig before, during, and after their years at M.A.C. are remarkable. Their stories reveal as much about how their educational experiences were inevitably shaped by America's first agricultural college as they do about who they became, obstacles and tragedies over which they triumphed, and what they accomplished during trying times. Unconcerned with their history-making and legacies, Warren, Thompson, and Craig paved the way for generations of Black students who followed in their footsteps. Their stories and those of ensuing generations of Black students, staff, and faculty enhance our understanding of MSU's robust history.

Chapter 2

Booker T. Washington and M.A.C.

On February 7, 2014, during the first full week of Black History Month, President Barack Obama visited Michigan State University to sign into law the Agricultural Act of 2014, commonly referred to as the U.S. Farm Bill. Obama opened his twenty-three-minute speech before approximately five hundred onlookers in the state-of-the-art Mary Anne McPhail Equine Performance Center by enthusiastically pronouncing, "Hello, Spartans!" In line with the customary MSU call-and-response tradition, he then proclaimed, "Go, Green!" In unison and with unbridled enthusiasm and pride, the excited audience of course responded, "Go, White!"

Obama expressed his delight being at MSU and in the Great Lakes State. The athletic six foot one president then threw in a shout-out to head basketball and football coaches, Tom Izzo and Mark Dantonio, for their recent success. In the remainder of his Farm Bill speech, an optimistic and habitually eloquent Obama discussed Michigan's auto industry, economic and job growth in the United States, and recent developments in the Motor City. Sampling from his recent State of the Union address, he mentioned his desire to collaborate with Congress and praised the efforts of Senator Debbie Stabenow, MSU alumna and the ranking member of the U.S. Senate Committee on Agriculture, Nutrition, and Forestry representing the final version of the Farm Bill. Obama underscored how the wide-reaching bill was "going to make a difference in communities all over this country," especially for "hardworking Americans" in rural and farming communities. Obama gave a deliberate nod to the institution's agricultural heritage and historic ties to the education of farmers. He commended the university for its innovative research dealing with "cutting edge biofuels," agriculture and disease-resistant crops, and livestock.[1] A memorable event, this wasn't Obama's first visit to MSU. During his first presidential campaign at a "Change We Need" rally on a cold rainy day in early October 2008, then Democratic presidential candidate nominee Obama spoke for about an hour and a half to an audience of thousands on Adams Field where more than a century ago M.A.C. students participated in military drills and athletic competitions.

Obama's visits were not the first times U.S. presidents spoke at MSU. In late May 1907, President Theodore Roosevelt delivered the commencement address and presented diplomas to nearly one hundred graduates, including the first Black woman to graduate from the institution, Myrtle Bessie Craig. Obama also wasn't the first major African American political celebrity or historical icon to speak on MSU's campus. On January 23, 1963, Malcolm X—who came of age in Lansing and nearby Mason—spoke in MSU's Erickson Kiva before a packed crowd of more than one thousand, and the campus police guarded the doors of the popular lecture hall. In his memorable speech, "The Race Problem in America" sponsored by the campus chapter of the NAACP and the African Students Association, Malcolm, then still a devout apostle of Elijah Muhammad, shared his famous "house Negro" vs. "field Negro" anecdote. While many continue to believe Malcolm first popularized this celebrated analogy at a famous speech he delivered in Detroit, Michigan, at King Solomon Baptist Church on November 10, 1963, titled "Message to the Grassroots," he rehearsed it at MSU nearly a year earlier. At the end of his fiery hour-long speech, to the chagrin of some of those in the audience, he bluntly indicted Blacks who voted for John F. Kennedy in the election of 1960 and called for "complete separation" between Blacks and Whites. He suggested the U.S. government give African Americans "part of this country," offering a simple and compelling argument for reparations. Skeptics in the audience peppered the Nation of Islam leader with questions, and as usual, he responded with great poise, confidence, and precision.[2] As revealed in Les Payne's *The Dead Are Rising: The Life of Malcolm X* (2020), one of his former White childhood classmates was shocked by how her friend, who she had remembered as being so gentle, had changed. Perhaps some of Malcolm's African American childhood friends whom he ran the streets with and encountered at Lansing's Lincoln Community Center back in the day were in the crowd and interpreted his message differently.[3]

Several weeks before Malcolm was assassinated, Martin Luther King Jr. visited MSU.[4] In the MSU Auditorium on February 11, 1965, before an eager crowd of four thousand, King delivered what was certainly a much less controversial oration than his counterpart whom he had met for the first and only time in Washington, D.C., about a year earlier.[5] The most highly recognized public figure of the modern Civil Rights Movement who advocated nonviolent direct action was invited to speak as part of a fund-raising event for MSU's Student Tutorial Education Project (STEP). This was a reform initiative through which a small group of MSU students sought to help Rust College in Holly Springs, Mississippi, the birthplace of antilynching crusader Ida B. Wells, during the pivotal summer of 1965. Citing well-known thinkers of the Western world, he called for nonviolent mass action programs, global thinking, and a civil rights immediatism.

Malcolm X speaks in the Erickson Kiva, January 23, 1963. Courtesy of Michigan State University Archives and Historical Collections.

King certainly gave his MSU audience what they lined up for, majestically concluding with his famous "We Shall Overcome" mantra. In early March 1966, King returned to MSU and delivered a speech before an audience of two thousand in the MSU Auditorium. This speech was also part of a STEP fund-raising campaign. MSU students sought to raise $16,500 for the summer program. Now leading the Poor People's Campaign, King believed that financial burdens were among Blacks' most pressing obstacles. He called for a higher minimum wage and the end of school segregation and housing discrimination. He also recounted the history of the challenges faced by the Black family.[6]

During the modern Civil Rights Movement, the visits of Malcolm X and Martin Luther King Jr. to MSU were momentous. They represent noteworthy events in the university's history and, without question, had special significance to many of the African American students, staff, and faculty who populated the campus at the time. Malcolm and King weren't the first African American luminaries and Black Freedom Struggle crusaders to speak at MSU. More than one century before President Obama delivered his brief remarks before signing the Farm Bill into law, arguably the most influential and power-wielding African American spokesperson of the Progressive Era delivered a much-anticipated commencement address at MSU, then interchangeably called the State Agricultural College and Michigan Agricultural College (M.A.C.).

This leader was Booker T. Washington (1856–1915), the first principal and founder of Tuskegee Normal and Industrial Institute.

Washington was as much a celebrity as he was an educational reformer, shrewd politician, an advocate of Black self-help and racial uplift, and a White-elected Black spokesperson and representative. At the turn of the century, when 90 percent of African Americans lived in the South and no more than 2 percent of African Americans were considered "professionals" (the vast majority of whom were teachers), Washington became the first African American to deliver a commencement address at MSU. The 1900 M.A.C. commencement exercises featured Washington as a representative of his race whose miraculous life "up from slavery" defied the ridiculous foundations of anti-Black stereotypes on campus. The historic ceremony began at 10:00 a.m. on June 15 at the College Armory, a building that "functioned as a center of campus life" from 1886 until it was demolished in 1939.[7] Located near the 300 block of West Circle Drive where the College of Music is located, it served as a gymnasium, lecture hall, ballroom, and facility for students' military activity. During Washington's speech, the armory was packed to capacity by students and members of surrounding communities. The commencement exercises opened with musical performances, an invocation, and a presentation by graduate Miss Robson, "Woman and Her Relation to the Outside World," as well as talks on food conservation, soil preparation, and engineering. President Jonathan L. Snyder offered some brief remarks before the conferring of the degrees to twenty-six graduates. Then Washington, the speaker of the hour, delivered his address titled "Solving the Negro Problem in the Black Belt of the South."

Black people and culture had never before been the subjects of a commencement address at M.A.C. More important, it was the first time a Black person held court at M.A.C. in this manner. The next African American to speak at an MSU commencement ceremony was one of Martin Luther King Jr.'s mentors, a Baptist minister, civil rights activist, and longtime president of Morehouse College. Benjamin Elijah Mays came to the banks of the Red Cedar at the end of the spring 1968 term. Other esteemed African Americans followed in Washington's and Mays's footsteps, delivering commencement addresses during the remainder of the twentieth century, including Vernon E. Jordan, Andrew J. Young, Ruth Simms Hamilton, the Reverend Jesse Jackson, Darlene Clark Hine, Abel B. Sykes Jr., Ernest Green (who also spoke at the 2023 African American Celebratory), Ingrid Saunders Jones, William H. Gray III, Branford Marsalis, Gregory Kelser, and MSU's fourteenth president Clifton Wharton Jr. who delivered three commencement addresses.[8]

The idea to invite Washington to M.A.C. was most likely the brainchild of the institution's seventh president, Jonathan L. Snyder, who served from 1896 until 1915, a period coinciding with the apex of the Tuskegeean's power broking. Like his predecessors Oscar Clute and Lewis G. Gorton, Snyder understood the magnitude of the Second Morrill Act of 1890, which created separate land-grant institutions in the South for African Americans. He was keenly aware of Washington's pathbreaking work at Tuskegee. Washington's and Snyder's strikingly dissimilar lives can be contemplated side by side. Both were born during the turbulent decade of the 1850s when the issue of slavery was the most polarizing issue in American politics and culture. They were socialized, albeit in totally different environments and under completely different circumstances, to appreciate working with the soil and the quotidian rewards and joys of country living. Washington and Snyder respected farmers, valuing and admiring farming communities' ways of knowing and living, and both interacted with farmers as their equals. Their institutions embraced new interpretations of "scientific" agriculture and served farmers through their institutes, short courses, conferences, and outreach and extension programs. Under Snyder and Washington, M.A.C. and Tuskegee attracted students who often came from impoverished backgrounds and from families that didn't necessarily perceive liberal and practical education as being paramount to their success. They worked extremely hard to expand their respective institutions. Engaged in serious fund-raising efforts, they traveled extensively during the Progressive Era, defending and spreading the gospel of agricultural and industrial education. While they were beloved by students, faculty, and alumni, they were not afraid to transform their schools in profound ways. Separated by several years, both met their premature deaths just shy of their sixtieth birthdays, each leaving behind widows and three children. Still, their lives couldn't have been more different.

Washington was born in Hales Ford, Virginia, in about 1856 to an enslaved mother, Jane, and a White enslaver who owned about two hundred acres of land and ten enslaved men, women, and children. Washington didn't know the identity of his father, famously remarking in *Up from Slavery* (1901), "I do not even know his name. I have heard reports that he was a white man who lived on one of the nearby plantations. Whoever he was, I never heard of him taking the least interest in me or providing in any way for my rearing." In 1909, according to a plantation record, he discovered he was valued at $400 in 1861. His mother, whose ancestors "suffered in the middle passage of the slave ship," took care of him. She was his bedrock. From the age of nine until sixteen, he worked in the salt mines in Malden, West Virginia. From 1872 until 1875, he attended Hampton Normal and Industrial Institute in Hampton, Virginia, and became the founding principal S. C. Armstrong's most prized and accomplished protégé. Prior to becoming the principal of Tuskegee Normal School for Colored Teachers in the summer of 1881 at the young age of twenty-five, Washington taught at a small rural school in Malden, considered becoming a lawyer, and taught at his alma mater.[9]

Educated at Hampton, Washington didn't have the educational background that Snyder did. Washington's education at Hampton was probably the equivalent of Snyder's high school education and early college years. As Washington explained in one of his several autobiographical accounts, *My Larger Education*, he learned a great deal about life through his "experience and observation." Washington reflected in 1911, "I have had unusual opportunities for example in getting an education in the broader sense of the word." He continued, "the most fortunate part of my early experience was that which gave me the opportunity of getting into direct contact and communicating with and taking lessons from the old class of coloured people who have been slaves. At the present time few experiences afford me more genuine pleasure than to get a day or a half day off and go out into the country, miles from town and railroad, and spend the time with a coloured farmer and his family." Washington further explained what he meant by a hands-on education:

> I have gotten a large part of my education from actual things, rather than through the medium of books. I like to touch things and handle them; I like to watch plants grow and observe the behavior of animals. For the same reason, I like to deal with things, as far as possible, at first hand, in the way that the carpenter deals with wood, the blacksmith with iron, and the farmer with the earth. I believe that there is something to be gained by getting acquainted, in the way which I have described, with the physical world about you that is almost indispensable. . . . I found that while I was at a certain disadvantage among highly educated and cultivated people in certain directions, I had certain advantages over them in others. I found that the man who has an intimate acquaintance with some department of life through personal experience has a great advantage over persons who have gained their knowledge of life almost entirely through books. . . . I made up my mind that I would try to make up from my defects in my knowledge of books by my knowledge of men and things.[10]

The book learning Washington critiqued was a relevant aspect of M.A.C.'s curriculum and culture. Even so, Washington's admiration of what philosopher and educator John Dewey would dub "learning by doing" was appreciated by Snyder and the M.A.C. community. In his 1900 "President's Address," Snyder, the enthusiastic M.A.C historical revivalist, declared farmers must "know history, civics and economics," receive an education "as thorough as that of any man's in any occupation or profession," and possess a "wealth of mind or mental strength."[11]

Washington's slightly younger contemporary Snyder was born in Butler County, Pennsylvania, in 1859, eight decades after the Keystone State abolished slavery. According to a tribute to the then president emeritus Snyder published in the *M.A.C. Record* several days after he died in his East Lansing home on October 22, 1919:

> He was one of eleven children. His early life was spent on a farm and among country people, and through it he gained an appreciation of the viewpoint of the majority of students and the farmers of the state. . . . He was a great believer in industrial education, and shortly after his graduation from college, introduced into the Alleghany city schools of which he had charge, courses in sewing and cooking for the girls, and manual training for the boys.

A product of public-school education, Snyder earned a bachelor of arts degree from Westminster College in his native state in 1886. Five years later, a decade after Washington founded Tuskegee, Snyder earned a doctorate in psychology and pedagogy from his alma mater. Before being elected president of M.A.C. on February 11, 1896, Snyder served as the superintendent of schools in his home county, became principal of a school in Allegany, and helped establish a state normal school in Slippery Rock.[12] Snyder had little to no contact with African Americans or Black culture during the formative years of his life.

Snyder helped increase the college's enrollment by recruiting "thousands of Michigan farmers" to "become students of the agricultural college." Through the college's "winter short courses" and Extension Division, Snyder sought to help Michigan agriculturalists become "more informed practical farmers." He "took great pride in farmers' institutes, which were held in every county" and routinely covered in the *M.A.C. Record* during his presidency. Snyder believed M.A.C. students "needed to have their minds stimulated intellectually, as well as learn practical skills that would enable them to find a place in America's emerging economy."[13] The student body thought very highly of him, and his contributions to the college were monumental. "Exclusive of President Kedzie there is probably no one connected with the college who has as wide an acquaintance among alumni and former students of M.A.C. and among farmers of Michigan as had Dr. Snyder." The heartfelt eulogy in the *M.A.C. Record* continued, "under Dr. Snyder's regime, a great many changes took place at the Michigan Agricultural College curriculum policy, and he was instrumental in helping the college grow from a small school to one of considerable size and influence."[14] A year after he died, on November 19, 1919, the college's State Board of Agriculture drafted resolutions to honor Snyder, praising him for his "aggressive energy that stopped at no obstacle," "unfailing hospitality," "simple belief in the virtues of living," and overall commitment to the growth of the college. "We are glad to officially recognize that service for its full worth and to place upon the permanent records of this Board this expression of our deep appreciation of the accomplishments of one whose life and work will be forever bound up with the progress and welfare of Michigan Agricultural College," declared the board on the motion of John W. Beaumont, '82.[15]

Michigan historian Roger Rosentreter's concise assessment of Snyder's presidency captures his impact on the university, an influence like Washington's on Tuskegee. "By the time Snyder's presidency ended in 1915, he had dramatically improved MAC's fortunes. The school's enrollment had quadrupled to sixteen hundred students, the teaching staff had expanded fivefold, nine major buildings had been added, including Agricultural Hall and the Women's Building (Morrill Hall), and admission into the school required a high-school diploma, not an eighth-grade certificate as in 1896. Most significantly, annual state funding had increased from $16,000 in 1896 to $560,000 in 1915."[16]

Washington's philosophy of education dovetailed nicely with Snyder's. Washington was a proponent of educating everyday farmers in the South, particularly in Macon County, Alabama. Beginning in 1892, Tuskegee annually hosted the Tuskegee Negro Conferences during which local farmers ventured to campus to learn about the latest developments in farming. In 1897, several years before Washington's visit to Collegeville, Herbert W. Collingwood, the managing editor of the *Rural New Yorker* and M.A.C. 1883 graduate, published an article on the Tuskegee Negro

Conference movement based upon his firsthand experience. Collingwood praised Washington, George Washington Carver, and Black southern farmers. "One single day at Tuskegee will convince any fair-minded man that the old theory that negro blood cannot absorb the principles of science or acquire skill has been thoroughly leached out of the ashes of old-time prejudices." The M.A.C. alumnus continued, "We were never able to attract so many working farmers as were found at Tuskegee, and we never entertained them so well." Collingwood compared M.A.C. extension programs during his college years with Tuskegee's, concluding, "so far as I can learn, the Tuskegee students are generally prosperous, while those who attend the Conferences show material progress from year to year." Collingwood wasn't the only Aggie to participate in the Tuskegee Negro Conferences. In the late 1920s, Michigan State's tenth president, Kenyon L. Butterfield, delivered a keynote address at the thirty-fifth annual meeting. His oration, "A Satisfying Country Life," aligned with Booker T.'s admiration of rural living.[17]

Like M.A.C., Tuskegee hosted farmers' institutes, offered "Short Courses in Agriculture," and in 1906 educated poor farmers in surrounding areas through the Jesup Agricultural Wagon (also referred to as the Moveable School and the Farmer's College on Wheels). George Washington Carver joined Washington's "Tuskegee Machine" in 1896, the year the U.S. Supreme Court's ruling in *Plessy v. Ferguson* (1896) upheld de facto and de jure racial segregation throughout the South. Carver was the first Black to graduate from Iowa Agricultural College and Model Farm (Iowa State University) with a bachelor's degree in 1894. Two years later, he earned a master of science degree from his alma mater and began serving as Tuskegee's humble guru in the agricultural department. He devoted his career to research, teaching, and outreach initiatives to farmers, programs that mirrored M.A.C.'s farmers' institutes. Carver was to Tuskegee what horticulturalist Harry H. Eustace, farmer's outreach advocate Kenyon Leech Butterfield, botanist William James Beal, and chemist Robert Clark Kedzie were to M.A.C.

Given Washington and Snyder's shared commitment to supporting farmers as well as "mental strength" schooling and "brain training and hand training," social uplift, family values, religious training, and moral codes of living, it is not surprising Snyder extended an invitation to Washington to speak at M.A.C. Washington was a leading thinker and practitioner of the M.A.C.-type philosophy, and Snyder wasn't alone in acknowledging this. After delivering his famous 1895 oration at the Cotton States and International Exposition in Atlanta, Georgia, Washington quickly became Black America's most sought-after orator in Black and White communities throughout the nation. In 1900, Washington reflected upon how he viewed the opportunity to take to the podium at venues like M.A.C. He wrote:

So far as I could spare the time from the immediate work at Tuskegee, after my Atlanta address, I accepted some of the invitations to speak in public which came to me, especially those that would take me into territory where I thought it would pay to plead the cause of my race, but I always did this with the understanding that I was to be free to talk about my life-work and the needs of my people. I also had it understood that I was not to speak in the capacity of a professional lecturer, or for mere commercial gain.[18]

Unlike his outspoken contemporaries such as W. E. B. Du Bois, Ida B. Wells, T. Thomas Fortune, Anna Julia Cooper, Henry McNeal Turner, and Mary Church Terrell, Washington didn't preach Blacks' civil and political rights when spellbinding his captivated White audiences. He wasn't going to ruffle anyone's feathers in Mid-Michigan by championing African Americans' rights or racial reform; he wasn't going to talk politics. Snyder's decision to invite Washington to M.A.C. wasn't necessarily a sign of his progressive racial politics or his admiration of object lessons of Black success. Still, it's worth noting that in 1902, some seniors of the University of Nebraska protested their president's decision to invite Washington to their campus. "Booker T. Washington must not be the commencement day orator," five of the seniors from Nebraska declared.[19] Washington was an exceptional Black man and "safe Negro" in Snyder's mind. Epitomized in his famous 1895 oration, Washington publicly advised against Blacks fighting for their political and social rights. Despite what his staunch detractors like Du Bois and *Boston Guardian* founder and editor William Monroe Trotter thought about Washington's approach to the monumental and life-and-death challenges African Americans faced during the Progressive Era, no one could deny that the Tuskegeean's accomplishments were extraordinary.

Washington boasted during his commencement address at M.A.C. in 1900 that Tuskegee owned 2,500 acres of land (approximately 700 acres of which were "under cultivation" by students and faculty), dozens of buildings that the students themselves constructed, and "fifty wagons and buggies and 600 head of live stock." Washington emphasized to Snyder's disciples that "the total property" value of Tuskegee was $590,000. Snyder and the M.A.C. community were in awe of Washington's and his coworkers' achievements. The year 1899 was a "record breaker" for M.A.C. with the largest freshman class having more mechanical than agricultural students.[20] In the 1899–1900 academic year, there were 627 students enrolled in M.A.C., and according to the State Board of Agriculture, at the end of the fiscal year, June 30, 1900, "there remained in the hand of the State Treasurer to the credit of the College Land Grant Interest Fund $45707.17" and "the cash balance at the College was $5386.49 making the total available assets for current expenses at that date $51093.66."[21] In 1900, Washington insinuated his institution had nearly double M.A.C.'s enrollment. "Beginning with thirty students," he asserted, "the number has grown until at the present time there are connected with the institution a thousand and more students from twenty-four states, Africa, Jamaica, Cuba, Puerto Rico, and other foreign countries. In all our departments, industrial, academic, and religious, there are eighty-eight officers and teachers, making the total population on our grounds of about 1,200 people."[22]

In 1899, when the first Black student who graduated from M.A.C. started taking classes, Snyder first reached out to Washington. The Tuskegeean was aware of M.A.C., deeply respecting the type of education its graduates received. In the early and mid-1890s, Washington contacted college presidents Oscar Clute and Lewis G. Gorton, inquiring if there were Black "Aggie" graduates trained in industrial education and "mechanical or agricultural work" who might be interested in working at Tuskegee.[23] This marked the beginning of a significant relationship between Tuskegee and M.A.C. that took root during Snyder's presidency. The theatrical John Wesley Hoffman was enrolled in M.A.C. for a semester or so, before leaving the college to teach at Tuskegee in 1894. Chances are President Gorton recommended Hoffman to Washington.

Sometime before mid-January 1899, Washington agreed to be the keynote speaker at M.A.C.'s graduation, a coup the *Detroit Free Press* publicized. In his popular and best-selling autobiography *Up from Slavery*, Washington shared with readers his fondness for delivering speeches at colleges and universities. He declared:

> Next to a company of business men, I prefer to speak to an audience of Southern people, of either race, together or taken separately. Their enthusiasm and responsiveness are a constant delight. The "amens" and "dat's de truf" that come spontaneously from the coloured individuals are calculated to spur any speaker on to his best efforts. I think that next in order of preference I would place a college audience. It has been my privilege to deliver addresses at many of our leading colleges, including Harvard, Yale, Williams, Amherst, Fisk University, the University of Pennsylvania, Wellesley, the University of Michigan, Trinity College in North Carolina, and many others.[24]

Anticipating Washington's 1899 visit, the *M.A.C. Record* announced: "the College has just received word from Hon. Booker T. Washington that he will accept our invitation to deliver the commencement address here the 16th of June." The announcement continued, "We tried last year to get this noted leader in the educational work of the South, principal of Tuskegee Normal and Industrial Institute, but were unsuccessful; we are fortunate in securing him this year."[25] The tone of this succinct statement is revealing. It referred to Washington with the title "Honorable," a designation used as a courtesy to highly respected politicians and public officials. This wasn't a common title granted to Black men during the late nineteenth century or at the turn of the century, with the possible exception of Frederick Douglass. M.A.C. granted Washington this mark of admiration. The college spokespersons considered the securing of Washington as the keynote speaker as opportune and even providential.

In April 1899, Washington informed Snyder he couldn't speak at the 1899 commencement because he and his wife, Margaret Murray Washington, were recently invited to visit Europe by some of their friends who believed he needed a vacation. Routinely spending nearly six months of every year fund-raising on the road, Washington was exhausted. "It is always a severe trial to me to ever disappoint an audience and I assure you that I should not do so did I not consider it absolutely necessary. At some other time I hope to serve you," he concluded his letter to Snyder.[26] This announcement, along with the letter Washington sent to Snyder, appeared prominently in the first column on the front page of the *M.A.C. Record*. Snyder was dismayed by Washington's decision. That he printed the Tuskegee president's regrets in the *Record* suggests he wanted to emphasize that Washington's choice had nothing to do with him or the M.A.C. community.

Several months after Washington pulled out of his speaking engagement, John W. Robinson, who graduated from Tuskegee's academic course, wrote to Snyder, asking if there were any resources for "poor" and "self-dependent" students like himself. Washington encouraged Robinson to pursue an agricultural education at M.A.C. Like Washington, Robinson came from a humble background. Born in Bennettsville, South Carolina, in 1873 on a farm, he began attending school at age nine. He was determined to get the type of education denied to his parents. He recounted his Horatio Alger–like story in the propagandistic *Tuskegee & Its People: Their Ideals and Accomplishment* (1906), edited by Washington. Robinson's request intimates that M.A.C.'s scientific agricultural training far exceeded what was offered at Tuskegee. Snyder mailed Robinson a college catalogue and responded to this Washington disciple in an encouraging manner, letting him know that poor students could work while going to school. "If you save up a little money to start with, it is probable that you could get along alright," Snyder counseled Robinson. "However, it would take a great deal of perseverance and self-denial on your part. If you come, we shall be glad to do the best we can for you but as I said before it will almost all depend upon your own energy and ability."[27]

Snyder's response to Robinson wasn't out of the ordinary. Countless poor young men and women wrote to him expressing their longing to attend his college. Such inquiries from Blacks, however, were rare. Though he didn't reference Robinson's race in his reply, Snyder knew Robinson was African American based upon his affiliation with Tuskegee. During the Progressive Era, M.A.C. still focused on serving Michigan residents, but Snyder could have used this opportunity to recruit a Black student to his college and perhaps to even establish some type of informal pipeline between M.A.C. and Tuskegee. As scholar David Pilgrim discovered, during the early twentieth century, Woodbridge Nathan Ferris's school in Big Rapids, Michigan, created informal Black student recruiting pipelines with HBCUs in the South.[28] Like most presidents of northern colleges prior to the modern Civil Rights Movement, Snyder's educational program, despite his support of underprivileged farmers and underdogs, didn't explicitly seek to muster up interest among Black communities. These communities were full of young people who, like Robinson, would have diversified M.A.C. and contributed to its scholarly and service-oriented ethos. Though he never attended M.A.C., Robinson went on to accomplish great things, including traveling to Togo, West Africa, on behalf of Tuskegee for a short-lived cotton-growing initiative.

Chapter 3

Black Culture Imagined in Collegeville

By late January 1900, the M.A.C. community seemed elated that Booker T. Washington had agreed to speak at the graduation ceremony in June. "Booker T. Washington has done more than any other living negro for the advancement of industrial education among negroes of the South," read an announcement on the front page of the *M.A.C. Record* on January 23, "and his address connot [*sic*] fail to be of great interest to the people of Michigan."[1] On the same day, the *Grand Rapids Herald*, one of the city's main newspapers, announced that M.A.C. had secured the "Brainy Negro Educator" as the commencement orator. When Washington agreed to speak at the 1900 commencement exercises, there existed a small connection between M.A.C. and Tuskegee. Between 1894 and 1896, John Wesley Hoffman, who claimed an affiliation with M.A.C., taught at Tuskegee, and in the fall of 1899, one of the first known full-time African American M.A.C. students, Charles Augustus Warren, began teaching horticulture at Tuskegee, where he remained for about three years.

Further hyping up the M.A.C. student body and the Lansing community for the visit of a Black celebrity, a month before Washington's scheduled address, the *Record* published a celebratory essay on the Tuskegee founder, deeming him a more influential leader than former abolitionist and idol of Washington, Frederick Douglass. The author of the essay was Morris Wade, a writer for the *Detroit Free Press* who in January 1899 wrote an article in the Sunday edition of the *Free Press* titled "Working for His People: Booker T. Washington and His Tuskegee Industrial School." He described Washington's philosophy in a manner that resonated with Snyder

Washington around the time he spoke at M.A.C. Courtesy of New York Public Library.

and the M.A.C. community, praising his pragmatism and promotion of industrial education. "It is Mr. Washington's theory that the education of the brain and hand should go forward together," Morris asserted, "and the education of the brain is not forgotten in the regular work at Tuskegee." Morris concluded by exalting the annual Tuskegee Negro Conferences, an initiative Snyder surely respected. Notably, this pro-Washington composition also featured a large, dignified portrait sketch of Washington, the first image of a Black person to appear in the *M.A.C. Record*.[2] It's likely that Washington himself, a master propagandist, requested such fanfare.

In an interesting article published in the *M.A.C. Record* several weeks before the second announcement alerting the campus community to Washington's visit, one student praised Tuskegee for advancing a solution to what he called "one of the most widely discussed problems of the day." This member of the Phi Delta Theta Society grossly stereotyped the culture of enslaved Blacks, even claiming that during slavery the Black man "could not turn to agriculture because he had never learned it." Yet he recognized the achievements of African Americans at Tuskegee. "The best plan for the uplifting of the negro, and really the final solution of the problem, is education. Without education he is practically nothing." The student went on, "at Tuskegee, Alabama, they have a school for negroes exclusively. They have a farm of 650 acres which is cultivated by student labor. The students are taught in agriculture, dairying, architecture, masonry, carpentry, turning, and, in fact, everything that tends to give them a chance to make something of themselves. But they are not only taught the practical part of architecture, for example, but also the underlying principles. They are taught how to bring their knowledge of the sciences into every-day life."[3]

One wonders if M.A.C. students learned anything substantial in their history, political science, civics, or other courses about Black history and culture. At HBCUs during the late nineteenth and early twentieth centuries, Black students were exposed to their ancestors' trials, tribulations, and achievements. M.A.C. students had the opportunity to learn about the history of the United States in advanced courses for seniors, which included discussions of slavery, the Civil War, and Reconstruction. What they learned was represented by White historians who tended to portray sub-Saharan Africa as the "dark continent" with no history worth writing about, slavery as a benign and civilizing institution, and Reconstruction as an experiment empowering formerly enslaved African Americans. Racism bound many White scholars in the U.S. historical profession during the Progressive Era. A decade after Washington's visit to M.A.C., Harvard University historian Albert Bushnell Hart, the so-called Grand Old Man of American History, insisted in his book *The Southern South* (1910) that African Americans were inherently inferior to Whites.

At the beginning of the 1900 academic year, history and political economy professor Wilbur O. Hedrick, '91, described the study of history at M.A.C. Like other historians of his age, Hedrick embraced a "famous adage"—"History is past politics; politics is present history." He highlighted history's role in helping to make sense of the present and the field's relationship to "other studies in the course" and explained the "pedagogical philosophy," an approach that explored the past by starting with the present. "From the present to the past is the order of our arrangement—required by curriculum exigencies," the history professor continued; "the Teutons—our immediate ancestors—by brevity of time are thus made one race of mankind given detailed study. Progress from the better known to the unknown is the order employed."[4] In Hedrick's and his colleagues' minds, "our immediate ancestors" clearly meant Whites' Teuton ancestors.

Though the campus library routinely acquired American history books, it's highly doubtful M.A.C. students read the recently published scholarship by Black historians at the time, such as George Washington Williams's two-volume *History of the Negro Race in America from 1619 to 1880* (1882), Joseph T. Wilson's *The Black Phalanx* (1888), Edward A. Johnson's *School History of the Negro Race in America from 1619 to 1890* (1891), Anna Julia Cooper's *A Voice from the South* (1892), Frances Ellen Watkins Harper's *Iola Leroy* (1892), W. E. B. Du Bois's *The Suppression of the Atlantic Slave Trade to the United States of America, 1638–1870* (1896) and *The Philadelphia*

Negro (1899), or William H. Crogman's *Progress of a Race* (1897). A handful of M.A.C. students in 1900 might have read Frederick Douglass's third autobiography, *Life and Times of Frederick Douglass*, published in 1881 and revised in 1892. By the dawning of the twentieth century, M.A.C. students, like those throughout the nation at predominantly White institutions (PWIs), were exposed to the types of books Carter G. Woodson condemned. In 1916, for instance, a M.A.C. professor planned on providing a reading and review of "'The Nigger,' a recent drama" by Edward Selden to members of Lansing's Woman's Historical Club.[5] This same professor may have used similar writings in his classes at the college.

Born to enslaved parents in 1875 in Virginia, Woodson was a Black history institution builder, a preeminent popularizer of the Black past. Known as the Father of Black History, he earned a doctorate in history from Harvard in 1912, cofounded the Association for the Study of Negro Life and History in 1915, launched the *Journal of Negro History* in 1916, created Negro History Week (the precursor to Black History Month) in 1926, authored countless books, and mentored generations of younger scholars. Like his M.A.C. counterparts, he embraced outreach and extension programs. In 1919, he described how Whites at M.A.C. probably learned about Black history. He observed:

> Speaking generally, however, one does not find in most of these works anything more than the records of scientific investigators as to facts which in themselves do not give the general reader much insight as to what the Negro was, how the Negro developed from period to period, and the reaction of the race on what was going on around it.... There is little effort to set forth what the race has thought and felt and done as a contribution to the world's accumulation of knowledge and the welfare of mankind.... The multiplication of these works adversely critical of the Negro race soon had the desired result. Since one white man easily influences another to change his attitude toward the Negro, northern teachers of history and correlated subjects have during the last generation accepted the southern white man's opinion of the Negro and endeavor to instill the same into the minds of their students.[6]

Though few in numbers, scattered throughout M.A.C. students' publications, namely the *College Speculum* and the *M.A.C. Record*, founded in 1881 and 1896 respectively, there are glimpses into how some students might have perceived African American people and culture on the heels of Washington's historic visit to their campus. In 1899, in the same issue of the *Record* announcing the cancellation of Washington's originally scheduled visit, the editors included librarian and poet Sam Walter Foss's piece entitled "Sambo's Prayer." Written in a belittling, southern Black dialect liberally using the n-word, this tale recounted a Black man praying to God to "sen' a chick'n." Foss blatantly evoked the stereotype that Blacks liked chicken, so much so that it entered their prayers.[7] In its debut issue, the editors of the *College Speculum* claimed their paper was going to be a "high-toned" publication produced by "a body of students who are earnest and desirous of making it a medium of instruction between alma mater and alumni, between the college and the tax-payers of the state."[8] In the October 1894 issue of this quarterly, a few months after "The Darkey's Dream" was performed as the closing selection at the M.A.C. commencement exercises, a student in the Delta Tau Delta fraternity shared his so-called research on Blacks and voting in the South. His paper, he noted, emanated "from observation and talks with people who have lived among the negroes and who do not think from any prejudiced opinions." The author portrayed Black people as the "tool of the Southern politician." Employing derogatory Black dialect, the author claimed: "There are at least a million old 'befo' de wah' negroes that are as ignorant of a spelling-book or newspaper as they are a life in Greenland." The author added, "Occasionally a phenomenal negro brain springs up, such as the Harriet Beecher Stowe description, and the Hon. Fred Douglas, who tried to remedy the ignorance of his race." Somewhat familiar with Douglass's life and seemingly comfortable with granting him the honorific title "Hon.," this student knew nothing of the travels of explorer Mathew Henson who ventured to Greenland in the early 1890s with Robert Edwin Peary. This M.A.C. student was paternalistically sympathetic toward southern Blacks and was critical of what he called "Southern corruption" and the "Ignorant South." He hoped "something better than the present condition of affairs" would emerge in the future. He also leveled insults at Blacks, claiming they were ignorant, politically uniformed, passive, easily cajoled by southern Whites, and dependent upon Whites. "It would be supposed that in communities where the negroes greatly outnumber the whites that they could carry the polls to their liking," professed the author, "but their old slavery discipline comes useful to the white man. In a certain sense they have the same fear of the present politician as they had of their old masters."[9]

Five years after this "leading" article appeared in the short-lived *College Speculum* and several months before Washington's scheduled visit, a junior wrote a brief piece titled "Our Colored Brothers" in the *M.A.C. Record*. "Perhaps the most widely discussed problem of the day is the negro problem," the M.A.C. upperclassman opined, "and I will endeavor to place before you a few facts for which you may draw your own conclusions as to the solution." While the student praised Tuskegee for its practical and self-help approach, he described Blacks' African ancestors as representing "the lowest type of humanity." He claimed Blacks had not made progress since the days of slavery. Following the Civil War, this uninformed student echoed Frederick Hoffman's popular and racist 1896 essay "Race Traits and Tendencies of the American Negro," alleging Blacks' limited opportunities and lack of self-motivation steered them to lives of crime and that Blacks showed no proclivity for hard work, self-development, and growth. He believed Whites could set the example for Blacks to, through imitation and following Whites' lead, acquire the values "which belong to the ideal of the white race." The haughty student—whose essay, as advertised by the *M.A.C. Record*, was "edited by the faculty"—concluded as unambiguously as he opened: "the best thing we can do is to first set a good example, then encourage them to do everything we can to help them so that they may lift themselves up to the plane where they will be of some use to themselves and to the country in which they live."[10] Shortly before summer vacation in 1898 on a Friday evening at a well-attended oratory contest at the armory, a student delivered a speech on lynching. The judges were impressed with his performance, awarding him the second-place prize. "In clear, ringing, earnest tones, the speaker denounced the barbarous custom of lynching, so common in our country," *M.A.C. Record* editors wrote. "He had a good oration and his delivery was excellent; he seemed to forget self entirely in the importance of his subject."[11] For many White Americans in the North, taking a stance against lynching was as much an indictment against White southerners as it was a plea to protect Black people. How did this student's classmates respond to his views? What motivated this student to take such a passionate stance against lynching? Was this something he was exposed to by one of his professors, perhaps by Wilbur O. Hedrick? Was this young man socialized by progressive parents? After graduating from M.A.C., did he go on to speak out against this grave injustice?

During Charles A. Warren's freshman year at M.A.C., two essays published by students in the *Record* reveal the potential variety of opinions M.A.C. students held about Black people around the turn of the century. In 1896, *Record* editors published a freshman student's paper he submitted to a rhetoric course. The faculty editors were apparently impressed with his racist prose. "To the Washington darky, Emancipation day is about the greatest day in the year," the student's essay opened. In the remainder of this short piece that was written as if the student witnessed this historic celebration in the nation's capital, the author evokes Black dialect, uses the n-word, and belittles Black culture. "There is nothing that I know of that so delights the average darky as pomp and show of any sort, the more gorgeous the better. He would rather be a drum-major of a band than president of the United States." The student fantasized further, "to me the crowds that line the streets are as interesting as the procession. Big and little darkies, fat darkies, thin darkies, men, women, and children, they chatter and laugh and are thoroughly happy."[12] Closing ranks with many Whites in the post-Reconstruction era, this student clearly felt empowered by using an offensive term to describe Black people.

About five months later, a much different essay, in tone and content, appeared in the *Record* pertaining to the so-called "negro problem." In the late fall of 1896, E. Dwight Sanderson, '98, a member of the M.A.C. Oratorical Association and the Hesperian Society, won an oratory contest held in Lansing's Congregational Church for what *Record* editors called "a thoughtful and impressive oration on the present condition of the negro in the south and the duty growing out of that condition."[13] Echoing the author of "Our Colored Brothers," this student was agitated by how African Americans in the South were systematically oppressed. "The Fifteenth Amendment, guaranteeing him suffrage, is ignored," he proclaimed. He celebrated White benevolence, but acknowledged Black agency and perseverance, observing, "but, although both personal and civil rights are denied him, he has, through schools supported by Northern beneficence and by his own ability, made in a single generation the most rapid intellectual advancement of any race in history." This student was most concerned with the status of Black people as it related to the White society and the nation. If Blacks were not granted their rights "under a republican government," reasoned this student, the entire "Nation is imperiled." His line of thinking echoed what other Whites of his times argued. Blacks, the argument went, should be uplifted because they posed a threat to the growth and prosperity of the nation. As he opined, "Sociologically, the depravity of the Negro is a disease infecting all society." He chastised the institution of slavery, attacked southern racism, and condemned Black disenfranchisement. Yet he too evoked the n-word and believed Black people needed to be "morally and industrially elevated" by sympathetic White Americans. He labeled Black men as being criminals, called the "modern Negro" a "spoiled child who has not learned self-reliance," and believed that "race extinction" was plausible. The student's closing remarks reveal his belief that Blacks' condition would only be improved by benevolent Whites. "Our duty to the Negro is unquestioned. He has suffered a great wrong; we owe him reparation."[14]

While these examples don't represent the thoughts of the entire M.A.C. community in the years and months before Washington visited M.A.C., they probably represent many of the students' views. These writings reveal that the college's papers circulated expressions of anti-Black, racist thought among a readership who lacked intimate interactions with African Americans and their culture. By-products of a period of heightened anti-Black sentiments throughout every major facet of American culture, Whites in the M.A.C. community were socialized to view African Americans as being inferior and subservient. Anti-Black sentiments on campus during the Gilded Age were common with rare exceptions.

In the fall 2020 issue of the *Spartan Alumni Magazine* that features a story on both botanist extraordinaire William J. Beal and Liberty Hyde Bailey, "the father of modern horticulture," there is a full-page, stately photo of Booker T. Washington under the header "Green & White: Spartans Connect." Acknowledging Washington's historic commencement day address, the caption reads: "It was a message that resonated with the student body and administration and one we continue to address today. Washington's connection to the college encouraged Black students, leading to their increased presence and success at MAC." While several African American M.A.C. graduates taught at Tuskegee, this stroll down memory lane innocently exaggerates Washington's relationship with the college. When Washington spoke at the college, there was only one known Black student on campus, William Ora Thompson, and it's impossible to precisely deduce how Washington's visit contributed to an increase in future Black Aggies' and Spartans' "presence and success." Washington's interactions with presidents Gorton, Clute, and Snyder represented, at least symbolically, a tangible relationship with a leading historically Black land-grant college in the Jim Crow South. Many of those African Americans who graduated from M.A.C. and MSC during the era of Jim Crow segregation taught for some time at one of the numerous HBCUs. About five years before Washington visited Collegeville, M.A.C. had a few links to HBCUs beyond Washington's correspondences with the college's leadership that offer further insight into possible perceptions of African Americans within M.A.C.'s White community.

In November 1895, Thomas J. Calloway, the fourth president of Alcorn Agricultural and Mechanical College in Mississippi, the nation's first Black land-grant college, replied to M.A.C. president Gorton concerning the potential of hiring a M.A.C. graduate to teach in the heart of the Deep South. "We will consider a white man for the place only in the event that we cannot find a colored man of the proper qualifications," Calloway told Gorton. It is unknown if a M.A.C. graduate filled this position. Given Calloway's background (he was a Black cultural nationalist and attended Fisk University with W. E. B. Du Bois), a White M.A.C. graduate would have probably been exposed to very unfamiliar world views. Prior to Washington's in-and-out visit to campus, at least one M.A.C. graduate taught at a land-grant HBCU. In the summer of 1895, T. B. Keogh—president of the Board of Trustees of the Agricultural and Mechanical College for the Colored Race, Greensboro, North Carolina, established by the Second Morrill Act of 1890—wrote to President Gorton, asking him if there was a M.A.C. graduate who could possibly teach at his institution. An attorney and real estate investor once referred to as being a "carpetbagger," Keogh didn't specify the race of the teacher he preferred. Gorton replied to Keogh that a "Mr. Stevens," '93, instructor of agriculture, would be an ideal candidate. In his initial response to Keogh, Gorton indicated that Mid-Michigander Ala T. (True) Stevens, "who was brought up on a farm" in Alaiedon Township in Ingham County, wanted to know "whether the instructors are colored or white." Keogh informed Gorton that though the president of the college was a Black man, a former slave turned Baptist minister, activist, and politician (John O. Crosby), the White-run board of trustees was in charge. He also assured Gorton that there were other White professors at the college and that Stevens could live apart from his students and colleagues. "In this country there is nothing like social association between the whites and negroes," Keogh continued; "the relations between the races are most friendly—but the social line is sharply defined."[15] Keogh was obviously talking about the color line, de facto and de jure Jim Crow segregation.

Keogh was willing to hire Stevens, without question, because he came from an agricultural institution that had "no superior anywhere." Though racist in this thinking, Keogh strove to hire an Aggie who could establish a rigorous agricultural program at this young college that served the Black community and was willing to compensate Stevens with a competitive salary. In Gorton's mind, Stevens filled "the bill exactly"; he was a "Master of the Tri-County Grange" who had sympathy "with the rural classes." The "strong and robust" thirty-year-old with expertise in "stock-feeding and breeding," Gorton assured, was "anxious and enthusiastic about the work with the colored people." Gorton also guaranteed that he himself was eager and willing to help Stevens succeed in the Piedmont Belt. In one of the last correspondences before Stevens headed South, in August 1895, Keogh expressed that the hire was a true blessing. "We have no such man among our people here. With the colored people he will be a pioneer in this new line of education."[16]

Stevens taught at this pioneering land-grant HBCU in Greensboro for at least a decade, from about 1895 until the fall of 1907.[17] In September 1907, he became a "Professor of Gardening" at

Connecticut Agricultural College (CAC), Storrs, where he remained for twenty-six years until he retired. Working on the East Coast, he earned a master of science from M.A.C. in 1908. At CAC, he was recognized not only for his expertise in pomology (the science of fruit), but for his service and "constant interest in helping worthy students."[18] Celebrated in numerous newspaper articles, Stevens was well known in Connecticut for his talents. Stevens shared his adeptness with his Black students in North Carolina. He wrote a letter to Gorton in early November 1895 explaining how he had been "very busy" starting "at the bottom." By this, he meant the school, with only twenty-five acres of land and meager resources, was underdeveloped and the students knew little about the science of farming and needed to learn, among other things, the intricacies of fertilizing. An optimistic apostle of M.A.C., he declared he would "show their farmers here how to do business."[19] Stevens also requested a copy of M.A.C.'s agriculture textbook to help bolster his pedagogy. Gorton encouraged Stevens and sent him a complimentary copy of the foundational primer. Stevens introduced his African American students to what he learned in Collegeville. Through Stevens, M.A.C. engaged in outreach service to African American learners. Raised on an isolated farm without African American neighbors, Stevens practiced his craft in a Black educational community for a significant part of his life. How this experience in a segregated North Carolina community shaped him, we will never exactly know. It's interesting to note that in 1930, a sixty-six-year-old Stevens traveled to the West Indies to study marketing practices on the islands.[20] Stevens died in Connecticut in 1943 and is buried in Williamston, Michigan. Curiously, there's no mention of his time at what became North Carolina A&T State University in his obituary.

One of the first M.A.C. graduates to deeply contemplate the status of Black people in America during the age of Booker T. Washington was Lansing native and M.A.C. 1889 alum Ray Stannard Baker. A prolific journalist who wrote for the *Chicago Record*, *McClure's Magazine*, and the *American Magazine*, Baker became known as a muckraker. In 1908, he published a popular book on African American life under the veil of segregation, *Following the Color Line: An Account of Negro Citizens in the American Democracy*. In 1909, the *M.A.C. Record* published a piece by Baker, "The Negro in a Democracy." He indicted the White South's oppression of African Americans and reprimanded Whites in the North for opposing Black freedom. "Lynching, mob-law, discrimination, prejudice, are not unknown today in the North," Baker proclaimed. "We of the North, do not, most of us, in any real sense, live in a democracy which includes black men as well as white men." Baker told *Record* readers that "the spirit of democracy" includes equality for African Americans.[21] One of the handful of White journalists who covered issues of racial relations objectively during the Progressive Era, the M.A.C. alumnus possessed relatively enlightened racial politics during his times. "State's most distinguished man of letters" was on friendly terms with Booker T. Washington during the years after the Black educator spoke in Collegeville. Baker often solicited feedback from the Tuskegean for essays he penned on race in America and his book *Following the Color Line*. Washington was candid with his criticism. In response to the proofs for an article Baker penned on the Atlanta race riot of 1906 during which dozens of African Americans were murdered and lynched, Washington wrote to Baker in early February of 1907: "Let me tell you how much pleased I am with the careful and impartial way in which you have chronicled events leading up to and succeeding the Atlanta riot. I do feel, however, that I ought to express my disappointment because you use the small N (n) for 'Negro' through it. I believe Negro should be capitalized." Washington continued, "Self-respecting Negroes who are not ashamed of the term Negro, are always very much disappointed when they find themselves treated as a common noun, instead of as a race variety carrying capital letters in publications, just as others of our citizenship."[22]

When Washington participated in the 1900 M.AC. commencement exercises, the vast majority of African Americans, merely thirty-five years removed from slavery, had made monumental progress through a variety of self-help efforts. Black communities throughout the nation—especially, but by no means exclusively, in the South—faced a range of challenges, including de jure and de facto Jim Crow segregation, disenfranchisement and political repression, exploitative employment, limited educational opportunities, and violence. In 1900, 90 percent of Blacks lived in the South, 80 percent resided in rural areas, and 75 percent of Black farmers labored as sharecroppers.[23] Between the passage of the Thirteenth Amendment in 1865 and 1900, W. E. B. Du Bois recorded that 390 African Americans had graduated from PWIs.[24] In 1900, there were approximately 27,400 bachelor's degrees awarded in the United States. Between the 1820s and 1900, there were approximately two thousand African Americans who had graduated from a college or university in the country, and most of these degree holders attended HBCUs.

In 1900, Tuskegee Institute had documented evidence, mainly from newspaper accounts, for at least 106 African Americans who were murdered by White mobs between January and early June. Starting in 1882, Washington tracked lynching that occurred often in public spaces throughout the nation. He was aware of the widespread racial terrorism facing his people. Washington, who traveled by railroad throughout the hostile Jim Crow South, lived under constant threats to his life. Even while on his own campus in late October 1905 when President Theodore Roosevelt visited Tuskegee, Washington faced real danger. "Threats against the life of Booker Washington had been pouring in for weeks," so much so that Pinkerton detectives from New York City were enlisted to protect him from potential assassins.[25] Washington traveled in his "private railroad car" and, when possible, used "a special train." A writer for the Wilmington, North Carolina, *Morning Star* commented that Washington was "always a rather expensive guest," often demanding in the range of $400 for entertainment.[26] It wasn't uncommon for him to be denied accommodations in Whites-only hotels. As noted in the *Detroit Free Press* in 1905, while he was in Wichita, Kansas, the "leading hotel" refused to provide him with a room. "He was informed that colored people were not entertained there" and "was compelled to accept the hospitality of a friend there."[27] Once, while staying in a hotel that allowed him to cross the color line, a White woman, mistaking him for being a porter, told him: "Why don't you bring me that glass of water? I've been ringing half an hour." Washington recounted he gave the woman a pitcher of water and then informed the manager of the hotel what happened. After learning of Washington's identity, the embarrassed woman apologized to him.[28]

In 1900, there were few Blacks in Lansing, East Lansing, or Ingham County to welcome "the Great Negro Educator." In 1900, 99.1 percent of Michigan's total population of nearly 2,421,000 was classified as *White* (native and foreign born) and the state's 15,816 African American residents accounted for 0.7 percent of Michigan's total population, 63 percent of whom lived in "urban" areas. In 1900, approximately 45 percent of African Americans ten years or older were considered "illiterate." In Ingham County in 1900, there were 410 Black residents of a total population of about 40,000 (39,402 of the county's residents were White). Lansing's total population in 1900 was 16,485, 323 of whom were African American (described as being "Black" and "Mulatto"), and only 85 African Americans at the turn of the century were men of voting age in the city.[29] In 1900, the Black population in what was identified as "East Lansing city" was not documented by the Department of Commerce and Labor Bureau of Census. With a total population of no more than eight hundred residents, one can assume that there were very few, if any, African Americans calling the city home. During more than half of the twentieth century, African Americans who sought to purchase or rent homes in East Lansing regularly faced discrimination. It wasn't until 1968, when President Lyndon B. Johnson signed the Civil Rights Act of 1968, which included the Fair Housing Act, that the East Lansing City Council passed an ordinance prohibiting housing discrimination. It's often been recounted that in the 1960s former MSU dean and professor and civil rights activist Robert L. Green "was the first Black man to purchase a home in East Lansing."[30]

Chapter 4

Praise Song for Tuskegee

Many questions come to mind when reflecting upon Booker T. Washington's 1900 visit to M.A.C. Were there any African Americans from Lansing's Black community among the crowd? Was William Ora Thompson, the first known M.A.C. graduate, in the audience? Did African Americans from neighboring Mid-Michigan towns venture to campus in hopes of catching a glimpse of this celebrity from the Black Belt? Did any Black Detroiters come to hear Washington speak? What was the nature of Washington's brief stay at M.A.C.? What were his accommodations like and with whom did he meet? Did he attend any of the festive events leading up to graduation? Did he meet with local Black leaders like the Reverend George R. Collins, the longtime pastor of Lansing's historic Bethel African Methodist Episcopal (AME) Church?

We know Washington did not remain in Collegeville for very long. According to an interview with him published in the Knoxville *Journal Tribune* on June 17, 1900, on the very day after M.A.C's commencement exercises, he passed through Nashville "en route from Tuskegee, Alabama to Cincinnati, and visited colored institutions of Nashville." Washington's entire speech to the M.A.C. graduating class of 1900 was printed in the *Thirty-Ninth Annual Report of the Secretary of the State Board of Agriculture and the Thirteenth Annual Report of the Experiment Station from July 1, 1899 to June 30, 1900* as well as in the June 26, 1900, issue of the *M.A.C. Record*. Washington's oration wasn't specifically composed for Jonathan L. Snyder's graduating class. Despite the clarity of his message and its relevance to the educational philosophy of M.A.C.,

Washington did not make a single reference to the college by name and, instead, focused on the importance of industrial education and Tuskegee's accomplishments. Between his famous Atlanta Exposition speech in 1895 and the summer of 1900, Washington delivered countless speeches throughout the nation. Less than two weeks before arriving at M.A.C., six thousand people, Black and White, crammed into the Memorial Hall at St. Paul AME Church in Columbus, Ohio, to hear one of these talks. Like many Progressive Era politicians and popular orators, Washington recycled his speeches, many of which he agreed to deliver on short notice. There wasn't a need to customize his messages to predominantly White institutions. His aura alone was sufficient. His remarkable rise "up from slavery" was known the world over. By 1900, Washington had written numerous essays and several books including his famous *Up from Slavery* that was serialized in the widely read New York–based weekly magazine *The Outlook*.

About a month before the 1900 M.A.C. commencement exercises, Washington delivered a speech at the Metropolitan AME Church in Washington, D.C., sponsored by the Bethel Literary and Historical Association and published in the Washington *Colored American* on May 26, 1900. This talk essentially included everything he shared with his Collegeville listeners. As was the case with his earliest speeches and writings, in his M.A.C. commencement address, "Solving the Negro Problem in the Black Belt of the South," Washington wholeheartedly championed "the advantages of industrial training for the negro." He stressed that industrial education went part and parcel with "mental and moral training" and underscored his people's relationship with "the soil." This resonated with those M.A.C. students from farming families. Washington's notion of industrial education mirrored a plea for this brand of instruction detailed in a lengthy article, "Industrial Education," that appeared in the first volume of the *M.A.C. Record*.[1] "From the beginning of time agriculture has contributed to the main foundation upon which all races have grown useful and strong," Washington asserted. He reiterated his steadfast beliefs that "a negro boy," the likes of whom was most likely absent in the crowd, should not be preoccupied with seeking an education "that has no bearing upon the life of the community to which he should return." Frowning upon urbanization, he warned that city life was plagued by "sin and misery." He endorsed a type of education related to "the everyday practical affairs of life," what Snyder in August 1899 similarly called "the everyday affairs of life." Washington proclaimed, "We want more than the mere performance of mental gymnastics. Our knowledge must be harnessed to the real things in life."[2] These sentiments resonated with Snyder's message to the incoming class of 1899: "Education should conform to the spirit and progress of the times."[3]

In contextualizing his assessment of the best path forward, Washington, plainly exaggerating the historical record for effect, told his White listeners, "the white man is three thousand years ahead of the negro." This was a common catchphrase Washington often uttered to encourage Whites to view Black people—who were three and a half decades removed from enslavement— with empathy, perspective, and sensitivity. Washington explained that industrial education, which he believed evoked values of thrift, hard work, property ownership, and economic prosperity (i.e., "a bank account"), would somehow lead to wealth followed by leisure and, citing from the famed former abolitionist Frederick Douglass, space for "thoughtful reflection and the cultivation of the higher arts."[4] Parts of his speech could be considered conciliatory and sympathy-evoking. Yet Washington was well aware that he was inevitably a representative of Black people, something that *Detroit Free Press* writer Morris Wade trumpeted in his tribute to Washington in M.A.C.'s student paper a month before he arrived on campus. "Since the death of Fred Douglass, Booker T. Washington has been the most prominent representative of the negro race in America, and it is unquestionably true that Booker Washington is doing greater work for the advancement and elevation of his people than was ever done by Fred Douglass," Wade maintained; "the work of Booker Washington is eminently practical and its results are felt all over the South."[5] Washington was a quintessential "representative of the race." One of the only Black people at this event and certainly the solitary Black person to hold court at this major occasion, Washington let his White listeners know he sought to prepare Black men to enter the U.S. economy on a level playing field with their White counterparts.

"I plead for individual development, not because I want to cramp the negro, but because I want to free him," Washington, who founded the National Negro Business League in 1900, explained. "I want to see him enter the great and all-powerful business and commercial world." This type of rhetoric roused white supremacist Thomas Dixon Jr. to issue a warning to readers of the *Saturday Evening Post* five years after Washington spoke at M.A.C. Dixon, who spoke at M.A.C. in March 1902, authored the novel *The Clansman* (1905) that laid the foundations for D. W. Griffith's racist film *Birth of a Nation* (1915). "Mr. Washington is not training negroes to take their place in any industrial system of the South in which the white man can control him. He is not training his students to be servants," exhorted Dixon in 1905. "He is training them all to be masters of men, to be independent, to own and operate their own industries, plant their own fields, buy and sell their own goods, and in every shape and form destroy the last vestige of dependence on the white man for anything."[6]

Washington concluded his brief remarks at M.A.C. by bragging about what his followers and disciples had accomplished in Macon County, Alabama, in a relatively brief period. His reflections exuded notions of growth, self-reliance, and perseverance, key characteristics of his own life's path. Building upon the 1900 *M.A.C. Record* article applauding his achievements, Washington's digression into his overview of Tuskegee's success was deliberate and must have shocked more than a few of his White listeners. "If for a brief moment you will excuse me for the seeming egotism," Washington signified before lauding the exploits and handiwork of Tuskegee faculty and students, "I will tell you what a set of colored men and women have done at Tuskegee, Alabama, during the past nineteen years." He then wasted no time in delivering his familiar pitch, pronouncing: "Beginning in 1881, with absolutely no property, the Tuskegee Institute now owns 2,500 acres of land." Washington let the M.A.C. community—whose college's annual income from the U.S. government was about $95,000—know the valuation of his school, emphasizing that proud Black students were the builders of their own monuments. "There are upon the school grounds forty-eight buildings, and of these all except four have been wholly erected by the labor of the students," Washington continued; "students and their instructors have done the work from the drawing of the plans and making of the bricks to the putting in of the electrical fixtures." He promised his White listeners, many of whom might have bought into stereotypical notions of Black men as "brutes" and lawbreakers: "Not a single one of our graduates have even been convicted by any court of a crime. Not a single one of our graduates have ever been charged with the crime of attempting an insult upon a woman." Washington ensured that Tuskegee students were "valuable citizens" who received industrial training as well as "mental and religious training." He concluded his speech rather abruptly with a straightforward declaration of African American independence and self-determination. "We can now erect a building of any kind without going off the grounds to employ a single outside workman."[7] This was Washington's subtle way of saying, as Dixon pointed out, that Black people at Tuskegee were not reliant on White Americans. In his mind, they were essentially a nation within a nation.

Though this historic speech, along with a large portrait of Washington, was published in the June 26, 1900, issue of the *M.A.C. Record*, there was not any coverage of Washington's visit or oration in the paper. The only account of Washington's speech was offered by a writer for the *Herald-Palladium* (Benton Harbor, MI) who acknowledged that two of the city's residents witnessed Washington's address. The author briefly summarized Washington's talk, highlighting his endorsement of industrial education and "mental and moral training." The author underscored that Washington "would not confine the negro to industrial life but would teach the race that the best foundation that can be laid and the best service that can be rendered to higher education is to reach the present generation to provide a material or industrial foundation."[8] The students, who rarely, if ever, interacted with African Americans, must have been blown away by him. While there were at least two Black students at M.A.C in 1899, Grand Rapids native Charles A. Warren and William O. Thompson, members of the M.A.C. community were accustomed to seeing Blacks in subservient positions. Based upon its celebration of industrial education and agriculture as well as its messages of character building, practical thinking, and hard work, it's reasonable to assume Washington's oration was welcomed. The "principle of education" featured in the 1900 Michigan Agricultural College Calendar undoubtedly overlapped with Washington's lessons: "to learn to see by seeing: to learn to do by doing." The "four-year Courses" at M.A.C. sounded much like Tuskegee's approach: "all must include general culture; all require manual training; all are practical."[9]

How Washington was described based upon a speech he delivered to an interracial crowd of six thousand in Columbus, Ohio, three weeks before he visited M.A.C. serves as a window into how Washington's oratory might have come across. He was known to be a very lively and engaging orator. Under the header "Exemplar Force of Character," a tabloid journalist described Washington as if he had superhero powers.

Dr. Washington's physique, his face, head, and gestures typify the indomitable will and strength that carried him from a position of abject slavery to a commanding position in the nation as a missionary, looked to by negroes as a Moses of their race. The phrenologist at a glance can see the lines that make him a successful president of Tuskegee institute, the largest colored school in America. Although born under conditions that would make the ordinary man a humble citizen, he is today accepted as a power among leading white educators.

Dr. Washington walked on the stage at Memorial hall with a firm, confident tread, as one sure of his ground. His shoulders are broad and his six feet of stature gives the strength and poise to command respect. His hair is close cut and gives him the aspect of a war dog with all its tenacious fighting spirit. The eyes, however, gleam with kindliness and they temper the appearance of the latent fighting forces. The man's forehead is broad, high and shapely, with enough space to contain a plentiful supply of reasoning powers. His lips are then, drawn tight across his molars. They show strength of character. His jaw has the firmness of one who has the courage to stand by his convictions.[10]

Echoing James Creelman's sensationalist account of Washington's famed 1895 oration in Atlanta, Georgia, in the widely circulated *New York World*, this over-the-top description is hyperbolic and overdramatized. Nevertheless, it suggests Washington left memorable impressions on many of his listeners.[11]

Was President Snyder as impressed as the melodramatic Creelman or the enthusiastic journalist who covered Washington's speech in Columbus in 1900? He was most likely pleased with the man whom the *M.A.C. Record* in May 1900 broadcast as being "the most prominent representative of the negro race in America." Snyder's Alumni Day address a day before Washington's commencement speech reveals how he valued and approved of Washington's plain speak. In his sermon-like oration, Snyder dubbed M.A.C. the "oldest agricultural college in the United States . . . After which all the others have patterned." As Washington routinely espoused, Snyder asserted that farming required "knowledge of all the sciences," that farmers be educated in the indispensable liberal arts allowing for a more wholistic understanding of society. His description of agriculture as the cornerstone of the American way of life foreshadowed and harmonized with what Washington articulated a day later. "From the beginning of time agriculture has constituted the main foundation upon which all races have grown useful and strong," Washington told M.A.C. graduates and faculty. Similarly, at the "last meeting of this association [the M.A.C. Alumni Association] for this century," Snyder declared: "Agriculture is the basic 'bread and butter getting' for the entire nation. . . . All business is dependent upon agriculture."[12] The precise details of Washington's momentary visit to M.A.C. will most likely remain a mystery. This African American celebrity-leader's presence on campus represents a significant episode in the university's captivating history ripe with tradition. In 2020, a *Spartan Alumni Magazine* contributor surmised his speech "was a message that resonated with the student body and administration and one we continue to address today." The next African American to deliver a commencement day address at MSU would not come to campus until nearly three-quarters of a century later during the incumbency of John A. Hannah.

Washington's visit to M.A.C. opened the door to future visits to the state. In late January 1901, he spoke at the University of Michigan to the Good Government Club, and he returned to Ann Arbor in April 1907 to deliver a lecture to the university's Students' Lecture Association. The talk was "one of the best attended" events sponsored by the group, and U of M's longest serving president, James Burrill Angell, had nothing but praise for the Tuskegee Institute principal. Several months after dining in the White House with President Roosevelt and his family, in late December 1901, Washington was among the keynote speakers for the annual meeting of the Michigan State Teachers' Association in Grand Rapids. There were at least a few educators with M.A.C. connections who listened to his talk on the "Industrial Education at the South."[13] The local press praised his speech, crowning him "the Moses of the negro race in America" whose name "should be writ large in the national hall of fame."[14] Between 1901 and 1910, he spoke at widely celebrated events in Detroit, Mt. Pleasant, and Battle Creek, a particularly fruitful speaking engagement for Washington. Accepting a personal invitation from nutritionist John Harvey Kellogg, Washington presented at his Battle Creek Sanitarium on March 16, 1911, and received $10,000 in securities from D. K. Cornwell and another $2,000 from other donors. "His address was so appealing," wrote a journalist for the Saint Joseph *Herald-Press*, that Kellogg himself "sprang up" during his oration to give him $200. Washington left Kellogg's city "$12,000 richer than when he came."[15]

As announced in the *Lansing State Journal* and the *M.A.C. Record*, in 1912 Washington made an eight-day tour of Michigan that began on October 14, and earlier in the year, he had popped into the state. On February 13, he spoke at the annual Lincoln Club banquet in Grand Rapids, and on August 24, he was one of the headliners for the Paw Paw "Chautauqua." Five months before visiting Lansing, Washington sent one of his disciples, teacher R. D. Taborn, to the city to let Lansingites know about his remarkable work, how Tuskegee had "improve[d] modes of living," and the accomplishments of the school's nine thousand graduates.[16] Washington's 1912 fall Mid-Michigan tour was highly anticipated. In early October, the *State Journal* joyously announced Washington would be visiting the state capital in two weeks. "Lansing is particularly fortunate to secure him because he is in such great demand," a writer for the *Journal* noted. A week later, another writer for the *Journal* imparted that Washington's visit to Lansing was part of a larger tour of the state that included stops in Detroit, Ann Arbor, Ypsilanti, Adrian, Kalamazoo, Grand Rapids, Grand Haven, Muskegon, and Saginaw.[17]

Sponsored by an endowment from industrialist and philanthropist Andrew Carnegie, Washington's speech in Lansing at the YMCA's Masonic Temple on October 16, 1912, was free to the general public. The collection "taken up at the gathering" supported Tuskegee's "extension efforts." The Masonic Temple was "completely filled" by the time Washington took to the podium before a for the most part White audience. A small fraction of Lansing's small Black population was in the crowd, hanging on Washington's words. Several hours before the speech, Washington and his small delegation enjoyed lunch with sixty-five invited guests at the Hotel Downey. Snyder and other M.A.C. leaders probably broke bread with Washington. Select Lansing African American leaders were in attendance, and Blacks who worked in the hotel were delighted to catch a quick glimpse of the Black dignitary. For those unable to attend the widely publicized event, the *State Journal* reprinted Washington's entire speech.[18]

As he did in his 1900 M.A.C. commencement address, he recounted the history of Tuskegee and waxed on about how his school had transformed during the three decades after its founding. As was his habit, he celebrated "practical farming" and "mental training and education through the study of things." Washington talked more about the progress Blacks made in the South than he did at M.A.C. a dozen years earlier. Sampling from his famous 1895 "Atlanta Compromise" speech, he kowtowed to his White audience of potential donors. "We are a young race. Life is a new experience for our people," Washington maintained. "Now is the time to save us and keep us on our feet." He claimed African Americans, forty-seven years removed from slavery, were still "ignorant" because of this oppressive institution. He critiqued African Americans who sought higher education. "There have been frequent instances in which a young colored man graduated from college and impressed with the new found advantages of a diploma have immediately affected patent leather shoes, and a top hat, and too frequently has been pointed out an example of what education does to the negro." Whites and Blacks interpreted this statement differently. While Whites perceived Washington as instructing Blacks not to be uppity, the Blacks in the audience viewed this anecdote as being a comical way of telling them to remain humble, to avoid letting one's education and book learning impact their disposition and abilities to relate with the "masses" of their race. Washington ended his concise oration with a plea to support Tuskegee and with a hint of racial pride. "I wouldn't change color with the whitest white man. My race has a problem and no member of it need to be ashamed that he is black."[19] Following his visit to Lansing, Washington sent several of his coworkers back to the city to raise funds for his school. In late October 1912, R. D. Taborn, bearing "a letter of credentials" from Washington, was in the state's capital "soliciting funds."[20]

The announcement published in the *M.A.C. Record* poignantly summarized the objectives of Washington's Michigan circuit. "The purpose of this campaign is to awaken wherever possible, a wider and more intelligent interest in the work that this school and others like it are doing for the education and upbuilding of the negro race."[21] Though brief, Washington's visit to M.A.C. in June 1900 was historic and laid the foundations for further relationships he established in the state. M.A.C. alumni Charles Augustus Warren and William Ora Thompson worked at Tuskegee, personally knew Washington, and were inspired by him and his all-Black faculty collective. Myrtle Bessie Craig was aware of Washington's monumental achievements and heard stories about his historic visit to campus. In 1907, President Snyder recommended her to Washington and his wife, Margaret Murray, for a teaching position at Tuskegee. Pinpointing precisely how Washington's momentary presence on campus impacted the community's perceptions of African Americans or the future Black experience at the institution is impossible, but captivating nonetheless.

Chapter 5

Historic Commencement Ceremony

To most spectators and participants, the forty-seventh annual commencement at Michigan Agricultural College held on Wednesday, June 22, 1904, was a familiar scene. At first glance, onlookers didn't notice anything out of the ordinary. The year's proceedings were like recent rituals. Occurring shortly after the United States gained control over the Panama Canal, this graduation ceremony, like those preceding it, would not hold a candle to the much anticipated and historic semicentennial commencement day several years later on May 31, 1907, when President Theodore Roosevelt, accompanied by secret service men and "plenty of militia," addressed a "crowd that was estimated at 20,000" in front of the popular College Armory.[1] Evoking the title of Booker T. Washington's 1904 book *Working with the Hands*, Roosevelt's talk-of-the-town, inspirational, and long-winded address, "The Man Who Works with His Hands," was fittingly a nod to M.A.C.'s commitment to the agricultural sciences and farmers.

Without the pageantry of the monumental 1907 affair, the "well attended" 1904 commencement followed the usual routine. Beginning at 10:00 a.m., the program featured an invocation, musical and vocal performances, reflections from students from each of the college's three "courses," a keynote address, and the conferring of the degrees. "The different events were pleasant and," observed a writer for the *M.A.C. Record*, "everything passed off successfully." Unlike in some past issues of the college's paper, the late June 1904 issue printed the names of the graduates who earned bachelor of science degrees.[2] Of the fifty-seven listed, "27 graduated from the agricultural course, 19 from the mechanical and 9 from the women's." Toward the tail end of the list that took up several narrow columns in the *Record* was the name of an atypical soon-to-be M.A.C alumnus. Occupying two lines was the following name: "Thompson, William O., a, Indianapolis, Indiana."[3]

Did anyone realize the significance of this bachelor of science degree recipient? Curiously, his name wasn't listed in the official 1904 commencement program. Five fellow graduates also went unacknowledged in this memento. The specific circumstances surrounding why Thompson and five of his classmates were excluded from the program, we will never know. But we do know something with more certitude. Thompson joined the ranks of a small and distinctive group of history makers at M.A.C.[4] On this jubilant summer day in 1904, William Ora Thompson became the first-known African American to graduate from M.A.C. and the "a" following his name indicates that he had earned his degree, like nearly half of his fellow graduates, in the agricultural course, "the heart of the academic program" and the most popular field of study at the college during the early twentieth century.[5]

Reasonably assuming he was present at this event, one wonders what this historic occasion meant to this slender, light-complected, medium-height, Kentucky-born twenty-eight-year-old African American man whose parents, Savannah and Violet Thompson, were once enslaved. Born in the contentious decade of the 1850s, his parents were very proud of their son who had accomplished something they could have only dreamed about when they were about his age twenty years prior. Thompson himself had much to be proud of. The overwhelming majority of Black men his age labored in low-paying, back-breaking, and often wearisome agricultural and industrial jobs throughout the nation, primarily in the Jim Crow South. In the dawning of the twentieth century, close to 90 percent of African Americans lived in the South, and those fortunate enough to go to college didn't attend predominantly White institutions like M.A.C.

In the same year the governor of his Kentucky birthplace signed into law the "Day Law" that prohibited Whites and Blacks from attending the same schools, Thompson defied the odds. His accomplishment challenged the arguments made by his classmates on the M.A.C. debating team who, in their victory against Ypsilanti Normal in late April 1904, were tasked with affirming anti-Black legislation in Mississippi. According to W. E. B. Du Bois, who himself made history by becoming the first African American to earn a doctorate in history from Harvard University in 1895, Thompson was one of approximately 139 African Americans who graduated from an American university in 1904. Thompson was one of very few Black students out of a total student population of 917 at M.A.C. during the 1903–1904 academic year. Myrtle Bessie Craig and a small handful of Black students enrolled as "special" students were also at the college. During the early 1900s, most African American college and university students attended the more than seventy HBCUs.[6] Like his contemporaries at HBCUs and elsewhere, Thompson was a member of what Du Bois popularized as constituting the "Talented Tenth." As suggested by decisions he made later in his life, he was committed to uplifting the masses of his people, to a life of service.

Presuming he didn't miss out on this milestone, how might Thompson have experienced the commencement activities? Did he attend the baccalaureate sermon on Sunday, June 19, 1904? Was he, his family, his bride-to-be Henrietta King, or his friends invited to the reception at President Jonathan L. Snyder's home on the evening before graduation? Did he and his loved ones enjoy the refreshments consisting of ice cream, cake, and punch? Was he able "get acquainted" and have an "enjoyable time" in the company of his White classmates? What happened when he walked across the stage? Did he experience the type of support that "a number of Negro graduates" more than seven hundred miles away at the University of Nebraska purportedly did during the first decade of the twentieth century? "On commencement days a Negro usually receives a little more applause than a white boy when he walks over the stage," a Cornhusker official responded to a survey prepared by Du Bois and his colleagues around the time Thompson graduated. "I presume some things happen in his personal relations with his fellow students that are not entirely pleasant, but they never come to the surface. I doubt if there is a school in the country which is freer from race prejudice than the University of Nebraska."[7] Perhaps this optimistic observer was reminiscing on the days of his university's first Black football player who graduated in 1894, the popular, handsome, and future Nebraska Football Hall of Famer George Flippin. The first African American football player at M.A.C., the talented Gideon E. Smith, arrived in East Lansing in 1912, two decades after Flippin set foot on the University of Nebraska's gridiron.[8]

There are numerous questions that can be raised about how Thompson experienced the 1904 commencement ceremony and what this special day meant to him, his fiancée, his parents and siblings, members of the recently renamed George R. Collins African Methodist Episcopal Church to which he belonged, and the small African American Lansing community in which he resided. Perhaps even more thought-provoking, assuming Thompson was at the commencement to receive his diploma, is what he made of the racial harangue spewed by the commencement speaker of the hour, internationally known agricultural chemist and the then president of Georgia's State College of Agriculture and Mechanic Arts, Dr. H. C. White.[9]

A leading spokesperson for scientific farming in the United States as well as an outspoken advocate of Charles Darwin's theory of evolution and the social Darwinism espoused by Yale professor William Graham Sumner, White praised M.A.C., the mission of land-grant universities writ large, and the necessity of intellectual inquiry. His commencement address also overflowed with rudimentary white supremacist ideologies and an unmistakably racialized vision of American patriotism and democracy. For him, there was a clear separation of the races and a firm racial hierarchy. Evoking concepts of "racial wealth," "racial necessity," and "American racial pride" while encouraging the graduates to "stand united and unshaken in their determination to make their common country a land of liberty, enlightenment and peace," this social Darwinist candidly shared his perceptions of Thompson and his people.

This college president and respected scholar of fertilizers trumpeted that "intellectual power" and ability "have been restricted in the past and are restricted in the present to one only of the races—the Aryan—and their lineal descendants." The "Greeks alone," in White's universe, were the world's culture bearers and thinkers; "only the lineal descendants of this same great Aryan race possess this habit and its consequence." He continued, "Gentlemen this intellectual basis is the real and substantial foundation for our pride in what we sometimes call our Anglo Saxon purity of blood. . . . The American people have made wide provision for the full developmens [*sic*] and abundant fruitage of this racial power." This member of Britain's prestigious Royal Chemical Society concluded his racist rant with sentiments that deliberately excluded Thompson and the nine White women graduates. "Truly, the Aryan-descended, English-speaking, self-reliant American college man has cause to regard his Alma Mater with personal affection, manly administration and patriotic pride." White carried on, "Gratefully, gentlemen, the stranger within your gates, moved to admiration for the many and mighty energies of your Commonwealth and for the high ideals and wise activities of this institution, recognizes kinship in purpose, in endeavor, in destiny, from Michigan to Georgia of the American citizen and the American college man."[10]

This drawn-out commencement address was a blatant verbal assault on Thompson's humanity. It was an affront to his, among others', accomplishments, intellect, and struggles. How did President Snyder, who four years earlier welcomed with open arms Booker T. Washington as a distinguished guest within M.A.C.'s "gates," perceive this fellow university president's anti-Black thought? For Snyder, the State Board of Agriculture, and the M.A.C. community, White was no doubt a logical and ideal distinguished guest. His renowned work in scientific agriculture, investigations into soil improvement processes, and leadership of the Georgia Experiment Station were acutely relevant to M.A.C.'s overarching mission. Since both were presidents of outreach-oriented agricultural institutions that belonged to the Association of Agricultural Colleges and Experiment Stations, Snyder on occasion rubbed shoulders with White. Three years after White spoke at M.A.C., at the 1907 historic graduation ceremony, M.A.C. granted him an honorary degree for his "distinguished" educational work and research. As historian Lester D. Stephens has argued, White's "distinguished standing no doubt made it difficult for critics to attack his position as an evolutionist." His "view was not unique; other contemporary American racial theorists, like Theodore Roosevelt, espoused the same idea."[11]

Other writers with racist tendencies spoke at M.A.C. commencements during the early twentieth century. Eugenicist David Starr Jordan, the author of *The Blood of the Nation: A Study in the Decay of the Races by the Survival of the Unfit* (1902), spoke at the 1915 graduation festivities. During Snyder's presidency several other types of outspoken Progressive Era reformers also held court at M.A.C commencement ceremonies. Jane Addams, settlement house activist, social worker, and women's suffragist, became the first woman to deliver the keynote commencement address at M.A.C. in 1908. Heard by those who crowded the College Armory to its "utmost capacity," Addams's speech was unquestionably different from White's. For whatever reason, in Addams's case, the *M.A.C. Record* sidestepped what appears to have been a tradition by not publishing her address.[12] Ida M. Tarbell, investigative journalist and author of the influential *The History of the Standard Oil Company* (1904), spoke in 1913, and Thomas Mott Osborne, the radical prison reformer and author of *Within Prison Walls* (1914), spoke in 1914.

Whatever might have influenced the powers that be at M.A.C. in 1904 to invite an outspoken advocate of Aryan supremacy to speak at graduation, the episode provides some insight into a microcosm of what Thompson had to endure, contend with, and sort out on this special day for him. He had much to prove as M.A.C.'s first-known Black graduate. The burdens of being a "Black first" were simultaneously joyful and overwhelming. Along with countless others, he was living proof that H. C. White was wrong. In a 1905 letter in response to an inquiry about the college's racial attitudes, Snyder, without specifically mentioning Thompson's feat or Craig's presence on campus, replied: "There is no antipathy in this institution against colored students or students from foreign countries. They would receive fair and cordial treatment from everyone."[13] We will never know if Snyder's claim rang true for Thompson. There's evidence that several M.A.C. students of color encountered some racism during the Progressive Era.[14] Stereotypes about African Americans seem to have been acceptable and not uncommon at M.A.C. during Thompson's years. Several months before he graduated, for instance, the Eclectic Literary Society sponsored a minstrel show with blackface performers who received "frequent" encores.[15] As a Black man who grew up in Indiana, Thompson was not naïve when it came to such anti-Black behavior.

Thompson's presence as a student was publicly acknowledged long before the June 21, 1904, issue of the *M.A.C. Record* printed his and his fellow graduates' names. On October 3, 1899, the *Record* listed Thompson among the 272 incoming students. This time listed as "Thompson, W. O.," he was one of the seventy-nine students in the "Agriculture Course."[16] The only freshman from Indiana and one of the less than ten not from Michigan, his arrival to campus was not met with any fanfare as was the case with another person of color, Louis Garcia de Quevedo from Cayey de Muesas, Puerto Rico.[17] As was the practice at M.A.C. in the early twentieth century, none of the college's records referred to Thompson's or other students' race. Similarly, the college didn't spotlight its Black firsts. The first reference to a Black student making history at the college came about a decade after Thompson graduated. In November 1913, the *Record* casually announced that football star Gideon E. Smith, '16, was the "first colored lad" to earn a M.A.C. monogram.

Chapter 6

Class of 1900
Honorable Mention

Thompson wasn't the only African American student cataloged in the *M.A.C. Record* in 1899. A revealing thumbnail sketch featured prominently on the front page of the October 31, 1899 issue of the paper under the header "A Senior Goes to Tuskegee" reads:

> C. A. Warren, a member of the senior class, has accepted the position of assistant in horticulture at the Tuskegee Normal and Industrial Institute in Alabama. Three years ago he entered the mechanical course at M. A. C. but after a year's work changed to the agricultural course, because he thought there were better opportunities in the south for *colored* young men trained along agricultural lines. His opportunity came before graduation. Mr. Warren went to Grand Rapids last week to spend a few days at home before going south.[1]

The decision of the faculty and student editors of the M.A.C. community's paper to publish this update about Warren's resolution to leave their campus for Tuskegee before graduating is intriguing. While alumni were invited to send the *Record* updates on their progress and achievements, the paper didn't regularly report on students who decided to leave before completing their degrees, unless, perchance, for military service or other important reasons. Warren's ability to land a job at Booker T. Washington's school was considered a major accomplishment that the paper wanted to publicize. Warren did what many M.A.C. students, especially those from poor and working-class farming families, hoped to. They enrolled in M.A.C. to acquire an education—the "brain training" and "hand training"—that would allow them to secure a job, make a living, and become leaders and model citizens within their communities. Months earlier, in January 1899, in anticipation of Washington's visit, the *M.A.C. Record* celebrated the work of the the famous Black leader, and Warren was headed to work with this celebrity. Jonathan L. Snyder no doubt recommended Warren to Washington who, years earlier, wrote to President Oscar Clute in search of potential teachers to serve African Americans in the Black Belt.

That Warren was able to land his job and embrace "his opportunity" before graduating was viewed as a success for many M.A.C. students who had left school prior to graduating for a host of reasons. The tenor of the paragraph is intriguing for another reason. Intimating Warren was a "colored" young man, whom they dignified with the title of "Mr.," this is conceivably the first time the editors of the *M.A.C. Record* indicated they had a Black student among their ranks. The man identified as "C. A. Warren" was Charles Augustus Warren. He was born in Saginaw, Michigan, most likely on December 25, 1871.[2] His father, an African American named Joseph Warren, was born in Virginia in 1830. In 1850, he was among the free Blacks in the 98th Regiment in Mecklenburg County, Virginia. He was a free Black when 88 percent of African Americans were enslaved and approximately 30 percent of Virginia's total population consisted of enslaved African Americans. Joseph's occupation was listed as an assistant on a farm. At age twenty, he was a farm laborer living with his parents and four of his siblings. In 1859 in Windsor, Ontario, about nine months before John Brown and his posse's raid on Harpers Ferry Armory in Harpers Ferry, Virginia, Joseph married Charles's mother, Michigan-born Sarah Miner Judson. Their marriage was unique for the time. It was an interracial union: Joseph was Black and Sarah was White.

Between 1860 and 1869, Charles's parents had two daughters and one son and lived in Windsor and Sarnia, Canada. Sometime between 1868 and 1869, Joseph and Sarah migrated to Saginaw where their fourth child was born. Born during the era of Reconstruction six months before President Ulysses Grant signed into law the Enforcement Act of 1871, Charles was the fifth of his parents' six children. In 1870, Joseph worked as a plasterer and owned real estate valued at $200. Sarah was a housewife busy taking care of her children. With his five siblings, Charles grew up in East Saginaw's Third Ward, and sometime between 1874 and the late 1890s the Warren family relocated to Grand Rapids, Michigan. Census takers variously ascribed race to Charles, though he clearly self-identified as a Black man. His 1902 marriage record lists his race as "Mulatto." In the U.S. federal census records for 1910 and 1920, he is also identified as being "Mulatto." In 1930, he is listed as being "Negro," and in 1940, while residing in Cassopolis, Michigan, he's listed as being "White" with three years of college education.

Because he was twenty-four years old when he applied to M.A.C. and began taking courses in the fall of 1896, he was probably admitted without having to take an entrance examination. As a resident of Michigan, he benefited from the free tuition offered to in-state students. He was required to pay for his lodging off campus and other living expenses. Listed as "Warren, C. A., Grand Rapids, Mich." in the "New Students" section in a fall 1896 issue of the *M.A.C. Record*,

Warren and members of the class of 1900. Warren is standing on the far right. Courtesy of Michigan State University Archives and Special Collections.

he was one of about one hundred incoming freshmen.[3] Warren was attracted to M.A.C. for a variety of reasons. Not only was he a Michigan native residing in his home state who reaped the benefits of "free tuition," but the celebratory advertisements routinely appearing in the *Record* appealed to his sensibilities. Located "fifteen minutes from Lansing by electric car," the college offered "pleasant and beautiful surroundings," low expenses, a "broad, thorough, and practical education," first-class faculty, and nearly $500,000 worth of equipment. The advertisements, however, failed to mention that African American students were apparently not welcome to stay in the dormitories and a ride from Lansing to the Beal Street entrance on campus cost a nickel.[4]

Warren entered the mechanical course track. Created in 1885 to expand M.A.C.'s scope, in 1896 this field of study was described as "comprising the general work in mathematics, language, etc., with special training in mechanics and electricity" and was "supplemented by practical application, in manual labor, of the principles taught in the classroom." M.A.C. promised that students would receive "thorough training" in the particulars of "steam engine[s], steam boilers, valve gears, machine design, strength of materials, kinematics, thermodynamics." When Warren entered M.A.C., he was being educated to participate in America's Gilded Age. Following in his father's footsteps, he soon changed his focus to the agricultural course. His desire to study agriculture was influenced by William James Beal's observation that "the agricultural division had the advantage of size of equipment" and a much longer tradition than the "engineering course." In the agricultural course, he was required to "devote twelve and one-half hours per week to manual labor on the farm or garden." This course of study included "all subjects in agriculture and horticulture, English language and literature, botany, chemistry, zoology, veterinary science, physical science and political economy."[5]

When Warren entered M.A.C., professors Howard Edwards, Clinton D. Smith, and Frank S. Kedzie conducted a study exploring why the college's enrollment was on the decline. They called for several changes and improvements, especially the offering of "more teaching of technical or practical subjects during the freshman and sophomore years."[6] Warren also entered M.A.C. shortly after Jonathan L. Snyder became president. During Warren's first year, Snyder initiated what he called "radical changes," introducing "a course for young women" and shifting the "long vacation" from the winter to the summer. In 1896, the academic year was subdivided into three terms, beginning on September 14. The last term ended on June 20. On the eve of Warren's arrival in Collegeville, the streetcar line had recently been extended to the college's west entrance, making his trek to campus from the Lansing area more convenient. M.A.C.'s extension efforts expanded during his time at M.A.C., and Warren later embraced such activities at Tuskegee Institute.[7] At M.A.C., Warren learned that "the study and teaching of agriculture and engineering trained practically minded people to serve society in both the country and the city."[8] This notion of service was also exemplified at Tuskegee Institute.

It's unknown why Warren decided to leave M.A.C. one year before graduating with a degree in the agricultural specialization. Was he frustrated with his coursework? Did he feel marginalized in this environment where Blacks were virtually absent? The twenty-seven-year-old Michigan native might have simply been ready for a change, to embark on a new phase of his life's journey. He wasn't unique. Nongraduates from M.A.C. "made up 82 percent of the total number of students who had enrolled by 1900." Unlike 75 percent of these nongraduates, after leaving M.A.C. Warren didn't reside in Michigan at the turn of the century.[9] Warren went to the Deep South to Tuskegee Normal and Industrial Institute to join its faculty sometime in late October or early November 1899. Washington recruited him. Warren thought long and hard about leaving Lansing and venturing to the Deep South six months after the brutal and widely publicized lynching of Sam Hose in the presence of two thousand people in Newnan, Georgia, located less than one hundred miles from Tuskegee, Alabama. Nationwide, the burning of Hose was widely covered by the press, including in numerous Michigan newspapers. "His ears and fingers cut off one by one, body saturated with oil and then cremated," appeared in all capital letters on the front page of the Monday, April 24, 1899, issue of the *Detroit News*. The *Livingston Republic* described in detail how Hose was tortured and how his body parts were procured by some as souvenirs.

Citing from U.S. Attorney General John W. Griggs, the article in this Livingston County paper pessimistically noted "that the case had no federal aspect and that therefore the government would not take action wherever in this case."[10]

Warren's three and a half years of education at M.A.C. was enough to secure him employment as a teacher of horticulture at a leading HBCU. M.A.C. provided its students with a noticeably more advanced and scientific education than did Tuskegee. About a decade before Warren accepted the teaching position at Tuskegee, Booker T. Washington delivered his famous Atlanta Exposition oration, putting his school on the map as a recipient of altruistic White philanthropic charity. Keenly aware of M.A.C.'s reputation in scientific agriculture, Washington was pleased to have Warren join him and his coworkers in the Black Belt. When Warren arrived at Tuskegee, it was in its seventeenth year and, as Washington would boast about a year later while speaking at M.A.C. in 1900, was doing quite well and growing. The population of the country-town city of Tuskegee was about two thousand, many of whom lived on Washington's sprawling campus. That Warren was recruited to teach at Tuskegee is noteworthy. As historian Crystal R. Sanders argues, between 1881 and 1915, Washington explicitly mobilized and employed a "highly educated," "service-oriented," and exceptional "all-Black academic corps," challenging white supremacy and showcasing Black excellence. Warren and his colleagues modeled "the capabilities of African Americans within a climate of racism and repression" and "implicitly demonstrated Black potential." With Warren and his colleagues, Sanders suggests, Washington abandoned elements of Hampton Institute's industrial education model and "assembled a form of Black power and Black intellectual heft."[11] Unlike in East Lansing, at Tuskegee Warren was surrounded by like-minded Black intellectuals and social reformers. His brief Tuskegee experience significantly molded his trajectory.

There are glimpses into Warren's brief stay in Macon County, Alabama, suggesting he found a type of Black community that eluded him at M.A.C. and the Black communities he called home in Michigan. In May 1900, the *Tuskegee Student*, the school's paper, reported that Warren performed in "a rendition of Shakespeare's immortal Othello" at Washington's newly constructed home, "the Oaks." Warren played the role of "Cassio."[12] In 1901, Warren was also listed among the ten Tuskegee Experiment Station staff who worked under the guidance of its director, George Washington Carver. Warren applied what he learned at M.A.C. and learned tricks of the trade from this genius who, like his counterparts at M.A.C., worked closely with farmers and employed scientific agriculture in practical ways.[13]

The breadth and range of Carver's knowledge "was a decisive factor in his being one of the most effective agricultural educators and scientific popularizers of his era." Through Carver's Tuskegee Experiment Station, Warren connected with Black farmers who received practical advice pertaining to fertilizers, cotton production, livestock raising, soil regeneration, and a variety of crops such as cow peas, sweet potatoes, and later peanuts. With limited resources and funds, Carver and his coworkers were determined to help farmers. Warren and his colleagues

George Washington Carver (*front row center*) with his staff at Tuskegee Institute in 1902. It's possible that Warren is in this photo (*far right front row*). Courtesy of the Library of Congress Prints and Photographs Division, Washington, D.C.

made enormous sacrifices. Carver remarked of the work in which Warren and his contemporaries were engaged, "neither time nor expense will be spared to make our work of direct benefit to every farmer." He and his team also distributed free bulletins to farmers, literature that translated complex agricultural science to laypersons.[14]

With his well-rounded education from M.A.C., Warren educated his students not only in horticulture, but also in the realm of what Washington called "character building," service, and racial uplift. Washington's employees worked under a strict system and often complained of being overworked and underpaid. On average, notes Crystal Sanders, Tuskegee "lost ten of its approximately fifty faculty members a year during the 1890s." "Teachers at Tuskegee dreaded the sound of the carriage wheels in the night that signaled the return of Booker T. Washington to the campus," surmised one of Washington's biographers, "for they knew that the following morning he would be out inspecting every nook and cranny of his institution with an obsessive detail."[15] Washington preached that his teachers' mission was centered on the notion of representing and uplifting their people. Warren and other Tuskegee faculty met with Washington during weekly meetings when he was on campus and were evaluated on an annual basis.

In June 1901, Warren, who seems to have been given honorary status as a 1900 graduate of M.A.C., "stopped at the college for a few hours on a short vacation" and became the first African American student to publish in the *M.A.C. Record*.[16] On June 11, 1901, his piece "Some Remarks on Tuskegee" was published. *Record* editors promised his remarks "will be of much interest to our readers." After humbly noting that Tuskegee "will not boast of equality with M.A.C., in its capacity for educational work," he celebrated Tuskegee's growth. "The work of the institution is indeed far reaching," Warren observed. "Character as well as knowledge is fostered by the institution and the aim is to send out men who will be leaders among men of their own race. They shall be men and women strong mentally, physically, and morally, placing the emphasis on the morals. Tuskegee stands as a living monument to the untiring, unceasing worthy founder and principal, of whom the country north and south is proud."[17] Six months after his short vacation from the Black Belt, Warren was among the more than sixty M.A.C. alumni and friends of the college to attend a reunion in Grand Rapids at the Park Congregational Church. Sponsored by the newly organized Grand Rapids M.A.C. Association, this supper featured about a dozen speakers, including President Snyder who was the keynote attraction. In his talk, "The College Transit—a Look Backward and a Glance Ahead," he praised the new organization, reflected upon the college's past and future, and celebrated industrial education. Immediately preceding the college's fearless leader, Warren, respectfully identified as being "with '00," delivered a talk titled "Students' Courtesy, a Pleasant Remembrance of College Life." Expanding upon his musings published in the *Record* in June 1901, he "briefly contrasted his experiences" at Tuskegee with "his career at M.A.C. and thanked his associates for the kindly courtesy shown him."[18] The association valued what Warren had to offer. He was one of the group's forty-one members to take to the podium at this formal event. He also opened for Snyder. Warren let his colleagues know how a Black man was carrying on the M.A.C. spirit. He represented his alma mater and race with dignity, grace, and success.

Warren left his post at Tuskegee sometime in 1902. According to a biographical sketch in *Michigan Manual of Freedmen's Progress* (1915), complied by the secretary of the Freedmen's Progress Commission and Charles's older brother, Francis H. Warren, Charles "was engaged as Professor of Agriculture at Tuskegee, Ala." And in "1902, Mr. Warren returned to Michigan and settled in Cass County, where he engaged in farming."[19] Warren participated in M.A.C.'s farmers' institutes in Cass County. Likewise, an announcement in the "Alumni Notes" section of the *M.A.C. Record* in January 1913 indicates he once again identified as a member of the class of 1900, had for ten years "managed a farm in Cass Co.," and had just been appointed a "messenger to the governor."[20] The historical record suggests Warren's claims of managing a farm for a decade might have been exaggerated. Why did Warren leave Tuskegee? Perhaps life in the Jim Crow South didn't appeal to his sensibilities. As a northerner, he was taken aback by what he witnessed there. It was a completely different world. Though Michigan was by no means absent of racial prejudice, the racial order in Alabama was more strictly enforced and explicit. In Alabama, he would have never been able to have participated in an event like the Grand Rapids M.A.C. Association supper. In Tuskegee, he lived on or near campus in an isolated Black world in the Black Belt. After spending a few years in Macon County, Alabama, the Midwest cities of Saginaw, Lansing, Grand Rapids, and Detroit seemed like urban centers. His later life also suggests he was more comfortable collaborating with African Americans who were more outspoken about Black civil rights than Booker T. Washington or his disciples were.

The 1902 city directory for Grand Rapids, Michigan, indicates Warren lived as a boarder at "346 Jefferson av." In early October 1902, in Cassopolis, Michigan, he married Edna B. Harris, described as being a twenty-six-year-old "Mulatto." His occupation was listed as "Agriculturalist." In 1908, he lived in the same residence and worked as a "porter" for Stickley Bros. Company. When Warren resided in Grand Rapids, the Black population numbered between 600 and 650, and his formal training in agriculture made him stand out in the city. In 1910, there were about a dozen Black farmers in Kent County who collectively owned 522 acres of land valued at $43,450. But in Grand Rapids there were hardly any Black men working in agriculture, forestry, or animal husbandry. Forty-seven percent of Black men worked in domestic and personal service, 31 percent in manufacturing and mechanical industries, 10.5 percent in transportation, 4.7 percent in trade, and 2.2 percent in clerical occupations. Only 3.3 percent were employed in the various professional service positions. There were three clergymen, one lawyer, and several professional musicians by trade.[21]

Warren returned to Lansing by 1910, securing a job as a janitor at the state capital. William O. Thompson, '04, was also in Lansing working in menial jobs. In 1910, there were 354 African Americans in Lansing, 300 of whom were ten years of age and older. Eighty-three percent of the Black male population was ten years of age and older, compared to 27 percent of Black women. While Lansing had the same Black population as Jackson and a larger Black population than Saginaw and Bay City, it had less than Kalamazoo and Grand Rapids and dramatically less than Detroit whose Black population in 1910 was 5,741. In 1910, 33.5 percent of the 17,115 Blacks in Michigan resided in Detroit, and most of Michigan's Black population labored in domestic and personal service (44 percent), followed by manufacturing and mechanical pursuits (23 percent), agriculture, forestry, and animal husbandry (16 percent), transportation (6.7 percent), trade (4.2 percent), and professional service (3.4 percent). According to the authors of the *Michigan Manual of Freedmen's Progress*, African Americans in the state "have demonstrated their ability to control the forces of nature." In 1910, there were 640 farms operated by Blacks, 27 percent of which were in Cass County. Only five of these Black-owned farms were in Ingham County.[22]

In Lansing, African American men like Warren and Thompson had limited opportunities. In 1910, among other occupations, 56 percent of Black men were working in manufacturing and mechanical industries, 27.4 percent in domestic and personal service, 5.1 percent in transportation, and 3.4 percent each in trade, clerical occupations, and professional service. In 1910 in Lansing, there was one Black man working in "public service" out of a total of sixty-six in the state, thirty-four of whom were in Detroit. Lansing's Black community was small and tight knit in 1910, representing 2 percent of the Black population in Michigan and 1 percent of Lansing's population. In 1907, the Lansing Afro-American Business Men's Association held an Emancipation Day celebration that drew people from throughout the state. Founded in the aftermath of the Civil War, during the early twentieth century, the African Methodist Episcopal (AME) church was a cornerstone of the community, "kept open every night and day." Its members, as Rev. Joseph W. Jarvis proclaimed, were "devoted to [the] racial uplift effort." The church represented "practically the nucleus of the race betterment movement in this part of the state."[23] Warren held various leadership positions in the church.

In 1913, the twenty-eighth governor of Michigan, Woodbridge Nathan Ferris, appointed Warren to a clerkship in his office. Ferris, who founded and led Ferris Industrial School, had a relatively progressive stance toward admitting Black students. Gideon E. Smith, the future Aggie football superstar, attended Ferris's school on the eve of arriving in East Lansing. By the mid-1910s, Warren had become an energetic Black activist and amateur historian. Months after he and his wife tragically lost their six-year-old son, Harold, in the summer of 1914, Governor Ferris appointed a delegation of African American citizens to attend the Lincoln Jubilee and Celebration of Half Century of Negro Freedom in Chicago from late August until mid-September 1915. Ferris singled out Warren to "issue invitations to 57 Negro citizens of Michigan, of various occupations, to meet with the Governor and discuss ways to gain legislative support," prepare for the Lincoln Jubilee, and then produce a book highlighting the accomplishments of the state's Black community since the end of slavery. Warren embraced this leadership position, strategizing with fellow Black activists from Lansing and the state in late February 1915 at Lansing's AME church.[24]

Warren's older brother, Francis, was a lawyer for the Detroit branch of the NAACP "who prosecuted many cases of race discrimination" and served as the editor of the *Detroit Informer: An Afro-American Journal of News and Opinion*. He helped get Act 47, Public Act 1915 passed. Introduced by Senator Edgar Allan Planck on March 2, 1915, with $5,000 of approved funding, this bill led to the creation of the Freedmen's Progress Commission in late April 1915. This group was responsible for assembling an enormous exhibit for the celebratory Lincoln Jubilee exposition and quickly preparing a history, "The Negro in Michigan." Along with his outspoken brother, Charles Warren was one of the seven members of the distinguished executive committee. William O. Thompson was among the many "Honorary Vice-Presidents." Charles, who helped write the 370-plus page *Michigan Manual of Freedmen's Progress* and manned the "Poultry; Farm Products" exhibit at the Michigan Exhibit of Freedmen's Progress at the exposition in Chicago, was a well-respected member of the Freedmen's Progress Commission as well as Lansing's and the state's Black activist community.[25] In October 1917, as reported in the *Lansing State Journal*,

Warren, the first African American in Michigan to hold the position of executive office messenger under both a Republican and Democrat administration, demonstrated his patriotism by receiving "the first liberty bond seen in the state house. It was of $50 denomination and of the first issue of 1917." There was another Black man with interesting M.A.C. connections who served as an officer of the Freedmen's Progress Commission. Born in 1868 in Van Buren County, Michigan, William Ross Roberts was "one of the best-known characters around the state capitol building." A resident of Lansing from 1901 until his death in 1924, he worked as a clerk for the secretary of state, Governor Fred M. Warner, the Board of State Auditors, the State Board of Corrections and Charities, and the Michigan State Penology Commission. He was one of Mid-Michigan's most talented engrossers. In his spare time, for approximately twenty years this prominent man in "colored Masonic circles" and skilled portrait painter engrossed, with fine-tuned calligraphy, the diplomas for Lansing's high schools, Central Michigan Normal School, and M.A.C.[26] Was Roberts aware that eleven of the names he inscribed on M.AC. diplomas belonged to African Americans? Warren and Thompson no doubt shared with him stories about what it was like to be Black at America's first agricultural college.

Like Roberts, who diligently served as a trustee for AME pastor W. P. Q. Byrd from 1905 until 1908, Warren was active in Lansing's AME church and Lansing's Black community. An accomplished soloist, he often sang Negro spirituals at church functions and from time to time was "in charge of the service." Given the title "Rev." by a writer for the *State Journal*, in 1919 Warren was one of the "seven delegates from Ingham County" to attend a "training conference" organized by the Interchurch World Movement in Detroit. By 1920, Warren owned a home in Lansing and through the early 1920s worked as a "Messenger" for the governor's office, serving both Governors Albert Sleeper and Alex J. Groesbeck. He was one of the only African Americans to hold such a position in the state capital, vexing at least some White Lansing residents. In March 1920, for instance, the *State Journal* called Warren the "colored messenger in the office of Governor Sleeper" who "was getting kind o' uppity" when he attempted to sign a requisition paper as "Gov. Albert E. Sleeper, by C. A. Warren." By the early 1920s, Warren's status as an activist, mover and shaker, and institution builder in his adopted city grew. He lived at 1224 W. St. Joseph Street, and on October 8, 1920, with his wife Edna, he founded a "colored community house." Located near his home at W. St. Joseph and Logan Streets, this building served as "a headquarters" and "center of activity" for Lansing's Black residents. It was the "only place of its kind." By 1921, the center had "hotel accommodations for 20 persons and a dining room." Many Black professionals stayed there, including civil rights activist and former U.S. representative for South Carolina, George Washington Murray. The Warrens didn't seek to financially profit from this establishment. Instead, they were driven by "humanitarian principles" and sought to provide Lansing's Black community with entertainment, social functions, and programs, such as debating and literary events. Serving the youth was also important, as revealed by the community house's Young Peoples Committee. In 1921, sixteen-year-old Mabel Lucas, who attended Lansing

Central High School and later graduated from Michigan State in 1927, was a member of the center's Sunday Afternoon Program Committee.[27]

In May 1930, the *State Journal* listed Warren as being one of the "leading colored citizens of Lansing" who was a member of the Lansing Colored Business, Professional and Civic League.[28] At the time, he was working as a caretaker for Michigan State College. Three decades after he left, the first African American to be identified with a M.A.C. graduating class worked as a manual laborer at his alma mater. How did he feel about being back on campus in this capacity? Did he offer any advice to the handful of Black students on campus at the time? It doesn't appear he worked at Michigan State College of Agriculture and Applied Science for very long. During the early to mid-1930s while still living in Lansing, he held various jobs, including working in real estate. By the late 1930s, four decades after stepping foot on M.A.C.'s campus, at the age of sixty-eight he lived in Cassopolis, Michigan, in a home that he owned on Okeefe Street. The first-known African American to attend M.A.C. full time lived a very long life. At the age of ninety-two-years-old, he died in Niles, Michigan in late June of 1964.[29]

When William Ora Thompson arrived at M.A.C. early in the fall of 1899, Warren had already made up his mind to leave campus for Tuskegee. Thompson crossed paths with Warren but didn't develop a deep relationship with his predecessor then. This took place later in 1915 when they worked together in the Freedmen's Progress Commission and on the National Half Century Anniversary of Negro Freedom and Lincoln Jubilee. In 1899, there were no college social organizations that would have brought the two men together on campus. The first Black fraternity at Michigan College of Agriculture and Applied Science, Alpha Phi Alpha (Gamma Tau chapter), was founded almost half a century later, and Thompson's son, William Horton Thompson, would fittingly be among its founding members. Unlike during the late 1960s when it was commonplace for Black Spartans to actively help recruit other Blacks to come to MSU, in 1899 there were no nurturing Black social networks on campus. The Black Students' Alliance didn't exist. Supported by his family, Thompson, like Warren, navigated M.A.C. without the support of a Black student community, something that's been vital to African American students at MSU since the assassination of Martin Luther King Jr.

Chapter 7

Alumnus Extraordinaire

The eldest of four siblings, William Ora Thompson, named after his paternal grandfather, was born on November 22, 1875, in Kentucky. His father, Savannah Paris Thompson, and his mother, Violet Dixon, were once enslaved. Savannah was born on October 2, 1853, and Violet was born in the same year on August 15. Savannah and Violet experienced the traumas of enslavement as children and were twelve years old when the Thirteenth Amendment (1865) abolished slavery. The 1870 U.S. federal census indicates Savannah was living in Vanceburg, Kentucky, with sixteen others who ranged in age from three to fifty-three, suggesting he worked on a plantation as a field hand or sharecropper. His occupation was listed as a day laborer who could neither read nor write. The 1920 census also listed him as being illiterate. Violet Dixon, who was born in Louisville, wasn't living with William's father at this time. In 1875, the year of William's birth and when a short-lived Civil Rights Act was signed into law by President Ulysses S. Grant, Savannah and Violet were married, and in about 1877 they moved to Indianapolis, Indiana. Thompson's family relocated to Indianapolis when Marion County was experiencing tremendous growth, and Savannah worked in a range of manual labor jobs, including as a laborer, driver, teamster, and butcher. Violet, who was literate according to the census reports of 1900 and 1910, spent a significant amount of time keeping house, raising and supporting her children—two sons and two daughters—born in 1875 (William), 1877, 1881, and 1895. Like many Black women of her generation, she worked at home as a seamstress and weaver, passing on her skilled trade to her daughters. The Thompson parents shaped William's and his siblings' world views with stories about their lives during slavery, the Civil War, Reconstruction, and the early years of the post-1877 nadir of Black life.

From 1860 until 1900, the Black population in Indiana increased dramatically, by more than five times. Several years after the Thompsons migrated to Indianapolis, in 1880, there were about 6,500 Blacks in the city. In 1900, the Black population in Indianapolis—the seventh largest African American population in a northern city—was 15,931, representing 9.4 percent of the city's total population. In 1900, the Black population in Indianapolis was equal to the entire Black population of Michigan (15,816) and almost four times the Black population of Detroit. At the turn of the century, African Americans in the Thompsons' adopted city were largely poor and working-class. Yet they lived in their own thriving communities with plenty of businesses, restaurants, neighborhoods, and homes, and an active professional class. There were more than fifty Black churches, and the congregation that Thompson might have belonged to, the Bethel African Methodist Episcopal (AME) Church, had six hundred members, double the total African American population in Lansing at the time. The city was also home to three Black weeklies, the *Indianapolis World*, the *Freeman*, and the *Indianapolis Recorder*. Although African Americans began attending school with Whites in the immediate post-Reconstruction era, in 1888, 35 percent of African Americans in Indiana over the age of ten were illiterate and by 1900 22 percent were. Thompson was among a select group of young Black men to attend and graduate from high school in Indianapolis. In 1901, about 69 percent of African Americans between the ages of six and twenty were enrolled in schools in Indianapolis.[1]

In 1893, at the age of eighteen, Thompson graduated from high school.[2] Six years later, in 1899, he enrolled at M.A.C. where he was a student for five years. Between graduating from high school and 1899, when he was between twenty-two and twenty-four years old, he worked various manual labor jobs to help support his family and helped look after his younger siblings, the youngest of whom, Savannah Paris, was born in 1895. When Thompson applied for admission into M.A.C., the college had just changed its admissions requirements, mandating that applicants from nonapproved high schools take an entrance examination. The college sought to heighten its reputation, and Thompson met the requirements. Some of Thompson's classmates were required to take an additional year of study, a "preparatory year," which meant it could take them five years to earn a bachelor of science degree.[3] A student in the agriculture course, Thompson gained valuable experience working with livestock, a skill he took with him to Tuskegee after graduating.

During his senior year, Thompson lived with some White classmates near campus. According to the 1903–1904 *M.A.C. Directory*, he lived with five other students at "Elderkin's" in Collegeville. As a boarder, he shared space with college employee Henry B. Elderkin and other fellow Aggies. The thrifty Elderkin rented out rooms to students because of his meager earnings. In 1900, his salary was changed from $32.50 per month to $25.00 per month. Thompson might very well have been the first African American to reside in what, by 1907, became East Lansing. Born in New York in about 1832, Thompson's landlord Elderkin, the tough and rugged Civil War

Veteran who while working at Lansing's Reform School in the late 1880s disarmed an intruder who had a revolver, was a janitor who was "responsible for the care and cleanliness of so much of M.A.C." One wonders about the nature of the relationships Thompson developed with Elderkin and his White housemates. Elderkin defied the "Jim Crow North" conventions prominent during the early twentieth century.[4] Living in Collegeville instead of Lansing certainly made Thompson's senior year easier to navigate. In late June 1904 immediately following his graduation, several issues of the *M.A.C. Record* reported that Thompson was placed in charge of the dairy work on Aggie professor of agriculture Herbert Windsor Mumford's farm in Dexter, Michigan. Born in Moscow, Michigan, in 1871, Mumford was a contemporary of Thompson. After graduating from M.A.C., Mumford taught at his alma mater from 1896 until 1899. When Thompson began working on Mumford's farm in Dexter, Mumford was early in what would become his long career at the University of Illinois. With expertise in Jersey and beef cattle (Mumford was also an accomplished livestock judge), he trusted Thompson to oversee the dairy operations on one of his farms. In early 1905, Thompson worked at Olds Motor Works in Lansing. One and a half years after Thompson graduated from M.A.C. with a specialty in agriculture, the *M.A.C. Record* congratulated him on his new job. Like Charles A. Warren whose achievement was similarly acknowledged by the M.A.C. community, Thompson headed for Booker T. Washington's Tuskegee Institute.

On December 19, 1905, under the routine "Alumni" section, the *Record* recognized the college's first Black graduate whose name didn't appear in the 1904 commencement program or the 1900 edition of the college yearbook, the *Wolverine*.[5] The update was brief, but brought an important phase in Thompson's life to light.

> W. O. Thompson has recently been elected to a position with Booker T. Washington's school at Tuskegee. He will be employed as instructor in live stock breeding and also have charge of the livery and transfer department. In this department are 112 horses and mules, 60 wagons and carts, and 30 carriages and buggies. Mr. Thompson begins his new work Jan. 1.[6]

This terse announcement intimates the impressiveness of Thompson's new position. Washington put him in charge of a well-rounded department, gave him a lot of responsibility, and trusted his judgment.

Thompson's new job opportunity was bittersweet for him. Less than a year after he graduated from M.A.C., he suffered a great tragedy. His wife Etta died unexpectedly at age twenty-eight. Like William's mother, Etta's mother was a seamstress by trade. Etta's mother was mixed-race. Her father was a Black man from Maryland, and her mother was a White woman from Canada with Irish and English ancestry. William and Etta were married on June 29, 1904, and Etta died in her mother's home on March 30, 1905, shortly after giving birth to their son, Milton Ora, who was born on March 18, 1905.[7] Seeking a bachelor of science degree in the women's course, she enrolled in M.A.C. in the fall of 1903, a year after Myrtle Bessie Craig enrolled. The *Record* editors took note of Thompson's loss, extending to him "deepest sympathy" in early April.[8] A devasted Thompson was a widower at age thirty with a newborn. His decision to leave his ten-month-old son in Lansing when he ventured to Tuskegee was gut-wrenching. But he knew Milton would be looked after by Etta's family. Thompson's parents also moved to Lansing sometime between his graduation and 1906 and lived in the city's Second Ward at 1027 Allegan Street. William's father Savannah worked as a janitor at W. H. C. Co. (Wynkoop Hallenbeck Crawford Company), a printing company. Milton lived with his grandparents for a decade, and when Etta's widowed mother, Mary King, died on December 21, 1907, she was residing with the Thompsons. William's mother, Violet, signed as the informant on Mary's certificate of death, suggesting the parents-in-law were close and supported each other. While William was at Tuskegee, his parents and Etta's mother, until her death, raised Milton.

Thompson remained in Macon County, Alabama, for at least four years, between January 1906 and 1910 or 1911. He arrived at Tuskegee during a special time in the school's history. The year 1906 marked its twenty-fifth anniversary. When Thompson reached Tuskegee, Booker T. Washington embarked upon a major fund-raising campaign starting at New York City's Carnegie Hall. Numerous New York celebrities including lawyer Joseph Hodges Choate, businessman Robert Curtis Ogden, and writer and humorist Mark Twain heaped praises upon Washington's accomplishments at Tuskegee. "One has no right to pass judgement upon a people until he has taken the pains to see something of their progress, after they have had a reasonable chance," Washington declared to those jammed packed in the prestigious venue; "the negro in many ways has proved his worth and loyalty to this country. What he now asks is that through such institutions like Hampton, Fisk, and Tuskegee he shall be given the chance to render high and intelligent service to our country in the future. I have faith that such an opportunity will be given him."[9] Tuskegee was in the national spotlight when Thompson took his post. There were approximately 1,500 students enrolled, and the school had an endowment of at least $1 million. When Thompson arrived at Tuskegee, the school provided training in thirty-six industries, several of which—such as stock-raising, agriculture, and horticulture—were part of the recent M.A.C. graduate's repertoire.

During the early twentieth century, various reform movements swept across the nation. The Progressive Era was a period of great change and reform in response to massive industrial growth, immigration, urban transformations, and political double-dealing. Progressive Era reformers were a mixed bag. Often at odds with each other, they embraced many different causes, and their activism resulted in profound changes in American culture. During the Progressive Era, African Americans' day-to-day lives were under assault. As historian Rayford W. Logan argued in the mid-1950s, the Progressive Era was the lowest point of American race relations. From the end of Reconstruction through the early twentieth century, an American anti-Black culture prevailed. Disenfranchisement, segregation, economic exploitation, racism in academia, science, and popular culture, and especially acts of racial terrorism were common. Thompson was alarmed by the Atlanta race riot that occurred from September 22 until September 24, 1906. White mobs, numbering at least ten thousand, murdered at least twenty-five African Americans and destroyed businesses and homes in Atlanta's Black community. Tuskegee was only 130 miles away from Georgia's largest city and capital. A month after Thompson arrived in Macon County, Alabama, Bunk Richardson, a Black man accused of raping and murdering a White woman, was lynched by a White mob in Gadsden, Alabama. Richardson was one of at least four Black men lynched in Alabama in 1906, and while Thompson was at Tuskegee, at least thirty-eight African American men were lynched in the state. According to the NAACP's *Thirty Years of Lynching in the United States, 1889–1919* (1919), in 1906 at least sixty-four documented lynchings of African American men took place.[10]

When Thompson joined Washington's all-Black faculty, Tuskegee had an unmistakably clear mission: "to train men and women who will go out and repeat the work done here, to teach what they have learned to others, and to leaven the whole mass of Negro people in the South with a desire for knowledge and profitable operation of those industries in which they have in so large a means the right of way."[11] The highly propagandized "Tuskegee Idea" Washington and his disciples espoused when Thompson, and earlier Warren, was there mirrored what Jonathan L. Snyder preached at M.A.C. Though the two schools served distinctly different populations, they shared the overarching beliefs that education should be guided by high moral standards; well-rounded; practical and applied; forward-looking; respectful of nature, the land, and manual labor; and rich in character building. Like Washington's persona, "there was combined in his [Snyder's] personality," as members of the State Board of Agriculture proclaimed in 1919, "a triumvirate of qualities—unusual practical sense, keen penetrating analysis, simple belief in the virtue of living." Tuskegee shared the vision of the idealized land-grant philosophy as well—"professors instructing students who, in turn, learned how to impart their newly acquired knowledge to others."[12] Central to Tuskegee were the values of cleanliness, honesty, respectability, and timeliness, principles that were similarly championed at Snyder's M.A.C.

Washington held high and demanding expectations of teachers like Thompson and Warren. He expected his faculty members to embody and preach Tuskegee's ideals. According to Washington's right-hand man, adviser, and personal secretary Emmett J. Scott, teachers were vetted with great care. In 1905 and 1906, Tuskegee teachers were "carefully sought out and brought to Tuskegee, not only for their teaching ability," but so that they could demonstrate "what the highest culture can do" for "their own race." They were living object lessons. With his well-rounded education from M.A.C., Thompson learned that educated African Americans like him "were under constant pressure to defend the image and honor of Black men and women." Like Warren and Craig, he was responsible for passing along this approach to his students. "From this perspective," suggests historian Kevin Gaines, "to 'uplift the race' meant African American leaders combated stereotypes." It was a complex "anti-racist argument" and often "a call to public service" that may have assumed the Black masses needed "moral guidance." This approach was ultimately rooted in a struggle to help African Americans advance themselves while creating race representatives who might be able to, through their intellect and achievements, stand for the race.[13]

At Tuskegee, Thompson taught his students "pride of race" and to embrace the pillars of racial uplift. Teachers also helped their students to learn how to live more harmoniously with Whites. Thompson had plenty of experience in this realm, although he was not as well versed as his southern colleagues were about the rules of engagement with southern Whites. He earned between $800 and $900 per year with six weeks of vacation. If he was paid regularly, Thompson made enough money to survive and send small amounts of money to his parents who were looking after his son Milton. Very few existing sources shed light on Thompson's work at Tuskegee. He seems to have impressed Washington. "W. O. Thompson who has charge of the division of livery and transportation at the Tuskegee Institute, has under his charge 110 animals, of which 87 are mules. When he entered upon his duties some 10 or 12 of these were in the hospital, but as a result of careful care and feeding he has reduced this number so that at present only two are laid off on account of disability," a writer for the *M.A.C. Record* reported in May 1906; "in referring to the work of the division Booker T. Washington said that it had improved greatly since Mr. Thompson had had supervision of it."[14]

In a 2005 interview, Thompson's son William Horton Thompson, who graduated from Michigan State College in 1950 and was an early member of the campus's Gamma Tau chapter of Alpha Phi Alpha, recalled his father taught him how to read as a toddler and left Tuskegee because "he hated the Jim Crow laws." A decade later, MSU alum Phillip Lewis interviewed a lucid ninety-six-year-old William Horton Thompson who reflected upon his father's time in Alabama. "He went down to Tuskegee, Alabama when he graduated and worked under Booker T. Washington for a while." The younger William continued, "Then he came back to Lansing. The racism in Alabama was so bad, he couldn't handle it. He came back to Lansing and started medical school."[15] Thompson returned to Lansing after departing from Tuskegee sometime in 1910 or 1911. In 1910, he was listed in the census as being a teacher at a "Coloured College," and in the 1911 city directory of Lansing he was listed as working at the printer company where his father temporarily worked. He became active in the George R. Collins AME Church, serving as one of its trustees in 1912 who oversaw planning their activities, fund-raising, and improving the church's outreach activities. In November 1916, he married twenty-five-year-old Elsie Amanda Merchant, William Horton Thompson's mother. She was active in the AME church as suggested by her participation in the "special patriotic service" in January 1918. While residing at 1027 West Allegan Street, Thompson was an honest man. In July 1913, the *State Journal* reported that he found a "purse containing $2" and "turned the money over to the police department." Between 1911 and 1916, he had various forms of employment, including a one-year stint at M.A.C. "in an unknown capacity" and at the Segar Engine Works.[16] Dated September 12, 1918, his World War I draft registration card reveals he was employed by REO Motor Car Company. Six months later, Thompson and Elsie were pleased to share with *State Journal* readers the birth of their son William in Sparrow Hospital.[17]

After returning to Lansing, Thompson developed into a civil rights activist. In 1917, he held the position of chairman of the city's Negro Civic League and in February read with great pride excerpts of Frederick Douglass's speeches at the organization's Lincoln-Douglass celebration. Founded in about 1915 and led by C. A. Campbell, the league regularly met at the AME church and charged a host of committees with addressing pressing issues facing the Black community. The organization took a particularly vocal stance against negative portrayals of African Americans in films. Beginning in 1915, the league waged a campaign against the showing of films in the city that could in any way "intensify race prejudice." In addition to calling for a ban on a racist photo-play titled *The Nigger* playing at the Colonial Theater in May 1915, in November the league, with support from the Lansing Ministers' Union, called upon city officials to prohibit the showing of D. W. Griffith's popular *The Birth of a Nation*, a film that reinforced anti-Black stereotypes, featured White actors in blackface, depicted Reconstruction as a failure, celebrated the Ku Klux Klan, and included a lynching scene. In response to the league's demands, editorials in the *State Journal* flatly disagreed with censoring Griffith's long film, underscoring that race relations in Lansing were ideal and that no film could "inculcate race hatred" in the city. With a score played by a talented "symphony orchestra of 30," *The Birth of a Nation* played throughout Lansing theaters from 1915 until 1918. Governor Woodbridge Nathan Ferris may have "attacked" the film in February 1918, but the *Journal* concurred with countless Whites throughout the country who adored the racist screenplay. Contrary to the *Journal*'s assessment, the film fueled racism. In February 1916, for instance, "Rumor says racial prejudice heightened by witnessing 'The Birth of a Nation,' caused a small sized riot between 'white' and 'black' in the Looking Glass barber shop" located on East Michigan Avenue. Reacting to a racist slur from a White barber, an African American porter named Frank Burton confronted the barber who, in response to him "throwing out his chest," struck him in the forehead with a glass container of hair tonic, leaving Burton with a gruesomely "long gash" on his left cheek. Burton reacted by throwing the bottle through the shop's front window.[18]

While Thompson was active in the Negro Civic League, many of the organization's members joined a newly established branch of the NAACP in the state capital. The president of the league, C. A. Campbell, was the president of the new Lansing Black organization. Founded in December 1918 about a decade after the national branch was set up in 1909 by an interracial group of Progressive Era reformers, the Lansing branch of the NAACP had about one hundred members by the spring of 1919. Thompson's friend Charles A. Warren was among the new organization's chief recruiters. In January 1920, Thompson was elected vice-president of the organization and contributed to its growth. Like the National Urban League, while Thompson was in a leadership position, Lansing's NAACP embraced the national association's approach and philosophy. They sought to help African American "newcomers" to the city, invited African American major leaders to the city (including Walter White, William Pickens, and a spokesperson for Marcus Garvey's Universal Negro Improvement Association), and sponsored events, often held in the AME church. Thompson and his colleagues attended the NAACP's twelfth annual conference in Detroit where more than one thousand delegates discussed lynching, peonage, Black labor, the media, Pan-Africanism, disenfranchisement, and Black women's suffrage.[19] The Lansing branch included working-class African Americans among its ranks, and Black women were active in leadership positions. Restaurant keeper and cook Mrs. Ella M. Bell, and Mrs. Beulah Irons, a longtime janitress and custodian, served in leadership positions in the organization during the 1920s. Bell served as president, and Irons served as secretary. While Thompson was active in the organization for several years, his coworkers grew in numbers, coordinated various programs and events, and spoke out against lynching. Thompson died within several years of assuming a position of leadership in Lansing's activist Black community, leaving behind his thirty-two-year-old wife Elsie and four-year-old son. In January 1929, Elsie married Alonzo F. Seaton, and they lived a happy life together, celebrating their widely publicized fiftieth wedding anniversary in 1979.[20]

An obituary published in the *M.A.C. Record* in late February 1923, the longest and most detailed of the six notices, spoke to Thompson's educational background, membership in Lansing's AME church, community activism, and employment. It read:

> William O. Thompson, '04, died at his home, 1414 W. Ionia Street, Lansing on February 7 after a short illness. He had been employed by several Lansing firms after leaving college and at the time of his death had served Reo company over a long period. He was graduated in the agricultural course where the instructors found him a willing worker, anxious to keep abreast of his class.
>
> He was a highly respected member of the A. M. E. Church in Lansing and was well known and respected in his community. His life was devoted to service which he found at hand and his employers found his marked ability slightly handicapped by a reserved attitude. His funeral was held from the A. M. E. Church on Saturday, February 10.[21]

Curiously, the obituary didn't mention his work at Tuskegee. There was also no mention of this "highly respected" community man being the *first* African American student to graduate from M.A.C. Unlike the update on Warren in the *Record* in 1899 that identified him as being "colored," this statement neglected to mention Thompson's race.

Though concise, this death notice can be further dissected. Was it authored by his second wife, Elsie Amanda Thompson, by one of his siblings, by members of his church community, or by a writer for the *Record*? The text offers several interesting undertones and subtleties. To say he worked for "Lansing firms" could have suggested he was a business partner of some sort. His specific job as a janitor at Olds Motor Vehicle Company, as was the case in a February 1916 update in the *M.A.C. Record*, wasn't mentioned. Instead, the author of the passage praised him for his lengthy commitment to the company. Did the person(s) who crafted this statement speak to those who taught Thompson to be able to deduce that he was "a willing worker"? Was the supposed unease he felt while seeking to keep up with his classmates the by-product of him being an African American trailblazer who, like many Black firsts in White spaces, felt the burden of representing the race and inspiring future generations of Black students who would enroll in M.A.C.? Maybe this was simply a compliment to his work ethic. The second paragraph begins by asserting that Thompson was an upstanding man valued by his community. Then, the author of the text writes: "his employers found his marked ability slightly handicapped by a reserved attitude." Which employers said he was hindered by his guarded, withdrawn, restrained, and/or private disposition? If he did, in fact, exhibit such a "reserved attitude" in the White work environment in which he routinely operated, it may have very likely been a coping and survival mechanism. He could have worn what poet Paul Lawrence Dunbar so eloquently called "the mask." Or, following the advice of Booker T. Washington, he may have simply decided to live harmoniously with his White employers.

We can only speculate about what Thompson experienced at M.A.C. Did he find a community in the AME church while he was a student? Did he belong to any student organizations? Did he see the Fisk Jubilee Singers when they came to the Collegeville area in March 1902? Did he pay attention to the Debating Club's engagement with issues pertaining to Black life in 1903 and 1904? How was he treated by his classmates and professors? Was there truth to Snyder's claims during the early twentieth century that racial prejudice didn't exist at his institution? How many brushes did he have with racial incidents or, in today's terms, racist microaggressions? Such questions abound. In any case, Thompson and Warren did symbolically at least pave the way for the arrival of the first Black woman M.A.C. graduate, Myrtle Bessie Craig. They knew each other. Thompson had been at M.A.C. for three years when Craig came to campus, and Warren, Thompson, and Craig belonged to the George R. Collins AME Church and were members of Lansing's small community of college-educated African Americans. They probably met in this tight-knit community in or after 1907, unless they met when Craig was visiting her father who lived in the Lansing area.

Chapter 8

Of the Highest Qualities of Character

Known as Miss Myrtle Bessie Craig when she was a student in the five-year women's course at M.A.C. from 1902 until 1907, beginning in the 1970s, Myrtle Craig Mowbray was consistently celebrated as being "MSU's first Black graduate." She was first publicly given this honorific designation in 1972 by a writer for the *MSU Alumni Magazine*. A year later, a stately photo of Mowbray appeared on the cover of the *Grapevine Journal* with the following caption: "Myrtle Craig (now Mrs. Myrtle Mowbray) is the first known MSU Black grad, class of 1907. Since then, Black life on campus has grown in magnitude and complexity."[1] In the early 1970s, Mowbray reflected upon her decision to attend M.A.C. and her experiences in East Lansing. She recalled:

> My father worked in the capitol downtown, and I used to come up on weekends to visit him. When it came time for me to go to college, he said it was either Michigan Agricultural College or none at all, he couldn't afford anything else. I would've been delighted to go down to Ann Arbor, since M.A.C. didn't appeal to women then. My first thought was "What could I do at an agricultural school?"

Mowbray further reminisced: "I sold scissors for a clothing store after school and worked as a waitress catering in a club where often my pay was dinner and a dollar. . . . I didn't feel any different because of my race. . . . There were sororities for girls, but I was poor, I didn't have the time or money for those things."[2] The circumstances of her life didn't permit Myrtle to enjoy an active on-campus social life.

Based upon her keen recollections, Craig's experience at M.A.C. was positive. An eighty-nine-year-old Mowbray might have practiced what historian Darlene Clark Hine theorized as "the culture of dissemblance" in Black women's history. Like many Black women of her generation, Mowbray could have consciously created "the appearance of openness and disclosure but actually shielded the truth" to "protect the inner aspects" of her life from the broader MSU public.[3] Her life was full of various challenges, obstacles she overcame with great poise and determination. Shortly after her death on November 15, 1974, in a brief obituary nestled in the *Battle Creek Enquirer*, snippets of her later life's work were mentioned and, once again, she was dubbed "the first black graduate of Michigan State University."[4] Craig's place as a Black first in MSU's history would be reiterated in articles in the *Lansing State Journal* and elsewhere through the early 2000s. In 1990, the Myrtle Craig Mowbray Scholarship was established at MSU to honor her memory. While this award is open to "all students," today part of the program's mission is to support "students of color" in the Honors College with an award of $7,500. The website for the Mowbray Scholarship does not provide details about its namesake's biography. To date, the most extensive account of Mowbray's fascinating life is historian Keith R. Widder's concise sketch in *Michigan Agricultural College* (2005).

Mowbray was born Myrtle Bessie Craig on March 16, 1883, in Adrian, Michigan, near the spot where approximately fifty years earlier the first major antislavery society in Michigan was founded by a group of Quakers. Her father, Stephen Craig, was born in New Jersey in 1851 or 1852 though he spent most of his life in Michigan, in Adrian and Eaton Townships. Celia Kenner, Myrtle's mother, was born in about 1861 in Missouri. Stephen, a barber by trade, and Celia, a housewife, were married in Adrian on August 15, 1881. When Myrtle was four and a half years old, her mother died. A thirty-five-year-old widower with a young daughter, Stephen was devasted by this loss and overwhelmed by the responsibility of being the sole provider for Myrtle. Sometime between her mother's death and 1900 Stephen took Myrtle to Sedalia, Missouri, to be close to Celia's family. Known by many as the stomping grounds of ragtime king Scott Joplin, Sedalia boasted a vibrant and enterprising Black community. Between 1880 and 1900, the city grew from a population of 9,500 to 15,000. Though African Americans only made up about 5 percent of Missouri's population in the early twentieth century, African Americans in Sedalia boasted a thriving community. According to self-trained historian of Sedalia and longtime Missouri journalist Rose Nolen, during the Progressive Era, Sedalia's Black community resembled other Black communities throughout the nation that intricately carved out spaces within the oppressive system of segregation. Blacks in Sedalia had their own newspaper that Myrtle read, the *Sedalia Times*.[5]

Although not located in the Deep South, during the era of Jim Crow segregation, Missouri had established racial mores, conventions that sought to relegate African Americans to subservient and second-class positions in the established racialized social order. In Sedalia, Craig lived in a segregated city that allowed for Blacks to establish their own parallel communities, but they also lived under the constant threat of violence. Following Reconstruction, Missouri had the second highest number of lynchings outside of the Jim Crow South. Between 1889 and 1916, the NAACP reported on eighty-one lynchings in the state. In 1901 in Pierce City, Missouri, three Black men were lynched, and a Black community in the state was attacked, a travesty covered in major newspapers at the time.[6] As an adolescent and teenager, Myrtle learned to navigate coexisting with Whites and living in a segregated society. This prepared her for her life in the Lansing area, which was about the same size as Sedalia when she returned to her state of birth in 1902.

In 1900, eighteen-year-old Myrtle worked as a "servant" for a White couple, James and Olivia Richey. James, forty-four years old at the time, made enough money to employ a domestic servant, which didn't need to be much because "the poorest White families considered some sort of 'help' an affordable necessity." Myrtle's job at this point in her life was not unique. Black women like her often worked as poorly compensated wage laborers, as either domestic servants or laundresses. At the turn of the century, of the Black women who were wage earners, "fully 90 percent of them labored as domestic servants in private homes or in commercial settings such as hotels and boardinghouses." Oftentimes, "the younger the black woman, the more likely she worked in a white household." This was the case with Craig. With few other options, she had to accept "exploitative wages."[7] As a live-in domestic servant, she was constantly under the supervision of her White employer and was always on call, working between twelve and fourteen hours per day. Her responsibilities included cooking, housekeeping, and laundry. According to historian Jacqueline Jones, for Black women domestic servants of Craig's times, "the work environment remained heavily laden with the trappings of slavery." At the same time, Black women domestic servants like Craig escaped the drudgery of industrial manual labor jobs and "had potential power over their employers because they controlled the quality of their own labor" as well as "the supply of that labor."[8] Craig learned to navigate existing in this space where the male head of the household and mistress ruled. Like her contemporaries, she developed a repertoire of daily resistance strategies. She carefully calculated her daily activities. While working for the Richeys, Myrtle attended George R. Smith College, a historically Black college known for its music program. In 1902, John Wesley Hoffman, who briefly attended M.A.C. in the 1890s, was the chair of the college's Department of Chemistry, Biology, and Agriculture. Like other Black women of her socioeconomic class who attended school, Myrtle worked out an arrangement with her employer and balanced two distinctly different types of work: manual labor and academic work.

After graduating from George R. Smith College, she taught for a year at an elementary school. Black teachers like Myrtle usually made 60 percent of White teachers' salaries. By becoming a teacher, an occupation considered one of the so-called feminized professions, she became a Black woman professional and embraced what historian Stephanie J. Shaw called "socially responsible individualism."[9] At a time when most Black women of her generation labored as domestic servants and manual laborers, Myrtle possessed a sense of independence; she was an adventurer. While she was living and teaching in Missouri, her father resided in the Lansing area and plugged away at a variety of jobs, including as a laborer, janitor, and barber.

When Craig arrived at M.A.C. in 1902, the women's course was less than a decade old and Morrill Hall had recently been constructed for women students. Craig and her women classmates received an education overlapping with that of their male classmates. Yet it was ultimately carried out "in reference to the home."[10] The college advertised its women's course as an education that would not relegate them to the kitchen or traditional domestic sphere. In President Jonathan L. Snyder's vision, women at M.A.C. needed to be educated in a manner meeting "the challenges of life inside and outside the home." In addition to taking the courses her male colleagues took, Craig also studied cooking, sewing, and home economics, areas she had learned about firsthand as a domestic servant several years earlier. In the demonstration-oriented classes she participated in and from studying under the handful of women teachers at M.A.C., Craig learned the nuances of the teaching profession. She was a busy student with little time for leisure. Like many of her classmates, she worked while going to school to pay for her tuition. During her first year at M.A.C., she lived with the family of the secretary of the Board of Agriculture, Addison M. Brown. "She helped with meals, and learned cosmetology." During her second year, she boarded at the home of Chace Newman, an assistant professor of drawing in Lansing.[11] While living with these families Myrtle, a highly skilled domestic worker, paid for her board in exchange for helping around the house. Her experiences working for the Richeys prepared her for such an arrangement. While a M.A.C. student, she was a member of Lansing's George R. Collins African Methodist Episcopal (AME) Church and, along with William O. Thompson, "signed the contract for the church when it purchased its first piano."[12] Considering Sedalia's vibrant Black community Myrtle once called home, she made do with what Lansing's small Black community had to offer. Her identity as a Black woman inevitably made her experience at M.A.C. drastically different from that of Warren or Thompson. As reported several times by the *Adrian Daily Telegram*, Craig returned to Adrian for the holidays.

In 1903, one of her classmates penned an article for the *M.A.C. Record*, "The Anglo Saxon Society Woman," that offended Craig and her Black male contemporaries, claiming that White women were superior to women from other racial backgrounds. "It is but natural that from such a people there should spring a race, not merely physically perfect, but endowed with strong intellectual powers as well," this member of the college's Olympic Society wrote. "And that the Anglo Saxon woman should be more intellectual, and hence to wield a greater influence, to have higher ideals, strong personalities and greater ambitions than the women of other races must necessarily follow." Several years later, a group of M.A.C. "college minstrels" performed several times on campus, including a popular show sponsored by the Eclectic Literary Society at the armory. They also performed at other neighboring small towns in Michigan. "'The College Minstrels' [o]f the Michigan Agricultural College on their annual tour during the spring vacation," reported the *Belding Banner* (Belding, MI) in late March 1906, were "a fine attraction. Twenty-five people in the company."[13]

Craig was one of the several known Black students as well as the only known Black woman enrolled as a full-time student in M.A.C. during the first decade of the twentieth century. She was not the only Black woman taking classes at the college and experiencing a campus climate that somewhat normalized the denigration of Black culture. During the 1903–1904 academic year, William O. Thompson's wife, Etta, was enrolled in the women's course, and a Black woman and Michigan resident named Emma C. Baker was enrolled in the college under the "special student" designation. Baker was born in the village of Deshler, Ohio, in Henry County in about 1877 and as an adult claimed Findlay, Ohio, as her home city. Her father, Lewis H. Baker, was born in about 1842 in Virginia and worked as a barber and day laborer. Her mother, Eary Ann Baker, was born in Ohio in about 1845 and labored as a domestic worker. In 1899, Emma's mother died, and in 1900, a twenty-three-year-old Emma, the fourth of six children, lived with her father and two younger sisters, Mary, nineteen, and Lucy, sixteen, in the small Millbrook Township, Michigan, in Mecosta County located about eighty-two miles north of Lansing. In 1901, Emma's father died, and the saddened daughter signed the death certificate on behalf of the family. It is unknown exactly when Emma ventured to the Lansing area to attend MA.C. Her name appears in the 1903–1904 academic year college catalogue of students and officers. At the time, the college offered four primary courses or fields of study: agriculture, mechanical engineering, home economics (known as the Women's Course), and forestry. The college also offered five "special short courses" to help farmers, horticulturalists, and those engaged mainly in agricultural work improve their skills in the applied sciences of their chosen professions. The college didn't offer special courses to young women beyond those that were primarily designed for young men. Women like Baker could enroll as special students. A "young woman of previous training and maturity of judgement may enter as a special student and take cookery, sewing, and any other subjects for which she is prepared," M.A.C.'s 1903–1904 catalogue outlined. "She should plan to remain not less than two years in order to acquire good practical training." For a fee of between $2.50 and $5.00 and an additional $1.00 per term for laboratory fees for cooking, Baker had a range of courses to choose from. As one of the eighty-three women enrolled as a special student (out of a total of 120 special students), Baker took several classes in the women's course in 1903 and 1904.[14]

Sometime in 1904, Baker left the Lansing area to teach domestic science at the Joseph Keasbey Brick Agricultural, Industrial and Normal School in Enfield, North Carolina. In 1909, a writer for the *New York Age* acknowledged her affiliation with M.A.C., observing: "Miss Emma C. Baker, an ex-student of the Michigan Agricultural College, and who is teaching in the Joseph K. Brick School of Domestic Science, is visiting the Y.M.C.A. en route to her home."[15] After her more than five-year stint at Brick, Baker held numerous other positions at other normal and industrial schools for African Americans, including Straight University, New Orleans, Louisiana;

the State Colored Normal School at Elizabeth City, North Carolina; Ballard Normal School, Macon, Georgia; Beach Institute, Savannah, Georgia; Livingston College, Salisbury, North Carolina; Berry O'Kelly Training School, Raleigh, North Carolina; and Georgia Normal and Agricultural College. During the first several decades of the twentieth century, she traveled a lot, building upon what she learned at M.A.C. During the early 1910s and again in the early 1920s, Baker lived in New York City and took courses at Columbia University. In the City of Dreams in 1915, she found a supportive community of Black women by joining a branch of the YWCA.

Unlike Craig, Baker did not graduate from M.A.C. Like John Wesley Hoffman, who attended the college for a very brief period in the early 1890s, she publicized her affiliation with America's first agricultural college. In 1923, an announcement for Baker's visit to the Bleeks Dressmaking School in New York City highlighted her M.A.C. connection. "Miss Grace Haley was hostess at dinner at the Craig dining room 102 West 130th street, Monday evening, for Miss Emma C. Baker of the Michigan Agricultural College, who has been studying at Columbia this summer," wrote a *New York Age* journalist.[16] Baker claimed to be a bona fide M.A.C. alumna. During the 1920s, as a self-proclaimed member of the class of '05, she periodically wrote to the editors of the *M.A.C. Record*, updating her adopted alma mater about her accomplishments and whereabouts. In 1926, she provided *Record* readers with the following lengthy update.

> Emma C. Baker, on the home economics staff at the Berry O. Kelly Training school, Method, N.C., writes: "You have the correct information and if you will kindly mention it in THE RECORD I will thank you. That is the way I let my old professors and teachers know where I am and what I am doing. I left Livingstone college, which is one of the oldest and best schools in the country for colored folks. I was there five years. I resigned under very kindly feeling to all and accepted work here which is under the direct supervisions of the state. They are very much interested in and also exceedingly kind to us. They are especially anxious for us to have a strong H. E. Department and that is what I am trying to do. I found it in a splendid condition and if I can get along I hope to leave it better."[17]

Three years later, in June 1929, Baker informed the *Record* she "may be reached at Albany, Georgia." She had accepted a position teaching home economics at Georgia Normal and Industrial School working under the direction of Esther Tate Holley who graduated from M.A.C. in 1920 and managed the school's Home Economics Department. According to the 1930 U.S. federal census, a forty-nine-year-old Baker lived as a "lodger" in the Militia District 1097, Dougherty, Georgia, and was a teacher at Georgia Normal. Not much is known about Baker's actual experience at M.A.C. Yet it's clear Craig and Baker faced and overcame a different set of odds than Warren or Thompson. They faced triple oppression based upon their gender, race, and socioeconomic class. Craig was a poor Black woman who sought to use education as a form of self-transformation and racial uplift. Dispelling the myths of the "Anglo Saxon Woman" and the stereotypes of blackface performers, she proved herself as a student.

The graduating women of the class of 1907 sit for a senior portrait. Craig is standing in the middle row, far left. Courtesy of Michigan State University Archives and Historical Collections.

Craig graduated in 1907, participating in the historic commencement ceremony featuring President Theodore Roosevelt as the keynote attraction. She received her diploma from the twenty-sixth president of the United States and later reflected that she did not totally process the importance of her accomplishment at the time. W. Kim Heron, who interviewed Craig in the 1970s, noted, "graduation alone had her so excited that she cannot remember what Mr. Roosevelt said to her though several of her classmates told her afterwards that he had spoken to her." Craig was not the only African American at the ceremony. Charles W. Green, the head of the Department of Agriculture at Tuskegee, was among the many delegates from "other institutions and societies" who "assembled on the west side of the platform" and delivered best wishes to President Snyder. A close friend of Booker T. Washington dating back to when they were roommates at Hampton Institute, Green was sent to the commencement as his stand-in. A year after Washington spoke at M.A.C., in mid-October 1901, Washington, to the chagrin of many southerners, dined in the White House as the former New York governor and newly installed president's personal guest. He became Roosevelt's adviser on issues pertaining to African Americans. Whether or not Roosevelt paid any attention to Craig, President Snyder thought highly of the first Black woman to graduate from M.A.C. His respect for Craig reflected the values highlighted in the November 19, 1919, resolution upon Snyder's death. "He was unalterably committed to democracy of living and democracy of learning, and he successfully struggled with the problem of building up a great democratic institution and study body, where snobbery is unknown and where worth and honesty, in whatever guise they appear, are uniformly respected."[18]

Several months before Craig received her diploma at the historic graduation, Snyder reached out to Booker T. Washington with a strong recommendation for her. He sent similar letters to other schools. He wrote:

> We graduate from our institution this year a young colored woman of more than ordinary ability. She received her preparation for college work in the George R. Smith College, Sedalia, Missouri. She taught one year in an ungraded school. She entered our freshman class and has done very commendable work throughout her entire course. She will graduate at our next commencement. She has the respect and confidence of her teachers and associates. She is level-headed and I believe will, in the course of a few years, be capable of filling a very responsible position. She certainly is well prepared now to teach domestic science and art, or, in fact, any of the subjects she has pursued in college. In addition to her college work she has also completed certain lines of educational work which will entitle her to a state certificate issued by the Department of Public Instruction.[19]

In early February 1908, Booker T. Washington wrote another letter to Snyder asking him if any Black men trained in agriculture had recently graduated from M.A.C. and would possibly be interested in working at Tuskegee. Snyder, once again, evoked Craig, informing Washington that "a very capable young woman" had recently graduated and was teaching in Kansas. Washington's wife, Margaret Murray Washington, followed up with Snyder in hopes of recruiting Craig away from her position at Western University. "Will you be kind enough to give me the address of the young woman who graduated from your school last year?" Mrs. Washington inquired. "I understand that she is now teaching somewhere in Kansas." In his brief response, Snyder stressed she "is a young woman of rather exceptional ability." He added, "She is energetic, dignified and of the highest qualities of character."[20]

When Craig received her diploma, she was one of 133 African Americans to do so in the United States and was one of a handful of Black women to achieve such a feat. The first Black woman to earn a bachelor's degree in the United States was Mary Jane Patterson, who graduated from Oberlin College in 1862. By 1910, less than seven hundred Black women had graduated from what W. E. B. Du Bois designated a college in his study *The College-Bred Negro American* (1910). Like many college-educated women, Craig became a teacher. Shortly after arriving at Western University in Quindaro, Kansas, where she taught in the State Industrial Department, Craig began making a name for herself. "Miss Myrtle B. Craig, instructor of domestic science, served the university and trustee boards to a six-course dinner Thursday and Friday," reported Kansas City's *Rising Son* in mid-October 1907. "This is Ms. Craig's first dinner, and with the assistance of her senior girls she served the menu in an elaborate style." Unfortunately for M.A.C., the paper mistakenly wrote that she graduated from the University of Michigan.[21] The *M.A.C. Record* also recognized her accomplishments shortly after she graduated. Though they didn't mention Craig's history-making at the college, the editors included a letter she sent to Mrs. Linda

Eoline Landon, one of the first women to teach at M.A.C. who served as the college's librarian from 1891 until 1932. Known for being kind and a mentor to many students, Landon made a lasting impression on Craig who informed her former teacher as well as the *Record* readership about her post-M.A.C. life.

Craig wrote, "Our school is young, but growing and progressive. We have about 200 students, the majority of whom come from Kansas, Missouri, Indian Territory, and Oklahoma." The excited and prideful alum continued, "the state supports the industrial side of the work, and the literary department is under the A. M. E. Church. There are three buildings with a fourth in process of construction and our teaching force numbers fourteen."[22] Craig signaled to her mentor that her success represented an accomplishment for her people. Like Warren and Thompson before her, she was a representative of her race and as a teacher became a "race woman" committed to the National Association of Colored Women's motto, "Lifting as We Climb." Western University was an ideal place for Craig to cut her teeth. A small historically Black university, when she began teaching there the school's first Black president, William Tecumseh Vernon, had just been appointed the register of treasury by President Roosevelt. The author of *The Upbuilding of a Race; or the Rise of a Great People* (1904), Vernon, a Black cultural nationalist, used Booker T. Washington's Tuskegee Institute as a model. Considering what she was exposed to at M.A.C., Western was an ideal first job for an energetic, confident, and hard-working twenty-two-year-old Craig.

After leaving the only historically Black university in Kansas in 1910, Craig taught at Lincoln Institute in Jefferson City, Missouri. Lincoln was designated a land-grant university under the Second Morrill Act of 1890 and focused on agricultural and mechanical education as well as teacher training. Craig was eager to share this news with her alma mater. On January 12, 1911, she wrote to the editors of the college weekly, enclosing fifty cents for her annual subscription. After informing the M.A.C. community that she recently accepted a higher-paying position at Lincoln Institute in Jefferson City, Missouri, she praised the school's Domestic Science Department, especially the cookery and laundrying programs. "It was my pleasure to plan an entirely new equipment for both laboratories, and we are enjoying this year (what I am sure you would agree with me) is one of the best equipped domestic science departments in the country."[23]

On the center of the front page of the 1911 Thanksgiving issue of the *M.A.C. Record* appears Paul Lawrence Dunbar's famous poem "Sign of the Times," one of his many pieces penned using Black dialect. Black readers could decipher the beauty in this expression of Black southern culture. For White readers, this poem reinforced stereotypes about Black people as being simple-minded, folksy, and uneducated. In this same issue, *Record* editors saluted "Miss Myrtle Craig, '07, teacher of domestic and art at Jefferson City, a school for colored youth," one of "two M.A.C. girls" to win a prize at a Missouri state fair.[24] In 1912, the *Lansing State Journal* reported she had resigned from her job at Lincoln and was "taking a summer course in advanced work at the Agricultural college" (M.A.C.) and had recently accepted a position in a Domestic Science Department at a high school in Kansas City, Missouri.[25] Craig's father lived in Eaton Rapids, and Craig stayed with him while taking a summer class, or a "short" or "special" course, from M.A.C. in 1912 before heading for Kansas City in the fall. On M.A.C.'s campus five years after graduating, she still found herself as one of the only Black students. Her return suggests she felt comfortable at her alma mater.

In June 1915, Craig married William H. Bowen, a minister and public school teacher who was born in Kentucky in the early 1870s. From 1915 until the late 1940s, Myrtle taught at Sumner High School in Kansas City, at Lincoln Institute, and at an elementary school in Fulton, Missouri. Her father died in 1933 in Fulton. As Stephen did for her after her mother died, Myrtle had looked after her father. In 1951, Myrtle married Washington, D.C.–born George Hamilton Mowbray who was employed at Sumner High School. Now Myrtle Craig Mowbray, she remained active in her later years, participating in the Kansas City Model Cities program and the Conference on Aging. Her concerns about urban development and the treatment of elder Americans dovetailed with her lifelong commitment to educating, advising, and looking after young students. In 1972, Mowbray returned to her alma mater excited to meet President Clifton R. Wharton Jr. She expressed regret for not being able to witness his first commencement. "I so wanted to come back to see his first commencement, but I just couldn't make it. Dr. Wharton is remarkable, especially at a university this size and stature because Black folks just haven't held these positions before." She continued, "I constantly follow the news clippings about him to see how he's regarded and how his family is treated." Mowbray was amazed by the progress her alma mater had made over the last six-plus decades. During her last visit to MSU, she made her presence known, letting those in the Alumni Association offices know she was, as far as she knew, MSU's first Black graduate. For this, she wanted to be recognized. "I wanted them to put out the red carpet for me when I came back," she remarked, "and they sure did!"[26] She died two years later in 1974. Mowbray lived a dynamic and long life, outliving all African Americans who graduated from Michigan Agricultural College by 1920.

The lives and experiences of Charles A. Warren, William O. Thompson, and Myrtle Craig Mowbray before, during, and after their enrollment at M.A.C. are full of fascinating stories. They came from families who overcame the odds and supported their educational aspirations. They were inevitably impacted by the era of Jim Crow segregation. They left their footprints at M.A.C. After leaving campus, they became educators and selflessly served their communities. Had they come of age when their Blackness didn't automatically other them in the eyes of those who had some type of impact on their destinies, their lives would have without a doubt been different. They persevered. In a historical and spiritual sense, today's African American undergraduate and graduate students at MSU are the progeny of Warren, Thompson, and Mowbray.

Chapter 9

Spartan Superhero

n 2013, Michigan State University celebrated its five hundredth contest at Spartan Stadium during the ninety-eighth homecoming football game. "Creating Spartan Super Heroes" was the year's timely theme. The university saluted and memorialized a group of MSU alumni's "life changing" accomplishments. In the pages of the fall 2013 issue of the *MSU Alumni Magazine*, editor Robert Bao remarked it was "high time" to publicize the glory of the undefeated 1913 football team, a squad that included Gideon E. Smith, '16. Affectionately known as "Gid" back in the day, Smith was the first African American to play football at the university and earn a coveted M.A.C. monogram when MSU was still called Michigan Agricultural College. Gideon and his teammates were known as the Aggies and sometimes, as both a compliment and a diss depending on the circumstances, the "Farmers."[1]

Smith was one of the "Spartan Super Heroes" whose exploits were formally acknowledged. "The 100th anniversary of Smith's bold action was honored, along with his other achievements," during the 2013 "festivities commemorating the 500th game at Spartan Stadium."[2] Several days after the Spartans handily defeated the Indiana University Hoosiers in their sixtieth meeting, 42-28, *MSU Today* and the official website of Spartan Athletics highlighted how Smith "opened the doors for African American athletes at MSU" and featured reminiscences from Smith's grandson-in-law John Milton Belcher III, longtime Spartan and MSU's second Black athletic director Clarence Underwood, and Spartan alumni who knew of Smith's prowess.[3] Smith's place in MSU history, like that of Myrtle Craig Mowbray, was periodically lauded in the *State*

News and the *Lansing State Journal* several decades earlier. In 1994, he was inducted into the MSU Athletics Hall of Fame. The 2013 ceremonial acknowledgement of the dominant tackle was different. It more squarely placed him within the context of MSU's dynamic past, a history impacted by the contributions of many African Americans since the late nineteenth century.

Sixty years earlier, in 1953, some members of the 1913 M.A.C. team—Smith, Hugh Blacklock, George Gauthier, Blake Miller, Oscar Miller, and Faunt Lenardson—were invited to Michigan State College to be honored during the halftime ceremonies of the sold-out homecoming game against the Hoosiers. It was the fortieth anniversary of the college's first undefeated team, a squad that defeated the University of Michigan for the first time since the rivalry began in 1898. The Aggies had suffered some painful losses to Michigan, including in 1912 when coach John Macklin's team lost 55-7. The former gridders who contributed to M.A.C.'s unprecedented 1913 season and historic win against Michigan were presented with "special certificates as they were introduced to the crowd over the public address system." They were guests of the MSU Alumni Association at a "special stag celebration."[4] Below a photo with Smith and his teammates, a Spartan alumnus proclaimed in the November 1953 *M.S.C. Record*: "FIRST!—the first undefeated and un-tied Spartan gridiron team—the team of 1913." Smith's and his brothers in arms' visits to MSC were not in vain as coach Biggie Munn's team crushed Indiana at Macklin Field, 47-18.

The reunion in East Lansing took place during an interesting time for African Americans like Smith. In June 1953, several months after the end of the Korean War and during the early years of the Cold War era, the United States embarked on nuclear weapons testing. In Baton Rouge, Louisiana, African Americans in the United Defense League orchestrated a bus boycott that symbolically inspired the famous Montgomery Bus Boycott and ultimately introduced Martin Luther King Jr. to the world. In August, President Dwight D. Eisenhower signed Executive Order 10479 prohibiting racial discrimination in the assigning of government contracts. At the beginning of the next month, African American Women's Army Corps private Sarah Louise Keys launched her historic battle against bus segregation. The landmark *Brown v. Board of Education* case was also being reargued in the Supreme Court. A longtime resident of Virginia who came of age during the era of Jim Crow segregation, Smith was entirely familiar with African Americans' enduring struggles for social justice. His life was part of the long Black Freedom Struggle.

For the sixty-four-year-old Smith, his visit to East Lansing in 1953 meant something special. Others cherished the moment as well. Under the header "Smith to Rejoin 1913 Teammates at Spartans' Fete," a newspaper in his home state of Virginia, where he served for two decades as the head football coach for Hampton Institute, shared with its readership how their hometown hero, "the first Negro ever to play football at Michigan State, gathers with his teammates of Spartans' 1913 team at reunion in East Lansing Oct. 17." Even one of the most popular Black magazines, *Jet*, mentioned Smith's return to MSC, featuring a photo of him and his teammates and hailing him "one of the toughest linemen in Midwest football history."[5] The eight Black players on MSC's 1953 team felt especially proud to see their trailblazer Smith being honored.

Smith was a member of another immortalized M.A.C. football posse. Several months after President Lyndon B. Johnson signed into law the epoch-making Civil Rights Act of 1964 prohibiting racial discrimination in voting and upholding what was outlined in the Fourteenth and Fifteenth Amendments, the accomplishments of the 1915 team, which included another big win over Michigan, were honored during the pregame ceremonies for the 1965 MSU homecoming game.[6] Along with thirteen of his teammates, the retired seventy-six-year-old Smith attended the event that though important symbolically, didn't seem to have the same fanfare as the 1953 gathering. Many things must have run through Smith's mind, especially considering how the composition of the Spartan football team drastically transformed over the past fifty years. In 1965, there were eighteen Black players on the MSU roster, nine of whom hailed from the South.

Smith's first memorable visit back to his alma mater occurred several decades before the ceremonial 1953 and 1965 events.[7] In July 1930, the *M.S.C. Record* reported in the "Alumni Affairs" section that Gideon "made his first visit to the Campus in fourteen years." The paper added, "Gideon was one of the great tackles in State's football history. He was an important cog in the Macklin machine which made gridiron history on old College Field." Sixteen years later, in June 1946, Smith returned to Michigan State for Alumni Day. He was among the fifty members of the class of 1916 to gather for a luncheon in the Union Building, swapping stories about back in the day. Gideon shared "some of his old football experiences under Coach Macklin."[8] A year later, in 1947, Smith came back to East Lansing to take "some refresher courses" in physical education. While enjoying his sabbatical leave from Hampton Institute, he enrolled in MSC as a graduate student to further hone his skills as an athletic director. His return to MSC was covered in the *State Journal* and mentioned in other Michigan newspapers. "One of Michigan State's all-time greats, 53-year-old Gideon Smith, *a negro*, has returned to the Spartan school for a graduate course in physical education," wrote a columnist for a relatively obscure newspaper in the Upper Peninsula. "One of the most famous names in Michigan State's football history is back on the student roster," a *State Journal* sportswriter remarked. "It's that *colored* Gideon Smith."[9]

The author of the piece in the *Journal*, veteran local sports journalist George S. Alderton, didn't highlight Gideon's accomplishments as a pioneering African American football player during the oppressive era of Jim Crow segregation when Black men like Smith were routinely dehumanized. Like his colleague from the Upper Peninsula, he deliberately referred to Smith as being *colored*. The questions Alderton posed to Smith during an interview predictably centered on sports. Smith opted not to inject stories about the challenges he faced while playing football at M.A.C. As his grandson observed, Smith possessed a calm, amicable, cerebral, and unconfrontational disposition. In his estimation, his grandfather enjoyed football as an outlet. It was his passion, as revealed by his long coaching career. In engaging with his questioner, Smith "intentionally avoided talking about the difficulties he encountered while expressing a positive narrative of his time as a M.A.C. Player."[10] Perhaps unconsciously evoking caricatures of the stereotype of the happy-go-lucky Black man, Alderton commented on Smith's so-called characteristic grin, writing that Gideon "smiled broadly" and his "eyes lighted up" at one point during their lively discussion. Partly playing to the sensibilities of his interviewer, Smith focused on how much his alma mater had changed, his former teammates, and his professional football days. Reflecting on how the game had changed, he conjured up a Black masculinity that surely resonated with his interviewer and readers. "I don't think they tackle as well as they used to," surmised Smith. "There's more loose tackling now. Back 30 years ago when you hit a man you were supposed to take him down and hold him." Gideon concluded the interview by talking about his children, praising his son. In response to a question about his son's abilities as a football player, he signified and responded: "Well now he THINKS he is." Smith continued, "and I guess he is, too. Plays basketball and tennis also. He's smarter than his dad, though. Why, he's a halfback."[11] Gideon and his wife, Mildred, who was also a teacher, took great pride in their ability to provide more educational resources to their children than their parents were able to bestow upon them.

This brief 1947 interchange is noteworthy. Smith's voice comes through. A longtime Lansing sportswriter who covered MSU sports for forty years and came up with the "Spartans" nickname in 1926, Alderton respected Smith and allowed him to speak for himself. Smith was never extensively interviewed, if at all, by the media after his remarkable performances at M.A.C. from 1913 until 1915. When he was quoted or spoken for by mainstream reporters, he was routinely portrayed as being inarticulate, void of intellect, and simple-minded. In a similar manner to how many of Booker T. Washington's biographers portrayed him, Smith was reduced to being a "man of action." In October 1915, after M.A.C. defeated their in-state rivals by a score of 24-0, a writer for the *State Journal* wrote, "Incidentally, Gideon Smith when he rose to speak, hid behind a smile. Later he admitted that the man who fills his shoes when he retires from football will have 'some feet,' and he might have added, some smile."[12]

Four months before Smith graduated in 1916, a reporter for the *State Journal* quoted him in reference to a job offer he received from Tuskegee Institute to coach its football team. Recounting their exchange, the interviewer wrote, "'Ah'm considering the mattah very carefully,' the big boy remarked to his friends today, 'but ah just haven't made up my min. It looks like a good thing, but I suah do hate to leave Michigan. She's been mighty good to me.'"[13] This sportswriter's deliberate exaggeration of Smith's southern, Black dialect infantilized Smith, rendering him uneducated, simple, and childlike. He characterized Smith, despite his menacing presence on the gridiron, as being the stereotypical, loyal, subservient, and nonthreatening Black man. This was a gross caricature. In 1916, Gideon was a twenty-seven-year-old man who had been initiated into adult responsibilities during his childhood when he worked hard to help support his single-parent-led family. He was a leader in Lansing's small community and a member of several scholarly clubs at M.A.C., including the worldly Cosmopolitan Club, a very popular organization at the time, for which he served as treasurer during the 1916 winter term.[14] He was a dignified man. White sportswriters, especially those from the leading Michigan newspapers, habitually described Smith's play in racialized manners and refrained from calling him by his name, a first name that evoked much biblical and prophetic power, symbolism, and mysticism. The list of insulting names attached to Smith was never-ending. Sportswriters dubbed him "the Aggies' colored tackle," "the big colored fellow," "the giant colored tackle," "the negro tackle," "the big colored chap," "the chocolate-hued member of the Michigan Aggies," "the big Negro star," "the colored flash," "the coffee colored phantom," the "Aggies' Black Terror," "the dusky grid man," and even "the big colored boy," "the big Negro boy," and "a certain dark-hued boy."

These descriptions of Smith were expected. Such discourse dated back to the antebellum era when enslaved Black men were infantilized and racially inscribed in "runaway slave" advertisements and at sales by their captors. Black men during Smith's era were oftentimes reduced to their physical characteristics and attributes, criminalized, imagined as "brutes," and perceived as being inherently violent. Smith came of age as a star collegiate athlete when the first Black World Heavyweight Champion Jack Johnson, often called the "Galveston Giant," reigned. Johnson was the subject of White sports journalists' racial imaginations and intrigue throughout the world. A Black celebrity of some sort during his mid-twenties, Smith was the first African American M.A.C. student and graduate to gain fame and stardom. This notability made him an exceptional African American in the eyes of his White fans and classmates. He was a Black man who, despite his dark complexion and unmistakable African heritage, didn't represent the masses of Black people in their minds. On one level, he was different from the Black caricatures depicted in on-campus minstrel shows or in the *M.A.C. Record* during the first decade of the twentieth century. His experiences at M.A.C. reveal how his teammates and schoolfellows accepted him as a member of the college community even if he didn't reside within the campus walls. His White classmates and fans didn't speak out for African Americans' civil rights, but were often willing to stand up for "Gid" and call him "one of their own." According to a 1922 recollection of a M.A.C. graduate, "Blake Miller once threatened to lick a man five times his size because he had been slugging Smith during the scrimmage."[15]

Smith was worshipped for his athletic ingenuity and modesty. Whether he liked it or not, he became a popular ambassador for America's first agricultural college based upon his greatness, creativity, and fearlessness on the gridiron. At the end of his first year on the varsity football team at M.A.C., the *State Journal* deemed him "one of Michigan's most prominent representatives of the colored race."[16] Beyond the *State Journal*, the *Detroit Free Press*, the *Detroit News*, and countless other Michigan papers publicized Smith's gallantry, versatility, and skillfulness, including the *Muskegon Chronicle*, the *Jackson Citizen Patriot*, the *Kalamazoo Gazette*, the Adrian *Daily Telegram*, the *Grand Rapids Press*, the *Flint Daily Journal*, Ann Arbor's *Daily News*, the *Times Herald* (Port Huron), the *Saginaw Courier-Herald*, the *Escanaba Daily Press*, and many more. Sportswriters throughout the nation also covered Smith's virtuosity. Read critically with circumspection, the vast newspaper coverage of Smith's M.A.C. football career provides a window into not only how he was perceived, but how he challenged sportswriters to unconsciously rethink their notions of Black people.

Smith's circumstances were not unprecedented or solitary in the national context. He belonged to a small club of stouthearted African American men who integrated collegiate football during the late nineteenth and early twentieth centuries. They faced great adversity on and off the field. Born between the era of Reconstruction and the late nineteenth century, these young men were among the only Black students on their respective campuses and often bore the burdens of representing and vindicating the race on the athletic battlefields as well as in the classrooms. As a prideful writer for the African American newspaper the *New York Age* commented in 1915 when situating Smith's accomplishments, "in every university of [*sic*] college where there are colored students they invariably win honor and fame. Not only in the intercollegiate debates, the oratorical contests and high scholarship," the author continued, "but in the strenuous athletic battles, particularly football, some hero in ebony is continually bursting forth as a star of the first magnitude."[17] During his days at M.A.C., Smith, like his predecessors and spiritual disciples, found effective ways to cope with normalized racial prejudice and discrimination. African American football players like Gideon faced racism and racially motivated violence in stadiums across the country. "Racially motivated gridiron brutality was part of a 'long reign of organized terrorism' against African Americans that included rape, lynching, whitecapping, and similar abominations," kinesiology scholar Jaime Schultz argues. "Sports may seem trivial in the larger scheme of things, but it provided a prominent platform on which whites might exercise their racial animus."[18] The moment Smith first stepped on the field for the Aggies All-Fresh team in 1912, he was mindful of how some of his opponents perceived his presence. His teammates had his back, but he always kept his head on a swivel. He avoided serious injuries against opponents who often sought to take him out of games. He used the animosity his opponents had toward him as motivation. Like generations of African Americans who came of age during the era of Jim Crow segregation, he learned the core of his survival strategies during his early years, from his family and community. Smith's years at M.A.C. were narrated in numerous contemporary newspapers, and his success as a football coach for several decades at Hampton Institute with an impressive record of 97-46-12 has been ceremoniously chronicled. Very little, however, has been written about his life before and after his time at M.A.C. His illustrious football career and day-to-day life at the college has likewise remained underexplored.

Chapter 10

From Norfolk to East Lansing

n the 1916 M.A.C. yearbook, Smith identified Princess Anne, Maryland, as his hometown. This was not his birthplace. Smith was born on July 13, 1889, in Virginia. On his World War I and World War II draft registration cards, he indicated he was born in Norfolk, in (northwest) Norfolk County.[1] At the time of his birth, the city of Norfolk had a population of about 34,800, 16,200 of whom were African American (approximately 47 percent of the total population). Of the six wards, most Blacks lived in the Fourth Ward. From Smith's birth until 1910, "various aspects of Jim Crow society slowly enveloped daily life" in Norfolk, and the city "found itself in lockstep with the regional ethos, as the city divided along lines of black and white." As unearthed by historian Earl Lewis, African Americans in Norfolk responded to this increasingly entrenched racism by directly confronting racial discrimination through boycotts and other forms of day-to-day resistance. Members of Smith's community developed their own "institutional infrastructures" in the form of "churches, school, social organizations, and small businesses."[2]

Smith came of age in a segregated city where African Americans had an established presence, a community-based philosophy, and a vibrant culture. The larger Black community to which he belonged reinforced the possibilities of Black autonomy, psychologically empowering its members. Smith isn't listed in the 1890 Virginia census or the city register. He first appears in the 1900 U.S. census and is listed as living in Norfolk County in Pleasant Grove township. At age ten, he could read and write and attended elementary school. Along with a woman identified in the census as being his mother, fifty-year-old Patience Smith, and two older sisters Mary, thirteen, and Margaret, fifteen, Gideon's and his sisters' relationship to the head of the household is listed as "servant." Patience's occupation was listed as "housekeeper" for a forty-two-year-old farmer named W. L. Wilson who owned seven farms and claimed eighty-nine "farm schedules." Wilson's sister, eleven-year-old niece, and fifteen-year-old nephew also lived in the home.[3] Smith and his family lived in quarters on Wilson's large property and maintained a small farm of their own. A young Gideon, like the majority of his future M.A.C. classmates, was raised to be a farmer.

Despite the system of segregation characterizing Norfolk at the time, young Gideon most likely regularly played with Wilson's niece and nephew. Just as during the antebellum era when enslaved Black children often entertained and played with the children of their captors, it wasn't uncommon for the children of Black domestic servants and field laborers and the White children of the homeowners to play games together. From a young age during the era of Jim Crow segregation, Gideon learned how to interact with White children and adults, a skill he instinctively drew upon at M.A.C. He learned how to navigate the color line and, when necessary, wear "the mask" that poet Paul Lawrence Dunbar so eloquently described. In 1895, Dunbar published his famous poem "We Wear the Mask." He wrote:

> We wear the mask that grins and lies,
> It hides our cheeks and shades our eyes,—
> This debt we pay to human guile;
> With torn and bleeding hearts we smile,
> And mouth with myriad subtleties.
> Why should the world be over-wise,
> In counting all our tears and sighs?
> Nay, let them only see us, while
> We wear the mask.
> We smile, but, O great Christ, our cries
> To thee from tortured souls arise.
> We sing, but oh the clay is vile
> Beneath our feet, and long the mile;
> But let the world dream otherwise,
> We wear the mask![4]

In 1910, twenty-one-year-old Smith is listed as living with his sisters and mother who, as the head of the household, rented a property in the Pleasant Grove district and worked as a "farm laborer." Gideon wasn't listed as having a trade or profession.[5] When the census was taken, he was a student. He helped his elderly mother when he could, especially during his vacations away from school. In 1910, he graduated from Booker T. Washington's alma mater and his future place of employment, Hampton Institute. Founded in 1868 as Hampton Normal and Agricultural

Institute, the school stressed industrial education, manual labor, the Protestant work-ethic, political conservatism, and civilizationalist and missionary ideologies. Celebrating his 1981 induction into the Central Intercollegiate Athletic Association Hall of Fame, several accounts of Gideon's early years suggest he entered Hampton in 1905. Though feasible, he probably didn't take five years to graduate. One account also noted that he wasn't a standout football player, but did make his mark as a "sprint star" on the intramural track team.[6] According to historian James D. Anderson, the "Hampton model" during Smith's time didn't prepare him intellectually. Anderson argues that at Hampton during the early twentieth century, "academic education was of low quality." From its founding until several decades after Smith graduated, Hampton was not a trade school nor an academic school. It was an institution "that attempted to train a corps of teachers with a particular social philosophy relevant to the political and economic reconstruction of the South."[7] After several years at Hampton (the standard program included three years of study), Gideon was ready for a major change. He left Virginia and traveled nearly nine hundred miles northwest to pursue a more valuable education in Michigan, an education that overlapped a bit with the "Hampton model" but was profoundly different.

In 1910, Gideon enrolled in Ferris Institute (now Ferris State University). His new choice in schools was founded in Big Rapids, Michigan, in 1884 as the Big Rapids Industrial School by New York–born educator and future Michigan governor and senator Woodbridge Nathan Ferris. Gideon became Ferris Institute's first African American football player and joined the school's band. He didn't choose Ferris because of its football program, which was founded around the same time as M.A.C.'s. The school offered him a similar type of education he experienced at Hampton, minus the socialization of Black teachers to uplift their communities. According to founder and director of the Jim Crow Museum of Racist Memorabilia at Ferris State University, David Pilgrim, President Ferris created an informal recruiting pipeline program with Hampton during the early twentieth century that attracted a significant group of African American students like Smith to Big Rapids.[8] M.A.C. was attractive to Gideon for several reasons. Football became one of his means of self-expression and creativity, and the education and resources offered at M.AC. would provide him with a broader experience. Coach Chester Brewer transformed M.A.C.'s football program into a Michigan Intercollegiate Athletic Association (MIAA) and independent powerhouse from 1903 until 1910 and coach John F. Macklin's 1911 "Olive Green" squad was 5-1. Like Brewer before him, Macklin encouraged a culture of heartfelt teamwork. He demanded and expected that his superstars remain humble and lead by example. By the early 1910s, M.A.C. had benefited from President Jonathan Snyder's determination to expand the college's curriculum and improve its academic reputation. Gideon's desire to move from Big Rapids, whose Black population was almost nonexistent, was uncomplicated. While attending Ferris, Gideon was one of several Black people living in in Big Rapids. In Lansing, there was a small Black community, numbering about 350, that had several businesses, a small group of reform-minded Black professionals, and social organizations, including the George R. Collins

AME Church. In 1912, Gideon migrated 120 miles southwest from Big Rapids to East Lansing and enrolled in M.A.C.

During Snyder's presidency, Macklin's predecessors Henry Keep, Charles Bemies, George Denman, and Chester Brewer do not appear to have deliberately drawn the color line on the grid-iron. Before and during Smith's years, the Aggies competed against several squads that included a Black player. In 1901 on Thanksgiving Day at about 2:00 p.m. in front of more than one thousand spectators in Collegeville, Olivet College defeated the Aggies in the MIAA championship game, 23-18. It was a nail-biter decided in the final minutes. A *Detroit Free Press* writer dubbed it the "most fiercely-contested game of the season." Olivet's African American left halfback, Stephen Morgan, played a spectacular game, registering several long runs and scoring two touchdowns, one of which came from a twenty-three-yard scamper. M.A.C.'s all-White squad was defeated largely at the hands of Morgan's sensational play. In summarizing the game, the *M.A.C. Record* described Morgan's prowess without making any reference to his race. During the era of World War I, another Michigan school's football team, Western State Normal School (by 1957 known as Western Michigan University), had an African American superstar among their ranks. Known as "the Black Ghost," Sam Dunlap played right halfback for Western for four seasons between 1915 and 1919. During Gideon's senior year, Dunlap, who was also an exceptional kicker, scored nineteen touchdowns. In November 1916, the Aggie All-Fresh team was completely outplayed by William H. Spaulding's Western football squad by a score of 77-3. As the starting right halfback, Dunlap proved to be determined ground gainer. In October 1919, the undersized "Kazoo eleven" defeated the Aggies in East Lansing 21-18, and Dunlap was one of the "several individual stars." According to the *M.A.C. Record*, he "was hard to stop once he was started in a broken field" and successfully kicked all three extra points to win the game.[9]

Two years before Smith joined the M.A.C. All-Fresh team, in 1910, under Coach Brewer, racism peculiarly reared its head at a home football game against Olivet on November 19. At halftime of this blowout (M.A.C. trounced the visitors 62-0), there was a minstrel show–like performance during which, according to a writer for the *Record*, "the All-African team" and "an All-World aggregation" played a few downs against each other. The so-called All-African team, Whites adorned in blackface and costumes, defeated their opponents. The brief description of this halftime entertainment written up in the November 22, 1910, *Record* depicts Blacks as being ignorant and inarticulate "coons" and "Ethiopians" who were naturally gifted musicians. Black women were also targeted, insulted by the author who wrote that a "negro wench from the suburbs of Collegeville" refereed the contest. In the November 21, 1910, issue of the *Holcad*, the associate editor in charge of covering sports commented on the same halftime show. "Between the halves," wrote a member of the class of 1911, "a burlesque game between Lindy's Gartenhouse gridiron toughs and Jimmie Hay's dusky Booker T. Washington's furnished merriment distinctly melancholy-banishing." This last game of the season was attended by many Aggie fans, including coeds "dressed in *classy* regalia."[10] Several years prior to Gideon's arrival in East Lansing, African

Americans on the gridiron were openly mocked, to say the least. Gideon would unequivocally defy such blatantly racist characterizations commonly held at predominantly White institutions throughout the nation.

While such performances at halftime of football games were not the norm, during the early twentieth century, evidence suggests the existence of a short-lived M.A.C. student minstrel troupe while Myrtle Bessie Craig was a student. More than a few examples reveal the popularity of minstrel shows at the college. In 1908, a minstrel show was held in the College Armory that sold more than $180 worth of tickets. In early May 1909, a packed performance of the "Mississippi Wrinkle Eradicator" was held at the Ero-Alphian Opera House and included blackface performers, like "Dusky," "Topsey," and "Black Jack" and songs like "Let Me Be Your Lemon Coon." In February 1911, twelve members of the M.A.C. faculty performed in the play *Alabama* in the armory. A fund-raising effort for "a loan fund for women," the play was set in the plantation South. "The characters are all clean cut and interesting," observed a writer for the *Holcad*, "even to Decateur, the old family servant, who has little to say but who wins his way to the hearts of the audience only as an antebellum darky can." The role of Decateur was played by a twenty-eight-year-old, New York–born instructor who wore blackface. A month later, "hundreds of students flocked to the Bijou" to support their fellow classmates who performed in a range of vaudeville acts. Two of the students appeared in the "Holcad Bijou Night" that "took well, not only with the students, but seemed to afford the Lansing people a good deal of enjoyment." The *Holcad* celebrated the two young men who "came on first with their black face comedy stunt." A student continued his coverage of the performance, "They carried off their coon song and jokes in quite a professional way and did not seem 'fussed' nearly as much as the Coeds in the box to whom they paid little attention." Plays like *Uncle Tom's Cabin* performed at the 1912 "annual athletic carnival" further contributed to denigrating portrayals of Black culture on campus. In 1915, when Gideon played in his final spectacular season for the Aggie gridders, there were several major on-campus performances that reinforced denigrating stereotypes about African Americans. In January, sponsored by the YMCA, the Watermelon Jubilee Quartette performed in the armory, singing a variety of "plantation songs and melodies" and "their comedies 'brought down the house.'" Continuing this glorification of slavery, the 1915 Junior Hop for the class of 1916, Gideon's class, was a "cotton party." Held at Lansing's Masonic Temple, more than one hundred couples and M.A.C. personalities like President Snyder, Coach Macklin, college deans, and others were treated to what was described as "one of the most delightful occasions of its kind." To recreate "the realism of Dixie, Stone's colored orchestra and soloists of Detroit furnished the music." In addition to such performances, from time to time, stereotypical caricatures of Black people and Black culture appeared in the *Record* and the *Holcad*. In the mid- to late 1920s, racist ads like one for Dixon's Eldorado pencils included grotesque cartoons of Black men butlers.[11] Terms like the n-word, "darky," and "Rastus" appeared in the *Record*, and during the 1910s, cartoonists for the *Holcad* occasionally poked fun at Black people. While a few articles in M.A.C. papers, such as

"The Negro Preacher Eloquent" (1910) or "Aid for Negro Education" (1911) didn't necessarily denigrate Black people, other long pieces, such as the "Hai-Cut?" (1910) certainly did. In this lead article, a student, identified as "Jimmy, 1911," recounts an interaction he purportedly had with a Black barber named Nehemiah Phillips Brooks. Though the author called him "Mr." and "a gentleman of color," he creates a nonsensical dialogue for him in his poor rendition of Black southern dialect. In the student's tale, the man recounts to him how he used to grow tobacco. "I fell into a revery," wrote the student, "thinking of the old slave days in Virginia, and the J Hop."[12] Ironically, the student was characterizing Black life in Gideon's home state.

One of the most striking examples of the racism Gideon encountered appears in the June 15, 1914, *Holcad*, the last issue of the academic year. Toward the end of the issue, there is a large photo of the 1913 team with Gideon standing to the direct right of Coach Macklin. This is the first large photograph to appear in the *Holcad* with an African American student. On the very next page, there is a prominently placed cartoon with a grotesque looking Black man, hunched over shining a White man's shoes. "Gimme another shine," the White man tells the dejected Black man who is completely dark, except for one white eyeball. Underneath the cartoon, reads: "*Now That We Are Discussing Wearing Apparel.*" This was not the only time images of Black shoeshiners appeared in the *Holcad*. Several issues of the paper through the era of World War I included an advertisement for the popular Lansing shoe store Mac's with a Black man depicted with a large head and mouth holding shined shoes and a shoeshine box saying, "Dey Sho' is Beauties."[13] What did Gideon think about this portrayal of Black manhood?

Chapter 11

Merit Counts

I n 1912, frontpage articles in the *Lansing State Journal* covering the gruesome fate of some Black men in the South were common. Headlines such as "Negro Shot to Death by Mob," "Georgians Work Vengeance Because of Alleged Crime by Black," "Augmented Force Continues Hunt for Alleged Negro Shooters in South," and "Negro Is Lynched" reminded Gideon Smith of the dangers his southern brethren faced.[1] In October 1912 in front of a "crowd of about 200" in Lansing's Masonic Temple, New Orleans Black republican J. Madison Vance characterized what Gideon and his people were experiencing. "This is a crisis in the history of the colored race," proclaimed Vance. "We are facing future success or complete annihilation."[2] Gideon strove for future success.

The M.A.C. newcomer's arrival on campus sometime in the early fall of 1912 was not met with any fanfare. Coach John "Big John" Macklin—the former six foot seven University of Pennsylvania standout who began his illustrious coaching career at M.A.C. in early 1911 and strove to carry on Chester Brewer's winning tradition—did not recruit the outstanding tackle.[3] There are a few stories about how Smith made his way onto Macklin's field before making his first appearance rocking the Green and White on the varsity squad against Olivet College on October 4, 1913, a home game in which he registered his first touchdown. According to one MSU sports historian, when Smith attempted to join the freshman football team, Macklin supposedly "turned him away by refusing to issue him a uniform." A persistent Gideon, the story goes, "reported to practice anyway," wearing the old high-school uniform of a classmate, veterinary student Chuck

Duffy. Because of his "rugged play" and strong performance, "Macklin allowed him to stay on, and in 1913 made him the school's first black varsity student athlete."[4]

In 1934, a reporter for the national edition of the *Chicago Defender*, a popular African American newspaper founded in 1905, offered his own version of Gideon's journey to M.A.C. "Smith, so the legend has it, registered first at the Ann Arbor institution," Dewey R. Jones recounted with an air of confidence. "He was a natural born football player and sought to shine as a member of the Michigan eleven." Jones then claimed the University of Michigan's longtime and future College Football Hall of Fame coach Fielding H. Yost informed Smith "he could never aspire to a regular berth on the Maize and Blue." Jones charged Yost, "a southerner," with drawing the color line. Jones extolled M.A.C., at the time with African American Flint native James McCrary at the fullback position, for having "no such prohibition against a dark man." Smith, "sensing something rotten," Jones waxed on, "turned in his suit, quit his classes, and while Yost was congratulating himself on his moral victory in defense of the confederate states, signed on the dotted line in Lansing. From there on, life was different. . . . The next year after Smith registered at M.A.C., things started happening. In the first place, he promptly made the team." Evoking Psalm 118:22, Jones concluded, "Gideon Smith was the rejected stone that had become the cornerstone of another building and said building had confounded the master architect."[5] Who knows how this reporter for the *Chicago Defender* came up with this entertaining story or who might have shared with him this legend. We do know Smith was a member of the M.A.C. football team from 1913 until 1915, played in every game, and during his first year at M.A.C. played on the freshman team.

"George Brown, the only colored member of the football squad, who plays right tackle on the All-Freshman team, was at practice on the M.A.C. field yesterday, in spite of the fact that he has a badly injured nose. In the game with the Western State Normal school team in Kalamazoo last Saturday, Brown got mixed up in a bunch of tacklers and the bridge of his nose was crushed," reported a writer for the *State Journal* in late October 1912; "the injury undoubtedly was very painful, but Brown never uttered a word of complaint, and when a doctor set the break he took it coolly, showing real nerve." The article continued:

> Brown is the first colored boy who has worked out at East Lansing in some time. There are many difficulties in his way, and because of his color, there is a bit of prejudice against him. This is not openly shown at the school, but has been in all the games in which he has played in the surrounding towns. He never pays any attention to remarks made to him, and has won the favor of his teammates by his gentlemanly conduct.[6]

This incident sounds very similar to what happened to Paul Robeson in 1915 when he tried out for the Rutgers University football team. On the first day of practice, unlike "George Brown" at

The M.A.C. 1912 All-Fresh Team. Gideon is in the front row (*second from far left*). Courtesy of Michigan State University Archives and Historical Collections.

M.A.C. who received his blows from his opponents, Robeson's Scarlet teammates targeted him. Like "George Brown," Robeson's nose was broken, an injury that later impacted his rich singing voice. Robeson and other Black football players who integrated collegiate football were often verbally assaulted with racial slurs and targeted not only by their teammates, especially when they were trying out for their school's squads, but more often by their opponents.

Who was this "George Brown"? Was it Gideon Smith? Was "George Brown" a pseudonym for "Gideon Smith"? The answer to these questions is undeniably *yes*! A member of the M.A.C. All-Fresh football team in 1912, Gideon was the first-known Black athlete and football player at M.A.C. If there were two African American players on M.A.C.'s freshman team, the *State Journal* sportswriter would have certainly mentioned this. In the 1913 M.A.C. yearbook, Gideon, listed as right tackle, appears in a photo with his freshman teammates. With six other teammates, he's in the front row in his secure and confident stance, looking much more menacing than he did in a 1911 photo with his Ferris teammates that resembled the unintimidating photos of college football teams from the 1890s.

The description of "George Brown" fits how Gideon was later described. He was routinely applauded for his toughness, grit, determination, self-control, and humility. While the young man on the 1912 freshman team is listed as playing right tackle, Smith played left tackle, a position that Macklin decided to play him at because the right tackle position on the 1913 team was on lockdown by the fearless captain Chester Gifford. The 1912 M.A.C. All-Fresh team Gideon helped lead was hailed for having great promise. They lost 19-17 in a scrimmage with the varsity squad, leading a writer for the *M.A.C. Record* to conclude, "Several of these men are sure to get a monogram next year if they continue to improve." The coverage of the game in the *Holcad* reveals how much potential Gideon and his teammates had. "The Varsity-Scrub game played on Saturday was good in every respect. The Scrubs fought every inch of the way and were only defeated by the regulars after the hardest kind of play. The final score, 19-17, shows how nearly the teams were matched."[7] While Gideon's play was not highlighted, it's clear he played an impressive game. Listed in the lineup as starting at right tackle, he also stepped in as fullback and carried the ball. In this postseason game, he scored both touchdowns for the so-called Scrubs. Gideon's play was even more impressive considering that the 1912 varsity squad was considered the most successful team at the time. As a starter on the varsity between 1913 and 1915 at left tackle, he played in all twenty games and scored a total of nine touchdowns, including three against Marquette in 1915. One *Holcad* writer aptly described Gideon as being "a sure bet with the ball."[8] Macklin refereed the Varsity-Scrub game and was impressed with Gideon's defensive play and ball carrying. He knew he'd be an asset to the 1913 team. Gideon was a versatile player who held down the left tackle position and who, in certain formations, could be moved to the fullback position. During Gid's varsity career, the Aggies had an exceptional backfield, including George Edward "Carp" Julian, Blake Miller, and Neno Joseph "Jerry" DaPrato.

The fractured or broken nose Gideon sustained in the 1912 All-Fresh game against Western followed him throughout his career. Gideon's fractured nose was set by Dr. Edward J. Bernstein in Kalamazoo, and Coach Macklin paid ten dollars for the medical services.[9] Sports journalists' descriptions of Gideon don't mention him donning a nose guard, the rubber protective device with pieces of soft leather for gripping with back teeth that was first invented in 1892 to help protect players. Yet, in the 1913 clash with Michigan, and in other games, Smith sported nose armor. There is a photo of him, wearing a white nose mask, watching Julian make a headlong dive to cross the goal line for M.A.C.'s first touchdown in the first ten minutes of the 1913 game against Michigan. He sported the same nose guard in a game against Wisconsin. Given his injury from about a year prior, it made sense for him to wear this device, particularly in the rough game against Michigan. The stand-offs between these in-state rivals were particularly brutal. Toward the end of the first half of the 1913 M.A.C.–U of M contest, an unconscious Blake Miller had to be carried off the battlefield. He certainly suffered a concussion and, of course, there were no concussion protocols at this time. Rough tactics characterized collegiate football during the early twentieth century. Hundreds of players were seriously injured, and between 1900 and 1905 more than forty players died. In response to the particularly brutal 1905 football season, President Theodore Roosevelt mandated reforms to help decrease the dangers of stepping on the gridiron.

There are more than a few possible explanations why Gideon Smith was identified by the name "George Brown" in 1912 by the *State Journal*. It's conceivable that Smith, for whatever reason, told the reporter this was his name. Perhaps Smith's coaches identified Gideon as "George Brown" because they didn't want their tough player with a bright future to be poached by another team willing to field a Black player. As a freshman, Gideon showed exceptional promise, enough potential that a reporter for the *State Journal* commented on his performance during a scrimmage. This would not be the only time Smith played under an assumed name. In his debut in professional football several years later with the Canton Bulldogs, he adopted the pseudonym "Charlie" Smith. Other provocative questions are raised by the 1912 *State Journal* article. Who were the other African Americans who supposedly played football at M.A.C. before Smith? Were there other African Americans who tried to integrate M.A.C. football before Smith? It's possible, especially considering earlier appearances of African Americans on the gridiron in Michigan. George Jewett played for the University of Michigan in 1890, and Stephen Morgan was a member of the storied 1901 Michigan Intercollegiate Athletic Association championship Olivet football squad that defeated M.A.C. In any event, Smith was the first African American to play on the varsity M.A.C. football team, the first Black football "monogram man" at the college, the first Black to achieve celebrity status on campus and in Michigan, and the first African American Aggie to be widely known throughout the nation.

Though his place on the team wasn't mentioned among the "stars" in the September 30, 1913, issue of the *M.A.C. Record*, a week later, a writer for the paper made the first major mention of this new addition to the "Green machine." He wrote, "Smith, a giant colored boy, with speed to burn, was sent to left tackle."[10] The *State Journal* praised his play in the first game of the 1913 season against "the big, husky" young men from Olivet College. "Smith's work was perhaps the most noticeable. It was his first varsity game, and the big colored fellow covered himself with glory. He made his first touchdown, never failed to gain when he carried the ball, and [was] a tower of strength on defense."[11] Yet, readers of the *Record* editors' in-depth coverage of the game would have only known Gideon was on the team from the listed line-up, "L. T . . . Smith."[12] While the play of many of his teammates was mentioned, Gideon's contributions were ignored. Throughout most of his time in East Lansing this seemed to be the modus operandi of the *Record*'s editorial staff. They acknowledged Gideon from time to time but did not tend to consistently celebrate him until about 1915. By September 1913, the *Record* was taken over by the M.A.C. (Alumni) Association. As announced in the September 30, 1913, issue, the new focus of the paper became "to strengthen the bonds of friendship between all former students and the College."[13] The first issue of the *Holcad* was released on March 10, 1909, when most likely no African American students were enrolled in the college. The founders of the *Holcad* welcomed contributions from their fellow classmates and envisioned their new publication as being the first real student paper, that is, a paper that was produced by and for M.A.C. students. Writers for the *Record* and *Holcad* didn't wax on about Gideon's heroics but included several photos of him in action on the gridiron.

Why didn't editors of the *Record* and the *Holcad* continuously showcase Gideon's spectacular abilities and dexterity in the same way that they did his White teammates'? Did they not want to draw attention to their only Black player? Did they not want him to outshine his White brothers in arms? Were they placating to the racial etiquette of their times? Gideon wasn't totally absent from these papers. Of course, his name was included in the team lineups and there were a few photos of him. Still, unlike some of his teammates, an individual photo of him didn't appear in the *Holcad*. In late September 1915, the paper included a large and impressive photo of eight of Gid's teammates, "Some of the Veterans." Why Gid wasn't included in the photo raises some interesting questions. On November 11, 1913, the *Record* published a feature photo of the team. This was the first time that a photo of a full-time Black student appeared in this publication, and Gideon's blackness was unmistakable, unlike the drawing of Booker T. Washington that appeared in the *Record* in 1900, softening Washington's African facial features. In the 1913 team photo, a youngish-looking Gideon is clearly visible in the photo, standing in the top row, sandwiched between the noticeably taller left guard Pobanz and assistant coach Elmer "Chill" Gorenflo, the former Aggies captain. Gideon's arms are resting on his hips, a gesture suggesting his confidence, assertiveness, and preparedness.[14] With a heavy brow and a very slight smirk, he, like a few of his teammates, is looking off slightly to his right while Coach Macklin, seated in the center of the second row, peers off into the distance to his left. A year later, with his teammates, Gideon appeared on the cover of the October 20, 1914, *M.A.C. Record*, becoming the first Black student to do so. It would not be until more than three decades later that other Black students, student-athletes like Gideon, would appear on the cover of the *Record*. In September 1948, Horace Smith appeared on the cover of the paper with the football team, and two years later Fred Johnson, "probably the best all-around track star in America," graced the cover, in action in the low hurdles.

Gideon's toughness, skill, and athletic ability won over Coach Macklin, his teammates, the M.A.C. student body, and Aggie fans. According to one account, "If you wanted to have a bunch of aroused Aggies on your hands, all you had to do was make some slur at Gideon or throw a loose elbow his way. . . . Students used to walk Smith home on Friday nights before games to see that he arrived safely and got a good night's sleep." Gideon appreciated his teammates, especially his "old friend Del," left guard Adelbert "Del" VanDevoort who is seated to Smith's right in a team photo that graced the cover of the October 20, 1914, *M.A.C. Record* (Carp Julian is on Smith's left). According to the 1916 *Wolverine*, junior standout VanDevoort was a "doughty individual," and "visiting teams found a great deal of trouble handling" him. "Working with Gideon Smith, he kept holes plugged up and made others when they were needed." Smith respected his teammate's game. "Goodness me," Smith recalled in 1947, "he could tear a barn apart with his bare hands. I never did see a man who gave so much of himself to the game. If there's anything wrong with the present day football player, it's that he doesn't try hard enough—he saves himself too much. . . . It wasn't hard playing tackle when you had a guard like Del beside you. Oh, he was a terror!" On more than a few occasions, Julian and his teammates had Smith's back. Running back sensation Blake Miller "used to say the racial epithets hurled across the line of scrimmage by opponents at Smith were un-repeatable," and his teammates didn't stand for him being disrespected like that.[15]

After beating Michigan in Ann Arbor for the first time on October 18, 1913, 12-7, M.A.C. fans were elated. The 1912 loss in Ann Arbor 55-7 was humiliating for the Aggies. Governor Woodbridge Nathan Ferris addressed a crowd of proud Aggies following the 1913 game, and professors cancelled classes after 10:45 a.m. on the Monday following the victory. Students, professors, and Lansing residents, men, women and children, marched in unison to the steps of the Capitol, set off "Roman candles," stoked "the largest bonfire ever built in the streets of Lansing," and reveled with unrestricted jubilation in the historic win. On December 6, 1913, the Detroit M.A.C. Alumni Association treated the team, Coach Macklin, and the band, which included African American band member Everett Claudius Yates, to an all-expense-paid "complimentary smoker."[16] Again, the *Record* didn't mention Smith's performance in their detailed accounts.[17] But it's worth noting that a photo of Smith watching his teammate Julian score a touchdown was the only image of the game featured in the October 21, 1913, *Record*.

Others recognized Smith's play, including Michigan governor Ferris who was familiar with this former Ferris Institute baller. From his executive chamber in Lansing about nine months after he spoke to 1,300 students in the College Armory, Ferris wrote the following letter to Smith on October 30, 1913:

My Dear Mr. Smith:

I have been watching the reports of the M.A.C. Football team. I am glad to see that you are receiving the same consideration at M.A.C. that you received at Ferris Institute. I am glad that merit counts.

I want to congratulate you upon the splendid work you have been doing in the football team. Your friends at Ferris Institute read of your success with great delight.

I like you for two reasons. First because you are a man and you have a wholesome ambition for doing your work well. Second, I like you because you are a success in football. Go ahead. I am sure that you are now realizing in a measure your ambition, and I am also sure that the future is rich with promise for you. I might go further and say that I congratulate M.A.C. upon having a man of your ability in their team, a man who reflects credit upon himself and upon his fellow associates.

With best wishes, I remain, as ever.
Cordially yours,
Woodbridge N. Ferris, Governor.[18]

Published by the *State Journal* and other newspapers, including the African American *New York Age*, but not by the editors of the *M.A.C. Record*, this letter is intriguing at various levels. Smith was one of the only M.A.C. students to be publicly acknowledged by the governor during his time in office. The *Record* editors' decision to not publish Ferris's letter is perhaps somewhat baffling to the twenty-first-century observer. These accolades from the governor praised Smith, while elevating Jonathan L. Snyder's college. During Snyder's presidency, football became one of the most important features of the college's identity, and the White administrators may have been uneasy with letting this young Black man shine too much. Unlike sports journalists who often referred to Gideon as being a "boy" and always identified him in racial terms, Ferris addressed him as "Mr." and as a man. Ferris acknowledged M.A.C. for allowing Gid to don the Green and White and cast him as being a representative not only for himself, but for his "fellow associates," which may have been a double entendre. Gideon represented his teammates and classmates *and* African Americans. This letter meant a lot to Gideon. In a 1958 interview with sportswriter Wendell Smith, who is credited with recommending Jackie Robinson to Brooklyn Dodgers general manager Branch Rickey, Gideon expressed how much Governor Ferris's letter meant to him.[19]

The 1913 team's victory over Michigan had deeper significance. A year earlier, the *State Journal* featured a front-page article written by a White student from U of M who declared that African Americans in the South were inferior, calling them every name in the book ("savage," "criminal," "lazy," "shiftless"). Though the student didn't refer to him personally, the student demonized Gideon's southern and African heritage. Such sentiments resonated with some in the university's storied football program.[20] An African American, George Jewett, played for Michigan more than two decades before Smith arrived in East Lansing. But Michigan's legendary coach, Fielding Yost, forbade Blacks from playing on his teams from 1901 until 1926, and as athletic director resisted allowing African Americans to play sports at the university. Smith's abilities must have seemed unbearable to him. The Mid-Michigan press was critical of Michigan's drawing of the color line in sports shortly before Smith arrived on campus. "Because a certain element at Michigan seems inclined to object to the presence of a negro on one of the university's athletic teams the color problem may come up for solution in the near future," wrote a pro-M.A.C. sportswriter for the *State Journal* who echoed the sentiments by the NAACP's *Crisis* magazine edited by W. E. B. Du Bois. "The faction which does not care to have a colored man wear the Maize and Blue apparently means to make it unpleasant for the athlete in question, even if it is not successful in causing him to withdraw from the list of candidates. The stand is rather a novel one for a college located this far north and the would-be fuss-makers evidently have forgotten that Harvard, Pennsylvania, Amherst, Brown, Dartmouth, and a number of other eastern institutions have permitted negroes to represent them on the athletic field with great credit."[21]

The *State Journal* continued to cover Gideon's play during the 1913 season. Shortly after the *M.A.C. Record* and the *Holcad* included photos of him in action against Wisconsin, in early

November, the *Journal* featured a photo of Gideon, albeit a bit blurry and hard to decipher, in action carrying the ball against Buchtel. The photo resembles the photo of him in action against Wisconsin that appeared in the *Holcad* on November 3, 1913, with the title "Some Good Work by Smith." According to the *Journal* writer, in the game against Buchtel, he "played a grand game" and "was called upon many times to carry the ball, and nearly always responded with a large gain."[22] For one of the first times, the *Holcad* also gave Gideon his due. "A peculiar feature of the game was the success of the tackle around plays. A large percentage of the gains were made by the fleet footed Smith or Capt. Gifford's terrific plunges." Likewise, in passing, the *Record* celebrated Smith's history-making. "Gideon E. Smith has the distinction of being the first colored lad to win one of the coveted honors at M.A.C.," wrote one of Gid's fellow Farmers after he earned a monogram.[23]

Lansing's small and cohesive Black community was enamored by Gideon. They embraced his success as their own. It was empowering for them. He was their Jack Johnson. On a cold Friday evening in early December 1913, reportedly with an assistant coach Courtright and the team's rugged captain "Chet" Gifford, Gideon attended a banquet held in his honor at the African Methodist Episcopal (AME) church. "Members of the African Church," the *Journal* recounted, "were ardent and withal loyal supporters of Smith during all time he was helping M.A.C. show Western football experts new tricks."[24] The gridiron star was used to such soirees. On March 21, 1914, he attended "a banquet and social program" in Central Labor Hall sponsored by members of the L.Y.P.L.S.C. and he performed a "reading" before an audience of African American professionals, including Kalamazoo attorney E. J. Marshall, W. J. Lewis, honorary vice-president of the Freedmen's Progress Commission and officer of the Grand Lodge of the Free and Accepted Masons C. A. Campbell, and H. B. Wallace.[25] M.A.C. alumni Charles A. Warren and William O. Thompson were in attendance. Gideon participated in activities in the Black community and at the AME Church on a regular basis. In an "elaborate program" in celebration of Governor Ferris's visit to the church in late April 1916, Charles A. Warren performed a solo and Gideon performed for the governor in a quartet that included fellow M.A.C. classmate and percussionist Everett Claudius Yates.[26]

During his second season, at the end of which Macklin optimistically tried to test him out on the basketball court to no avail, Gideon appeared on the cover of the October 20, 1914, *M.A.C. Record* in a team picture. Unlike in the 1913 team photo, this time he was positioned in the second row from the front, sitting in between left guard VanDervoort and star fullback and captain Carp Julian. Based upon how Gideon is sitting, he appears to be smaller than his teammates. He also appears to be unassuming. During the 1914 season, he received minimal attention from the *Record* editors. Of a spectacular and arguably record-setting run, a writer for the *Record* commented in passing: "Smith upon one occasion taking the ball at M.A.C.'s 5-yard line on a tackle-round play for a 95-yard run."[27] This underwhelming description was strikingly different from the headline in a November 1914 issue of the *Saginaw Courier-Herald*, "Julian Makes Seven

Touchdowns, While Negro Lineman Furnishes Thrill with Sprint for 95-Yard Gain," and the *New York Age* writer's assessment of Smith's stunt: "Only three men in the history of the game, as the records show, have made longer runs from scrimmage. Smith ran for 90 yards for a touchdown in a game against Akron College in 1914."[28] Though the writer took away five yards from Smith's awe-inspiring run, his message was clear: Gideon's name was added to the record books.

In 1914, two articles on Gideon stand out, one from the *New York Age*, a widely read African American weekly that was founded by civil rights activist and journalist T. Thomas Fortune in 1884 as *The Freeman*, and another from the *State Journal*, which came into existence three decades before the *Age* as the *Lansing Republican*.

In early January and mid-February, Phil Waters, a correspondent of the *Sporting News*, introduced Smith to New York readers. Accompanying the article in the *New York Age* is a stately photo of Gideon looking directly into the camera with a confident swag and faint smile. He proudly sported a thick, white turtleneck sweater with a large "M.A.C." logo. He purchased this sweater with great pride from Larrabees Sport Shop at 325 S. Washington Avenue. Waters's facts about Gideon are a bit off. He thought, for instance, 1914 was his "first year of college football." But he praised him for never failing "to advance the ball when called upon by his teammates." Waters cited Walter Eckersall, former University of Chicago football star, referee, and sportswriter for the *Chicago Tribune*, who said the African American Aggie "will develop into the most famous tackle that ever played on a Western gridiron." Sharing the entire letter from Governor Ferris with his readers, Waters closed by noting that Smith had support from "the entire student body" and that he was humble. "Smith is modest and unassuming," observed Waters, "despite his success on the gridiron."[29] Other Black papers picked up on this story years later. The Indianapolis *Freeman*, for instance, reprinted this piece on New Year's Day in 1916.[30]

"This Is Gideon Smith—M.A.C.'s Great Left Tackle: How Would You Like to Face Him on the Gridiron?" This was the headline for a feature article on Gideon published on the front page of the sports section in the *State Journal* in late September 1914 in anticipation of the season that was right around the corner. Beneath the title that appeared in elegant, bold, and large font is a photo of Gideon that is much different from the one that appeared in the *Age*. In this photo, a front-leaning Smith suited up in full uniform is getting ready to block his opponent or make his way downfield. His gaze is menacing, yet focused. Staring directly into the camera, this time he is ready for war. While the "entire crew of the first team men" is overviewed to the left of the sinister photo of Smith, he is the focus of the article. The brief preview of Gideon, who, writes the author, "is not worried about his job," highlights his strategic and measured approach to the game as well as his strength.

> As a tackler Smith has achieved a reputation for being about the most difficult man to get away from the Aggie line. He seems to move slowly, but up to the present time there isn't a man on the Farmer squad who on a dash down the field with the ball has been able to outrun him. When he

Smith posing for the menacing photo that appeared on the front page of the "News and Views of Athletic World" section in the *Lansing State Journal* on September 26, 1914. Courtesy of Michigan State University Archives and Historical Collections.

arrives at the heels of his man, Smith just wraps his long arms about the runner, and the procession stops suddenly.

Smith has shown a knack too for foiling the "stiff-arm," or the warding-off tactics employed by a man with the ball against the oncoming tackler. Usually the runner suddenly shoves an open hand into the face of the tackler and so keeps the latter away, but that sort of thing does not count at all with Smith. His trick is to grab the out-stretched hand, if necessary. Usually that is sufficient. The runner has a choice of downing the ball or having an arm pulled out by the roots.

Smith weighs 176 pounds stripped. That means about 185 pounds in high football clothes. Coach Macklin is depending upon him to serve as one of the big defences [*sic*] this fall in the Aggies forward division.[31]

Smith's game, the author opines, was defined by his innate speed, "long arms," and brute force. The author also acknowledges there was a scientific and intellectual side to Gideon's approach. His "knack" could have been considered his genius, methods, techniques, expertness, and adroitness as much as an instinct, gift, or flair. Others echoed such sentiments.

Gideon's play during his second season won him second All Western Eleven honors. In 1915, his last year, he was named to the All Western Eleven, leading one Black journalist to remark that the "leading experts of the West" showed "color blindness." Gideon's final year was much anticipated by Aggie fans, Coach Macklin, and the local and national press. Along with veteran Hugh Blacklock, Gideon reported to the Aggies training camp at Pine Lake in mid-September after "a line composed of veterans and promising recruits" battled in a scrimmage. In 1915, there were more than fifty young men from whom Macklin had to choose. Gideon reportedly spent the summer building up his strength with farm work in the "Adirondack Mountains," apparently an analogy for the South or a country area. He weighed in at about 190 pounds. Reporting on a practice before the 1915 season opener, a writer for the *Detroit Free Press* observed, "the day's work, however, did not close without its rewards. Gideon Smith, the big Negro, made his first appearance at the afternoon practice. He jumped right into the work without any preliminaries. A summer's hard work in the Adirondacks has rounded him into fine shape." In less theatrical terms, the *M.A.C. Record* noted, "the return of Hugh Blacklock and Gideon Smith were the big features of the easy feeling indulged in last week."[32] Sportswriters for the *State Journal* were even more optimistic. "Five of the 1914 veterans of the line have been returned to their positions by the coach," the state capital's newspaper observed. "Gideon Smith, the big colored chap, is playing the left tackle position in a fashion that threatens to even outdo his records of other years."[33]

On the other hand, a writer for the *Detroit News Tribune* mocked Smith and, in the paper's usual fashion, stereotyped him as a happy-go-lucky Black brute. None of the other M.A.C. players were described based upon their physical attributes. Under the attention-grabbing header "COFFEE COLORED PHANTOM RETURNS: Gideon Smith, Aggies' Black Terror, Back with Grid Squad," this Detroit paper printed: "Gideon Smith, the dusky left tackle of the Michigan Aggies, hearkened to the call of the gridiron today, and lined up with the squad this morning for his first practice of the season. Gideon, as the only colored foot ball star among the bigger schools, came back with his usual 16-inch smile and his 180-pounds of beef-hardened into muscle by a summer spent on the farm back in Maryland."[34]

During Smith's final year in an Aggie uniform, the *M.A.C. Record*, unlike in 1913 and 1914, mentioned Gideon's consistent play. The paper alluded to his "plunging" and plowing for yards, his touchdowns, and his sturdiness and dependability.[35] They recognized him as "the star on the line." The writers for the *Record* gave him his due credit for his performance in the 24-0 "beating down" of Michigan on Saturday, October 23, 1915, in Ann Arbor. After losing in 1914 to Michigan in a very low scoring defensive battle, 3-0, M.A.C. was out for revenge and Gideon was, as usual, hyped up for this annual battle. The previous year's loss left a bad taste in his mouth, as well as on the tastebuds of countless Green and White rooters, his teammates, and the prideful and shrewd Coach Macklin. "Gideon Smith was a real star," the *Record* noted. "It was he who balled-up Michigan's attack when they did get the ball, and again, Gideon got over half of the tackles." A writer for the *Holcad* shared these sentiments, boasting: "Gideon Smith added to his enviable record by stopping play after play besides making a few needed yards through the line. He seemed to be in every play and his presence meant death to Michigan's efforts."[36] Before and after the Aggies' victory over their archrivals, newspapers in Michigan and elsewhere celebrated Smith's play, shedding light on how he was perceived on campus as well. After M.A.C. pounded Carroll 56-0, the *Detroit Free Press*, under the header "Work of Smith Is the One Redeeming Feature," might have called him "the big colored boy," but concluded, "had it not been for him," the Aggies "might have gone into the final period with a count of two."[37] Sportswriters for the *Holcad* also gave Gideon more props during his last season with the Green and White, celebrating, for instance, his performance against Carroll, which included several long runs and two touchdowns. Gideon, who "again occupied the limelight throughout the game," was also applauded for his protection of the football as a ball carrier and his tenacious defense.[38]

The cover of the *Detroit Free Press*'s "Sporting Section" on Sunday, October 24, 1915, features an image of Gideon in action as "Jerry DaPrato obliges with a few yards straight through the Michigan line." The writer extolled Gideon as a key contributor. "When it came to the defense Smith was there. The score card shows there was only one Smith in the game, and to the spectators it seemed as though there were twenty of his kind right on the heels of the Michigan plays [*sic*]. Not only did Smith pulverize the Michigan defense, but he carried the ball on several occasions and got away for good gains," the popular Detroit paper continued. "This large person is a decided brunette as to complexion, but as a football player he is pure gold all the way through. No matter where the Maize and Blue sent its plays, there always seemed to be a dark man in the way."[39] Under the header "Gideon Smith, M.A.C. Colored Tackle, Was Game's Hero, as Were His Mates on the Line," a writer for the *Adrian Daily Telegram and Times* was concise in his assessment of Gideon's play, concluding that "the great colored tackle for the Aggies was the stellar player of the day."[40]

Citing from the *Free Press*, the *Chicago Defender* minced no words in their belief that Smith was the "shining light" of the game. The *Defender* declared Gideon "was far and away the best man of the game." They added, "Gideon Smith, star tackle for Michigan Agricultural School, was a shining light in the defeat of the Michigan University game last Saturday on Ferry Field. This is the second time in ten years that Yost's machine has been humbled by this school." The *Defender* also claimed after the game Smith was "carried on the shoulders of white teammates as 10,000 Michigan rooters look on."[41]

Smith, no doubt, took part in the celebrations following the game against Michigan. On October 25, 1915, the Monday after the game, 1,500 M.A.C. students, band members, and coeds along with ten thousand to fifteen thousand Lansing residents celebrated their team's second victory over their rivals. They started a large fire in front of the capital building, marched in unison, and set off "Roman candles." The scene was reminiscent of the mayhem following the 1913 win over their archrivals. Despite the "delirious" nature of the "Aggie students," as well as the fact that the Lansing firemen had to extinguish a blaze near a street car wire, Earl R. Trangmar of the *State Journal* reported that "it was an orderly demonstration. Scarce a policeman lost a smile." From the "poopdeck of a motor truck" some of the Aggie Eleven addressed the large crowd, thanking them, as team captain Blake Miller did, for their unwavering support. "We want to thank you all for the great support that you have given us these many seasons," an appreciative and elated Miller shouted like a coach after winning a championship game. "It's what put the pep into a team." Beaming with pride and the hopes of Lansing's Black community behind him, Gideon rose to speak and instead supposedly "hid behind a smile."[42] His smile said everything. He was a humble man of few words. He let his and his teammates' performance speak for itself. Like Blake and Hewitt Miller, Gideon was among those players who "stood up and faced the music" while others, perhaps overcome by the moment, ducked away from the limelight and privately enjoyed the festivities with their fans. Like his teammates, Gideon took part in countless brief interactions and was swarmed by fans, embraced, and patted on the back, shoulder, and head. Gideon might have even been able to cross the color line at the Bijou movie and vaudeville theater where the upperclassmen gathered for more whooping it up and where earlier in the year "Comedy Colored Comedians" Irving Jones and Johnson Roy performed "Dice, Gin and Chicken."[43]

Following the 1915 victory against Michigan, Macklin's second win against Yost in Ann Arbor in three years, Gideon finished the season strong. He was very tough, never missing a game during his career. After a game against Penn State at State College in front of a hostile crowd, a reporter remarked, "Gideon Smith limped, an unheard-of thing for Gideon, for while most of the men have in the past borne bruises and contusions galore following a battle, Gideon has come through with a smile and little else. At Penn State, however, he was badly bumped in the leg."[44] He suffered a significant injury in the game against Michigan in the second quarter. In early November 1915, the *Detroit Free Press* reported he fractured a rib after he received a "hump."[45] Was Gideon targeted because of his complexion, as was the case with Fritz Pollard, the

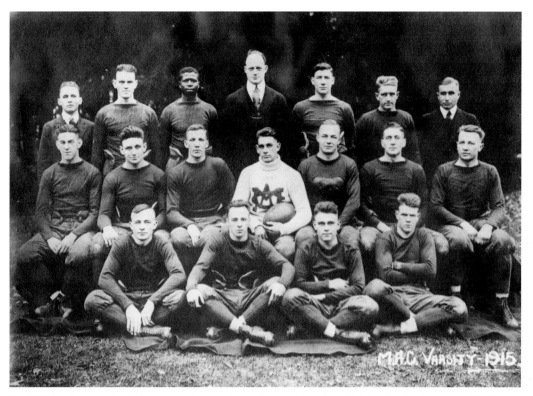

The 1915 M.A.C. varsity football team. Smith is standing right next to head coach John Macklin. Courtesy of Michigan State University Archives and Historical Collections.

first African American to play football at Brown University who was constantly the recipient of cheap shots? Was this what a *State Journal* writer referred to in September 1914 when he remarked that Gideon was destined for greatness "provided of course that some rough footballer doesn't kick him in the ribs or otherwise incapacitate him before the season's games begin?"[46] Smith played the remainder of the 1915 season following the game against Michigan with a fractured rib, shining against Marquette in M.A.C.'s 68-6 thrashing. He and the multitalented and dexterous Jerry DaPrato accounted for seven of the squad's ten touchdowns.[47]

At the time considered "MA.C.'s greatest football machine" marshalled by Macklin and assistant coaches G. E. Gauthier and C. W. Gifford, the 1915 team lost five key contributors at the end of the season, captain Blake Miller, Hewett Miller, Jerry DaPrato, Howard Beatty, and Smith. Of Gideon's career, the *State Journal*, echoed by Ann Arbor's *Daily Times News*, concluded, "the Farmers will lose Gideon Smith who probably recovered more fumbles than any other man on the team."[48] Along with his teammates, Smith was heralded at the football banquet in late November 1915 and was among the small group of players who offered "a few words" at Lansing's most upscale hotel, the Hotel Downey, before the delegation "migrated to the Bijou" for further festivities. The M.A.C. community was sorry their hero Gid was no longer eligible to sport an Aggie uniform. He and his graduating classmates were among the most accomplished athletes in the history of the college. The students were especially appreciative. Gideon was one of the most popular football players, and athletes, who ever played at M.A.C. and even appeared in one of the first musical comedies ever staged at M.A.C. in 1915 along with several of his teammates, including Julian, and the Miller brothers. He was popular not only with students, "but [with] alumni and residents of Lansing as well." As noted by a writer for the *Times Herald* of Port Huron, Michigan, the "college students have purchased him a gold watch with a popular inscription to be presented to him at a football banquet."[49] The students raised money to give a gift to Smith for his performance. In his coverage of the event, a White sportswriter for a Detroit paper evoked the stereotype of the happy-go-lucky and deferential Black man. "Lansing and East Lansing rooters, more or less fascinated by Gideon's faculty for playing football and somewhat entranced by his 16-inch smile, are contributing to a pot to buy him a present. This gift will be in the form of a time piece, though a considerable number of rooters hold that when a football is around loose anywhere the big fellow seems to be always on time without the aid of a chromometer."[50]

Gideon Smith's extraordinary talent on the gridiron was the main reason members of the M.A.C. community, especially the students, adored him so much. Because of his otherworldly skills, ability, toughness, and warrior-like mentality on the gridiron, his coaches, teammates, and classmates saw beyond his race. Macklin was not the first coach at a predominantly White institution to give an opportunity to an African American football player. But there were many coaches of his era who didn't defy the de facto segregation that prevailed in collegiate football during the era of Jim Crow segregation. A Black *New York Age* journalist gave credit to "Big John" for recognizing Gideon's raw talent. "Johnny Macklin is one of the few great gridiron generals who believes in giving every candidate for his team an equal show regardless of color, race or his pocketbook."[51] Smith respected Macklin. When he visited M.A.C. in 1946 for Alumni Day, he shared fond memories of his former coach. The feeling was mutual. He probably regretted not attending the 1935 homecoming game where his former coach was honored with the dedication of Macklin Field. To the chagrin of a Maize and Blue reporter for the *Detroit News*, Macklin placed Smith, along with M.AC. halfback DePrato, on his All-American Team.[52] In the official 1913 and 1915 team photos, Smith is standing in the back row right next to Macklin, even though he was not one of the two tallest players on the team. The placement of Gideon next to the towering soon-to-be-legendary coach was a sign of respect granted to the team's first African American football player. Smith told a reporter from the *New York Age* that "he gives all credit to his unprejudiced coach." Macklin, it has been said, looked after Smith, especially when the team traveled to away games and had to obey the de facto rules of segregation. Between 1913 and 1915, the team ventured outside the state to Lincoln, Nebraska; State College, Pennsylvania; and Madison, Wisconsin. "Not allowed to check into the team's White-only hotel on road trips, Smith would get off the train and ask Macklin what time practice would be held," Steve

Grinczel recounts; "with money provided by Macklin to pay for food and lodging in the local black community, Smith would not be seen by the Aggies again except at practice, at the game and on the train ride back to East Lansing."[53] This involved significant forethought and planning.

As many mentioned, Smith was humble and modest, something he learned growing up. His disposition was key to his success and even his survival. In this sense, he had a similar disposition to future boxing heavyweight champion Joe Louis. In 1916, Gideon is noticeable in the large centerfold class photo in the *Holcad*, and the students gave Smith a fitting tribute in the yearbook, the *Wolverine*. This was the first time an African American was honored in such a manner.

> Gideon's playing of his position was one of the notable things of the year in central western football. He was a mountain of strength in the line, but his greatest value to the team lay in his almost uncanny faculty for doping out the other fellow's intentions. If close tab had been kept in the matter, it would undoubtedly have been demonstrated that Gideon broke up more enemy plays before they were started than did any other man on the team. Coach Macklin paid him the tribute of classing him with the best tackles he has ever seen, while critics generally accorded him favorable mention.[54]

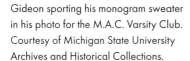

Gideon sporting his monogram sweater in his photo for the M.A.C. Varsity Club. Courtesy of Michigan State University Archives and Historical Collections.

Chapter 12

Of Football Fame

In the years following Gideon Smith's graduation, alumni echoed the praise for him in the *Wolverine*. This is most poignantly revealed in a letter to the *M.A.C. Record* from William Carl Chapman, '05. This New York City resident was livid about the Aggies' poor 1922 season, especially the 0-63 loss to the University of Michigan. "We had a colored boy a few years ago—one Gideon Smith. Prejudice kept him off the squad for a year. Finally he appeared in a tattered old suit that he paid for himself out of his scanty earnings. The coach said that if he had that much spirit he was going to get a square deal. Smith turned out to be one of the greatest tackles in the country. He not only was a marvelous player but one of the cleanest sportsmen that ever wore the monogram. Many was the time when the opponents, failing to gain through Gideon's side of the line resorted to the dirtiest kind of rough stuff, but Smith never lost sight of the fact that he was a sportsman and a monogram man." Chapman ("Chappie") continued, "Some of the present generation could well emulate Smith in his honest desire to give the best talent he had to his Alma Mater."[1] Even though he referred to Gideon as a "boy" (and Gideon was a grown man when he played for the Aggies), Chapman's veneration of him is unmistakable, and many of his fellow alumni shared his sentiments. Gideon, "who helped 'beat Michigan,'" provided those who watched him play with a treasure trove of fond memories. His sportsmanship was echoed by those outside of the M.A.C. community as well. In 1930, a former Penn State gridder who played against him, Coach Albert M. Barron, called Gideon "one of the hardest men—and cleanest—he ever opposed." Gideon "showed him several new pages in the gridiron volume."[2]

Six months before graduating and three weeks after the 1915 team's final game against Marquette, Smith became the fourth African American player to play professional football. On November 28, 1915, John Cussack, the coach of the Canton Bulldogs, acquired him. He played under the assumed name "Charlie" Smith. One account suggests that Smith's friend George Edward "Carp" Julian, who played for the Bulldogs in 1915 and 1916, recommended him to the coach. His career was very short lived. He only played in one game.[3] Smith had fond memories of his professional debut. He recalled:

The coach looked at me kind of funny when he came into the dressing room. . . . He didn't start me. That was all right, because I never had seen much football from the stands and I was enjoying it. But he sent me in to start the second half, and I stayed. After the game Jim Thorpe, who was on my team, came over and said: "Boy, I wish you was in there all the time. They don't pay quite so much attention to me when you're in the game." I guess . . . that was about the nicest compliment I ever had, coming from an athlete like Jim Thorpe.[4]

After the 1915 football season came to a close, the Michigan sportswriter community continued to follow Smith's career. Tuskegee Institute heavily recruited him to be their head football coach in the summer of 1916, and the *Free Press* even claimed he was coaching there in October. This was not the case. In October 1916, he was among the large group of former Aggie stars to hold an informal position for M.A.C. coach Frank A. "Dutch" Sommers's camp at Pine Lake. Sometime in the early fall of 1916, after graduating with about 250 others and his brief stint playing professional football, he accepted a job at West Virginia Collegiate Institute, one of the original HBCU land-grant universities founded as West Virginia Colored Institute in 1891 as a part of the Second Morrill Act. A small African American weekly in Keystone, West Virginia, introduced Smith to its readers, letting them know that he was going to be paid eight hundred dollars per year.[5] In the fall 1916 semester, Smith arrived at the school during a time of significant transformations. Under the leadership of Booker T. Washington disciple Byrd Prillerman, M.A.C. student Delbert M. Prillerman's father, in 1915 the school changed its name from West Virginia Colored Institute and became a more rigorous college. The school was very small with an enrollment of 368 students, and Smith served as the "New Commandant of Cadets, and a teacher of chemical science." He also coached the school's football team that only suffered one loss during his brief pitstop in West Virginia. The college officials took pride in introducing him as "one of the few Negroes of the United States, who has made his name a phrase of charm with wherever football is known." The institute's administrators continued, "to this eminence he adds more commendable virtues of a gentleman and scholar."[6]

In June 1917, Smith registered for World War I, and like more than 350,000 African Americans served his country in a segregated U.S. military. After being discharged, beginning in 1919, he taught and coached football at Virginia Normal and Industrial Institute in Petersburg, Virginia, and at Princess Anne Academy in Princess Anne, Maryland, where he also taught "science and art as Commandant."[7] He then joined Hampton Institute where he served as the head football coach from 1921 until 1940. He also coached track and mentored Hampton athletes. His approach to football was inspired by Macklin. A reporter for the *Washington Tribune* described Smith's straightforward stratagem and outlook in the mid-1930s. "Gideon Smith, likewise, knows football and believes in the straight, solid game, ignoring all of the fancy frills and foibles which each year find their way into football. Hampton teams are always strong, both in the line and in the backfield, knowing their football as they should know it."[8] The *Detroit Free Press* took note of Smith's retirement in 1940, highlighting his connection to Michigan State College, this time without calling attention to his race as they routinely had done twenty-five years earlier: "Gideon E. Smith, one of the greatest linemen in Michigan State College football history, has retired as head coach at Hampton Institute in Virginia but will stay on as line mentor."[9] Smith remained on the staff until he retired in 1955, and his service was formally recognized at Hampton's annual Varsity Day banquet and later at a 1958 homecoming game sponsored by the Hampton Athletic Committee. Once again, his Michigan State connection was a part of his impressive résumé. At the 1955 celebration, he was introduced to the community as being an "ex-star" who "gained national fame" while playing "60 minutes of every game for the MSC gridders."[10] In 1981, he was the winningest coach in the history of Hampton with an overall record of 97-46-12, including five championship football teams and ten championship track teams.

At Hampton, Smith was multidimensional. In addition to coaching generations of football players, students and athletes, he also served as assistant athletic director, helped coach baseball and basketball, directed intramurals, taught physical education, and actively participated in the Central Intercollegiate Athletic Association (CIAA).[11] He was a well-known community man who often spoke on campus and in the community about sports and character building. In the early 1930s, he was vocal about achieving justice and equal treatment for players whose eligibility was being questioned by the reformist CIAA. A passionate speech he delivered at the annual CIAA meeting in December 1932 was cited in its entirety in a widely read Black newspaper. His words were precise and measured. Their star player, Ivory W. Richmond, was declared ineligible for two games during the 1932 season. In defense of his school's program that was facing challenges pertaining to eligibility requirements, Smith declared, "We at Hampton Institute want the same benefits and same privileges according us as those accorded to other institutions in the association. We do not wish any favors nor do we wish any privileges that are not accorded the other members of the association. As a member of the CIAA we demand equal treatment as long as we are members."[12] Smith maintained Richmond was indeed eligible in 1932. He was also vocal about how sports could help African Americans in practical manners. In 1943, "Coach Gid," as he was affectionately referred to, spoke in Norfolk, Virginia, on the topic of "Athletics in the Post World War."[13]

Smith was not only what a writer for the *New York Amsterdam News* called in 1929 "the brains behind Hampton's offensive," but was also the scholar West Virginia Collegiate Institute introduced him to be in the fall of 1916.[14] In 1924, the Alumni Association of Hampton Institute released the first issue of its alumni journal, and Smith penned an article whose title, "Are You an Asset or a Liability?," tells us something about his world view.[15] In 1932, he played the role of amateur historian, producing with George Lyle a brief history of twenty years of Hampton athletics published in the *Washington Tribune*.[16] In 1941, a writer for the *New York Age* suggested the more than "qualified" Smith be promoted to the position of chair of Hampton's Department of Agriculture. This was on account of his intellect and knowledge in agriculture, something he intensely studied at M.A.C.[17] In the early 1940s, Smith conducted a survey of Hampton graduates who participated in athletics to determine how their experiences in sports impacted their educational pursuits. He was pleased to discover that most of his respondents found their participation in sports at Hampton to be fulfilling and beneficial to their future endeavors as coaches, teachers, and professionals. "The men," concluded Smith, "proved conclusively that both brains and brawn are found in Negro college stars." For Smith, this work was a self-study of some sort. The responses of Hampton alumni resonated with his own experiences at M.A.C. Like many of his respondents, he used football as an "outlet to relieve" himself "of excess energy," to learn the "fundamental techniques" of football, and to express his values of "fair play, honesty, sportsmanship, courage, cooperation and stamina" that followed him in his life after he graduated from M.A.C.[18] Smith advocated for African American autonomy and leisure, as revealed by his service with the New Bay Shore Corporation during the 1940s and 1950s.

Smith was a respected and admired member of the Hampton Institute community. In the mid-1980s, one of his former players, scientist and educator Carl McClellan, shared only his fondest memories of Coach Smith. "One of the highlights was coach Gideon Smith. He was a man of such integrity. And I learned so much football and character from him," McClellan reminisced. "When I first went out for the HI football team, coach Gideon Smith didn't want to give me a uniform. As a matter of fact, he gave me a football and lined me up against some big ends and tackles. I had to run for my life to get through them. But I did. That impressed Smith."[19] McClellan's rite-of-passage story sounds very much like what Smith overcame on Macklin's practice field. After retiring from Hampton, Smith continued to work, serving as an instructor of health and physical education at Virginia Theological Seminary and College in Lynchburg, Virginia. In 1961, Ferris State University honored Smith as an alumnus. The school's Alumni Association presented him and two others with a Distinguished Alumnus Award, a trophy for those who "distinguished themselves in their fields of endeavor." Ferris claimed him as one of their own, but also acknowledged what he accomplished at M.A.C.[20]

In 1968, the year that Martin Luther King Jr. was assassinated, Gideon E. Smith, seventy-eight, died at the Veterans Administration Hospital in Salem, Virginia. He passed away about eight months after his beloved wife and fellow Hampton teacher Mildred George Smith died. He was survived by his two children, Mildred S. Belcher and Gideon E. Smith Jr., and his funeral rites were fittingly held in Hampton Institute's Memorial Chapel. Once again, his immortal title as an African American first at Michigan State University was broadcasted in all of his obituaries.[21] On May 30, 1981, in Fayetteville, North Carolina, he was posthumously inducted into the CIAA Hall of Fame. "For the 1913–15 seasons, Smith was the heart of the Spartans defense at tackle. He was the first Black athlete to ever play at Michigan State and was a member of the first Michigan State team to beat archrival Michigan."[22] In 1994, two years after Charles "Bubba" Smith, Don E. Coleman, Earvin "Magic" Johnson, Johnny Green, and Gene Washington, he became the sixth African American to be inducted into the MSU Athletics Hall of Fame. The only other player from the 1915 team to be inducted, the sensational scorer and extra-point kicker Jerry DaPrato, joined Smith in 2001. In 2017, for the first time, Smith was on the College Football Hall of Fame ballot. In 2019, for the third time, Smith was on the ballot in the divisional coaching category.

Gideon Smith's years on the M.A.C. varsity football team from 1913 until 1915 were remarkable. For decades after he graduated, beginning with the comparisons made between him and Kansas-born fullback Harry C. Graves who arrived in East Lansing in 1918, he was a living legend. In the "Alumni Notes" of the October 10, 1919, issue of the *M.A.C. Record*, Smith was described as "'Gid,' of football fame, who helped 'beat Michigan,'" and in October 1920, a throwback photo of him trotting onto the field before the battle with Michigan in 1914 with his teammates in his thick, white, turtleneck monogram sweater was published in the widely read by alumni paper. Under the header "How They Looked in '14," the photo was also reprinted in the *Holcad* in 1921. In 1934, a writer for the *Chicago Defender* reinvoked the lore of Smith's days at M.A.C. and his performance in the first victory over Michigan. "Everywhere one looked, there was one Gideon Smith. He carried the ball, punted, he pitched, he caught, he tackled and called the signals. The result was obvious—there was just too much Gideon Smith for Ann Arbor, so the lowly Aggies walked away with all honors, to say nothing of the goalposts and the bleacher seats."[23]

At M.A.C., Gid was more than simply an amazing football player who helped the college avenge a losing streak against their foes. He was a student and intellectual. He was popular and beloved by his classmates. He belonged to the Cosmopolitan Club, assuming leadership positions from 1914 until 1916 (positions to which his classmates elected him), the Farmer's Club, and the M.A.C. Varsity Club. He was also active in Lansing's Black community. Gideon encountered racial prejudice on occasion at M.A.C., especially during his freshman year in 1912 before making varsity a year later. He watched his back and endured glaring stares while navigating his way around Lansing and traveling to different cities and states when the Aggies traveled for away games. He was not defined by his detractors or totally bound by his times, and he did not speak publicly about these inevitable realities. As his great-grandson recalled, he loved MSU and fought tirelessly "for the only colors, Green and White!" Years after he graduated, Gideon wrote to the editors of the *M.A.C. Record* eager to share with his former classmates milestones in his life, including his new jobs, his marriage, and the births of his children. He wanted to stay in touch with his alma mater. In March 1920, the "warrior of the grid" wrote to the alumni paper, "Just keep sending *Records* to the same old address. I don't want to miss any of them, for it is the only way I have to keep up with the great happenings at the dear Old School. A failure to receive one is equivalent to being absent from the college for a week." In 1923, he shared his disappointment with *Record* readers about not being able to return for homecoming. In February 1926, he assured his fellow alumni he'd "kept up with the college through the record." In November 1934, he wrote to the class of 1916 secretary, "It is a great joy to me to read each Sunday of the wonderful success of the M.S.C. Football team. I hope it will keep up the good work."[24] His appreciation for his alma mater was revealed by his contributions to the college's alumni fund as well as by his memorable visits back to East Lansing in 1930, 1946, 1947, 1953, and 1965. He was in no way obligated to return. He did so because his experiences at the college and in East Lansing and Lansing meant something to him. MSU was part of his personal history and identity.

Affectionately known as "Gid," Gideon E. Smith was among the few first African Americans to graduate from M.A.C. in the decade after Myrtle Bessie Craig did so in 1907. Just as Charles A. Warren, William O. Thompson, and Craig paved the way for him, Gideon opened the doors for those African Americans who enrolled in M.A.C. in the late 1910s and 1920s and stepped foot on the gridiron. Symbolically, he reopened the doors for African Americans to enter the college. He made it easier for those who walked in his footsteps to hold their heads up high. Smith was not the only African American student at M.A.C. during the early to mid-1910s. Another African American student also graduated in 1916. A close friend of Gid's, Everett Claudius Yates, was at M.A.C. for four years with Smith. Yates was an accomplished percussionist in the M.A.C. orchestra and cadet band who performed with his classmate B. D. Jones and Charles A. Warren in a reception in honor of Governor Ferris's visit to Lansing's AME church in late April 1916. While Smith won battles on the dangerous gridiron, exhibited his athletic creativity, and demonstrated that Black athletes were intellectuals and could compete with Whites, Yates represented the race and broke down barriers within M.A.C.'s more highbrow artistic spheres.

Chapter 13

Between the Wars Pathfinders

From 1916, when Gideon E. Smith graduated, until President Franklin D. Roosevelt's signing of the Neutrality Act of 1939, at least twenty-three African Americans graduated from M.A.C. and what in 1925 became Michigan State College of Agriculture and Applied Sciences.[1] While the vast majority of the college's White students from the era of World War I through the 1930s were Michiganders, only a handful of the Black students were from the Wolverine State. These groundbreakers were born during the nadir of U.S. race relations. Three-quarters of these Black Aggies and Spartans came of age in the South to parents who were born between the antebellum era and Reconstruction. In addition to Smith, this diverse, yet mostly male, group of M.A.C. and MSC graduates includes Everett Claudius Yates, '16; Delbert M. Prillerman, '17; Clement C. Johnson, '18; Oliver Meakins Green, Herbert McFadden, and Esther I. Tate, '20; McGlenard Williamson, '21; Harry C. Graves, '23; Margaret Elizabeth Collins, '24; Benjamin L. Goode, '25; Clarence E. Banks and Aeolian E. Lockert, '26; Mabel J. Lucas, '27; Clarice A. Pretlow and Chester Smith, '30; Stenson Broaddus and James L. McCrary, '35; Albert H. Baker, Herschel L. Irons, and Arthur M. Bowman, '36; and William H. Smith and Frances Langford, '37.

Like their White classmates but in significantly different ways, they were inevitably shaped by their individual backgrounds and upbringings, what they experienced on campus, decisions they made during and after their college years, and the eventful times during which they lived. The college transformed drastically during the dynamic era of World War I through the 1930s, what U.S. historians refer to as "Between the Wars" or the interwar period. As Keith Widder underscores, World War I "seriously disrupted the lives of M.A.C. students and faculty, changed the physical and social landscape of the campus, and brought new opportunities for the college to carry out its land-grant mission."[2] The influence of the Great War was symbolized by the War Department's establishment of a Student Army Training Corps unit on campus. Following President Jonathan L. Snyder's retirement in 1915 until the beginning of John A. Hannah's long and impactful term in 1941, there was what historian Madison Kuhn called "a lack of continuity" in college leadership. Four presidents led the college, and as journalist David A. Thomas has pointed out, several of their terms were controversial. Frank S. Kedzie, 1915–1921, and Robert S. Shaw, 1928–1941 (who served as interim president three times prior to becoming the college's eleventh president), held the longest terms during the interwar period, shaping the college's evolution in noticeable ways.[3]

The changes on campus were symbolized by the much debated renaming of the college in 1925 from Michigan Agricultural College to Michigan State College of Agriculture and Applied Sciences. "A new name," observed Madison Kuhn, "precipitated changes in college titles and symbols."[4] A year later, the college adopted a new nickname. The "Aggies" became the "Spartans." During the 1920s, the curriculum expanded far beyond the agricultural, forestry, mechanical (engineering), veterinary, and women's (home economics) courses. Under President Shaw, the college created new courses of study including the applied science course, liberal arts, business administration, nursing training, medical biology, hotel management, and applied music. Teacher training also expanded. "Of the liberal arts seniors who graduated in 1930," for instance, "one-half earned a secondary certificate in the department of education."[5]

By the 1925–1926 academic year, there were eight courses of study and more than thirty departments of instruction. The fees to attend the college also increased from $7.50 per year during its first fifty years to $105.00 by 1925.[6] In the mid-1920s, the number of graduate students significantly increased and doctoral programs in seven disciplines were inaugurated. The construction of a new library contributed to the evolving scholarly and intellectual landscape.[7] By 1925, the college's continued commitment to outreach and extension "confirmed the wisdom of its founders and fulfilled their vision in an amazing fashion."[8] Other noteworthy changes included the construction of many new buildings from the mid-1920s until the late 1930s. In 1939 alone, more than five major building projects were completed. During the interwar period, less strict social rules governed student life, fund-raising efforts increased, and on-campus healthcare and student services, communications, and public safety improved. College leaders evoked expressions of historical revivalism by celebrating the institution's growth. After declining during the early 1920s, the football program with its upgraded facilities made great strides. The overall scope of what campus life entailed expanded, and in 1931 the college became a member of the Association of American Universities.[9]

During the 1920s, in the wake of the passage of the Nineteenth Amendment, White women made significant inroads in the college's leadership and their educational opportunities. The

Human Ecology Building, erected in 1924, provided a state-of-the-art site for women's instruction in home economics. A year later, the college's Women's Athletic Association allowed women to compete in interclass women's sports and earn monograms, awards, and recognition. In 1929, the first woman was permitted to enroll in the engineering program. In 1931, 1937, and 1938 respectively, Mary Mayo, Sarah Langdon Williams, and Louise Campbell Halls—all named in honor of the college's standout women leaders—opened for women. "The Great Depression of the 1930s," David A. Thomas suggests, "affected life at Michigan State much as the downturn affected life throughout the United States." President Shaw strategically navigated the economically trying times as the college acquired more land, constructed new buildings, and saw the student population increase dramatically.[10] There were slight decreases in student enrollment between the 1921–1922 and 1923–1924 and the 1931–1932 and 1933–1934 academic years. But by the end of the 1920s, there was an enrollment of approximately 3,800, and by the 1938–1939 academic year, there were 7,658 students enrolled at Michigan State College.

The "Between the Wars" African American students did not necessarily benefit from this growth and reform. Despite college spokespersons' claims that MSC was a "very democratic institution," it wasn't until the early 1940s that the dormitories were officially desegregated. As the campus expanded and the student population increased by about 280 percent between 1916 and 1939, Black students on campus blazed new trails on their own terms. They didn't have an established Black campus community to turn to for comfort, moral support, and encouragement. As 1944 MSC graduate and Lansing native Jennie Washington reminisced, "There were virtually no Blacks on campus in those days."[11] They were habitually the only Blacks in their classes and the college's clubs, organizations, and sports teams that a handful of them integrated. Though in the early 1940s two African American men (cross-country star Harry Butler, '40, and track sensation Walter Arrington, '41) served as captains of varsity sports teams, when the young men lived in the dormitories, they roomed with each other or alone in designated spaces. Like their predecessors, the "Between the Wars" African American students had to watch their backs, especially while moving about the Lansing area and Mid-Michigan. This took psychological tolls on them. Black women and men faced racial discrimination, imagined and real threats of violence, and racial profiling. In 1921, for instance, the *Lansing State Journal* published a brief "special" story about an innocent Black man, called "Mr. Darky," who was accused by the sheriff of "being a bold, bad n——r, bent on holding up the railway mail" in Charlotte, Michigan.[12]

The presence of the college's African American students in public spaces was conspicuous. East Lansing was not noticeably integrated until after the modern Civil Rights Movement, and the Black population in Lansing was small during the interwar period, averaging about 1.6 percent of the city's total population from 1910 until 1940. In 1910, there were 354 African Americans in Lansing. Following World War I, the number of African Americans who migrated to the city from the Deep South increased. The U.S. census of 1920 lists 698 Blacks in Lansing. The local NAACP, founded in 1918, claimed that 75 percent were "owners of their own homes" worth a total of $330,000.[13] In 1930 and 1940, respectively, there were 1,409 and 1,638 Blacks living in the state capital. The White student population at Michigan State grew at a much swifter and steadier pace, from approximately 4,500 in 1930 to 8,400 in 1940. The "greatest relative increases" in Lansing's Black population occurred after 1940. Between 1950 and 1960, the Black Lansing population grew by more than 120 percent, from 2,971 to 6,745. Some of Lansing's Blacks lived in integrated neighborhoods, but most of the Black population between 1915 and the late 1930s lived in west-central Lansing in the city's Third Ward. While there was a small middle-class Black community in Lansing, the vast majority worked in service and common labor positions.[14] White Michigan State students were accustomed to seeing African Americans in service occupations engaging in menial common labor. The first Black employees were most likely hired by the university during the late nineteenth century and early twentieth century, and through the 1960s, they were very cognizant of their racial identities while on campus. They understood the informal racial etiquette of their times. In the late 1920s, many White students noticed the African American Bob Allen, who was employed as a "Truck Driver" by "State College." An editorial in the *M.A.C. Record* recounts how Allen helped eighty-year-old Scottish immigrant Robert Burns who performed "odd jobs" on campus and worked for horticulturalist Thomas Gunson. Allen collected "rubbish with his truck" and, like Burns, gave "his all to an institution he loves," representing "a true loyalty to the cause."[15] As revealed in several yearbook photos, it was common to see African Americans in service positions at students' campus events like dances.

Beyond seeing and perhaps interacting in passing with a handful of Blacks in service-oriented positions, the closest most White students came to experiencing aspects of Black culture during the interwar period was through entertainment. During the era of Jim Crow segregation, hundreds, if not thousands, of minstrel show performances took place in Ingham County communities. In Lansing, theaters such as the Continental, the Gladmer, and the Bijou regularly featured amateur and professional vaudeville and blackface performers who belittled and insulted Black people. An October 1919 ad featured in the M.A.C. student newspaper, the *Holcad*, declared in bold print that for three days the students could see Addam & Guhl "Now in Black Face." As reported in the *Holcad*, a blackface performance was welcomed in 1920 at one of the biggest events in the college's history to honor athletes. Similarly, during the era of World War I, the *State Journal* featured photos of prominent White performers, like Charles Rozell and George Primrose, wearing carefully applied blackface makeup. Active in Lansing's theater culture, M.A.C. and MSC students were among the thousands of Lansing's minstrel show goers. Minstrel shows were customary features of popular culture in Lansing as late as the 1950s and 1960s. In January 1950, there was a "Benefit Minstrel show," a "'blackface' extravaganza," in the J. W. Sexton High School auditorium. A decade later, the *Journal* announced, "the old time minstrel show is coming back to Lansing." In early March, "with all of its color, gaiety, songs, and end men," the much-anticipated show, sponsored by the Holy Cross parishioners, took place once again in the Sexton auditorium.[16] Scores of M.A.C. students also viewed D. W. Griffith's *The Birth of a Nation* (1915). This racist film was shown from 1915 through 1918 at the Gladmer Theater and the Bijou and then again in 1924 at the Continental and in 1925 at the Plaza Theater. In October 1924, a writer for the *Journal* concluded that its treatment of history was "thrilling," "magnificent," and "interesting," introducing America's past to a "new clientele," among them being some impressionable M.A.C. students.[17] Though keenly familiar with America's racial climate, the small group of African American students between 1915 and 1924 were appalled and personally threatened by such depictions of their people.

From the early twentieth century through the Great Depression, African American entertainers, like Parker's Colored Entertainers of Columbia and Fletcher Henderson's thirteen-piece orchestra from New York City, routinely performed for White students on campus at J-Hops and other events. On January 23, 1935, concert artist extraordinaire and one of the first Black artists to record with Columbia, Roland Hayes, participated in the college's concert course. "Hayes presented a varied program to a large audience which called him back for encores time and again," observed a writer for the *M.A.C. Record* in February 1935. Several years later, Marian Anderson, along with three White artists, performed a series of concerts for Michigan State students and faculty at the Peoples Church. African American artists continued to perform at J-Hops during the civil rights era. In early February 1959, Ella Fitzgerald kept the crowd wanting more, and in February 1962, Count Basie and Sonny Payne had the students and many enamored fans doing the twist.[18] These dignified Black performers demonstrated African Americans' professional and scientific musical and artistic talents to their White audiences.

Still, into the mid-1950s, members of the college community were still supporting blackface portrayals of African Americans. In 1930, an alumni event in Flint featured entertainment from a company "impersonating the colored boys of the air," and as a part of a Fourth of July parade in 1932, "students dressed to represent the various races which compose our nation," including a student who played "the American negro."[19] Despite the progress the university made as a result of Biggie Munn's recruiting of Black players, the members of the White MSU student community continued to revitalize denigrating stereotypes of African Americans. In the centennial edition of the *Wolverine*, yearbook editors included a 1904 photo of two White male students with a life-sized "Topsy" doll and a couple in blackface from head to toe performing in a talent show as *Brown v. Board of Education* was in the courts. In 1955, the Michigan State Children's Theater toured East Lansing, Lansing, and ten out-of-state cities staging *Huckleberry Finn* to more than ten thousand children. Playing Jim, an amateur White thespian was done up in blackface with black wooly stuff glued to his scalp for these performances, and two photos of him in action appear in the 1955 yearbook. One wonders how the more than forty members of Alpha Phi Alpha and Alpha Kappa Alpha Sorority, Inc., as well as Bill Reid, the only Black member of the Senior Council, reacted to these insulting representations. White students performing in blackface at the college was a tradition that dated back to the early twentieth century and probably earlier. Several existing photos corroborate this. In the 1915 *Wolverine*, a White male student appears in blackface dressed as a waiter. In February 1923, another White male student performed in blackface for the third annual campus night revue. And in the 1925 *Wolverine*, there is a photo of a White female student blackened up from head-to-toe sporting a wig braided into pigtails. She embraced her role as "Topsy" in the college's rendition of *Uncle Tom's Cabin*. "Topsy" also appeared in earlier M.A.C. yearbooks. In 1920, a drawing of two blackface girls appears above the heading "A Man's Impression of the Co-ed Prom."

Despite the clear divide between the college town of East Lansing and Lansing as well as the de facto segregationist patterns that characterized the greater Lansing area, some White students interacted with working-class African Americans in Lansing's small-town nightlife. This was certainly the case with one White student who attended Michigan State from 1931 until 1935 and kept a detailed diary. In mid-January 1935, this prolific liberal arts major reminisced on an exciting night out he had "slumming" with an "intellectually brilliant," Left-leaning "true Bohemian" classmate after attending the Civic Players' *Elizabeth and Essex*. "After the play he took me to a Black and Tan club in an old brick house on North Cedar St. I felt queer at first. John knocked and finally we were admitted, passing through two doors into a stuffy room with negroes and whites sitting at tables." He continued, "There were some good looking colored girls and the music quite appealing. John exclaimed over the beauty of the negroes and pointed out one wench he had gone with the week-end before. She was very attractive. Then mixed couples began to dance. I found the amorous play of men to colored gals rather revolting at first, but after a time thought little about it."[20]

Though he didn't indicate whether or not he himself attempted to pursue any of the "good looking colored girls" and seemed to have been initially appalled by the interracial sexual liaisons, this Michigan State liberal arts student was attracted to some of the Black women in the club. He wasn't shocked by his pleasure-seeking classmate's claim of having sex with a Black woman. In his exhaustive diary, the voyeuristic student referred to Black women in hypersexualized, stereotypical, and racist manners. As scholar Carissa Harris has pointed out, beginning during the antebellum era, the term "wench" became a "gendered racial slur," namely "a tool for dehumanizing black women, insisting on their sexual availability to white men, and facilitating their exploitation." Harris adds, "the term's derogatory connotations work to overshadow the very real and constant violence that black women suffered as a result of their intersecting disadvantages. When a woman is called a wench, we are prepped by centuries of connotation to see her as something intended for sexual use."[21] Unaware of the long, racialized history of the term "wench," this student probably was not alone among his contemporaries in his characterization of Black women. Beyond being tourists in Black and interracial spaces, during the interwar period there were inevitably White students who established amicable relationships with African Americans on and off campus and didn't embrace popular assumptions of Black inferiority. A small group of M.A.C. students learned first-hand about the fallacies of notions of Black intellectual inferiority. In May 1923, the M.A.C. debate team were defeated on the road by a group of young Black men from Wilberforce University, a small HBCU in Xenia, Ohio. The Wilberforce squad successfully "defended the negative side of the subject, 'Resolved, that labor disputes in the public utilities should be settled by compulsory arbitrations.'" As was the case at most predominantly White institutions, there were not any White student-led movements at the college that focused on dismantling anti-Black racism during this period.[22]

Those few African American women who attended Michigan State before and during the 1930s were aware of the all-too-familiar, harmful stereotypes the aforementioned Michigan State student expressed in 1935, and they directly challenged them through their actions and achievements. Like their predecessors, the "Between the Wars" Black students encountered subtle and overt forms of racial prejudice and assaults upon their humanity. They turned within and created, seized hold of, and maximized opportunities during a period when African Americans throughout the nation were routinely demeaned and treated as second-class citizens. They were constantly reminded of how many of those in the White community perceived them. Between the early 1910s and the late 1930s, the *Lansing State Journal* often exaggerated claims of Black criminality, reported on anti-Black violence throughout the country, and published racist advertisements. From 1911 until about 1939, the *Journal* used the n-word racial slur quite liberally (more than 250 times in a range of contexts).

In the late summer and early fall of 1924, more than fifty thousand Whites attended the "the first Klonvocation of the Ku Klux Klan"—"the first spectacle of its kind"—in Lansing. Whatever their motivations, members of the East Lansing and M.A.C. communities attended some of the events. Along with the more than seven hundred African American Lansing residents, the few Black M.A.C. students were disturbed by this public display of racial hatred. As historian Craig Fox points out, during the 1920s the Klan expanded far beyond the "borders of the old South." Most scholars concur that by the mid-1920s, there were approximately eighty thousand members in Michigan. In 1925, the *Washington Post* claimed there were more than eight hundred thousand members in the state. Whatever the case may have been, it's clear that during the 1920s most of the state's Klan members lived in Detroit, and about ten other major cities, including Lansing, had active chapters. According to Fox, various classes of Whites throughout the state were drawn to this clandestine group. It was not considered a "fanatical fringe group"; it possessed "an accepted mainstream presence, largely populated by 'average' or 'ordinary' citizens."[23] The Ingham County branch of the Klan organized the 1924 gathering that was called "one of the largest the country has witnessed." About fifteen thousand Klan members participated in the parade. The "robed hordes" of men, women, and children from all over the state marched throughout downtown Lansing celebrating Labor Day. The Michigan Electric Railway company and motor buses provided special transportation to and from the various events. Members of the Klan "were posted about the city to guide newcomers." The *State Journal* enthusiastically dubbed it an "impressive spectacle." Klan members felt welcomed enough that their spokespersons sent a letter to the Lansing police chief "complimenting the local police department on the co-operation" afforded to them.[24]

Several years after these racist xenophobes marched in Lansing, in a section toward the end of the Michigan State yearbook titled "1927 Bullverine," a student cartoonist offered readers a comic strip depicting a gross caricature of a Black man fleeing in fear from a hooded Klan member with an "X" on his robe. The caption reads: "Whooie!! Look lik' de klu kluxers!" Authored by members of Excalibur, a senior men's honorary society "made up of men giving the greatest service to the College," the commentary, whether in jest or not, suggested the group's affiliation with the Klan. "No! don't get us wrong, these boys are quite democratic even though they rate among the elite of the popular set here. We ask you how can they help it if they're lucky enough to get into the East Lansing Chapter of the Ku Klux Klan?"[25] Though not as brazen as the makeshift Ku Klux Klan regalia three students wore in mid-February 1976 as they marched toward South Complex in protest of affirmative action policies and support given to Black caucuses and culture rooms, the robes members of this "honorary society" wore in a 1929 photo in the *Wolverine* resembled the one sported by the hooded man in the cartoon.[26] This cartoon appeared in the volume of the *Wolverine* that included Black woman Mabel Lucas's graduation photo. What did she think about this being included in her graduation memento? Like her Black classmates Clarice Pretlow and Chester Smith, she was accustomed to such behavior. Similar racist cartoons, depicting African Americans as dishonest, shiftless, and ignorant, appeared in previous issues of the *Wolverine*.

Cognizant of what their presence on campus symbolized and entailed, without their consent, the "Between the Wars" African American students served as representatives of African Americans to their White classmates, professors, advisers, and coaches. Their matriculation through the college might have been perceived by the White East Lansing community as representing the accomplishments of "exceptional" African Americans. When they walked across the stage at commencement, they slowly chipped away at the widespread notion that African Americans were intellectually inferior. Like countless other Black students and graduates during their times, they were living proof to the contrary. Their abilities to persevere contributed to the future Black presence at America's first agricultural college. As Julius Smith, the son of William H. Smith, '37, said of his father, "He was a man before his time. He was a trailblazer."[27] While a diverse group based upon their identities, birthplaces and hometowns, scholarly and extracurricular interests, and future career trajectories, they all became professionals after graduating. More than three-quarters of them became teachers, mentors, and role models to African American children, adolescents, and young adults in a variety of settings. Those who went into teaching worked at HBCUs, a group of which were founded because of the Second Morrill Act of 1890. An extension of the Morrill Act of 1862, this act led to the creation and growth of land-grant colleges and universities that served African Americans.

Embracing the service ethos and self-help philosophy that HBCU students were socialized to take up, many of the early African American graduates from America's first agricultural college became involved in civil rights struggles and progressive reform by participating in organizations seeking to improve the conditions of their communities. The two who became lawyers, Oliver

M. Green and Chester Smith, served African American clients. Longtime civil engineer for the state of Michigan William H. Smith, like several of his fellow graduates, was active in the NAACP. The majority of the "Between the Wars" Black students at M.A.C. and MSC were men, 50 percent of whom served in the U.S. Armed Forces and more than a few of whom were student-athletes. Graves, Benjamin Goode, Clarence Banks, Jim McCrary, and William H. Smith earned varsity letters in sports. In 1936 and 1937, graduate of Detroit Northeastern High School Roosevelt Barnes, who arrived in East Lansing in the fall of 1934 and developed into the college's star featherweight, contributed to the new boxing program's growing popularity. The "Between the Wars" Black students' identities and talents as athletes didn't define them but, undoubtedly, helped them persevere. Despite the prejudice they faced, like Gideon E. Smith before them, they used sports as effective outlets. Through the quasi-level playing field collegiate sports offered, they cautiously performed their Black masculinity, demonstrated Black athletic excellence, and found ways to add balance and pleasure to their stressful lives.

Young Black women's experiences on campus were especially alienating. The next Black woman to graduate from M.A.C. after Myrtle Bessie Craig, '07, was Lansing native Esther I. Tate, '20. She was followed by Margaret Collins, '24, Mabel J. Lucas, '27, and Clarice A. Pretlow, '30. The last known Black woman graduate in the 1930s was centenarian and graduate Frances L. Langford, '37 (later Frances Langford Owens). A handful of Black women attended Michigan State during the 1920s and 1930s without earning degrees.[28] Negro History Week enthusiast Lila May Barnett, who was head of the History Department at Rust College in Holly Springs, Mississippi, in 1928 and taught at Baltimore's Morgan College, did "special work" at M.A.C. during the 1920s. Mary Elizabeth, a "young dramatic soprano" from Jackson, Michigan, enrolled in the college in the early 1930s and after her first year transferred to Wilberforce University where she earned her bachelor of science degree in music in 1936. Exuding Black excellence, this private HBCU in Ohio provided her the educational experience she needed. Hailed the "new voice queen for Michigan" by the *Michigan Chronicle* in the summer of 1945, during the World War II era she settled down in Detroit and taught music in the public school system. Unlike some of their male contemporaries, "Between the Wars" Black women, except for Lucas who earned an interclass monogram in women's volleyball, did not make their marks in sports. They encountered obstacles based upon their race, gender, and in some cases, class. In Lansing during the 1920s and 1930s, most Black women labored in service positions and as domestic servants, something that Pretlow, who worked as a live-in housemaid for a White East Lansing family in the late 1920s, knew all too well. They engaged in what historian Evelyn Brooks Higginbotham theorized as Black women's "politics of respectability" during the Progressive Era.[29] Through their calculated daily behavior and academic achievements, they battled against the stereotypes that sought to define and denigrate them in the eyes of White America. They contested and flatly defied the familiar "Topsy" stereotypes that many of their White classmates accepted.

Why was there such a large span of time between the graduations of Craig and Tate, and why did so few Black women attend the college during the interwar period, especially considering the progress made in the education of women at the college? One possible explanation is that Black women could have received high-quality, Black-centered preparation in home economics at HBCUs. In such spaces, Black women teachers had their students' best interests and welfare at heart. They schooled their protégés about racial etiquette, maintaining a home, "the politics of respectability," and the intricacies of Black womanhood. America's first agricultural college didn't offer them the varied opportunities of which their male counterparts could take advantage. Black women from the South were also reluctant to relocate to another state where they didn't have the types of "female networks" that, as historian Deborah Gray White theorized, existed in Black communities since the antebellum era.[30] Three of the four Black women who attended the college during the 1920s—Esther I. Tate, Margaret E. Collins, and Mabel J. Lucas—and the only Black woman to graduate from MSC in the 1930s, Frances L. Langford, had close Michigan ties.

The "Between the Wars" Black student pathfinders' presence not only constituted much of the racial diversity on campus, but helped transform what we now call campus climate issues. In June 1935, the efforts of James McCrary, '35, and Albert H. Baker, '36, moved the State Board of Agriculture to publicly declare that Black and White students would be treated equally, that "equal opportunity" would be granted to "all students, regardless of race or color." The "Between the Wars" graduates from the college shared a common vision of the deeper significance and meaning of their education. In part limited by the constraints of Jim Crow segregation and U.S. race relations throughout the nation, the majority of these educated and driven graduates secured positions at HBCUs in the South and became involved in their communities and a wide array of social reform movements. They embraced an African American version of their alma mater's deeply rooted commitment to service.

Chapter 14

It Is More Blessed to Give than Receive

On June 14, 1916, Gideon Edward Smith, as he was listed in the commencement program, was one of two African American students to graduate from M.A.C. Among the more than two hundred members of the 1916 graduating class was another young Black man, Everett Claudius Yates, Gideon's roommate during the 1912–1913 academic year. As historian Keith Widder discovered in 2005, Yates was the "first known African American student to play in the college's cadet band and orchestra." While at M.A.C., Yates did not spend much time contemplating the implications of his historic accomplishment. In his own way, he paved the way for the first co-drum majors in MSU history. These young men were Robert James and honor student and Jackson, Michigan, native Henry Baltimore who mysteriously disappeared from his East Lansing apartment in the early summer of 1973. Revisited by a reporter for the online magazine *The Root* in 2022, the multitalented Baltimore's mysterious disappearance at the end of his junior year remains a cold case.[1]

A talented percussionist who was in East Lansing six decades before James and Baltimore entertained thousands of spectators in Spartan Stadium, Yates charmed Aggie fans as a band member and member of the college's small orchestra who "provided music for dances on campus."[2] He wasn't a major public figure or household name like Smith. Yet he was in no way an anonymous figure on campus. Like his spiritual descendants James and Baltimore, he too stood out. To overcome the odds, he knew he had to be an exceptional musician with a nuanced approach to interacting with Whites. Yates enrolled in M.A.C. because of his interest in studying agriculture and the growing reputation of the M.A.C. band. "The band was organized and installed shortly after the establishment of the military department at M.A.C.," recounted the 1912 *Wolverine* yearbook. "Since then it has flourished with more or less vigor until at the present, it has the deserved reputation of being one of the finest college bands in the country; made manifest by the receipt of the highest possible grade at the last government inspection."[3] Like the vast majority of his African American contemporaries, he could have gone to his choice of HBCUs or a college or university closer to home.

Yates was born in Lawrenceville, Virginia, on February 3, 1892. His parents were born in Virginia during the antebellum era. His father, Nicholas Yates, was born sometime between 1840 and 1844, and his mother, Lucy Henry Walker, was born to free parents in Virginia sometime between 1846 and 1853. In 1870, Nicholas, a laborer, and Lucy, a homemaker, lived in Red Oak, Virginia, in Brunswick County with their one-year-old child. Between 1872 and 1892, Nicholas and Lucy had eleven children, nine daughters and two sons. Everett was the youngest child whose oldest sibling was twenty years his senior. At the age of two months, he moved to Boston. His parents, like countless other African Americans, searched for a better life outside of the South. In Boston, his father continued to work as a manual laborer. In 1900, eight-year-old Everett attended Sherwin Grammar School in Roxbury that was founded in 1870. During Yates's childhood in the City on a Hill, African American parents were involved in the education of their children as evidenced by their participation in the Sherwin-Hyde Parents Association.[4] As a youth, Yates lived with his parents, six siblings, a brother-in-law, three nieces, and a twenty-year-old woman who worked as a domestic servant and boarded with the large and tight-knit family. Young Everett benefited from being the youngest son and having older siblings who looked after him, teaching him by example.

On June 21, 1911, as noted in the *Boston Globe*, Yates was one of the more than 150 students to graduate from English High School, a well-known, predominantly White public school in New England. In the fall of 1911, a year before Gideon was scrimmaging with the freshman football team, the eager and driven Yates arrived in East Lansing. Based upon his educational background and high school credentials, he was more than prepared for M.A.C.'s curriculum. Nevertheless, he matriculated as a "sub-freshman." He enrolled in the agricultural course and actively participated in extracurricular activities, including the military band, the orchestra, the Horticulture Club, the New England Club, and the Cosmopolitan Club.

The description of the M.A.C. band's director, Professor A. J. Clark, as being "a man who shows but little partiality" rang true in Yates's case. The band was "indispensable to the social and athletic phases of college life," continued a description in the 1912 *Wolverine*. "Mass meetings, the barbecue, cap night and other functions would be incomplete without its presence. During the winter term fortnightly sacred concerts are given in the armory, and in the spring term the midweek open air concerts. Besides all this, the band finds more time to give a promenade concert and a dance once a term, and to make short trips about the state during the year."[5] In addition to

The Michigan Agricultural College Military Band. Yates is conspicuous in the front row, fourth from the left. Courtesy of Michigan State University Archives and Historical Collections.

regularly performing on campus and participating in various competitions, the respected college band was especially busy during commencement weeks and alumni events. The band's "sacred concert" performances were always well attended and greatly appreciated by the students. With their regular performances, they were integrated into the college's culture. During Yates's time at M.A.C., the band became increasingly competitive and was dubbed by those in Mid-Michigan as being "The World's Best College Band."[6] The October 1915 ultra-competitive band tryouts broke a record with more than eighty students trying out. Yates was among the fifty selected to be in the company and was one of the six members of the drumming corps. The *Holcad* proudly announced, "M.A.C. Military Band Is Better Than Ever."[7]

During the 1912–1913 academic year, Yates and Gideon Smith lived together in Lansing at 164 Michigan Avenue. Yates performed at home football games and from time to time accompanied the team to away games. The band's trips were financed by team boosters and donors who raised more than one thousand dollars to send the band to Penn State. The Aggies won the low-scoring contest, 6-3. In 1913, at a "mass meeting," students, faculty, staff, band members, and other M.A.C. "loyal rooters" discussed the possibility of traveling to Madison, Wisconsin. For about ten dollars per person, more than one hundred Aggie fans traveled on a "special train" to St. Johns to Grand Haven and then to Milwaukee "via the Crosby Transportation Co.'s boat." Another "special train" took them to Madison. The return trip was the same and "electric cars" ran "as far as the campus."

Yates was one of the 175 Aggie supporters to travel to Madison to witness their team's victory. Following the victory over the "Champions of the West," students were given a holiday break on Monday. "Due credit was given to the team, the band and the rooters, and the faculty speakers showed that they were with the students with a real live brand of enthusiasm and pep."[8] Featured in the *Holcad*, a photo exists of Yates among the large entourage. The only African American in the photo, he looks comfortable and at home. At least one other photo of Yates appeared in the student paper. Sitting in the front row with a drum between his legs, Yates is in a photo on the front page of the *Holcad* on January 11, 1915, making him the first Black student to grace this paper's cover. Like his classmates, he is identified in a simple manner: "Tympani—Yates."

Yates was active in Lansing's African Methodist Episcopal (AME) church. In 1914, he performed with a choir at a "special feature service" and in 1916, he performed at the church's celebration for Governor Woodbridge Nathan Ferris.[9] Yates took great pride in his experiences and service at M.A.C. On his World War I registration card from June 1917, he indicated he had four years of "military service" as a "Sec. Lieutenant" at "Michigan Ag. College."[10] A proud Yates referred to his membership in the band that was organized "strictly on a military basis" with officers, including a drum major, a principal musician, as well as first and second lieutenants and sergeants and corporals.

When Yates arrived at M.A.C. in the fall of 1911, he met a fellow young Black scholar, Claudius Augustus Reid. Born in Newcastle, Kentucky, on November 29, 1889, Reid migrated with his family to Detroit sometime during the early twentieth century. According to the 1910 U.S. census, he lived in the city with his father, a West Indian immigrant preacher, and his mother, a dressmaker, and a younger brother.[11] Between 1908 and 1910, Reid worked as an elevator operator and a porter. With about 150 others, he enrolled in M.A.C. in September 1910 as a member of the "sub-freshman class." As was the custom, as one of the "Preps," he had to sport the "Black-sheep, peanut-like cap." Like his ridiculed yet encouraged classmates, he came to M.A.C. "with the determination to win" and overcome "all obstacles."[12] During the 1910–1911 academic year, Reid was an active member of the Cosmopolitan Club. A year later, Yates joined him in this organization. They were in the group's photo together in the 1912 *Wolverine*. Reid is also pictured in the 1912 *Wolverine* among his freshman classmates. Residing in Lansing, Reid remained at M.A.C. for several years. From 1910 until 1912, his father, T. A. Reid, served as the pastor of Lansing's George R. Collins AME Church. Claudius founded the church's short-lived Usher's Association. In the words of Rev. Joseph W. Jarvis, he "saw a great need of something for the young people to do and work to give them an up-to-date institution." Under Claudius's leadership, the youthful association raised $45 for renovations. In 1913, he lived in Detroit working as a porter. On his World War I registration card dated June 2, 1917, he indicated he engaged in "2 ½" years of military service at "Agricultural College Michigan" and was employed as a "moulder" for Winslow Brothers Co. in Chicago.[13] Evidence suggests he worked in Chicago by 1914 and developed into a cultural mover-and-shaker and activist in Chicago.[14] Yates was dismayed by his friend Reid's departure.

On October 17, 1916, the "Alumni Notes" section of the *M.A.C. Record* acknowledged Yates's postgraduation move. "Everett C. Yates . . . is pursuing studies in Boston Normal School preparatory to teaching in that city." After about a year, he accepted a position at Tennessee Agricultural and Industrial State Normal School in Nashville, a Black land-grant institution founded in 1911. Between 1919 and the early 1920s, Yates regularly shared updates with the editors of the *Record*. While working as an "assistant agriculturalist" at State Normal School, he actively engaged in extension division work, visiting "nearly all of the colored schools of the state." In April 1920, Yates shared with his alma mater how he was enjoying "working here in the south" and "had the good fortune of meeting a few M.A.C. graduates" who were also engaged in agricultural work. In 1921, he was promoted to the position of "State Teacher Trainer." A Black New Englander at heart, he had similar impressions that Massachusetts native W. E. B. Du Bois had when he ventured to Fisk during the era of Reconstruction. Black life in Nashville was noticeably different for Yates than in Boston and certainly Lansing. Nashville was home to a thriving Black southern elite community with a dynamic musical culture and four HBCUs.

In 1922, Yates returned to Boston and began his long teaching career at Rice School. According to one account from 1967, he "was believed to be the first Negro ever to teach in the public schools here."[15] By the mid-1920s, Yates stopped sharing updates with the *Record*. In 1925, his name was among those in the paper's sections, "Help! These People Have No Addresses" and "Do You Know Where These People Are?" In 1933, he became Rice's first African American "submaster" and soon developed into a social activist. In 1937, for instance, he was the keynote "orator" for an event sponsored by Boston's War Veteran's Council and the Colored Citizen's League in honor of Edgar L. Reed. The next year, as a supporter of the NAACP, he lobbied Massachusetts senators David I. Walsh and Henry Cabot Lodge Jr. to support the Anti-Lynching Bill. In the late 1930s, he embraced causes relevant to the improvement of the Black community. In 1939, at Arlington St. Church, Yates spoke to the "College Age Group" on the topic of "international race relations."[16] In 1946, he was elected to a position of leadership in the American Church Union's New England Branch. Beginning with his appointment by the governor in 1954, he served on the Advisory Committee on Service to Youth. Along with his colleagues, Yates called for immediate and comprehensive state support in addressing the pressing problem of "juvenile delinquency," a problem that disproportionately impacted Black youth. They called for "a joint state-community program" with adequate financial resources. Though diplomatic, there was a militant tone to Yates's and his coworkers' report. In 1960, Yates retired from South End's Rice School. He had dedicated his life to educating and mentoring young people and remained committed to the mission of one school for the bulk of his career. His impact was large scale enough that in honor of his retirement, the *Boston Globe* featured a story on him. He was admired and respected by his community and former students. "During the 38 years" of his career "he worked with literally thousands of troubled students." In 1967, Yates died, and the lengthy obituary in the *Globe* mentioned that Michigan State University was his alma mater.[17]

Yates and Smith were the only African Americans to graduate from M.A.C. in 1916. In the fall of 1914, they were joined by Delbert M. Prillerman who was, in more than a few ways, better equipped for the college than his comrades. Prillerman was born on October 19, 1894, in Charleston, West Virginia, to Byrd Prillerman (1859–1929) and Martha "Mattie" Eugenia Brown (1869–1921). The oldest of four children, he grew up in West Virginia in Kanawha County where Booker T. Washington worked in the coal mines as a child. Prillerman's parents were highly educated for their generation. His mother graduated from Wayland Seminary and his father, who earned degrees from Knox College, Westminster, and Salem University, was a longtime educator and social reformer. Byrd helped found West Virginia Colored Institute in 1891 under the Second Morrill Act, served as the school's president from 1909 until 1919, and helped transform the institute and elevate its academic reputation. As a result of the changes in curriculum initiated by Delbert's father, in 1915 the school's name was changed to West Virginia

Yates and Prillerman pose with classmates in front of Williams Hall, 1915. Yates is about three rows from the bottom, third from the right. Prillerman is about four rows from the top, third from the left. Courtesy of Michigan State University Archives and Historical Collections.

Collegiate Institute. Byrd maintained friendships with leading African American educators and scholars such as Booker T. Washington, W. E. B. Du Bois, Kelly Miller, George Edmund Haynes, and Nannie Helen Burroughs.

On June 4, 1909, the West Virginia Colored Institute staged an elaborate graduation ceremony for its largest class in its history. Among those marching behind the school's band to "Hazelwood assembly hall in the academic building" was Byrd's firstborn, fifteen-year-old Delbert who earned his diploma and certificate in agriculture along with two other young men.[18] Under his father's close gaze, Delbert took courses in agriculture, horticulture, mechanical arts, military drilling, and teacher education. Five years later, he enrolled in M.A.C. Delbert's father encouraged his son to attend M.A.C. As chairman of the Conference of Negro Land Grant Colleges, Byrd appreciated the college's commitment to scientific agriculture. Seeking to win over White philanthropists, Byrd celebrated land-grant legislation. Under his presidency, Senator Justin Smith Morrill's birthday was an annual celebration sponsored by the school's Morrill Agricultural Club.[19]

Delbert came to East Lansing to build upon his high school equivalent education. He knew M.A.C.'s established, scientific, and hands-on agricultural course would amplify his knowledge. A member of the Horticulture Club, he was also a talented tennis player, something unique for a young Black man of his generation.[20] Delbert was a confident young man, especially in terms of his Black consciousness. He grew up with a father, a president of an HBCU, who was an outspoken advocate of African American uplift and education. He taught his children and students to serve their communities. In a long-winded speech he delivered in May 1918, "Responsibility of the Educated Negro," Delbert's father encouraged young African Americans to uplift themselves, strive toward home ownership, embrace the highest moral standards, know the history of their country and be patriots, and become "an intelligent citizen." Echoing Booker T. Washington and Jonathan L. Snyder, Byrd endorsed the type of education his son pursued. "Our material wealth exists mainly in the soil," he declared. He had a clear message for his son and his contemporaries. "The Negro who returns from college is in great measure responsible for the moral and religious life of the community. He should be a creator of sentiment and a moulder of character." Delbert's father concluded this oration by celebrating Black historical icons Crispus Attucks and Frederick Douglass and evoking race pride. "The progress of your race is unparalleled in history. Fifty years ago, this race came out of slavery ignorant and homeless, without credit and without money. Today this same race owns more than 20,000,000 acres of land, and pays taxes on more than 900,000 homes. Its students have taken honors from our leading colleges and universities."[21] Delbert and his siblings heard this message daily, helping them better navigate the White spaces they traversed.

Byrd Prillerman visited his son in East Lansing. While in Detroit in the spring of 1916 for a meeting of the National Education Association, Byrd came to M.A.C. and delivered a lecture. The *Denver Star* reported the following:

He visited the Michigan Agricultural College at Lansing where his son, Delbert McCullough, is a junior in the agricultural course. There were three other colored students in attendance, but none from the state of Michigan. He was treated with every courtesy by the president and the professors of the institution and by invitation of the president spoke at a banquet given by the agricultural students.[22]

A very capable student, Delbert graduated in three years. Before graduating, he registered for World War I and was eager to serve his country's armed forces. Like the nearly four hundred thousand other African Americans who served in the army during the war, he defended his birthplace in a segregated military. After serving in the Great War, he became a teacher, securing a position as an instructor at West Virginia Collegiate Institute. "An army veteran of World War I and a graduate of MSU," his obituary in 1979 indicated, "Mr. Prillerman was a teacher for many years at West Virginia State College and Bluefield State Teachers College. He was a member of Kappa Alpha Psi fraternity."[23] A decade before his death, he kept abreast of what was happening at his alma mater. After hearing the news of Clifton R. Wharton Jr.'s appointment as MSU president, seventy-five-year-old Prillerman wrote to the fourteenth president, letting him know how proud and happy he was to live to see a Black president of his alma mater.[24]

Delbert was at M.A.C. with Gideon Smith and Everett Yates throughout the 1914–1915 and 1915–1916 academic years. During his senior year, in 1916, McGlenard "Bill" Williamson was among the "sixty Lansing freshman" of 523 incoming M.A.C. students.[25] Born on August 25, 1893, in Caswell County, North Carolina, in 1910 Williamson, the son of a coal miner, lived in McDowell County, West Virginia, not too far from his classmate Prillerman. He studied agriculture at M.A.C. and during the 1917–1918 academic year lived in Williams Hall with another young Black man, freshman Herbert McFadden who was also in the agricultural course. Williamson and McFadden were probably the first African American students to live in M.A.C.'s men's dormitories. Following his second year at M.A.C., Williamson served in World War I as a corporal in Company B 543d Engineers. After his service in the U.S. Armed Forces, he returned to M.A.C. and lived in Wells Hall. In 1920, he was a member of Sigma Tau Pi, and in 1921, he was in the Detroit Club. He graduated in 1921, and his accomplishment was acknowledged, with an accompanying photo, in a lengthy report on Black college graduates published by the NAACP's *Crisis* magazine.[26]

In 1913, when Gideon Smith began his first year on the varsity M.A.C. football team and Claudius Everett Yates was a member of the college's highly touted cadet band, a young man named Clement Charles Johnson eagerly applied for admission into M.A.C.'s engineering course. Johnson was sure about what he wanted to study. "You'd be wiser to major in agriculture, then go to the South to teach your people," President Snyder counseled Johnson. Snyder's advice to Johnson emanated from his understanding of U.S. race relations and conventional notions of African Americans' place in American society. He believed a Black man like Johnson would have

Clement Charles "Chas" Johnson.
Courtesy of Michigan State University
Archives and Historical Collections.

a hard time securing employment in the nonagricultural sector. His inclination was reasonable, but Johnson was determined to follow his dreams; he was convinced he could overcome racial discrimination in his chosen profession. "No sir," a self-assured Johnson responded to Snyder. "I'm strong in math and physics and I want to follow in my daddy's footsteps. I want to be an engineer."[27]

In 1918, Johnson became the first African American to earn a degree in engineering (mechanical) from M.A.C., a distinction that for some time had been granted to William H. Smith, '37. Johnson was born in Findlay, Ohio, on October 30, 1893. His father, Charles (b. 1868), was a metalsmith well-versed in the craft of manufacturing nails, and his mother, Anna (b. 1873), was a housewife. When Clement arrived in East Lansing, his six siblings were ages seventeen, fifteen, thirteen, eleven, eight, and four. While a student, he lived in several different locations in East Lansing, including in a home on Grand River Avenue, the Peoples Church, and, during his senior year, in 15A Wells Hall. In the 1915–1916 academic year, Clement stayed in a large home at 460 Grand River Avenue right across from campus that was owned by former abolitionist and Civil War veteran Henry Payson Kinney who died in June 1914. Following Kinney's death, the home was advertised as "nice 10-room house . . . Suitable for roomers" that "will pay for itself." Like William O. Thompson before him, Johnson was among the only African Americans living in East Lansing during the early twentieth century, sharing space with White students and borders.[28]

In December 1917, Clement married a music teacher from Lima, Ohio, Edith Mae Adams. Also known as "Johnny," Johnson was quite a student-athlete. He was a member of the interclass football and baseball teams. He was the first African American to participate in a form of competitive baseball at the college (in the early 1950s, shortstop phenom and Flint native Stan Turner became the first African American to play varsity baseball at MSC). After graduating, Johnson "made an army-financed round trip to France near the end of World War I." As he shared with *M.A.C. Record* readers in mid-January 1920, he then settled down in Detroit and secured a job as a "tool designer and draftsman" for Ford Motor Company in Highland Park. He informed his alma mater that he, his wife, and "little daughter" resided at 942 24th Street in Detroit. Johnson joined thousands of African American men who worked for Ford's enterprise and often encountered discrimination in the workplace. After he was hired, more than one hundred White workers "signed a petition asking for his removal." Unpersuaded by these racist antics, Johnson's manager refused to fire him because of his "satisfactory" work. During the early years of the Great Depression, Johnson briefly left Ford to work as a state highway surveyor. Between the mid-1930s and the mid-1940s, he worked at Ford's Ypsilanti starter and generator plant. In 1944, he was transferred to the Rouge plant and became "one of America's first rocket-research engineers." Johnson holds the distinction of being "the first Negro engineer hired by Ford Motor Company." His specific expertise was in the realm of "checking designs of tools for engine making."[29] A widowed father, Johnson retired from Ford in 1958 at the age of sixty-five and committed much of his time to his hobby of repairing watches and televisions. Johnson, who was a member of Alpha Phi Alpha fraternity and was active in neighborhood beautification efforts, died in Detroit in 1966 and was laid to rest at Elmwood Cemetery.[30] Clement was not the only male African American student at M.A.C. from 1913 until 1918. At least four Black men—Smith, Yates, Prillerman, and Herbert F. McFadden—were on campus at one point with Johnson. During the 1916–1917 and 1917–1918 academic years, Esther I. Tate was also one of Johnson's classmates.

About fourteen years after Myrtle Bessie Craig arrived in Collegeville as a first-year student in the budding women's course, on June 13, 1916, Esther Isabelle Tate was a member of the "largest class in the history of Lansing high school" to graduate. In the fall of 1916, Tate was one of the sixty incoming M.A.C. students from Lansing and East Lansing.[31] For many years, she remained the first Black Lansing native to graduate from the college. She went on to live an enterprising and eventful life that most of Lansing's Black women could not imagine nor relate to. Tate was born in the state capital in 1899. There were approximately 320 African Americans in the city out of a total population of more than 16,400 residents. Her parents, William L. Tate (b. 1861 in Ohio) and Esther T. Jackson (b. 1869 in Canada), were married in 1894 in Ingham County. William was a boilermaker, and his wife was a schoolteacher. When Esther attended M.A.C., her father was a foreman at Jarvis Engineering Company. A middle-class family, the Tates raised their only daughter in Lansing's Third Ward, and Esther was a gifted child who was involved in a range of extracurricular activities, many of which were covered in the pages of the *Lansing State Journal*. As early as 1911, the paper recounted recitals she participated in with teachers from Kalamazoo Street School. During her years at Lansing High School, she delivered readings at churches including Hillsdale Baptist Church and Lansing's AME church. The fruit didn't fall far from the tree. Esther's mother was quite an orator and community leader, often delivering speeches and readings at local churches. A friend of Charles A. Warren, Esther's mother was also active in the liberty bonds buying movement during the era of World War I and served as a "prominent" secretary for the AME church's Sunday school.[32]

Unlike Clement C. Johnson and her African American male predecessors, Esther lived at home, 827 W. Lenawee, while a M.A.C. student. But this didn't protect her from expressions

Esther I. Tate. Courtesy of Michigan State University Archives and Historical Collections.

of racism on campus. Also known as "Tatie," she graduated with a bachelor's degree in home economics on June 16, 1920, with African American classmates Oliver Meakins Green and Herbert F. McFadden. To graduate with a specialization in teaching, she was required to travel throughout the state a bit, visiting Michigan secondary schools. In April 1920, the *Chicago Defender* mentioned her visit to a junior high school in Jackson, Michigan. A few days before graduation, five hundred M.A.C. students participated in a "historic and patriotic pageant." The *State Journal* advertised that the play, *The Triumph of a Nation's Faith*, offered a "history of the nation." Along with many other senior coeds, Tate was assigned a minor role in the much-anticipated pageant. How did she, Green, and McFadden respond to the college's ROTC who rode "in the play as members of the Ku Klux Klan" and "seemed from their efforts in the rehearsal well equipped to reproduce the wild rides of the body they represent?"[33] Such offensive performances were common during the 1920s. Five months before Tate graduated, the "first Annual Co-Ed Prom" was held in the gymnasium on January 23. There were more than three hundred "co-eds, alumni and faculty ladies" dressed in a variety of costumes. "Martha and George were there in triplicate," observed a writer for the *M.A.C. Record*, "and several pairs of gold dust twins, each blacker than the ones before, were out with gold dust and scrub clothes." At the end of the event, the "second prize, a three-pound box [of candy], was awarded to Irene Dale and Osee Hughes, the blackest 'Gold Dust Twins.'"[34] They appear, face blackened and all, in the 1920 *Wolverine* yearbook. Blackface performances continued through the 1920s at events beyond the coed prom. Late in 1920, the "biggest meeting in the college's history," where prominent M.A.C. alumni discussed "the betterment of the college," featured a "Black Face Vaudeville." On November 12, 1920, the *Holcad* widely advertised this event. "Every student should be there. This is a meeting for alumni and active students." Years later in the summer of 1926, students continued this tradition, holding the fourth annual water carnival and festival. In addition to the customary "races on the Red Cedar course," there were a series of "vaudeville acts" that took place on a "specially constructed stage on the opposite bank of the river. Put on by the students of the College," these acts included "dances, black face acts and humorous stunts."[35] During the 1920s, one alumni continued a tradition he took part in when he was a student in the early 1890s. "As in his college days he is mixed up with singing in various organizations—a choir, an opera, a minstrel show, and a choral society," documented the *M.A.C. Record* in 1924 in reference to a member of the class 1895. "Some of the songs that were sung by no one else on the campus during his college days are, he says, 'still wearing well.' They always bring a laugh as does also the anecdote of the 'two little boot blacks, one white and one black.'"[36] Several years later, in late May 1926, one of this alumnus's classmates, Charles H. Alvord, '95, didn't belittle African Americans like his classmate. Instead, he educated *M.A.C. Record* readers a bit about "June 'teenth."[37]

Following in her mother's footsteps, in the early 1920s Esther entered the teaching profession. In 1921, she started working at Virginia Normal and Industrial Institute in Petersburg, Virginia, helping provide disabled African American veterans with industrial education.[38] In 1925, she was back in Lansing working as a schoolteacher. In 1927, twenty-nine-year-old Tate married forty-year-old minister and educator Joseph Winthrop Holley. Born in 1874 in Winnsboro, South Carolina, to former slaves, Holley founded the Albany Bible and Manual Training Institute in 1903. Recognizing the value in both industrial and classical education, Holley was an ideological disciple of both Booker T. Washington and W. E. B. Du Bois. As Tate completed her first year at M.A.C., Holley's school became a two-year college and was renamed the Georgia Normal and Agricultural College. Holley remained president of the school until he retired in 1943. As the wife of the school's president, Esther was in a respected position. She taught at the school, heading the Home Economics Department. While living in Georgia, she regularly returned to visit her parents in Lansing. During these vacations, she often participated in social events. In 1929, she took part in a "Collegiate Night" for her alma mater at the George R. Collins AME Church. Esther delivered a talk titled "The Negro in the South." She shared with her Lansing colleagues the day-to-day conditions of the majority of African Americans, approximately 80 percent of whom resided in the South. As reported in the *Record* in February 1929, she also spoke at the AME church about her experiences at the international conference held in Leopoldville, Congo Free State, in her talk "A Message from the Fatherland." A year later, she spoke at Hillsdale Baptist Church.[39]

Contributing to the academic reputation of Georgia Normal, in 1933 Mrs. Holley earned a master's degree in home economics from Columbia University. She was among the "women of the Race" applauded by the *Chicago Defender* and *New York Age* for earning advanced degrees during the peak years of the Great Depression. During the 1940s, Esther lived in Philadelphia and worked as a schoolteacher. She continued to return to her hometown of Lansing to visit her widowed mother (Esther's father died in 1935) and participate in community functions. In 1944, she lived in Philadelphia, "spending the winter with her mother" and delivering numerous talks in Lansing. In late February, she spoke about "Women of Africa" in the Peoples Church and "The Negro in the Lansing Community" at a meeting of the city's Altrusa Club. Her philosophy of race relations was straightforward. Like Booker T. Washington, she believed if Whites had "better understanding" of Black people, racial prejudices could be eliminated. "Racial understandings," she noted, "are necessary if we are to have the right kind of peace." She characterized her people as wanting to live a simple life. "The desire of the race," observed Esther, "is a 'decent' home and suitable surroundings for his family." She was often called upon in Lansing to speak about interracial problems, and in May 1944 spoke in the city about the 1943 Detroit race riot and the "animosity of Whites toward the Negroes prevailing in many sections of this country." In September, she was one of the keynote speakers at Lansing's "first health institute for Negroes." She also played a key role on the "Recreation committee" for "a Lansing Citizen's league to promote better health among Negroes."[40]

In 1948, Esther's mother died, and Esther continued to visit Lansing from Philadelphia. In the early 1950s, she was a featured speaker at "a youth conference" at Lansing's Lincoln

Community Center. About two decades after her husband died, Esther Tate Holley died at the age of seventy-eight in Philadelphia. According to a brief obituary in the *Philadelphia Inquirer*, she taught home economics to students with "special needs" for "many years" at Burke High School, retiring in 1963. The account also indicates that before her stint at Georgia Normal and Agricultural College, she taught at Old Dominion in Virginia and Florida A&M. She was buried in her home state, in Charlotte, Michigan. Tate lived a dynamic life, teaching in a range of educational institutions in the Midwest, the South, and the Northeast, engaging in graduate studies, wearing the hat of a social activist, and helping those in need, especially those with intellectual disabilities. Her connections to her alma mater were often conjured up. She was routinely introduced during speaking events in Lansing as being a proud M.A.C. graduate. Her obituary also highlighted this. "Mrs. Holley was a native of Lansing, Mich. She graduated from Michigan State University."[41]

Two African American men graduated from M.A.C. in 1920 with Tate, Herbert Floyd McFadden and Oliver Meakins Green. A World War I veteran like Williamson, Green arrived at M.A.C. sometime after serving overseas between June 10, 1918, and February 17, 1919. McFadden most likely arrived at M.A.C. in the fall of 1917. He was born on January 11, 1891, in Waycross, Georgia, and received his early education at Florida Agricultural and Mechanical College for Negroes and also worked at the school prior to coming to East Lansing.[42] Founded in the late 1880s as the State Normal College for Colored Students, Florida A&M (now commonly called "FAMU") was supported by the Second Morrill Act. When McFadden was there, former Tuskegee Institute academic department head and Booker T. Washington disciple Nathan B. Young served as president. Well versed in agriculture based upon his coursework and his employment at Florida A&M, McFadden came to M.A.C. to broaden his knowledge in scientific agriculture. Living with Williamson in room 16 Williams Hall, they were friends, helping each other navigate the unfamiliar environment in which they found themselves. They had spirited and penetrating conversations.

After graduating in 1920, McFadden taught at two HBCUs, Virginia State College and Lincoln University in Jefferson City, Missouri. At Virginia State College, he met his wife who taught home economics. In the mid-1920s, he settled down in Detroit and worked as a clerk for the U.S. Postal Service for thirty-five years. While in Detroit, he continued his education, earning a master's degree in sociology from Wayne State University in 1949. Embracing an array of social justice causes, he was an activist of some sort. He was a lifetime member of the NAACP, a charter member of the Detroit chapter of Omega Psi Phi fraternity, and a member of the Detroit branch of the Association for the Study of Negro Life and History, the leading scholarly organization of its kind founded by Carter G. Woodson, the Father of Black History, in 1915. McFadden's son, Herbert McFadden Jr., a Detroit city councilman from 1977 until 1981, remarked about his father after he died in 1981: "He always talked to me about education, and the importance of schooling."[43]

In addition to rooming and bonding with Williamson, McFadden knew Green who rolled up to M.A.C. in 1919 after serving in World War I as a member of the infantry band. Green's time at M.A.C. was brief; he graduated in one year. He previously enrolled in Cornell University and Syracuse University. Born on September 12, 1894, in Gadsden, Alabama, Green spent some of his early years in upstate New York.[44] He attended Ithaca High School and then enrolled in the nearby Cornell University. The first Black students graduated from this prestigious ivy league college that was founded in 1865 in the 1890s. Alpha Phi Alpha fraternity, the first Black intercollegiate fraternity, was founded on its campus in 1906. In the early 1920s while he attended law school at the University of Michigan, Green became a member of this fraternity. Like McFadden and Williamson, he lived in M.A.C.'s dorms. In the 1919–1920 academic year, he resided in 7D Wells Hall. In mid-June 1919, Green participated in a "mass meeting" in the gymnasium in honor of M.A.C. students who returned from their service in World War I. "Oliver Green, '19," noted the *M.A.C. Record*, "of the 367th Inf. (colored) gave an original poem written while he was in France that made a decided hit."[45] He was a passionate orator.

After graduating in 1920, Green enrolled in law school in Ann Arbor. While at M.A.C., he developed a friendship with longtime Lansing resident Miss Marie Dorsey (also known as Maria Dorsey) who lived on Division Street.[46] The native upstate New Yorker listed her as his parent or guardian on his registration forms for law school at the University of Michigan. While in law school, Green lived in Ann Arbor, Lansing, and Grand Rapids. He maintained connections with Lansing's Black community that helped sustain him while he was at M.A.C. Mr. Charles Campbell, a "Mr. Roberts," and Reverend Walker of the Lansing AME church on Pine Street were among his closest friends. After graduating from law school in 1924, Green settled down in Grand Rapids. In the late spring of 1924, he was identified as a Grand Rapids resident who served as the "toastmaster" for a program sponsored by the Alpha Phi Alpha fraternity called "Go-to-High School, Go-to-College" at the AME Community Church.[47] In late 1924, he was among the 179 who took and passed the Michigan bar examination, a feat recognized by the *Detroit Free Press*.[48] A year after Green completed law school, Black lawyers founded the National Bar Association to support, represent, and advocate for African Americans in the legal profession. At the time, there were only about one thousand African American lawyers in the United States.

Green participated in a Black radical tradition. In part influenced by his service in the Great War, in the early 1930s he wrote several letters to the editors of the *Detroit Free Press*. In 1931, he defended members of the Pontiac Unemployed Council and a local Communist leader against the charge of disorderly conduct. He publicly argued that "Communism seems to offer a program of relief to millions of workers in the United States against starvation, misery and hardships. It may not offer the best possible program, however, and when the other political parties offer a better one Communism will cease to spread." Green continued, "When the Democrats and Republicans give less time to bankers, manufacturers and political hirelings and more time to the masses of the workers, who, by the way, elect them to office, there will be no need to worry about Communism. The workers in America want only work so that they may earn a livelihood, and they don't care whether you call it Republicanism, Socialism, Communism or no ism at all."[49] A year later, he submitted a Communist-leaning think-piece addressed "to the Editor" titled "Asserts Poor Men Pay for Rich Men's War," which he signed "Oliver M. Green, (Disabled Veteran of World War) Pontiac, Mich." In no uncertain terms, he mocked the pope's prayer "for peace" and questioned the economic motivations of war. Green proclaimed: "Most wars are rich men's wars, but poor men's fights. The World War contributed no material benefit to any single citizen who was not a war contractor." After listing the massive wartime profits of the Bethlehem Steel Corporation and the Anaconda Copper Mining Company, he concluded, "These figures give a picture of bloody butchery in the World War, which was nothing more than a sacrifice of the workers on the altar of big business for greater profit. Instead of worrying God over it, why not use our persuasion on those who really cause war and benefit therefrom?"[50]

A month after this concise broadside was published, Green's life came to a sudden and tragic end. Thirty-eight-year-old Green was killed on March 20, 1932, at about midnight on Woodward Avenue and Lone Pine Road in Bloomfield Township, Michigan. While traveling home to Pontiac with a friend, his car's engine stopped. Green exited to check if they had run out of gas. A car traveling at a high speed struck him, launching his body ninety feet. He was pronounced dead at St. Joseph's Mercy Hospital. The driver of the vehicle was charged with negligent homicide and found guilty of driving carelessly. A recognizable and highly respected figure in the African American professional community, Green's death was covered in several papers in Michigan outside of the Detroit metropolitan area. In a lengthy story under the header "Oliver M. Green Killed in Crash—Pinned Between 2 Cars on Woodward Avenue—Veteran of World War," the *Pontiac Daily Press* reported, " Attorney Green had been in practice in Pontiac for several years with an office at 40 South Saginaw street. He was one of the city's two Negro lawyers. . . . He was graduated from Michigan State College and the University of Michigan. He practiced law in Grand Rapids before coming to Pontiac."[51]

Chapter 15

Chief

While Oliver M. Green, '20, Herbert McFadden, '20, and McGlenard Williamson, '21, were in East Lansing, the most widely known and revered African American student on campus since Gideon E. Smith arrived in East Lansing. Football player Harry C. Graves's potential on the gridiron was trumpeted soon after he stepped foot on campus in the fall of 1917. Under coaches George E. "Gooch" Gauthier, Gideon's former teammate who played quarterback from 1911 until 1914, and Penn State graduate Albert M. Barron, Graves played varsity football during the 1918, 1921, and 1922 seasons. He was on campus during the 1917–1918, 1918–1919, 1921–1922, and 1922–1923 academic years and was a bright spot for the football program during these down years when the varsity's winning percentage was less than 50 percent. He returned home between the fall of 1919 and the summer of 1921.

Graves was born around Denver, Colorado, on April 28, 1898. His literate parents, Henry and Mary, were born in Missouri during the era of Reconstruction. In 1900, Graves's mother died unexpectedly at age twenty-nine. In his early thirties, Henry became a widower with a toddler son, Harry, and twin four-year-old daughters, Mattie and Margaret. Mary's death devasted Henry, who had married her four years earlier. Henry and Mary strove to provide their children with better lives than they were able to enjoy. Sometime after 1900, Henry, Harry, Mattie, and Margaret migrated to Kansas. Harry and his sisters grew up under the watchful eyes of their father and paternal grandmother, Landonia Graves, who was born in about 1828 in Virginia. Sometime between 1915 and 1920, Graves's father married widow Sallie (or Sally) Hall. Without a mother during his childhood years, Harry established a tight bond with his father. He worked on his father's farm, and his grandmother routinely shared with him stories about Black life during slavery. They instilled within him values of perseverance, self-determination, hard work, self-reliance, and leadership that would serve him well in the future at M.A.C. Harry followed in his father's footsteps by becoming a farmer. A popular student identified as "a manly man" in his high school yearbook, Graves graduated from Pratt High School in the summer of 1917 and then traveled more than 970 miles to enroll in M.A.C. to study agriculture in the fall. Like McFadden, Green, and Williamson, he lived in the men's dormitories, in room 39 Williams Hall, during the 1917–1918 academic year with another African American freshman studying agriculture, Fred Douglas Carter.

In 1917, Graves started at fullback and right halfback on the All-Fresh football team coached by Gideon's former teammate Howard E. Beatty, '15. A writer for the 1918 *Wolverine* praised Graves's gritty play during the 1917 season. The 1917 All-Fresh team photo in the 1918 yearbook included a handsome, fit, and jovial Graves standing directly next to Coach Beatty. Graves's smile exudes confidence, coolness, and swag, and he looks as if he was one of the larger players on the squad. The team had a losing record (2-3), but Graves's unmistakable talent and potential was recognized by Aggie fans. The "colored full back, was one of the features of the game," the *Holcad* remarked on November 6, 1917, about Graves's performance against Notre Dame. "He was responsible for stopping Notre Dame's backs time after time and seldom failed to gain when called upon to make a few yards. His punting was exceptionally good, putting his spirals fast and far." By the end of Graves's freshman year, Coach Brewer was impressed by his play and looked forward to replenishing his depleted backfield. Brewer longed for the days of "famous line-smashers of the DaPrato, Julian, and Miller type" who struck fear into opposing defenses. The *Lansing State Journal* agreed with Brewer, considering the multipurpose Graves one of the up-and-coming gridders with great varsity potential.[1]

In 1918, onlookers greatly appreciated and heralded Graves's presence on the football field. The 1918 influenza pandemic, also known as the "Spanish flu," hit the M.A.C. campus hard. In mid-October 1918, the *M.A.C. Record* announced, "Every effort is being put forth" to "control and stop the spread of the epidemic." Several football games were postponed, and the college instituted a six-week quarantine and created "makeshift hospital wards." Graves's and his teammates' performances on the gridiron served as a welcomed diversion from the disruption caused by the devastating pandemic. Several weeks after a breakout game against Albion in October 1918 in which he consistently ran for gains of five to fifteen yards, scored two touchdowns, and kicked two goals, Aggie fans sang his praises even more. The November 1918 homecoming edition of the *Record* dubbed Graves one of the "Stars of the 1918 Varsity" and the "Fullback Who Ranks with Best." Along with quarterback Dean Ferris and captain and veteran center Larry Archer, there is a large menacing photo of Graves in full uniform carrying the ball in this widely read edition of the alumni paper. Like Gideon E. Smith who was given the assumed name "George Brown" during his freshman year, Graves was also assigned a pseudonym and portrayed in highly racialized manners by the local press. "Mistah Johnson, colored," reported the *State Journal* in April 1918, "is well on his way to becoming another Gideon Smith." Five months later, a writer for the *Journal* further compared Graves to his predecessor: "Graves possesses a chocolate complexion of about the same general density as that of much renowned Gideon Smith," the writer waxed. "He also possesses numerous other of Mr. Smith's qualities. Graves is a backfield man, carries himself along a pace better than 100 yards in 11 seconds." Graves performed well enough in the 1918 season that he was one of the eleven Aggies who was awarded a varsity monogram to be worn on his sweater, "the highest award bestowed by the college for athletics."[2]

Graves's performance against Michigan in November 1918 failed to meet his critics' expectations. Yost's team shut him down and defeated the Aggies 21-6 in Ann Arbor. Graves's glory and stardom materialized after he helped the Aggies defeat Notre Dame, 13-7, in their twelfth meeting on November 16, 1918, in East Lansing. He was directly involved in both of his team's touchdowns. Not only did he complete a twenty-yard pass for a touchdown when the game was predominated by the running game, but he also plowed across the goal line. He played an all-around complete game on offense and defense. His second touchdown became the defining moment of his peculiar M.A.C. football career. "Notre Dame still remembers how Harry used his 'tank' methods on them and smashed through their entire team for a touchdown that won the game for the Aggies," the *Wolverine* boasted in 1919. Graves's performance became legendary, especially within the Black community. As late as the 1930s, African American newspapers recounted with pride how Graves was Notre Dame coach Knute Rockne's "jinx." Echoing the Baltimore *Afro-American*, in 1932, a writer for the *Pittsburgh Courier* recalled, the fact that Graves

> once stopped the victorious march of an unstoppable Notre Dame eleven back in 1918, would never be known if he were to tell it. . . . It was Grantland Rice, nationally known sports writer, who recalled that the late Knute Rockne considered Graves his jinx. In an interview with Notre Dame mentor, Grantland Rice was told that Harry C. Graves made a blot on his clean record of two years in the game against the Aggies in 1918. . . . On the fourth down, Graves carried the ball over, eluding even the mighty George Gipp, who is probably the greatest backfield star in Notre Dame history. . . . This incident had a prominent place in Rockne's memory and afterwards sent Graves complimentary tickets to all the games.

Several years later, the *Courier* added to the tale: "Recalling Graves' sensational performance while a back at Michigan State, it is a fact that Harry once carried the pigskin through the mighty Notre Dame line to score a winning touchdown for his Michiganders over the famous Ramblers. Reminiscing on the incident, Rockne once said over the radio airwaves, 'the only nemesis I ever had was a little colored lad out at Michigan State.' And the player he referred to was Graves!"[3]

Graves finished the 1918 season strong. A staff member for the 1919 *Wolverine* commented in the yearbook that his game was defined by his weight, speed, and so-called natural ability. He was an all-around athlete. Pictured with the varsity track team in the 1919 *Wolverine*, he was the first African American to integrate this sport at M.A.C. He also played interclass baseball for several years. In late September 1919, to the delight of athletic director Chester Brewer, Graves reported to varsity football practice. He was one of the more than a dozen players trying out for the coveted backfield positions. Graves, however, did not play during the 1919 or 1920 football seasons. It seems he may have been suspended from the college for some reason early in the fall of 1919. He returned home to plod away on his father's farm in Pratt, Kansas, working with his twenty-year-old twin sisters and a nineteen-year-old roomer.[4] Shortly before the beginning of the 1920 season, Lyman L. Frimodig, '17, who coached the 1919 All-Fresh football team and varsity basketball, informed Coach George "Potsy" Clark that he wrote personal letters to more than twenty "of the boys we expect back this fall." Of Graves, "Frim" wrote, "Harry Graves—180-185—fullback—*colored*. . . . Expect him back this year—if you have no objections to a colored man you will find Graves a good man—quickest starter on the squad and is usually going at full force before the opposition is set—mighty strong on defence and a good worker for a colored man."[5] Of the more than twenty players Frim previewed, Graves was the only one referred to in racial terms. Frimodig played with Gideon Smith and often told stories about how he and his teammates "looked out for" Smith.[6] Yet Frimodig also believed in the prevailing stereotype that Black men were lazy. Did other M.A.C. coaches and players share his sentiments? Frimodig recommended Graves with caution, seemingly unaware of Clark's racial politics. Previous M.A.C. coaches, namely Chester Brewer, John Macklin, Frank Sommers, and George Gauthier, didn't explicitly draw the color line on the gridiron. Based upon the legend of Gideon, not to mention Graves's stellar play during the 1918 season, Clark would have been foolish not to be excited about Graves's potential return. Graves was aware of how many Whites on and off campus perceived Black people and culture. Was his possible suspension and decision to take a break from M.A.C. related to the campus's racial climate? Did he encounter overt or subtle racism on the gridiron or "on the banks of the Red Cedar"? Graves wasn't the type of Black man who "turned the other cheek."

Whatever the case may have been, Frimodig's prediction that Graves would return for the 1920 season was wrong. The powerful, fleet-footed, and confident fullback didn't return to East Lansing until the fall of 1921 when, as announced on the front page of an October issue of the *Holcad*, the "largest student body ever" (1,771 students) was enrolled. Graves was excited to suit up again, and Aggies fans were elated. In mid-October of 1921, the *Holcad* published a wonderful and prominently positioned photo of Graves. Looking off into the distance with his hands confidently placed on his hips, Graves looks focused, poised, and self-assured. In his dark practice jersey without his pads on, the size of his upper body can't be fully appreciated. The two years of farm work paid off. He bulked up and stayed in shape working on his father's farm in Pratt, Kansas. Above the photo reads: "STAGES COMEBACK."[7] This photo has deeper significance than simply celebrating Graves's much anticipated homecoming. This is the first

This photo of Harry C. Graves appeared in the *Holcad*, welcoming him back to campus after his brief hiatus. Courtesy of Michigan State University Archives and Historical Collections.

time an individual photo of an African American student appeared in either the *M.A.C. Record* or the *Holcad*. Perhaps the attention the student journalists afforded to Graves inspired him to play the amazing game that he did against Western State Normal.

Graves's 1921 homecoming was welcomed with a bit of skepticism. A sportswriter for the *Lansing State Journal* concluded that Graves, overall, played a "brilliant but inconsistent game."[8] In a September 30, 1921, article in the *Record* previewing the season with the new head coach, "clean-cut" Albert Barron, the writer questioned what Graves could contribute following his long hiatus. "Harry Graves, star fullback of the S.A.T.C. Team in 1918, is back and bids fair to win back his old place. Graves is heavy and fast, and has real football ability, although inclined to be somewhat erratic." Fans were elated to have Graves back, knowing he was tough as nails, a dual-threat, and experienced. Upon his return, he was in great shape from all of the work he performed on his father's farm. Many hoped he would replace John Hammes, the "big fullback" whom *Chicago Tribune* sportswriter Walter Eckersall picked for the All-Western Team in 1919.[9] Coach Barron's first year was a challenging one. His squad had a disappointing record of 3-5. Graves, however, proved his critics wrong, and his stellar play during the 1921 season was celebrated, earning him another varsity letter.

He played wonderfully in the Aggies' season opener against Alma on October 1. Starting at fullback, Graves scored two touchdowns in the second quarter. After losing to Albion on October

8, 1921, 7-24, the Aggies prepared for their matchup against their favored in-state rivals. Though M.A.C. was shut out by Michigan in front of more than twenty-three thousand onlookers at Ferry Field, 0-30, the Aggies' defense showed some grit, tallying five interceptions. Graves was a bright spot on the defensive side of the ball. In the blowout loss to U of M, Graves was a defensive power who "was accountable for at least half of the M.A.C. tackles."[10] In late October, Graves played an important role in the Aggies come-from-behind win over the strong Western State Normal team. His performance was nothing short of heroic. A sportswriter for the *Lansing State Journal* praised the courageous Aggie, declaring, "The story of the last half is the story of Graves' performance." It was "very much like the feats football heroes of fiction."[11] The account from the *Record* captures the essence of Graves's bravery and determination:

> The second half found the varsity returning with the score board reading 14-7 against them, and the bleachers pleading for a comeback which would sew up the game. Graves, regular fullback, spent several days last week in the hospital suffering from acute indigestion. Discharged Saturday morning, he came to the game in civilian clothes as a spectator, but the sight of the last Normal touchdown was too much, even for a sick man's nerves. To the surprise of everyone Graves appeared on the field in uniform at the start of the second half and was promptly sent into the lineup.
>
> With Graves carrying the ball on almost every down, the varsity took up an uninterrupted march down the field for their second touchdown, Graves going over on a line buck. Brady again goaled with the tying point.
>
> The final quarter found the teams battling in the middle of the field, the Aggies finally getting deep into the visitors' territory. Line plays failed here, however, and the team was forced to resort to a kick, Graves scoring via the dropkick route from the 33 yard line. These three points proved to be the margin of victory, the final whistle stopping another M.A.C. march toward the Normal Goal.[12]

Following the Aggies' thrilling win over Western orchestrated by an unhealthy but determined Graves, Barron's squad lost three of the four remaining games of the season, going scoreless against Marquette and Notre Dame. One of Graves's last spectacular performances for the Green and White was against South Dakota on November 5, 1921, at College Field in East Lansing. It was a homecoming Saturday. Before a crowd of seven thousand, Graves played an excellent defensive game. "Graves was the power behind the line in the Aggie defense," recounted the *Record*. "Roving behind the Green forward wall the big fullback kept his eyes glued to the ball, and when linemen were busy taking Scarlet-clad forwards out of play he was almost always in position to throw himself into the hole and ground the runner without gain." On the offensive side of the ball, "Graves had to be ridden by more than two opposing players to be stopped in his plunges."[13]

The 1922 *Wolverine* paid tribute to Graves's impressive 1921 season. He is pictured four times, suggesting he was a popular student. In his class of '23 photo, he claimed Detroit as his hometown, underscoring his imagined connection to the growing Black population in the city that boasted more than forty thousand Blacks at the time. He deliberately identified with this thriving Black community. Like many of his classmates, he actually came from a small town. In 1900, about five thousand people lived in Pratt, Kansas, and the Black population was miniscule at less than 1 percent of the total population. In the yearbook, he also adopted the nickname "Chief," intimating his leadership abilities. He may have been given this moniker by his teammates because of his take-charge attitude exemplified in his performances against Notre Dame in 1918 and Western State Normal in 1921. Although Graves was known for his offensive talents, the *Wolverine* also celebrated his defensive play and intellect. He demonstrated he was what we today call a student of the game. "Graves' greatest feats during the 1921 season were his performances in secondary defense," noted a writer for the *Wolverine*. "Playing close behind the line, he solved almost every play attempted by an opposing team soon after it was started, and it was more often true than otherwise that when the runner was brought down, Graves was in the midst of the movement to stop him." There is also a vivid photo of Graves in action running around the end against South Dakota. Holding the ball securely in his left hand, the determination on his face is evident. "It takes a low tackle to drop 'Harry,'" concluded one of Graves's classmates.[14]

During the 1922 season, Graves was moved from the coveted fullback position to right tackle and started in about half of the games. Football was a dangerous sport at the time, and he suffered from injuries because of his aggressive running style. Graves was eager to play against Michigan despite his nagging knee injury. He played one of his best games of the 1922 season against Albion in October. According to a writer for the *Record*, Graves "added the best bit of work to the day's grind by blocking a punt on the enemy's 30-yard line. . . . Graves and Eckert were the shining lights for the Aggies." In the game against Alma, Graves played the entire time. About four months after the end of the 1922 season, at a "mass meeting" on March 1, 1923, in

The determined Graves in action carrying the ball in 1921. The headline in the *Wolverine* reads, "It takes a low tackle to drop 'Harry.'" Courtesy of Michigan State University Archives and Historical Collections.

Harry Cornelius "Chief" Graves's 1923 handsome graduation photo. Courtesy of Michigan State University Archives and Historical Collections.

the gymnasium, Graves was one of six seniors to get a "gold football" in recognition for his three years of varsity play. One wonders if footage of Graves was included in the "reel of alumni moving pictures" showing "the strongest of the Green and White football stars in action" that was released in 1923 and 1924.[15]

After graduating on June 18, 1923, Graves became the head football coach at Virginia Normal and Collegiate Institute "with an unusually large and enthusiastic squad."[16] In February 1924, he let the *Record* know he was also the school's director of athletics. A year later, after a successful season of coaching behind him, in September 1924 he accepted a position as head football and baseball coach at Wilberforce University in Xenia, Ohio. After six years of great coaching, Graves's career at Wilberforce was in jeopardy. University president Gilbert H. Jones suspended him "for unknown reasons" in late October 1930. In the end, Jones made the right decision in retaining the "Chief." In 1931, Wilberforce became "national football champions," and numerous newspapers covered Graves's prowess as a coach. Between 1924 and 1931, Graves's record was seventy-one wins, seven losses, and eight ties. His teams were known for their "machine-like precision" and clever and aggressive offensive schemes, including a modern and sophisticated passing game. In June 1933, Graves resigned as head football coach and the supervisor of the Department of Health and Physical Education. His overall record at Wilberforce was impressive, 84-11-8. When Graves decided to leave Wilberforce, he, along with Gideon Smith, was one of the three longest serving Black coaches who spent their careers at one university. "I am rather inclined to say that nine years is long enough for any coach at the same institution," Graves reflected upon his career at Wilberforce, "It is human nature to like to see new faces and new methods." One of Graves's assistant coaches admired his boss. "We thought the world of him. No one better than we do, realize how much he really did and what handicaps he had to overcome," Henry "Hank" Corruthers testified. "I have never seen Graves' superior as an organizer. He is wonderful at it."[17]

Graves's retirement was influenced by his desire to apply his knowledge and experience in different ways. In 1933, he earned a master's degree from the Ohio State University. His thesis, titled "The Construction of a Curriculum for the Preparation of Teachers of Health and Physical Education for Wilberforce University," explored "the health and physical education curricula of the Negro high schools of the United States, and constructs a curriculum for teachers of health and physical education for Wilberforce university."[18] Graves's scholarly approach to sports and physical education dovetailed with and intimately informed his coaching. As historian Derrick E. White points out, African American coaches and athletic directors at HBCUs, like Florida A&M's longtime football coach Jake Gaither, earned master's degrees as a part of their continual professional development. Graves's postbaccalaureate education opened some doors for him. In 1934, he was appointed one of the eight newly selected "colored camp advisers" in the Civilian Conservation Corps, making him one of twenty-nine African American advisers in the country at the time. This was indeed a prestigious position. "High standards" were maintained "throughout the whole personnel." The biographical sketch of Graves printed in the *New York Age* on December 22, 1934, took note of his M.A.C. roots. "Harry Cornelius Graves: Age 36, B.S. Michigan State College; M.A. Ohio State University, 1933; Teaching experience, Wilberforce; Superintendent of Health and Physical Education."[19]

After leaving Wilberforce, rumors surfaced Graves was going to become the next head football coach at Howard University. An article from the Washington, D.C., *Evening Star* even quoted Howard's chairman of the Board of Athletic Control as confirming this hearsay. With his wife and fellow educator Nellie Love Bundy, he moved to the nation's capital, but not to join Howard. He became the athletic director at Armstrong High School. In Washington, D.C., Graves became a multidimensional community man. While working at Armstrong, he managed a singing group, briefly coached the Washington Lions football club, and spoke in a variety of venues. As late as the 1950s and 1960s, his accomplishments as a player and coach on the gridiron continued to be celebrated by the Black press. In 1950, Dan Burley of the *New York Age* praised "Harry C. Graves and Ben Goode of Michigan State" as "outstanding business and professional men" with "collegiate football backgrounds." A year before his death in 1966, the *Pittsburgh Courier* paid tribute to Graves and Gideon Smith as being among the exceptional Black football coaches who attended predominantly White institutions before the mid-1920s.[20] Graves was one of the greats in the history of M.A.C. football.

Chapter 16

Gridiron and Dairy Farm

Whem Harry C. Graves returned from his father's farm to M.A.C. in the fall of 1921, he was not the only African American football prospect on campus. In 1922 when Graves was switched from fullback to right tackle, Benjamin L. Goode joined the Aggies. Goode was born on April 19, 1899, in Harvey, West Virginia. He received an early education in Charleston, West Virginia, and, like Delbert M. Prillerman before him, attended West Virginia Collegiate Institute. He enlisted in the U.S. Army in mid-October 1918 and was discharged in late December 1918. He arrived at M.A.C. in the fall of 1921. "It is announced that Goode, the colored boy sent to M.A.C. by Gideon Smith, former star tackle, is now eligible to play and is rounding rapidly into shape. He is a fast man in the backfield."[1] Smith coached Goode briefly at West Virginia Collegiate Institute from 1916 until the summer of 1917 and encouraged him to attend his alma mater. A writer for the *M.A.C. Record* declared the 1921 All-Fresh team, on which Goode played right half, the strongest All-Fresh team in the history of the college. The young squad had "a lot of mighty fine" future varsity gridders. Gideon's protégé Goode was key to the team's backfield and played a key role in the All-Fresh's victory over Notre Dame in November 1921, scoring the only Aggie touchdown. On the M.A.C. varsity squad, Goode had little playing time in 1922 and saw the field for a total of less than forty minutes in 1923.[2]

In 1923, Holloway Smith, another Black gridder, played as many minutes as Goode during the Aggies' disappointing 3-5 season. Smith substituted in a few varsity games and started for the freshman team. Born on November 19, 1896, in Spottsville, Kentucky, located in Henderson County, Holloway grew up on his father's farm. In 1910, a thirteen-year-old Holloway was a farm laborer and one of ten children of Kentucky-born James and Harriet Smith. Considering his upbringing, M.A.C. was a logical choice for him. When Holloway arrived in East Lansing in the fall of 1923, he was a grown man, a twenty-seven-year-old World War I veteran who had grown up on a farm. Like Graves, Holloway was compared to Gideon Smith by a writer for the *Record*. "Holloway Smith, a prototype of Gideon Smith, M.A.C. marvel of ten years ago, saw duty at tackle for part of the contest" against Lake Forest on October 6, 1923, as a substitute in the varsity's game "and acquitted himself creditably."[3] This was an important game, the first in the newly constructed College Field. Before a crowd of "nearly 7,000 people," first-year coach Ralph H. Young's team won the contest 21-6, and Aggies' fans saw the team's fourth Black player, Holloway, don the Green and White. The comparison drawn between the Kentucky native and Gideon had much to do with Holloway's appearance. His complexion was dark, and he stood 6 foot 3 and weighed between 195 and 219 pounds. He was an imposing figure. In the 1923 loss to Wisconsin at Camp Randall Stadium, Holloway played left guard in the fourth quarter, substituting for starter V. J. Hultman. In the 0-37 loss to Michigan in Ann Arbor on October 27, Holloway saw some time at left tackle. In early November, he started at guard in the freshman team's game against Assumption College, and at the end of the season he, like Goode, had not played enough to earn a monogram. Instead, they were granted heavy green V-neck sweaters for their contributions. Holloway didn't return to M.A.C. the following year.[4]

In 1926, at age thirty, he became the second African American to play varsity football at Iowa State College of Agriculture and Mechanical Arts, another early land-grant institution. He had big shoes to fill. Jack Trice, who died on October 8, 1923, from injuries he sustained in a violent game against the University of Minnesota, was respected for his grit and mourned by his classmates. Holloway was benched in several games against southern opponents. But he was undisputably a "star for the Cyclones" at right tackle. Just as Gideon was depicted in Michigan newspapers in racialized terms, the Iowa press routinely described Holloway as the "giant negro" and "colored tackle." His Michigan and M.A.C. connections were also conjured up. He claimed Detroit as his hometown (an affiliation with the Black city of Detroit brought much more swag than his hometown of Spottsville, Kentucky), and the local Iowa press took notice of his brief M.A.C. career. "On the line Holloway Smith of Detroit will also appear before the home crowd for the last time Saturday," recounted the *Courier* (Waterloo, Iowa) on November 14, 1927. "Smith has starred two years at tackle for the Cyclones, and also has one year of competition at Michigan State chalked against him." Holloway graduated in 1928 with a bachelor's degree in agricultural education and became a longtime educator in Arkansas. One wonders exactly why he left M.A.C. and how he could have helped the Aggies who struggled under Coach Young from 1923 until 1927.[5]

In the 1924 season, Benjamin Goode, who probably counseled Holloway about racial etiquette at M.A.C., was a "consistent starter" on the varsity and, according to historian Johnny Smith, faced discrimination when he didn't accompany the team to an away game against St.

Benjamin Goode in the *Wolverine* (1925).
Courtesy of Michigan State University
Archives and Historical Collections.

GOODE
Half Back

Louis. This incident, according to Smith, "was the first instance where Michigan State excluded its Black players against a southern team."[6]

Goode didn't achieve the fame on the M.A.C. gridiron Gideon Smith or Graves enjoyed. But the Black press took notice of him in his last season. The *Pittsburgh Courier* and the Baltimore *Afro-American* were enamored with him. The writer for the *Courier*, who also most likely penned the strikingly similar piece in the *Afro-American*, provided a brief biography of Goode with a large and handsome full-body photo of him in his practice uniform. He was smiling and exuding pride. The author exaggerated his status on the team, insinuating he started at fullback for three years. After graduating from MSC in 1925, Goode coached four sports, including football at South Carolina State College in Orangeburg, South Carolina. In 1927, he returned to his home state where he "served as assistant coach in all sports" and taught agriculture, his specialization at M.A.C., for close to twenty years. He earned a master's degree from Iowa State College and lived in Ames, Iowa, for several years. He was elected "senior grand vice polemarch" of Kappa Alpha Psi fraternity in 1939, and the description of him in the *Chicago Defender* noted underneath his photo, "football star at Michigan State, his alma mater." A skilled chess player among other hobbies, he was active, with Gideon Smith, in the Central Intercollegiate Athletic Association and was the vice-commander-at-large of the West Virginia American Legion as well as a member of Charles Young Post 57.[7]

A year after Goode graduated, two African American men graduated from MSC, Aeolian E. Lockert and Clarence E. Banks. Born on March 6, 1897, in Clarksville, Tennessee, Lockert was destined to become an educator. In 1900, his father, Henry, was a teacher and a proud homeowner. The oldest of five sons, at age sixteen, Lockert lost both of his parents.[8] As the eldest son, Aeolian helped look after his younger siblings. After being called into service for World War I, in 1923 he earned a diploma in agriculture from Tennessee Agricultural and Industrial State Normal School for Negroes, a public, land-grant HBCU in Nashville.[9] A year later, he became a member of "the first class to receive the baccalaureate degree" from what became Tennessee Agricultural and Industrial State Normal College.[10] Lockert then enrolled in M.A.C. to study agriculture in either 1924 or 1925. During the 1925–1926 academic year, he lived on the fourth floor of Wells Hall, and his classmate Banks lived in 15C Wells Hall. He didn't appear in any of the college's yearbooks before 1926 and may have only attended MSC for one year.[11] After graduating, Lockert returned to his home state and in the fall of 1926 began teaching agriculture at Tennessee Agricultural and Industrial State Normal College. When he returned to his alma mater, it was undergoing significant changes and great growth: $400,000 worth of buildings were being constructed, and part-time and night school students were being integrated into the school.[12] The 1930 U.S. census lists Lockert as being a high school teacher, and by the early 1940s he taught within the Fayette County public school system. Lockert's experience on campus differed from his fellow 1926 graduate Clarence E. Banks's. Lockert lived in the men's dormitories and socialized with Banks, Benjamin D. Jones (who attended M.A.C. for several years), and Clarice A. Pretlow, '30, among others. Because he was only in East Lansing for a year or two and was almost thirty years old when he graduated, he probably didn't extensively fraternize with those students who were in their early twenties. Banks, on the other hand, was involved in a range of activities on campus. Not only did he live in Wells Hall, but he was a cross-country runner and joined the YMCA, the Student Citizenship League, and, most importantly, the Dairy Club.

The child of tenant farmers, Richard and Clara, Clarence Banks was born on February 3, 1901, in Henderson County, Kentucky. Throughout his life as a sharecropper and manual laborer, Richard encountered a great deal of racism, profoundly shaping his children's world views and his perceptions of Whites. Like most Black women of her generation, Clarence's mother, who married Richard before she completed high school, worked as a laundress, seamstress, and domestic servant. She was also an independent business woman, selling milk, eggs, and chickens that they raised. Like her husband, she instilled within her children a sense of self-sufficiency. Clarence spent part of his youth on an isolated, twenty-five-acre farm in a small, majority-White town, the "village of Geneva." Until about age ten, he lived in a small, raised four-room house in an area known as the "bottom-lands" that often flooded. As a child, Clarence attended a one-room school, and his later participation in a religious organization at MSC was influenced by his being "taken into the church" at a young age. The Banks family grew and harvested corn, oats, and hay for sale. Sharecropping was oftentimes exploitative and could result in Black families being indebted to landowners. The Banks family carved out some autonomy and supported themselves, raising their own chickens, hogs, mules, horses, and cows, and growing vegetables. Clarence gained valuable experience tending to livestock, working six days a week from sunup to sundown. Banks's brother William Venoid Banks—founder of "the first Black-owned and Black-operated [radio] station in the United States" in Detroit, Michigan—shared stories about their childhood, shedding light on how Clarence was raised to live off the land, appreciated the rhythms of nature, and coexisted with livestock. "I learned a new lesson every day. Some lessons involved caring for the animals we raised, which included horses, mules, cows, hogs, chickens, geese, turkeys, and ducks," William recalled. "I had to know how to care for them from the time they were born or hatched."[13] The Banks siblings learned the value of hard work, respect for nature, education, self-reliance, and even self-defense. Clarence's adolescence and young adulthood prepared him to venture to East Lansing.

Clarence's family migrated from Geneva to different places seeking a better life, including to bigger cities in Kentucky; St. Louis, Missouri; Evansville, Indiana; and Little Rock, Arkansas. At about age fifteen when his family was living in Little Rock, Clarence attended Lincoln Institute, a Black vocational boarding high school in Lincoln Ridge, Kentucky, where his uncle taught. His mother pinched pennies so that Clarence could attend Lincoln where he worked on the school farm milking cows.[14] After graduating from Lincoln Institute and returning briefly to Evansville, Indiana, nineteen-year-old Clarence arrived at M.A.C. in 1922. While in East Lansing, Banks visited his parents and brother in Detroit. His parents migrated to the Motor City in about 1919, his brother worked at Ford Motor Company, and his mother Clara was active in Detroit's Black community. Active in the city's historic Second Baptist Church, the Eastern Stars, and the Credit Union of the International Masons, Clara developed local legendary status from "her downtown Brush address." During the Civil Rights Movement, the *Michigan Chronicle* named her "Mother of the Week," celebrating her life of service. "For nearly 40 years this mother of three has been making contributions to the Detroit community," the popular newspaper continued, "Each day the physical and spiritual needs of some of her fellow members and friends." This explains why Clarence listed his hometown as Detroit in the 1926 *Wolverine*. In 1923, Banks became the first African American to be on the varsity M.A.C. cross-country team. He found his calling in the Dairy Club. This "professional club," promoting dairying and annually competing in the National Dairy Show, participated in Farmer's Week activities and was one of the most active clubs on campus. Beginning in the late nineteenth century, the college took great pride in its prize-winning cows such as Belle Sarcastic and her offspring Sarcastic Lad.[15]

What Banks learned at his alma mater served him well in the future. He had a passion for livestock from his early years and further honed it at MSC. In November 1926, Banks informed the college's alumni newspaper that his new address was "M. T. and I. School, Bordentown, New Jersey." Immediately after graduating, he began working at New Jersey State Manual Training and Industrial School for Colored Youth. It was a boarding school that provided students with "special vocational training" to support the "school work." Banks was one of about twenty-seven faculty and staff.[16] In the mid-1920s, the *Pittsburgh Courier* reported that he oversaw the school's

Banks as an active and proud member of the Dairy Club in 1925. Courtesy of Michigan State University Archives and Historical Collections.

dairy and hailed from Michigan State College. Commonly known as the Bordentown School, the school was founded in 1886 by minister Walter A. Rice who was once enslaved. His goal was to teach young African Americans how to become self-sufficient. Referred to by some as the "Tuskegee of the North," by the time Banks began working there, the state of New Jersey had taken control of the school. In 1928, the school enrolled students from the sixth through high school.[17]

Banks developed a reputation for being an excellent teacher and "herdsman." In 1936, the popular *Opportunity: A Journal of Negro Life* praised his skills: "We hail the achievement of the Bordentown Manual Training School for Colored Youth at Bordentown, New Jersey." The Harlem Renaissance literary magazine continued, "We offer our congratulations to W. R. Valentine, Principal, and to Clarence E. Banks, herdsman, and to the young men who brought to Bordentown an important national championship." Under Banks's leadership, the Bordentown school won "first place among Holstein herds" in New Jersey, and "an individual cow in the herd received top ranking among cows in her class." The Holstein-Friesian Association of America remarked that this cow "gave 8,000 quarts of milk and seven hundred fourteen pounds of butter[fat] in 305 days." *Opportunity* dubbed Banks's and his students' accomplishment "amazing" and concluded: "at a time when the problems of agriculture are in the forefront of the world problems demanding the attention of state and national legislatures, it is inspiring to know that a school devoted to the training of Negro youth has attained national distinction in one of the most important phases of farm life." Banks's abilities were praised by others in the Black community. According to a reporter for the popular *New York Amsterdam News* in 1937, Banks was "frequently called in as a consultant buy fancy breeders, and was recently awarded a certificate of honor by the New Jersey Guernsey Breeders' Association for his superior skills as a herdsman in charge of Alyukpa Golden Princess."[18] In the early 1940s, Banks continued to demonstrate his prowess as a teacher and award-winning "herdsman." In 1941, a Bordentown School three-year-old Holstein cow, Alpha Piebe Homestead, produced a record-setting number of pounds of milk with "767.62 pounds of butter[fat]." Bordentown won several state championships for three-year-olds milked twice daily. This prize-winner and the Holstein herd at the school were bred and raised "under the direction of Clarence E. Banks," noted the *Chicago Defender*, who taught his students about the "development of live-stock."[19] The Bordentown School closed its doors in 1955, and it remains unclear what Banks, age fifty-four at the time, did for the remainder of his life. He died in Pennsylvania in 1979.

Chapter 17

In Myrtle's Footsteps

I n H. A. Scott's brief 1924 feature story on Benjamin L. Goode's accomplishments in the backfield of the Aggies' "varsity eleven" published in the Baltimore *Afro-American*, he mentioned Banks's participation on the M.A.C. cross-country squad as well the presence of another noteworthy African American student. "At the present time, there are but four colored students at Michigan State College and as a result of the comparative lack of racial friction, all are engaged in campus activities." Scott continued, "Mabel Lucas, of Lansing, the only colored girl in the school, is a trap drummer in the Co-ed orchestra."[1]

Several months before Scott's article appeared, another young Black woman was finishing her degree at M.A.C. At the end of Mabel's freshman year, in mid-June 1924, Margaret Elizabeth Collins graduated, becoming the third known Black woman to graduate from the college.[2] She did so close to two decades after Myrtle Bessie Craig made history and four years after Esther I. Tate graduated. Black women students' presence on campus was not collectively recognized until three decades after Collins graduated. In 1954, the Delta Zeta chapter of Alpha Kappa Alpha Sorority, Inc. was chartered, providing nearly twenty young Black women a sense of belonging. A decade later, a student journalist showcased several Black women students' perspectives on range of issues, including interracial dating, in a first-of-its-kind write-up in the *State News*. A first-year young Black woman from Detroit shared how it felt to be Black. With a bit with witticism, she responded, "Life could be worse. I know that anything I've accomplished has been on my own merit. Perfect equality will never occur in this generation."[3] Collins could have certainly imparted the same rejoinder, and then some. Unlike their spiritual protégés who came of age during the modern Civil Rights Movement, Collins and her Black women classmates did benefit from on-campus organizations that were created by and for them. They had to create community for themselves, and this usually took place off campus. Like Myrtle Bessie Craig before her, Collins found moral support and fellowship in Lansing's modest Black community.

Collins was born on December 11, 1900, in Lansing, Michigan. Her father was Rev. George R. Collins, the long-serving pastor of the African Methodist Episcopal (AME) church.[4] Margaret was raised by her mother, Lucy R. Collins, a hairdresser by trade, who was born in about 1871. A decade after her husband died, in 1913 Margaret's mother married Charles A. Campbell, a clerk who was an honorary vice-president of the Freedmen's Progress Commission along with William O. Thompson, '04. A leader in the organization, Charles Augustus Warren, '96–'99, knew Margaret's stepfather very well. In 1915, Campbell, who settled down in Lansing in about 1907, was an officer in the Grand Lodge of the Free and Accepted Masons of Michigan.[5] In 1920, Margaret lived with her stepfather, mother, and two boarders and was employed as a domestic servant. There were about seven hundred African Americans living in Lansing out of a total population of more than fifty-seven thousand; most African Americans in the city labored in service-oriented jobs, and many young Black women like Collins worked as domestic servants.

Collins enrolled in M.A.C., focusing on home economics. She lived in Campbell's well-known and spacious residence at 1111 West Main Street and spent much of her time in the Lansing community. She had to overcome some obstacles while in college. In the spring of 1922, the *Chicago Defender* reported that she "underwent a very serious operation" in Sparrow Hospital. After graduating, she became a teacher in Lansing, and in 1930, she was a faculty member at Georgia Normal and Agricultural College where Esther Tate Holley, '20, worked. Holley helped recruit Collins to her husband's school.[6] Between the 1930s and her death in 1994, Collins was married several times and lived in Lansing; Marion County, Florida; Pine Bluff, Arkansas (where she may have worked with her husband at Arkansas Agricultural, Mechanical and Normal College); Jackson County, Missouri; and Chicago, Illinois where she and her husband William M. Henderson ran a funeral home on the city's South Side.[7]

At the beginning of Margaret E. Collins's senior year at M.A.C., Mabel enrolled in the college. Mabel sought council from the more seasoned senior. As Lansing residents whose families belonged to the AME church named in honor of Margaret's father, they knew each other. Collins served as the secretary of the church's Sunday school as a young adult, and Mabel, an active member of the AME's Children's Division and a skilled vocalist, attended many of these meetings.[8] Mabel was born on August 29, 1904, in Chicago, Illinois. Her father, William Lucas, grew up on a farm in Caledonia County with six siblings, became an insurance salesman, and spent most of his time in Chicago. In 1925, during her sophomore year at MSC, William died. Mabel's mother, Rosetta "Etta" Hurst, was born in Allegan, Michigan, on September 26, 1880, and lived in Lansing for most of her life working as a hairdresser and domestic servant. Mabel's parents were married in Owosso, Michigan in August 1903 and split up sometime before 1911 when her mother remarried in Detroit. Mabel was a well-traveled child, developing the capacity to adapt to different environments early in her life. She spent her childhood in Chicago, Detroit, and Lansing. The time she spent in Chicago and Detroit exposed her to different dimensions of Black culture. Between 1910 and 1920, the Black population in Lansing increased slightly from 354 to 698, and the vast majority were relegated to working in service-related industries. While not monolithic, Lansing's Black population did not have the diverse Black subcultures of Chicago or Detroit. The Black populations in Chicago and Detroit skyrocketed during the first phase of the Great Migration, from about 5,700 to 41,000 in Detroit from 1910 until 1920 and about 44,000 to 109,500 in Chicago. Many African Americans who populated these cities migrated from the Black Belt South and brought with them their distinctive cultural mores and ways of living. A young Mabel interacted with Black children her age whose parents hailed from all over the Deep South and the nation.

The *Chicago Defender* routinely offered "ordinary" African Americans space to share with readers quotidian events in their lives. In 1917, the paper noted: "Little Mabel Lucas, niece of Stephen Lucas, will return to Detroit to remain during school vacation, accompanied by Mrs. S. Lucas."[9] When the United States entered the Great War, a teenage Mabel lived in Lansing with her father's older brother, her uncle Stephen Lucas. Born in 1861, Stephen moved to Lansing sometime during the late nineteenth century. In 1900, he worked as a waiter in Lansing and later held various jobs in the city until he died in 1937, including plodding away as a clerk, messenger, janitor, and laborer. Between 1912 and 1917, he served as secretary of the AME church. During World War I, he was recognized by Lansing's White community for his patriotism. Contributing to the cause, he purchased Liberty bonds. "Stephen M. Lucas," noted the *State Journal*, "the first Lansing Negro to get a 'V' walked into headquarters of No. 11 at 6 o'clock Saturday morning just as the siren whistle announced the opening of Liberty day. Mr. Lucas is the owner of bonds of the first and second Liberty Loan."[10] In 1920, Mabel lived with her uncle Stephen, his wife Persula (Sula), Sula's son and his wife, and three "roomers" between the ages of twenty-two and thirty-seven. In 1922, when Mabel was eighteen years old, Stephen married her mother, his sister-in-law Rosetta Hurst Williams. Mabel lived with her uncle and mother at 522 S. Sycamore while she was attending M.A.C. This was an interesting arrangement. After graduating from Lansing Central High School in 1923, Mabel enrolled in M.A.C. and defied the odds. She specialized in the sciences. While a writer for the Baltimore *Afro-American* mentioned in passing that she was "a trap drummer in the Co-ed orchestra," a writer for the *Chicago Defender* mentioned her talents as an athlete, observing: "She has excelled in hockey and baseball as well as participating in tennis and swimming." A writer for the *Pittsburgh Courier* added that Mabel was "a member of the famous Co-ed Orchestra at the college . . . has displayed exceptional scholastic ability in her courses, and is exceedingly popular with the entire student body."[11]

A photo of her appears among the graduating seniors in the 1927 *Wolverine*. Next to her photo appears: "lucas, mable [sic], Science. *Lansing*." Another photo shows her as a member of

Mabel Lucas on the women's interclass volleyball team. She was the first known Black woman to participate in the college's women's athletics program. Courtesy of Michigan State University Archives and Historical Collections.

Lucas during her senior year with other members of the Tau Sigma, Local Honorary Science Fraternity. Courtesy of Michigan State University Archives and Historical Collections.

the class of 1927 "Winners of Interclass Volleyball." The first Black woman to major in the applied sciences, Mabel was also the first known Black woman to be a member of the college's Women's Athletic Association (WAA). Organized in the spring of 1925, two years later the association had ninety active members, one of whom was Mabel. In the fall 1926 term, she earned a class monogram for her active participation on the interclass women's volleyball team. Volleyball was a popular women's winter sport, "second only to basketball." According to the association's "system of awards," Mabel earned the total five hundred points making her eligible for a WAA class monogram. In December 1926 at the "term-end banquet," she and eleven of her classmates received their monograms "for 500 points under 'W. A. A.' ruling."[12] Mabel's participation on the volleyball team spiced up her on-campus social life. Like Collins, she spent most of her time on campus in the classroom, and her family and Lansing's small Black community sustained her during her four years at M.A.C. In mid-November 1926, the *Pittsburgh Courier* proudly announced that she was elected to the college's Tau Sigma fraternity, "a national honorary society to which but few members of the colored race have been elevated and given in reward for exceptional ability and scientific fields." The *Courier* went a step further, praising Michigan State for maintaining "democratic principles" by promoting Black women's scholarly excellence.[13] After earning a bachelor of science degree in applied sciences, she accepted a position teaching chemistry and biology at Prairie View State Normal and Industrial School in Prairie View, Texas. Founded in 1876, Prairie View, a land-grant school, was the first state-supported school of its kind for African Americans in Texas. During Mabel's career there, the school offered four courses: agriculture, mechanical arts, home economics, and education.

The principal, W. R. Banks, stressed to Mabel and her colleagues "the importance of character, of the noble and simple life." He proclaimed, "We want a greater Prairie View. Prairie View cannot be stronger than its faculty. We must emphasize scholarship and orderly conduct." In a fall 1927 newsletter, the institution took great pride in having "exceptionally strong" professors from "leading institutions." Under the header "Prairie View College Strengthens Force, Able Faculty," there were the names of about twenty new faculty, including "Miss Mabel Lucas, B. S., MSC, Professor of Mathematics."[14] The standards at Prairie View were aspirational. Mabel and her colleagues were encouraged to pursue master's degrees. Banks stressed, "our faculty must be strengthened, more masters must be added in order that we may meet the approval of the Southern Association of Colleges."[15] Mabel was proud of her new position, updating her alma mater. "Mabel Lucas will teach chemistry at the Prairie View State college at Prairie View, Texas this coming year," the *M.S.C. Record* documented in September 1928. "Miss Lucas was in the mathematics department last year. She remarks that she will be glad to hear from any of her classmates." Several years later, in July 1930, she wrote to her alma mater, reiterating: "I would be glad to hear from any of the class of '27." She added with pride, "I have been awarded a fellowship from the General Education board to study at the University of Chicago during the year 1930–31. I expect to receive my master's degree in chemistry."[16]

While at Michigan State, Mabel was mentored by former college president and chemistry professor Frank S. Kedzie, or "Uncle Frank," as the students commonly knew him. An encouraging adviser to many who served as dean of the Division of Applied Science from 1925 until 1927, Kedzie respected Mabel's work ethic and gave her moral support during and after her time at MSC. In 1930, she wrote several letters to her former professor. In May, she joyfully informed him that she received a graduate fellowship to attend the University of Chicago. Though she shared with him her plans to return to East Lansing for graduate school, she could not turn down this special opportunity. "I want you to know that just as I have kept Michigan State in my mind in all my efforts, in the past three years, just so will I go to the U. of C. to make a record not only for myself but Michigan State also." Kedzie was delighted by Mabel's success, offering her only words of sincere encouragement.[17]

Kedzie's championing of Mabel could be considered an extension of support he previously expressed to Lansing's Black community. In 1917, he delivered a keynote address at the golden jubilee celebration for the AME church. He was one of the handful of Whites at this historic event. He was comfortable hanging out with members of the Black community, listening to orations like Rev. Joseph W. Jarvis's "The Negro's Patriotism in the Crisis of the Nation." Mabel received a fellowship from one of the leading institutions of higher learning in the United States, and Kedzie shared this news with the *State Journal* whose editorial staff published an update about Mabel in the "City in Brief" section. "Miss Mabel J. Lucas, 522 South Sycamore street, who has been teaching science at the Prairie View State Normal and Industrial college, a negro institution in Texas, has been awarded a fellowship by the general board of education at the University of Chicago, according to Dr. Frank S. Kedzie, historian at Michigan State College."[18]

Mabel left Prairie View at the end of the 1929–1930 academic year and enrolled in the master's program in chemistry at the University of Chicago in the fall of 1930. The transition from life in Texas to Chicago and from the Prairie View to the University of Chicago was a massive shift. Mabel was familiar with this large metropolis. While there, she probably lived with her aunt Julia Brown, her father's older sister. In the spring of 1931, she told *Record* readers her new address in Chicago was 4555 South Parkway and, like Gideon Smith, contributed to the annual MSC alumni fund. In the late spring of 1932, Prairie View's leader W. R. Banks was under the impression that Mabel would return to her work at Prairie View after completing her master's degree. She didn't return to Banks's school. She remained in Chicago and by 1934 secured a position as a supervisor for the Chicago Relief Administration founded during the leadership of longtime Chicago mayor Edward J. Kelly. Mabel's last communication with her alma mater was in March 1935 when she informed her former classmates she was employed as a caseworker in Chicago for Illinois's Emergency Relief Commission and lived at 5929 S. Michigan Avenue. On September 15, 1941, at the young age of thirty-seven, Mabel died in her home in Chicago. After the funeral at St. Edmund's Episcopal Church in Chicago, she was laid to rest in Lansing's

Mt. Hope Cemetery. She was remembered by her alma mater. A brief obituary was published for her in the *State Journal* as well as in the *Record*.[19]

In the fall of 1925, the fifth Black woman to graduate from MSC, Clarice Arinthia Pretlow, joined Mabel, Benjamin L. Goode, Clarence E. Banks, Aeolian Lockert, and B. D. (Ben or Benjamin) Jones at the college. Pretlow was born in Virginia on September 1, 1905, and grew up on her parents' farm in Newport, Virginia, in Isle of Wight County. Unlike most African American men of his generation in the South, Pretlow's father, Kenneth Wesley (or Westley) Pretlow, owned the farmland on which he worked. His family's livelihood depended upon their connection to the land and soil. Kenneth was born in Virginia in November 1874. In the spring of 1900, he married Arinthia Missouri Tynes who was born in October 1874 in Isle of Wight County. Clarice was the second daughter and third child of Kenneth's and Arinthia's seven children.[20] As mothers during the Progressive Era customarily did, Clarice's mother took care of the children and managed the day-to-day operations of the household while Kenneth farmed the land with the help of his three sons. All the Pretlow children, including Clarice, were intimately acquainted with the farm's daily rhythms and chores. Children of farmers worked alongside their parents, especially after the school year ended.

Kenneth and Arinthia, both of whom could read and write, passed the core value of education on to their children. Clarice's younger sister Jocelyn was especially successful as a scholar. After earning a bachelor of arts degree in English from Fisk University and a master of arts degree in English from Columbia University, she became a college professor and published several books. Like Jocelyn, Clarice received her early education in her hometown and attended Virginia State College for Negroes founded in the early 1880s. When Pretlow came to MSC in 1925 to study home economics, she had a solid foundation that began during her childhood. Clarice's mother shared with her vital hands-on and transgenerational knowledge pertaining to cooking, housekeeping, family life and child-rearing, sewing, and financial household planning. Clarice perfected these skills at Virginia State College. Like Myrtle Bessie Craig two decades earlier, while taking classes at MSC, Clarice worked to support herself. In 1928, the Lansing city directory listed her as being a "maid" for Owen Knapp, an "assistant manager of the Reo Service Station in Lansing."[21] While a student, Clarice lived in Lansing, successfully balancing going to school full-time and working. On campus, she socialized with the small group of Black students.

In 1926, she attended a get-together—an event mentioned in the local section of the *Pittsburgh Courier*—at the home of a fifty-nine-year-old Black woman named Mary Dillard who had migrated from South Carolina to Lansing with her three daughters. Sara Dillard, Mary's seventeen-year-old daughter, a domestic servant, "entertained a number of friends" at her mother's home on Williams Street. Among those "friends" was Clarice, along with MSC students Clarence E. Banks, B. D. Jones, and Aeolian Lockert as well as Sara's two sisters, also domestic servants, and a twenty-three-year-old porter from Missouri named Harold Lindsay Tutt and another man named H. Edwin Jackson.[22] Not only is it intriguing that this gathering of ordinary, working-class people made its way into the pages of the *Courier*, but it suggests Clarice and her classmates weren't elitist. She met Sara and her sisters, fellow domestic servants, in their social circles.

Like the other Black M.A.C. students before her, Pretlow participated in the activities of the George R. Collins AME Church. In July 1926, African American MSC students presented "the program for 'Collegiate Night' services" at a Sunday evening event at the church. Clarinet player Ben (B. D.) Jones and Pretlow, among others, provided the music for the program that featured a presentation from a teacher from Albany Normal School in Albany, Georgia, where Margaret E. Collins, '24, would briefly teach the following year and where Esther Tate Holley, '20, led the economics program.[23] Six months later, Pretlow and her Black classmates put on "an emancipation celebration" program at Hillsdale Baptist Church. Pretlow completed her requirements for graduating from MSC before the end of the 1929–1930 academic year because she was residing in the Phyllis Wheatley Association in Cleveland, Ohio, in April 1930 and working as a dietician and teacher at Hunten House.[24] For some time during the 1930s and 1940s, Pretlow lived at her parents' home in Virginia and worked as a public school teacher. In the 1940s, she became the first African American to become a home demonstration agent in Isle of Wight County, Virginia. In this position, she helped Black women manage their homes by applying what she learned from her mother and from her home economics training at Michigan State College. In the late 1940s, the *Pittsburgh Courier* featured a photo of Pretlow in the kitchen with a Black woman who was slicing off "a piece of home-cured ham for her home demonstration agent, Mrs. Clarice Pretlow."[25] In 1949, she led a tour of successful farms to residents of Isle of Wight County and "from as far away as 20 miles."[26] She educated countless African Americans in a manner that carried on the tradition of MSC's experiment station and extension work.

In the mid-1950s, Pretlow lived in New Jersey and worked for Clinton Farms, a "reformatory for women."[27] Built in 1909, by the early years of the Great Depression, Clinton Farms had developed educational programs for women—including home economics, vocational training, and farming—and many of the attendees were Black women. Pretlow died on August 10, 1976, in her hometown of Smithfield, Virginia. The services for her funeral were handled by Pretlow & Chapman, founded by Clarice's younger brother Richard C. Pretlow in 1937. Clarice A. Pretlow lived a full life, taking on a range of jobs and causes linked to the education she received at MSC. The simple obituary for her in the Newport News *Daily Press* is succinct, highlighting her pioneering work in extension and outreach. "Miss Clarice Arinthia Pretlow, of Route 2, Smithfield, died Tuesday in a Portsmouth hospital. Miss Pretlow, a retired educator, was the first Black home demonstration agent in Isle of Wight County. She was a graduate of Virginia State College and Michigan State University. She had taught at Florida A & M College and Hunten House in Cleveland, Ohio."[28]

The last known Black woman to graduate from MSC during the interwar period, a centenarian, lived a full and nothing short of phenomenal life. She was a nontraditional student who, beginning early in her life, overcame a host of obstacles. At the age of thirty-four, Frances Llewellyn (also spelled Lewellen) Langford earned a bachelor of science degree in home economics. By the time she arrived in East Lansing, Langford had lived a life to which very few, if any, of her classmates or professors could relate. She was born on March 24, 1903, in Marianna, Arkansas, a small city whose economy depended largely upon cotton production. Her parents, Louis Lewellyn or Lewellen, and Joanna or Johanna Newsom(e), were born during the Civil War. According to her great-niece, when Frances was about twelve years old, her parents died, and she moved to Detroit to live with her older brother Joseph Hatfield Baugh who was eleven years her senior. In 1922, she married World War I veteran Wade A. Langford in Charlevoix, Michigan. Eight years later while living in Detroit, Wade, a porter and machine operator who had attended the University of Michigan, died following a tragic accident. The early 1930s were very stressful and arduous for this young widow. Her perseverance did not go unrecognized. "That was an awful shock and blow to the young wife, and for a while the future seemed dark," observed a writer for the *Tribune Independent of Michigan* (the *Detroit Tribune*); "however, this courageous young woman determined to pick up the threads of life and carry on, just as in the days of old."[29] Education was her source of salvation in moments of despair. Frances's high school yearbook quote had deep meaning for her: "Education is the golden road to success."

After graduating from Detroit's Northern High School, thirty-year-old Langford enrolled in MSC to study home economics.[30] To help fund her education, she received a "scholarship

Frances Langford. Courtesy of Michigan State University Archives and Historical Collections.

for outstanding scholastic achievement" from a Delta Sigma Theta chapter in the Motor City. In 1934, she lived in Lansing on South Logan Street, and during her junior and senior years, she lived close to campus in East Lansing in a new three-bedroom home at 1033 Cressenwood Road. She crossed paths with another Black woman enrolled in classes in the early 1930s, Mary Walls. In 1933, Walls was a student in the music department and left MSC to live in Jackson, Michigan, where she continued to sing and in 1939 even won the praises of Marian Anderson.[31] Like Myrtle Bessie Craig and Clarice Pretlow, Frances worked as a domestic servant for a White family in exchange for room and board. As a nontraditional student in her early thirties, Frances probably did not participate much in campus life beyond her academic work, and she was among the only Black women on campus. During the summer of her first year, she caught a glimpse of eight Black women from Detroit who briefly attended a special course for social workers at the college. In 1937, Langford graduated from MSC and returned to Detroit to work as the lunch room manager at Garfield Junior High School from the late 1930s until the early 1940s. About a decade after her husband's tragic death, she married Theodore R. Owen, a printer from Detroit. While working at Garfield, Frances served as the director of food services at the Gotham Hotel, a renowned hotel founded in Detroit in 1924. In the early 1940s, the hotel was purchased by three businessmen who made it an establishment catering to Detroit's growing Black community. In this famous building, Langford interacted with wealthy African Americans and celebrities.

"Mrs. Frances Langford Owens has been appointed food service director at the legendary Lucy Thurman Branch YWCA," announced the *Detroit Free Press* in early January 1942. "She is a graduate of Michigan State College, where she specialized in home economics, and for the past four years has been lunch room manager at the Garfield School." Langford had many responsibilities from personnel matters to planning the creative menus for YWCA residents and guests. The cafeteria in Thurman "Y" was an important "gathering place" for Detroit's movers and shakers. Regular patrons knew of its "famed 'Round Table,'" that attracted "politicians, ministers, physicians, lawyers, and business men" to discuss "local, national and world problems." For more than a decade, Frances exhibited her talents in the realm of home economics, a branch of knowledge she explored in great depth at Michigan State. "Mrs. Owens has many secret formulas for recipes that have been in her family for generations. Many patrons have tried to get them," a reporter for the *Michigan Chronicle* observed in early May 1947. "Mrs. Owens' huge kitchen in the cafeteria is spotless," and "she leads an active community life." Active in Detroit's NAACP branch, from 1947 until 1949, she served as president of the Detroit Alumnae chapter of Delta Sigma Theta Sorority Inc., an organization she continued to support through the late 1990s. Owens's educational aspirations and journey did not end with her education at MSC. When she worked full-time at the Lucy Thurman YWCA branch, she toiled away in a master's program in home economics at Wayne State University. In 1961, a fifty-eight-year-old Owens completed the requirements for her master's degree by submitting her thesis, "A Correlated Unit of Study between Homemaking and Social Studies for the Seventh Grade, Neinas Junior High

School, Detroit, Michigan." With this additional academic credential, she secured a position as a teacher in the Detroit public school system, teaching home economics to generations of young African Americans. In 1972, she retired and died in 2004. In honor of her "100th birthday centennial jubilee," the Detroit City Council passed a testimonial resolution acknowledging her miraculous life. The *Detroit Tribune* was spot on in the spring of 1935 when they predicted "for her a brilliant future."[32]

During the late 1930s as the Great Depression came to an end, the Black student population at Michigan State grew at a snail's pace, especially considering the sizeable increase in White student enrollment from about 5,700 at the end of 1937 (when Frances graduated) until the 1939–1940 academic year when the total M.S.C. enrollment was about 8,500. During the 1930s, there were at least a dozen Black students on campus who paved the way for those Black students who arrived in East Lansing as the Great Depression came to an end. Frances Langford Owens's great-niece Karen Lewellen reflected that her great-aunt had a "passion for life" and personified "the essence of moxie, grace, wisdom and dignity."[33] Indeed, many of Frances's fellow Black Spartans possessed these same characteristics, helping them survive and thrive "on the banks of the Red Cedar" and beyond.

Chapter 18

Demanding Equal Opportunity, Serving Others

I t's likely that Clarice A. Pretlow wasn't the only African American to graduate from Michigan State in 1930. Born on November 30, 1908, in Birmingham, Alabama, and raised in Detroit, Chester Smith arrived at MSC in the fall of 1926 and roomed with B. D. Jones in Wells Hall. Jones was an exceptional musician who was embarking upon his junior year, and Smith was a promising athlete focusing on liberal arts. In 1927, as a nineteen-year-old sophomore, Smith earned a starting position at tackle as well as a varsity letter. His football career was short-lived; he only played one season. This did not diminish his contributions in the eyes of his fans. "He will be remembered for his exploits on the gridiron and he was the first Negro football player to play in the new stadium at Lansing," the editors of the *Michigan Chronicle* pronounced in late October 1942. Smith enjoyed at least one moment in his brief football career. On April 3, 1954, he shared with *Detroit Tribune* readers his "Greatest Sports Thrill." For him, this was kicking off for his alma mater in a battle in Ann Arbor on October 8, 1927. "My many friends from Detroit were present in the stands giving out cheers of encouragement," he recalled. "Truly it was a warm heartfelt occasion. One that has always supplied a fond remembrance over the years."[1] After earning a bachelor's degree from Michigan State in liberal arts, Smith returned to Detroit. He was admitted to the Michigan bar and spent "spare time" at one of the city's earliest law firms, Lewis, Rowlette & Brown. He attended and graduated from the Detroit College of Law and went on to practice law in the city for more than four decades, handling a range of cases. He

Chester Smith's roommate, B. D. Jones, featured prominently with the Michigan State Orchestra in 1925. An accomplished clarinet player, Jones attended the college during the mid-1920s and didn't graduate. He was the first standout African American student in the college's orchestra. Courtesy of Michigan State University Archives and Historical Collections.

was respected as a leader in Detroit by local politicians. In 1948, Mayor Eugene Van Antwerp appointed him to the Interracial Committee. Following his death, MSU established the Chester S. Smith Memorial Fund.[2]

In 1933, two African Americans, Alvin F. Jackson and James McCrary, played on the varsity football team. Twenty-one-year-old Jackson, from Gary, Indiana, enrolled in 1932. In the winter of 1933, the six foot six graduate of Gary's Froebel High School played center on the freshman basketball team, and at least one local sportswriter "touted" him as "the best-looking pivot man to wear the first year togs at State in several seasons."[3] In the spring of 1933, while on the track team, he excelled at the long and high jump events and the hurdles. In the fall of 1933, Coach Charles "Charlie" Bachman Jr. invited him among sixty potential gridders to attend the preseason camp. In mid-October, he was injured but still earned a varsity letter. He didn't play football or basketball in 1934. Instead, he shifted his attention to track and participated in five events at the "iron man" event at the annual University of Pennsylvania Relay Carnival in late April.[4] Jackson stopped attending MSC following the 1933–1934 academic year. In the summer of 1934, he worked at Gary's Riverside Park. Several years later, he played basketball for the Chicago Crusaders, a barnstorming basketball team that played exhibition games throughout the nation from 1933 until 1937. Jackson's style of basketball clashed with the conservative approach to collegiate basketball at predominantly White institutions (PWIs). By 1938, Jackson was a police officer in Gary, Indiana, a job he held for about two decades.[5]

During the early 1930s, African American football players, including Jackson, faced expressions of racial prejudice that Gideon Smith did not two decades earlier. The 1930s was a particularly challenging decade for African American football players at PWIs in the Midwest and Northeast. Like many other northern schools during the long era of Jim Crow segregation, Michigan State adhered to some of the southern schools' segregation policies on the gridiron. In promoting the 1934 team, which had three Black players (James L. McCrary, Albert H. Baker, and William H. Smith), Coach Bachman, who on the eve of arriving in East Lansing had coached at the University of Florida from 1928 until 1932, had two photos of his squad taken—one that included the African American players and one that didn't. According to historian Johnny Smith, during the 1934 season when the Spartans played in away games, McCrary and Baker roomed together, "leaving Smith without a roommate, and therefore sitting in East Lansing." As he recounted in 1996, William H. Smith quit the football team as a form of protest and joined the track team at the request of athletic director Ralph Young.[6] Born in Talladega, Alabama, in 1912, William Howard Smith grew up in Hamtramck, Michigan, and graduated from MSC with a bachelor of science degree in civil engineering. He then became a field engineer for the Michigan Department of State Highways, a position he held for forty years. The well-known "highest ranked Black engineer" to work for the state of Michigan during his times, he was a member of Lansing's NAACP chapter and was an active community organizer, serving as president of the Lansing Model Cities program and vice president of the Lansing West Side Neighborhood Association. He was also a member of the Tri-County Advisory Committee.[7]

McCrary and Baker were also humiliated on the road. In late October 1934, Bachman's team traveled to New York City to compete against the Manhattan College Jaspers. The Spartans pummeled their opponents, 39-0. McCrary had a dazzling performance. "Jim McCrary, powerhouse of strength, played like an All-American at fullback. He charged the Manhattan line into submission," wrote a respected *Lansing State Journal* sportswriter. Perhaps McCrary's experience with Jim Crow North the night before the contest inspired his breakout, two-touchdown game. McCrary and Baker were denied their basic right to stay with their White brothers in arms in the Hotel St. George, Brooklyn's largest and most popular hotel at the time. Instead, they were accommodated in the Brooklyn Colored YMCA. The Brooklyn branch of the NAACP, stewarded by Alexander Miller, the Crispus Attucks Community Council, and the Brooklyn branch of the Urban League demanded justice for the Black Spartans.

Shortly after the Hotel St. George incident, McCrary and Baker were once again degraded. This time it was by their coach.[8] When the Spartans played Texas A&M in early December 1934, Bachman and the Michigan State administration forbade Smith's classmates McCrary and Baker from making the trip. "After gaining recognition with the African American community as a school open to Black players," observed Johnny Smith, "MSC acquiesced to Jim Crow." The University of Michigan's football program drew the color line under the leadership of Coach Fielding Yost who prohibited Blacks from joining the football team from the days of George

Jewett until track phenom Willis Ward made the team in 1932. Yet, from the early 1930s through the early 1950s, U of M refused to compete against southern teams that endorsed Jim Crow segregation on the gridiron. During the interwar period, MSC acquiesced to southern gridiron segregation and from 1935 until 1945 "had only one season in which a Black player made the varsity squad," a phenomenon that "overlapped with the resegregation of the National Football League from 1934 until 1946."[9]

During the 1934–1935 academic year, McCrary and Baker encountered racism and differential treatment off the football field, as students seeking to fulfill their basic academic requirements. In the spring of 1935, they were enrolled in social science courses requiring them to engage in "practice teaching" at East Lansing High School and Lansing's Central High School. McCrary and Baker had experience working with youngsters and were eager to teach. In 1934, they both participated in leadership capacities in the "first negro boy's camp" in Lansing at Mystic Lake Camp.[10] "Each student," reported the *Pittsburgh Courier*, was "supposed to take his turn in actual teaching," but they "were prevented from doing so and allowed only to sit and 'observe.' One teacher frankly admitted that a colored student could not actually teach."[11] When McCrary and

Most likely the first African American to play competitive basketball at Michigan State, Albert Baker was a member of the freshman basketball team. Courtesy of Michigan State University Archives and Historical Collections.

Baker reported this to MSC leadership, President Robert S. Shaw's solution was to send them to Detroit to do their student teaching in Black schools. This was a humiliating experience for McCrary and Baker, and they refused to passively accept this ill treatment.

Baker reached out to his father who was a lawyer, in the words of the *New York Age*, "one of the best known attorneys in Michigan."[12] Albert Harrison Baker was born in Bay City, Michigan, in 1912. Baker's mother, Ida Baker, was born in Ohio in about 1884; his father, Oscar W. Baker Sr., was born in Bay City in 1879. In 1902, Oscar became the first African American to earn a law degree from the University of Michigan and in the same year founded a law firm in Bay City. Until his death in mid-December of 1952, he held a range of state and civic positions and engaged in civil rights activities.[13] In 1915, he served as the president of Michigan governor Woodbridge Nathan Ferris's Freedmen's Progress Commission and knew M.A.C. alumni Charles Augustus Warren and William O. Thompson well. After speaking with his son and McCrary, in early April 1935, Oscar W. Baker Sr. publicized the matter in Detroit's Black community and enlisted help from the NAACP. Later that month, Snow F. Grisby, chair of Detroit's Civil Rights Committee, spoke at the People's Church in East Lansing and chastised the university for its mistreatment of McCrary and Baker. William Pickens, the prolific national field secretary who was no stranger to higher education, visited East Lansing during a membership drive in Michigan and confronted President Shaw. Pickens used his pulpit to put MSC on blast. "I was not fair to the south for I should have mentioned the fact that in Michigan right now the Negro is being forced to fight for his equal right to higher education," Pickens wrote in the *Atlanta Daily World*. "When I was there I found the active opposition to the Negro students coming from two southerners who were heading up the educational department." Pickens and Baker let the State Board of Agriculture know that the college had no right to "treat them in any other manner than the other students." Knowing his clients' case was flawless, Baker warned the college that if any Black students were discriminated against like this in the future, he would "make a test of this in the Circuit Court of the County of Ingham, and subsequently the Supreme Court." Baker was not playing. At a meeting with the State Board of Agriculture on May 16, 1935, the "communication" from Baker was read "relative to alleged discrimination against colored students at Michigan State College." According to the *Pittsburgh Courier*, Shaw "completely evaded the issue." Baker then reached out to the Lansing branch of the NAACP who investigated and protested what happened to McCrary and Baker.[14]

On June 10, 1935, the State Board of Agriculture met and discussed the communication from the NAACP and attorney Baker. The following was recorded in the minutes for the June 10, 1935, board meeting:

12. The Chairman of the Board read communications from the Lansing Branch of the National Association for the Advancement of Colored People, from Oscar W. Baker of Bay City, and from the State Attorney General addressed to the N. A. A. C. P. On the motion of Mr. Berkey, seconded

by Mr. Brody, *it was voted* that the following statement be included in the minutes of the Board and be made public:

"The communications of June 1, 1935, from the National Association for the Advancement of Colored People, and of May 31, 1935, from Oscar W. Baker of Bay City relative to alleged discriminations by the College against colored students were received and placed before the Board, and after due consideration the Board is of the opinion that there is no agreement on the part of the College to withhold or deprive any colored student of any privilege given White students.

"The Board wishes hereby to make it clear that it has at no time sanctioned or advocated that there should be any discrimination in any department of the College, and declares its policy, both past and present, to be such as to provide equal opportunity to all students, regardless of race or color."[15]

McCrary and Baker's refusal to turn the other cheek as well as Oscar W. Baker Sr.'s and the Lansing NAACP's persistence influenced Michigan State to take a public stance on policies regarding the well-being of their Black students. This is the first time the university and the State Board of Agriculture issued an explicit and public statement against anti-Black discrimination. Throughout the nation, the Black press commented on McCrary and Baker's fight. In late June 1935, editors for the *Pittsburgh Courier* brought up the State Board of Agriculture's "order of 'equal opportunity' for Negro students" among a long list of major civil rights activities—including Charles H. Hamilton and Thurgood Marshall's attack on "educational jim crowism" and antilynching campaigns—that demonstrated that "Negroes CAN do something about their plight." Baker and McCrary's case slowly chipped away at East Lansing's racial order. In July 1963, MSU graduate, Delta Sigma Theta soror, president of the Spartan Wives, and Detroiter Sharon Wilson Cardwell finally became the first "full-time classroom teacher" in the East Lansing public school system. The first Black administrator in city's public school system was hired in 1971 when the Black student population was approximately 4.5 percent.

Oscar Baker Sr.'s outrage toward Michigan State did not last forever. After graduating from Bay City's Central High School in 1943, his youngest daughter, Elaine, enrolled in the college to study music with Fred Patton, baritone, professor of music, and head of the voice department. She was a very talented soprano whose gift for singing was discovered when she sang as a youth in the church choir. At the beginning of her sophomore year, she traveled to Philadelphia to compete in a competition for a music scholarship sponsored by famous contralto Marian Anderson. On campus, she broke down barriers for Black women vocalists, performing as a soloist for the college's Women's Glee Club. Recognizing the limitations of pursuing her singing career in Mid-Michigan, in the fall of 1946 she left MSC for New York City to study at the American Theatre Wing. In the Big Apple, she studied with opera singer and producer Leopold Sachse and performed with the Metropolitan Opera.

After graduating in 1936, Elaine's older brother Albert worked for some time as an assistant football coach, an "end coach," at Wilberforce University.[16] Of the four African Americans who

James McCrary as featured in the *Wolverine*. Courtesy of Michigan State University Archives and Historical Collections.

played football at Michigan State College during the 1930s, McCrary had the most dynamic career. Born in Georgia on March 10, 1911, he grew up in Flint, Michigan, and attended Flint Northern High School where he excelled at football and baseball. McCrary played on the Spartan varsity football team during the 1933 and 1934 seasons. In December 1932, along with Albert Baker, he earned a Service Award. Like Gideon Smith and Harry C. Graves before him, his prowess was routinely covered by the Michigan press and was also described in highly racialized language by the *Lansing State Journal* and *Detroit Free Press*. In 1934, Lansing sportswriter George S. Alderton, who was very fond of McCrary, promoted a stereotypical characterization of him, calling him "Jimmy McCrary, the grinning colored boy who plays fullback for the Spartans."[17] Among the other monikers given to McCrary were the "dusky Flint junior," the "dusky Spartan fullback," "the Flint colored youth," "the Negro star," the "stocky Negro fullback," and even "the negro boy." Writers for the *M.S.C. Record* distinguished him from his teammates, calling him "McCrary, Negro back for State."[18]

The *State Journal* also described McCrary in partially laudatory terms. "This fellow Jim McCrary is one of the best all-around fullbacks Michigan State has seen in many years. The colored boy from Flint is fast, can run like a ghost in an open field and is powerful defensively." The blurb below a picture of a graceful McCrary in action continued, "He is grooming himself for the game of his life in Ann Arbor Saturday. Jim is held in high esteem by all rivals, he's a good football player and a good guy."[19] Though McCrary's performance didn't match that of Gideon Smith against Michigan in 1913 and 1915, he did average several yards per carry, and the Spartan team McCrary played on in 1934 beat Michigan for the first time since 1915. McCrary won over his teammates and Spartan fans. In 1933, he got some playing time and a year later turned into a star who not only ran the ball with purpose, but was also a proficient kicker, "defense stronghold," and effective leader. (He was also an accomplished outfielder on the baseball diamond.) In the middle of the 1934 season in a game against Marquette on November 3, McCrary suffered a career-ending "spine injury," a chipped vertebrae that he played with "in pain" in a game against Syracuse a week later. He even wanted to play in a game against Detroit on November 17.[20]

"The Flint senior has a spine injury that has tabled him for keeps," observed George S. Alderton in late November 1934, "He has exactly as much interest in the team as before and is still trying to talk Coach Bachman into using him."[21] McCrary was a leader on the 1934 squad despite his injury. "It may be that McCrary can do something useful on sentimental grounds," noted the *State Journal*. "If the 'going' is tough the Negro star, who is well liked by his teammates, can be expected to be called upon to make a 'fight' talk to the team."[22] The Black press, especially the *Pittsburgh Courier*, celebrated McCrary's career. In late November 1934, he and four other African American collegiate football players, including his teammate Albert Baker and the University of Michigan's Willis Ward, were guests at the Thanksgiving game between Wilberforce University and West Virginia State College held at Hamtramck Stadium in Hamtramck, Michigan.[23] McCrary faced adversity during his playing years. While productive on the gridiron, he struggled to pay for his education. "Jim McCrary, State's colored fullback," announced Alderton in February 1934, "is still looking for a part-time job to help pay his way. . . . Anything at all, he says."[24] McCrary's "good guy" reputation persisted. In 1934, the Lansing Inter-racial Council with the YMCA sponsored a camp for Black youth, mainly "needy youngsters," at Mystic Lake, and McCrary was in charge of the camp's athletic programming.[25] This experience served as an impetus for his later work with youth that by the mid-1970s earned him recognition from the Michigan House of Representatives.[26]

After graduating from Michigan State in 1935, McCrary became the first-known African American to serve in some type of coaching position at his alma mater. Two decades after he graduated, the *Michigan Chronicle* erroneously called him "an assistant football coach."[27] Though from 1935 until 1937, the Flint native assisted Coach Bachman and Frank Leahy, it was in an unofficial capacity. He was not listed in university promotional material as being a verified assistant football coach. In a more recognized role, after graduating he worked as a columnist for the *Detroit Tribune* covering the conditions faced by Black college football players. In 1937, he became the head football coach at Wilberforce University, a position Graves previously held. He was fired from this position in 1939 and later rehired as an assistant coach. After being released from his duties as head football coach at Wilberforce, in the summer of 1940, McCrary was "called back to his Alma Mammy" to help with the football program. "While it does not spring from an authentic source," wrote the *Detroit Tribune* in June 1940, "the information has come down from Lansing that Coach Bachman was well satisfied with the work of the hard-muscled McCrary, and prospects are bright that he will return to the Lansing institution this Fall to lend a hand in coaching the pigskin handlers." McCrary was "called back" to help coach "aspirants of the fullback position" by Coach Bachman. "These young upstarts were fortunate in having the wise counsel of McCrary," opined a writer for the *Tribune*.[28]

McCrary also coached at Arkansas A&M and worked at Central State University. Working with youth became McCrary's passion. From about 1944 until 1973, he taught "difficult children" at the Moore School for Boys in Detroit. "It was estimated that between 40 and 50 percent of the boys at the Moore School had been on probation."[29] McCrary was active in a range of organizations, including the Southeastern Livingston County Human Relations Council (which he cofounded), the Comprehensive Health Program of Howell, the Motor City Lodge of the Benevolent and Protective Order of the Elks (for which he was "past exalted ruler"), the Detroit Federation of Teachers, the Brighton Gardens Association Inc., the Brighton Kiwanis, and the Detroit Alumni Chapter of Kappa Alpha Psi.[30] Football served as McCrary's entry into Michigan State, and he made a living after graduating by coaching like his predecessors Smith and Graves. The several obituaries for him highlighted he was an "ex-MSU football star" and "star of the Bachman era." He was not, however, defined by his legacy as a fleeting Spartan football star. From the mid-1940s until his death in 1975, he committed himself to working with and on behalf of disadvantaged youth.

Because they were high-profile African American varsity student-athletes, McCrary and Baker were recognizable figures on campus. With their charge of discrimination against the college in 1935, they became household names to President Shaw and the State Board of Agriculture. Ultimately, they obviously stood out because of their race. But they weren't the only African Americans to graduate in 1935 and 1936 respectively. They were joined by Stenson Eften Broaddus, '35, and Arthur Moses Bowman and Herschel L. Irons, '36.

Stenson was born in Leitfield, Kentucky, on January 25, 1903. His father, Robert F. Broaddus, was a Methodist pastor, and his mother, Mary Catherine Dill, was a public school teacher. Faith and education formed core twin pillars to the Broaddus family. After graduating from Kentucky State College in 1923, twenty-year-old Stenson moved to Detroit to work in the industrial sector. Unfulfilled by the drudgery of factory work, he enrolled in MSC to study agriculture. Living in Lansing, he was active on campus in the YMCA and the Bee Seminar. After graduating, he taught agriculture at Kentucky State College from 1936 until 1943, and from 1947 until 1952, he served as the director of veteran's affairs at Lincoln Institute in Kentucky, high school alma mater of Clarence Banks, '26. Active with his wife in the NAACP, in the late 1940s, he lived in a home he built in Harrods Creek, Kentucky, valued at $7,000, worked "on the Farm Training Program for World War II veterans," and owned an "up-to-date" poultry farm with eight hundred chickens. From 1952 until 1965, Broaddus was a manager with the Louisville Municipal Housing Commission, and later he worked for the Louisville and Jefferson County Community Action Commission and the Greater Kentucky Community Action Commission. In these roles, he sought to address issues pertaining to urban development, including the conditions faced by the city's poor and needy populations.[31] Dubbed "Kentucky's Favorite Son" by members of his fraternity, Alpha Phi Alpha, he was very active in the organization and served in Louisville's NAACP and Urban League branches, the United Way, the YMCA, and the Boy Scouts. For decades, he was a religious, business, and educational leader in Louisville. Toward the end of his life, like Myrtle Craig in her later years, he became an advocate of the elderly, as revealed by his management of the J. O. Blanton House, "a community for senior citizens" that was embraced by Louisville's Black community.[32]

Arthur Moses Bowman was a proud Black Detroiter who attended MSC and went on to have an impact on his city. He was born in Augusta, Georgia, on September 8, 1915. His family participated in the Great Migration, moving to Detroit in about 1916. His father, Charles, secured a job as a machinist in one of the Big Three automobile factories. Sometime after graduating from Northeastern High School in 1931, Bowman enrolled in MSC. He graduated with a bachelor of science with honors in applied sciences in 1936. In 1940, a writer for the *Michigan Chronicle* reported that Bowman was not only "the first Negro to be commissioned as an officer in Reserve Officers Training corps in Detroit high school" but also the "first to work as a chemist for Michigan State college." Bowman's son remarked that he loved boxing and "used to be a boxer at Michigan State." If this was the case, he did so informally. Boxing as a varsity sport wasn't reintroduced at MSC until 1938.[33]

After graduating, Bowman became involved in politics, serving as a secretary for the Richard W. Reading for Mayor Booster Club in 1937. A year later, Bowman ran on the Republican ticket for State Senate, Third District. He was endorsed by the Michigan Colored Mayor's Association, the *Detroit Tribune*, and some ministers in the city. "We are not supporting this man because of his youth, but because of his qualifications," Reuben J. Patton declared. "He has always distinguished himself in everything he has attempted. He has learned the psychology of other races through association with them in Detroit elementary and high schools and at Michigan State College." In reference to Bowman, a writer for the *Tribune* added, "the Progress of the Race is Never Greater than the Progress of Its Youth." A group of progressive Detroit Black ministers echoed such sentiments, declaring a vote for Bowman "is a vote for the progress of the race." Unsuccessful in his campaign, in 1942, Bowman ran again. "We must have a representative in the State Legislature," pronounced the *Tribune*'s editorial staff, "and Arthur M. Bowman is our own young man seeking your vote for this office."[34] Following his political campaigns, Bowman served in the navy from 1943 until 1945. He then attended the Detroit College of Law and later became a judge. His previous experience as a clerk in the Common Pleas court exposed him to the complexities of judgeship. Described by his wife as being a "workaholic," during the Civil Rights Movement, Bowman helped secure "the marchers free legal help as director of Neighborhood Legal Services." After he died in 1988, his wife recalled, "he just loved helping the poor. That's one of the main reasons he became interested in legal services."[35]

A year after Broaddus graduated from MSC, Lansing native Herschel L. Irons graduated and continued to live a life of service. Following in the footsteps of Esther I. Tate, '20, and Margaret E. Collins, '24, he was the first known Black male Lansing native to graduate from the college and lived most of his life in his hometown. His service-oriented career as an educator received a fair amount of attention from the *Lansing State Journal*. Irons was born on June 21, 1911. His father, George, was born in Canada in 1883. After immigrating to the United States, he worked as a gardener, a farmhand, and as a laborer at Olds Motor Works. He died in 1915, and Herschel was raised by his mother, Viola, a Lansing native born in 1886. Her parents migrated to Lansing from Canada. In the 1920 U.S. census, Viola's occupation was listed as "missionary" for the "Church of God," and in 1930 she labored in domestic service as a "laundress" in "private homes." Herschel attended Lansing public schools and as a teen helped support his mother by working as a "boot black" at a shoeshine stand in the Olds Hotel. While attending Central High School, he was active in a range of activities. A member of Central Senior Hi-Y Club, in 1928, he was one of four Lansing high school students selected to attend the "training" workshop at Camp Hayo-Went-Ha at Torch Lake. With his classmates, Irons was active in a range of Black community functions.[36]

After graduating from Central High School in 1930, he enrolled in MSC with the goal of becoming a science teacher. Irons's decision to attend MSC was supported by Lansing Black educational activists like Harold Jackson, founder of the Lansing Young Peoples Movement (LYPM). During the early years of the Great Depression, the LYPM brought Black high school students together for a range of extracurricular activities, celebrating their accomplishments and encouraging them to attend college. The organization recognized the value of their proximity to a major college. In the summer of 1932, they held a reception for graduates from Central and Eastern High Schools in the MSC Union Building. When asked in an interview in 1973 how many Black students were on campus during the early 1930s, Irons remarked, "There were maybe not more than half-a-dozen."[37] Like Stenson Broaddus, he was a member of the YMCA. Irons faced racial discrimination as a student, maltreatment he overcame but that remained with him into his later adult years. When participating in ROTC, he was "denied an appointment for officer training," and his professors discouraged him from participating in the college's "practice teaching" program, an initiative McCrary and Baker challenged on the eve of Irons's graduation. Irons was instructed by his advisers "to take all the science courses" to prepare himself for a teaching career "in Black colleges in the South."[38]

Herschel Irons. Courtesy of Michigan State University Archives and Historical Collections.

After earning his bachelor of science degree in the applied sciences in 1936, Irons continued his education at MSC as a graduate student. Although he was initially interested in conducting research in genetics, the college's professors did not support him. Early in his program, he was assigned to work in a "rodent laboratory" as nothing more than a "nursemaid to mice." Unlike his White counterparts, his professors did not give him a traditional research assistantship that would have allowed him to work in a lab with a mentor, engage in his own independent scientific research, and run experiments with his professors.[39] Irons persevered and in 1938 earned a master of science degree in zoology. One of only six men to earn this distinction from the college in 1938, he was among the first African Americans to earn a graduate degree from the college. In the summer of 1937, thirty-year-old Alabama born Claude Edward Tellis—who married M.A.C. graduate Margaret E. Collins, '24, in late September 1937—was one of nineteen graduates to be presented with a master of science degree from Michigan State legend Dean Ernst Athearn Bessey. Tellis earned his master's degree in agriculture and immediately helped create the Extension Division at West Virginia State College. He was committed to the Black 4-H movement, sparking within Black boys "a greater interest in farming." He later secured a position promoting extension work and teaching agriculture and economics at several historically Black land-grant universities, including Alabama A&M, Delaware State College, and Alcorn A&M. Tellis's contemporary, twenty-seven-year-old Irons, became one of the most highly educated young Black men in Lansing, joining the ranks of W. E. B. Du Bois's "Talented Tenth." Along with Tellis, he broke down barriers in graduate education at MSC, demonstrating to the campus community that African Americans were more than capable of carrying out rigorous scientific research and scholarship.[40]

During his undergraduate and graduate years at MSC, Irons was active in Lansing's Black community. In the early 1930s, he supported the NAACP's membership drive and was credited with "having done outstanding social and financial work so far this season." In 1934, he delivered several lectures at Pilgrim Congregational Church. With provocative titles such as "The Contributions of the Negroes" and "The Negro in Education, Music, and Arts," Irons incorporated the study of African American history into the early Black Freedom Struggle. From 1934 until the late 1930s, he served as the director of Lansing's "first negro boy's camp" at Mystic Lake, sponsored by the YMCA. Beginning in his early twenties, Irons managed the activities of more than twenty Black youths, and his classmates Albert Baker and James McCrary, as supervisors of athletic activities, reported directly to him. While in graduate school, Irons wore the hat of a community activist. In 1936, he was the "chairman of all music" at Lansing's Black community center, the Colored Christian Community Center, at 916 William Street. This spot was very popular; it was "becoming a point of interest and social activity" for the city's small but energetic Black population.[41]

By 1937, the community center, sponsored by the Lansing Board of Education and City Council, was relocated to the "new Lincoln school building" on South Logan Street and appropriately renamed the Lincoln (School) Community Center. Irons was a member of the center's board of directors. Shortly after its founding, the Lincoln Community Center became a vital feature of Lansing's Black community. During its early years, it offered a wide selection of programs to an average of five hundred attendees—"children, young people, and adults"—per week. By the early 1950s, the average weekly attendance was approximately 2,500. Through the modern Civil Rights Movement, this "group work agency" provided services "in the fields of recreation, social adjustment, civic improvement and human relations," and more than a few Black students during and after Irons's time at MSC volunteered there. Represented by a competitive basketball team, the center offered indispensable space, however limited, for many organizations' meetings (from the NAACP to the Boy Scouts and Brownie Scouts), conferences such as the "area-wide Youth Conference," an assortment of social events, and a collection of afterschool programs for children and young adults. In addition to churches, African Americans who migrated to Lansing from the South during the era of World War II found Lincoln Community Center to be a familiar and nurturing space that helped them transition into new environments.[42]

In the first half of the twentieth century, African American social reformers throughout the nation advocated for the construction of more playgrounds for Black youth. In 1938, Irons was among such activists, pushing for the creation of the Lincoln Street playground. In the late 1930s, Irons was appointed director of adult education at the Lincoln Center, and in 1940, he organized courses in "current events, youth leadership, negro history, and adult courses in the fundamental subjects." During the 1930s, he was also active in Lansing's NAACP branch. In 1936, he participated in the organization's "Youth Day program" at the African Methodist Episcopal church and five years later served as the NAACP's vice-president. Like Herbert McFadden, he believed knowledge of African American history could psychologically empower Black people while, as historian and scholar-activist Carter G. Woodson underscored, helping inform Whites about African descendants' contributions to American culture and world civilization. In 1941, he organized the observance of the sixteenth annual National Negro History Week celebration. Kicked off at Lincoln School, the opening event featured a former employee of Booker T. Washington and colleague of George Washington Carver at Tuskegee Institute, Miss Beatrice Graine. Forty-seven-year-old Alabama-born Mrs. Beulah Irons, of no apparent relation to Herschel, presided over the community's discussion of Lansing's Negro History Week activities.[43]

During his thirties and forties, Irons was constantly on the move, migrating between Lansing and several locations in the South, especially during the summer months. In the late 1930s, the 1940s, and the 1950s, he taught at several HBCUs. Toward the end of the Great Depression, he followed in the footsteps of Mabel Lucas, teaching at Prairie View State College. During several summers, he returned to Lansing to work on a doctorate degree in bacteriology, an undertaking to which he remained committed through the late 1940s. After teaching biology at Storer College in West Virginia for six years, in 1946, Irons began his seventeen-year career at Shaw University in Raleigh, North Carolina. After serving as the chair of the Department of Biology for one year, in 1947 he was elevated to the position of chairman of the natural science and mathematics division. The *Lansing State Journal* acknowledged Irons's accomplishment, observing: "Lansing Man Promoted at Southern University." Irons took great pride in his new appointment, sharing the news with the *M.S.C. Record* in January 1947.[44]

He initially left Lansing to teach at Prairie View after earning his master of science degree because he was denied job opportunities in Lansing matching his educational qualifications. As he observed in 1977, he "was not permitted to move ahead because he was Black," despite the fact he earned degrees from MSC in 1936 and 1938.[45] In 1955, the *New Journal and Guide* (Norfolk, VA) reported that Irons had "completed his residence requirements in Bacteriology for the Ph.D. degree" and received a fellowship to complete his dissertation at MSC on "the sustainability of bacterial flora of market milk." Irons returned to Lansing in 1963 during the waning years of the modern Civil Rights Movement and became "among the first dozen minority teachers" in the city, teaching at Everett High School, Sexton High School, and Otto Middle School. In 1970, he began working with the Michigan Education Association, and after retiring in 1976, he served as the president of the Lansing Schools Education Association. Until his death in 1993, Irons found solitude in collaborating with a handful of religious and secular organizations. A year before his death, one reporter was spot-on in describing Irons's personality. "His key to happiness is in his contacts with people as he quietly and effectively serves others, leading them to better lives themselves."[46]

Chapter 19

And to Happen, of All Places, in Our Own State School

Franklyn Verlett Duffy was born in Toledo, Ohio, on March 27, 1918. He was the eighth of nine children and firstborn son of Mississippi-born Joseph and homemaker and native Tennessean Mamie Duffy. His parents owned a small single-family home, built in 1909, on Woodland Avenue, a few blocks away from the Toledo Lucas County Public Library where Joseph, at the time of Franklyn's birth, worked as a janitor. After graduating from Toledo's Edward Drummond Libbey High School, a well-known local public school with a curriculum of industrial and academic education, Franklyn briefly attended West Virginia State College led by 1917 M.A.C. graduate Delbert M. Prillerman's father, Byrd Prillerman. At this historically Black land-grant college, like Delbert, Franklyn developed a keen interest in studying agriculture. After much thought, in mid-September 1940, he made a measured decision to transfer to Michigan State College. He was convinced he would receive a top-notch education and learn more about cutting-edge advancements in scientific agriculture and practical extension work to farmers.

Three years later, on June 12, 1943, Duffy earned a bachelor of science degree in agriculture from MSC and then settled in Raleigh, North Carolina, where he applied the knowledge he acquired in East Lansing. Committed to his alma mater's outreach tradition, he worked closely with farmers "to improve their agricultural skills using soil and crop rotation and new methods of farming for more efficient use of the land." After serving in the U.S. Navy during World War II, he attended the College of Dentistry at the Ohio State University and graduated as a doctor of dental surgery in 1956. He then returned to his home city of Toledo to practice dentistry,

Franklyn Verlett Duffy, the catalyst behind President John A. Hannah's desegregation of the men's dormitories. Courtesy of Michigan State University Archives and Historical Collections.

becoming the director of the Dental Health Division of the Toledo Health Department. He dedicated much of his career to a movement to reduce tooth decay in children. A social activist and Black professional who used his expertise and vocation to directly help those in need, Toledo's Black community soon recognized Dr. Duffy as being a living legend.[1]

One wonders how Duffy's life might have been different if he had not attended Michigan State. After all, he almost didn't because of the university's hidden-in-plain-sight segregationist practices in student housing. On July 2, 1940, Michigan State received Duffy's application, along with a deposit of ten dollars and his basic request to live in Mason Hall or Abbot Hall. Like many incoming students, Duffy wanted to live on campus for the convenience of being able to walk to and from his classes and to enjoy campus life that, by then, had much to offer students. He had no intentions of commuting from Lansing like some of his soon-to-be Black classmates and predecessors. Mason Hall, named in honor of Michigan's first governor, Steven T. Mason, had recently been completed. The new dormitory had three stories including a ground floor with a "recreation center with game rooms and lounges." The dorm had enough rooms to house approximately 440 male students, and Duffy intended to be among these residents.[2]

Before Duffy was officially admitted, on July 10, G. R. Heath, housing director for men, wrote to Duffy "concerning living facilities." As Fred T. Mitchell, education professor and dean of men, further explained to one of Duffy's supporters, Hazel Marshall, on July 23, the college could not provide housing for him because the "space reserved for Negro men students" had "all been assigned." Mitchell added that Duffy, once admitted, had the right to apply for a room in the "Wells Hall area set apart for Negro students" and "would have an option on the first vacancy occurring in the said area."[3] In mid-August, Heath followed up with Duffy who hadn't responded to his explanation of the housing department's de facto segregationist student housing culture. "Since I have not heard from you, I am taking it for granted that you do not wish us to hold this deposit. I must say that the area in the residence hall for colored students is still completely filled up." Heath continued, "If you come to Michigan State College, it will be necessary for you to live in Lansing, as I suggested before. I am returning your $10.00 money order herewith."[4] A city whose homeowners collectively accepted racially restrictive covenants, East Lansing was not suggested as a viable option.

Duffy had none of this nonsense. Whether or not he was aware that African American male students were customarily assigned to rooms in a space in Wells Hall that was set aside for his people is unknown. It's clear Duffy refused to accept the college's Jim Crow North segregationist practices. Like two Black women students at the University of Michigan who were denied living arrangements in Mosher Jordan Hall in 1931, Duffy refused to be silent about this injustice. With the backing of his parents, Senator Charles C. Diggs Sr. of Detroit, and president of the Detroit NAACP branch James J. McClendon, he decided to openly contest this discriminatory and dehumanizing policy. Duffy's embroiled battle with the Michigan State administration lasted from mid-July through mid-September 1940. One can only wonder how many other Black students had made similar requests to Duffy's, but opted not to challenge the racialized verdicts they received.

On September 4, 1940, on Duffy's behalf, Senator Diggs wrote directly to President Robert S. Shaw, chastising and disputing this Jim Crow North practice in no uncertain terms. Diggs included Mitchell's response to Duffy that he deemed "self-explanatory." He called Mitchell's letter to Duffy "a glaring and vicious example of segregation and un-Americanism," stressing that such practices in discriminatory housing were unequivocally violations of "the letter of the State Laws." Diggs demanded Mitchell's resignation. If this was not carried out by Shaw, Diggs warned and threatened, he would (1) "have a suit brought against him" for violating Michigan laws, (2) distribute "thousands of photostatic copies" of his letter to the public, (3) call for Mitchell's resignation on the floor of the Senate, which he deemed "a foregoing conclusion," and (4) formally request that the federal government "withhold any further appropriation" for dormitories at MSC until African Americans were allowed to live in the college's dorms "as other Americans." Diggs, who "weighed only 135 pounds when soaking wet," closed his bold and no-nonsense letter of condemnation by requesting that the State Board of Agriculture explain the college's policies. He also reiterated that part of the situation could be "corrected immediately" by Mitchell's dismissal.[5] A day after he wrote President Shaw, Diggs traveled to East Lansing to meet with the board and the president to "demand the removal of the dean from office." Upon his return, he shared his concerns with the *Detroit Tribune* who publicized the case, sharing with Black Detroiters the letter Mitchell sent to Duffy. "This is the most outrageous violation of the Diggs Civil Rights law that ever occurred," Diggs told the *Tribune*, "and to happen, of all places, in our own state school, supported and financed by all citizens of Michigan."[6]

As secretary of the board, future Michigan State president John A. Hannah responded quickly to Diggs with a lengthy letter. President Shaw's son-in-law, Hannah had to be strategic with his reply. The measured stance Hannah adopted became part of his repertoire when navigating issues of race and African Americans' rights and demands on campus during his presidency. He said nothing about Diggs's call for Mitchell's resignation. Mitchell, a respected administrator and native of Clarksville, Mississippi, who arrived at MSC in 1931 to oversee the teacher-training program, didn't resign. He remained dean until 1944 and a year later left East Lansing to become the president of his alma mater, Mississippi State College, Starksville. There, he could openly endorse his segregationist views and practices. In an announcement of his departure, the *Record* observed that as dean he "soon earned the reputation of being a real friend of all men students."[7] Duffy wasn't considered one of those friends. Hannah's response to Diggs was diplomatic, somewhat deferential, and sympathetic in tone. "I am sure that you are sufficiently well acquainted with Michigan State College to know that it is a very democratic institution where every effort is made to eliminate racial and religious prejudices and to provide educational opportunities on a democratic basis for all qualified students coming from the state of Michigan without reference to race, creed or color," Hannah began his calculated response to Diggs. "I think if you will visit with the students of this college that are members of your race, you will find that they are very happy here. Several of them have told me at various times that they believe colored students are more fairly treated here than at any other College or University with which they are acquainted."[8]

As evidence for his claim that Michigan State modeled progressive race relations, Hannah mentioned a handful of outstanding Black students he knew who had recently distinguished themselves at the college, including track star and Varsity Club member Walter Arrington; Harry Butler, who graduated in 1940 with a bachelor of science degree in veterinary science (perhaps the first Black Michigan State student to do so); highly talented orator Julia Cloteele Rosemond; and Lansing Central High School graduate and incoming freshman football star Hugh Davis. Hannah maintained the college made "every effort" to even help its Black students find jobs on campus to cover "their expenses" because they often faced challenges "finding employment elsewhere." Once again injecting himself, Hannah pointed out how he helped Black male students. "I have personally made very substantial loans to colored students who were up against it so they might continue in school," he testified.[9] These sincere Good Samaritan deeds Hannah enlisted as being indicative of Shaw's and the board's support of Black students were prototypical of the numerous private gestures and acts of good faith he offered in support of African American students during his long reign at Michigan State. Among those of his beneficiaries he amplified were football star

James L. McCrary, '35, and engineering major and student-athlete William H. Smith, '37. What Hannah failed to mention was that McCrary and Smith encountered daily microaggressions and more blatant racial prejudice at MSC, specifically in Mitchell's teacher-training program. Like McCrary and Smith, Duffy refused to accept second-class citizenship.

Hannah's response to Diggs was framed within the notion that Michigan State's so-called overarching commitment to racial equality was reflected in his personal compassion for Black students. "I tell you all of this only for the purpose of indicating to you my desire to be helpful to the colored boys and girls that are making a struggle to improve themselves by getting college training," wrote Hannah. "I appreciate the many obstacles they face. I know President Shaw and all the members of the State Board of Agriculture have the same attitude as I have toward colored students and feel with me that they should be given every encouragement possible." Extending an olive branch, Hannah invited Diggs, whose support of the college and personal "courtesies" he deeply appreciated, to come to MSC to "visit over this entire matter" at his earliest convenience and enjoy a "little luncheon with President Shaw."[10] Hannah also reassured Diggs that living arrangements had "already" been secured for Duffy in Wells Hall. Seeking to avoid a publicized racial controversy, Hannah and the college's power brokers wasted no time in accommodating Duffy's request.

On September 6, the same day Hannah wrote back to Diggs, Mitchell wrote to Duffy letting him know that when he initially requested to live in the dorms, there were no vacancies, but since then "vacancies have occurred" and the college was holding a room for him while awaiting his confirmation. On September 10, Mitchell sent a memo to Shaw reiterating what he shared with Duffy, adding that the Toledo native was assigned to a "four room suite, comprising of a living room, sleeping room, study room and private bath, with two large closets." Mitchell included the floor plan for this spacious room in Wells Hall that could have accommodated three to four students. Sometime shortly thereafter, most likely on September 9, 1940, "a delegation from Detroit interested in Mr. Duffy," as recorded by Hannah, visited MSC to discuss the case further. Among them was president of the Detroit branch of the NAACP James McClendon.[11]

Following Hannah's advice that McClendon, as he requested, be kept abreast of Duffy's case, on September 13, Shaw tried to further explain the situation to the president of the NAACP Detroit branch. Without acknowledging that MSC did in fact segregate Black students in the men's dormitories, Shaw claimed Duffy was initially denied housing because there was a "waiting list of eleven persons" when he applied in early July. Shaw informed McClendon that those in charge of housing had gone through "a great deal of trouble in order to accommodate" Duffy. While Shaw promised McClendon that "no discrimination" against Duffy would take place in Wells Hall, he implied that MSC reserved the right to run its dormitories how its administrators wanted to. Wells Hall, he noted, was "the only residence hall for men owned outright by the College and in which we have perfect rights and freedom to make such arrangements as we may deem best."[12] To keep all parties in the loop, Shaw sent a copy of his letter to McClendon to Duffy and Diggs. His comportment toward Diggs was, understandably, given his status as a respected and influential senator, quite deferential. "I regret exceedingly that a controversial issue has arisen and feel that I can assure you that we shall try to make the very best impartial arrangements we can for Mr. Duffy if he should accept our offer," he told the Michigan senator.[13] Shaw's strategic message somewhat backfired.

Diggs did not follow up with Shaw. But McClendon wasted no time at all in crafting his calculated response. Unsatisfied with how Shaw characterized Mitchell's correspondences with Duffy and disappointed that the MSC president seemed oblivious to what they discussed upon his delegation's visit to campus, on September 16, McClendon repeated that Michigan State had no right to bar Black students from any men's dormitories, that such actions were "against the laws of the State of Michigan." McClendon concluded: "When our committee waited upon you we left with the definite understanding that efforts would be made to secure room in Mason or Abbott Hall for Mr. Duffy. The committee is definitely opposed to the segregated set-up in the Wells Hall." Rubbing salt into the wound, McClendon continued as if he was unaware of the compromise that had been reached, "We certainly feel that Mr. Duffy has been discriminated against because of his color, when he made a [sic] application in time for a room in one of the new men's dormitory [sic], and that he has not been treated justly. The committee is not satisfied with the disposition of this case to date."[14] The last written exchange in this contentious back-and-forth characterizing the compelling Duffy case is Shaw's defensive response to McClendon's indictment. On September 19, 1940, Shaw objected to McClendon's "insistence" that discrimination against Black people existed at MSC and professed that while Black male students "are grouped in one of the wards in Wells Hall, that action was taken specifically at the request of the colored students themselves." Like southerners who claimed Black people benefited from and consented to being segregated, MSC's eleventh president insisted that the school's miniscule Black male student body preferred self-segregation. He concluded his self-congratulatory comeback by emphasizing the immense amount of work his staff had done on Duffy's behalf. "We are going to considerable extra trouble and expense in order to recondition the only unused room in Wells Hall in order to accommodate Mr. Duffy."[15]

In mid-September 1940, a mature twenty-two-year-old Duffy offered his own clapback to Hannah's explanation and Mitchell's compromise, indicating that even though he specifically requested to live in either Mason or Abbot Hall, "a *single* room in Wells Hall would be satisfactory provided that it is not in that section of the dormitory, which in Dean F. T. Mitchell's language would be that 'area set aside for Negro students,'" the "undesirable basement rooms" as one on-looker described.[16] Cc'ing McClendon, a seemingly frustrated Shaw replied to Duffy, confirming he had been assigned to a single in Wells Hall "entirely separate from the ward in which other colored students reside." He stressed the great lengths that MSC went to for him. "As there have been no vacancies in any of our halls for several weeks, in order to provide for you we have had to make readjustments which will undoubtedly affect individuals either on the waiting list or to whom space has already been assigned," he wrote.[17] With this, Shaw essentially told Duffy that he should be grateful; that he, as an incoming *Black* student, was given special treatment. His arrangements, he was alerted, even adversely impacted his classmates. This was quite a welcome and orientation to Michigan State. A week after Shaw's final retort to McClendon, Shaw briefed the State Board of Agriculture on the results of the controversy. The minutes for the meeting do not provide any details into what transpired. "The President reported on the correspondence that passed between those interested in Franklyn Duffy, a student, and the members of the Board." Under the header "Race Students Admitted to Michigan State Dorms," on September 21, 1940, the *Pittsburgh Courier* credited "a protest by a committee from Detroit" with the win.[18] Diggs took great pride in Duffy's victory. In running for reelection in 1944, Diggs publicized his fight against segregation at Michigan State as part of his storied record of challenging racial discrimination in Michigan.

While the tone of Shaw's and Mitchell's letters to Duffy, McClendon, and Diggs are quite revealing, secretary of the board Hannah's September 6, 1940, response to Duffy's complaint and Diggs's letter is thought-provoking in more than a few ways, raising a host of relevant questions. What did Hannah mean when he testified that his alma mater was making "every effort" to "eliminate" racial prejudice and treat all students equally regardless of race or color? What was the nature of these supposed efforts? Given that the college endorsed segregated housing facilities on campus in 1940, how did Hannah expect Diggs and Duffy to accept this apologia? Did Hannah have plans in mind? Who were the Black students who told Hannah they believed Michigan State was more progressive, vis-à-vis its treatment of Black students, than other institutions "with which they are acquainted"? How did Hannah know the Black students on campus were "very happy"? If some Black students did offer such observations, what were the contexts of the exchanges between Hannah and the college's miniscule Black student population? Were these students practicing African American history-centered emotional intelligence and social awareness when interacting with Hannah, someone who was clearly in a position of power over their well-being? How were the generous "substantial loans" he made to Black students arranged? Lastly, beyond the success stories of six African American students Hannah referenced to demonstrate the college's commitment to African American equality, what specifically had the college done to noticeably fight against and denounce anti-Black prejudice?

When Hannah responded to Diggs and Duffy, the men's dormitories were segregated and Black women did not reside in the women's dormitories. Five years earlier in 1935, when James McCrary and Albert Baker called out discriminatory practices in the college's teacher-training program, Shaw initially ignored the charge. This changed when Albert's father, attorney Oscar Baker Sr. from Bay City, Michigan, publicized the case and got the Lansing NAACP chapter involved in the mix. In other words, when Hannah crafted his response to Diggs and Duffy, MSC's posture toward civil rights and the treatment of African American students was, like many predominantly White institutions outside of the South, ambivalent rather than extraordinary, liberal, or avant-garde.

About a year after the controversial Duffy incident began, John A. Hannah became the twelfth president of Michigan State, serving from July 1, 1941, until April 1, 1969. In 1951, the student-run *State News* dubbed him "a symbol of the greatness that is Michigan State college." A decade later, in the "Welcome Week" issue they declared that his twenty years in office were "the most significant period in the 106-year history of the university." Most would agree with the assertation of one of his biographers, David A. Thomas: "the Hannah years were arguably the most significant in MSU history." Thomas continued, "When John Hannah took charge in 1941, Michigan State College was basically an agricultural school with an enrollment of around six thousand. When he left in 1969, it was a world-class university with a student population of more than thirty-nine thousand."[19] During his unparalleled two and a half decades as president, Hannah significantly transformed, reinvented, and reimagined the college and university. Under his watch, many important changes took place. Hannah's accomplishments as president and the growth of MSC and MSU during his presidency have been detailed and celebrated in Thomas's *Michigan State College: John Hannah and the Creation of a World University, 1926–1969* (2008) and Richard O. Niehoff's *John A. Hannah: Versatile Administrator and Distinguished Public Servant* (1989). In his characteristically humble manner, Hannah also reflected upon his career in his 1980 memoir. His place in MSU's history is embodied in the seven-foot statue of him erected in front of the university's Administration Building in 2004 that had already been named in his honor.

During Hannah's presidency, Michigan State underwent a carefully orchestrated transformation process that appreciably influenced its future. The scholastic opportunities offered to students, as manifested in the dramatically expanding curriculum, provided students with more well-rounded educational experiences. MSC became a *multiversity*. There was, for instance, the creation of the Basic College program, the democratic MSC Evening College, the Honors College, a medical school, and several residential colleges. Hannah adjusted Michigan State's land-grant mission to meet the demands of the changing times. Striving for academic excellence, he was instrumental in recruiting talented professors, scholars, and administrators and supported the creation of a university press that soon became a member of the Association of American Presses. In the mid-1950s, he invested in a new library. Perhaps most noticeable by onlookers, Hannah expanded the campus by investing in massive construction projects. "John Hannah's greatest obsession," remarked one of his friends after his death in 1991, "was to make Michigan State the biggest place in the country."[20] By the end of his presidency, Michigan State's student enrollment had increased by more than 500 percent. The city of East Lansing benefited mightily from the institution's expansion. As a result of Hannah's and others' campaigning, Michigan State officially joined the Big Ten Conference in late May 1949 and won the Rose Bowl games in 1954 and 1956 and national championships in 1965 and 1966. Hannah, who ritualistically attended Spartan football games and served as the head of a committee to study intercollegiate athletics for the American Council on Education, supported and expanded the institution's athletic programs and approved the hiring of legendary head football coaches who supported the recruitment of African American players, Clarence L. "Biggie" Munn (who boasted a 54-9-2 record) and Hugh "Duffy" Daugherty (109-69-5).

Michigan State gained an international reputation under the direction of the well-traveled, folksy, and worldly Hannah. He fostered the emergence of a commitment to global studies and projects. When the institution enthusiastically celebrated its centennial anniversary, MSC's national reputation had grown exponentially. All the restyling, remodeling, and innovative changes Hannah catapulted were symbolized in the institution's widely discussed and debated name changes from Michigan State College of Agriculture and Applied Science to Michigan State University of Agriculture and Applied Science in 1955 and eventually, in 1964, to simply Michigan State University. Beginning with the Duffy case on the eve of his epoch-making presidency, Hannah became the institution's first executive leader to dedicate pensive thought to the Black experience on campus and to develop a nuanced approach to issues of race relations on and off campus. In MSU lore, he is a sort of civil rights icon.

Chapter 20

Making of a Civil Rights Icon

President John A. Hannah's intriguing legacy as an ardent supporter of African Americans' civil rights is firmly rooted in MSU legend and oral tradition. It's a prevailing storyline that has been routinely celebrated by his successors and acknowledged by some outside the Spartan community. After he was appointed chair of the U.S. Civil Rights Commission (CRC) in late 1957, journalists nationwide lionized the fifty-five-year-old for having previously "expressed strong feelings" on civil rights. The local media lead the charge. "The background and performance of Michigan State university's President John A. Hannah leave no question about his position on matter of racial integration," asserted a staff writer for the *Lansing State Journal* in November 1957. "One of Hannah's first acts when he was appointed M.S.U. President in 1941 was to integrate white and Negro students in the campus dormitories." This optimistic journalist added that "Hannah's integration order brought gasps of dismay for some of the top members of his staff and faculty, but their prediction of strife and doom were soon forgotten as white and Negro students melted into one student body."[1] Thirty-four years later, in an obituary for MSU's longest serving president, a prominent *New York Times* contributor wrote, "He directed the integration of dormitories, ordered racial descriptions struck from student records and refused to allow athletic teams to play in places where minority players might be deprived of equal rights."[2] Such glorious accounts of Hannah's on-campus racial reforms are incomplete and oversimplify his legacy. Though more progressive than many of his colleagues and fellow White college and university presidents, Hannah was persuaded to take a bolder stance for African Americans' rights by African American students and activists. While notable, Hannah did not publicize his decision to desegregate the dormitories in real time during the early 1940s, a decision that was made by President Robert S. Shaw in September 1940 when he informed Black activists from Detroit that Black students, moving forward, would be democratically assigned to dormitories. This move was reactionary and sparked by Franklyn V. Duffy's and his supporters' resolute refusal in 1940 to accept second-class citizenship. Likewise, in the late 1960s on the eve of Hannah's resignation, Black students and faculty pressured him to act.

More than three decades before Hannah attempted to shore up his alma mater's progressive stance toward Black students to incoming freshman Duffy and Senator Charles Diggs Sr., in 1905 President Jonathan L. Snyder professed, "There is no antipathy in this institution against colored students."[3] Under varying degrees of pressure, some of Hannah's predecessors like Snyder maintained in good faith that the college did not discriminate against African Americans. The twelfth president was beyond question the first of this special club to take a prudent stance on race relations and thoughtfully consider the nuances of Black student life on campus. Especially after being appointed chair of the CRC, Hannah demonstrated a particular type of commitment to African Americans' struggle for civil and human rights. As cautious and moderate as it was at times, it extended beyond rhetorical gestures and symbolic acts. His civil rights pursuits were earnest and far superseded what any of his predecessors had done. To be fair, his Farmer, Aggie, and Spartan forefathers were not appointed by the president of the United States to lead a civil rights delegation and did not shepherd the institution when a chapter of the enduring Black Freedom Struggle was among the United States' most high-priority domestic concerns. Hannah's views of racial equity naturally evolved during his presidency.

His civil rights world view was quite limited on campus during his first dozen years in office, and like Snyder before him, he defended the college when questioned about its racial climate. One instance took place several months before he was sworn into his position in the Eisenhower administration. In the fall semester of 1957, a fight broke out when three White male MSU students "began 'pushing around' a Negro who was talking to a white girl" in the Union Building grille. University officials, reported the *Lansing State Journal*, "refused to comment on the incident, but declared that MSU had 'outstanding' race relations." Hannah added, "the school has never had a serious racial problem in the 17 years he has been head of the institution."[4] The *State News* briefly discussed the incident, but the affair did not prompt any protests in East Lansing. Had the episode taken place several years later after the founding of the campus NAACP, Hannah might have found himself in a tight spot, at least temporarily. Less than a year after the racially motivated scuffle in the Union Building, at a Spartan Roundtable event, he was told by a Black student attendee that some public schools in the state refused to allow Blacks to do their student teaching there. As was Hannah's practice, he doubled down on the belief that the university didn't permit contracts with school systems that practiced discrimination. According to historian David Bailey, Hannah "made no major pronouncements on civil rights in his early years as president." Likewise, David A. Thomas concluded, "on campus, Hannah was not outwardly aggressive in the field of civil rights, nor did he seek publicity for the positive things he did for African-Americans."[5] Considering his background and especially when viewed within the context of his White male contemporaries, Hannah was shrewdly reformist when it came to African Americans' civil rights. He did and especially said enough to avoid major controversy until the late 1960s when a new generation of "militant" Black students arrived on campus demanding a version of culture change that he had trouble understanding.

The origins of Hannah's distinctive posture toward the Black Freedom Struggle and African American culture are difficult to precisely identify. He didn't speak extensively or deeply about the foundations and evolution of his racial philosophy. In his peculiar 1980 memoir, he did not get nostalgic about his civil rights activities or his relationships with African Americans on campus. Mulling over his days as an "extension poultryman" from the early 1920s through the mid-1930s, he remarked, "I came to believe that not much of lasting importance is likely to be settled on the battlefields. The only real hope for the human race, I am convinced, is to find a way for peoples of all colors, all races, and all religions to agree . . . on how to get on with peaceful efforts at solving the most important basic human problems."[6] Hannah's childhood and humble beginnings shaped his respect for farming and working-class culture, his commitment to outreach, extension, and the "land grant concept," and his belief that "formal education" wasn't the most important key to success. As president of MSU, he traveled around the country and the world, frequently interacting with unfamiliar cultures. In the late 1950s, while visiting Nigeria to establish the University of Nigeria, Nsukka, he existed, albeit temporarily, in a Black world for the first time in his life. This was not the case growing up.

Hannah was born in the fall of 1902 in Grand Rapids, Michigan. During his childhood, the Black population in the city with an "abolitionist legacy" was miniscule at less than 1 percent. Historian and MSU PhD alumnus Randal Maurice Jelks argues that because of this small Black population in the Furniture City during the early twentieth century, Blacks and Whites lived "in relative harmony." But African Americans in Grand Rapids during Hannah's childhood still "lived with the humiliation of being segregated." Coping with segregation and embracing the philosophy of Booker T. Washington, who visited the city several times, Blacks created their own communities, institutions, and organizations. Like their counterparts in Lansing, most Black residents labored tirelessly in low-paying service and industry jobs. When Hannah was born, there was only one Black teacher in Grand Rapids, and in 1915 there was only one Black physician. Before and during the Progressive Era, Grand Rapids newspapers routinely denigrated Black people. In 1919, the Ku Klux Klan created a "club" in his high school, Grand Rapids South.[7] There were sixty-five African Americans in the entire city between the ages of fifteen and nineteen when Hannah was a high schooler.

Football star Harry C. Graves graduated in the same M.A.C. class, '23, as Hannah, and the avid football fan must have been impressed by the "Chief's" gritty performances during the 1922 season. While an extension poultryman at his alma mater, Hannah watched a small group of talented and memorable young Black men compete on the gridiron for the Green and White. On January 1, 1935, Hannah became secretary of the college and secretary for the State Board of Agriculture. His first real encounter with Black student resistance was the discrimination encountered by James McCrary and Albert Baker in the college's teacher-training program in the spring. He met with them and their Black delegation, which included Baker's tenacious attorney father. Five years later, the Duffy case stretched him, requiring him to morally reexamine his alma mater's de facto segregationist practices. Once again, as a spokesperson for his father-in-law President Shaw and the university, he met with Black equality-demanding emissaries and tapped into his empathic disposition. The Black student population on campus was very small during the first decade of his presidency. Hannah, who even as college secretary knew countless students by name, was of course aware of the Black presence in East Lansing. Black students stood out. They were the "only ones" in their classes. During the late 1930s, as he testified to Senator Diggs, he personally helped support the handful of Black students at MSC. While president, Hannah knew Horace Smith, Don Sherrod, J. C. Williams, Jesse Thomas, Don E. Coleman, Willie Thrower, Arthur Ingram, Jim Ellis, Leroy Bolden, and the more than seventy other Blacks who played football on Biggie Munn and Duffy Daugherty's valiant squads. He was a keynote speaker at the MSU Alpha Phi Alpha chapter's 1948 chartering. He took great pride in helping recruit Black celebrity Ernest Green to campus in the late 1950s. After becoming chair of the Civil Rights Committee, Hannah's interactions with Black people dramatically increased. Armed with his experience in extension work, he visited numerous Black communities throughout the Deep South and practiced compassionate listening.

A Michigander at heart, Hannah was committed to America's first agricultural college. Except for a leave of absence for two years when he directed the Hatchery Coordinating Committee for the federal government, he worked continuously at Michigan State for nearly five decades. From 1935 until 1969, he never missed a regular Board of Trustees meeting and as president lived in Cowles House, the oldest building on MSU's campus. He was very hands-on, knew people "from all walks of life," and, to the best of his ability, had an open door policy. "I walked over the farms and through the laboratories and tried to know what was going on throughout the institution," he reminisced in the late 1970s. MSU president John DiBiaggio proclaimed at his funeral, "He may have talked with presidents and kings, but he walked with students and farmers."[8] Hannah regretted not having a PhD. What he lacked in academic credentials, he made up for with hard work, persistence, empathy, and a service ethos. It was his openness, social awareness, and modesty that allowed him to mingle with diverse groups of students, faculty, and staff. Until the assassination of Martin Luther King Jr. on April 4, 1968, African American students were among those to profoundly influence his effective leadership style.

Hannah's actions and rhetoric should not be perceived solely as a heroic individual's subjective ideas and world view, nor should they be viewed in a political, social, and cultural vacuum. They should not be overexaggerated or underappreciated. Like all historical figures, Hannah was a product of his times. As the president of a major college and university, he wore many hats. He had to walk a tight rope when it came to race relations, simultaneously navigating the politics of his relationships with various stakeholders and constituencies. Hannah's most important civil rights activities did not take place on Michigan State's colossal campus. They transpired throughout the nation, particularly the South, and in Washington, D.C., when he served as the chair of the CRC, a group composed of six male scholars, politicians, and legal experts, only one of whom in 1957, J. Ernest Wilkins Sr. of Chicago, was African American. During Hannah's lengthy leadership of the CRC, several other African Americans joined the group after J. Ernest Wilkins Sr. George Marion Johnson replaced Wilkins, and Spottswood William Robinson III and Frankie M. Freeman, the first woman to secure a spot on the commission, served under Hannah's captaincy.

As indicated in the Civil Rights Act of 1957, Hannah and his colleagues were charged with investigating "allegations under oath or affirmation" into certain cases where U.S. citizens were being denied their voting rights "by reason of their color, race, religion, or national origin"; studying and amassing "information concerning legal developments constituting a denial of equal protection of the laws under the Constitution"; and assessing "the laws and policies of the Federal Government with respect to equal protection of the laws under the Constitution." As reported in the press, they got off to a slow start, and Hannah was unjustifiably mocked for this. Eventually, they boldly traveled across the country holding numerous hearings in communities. While chairing the CRC for more than a decade, Hannah spent, in total, more than a year away from campus. They were ultimately responsible for submitting an initial comprehensive report on civil rights recommendations by August 1959. Much of the commission's work, Hannah pointed out in 1959, focused on voting, education, and housing.[9] Hannah strongly believed education, "not the laws or court orders," was most responsible for convincing many Whites to view civil rights in more enlightened and impartial manners. He optimistically maintained and theorized that education, unlike laws and court orders that tended "to stir up 'intolerance against tolerance,'" was a key ingredient to curbing the currency of intolerance and racism.[10] Interestingly, during the last decade of Hannah's presidency, courses on race relations or the Black historical experience at Michigan State weren't strategically developed. The first discernable courses centering the Black experience were introduced by the first critical mass of African American professors during the late 1960s and early 1970s.

A think tank and data-collection syndicate, the commission collaborated with others, established state advisory committees, and, often in the face of blatant resistance, actively solicited input from Black communities. As Hannah often reiterated, the commission did not have the prerogative to impose sentences upon those who violated the Civil Rights Act of 1957 or the Fourteenth Amendment ratified nearly ninety years earlier. He was quick to point out to White southerners that his commission was objective and had no intentions to "punish anyone." In describing what the commission's hearings in Mississippi would entail in 1962, he announced:

Hannah and members of the U.S. Civil Rights Commission. Courtesy of Michigan State University Archives and Historical Collections.

"the Commission's purpose in holding this hearing is to obtain a balanced picture of the status of civil rights in Mississippi. The Commission is not," he assured Mississippians, "a prosecuting agency; it cannot and does not seek to punish anyone. Our job is to find the facts and report them to the President and Congress, with recommendations for any corrective action which seems necessary." Hannah put the onus on Whites to address civil rights in their state, noting: "the Commission also hopes that a hearing conducted in this manner will assist responsible Mississippians in finding solutions to the problems in their State."[11]

Hannah's work and extensive travels with the commission directly exposed him for the first time to the harsh realities of racism in the Jim Crow South. He and his White colleagues heard many firsthand testimonies from African Americans who suffered the injustices of Jim Crow segregation and racialized violence. Southern White politicians were resentful toward northern members of the commission. While holding hearings in Montgomery, Alabama, pertaining to Blacks' voting rights, Hannah and his team were denied hotel accommodations because of the bold presence of the commission's outspoken Black member with an impeccable legal background, J. Ernest Wilkins. Obeying Alabama's dehumanizing Jim Crow laws, the group decided to stay at the Maxwell Air Force Base. Hannah opted not to "spend the first day of the hearings arguing about whether a Negro could stay in a white hotel."[12] The brevity and tone of his refusal to publicly comment on the mistreatment of Wilkins conveyed or at least suggested his disapproval.

Why was Hannah selected to be a member of this commission, and chair at that? This is a reasonable question. Hannah, wrote David A. Thomas, "was a somewhat unlikely candidate to head a civil rights group." Historian David Bailey added that Hannah lacked expertise in the field of civil rights and firsthand knowledge on the subject that scores of African American leaders possessed. While meeting with Dwight D. Eisenhower, Hannah, as he himself recalled, confessed he "didn't know much about Civil Rights." Hannah used his unique appointment as an opportunity to learn from other experts, a tactic he employed in other realms of his leadership. After the sudden resignation of former Supreme Court Justice Stanley Reed, Hannah was most likely elevated to the position of chair of the commission because of his previous service as assistant secretary of defense for manpower and personnel in Eisenhower's administration from February 11, 1953, until July 31, 1954, during which he took a sabbatical leave (although he was still active in leading MSC during this short term as a public servant). On July 26, 1948, President Harry S. Truman signed Executive Order 9981, declaring "all persons of the armed forces" would be treated equally "without regard to race, color, religion, or national origin." Hannah's responsibilities included dealing with the integration of the armed forces. He was guided by the spirit of EO 9981, reiterating in 1953 that "all races and colors" of Americans should enjoy "social justice, economic justice and political justice." In the eyes of the thirty-fourth president of the United States and others, Hannah's service in the Department of Defense was exemplary. In 1954, he was awarded the Medal of Freedom, the nation's most prestigious civilian award. During the presentation of the award at the Pentagon, U.S. secretary of defense Charles Erwin Wilson applauded Hannah for "his contributions to the formulation of policies which will have a major impact upon the security of the free world."[13]

Hannah received some criticism for his approach to civil rights while he was assistant secretary of defense and chair of the commission from a few writers for the *Chicago Defender*, a leading Black newspaper founded in 1905. In 1953, Hannah announced that complete integration in schools operated by southern states on U.S. Army bases would be achieved by the fall of 1955. One writer asserted that this was a sign of "intolerable weakness" from the U.S. military and critiqued Hannah for making claims of progress while also acknowledging, despite several years of pressure from the NAACP, "that there are many problems which must be ironed out."[14] When Hannah was in his first year as chair of the CRC, Enoc P. Waters of the *Defender* juxtaposed attorney and Assistant Secretary of Labor for International Affairs J. Ernest Wilkins's "adroit questioning" of Black witnesses in Montgomery, Alabama, during hearings as well as his "insistence in bringing out in full unsavory details" with Hannah's seemingly passive approach. "Chairman John A. Hannah," Waters observed, "asked a few sympathetic questions that indicated the practices described by Negro witnesses seemed almost incredible to him." Given the pride Hannah took in empathizing with African Americans and the fact that the four southern senators on the Senate Judiciary Committee voted against his appointment, this assessment no doubt disturbed him.[15]

Hannah's stance on civil rights was also applauded by writers from leading Black newspapers including the *Defender*, the *Pittsburgh Courier*, the *Norfolk Journal and Guide*, and the *New York Amsterdam News*. The *Defender* credited him for speaking up against the ruling in the 1959 Mack Charles Parker lynching case in Mississippi, being a man of "unquestionable administrative competence and intellectual integrity," having experience with "the problems of race relations and civil rights," and instituting changes impacting the lives of Black Michigan State students during the 1940s and 1950s. Under the header "New Rights Commission Head Optimistic about Job," the *Norfolk Journal and Guide* echoed the sentiments of the *Defender* and the *New York Times*, reiterating that "in the field of racial discrimination, Hannah, shortly after being named president of Michigan State in 1941, ordered integration of colored and white students in campus dormitories. Then he ruled that all racial designations be stricken from student records."[16] In 1960, Albert J. Dunmore and Luther Webb of the *Pittsburgh Courier* credited Hannah for his observation following the commission's visit to Detroit that the city "like most Northern cities, must face up to its racial problems quickly." Though Hannah stressed that the commission couldn't "solve the problem," he ensured his listeners "he would try to put the facts on the table." As reported by the *Courier*, he also intimated that Whites would be in part responsible for helping solve the city's problems stemming from racial discrimination. "The problem won't be solved until more than half the people in Detroit decide that there is a problem and something ought to be done about it," Hannah declared.[17]

Under Hannah's leadership, the group performed environmental scans, held public forums, and offered proposals for legislative changes. The facts the commission assembled were to be used to help promote change. A civil rights specialist and representative for Presidents Eisenhower, John F. Kennedy, Lyndon B. Johnson, and Richard M. Nixon, Hannah didn't claim to be an authority on civil rights as chair of the CRC. Yet, he did publish a scholarly essay on the subject, focusing on the negative impact discrimination in education, voting, and housing had on African Americans throughout the nation. In 1961, his densely footnoted, thirty-page article "Civil Rights—A National Challenge" appeared in the *South Dakota Law Review*. Hannah spoke on the topic of civil rights to countless different audiences, including to African American crowds. He seems to have been quite comfortable around Black people. During the Civil Rights Movement, he spoke at West Virginia State College, the eleventh annual United Negro College Fund conference, and the 1962 national Urban League conference, among other Black venues. While at times members of the Black press called him out for his shrewd approach, many Black social commentators acknowledged the sincerity behind his efforts. The commission Hannah headed contributed to laying foundations for the Civil Rights Acts of 1960 and 1964 and the Voting Rights Act of 1965. His leadership of the commission symbolically elevated MSU as a pro–civil rights institution.

Hannah's reputation as a civil rights advocate and a friend to Black Spartans did not emerge during the first half of his presidency. It came after his appointment to the bipartisan CRC in 1957 and was largely shaped by integration on the gridiron during Munn's and Daugherty's tenures. Shortly after unceremoniously desegregating the dorms, allowing the small handful of Black students opportunities to live interspersed among their White classmates, Hannah directed "that all racial designations be stricken from student records." With this gesture, he sought to signal the elimination of racial bias. If the college did not know the racial identities of its applicants and student body, how could it be accused of engaging in racial bias? This seems to have been part of Hannah's reasoning. In 1957, he noted, "It would be impossible for us to make any racial analysis of our student population today or to distinguish a white from a Negro from any university record."[18] While understandable and symbolically significant, this decision in the 1940s to remove students' race from their records suggests his lack of concern with methodically analyzing the number of Black students on campus with the goal of increasing their representation and diversifying the campus community. With this new policy, MSC had no data on African American students. Students like Duffy were rendered more invisible.

The 1940s didn't witness a significant increase in the Black student population, especially considering that the total student enrollment increased exponentially during the decade. Between 1940 and 1950, the 250 percent blossoming of East Lansing's population epitomized this growth. Hannah's resolution to eliminate students' racial identities from their records resulted in the university facing challenges in identifying the number of Black students in the future. In 1961, the CRC asked MSU to report on the status of minority groups within the student body. Hannah indicated this was not possible because the university didn't record these statistics. In defense of this practice of not recording students' race, he stressed that MSU was solely concerned with Spartans' academic abilities and moral character. It would not be until 1967 when MSU began systematically attempting to track the race of its students. In the fall, the university asked students to indicate their race and national background on a separate card attached to their housing registration cards to "prove that it is complying with the Civil Rights Act of 1964" and so the university could seek federal assistance and grants from the Office of Economic Opportunity. Students were asked if they were "White," "Negro," or "Other." The response rate from students was terribly poor. According to the *State News* in early December 1967, nearly six thousand students "failed to provide this information." The Black Students' Alliance posted flyers beseeching Black students not to fill out the university's racial identification cards, insinuating that this information could be misused.[19] The university's first major study of the Black student population occurred several years after MSU officials began attempting to track students' ethnicities. Completed in October 1970, this study, "The Admission of Minority Students: A Framework for Action," specifically sought to identify the racial backgrounds of "minority" students. The report was presented to the Presidential Commission on Admissions and Student Body Composition on October 22 by Robert L. Green, then assistant provost and director of the Center for Urban Affairs, the center's administrative team Larry Lezotte, John Scheitzer, and Donald Biskin, and "resource consultants" Joseph McMillan, director of the Equal Opportunity Programs, Thomas Gunnings, assistant professor, Counseling Center, and John Winchester, coordinator, American Indian Programs.

Beyond initiating several peripheral reforms at the outset of his presidency relevant to MSC's minute Black student population, during the remainder of the 1940s, Hannah did not introduce any cutting-edge policies directly addressing racial discrimination on campus. While growing the institution from 8,024 students in the 1941–1942 academic year to 20,000 by 1948–1949, he was not explicitly concerned with racially diversifying the student body. He did not create programs to recruit African American students. "When asked directly about discrimination," one of his leading biographers deduced, "Hannah would usually respond by reasserting the college's position on equal opportunity: everyone was treated the same."[20] Beginning in the first decade of his presidency, he was reluctant to endorse racial justice measures on campus unless he was directly pressured to do so. This was plainly the case with a controversial set of circumstances surrounding the ascending MSC football program in the immediate aftermath of World War II.

In 1947, first-year coach Clarence "Biggie" Munn benched sophomore star halfback Horace Smith at home when the Spartans played the Mississippi State Maroons on October 4. A week after suffering an embarrassing loss in the season opener to U of M 0-55 in Ann Arbor in front of seventy-two thousand onlookers, Munn's squad won the close game against the Maroons 7-0. The other Black player on the roster, Jackson, Michigan, native Don Sherrod, also did not see the field against the visitors from the Magnolia State on the cold fall day. Munn's shoddy choice did not come as a total surprise to Smith. A year earlier on October 12, 1946, when the Spartans lost to Mississippi State 0-6 in East Lansing, Coach Bachman—who had coached six Black players in East Lansing since 1933 and was charged with racism by William H. Smith—deliberately benched Horace Smith. He tried to save face by enjoining Smith to tell reporters he was injured. In early November 1946, Bachman also didn't take Smith, the rugged and productive number two right halfback, to Lexington for their game against the University of Kentucky, which the Spartans ending up losing by more than three touchdowns. Smith was in tip-top condition at the time and was disappointed by his coach's decision. Bachman and university officials did not directly respond to disgruntled *Michigan Chronicle* editors' repeated requests for a statement explaining why Smith was left behind for the Kentucky game and benched at home against Mississippi State. Unlike the 1,500 U of M students and faculty who signed a petition in support of playing Wolverine track star Willis Ward at home against Georgia Tech in 1934, MSC students and faculty did not protest or even seem to notice anything peculiar with the racist mistreatment Smith received. The football program's choice to humiliate and dehumanize Smith not only defied the college's 1935 policy to provide equal opportunity to all students, regardless of race or color, but went counter to the gridiron conduct of some other Big Ten schools. Penn State officials took a principled stance against segregationist practices by canceling their away game scheduled for November 29, 1946, against the University of Miami whose officials said they would not allow the Nittany Lions' two Black players to grace the field in Burdine Stadium.

Playing southern teams was not totally new for Michigan State coaches before the 1946 matchup with Mississippi State. From the early 1920s, during the days of Albert Barron and Ralph H. Young, until 1946, the Spartans played St. Louis, North Carolina State, Mississippi A&M, Texas A&M, Missouri, Kentucky, Auburn, and Miami. It does not appear that the Black Aggies and Spartans on the teams' rosters played in these contests. Despite it being the last game of the season as well as the final game of Harry C. Graves's storied career, the fierce senior fullback and tackle was not among the twenty-two Aggies Barron enlisted to go to the St. Louis University on November 30, 1922. They certainly could have used him on both sides of the ball in the 7-7 tie. For five seasons during the twenties, Blacks didn't play varsity football at Michigan State. In the final game of the 1934 season, the Spartans traveled to San Antonio to play Texas A&M. Bowing to Texans' segregationist beliefs, Bachman left James McCrary (who was injured but could have traveled with the team for moral support), Albert Baker, and William H. Smith in East Lansing, nonchalantly telling the *Lansing State Journal* they were "unable to make the trip."[21] After graduating in 1935, McCrary might have helped Bachman cajole talented African Americans to play at MSC, yet from the 1935 season through the 1940 season, Bachman did not recruit any Black players to East Lansing. On November 1, 1941, when Missouri put a blemish on MSC's homecoming festivities by beating Bachman's squad who barely rushed for one hundred yards, Hugh Davis was listed as the number two halfback but didn't see the field. The next week, Hughie made the trip to Purdue.

Though it did not take place on a homecoming Saturday, the Spartans' highly anticipated 1947 game against the tough and fast Mississippi State Maroons was more significant than the previous year's matchup. It was MSC's first home game of the year at Macklin Field. It ended up breaking an attendance record with 22,500 spectators. It was also Munn's first year as head coach, and the halftime festivities featured a meticulously choreographed performance from the 106-member MSC band in honor of the thirtieth anniversary of Leonard V. Falcone's service as director. The day before the contest, Michigan governor Kim Sigler personally welcomed the Mississippi State squad at the Capital City airport as they ceremoniously exited the massive, four-engine DC-4. Among the patronizing southern entourage was the university's president, segregationist Fred Mitchell, the former MSC dean of men who endorsed racial discrimination in the men's dorms and teacher education training program. Convinced that "Smith was withheld from the game in deference to the request of Mississippi officials," less than a week after MSC defeated its Southeastern Conference opponent, African American activists from the Detroit metropolitan area clamored for justice. A Detroit pastor was unambiguous with his displeasure. "What right has Michigan [State College] to set the hands of the clock of democracy [back] by bowing to the policies of a semi-fascist state like Mississippi," Horace White penned in the *Michigan Chronicle* in October of 1947.[22] The executive director of the Detroit NAACP branch Edward M. Swan called upon Governor Sigler to intervene, investigate, and rectify the situation.

While the *Detroit Free Press* and the *Lansing State Journal* largely ignored the controversy, the Black-run *Michigan Chronicle* and later the *Detroit Tribune* publicized the college's deference to their segregationist foes. One Black sportswriter was behind broadcasting MSC's acquiescence to southern racism on the gridiron. In 1946, several months after graduating from the University of Michigan where he ran track and majored in journalism, brilliant twenty-two-year-old World War II Air Force veteran Bill Matney (William C. Matney Jr.) began his long and illustrious career at the *Michigan Chronicle*, a path that opened the door in the early 1960s to him becoming the first Black reporter for the *Detroit News* as well as the first Black *NBC News* correspondent. His first taste of investigative reporting as the *Chronicle*'s sports editor was Bachman's 1946 benching of Smith against Mississippi State. A year later after Smith was sidelined again on October 4, 1947, Matney relaunched his attack on MSC's discriminatory practices. "Time and time again we have railed against the ugly practice, and yet our tax-supported State College persists in flouting in the face of Negroes this example of outright discrimination," he declared in an editorial, "Wake Up MSC," on October 18, 1947. "Michigan State is not only paying deference to the 'white supremacy' myth, it is also out of step with colleges of similar rank." Matney concluded his rebuke, "the attitude of Michigan State College seems absolutely scandalous. The time has come for the powers that be at Michigan State College to wake up and remember this is 1947, not 1847."[23] Not all African Americans shared Matney's militant and damning sentiments. Former Spartan gridder James McCrary—who in 1935 helped force Michigan State to issue its first public antidiscrimination pronouncement and later served as an unofficial assistant coach to Bachman—spoke cautiously in defense of athletic director Ralph Young and Coach Munn, suggesting those who set the college's overarching policies were to blame.

Hannah and Young denied the existence of any formal agreement between the schools about not playing Smith or Sherrod on October 4. They claimed, "they would have played if their service had been necessary." Future All-American Lynn Chandnois, they insisted, was taking care of business at the halfback position. In response to the pressure from African American activists and the *Michigan Chronicle*, notes historian Johnny Smith, Munn finally decided to play Smith in the home game on October 25, 1947, against the University of Kentucky. Munn's boss Hannah "made it clear that he would no longer bow to the demands of their opponents from segregated institutions."[24] According to one of Horace Smith's friends, Ray Uribe, "the University of Kentucky football team staged a protest on the sidelines" in response to Smith's presence. "They wouldn't come on the field," recalled Smith's longtime friend in 2006. "It took quite a while before they agreed to play the game."[25] Though the Spartans lost 6-7, star left back George Guerre left the game with a broken leg, and Smith threw an interception, Bill Matney, putting his Wolverine pride aside, celebrated the symbolic victory. "The year-long campaign of *The Michigan Chronicle* to crack the discriminatory sports practices at Michigan State College came to a successful close last Saturday when Halfback Horace Smith played against University of Kentucky at East Lansing," Matney proclaimed on November 1, 1947. "This event marked the first time in the history of MSC that one of its Negro players had been allowed to compete against a southern school. . . . *The Chronicle* launched a state-wide campaign to force MSC to take a stand one way or the other. . . . Facing a public ultimatum, Michigan State finally took a firm stance." The *Detroit Free Press*, who had been silent compared to the *Chronicle* about the year-long controversy, mentioned the historic nature of the game, that Smith became "the first Negro to play for State against a Dixie team."[26]

Horace Smith watching from the sidelines. Courtesy of Michigan State University Archives and Historical Collections.

A year after the game, Smith still had a bad taste in his mouth. The humiliation he endured in 1946 and 1947 was in the back of his mind when he briefly quit the team in October 1948 before the Spartans faced off against Arizona. In a public announcement from Munn published in the *Lansing State Journal* under the headline "Star Admits Mistake, Received by MSC Coaches and Players," it was reported that Smith, the leading scorer in the previous season, quit because of his limited playing time on offense. Munn's statement intimated that Smith came back to the squad with his tail between his legs. This was probably not the case. The fourteenth Michigan State football coach needed the fleet-footed Jackson native, especially on the defensive side. A week earlier, the Spartans lost 7-26 to Notre Dame in front of fifty-eight thousand. Three games into the season, they were 1-2. Smith did not necessarily need football. He was an All-American hurdler, setting Jenison Fieldhouse track records under the mentorship of a supportive coach in Karl A. Schlademan. Smith eventually let sleeping dogs lie. Like generations of African American Aggies and Spartans before him, he came to grips with the obstacles he faced, refusing to allow racial trauma to define his future. In 1962, while working in Flint's public schools, he earned a master's degree in education from his alma mater.

In the six years following the 1947 season and with Hannah's blessings, Munn recruited a dozen Black players, half of whom were from Michigan, four hailing from Flint. These student-athletes included Jesse Thomas, Coleman, Willie Thrower, Leroy Bolden, J. C. Williams, Jim Ellis, Ellis Duckett, Embry Robinson, John Lewis, Jim Hinesly, Alvin Lee, and Travis Buggs. In recruiting Thrower, considered one of the best, if not the best, college quarterback prospects during his time, Michigan State made history. The New Kensington, Pennsylvania, native was the first Black quarterback to play in the Big Ten and later the NFL. Because of his highly coveted position, Thrower, who was often called "a colored boy" by sportswriters, faced many more challenges than his Black teammates in getting playing time. Heralded for his "king-sized" hands, "almost perfect" aim and timing, and unbelievably strong arm, Thrower had to battle for playing time throughout his brief career in East Lansing. His struggle was compounded by other factors. In the fall of 1950, he dislocated his shoulder in a scrimmage, and in January 1951, he was racially profiled by the Lansing police. In this case of "driving while Black," his identity as one of Munn's players probably helped him get off the hook. In the 1952 season when MSC won the National Championship, he was disappointed being named the second string quarterback. But he didn't disappoint in his last year in a Spartan uniform. He had a breakout game against Texas A&M, 7-for-9 passing for 107 yards and contributing to two touchdowns. Katie Koerner and Ben Phlegar suggest that Thrower's "finest game as a Spartan" was his clutch performance against Notre Dame on November 15, 1952, when he led his team to a 21-3 victory in front of a record-breaking crowd of 52,472 in Macklin Field. Of Thrower's performance, the Associated Press noted, "the story of Michigan State 21-3 victory over Notre Dame is the story of senior substitute quarterback Willie Thrower and his first big chance in college football." He had "been ignored in crucial games since he enrolled in State in 1949," the AP continued, "but, things are different now." In the fall of 1953, a Black sportswriter penned an article "M. S. Loaded with Negro Grid Talent" for the *Pittsburgh Courier*, praising MSC and Munn for having more "beige talent on their roster than any other major school in the country."[27] Featuring photos of eight Black players, Will Robinson waxed on about the stellar play of LeRoy Bolden, Ellis Duckett, John Lewis, Travis Buggs, and Jim Ellis, the first Spartan to earn All-American honors in consecutive seasons and who was captain of the 1953 Big Ten and 1954 Rose Bowl Championship team. Several years later, in 1955, Coach Duffy Daugherty actively recruited the first Black football player from the South, Mobile, Alabama, native Karl Perryman, who played only in the 1955–1956 season. That year, MSC had ten Black players while the University of Michigan had three. With twelve and eleven Black football players respectively, Indiana University and the University of Illinois were the only major, predominantly White institutions (PWIs) to have more Black gridders than MSC. Several years after Daugherty appeared on the cover of *Time* magazine (October 8, 1956), the college took great pride in broadcasting that they had nine Blacks in their grid squad.

According to historian Johnny Smith, "In calling attention to the number of Black players on the team, the university and the football program were aware of the potential benefits of being known as the Brooklyn Dodgers of college football. What better way could the university promote itself as an institution that believed in and supported equality than by fielding an integrated football team that millions of viewers could see on television?" During the early 1960s, the Black press began to take notice of Daugherty's and MSU's efforts to recruit Black players. Not only did the Nation of Islam's radical *Muhammad Speaks* newspaper mention the college's novel stance toward Black football players, but a writer for the *Michigan Chronicle* even suggested Daugherty would be a "good candidate" for the NAACP's prestigious Spingarn Medal. Notwithstanding such admiration from members of the national Black community, the recruiting of Black football players to Michigan State under Daugherty's leadership that Hannah endorsed and supported should not be read primarily as a civil rights struggle. As Smith observes, though his decision to integrate his team could have placed his career in jeopardy if it backfired, "Daugherty played African Americans to win, not be to known as a civil rights activist."[28]

To be clear, what Daugherty accomplished with Hannah's blessings in East Lansing was unique, contributing to the university's unabating reputation and legacy as a flagbearer for forward-thinking race relations. Daugherty was downright liberal and enterprising compared to the majority of those in his peer group of head football coaches. The teams he fielded during the later years of the modern Civil Rights Movement were much more visibly integrated than the vast majority of other squads at PWIs throughout the nation. His teams were extremely talented and united across racial lines, loaded with outstanding Black student-athletes who represented the Spartans as much as they did Black communities across the country who were inspired by their accomplishments. As part of his unconventional recruiting strategy, Daugherty fostered genuine relationships with Black high school football coaches in the South, like Charles "Bubba" Smith's father Willie Ray Smith Sr., and recognized the potential of acquiring excellent Black gridders from the segregated South whose main options were playing at HBCUs. From the late 1950s through his retirement, this humble son of a Pennsylvania coalminer mustered more than forty Black players from the Jim Crow South. In 1964 the Spartans had twenty-one Black players, half of whom were from the South and more than ten of whom were sophomores. A year later, there were twenty-three Blacks on the team, and among them were key contributors on defense, including Harold Lucas, Jesse Phillips, Bubba Smith, Jim Summers, Charles Thornhill, and George Webster. Given that by the mid-1960s there were no more than approximately 120 Black students at MSU, the Black football players accounted for about 16–18 percent of the total MSU Black student population. In 1965, MSU started six Black players on defense. In 1966, the Spartans had many Black starters, leading several African American sportswriters to jestingly compare the Spartan squad to HBCU teams. As Maya Washington observes, "the visibility of the Michigan State football program had the potential to further the doctrine of equal opportunity by recruiting Black players from the South."[29]

The 1966 team opened the door to some "Black firsts." Not only were George Webster and Clinton Jones co-captains, but Jimmy Raye started at quarterback, becoming the second Black quarterback in Spartan football history. Unlike Willie Thrower, Raye was the number one play caller. Starting a Black quarterback in the 1960s was truly monumental. On the national scene, with one of the largest television audiences in the history of collegiate football, the Black players represented the university in "the game of the century" against Notre Dame. On November 19, 1966, more than eighty thousand fans crammed into Spartan Stadium to watch this game that had undeniable racial undertones. Some Fighting Irish fans, whose team had one Black player, were forthright with their racism. At a pep rally several days before the game, from the rafters in the school's fieldhouse they hanged an effigy of Bubba Smith with a sign that read "LYNCH 'EM."[30]

Johnny Smith offered the following insightful appraisal of MSU's integration of their football team during the mid-1960s and a bit beyond:

> Michigan State's squad was an example of what a fully integrated team might look like. While many northern football programs firmly believed that it would be dangerous to play more Blacks than whites, in 1966 Michigan State's defense started eight Black players and three whites. The offensive backfield started two Black running backs and a Black quarterback, and the team's two captains were Black. In an era that accepted without question the myths that teams could not win by playing more Blacks than whites and that Black players did not have the intelligence to handle leadership positions, Michigan State's 1965 and 1966 football teams were unlike any others in the prior history of integrated college football. Not only were Michigan State's teams in those two years fully integrated, but also they were the best that the school's head coach Hugh "Duffy" Daugherty had ever fielded, finishing a combined 19-1-1 as well as sharing the 1965 national championship. What separated these MSU teams from others in the country was a nucleus of talented Black players, many from the South.... Examining the fully integrated Michigan State football teams of the mid-1960s allows us

to understand better the struggles against racism in that era. Michigan State's greatest teams, replete with talented Black players, became a dominant force in college football, silencing racist critics by defying playing quotas for Blacks. Although Duffy Daugherty created a progressive roster, his own Black players took the lead in demanding equality beyond the playing field.[31]

Several years after he left MSU, Raye reflected on growing up in the segregated South, the disappointing 1967 season, his support of Black student activism at MSU, and the integration of MSU football. "Let's face it, MSU couldn't put a team on the field and win without any black guys on it. No college in the country could. You got to have the good black athletes to win. That's why they're recruiting them in the South now," Raye said in 1969, several years before returning to his alma mater to serve as an assistant coach.[32]

In 1968, as Hannah's presidency approached its end, MSU's Black students, including student-athletes, and faculty challenged the scope of the university's commitment to integration on the gridiron by protesting the lack of Black representation on the Spartans' coaching staff. This struggle was part of a larger movement and resulted in the expeditious hiring of the university's first African American assistant football coach, Spartan 1951 All-American Coleman, and assistant track and field coach Jim Bibbs. Several years later in January 1972, Raye was hired as an assistant offensive coach for receivers. While Coleman's career as an assistant football coach was very short-lived, Bibbs, whose specialty during his collegiate days was the sixty-yard dash, had a long career in the track and field program. "Jim Bibbs presents the father image for Black students and athletes at Michigan State University," a Black student commented in the early 1970s. While an assistant coach, Bibbs "has gained a reputation as a father, counselor and friend to the Black community on campus." In 1975, Ernie Boone penned an article on Bibbs in the *Michigan Chronicle*, echoing the realness that Bibbs brought to the table. "He's really warm and genuine," Boone noted. "He's a whole lot of man." Countless Black students praised the Ecorse, Michigan, native and former track star at Eastern Michigan University. "When I was depressed he always had time for me," Franceen Adel recalled. Star MSU sprinter and head women's track coach Karen Dennis recalled, "Without him, I wouldn't have had the athletic experience I've had or the opportunity of going to school and coaching. So, he introduced me to athletics and afforded us, as young girls, an opportunity. Then once I started coaching, he became my mentor. He's been at the forefront of everything I've done." After serving as acting head coach of the track and field program for several years, in 1977 he became the second African American head coach in the history of MSU. Upon Bibbs's retirement in 1995, an MSU athletics administrator remarked, "The name Jim Bibbs is synonymous with Michigan State track and field. His reputation is one of having developed individuals on a national scale and has left a legacy that will forever be a part of the history of the MSU track and field program." Lansing sportswriter Fred Heumann added that Bibbs was one of the greatest coaches in MSU history. The recipient of numerous awards, Bibbs accomplished much during his long career and life of service.[33] In 2022, his contributions to MSU history were recognized when he served as the homecoming grand marshal.

By the late 1950s, Hannah was challenged by his own rhetoric and highly visible role on the CRC to take a closer look at the Black experience at MSC beyond the gridiron. In the late 1950s, he repeatedly identified racial integration as being the most important problem for the United States and invited members of his commission to campus for meetings and conferences. In the early 1960s when the campus NAACP challenged the racial discrimination openly practiced by landlords who were registered on MSU's approved off-campus housing list, Hannah returned to his familiar repudiation of racial prejudice. He was in a position to wield his power and influence as the city grappled with fundamental issues concerning African Americans' basic civil rights. The city would not have experienced growth without the university Hannah expanded by leaps and bounds. A *Detroit News* poll in March 1964 suggested he "towers above all others seriously mentioned" as a possible candidate for U.S. senator from Michigan in a mock four-way primary. Based upon this poll, however, he was not popular with the state's Black population. It was predicted he would have received about 26 percent of the Black vote, slightly less than State Board of Education member James F. O'Neil. Though he was not available for an interview with the *State News* and was understandably measured with his comments, during the later years of his chairmanship of the CRC Hannah offered his support of MSU student-activists who protested the East Lansing City Council's controversial vote on June 1, 1964, against an open housing ordinance. "I *personally* regret the action taken by the East Lansing City Council," Hannah told the *Lansing State Journal*. "I feel it's important that East Lansing take whatever action is necessary to make it possible for faculty and employes [*sic*] of the university to buy or rent the kind of property they want. There are many Negro members on the faculty now and there will continue to be other minority group members here. The university must remain color blind and religion blind and so should the community."[34] Members of the campus NAACP were not satisfied with Hannah's public pronouncements. His comments intimated that freely residing in East Lansing was not one of their—Black students'—major rights or concerns. Despite Hannah's claim that there were many Black faculty at MSU in 1964, there were very few Black faculty and academic staff, and nearly all African American employees lived in Lansing. Hannah's relationship with the city was practical and prudent and was not conducive with vigilantly supporting the movement for open housing in East Lansing.

During his decade of service on the CRC, he symbolically placed MSU on the Civil Rights Movement map. When writers for *Ebony* visited East Lansing and featured a story on Ernest Green in 1961, members of the Black community nationwide thought highly of what Hannah had accomplished. Three years later, camera crews descended onto Hannah's campus to get some footage of Green—who was working on his master's degree—for a film on the Little Rock Crisis that was going to be shown outside of the country by the United States Information Agency.

Though the film focused on the lives of those who "went through the 1957 crisis in Little Rock," it would also inevitably serve as publicity for MSU abroad, portraying Hannah's school as a progressive, integrationist university.[35] The fact that Hannah was able to lead the CRC (as well as chairing the U.S. Section of the Permanent Joint Board on Defense) while being in command of a university that increased from approximately twenty thousand students in 1957 to thirty-one thousand in 1964 speaks to his Herculean work ethic. The Black student population did not witness significant growth until the late 1960s as his presidency came to an end. Hannah was a sympathetic gradualist when it came to the issue of civil rights. A realist, he believed and acted as if racism would take time to eradicate. As he was often quoted as remarking during the late 1950s and early 1960s, "Prejudice is like a congenital disease that is passed on from generation to generation. Unfortunately, we cannot hope to discover a vaccine overnight that will wipe out the disease."[36] In the February 10, 1969, "special section" of the *State News* commemorating Hannah's contributions, the paper's editor-in-chief interviewed the departing president. In response to a question about the university's responsibility to the Black community, he deflected a bit and commented that the "old Committee of 16 report" should be implemented "making it possible, particularly for blacks, to develop whatever they have in the way of potential, so that they can not only make contributions to society, but to live themselves in society, and I won't continue that speech."[37]

Hannah's legacy of being an advocate of civil rights is embodied in his long service on the CRC while serving as president of a major research institution. This was no easy feat. During his long and eventful presidency, he mastered the art of balancing his public persona with his more private life, especially when dealing with delicate issues surrounding civil rights on campus. The public Hannah delivered carefully calculated messages. The private Hannah took great pleasure and pride in helping African American students behind the scenes. On campus, he desegregated the dormitories and performed random acts of kindness to individual Black students like "Little Rock Nine" member Ernest Green who received an anonymous scholarship from him. Hannah hired the first Black Michigan State faculty members and in the early 1960s vowed to hire more. Beginning in the late 1940s, he refused to allow the college's athletic teams to compete against southern colleges who sought to draw the color line. In the spring of 1948, several Black male students were denied service at the barbershop in the Union Building. The students and their sympathizers urged Hannah to "create a Civil Rights Committee under the jurisdiction of the Student Council." Hannah decided to handle it on his own by accompanying the aggrieved students to the barbershop, getting a haircut with them, and then declaring the shop integrated.[38] Hannah verbally supported on-campus civil rights protests like the campus NAACP's marches against housing discrimination in the mid-1960s and backed the integration of the college's football team during the Duffy Daugherty era, a strategic move that resulted in a Rose Bowl appearance and two national championships. David Bailey's thoughtful and balanced characterization of Hannah's approach to civil rights is worth considering.

He preferred specific actions. In small, practical gestures, he signaled to the administration that the future of the university he imagined would have to include African-Americans as part of the transformation he sought. . . . He preferred to work by changing the system or fixing abuses on a case-by-case basis. . . . Perhaps Hannah was a somewhat reluctant activist on civil rights, as some of his critics insisted. Or perhaps he viewed his role as guiding the university and the community toward a gradual end of official bigotry. He would have insisted that the best way to judge an institution is not by what it says but by what it does. Equally important, in his view of academic leadership, he believed that his personal opinions mattered less than those actions which advanced the cause of Michigan State, the state of Michigan, the country and the world.[39]

Chapter 21

Forgotten Firsts from the Forties

After he desegregated the dormitories and removed students' racial identities from their records, Hannah became a member of the Board of College Scholarship Fund for Negro Students that in 1948 "issued a call to colored students" to apply for ten thousand available scholarships.[1] This did not result in any conspicuous changes in the demographics of the MSC student body during the 1940s. African American students in no way contributed to the massive increase in the college's enrollment from about 8,500 in the fall of 1940 to 20,000 in the fall of 1949.

In the early 1940s, the largest group of Black students until the modern Civil Rights Movement—a nontraditional fellowship—arrived on campus to take a specific set of classes. As reported by several Black newspapers, in the late summer of 1943, forty-three enlisted Black men in the Ninety-sixth Service Group and the 332nd Fighter Group, 302nd Fighter Squadron (also known as the Tuskegee Airmen) who were stationed at Selfridge, Michigan, were "ordered to take preliminary courses in the Army Specialized Training Program at Michigan State College." They were briefly in East Lansing studying in the medical and veterinary fields. Lansing native Jennie Howard Washington, who probably noticed these dignified Black men on campus and graduated from MSC in 1944, reminisced that she did not feel she was mistreated on account of her race by her classmates or professors. "I didn't feel any discrimination by the white students, but even if there was, there weren't enough of us to raise any Cain," she added. "There were virtually no Blacks on campus in those days. Almost all the Black males were in the armed forces."[2] She had very few Black women classmates. Lillian Williams from Detroit graduated in 1943 and then taught physical education in the Motor City. In 1944, Elaine Baker, Albert Baker's younger sister, was a sophomore studying music, and talented orator Sally Margerette Cornwell was a first-year speech major. Washington probably crossed paths with Dorothy Jeter Montgomery and Diane Hoiston, Detroiters who roomed together, and Ina Jane Smith who was a senior in 1946 majoring in Spanish.

Washington's observations based upon her years at MSC from 1940 until 1944 appear to have applied to the decade as a whole. The largely unnoticeable integration of African American students into the MSC community during Hannah's first decade as president was in part reflected in the composition of the football team. During the 1930s, four Blacks played on the varsity squad. In November 1938, the *Detroit Tribune* reported that a star Mt. Clemens High School running back was enrolling in MSC to play football. This never happened. During the 1940s, from Hugh G. Davis, who played in 1941, to Jesse Thomas and Don E. Coleman, who joined the Spartans at the end of the decade, only six African Americans rocked the Spartan Green and White. From 1942 until 1945, no Black players were on the roster. On the other hand, during the 1950s, thirty-two African Americans played on Biggie Munn's and Duffy Daugherty's squads. In the late 1940s, the corresponding secretary of the Alpha Phi Alpha fraternity at MSC estimated that there were between forty and fifty African American students at the college. Between 1940 and 1949, at least eighteen African Americans graduated from Michigan State, and in 1944 perhaps the first known African American earned a PhD from the college. When Franklyn V. Duffy arrived on campus in 1940 after launching his campaign to desegregate the men's dormitories, there were at least six African American students enrolled. In June 1940, at least two African Americans had recently graduated, Booker T. Holmes and Harry Butler.

Named in honor of the Black leader who spoke at the 1900 commencement exercise, Booker T. Holmes was born in 1914 in Oxmoor, Alabama. He was one of fourteen children who was supported by a father who was a coalminer and a mother who was a housewife. At age six, Booker T. moved to Ecorse with his family. Like numerous Black men during the era of the Great Migration, his father secured a job working as a laborer at Ford Motor Company. After graduating from Ecorse High School, Holmes enrolled in MSC to study agriculture. Like many of his predecessors, after completing the requirements for his degree in 1940, he received a job at Southern University, an HBCU in Louisiana, where he taught for several years. He served in World War II in the Philippines from December 1943 until the spring of 1946 and was promoted to the rank of staff sergeant in late 1945. There were more than a few other Black Michigan State students, younger than Holmes, who also served during the Second World War like graduate student Joseph Jenkins who in 1943 was an ensign in the U.S. Coast Guard and Lansing native Silas M. Jenkins who in 1944 trained at Tuskegee Army Air Field. From 1944 until 1947, Cass Technical High School graduate Richard D. Trent served in the U.S. Army. He enrolled in Michigan State as a clinical psychology major in the fall of 1947 and became the first Black in several student organizations including the Forensic Society. The veteran Holmes then returned to Detroit, working as a bus driver for the Department of Street Railways until 1974 when he opened his own landscaping company. One of his sons recalled how he, in the tradition of his namesake, was a hard worker. "His hobby," his son remarked, "was work."[3] In this sense, Booker T. Holmes was like his predecessors. Those African American students who graduated from M.A.C. or MSC before and during the interwar period worked very hard to succeed on a campus that was not founded or designed with them in mind. They had to create their own support networks. They had to chart their own paths. Holmes's family was less than one hundred miles away, and he lived in Lansing's Black community. Beginning in his first year, he lived at 1111 W. Main Street, the former home of Charles A. Campbell, a historic home that by 1949 was being marketed to "colored buyers."[4]

A classmate of Holmes, Butler, who was born in Decatur, Georgia, in 1915 and arrived at Michigan State from New York City in 1935, was named "honorary captain" of the freshman cross-country squad. He had a remarkable freshman season, finishing first in "every event he entered."[5] In June 1936, the cross-country coaches believed Butler, a member of the Intercollegiate Association of Amateur Athletes of America cross-country championship team, was among the four distance runners to be considered "possible Olympic material." In 1938, during his fourth year as a Spartan, Butler was named captain of the varsity team by legendary coach and college alumnus Lauren Pringle Brown, becoming the first African American to serve as captain of any varsity team at the college. According to scholars and MSU alumni Mark E. Havitz and Eric D. Zemper, Brown ("Brownie") was "synonymous with cross country at Michigan State from the mid-1920s to the mid-1940s" and his "stance with respect to racial parity was consistent."[6] He supported Butler who, like many of his predecessors and classmates, was also active in Lansing's Black community. In 1936 and 1937, Butler volunteered at the Lincoln Community Center, working closely with Black male youth. In 1937, under the auspices of the National Youth Administration and longtime director of the MSC alumni office and member of the Education Policies Commission of the National Education Association Glen O. Stewart, he mentored "30 out-of-school colored boys." "The Lincoln school with Harry Butler, Michigan State College track man, as director of activities," the *Lansing State Journal* announced, "an effort is made to develop manliness as well as muscle, and sportsmanship as well as just sports."[7]

After becoming the first African American to earn a degree in veterinary medicine in 1940, Butler soon began working for the U.S. Department of Agriculture after graduating. An active member of the Michigan State Alumni Association's Rochester, New York, chapter, Butler died in 1963 on Martin Luther King Jr.'s birthday at age forty-seven. Several years after Butler graduated, W. A. Ezell, who once taught physiology and pharmacology at Tuskegee Institute, became the second African American veterinarian to graduate from MSC. In the late 1940s, he settled down in Detroit and advertised his services in the *Michigan Chronicle* and *Detroit Tribune*, highlighting that he was a graduate of MSC's School of Veterinary Medicine. In 1949, Frederick D. Smith earned a bachelor of science degree in veterinary medicine from Michigan State and went on to work at at Tennessee State University for a very long time after starting his career at North Carolina Agricultural & Technical College. Other Black students at MSC who studied animals during the 1940s might have had different goals. In 1945, for instance, Major Harris, who studied poultry at the college, joined forces with two brothers from Detroit to create the 3-H Poultry and Produce Company. They had ten thousand chickens on their farm in Dundee, Michigan.[8]

As John A. Hannah boasted in his letter to Senator Charles C. Diggs Sr. in early September 1940, Duffy was not the only known incoming African American student. Hannah mentioned another Black male incoming freshman, Hugh Davis. For whatever reason, Hannah neglected to mention Davis's fellow Lansing Central High School graduate Jennie Mae Howard, a young African American woman with a bright future who was born in 1922 in South Carolina to Abraham and Celia. When Jennie was about seven years old, the Howard family migrated to Lansing and Abraham secured a job at Olds Motor Works. Like many African American men from the South, Abraham was drawn to Lansing's booming auto industry, in hopes of escaping the Jim Crow South. Between 1920 and 1930, the Black population in the state capital increased from 698 to 1,409, and the majority of African Americans lived in the Third Ward. Job prospects for Howard's parents were certainly limited. "Only in foundry work did Blacks make any kind of inroads, particularly at Lansing Drop Forge and Nova Foundry." During the 1920s, "Oldsmobile hired a number of Negroes for custodial work, but entrance to higher status jobs did not open significantly." Through the 1930s, "the proportion of Lansing's Blacks in service and common labor occupations remained high."[9]

Jennie attended Lansing's integrated public schools, graduated from Lansing Central High School in 1940, and enrolled in MSC in the fall. She was an outstanding student with clear leadership potential. One of the handful of Black students in her class, she was awarded Central's 1940 Home Economics Leadership Award and four years later, in 1944, graduated from MSC with a bachelor of arts degree in liberal arts, becoming the seventh known Black woman to graduate from the college and the fourth known African American to come of age in Lansing and graduate from the college. There was another Black woman enrolled in MSC in the early 1940s. Born in Forest City, Arkansas, in 1919, Ivory Clinton graduated from South High School in Grand Rapids in 1936 and then enrolled in MSC. In high school, she was a standout student, a member of the student council, the National Honor Society, the Latin Club, the orchestra, and the math club. She graduated from MSC in 1941 with a bachelor of science in applied science and later became a became a biochemist.

Like her African American classmates, Jennie Howard found fellowship and well-being in the Black community. While at Michigan State, she was active in the Lincoln Community Center, often helping young girls such as those in the Girl Scouts and Brownies. With MSC graduate Herschel Irons, '36, Howard was active in Negro History Week commemorations as well as interracial collaborations. In 1943, she joined a group of Lansing's leading social reformers from the city's "Inter-racial Committee" to solve "the race issue" through "education

Jennie Mae Howard.
Courtesy of Michigan
State University
Archives and
Historical Collections.

and organization."[10] While a student, she participated on panel discussions concerning "Race Relations" in Lansing. On campus, Jennie was active in Pi Alpha, an organization for sociology majors concerned with addressing social ills. Shaping the intellectual scope of the organization, she served as the program chairperson. Several days before graduating, she married Thomas L. Washington who served as an aircraft mechanic for the famous Tuskegee Airmen. Thomas served in the U.S. Air Force from 1941 until 1967, and the Lansing chapter of the Tuskegee Airmen was named in his honor. Jennie Howard Washington lived a long and fascinating life. She mastered balancing life as a homemaker and career woman. In what historian Ula Y. Taylor has dubbed the helpmate tradition in her brilliant *The Veiled Garvey: The Life and Times of Amy Jacques Garvey*,[11] Washington similarly supported her husband and family while working in the public sphere and engaging in civic activism.

A mother of three children who were born during the mid- to late 1940s, Washington was a longtime employee of the state of Michigan's Civil Service Department, retiring in 1978. Active in politics and civil rights, in the early 1970s, she helped found the Black Associates in State Employment. In 1994 in celebration of its twentieth annual conference, the organization awarded Washington the group's "first Image Award." In addition to being a leading figure in this organization, serving as its executive secretary and "resident agent," she was active in the Trinity African Methodist Episcopal (AME) Church, Alpha Kappa Alpha Sorority, Inc., the Tuskegee Airmen, Inc., and the Kingsley Community Center. Throughout the 1980s and 1990s, Washington also regularly sent letters to the *Lansing State Journal* sharing her unapologetic opinions on a range of topics, including coverage of Black history events, the rights of minorities in Michigan, equal treatment of Black state employees, affirmative action, and voting rights. About four years before her death in 2015, Washington was recognized for her decades of selfless service. In November 2011, U.S. Representative Mike Rogers presented her a Congressional Gold Medal replica for "her service as a civilian employee in the personnel department at the Tuskegee Airmen's Army Air Corps base in Alabama during World War II" as well as for her "decades of involvement in the Lansing community." Washington's son Gary fittingly summarized his mother's disposition. "Growing up, my folks were so humble, that I didn't realize how special they were to so many other people until I got to be in my teens."[12]

After graduating in January 1940 from Lansing Central High School, Jennie's classmate, all-around athlete and football star Hugh Grayson Davis, enrolled in MSC in the spring. Davis was born on November 21, 1920, in Jonesboro, Georgia. Part of a noticeable post–World War I Black migration to Lansing and other Midwest cities, like Jennie's family, the Davis family migrated to Lansing in the 1920s. By 1940 when Davis enrolled in MSC, nearly 40 percent of the African Americans lived in blocks that were 50 to 100 percent Black. In search of new opportunities, Hugh's parents, Joe and Nellie, were thrifty and ambitious. Sometime in the early to mid-1920s, they purchased a home on Olds Avenue where Hugh grew up with his older siblings, Ionia and Joseph. With a second-grade education and experience as a farm laborer in Georgia, Hugh's father worked a variety of jobs in Lansing, including holding positions as an engineer for Sand Travel Company and as a pump operator. Like many Black women in Lansing during the first half of the twentieth century, Hugh's mother labored as a domestic worker and cook. Moving to Lansing opened many doors for the Davis family, and Joe and Nellie envisioned a brighter future for their children. They knew their children could receive a better education in the integrated public schools in Lansing than they could in the separate and unequal schools in the Jim Crow South.

With classmate Jennie Mae Howard, Hugh attended Lansing's integrated public schools. While Jennie distinguished herself in home economics, Hugh was a stand-out athlete at Lansing Central School. Inducted into the Greater Lansing Area Sports Hall of Fame in 1997, the 1939 Lansing Central football team was undefeated and untouchable. The 1939 Big Reds won the city championship and the state 5-A League. It was a well-rounded squad, and Davis was vital to head coach Deane Burham's success.[13] In November and December 1939, Davis was covered by the *Lansing State Journal* perhaps more than any other high school athlete in the city. His dynamic and creative running skills captured local sportswriters' attention and imaginations. He was arguably one of the city's most well-known and celebrated Black high school athletes before Lansing-born Everett High School basketball phenom Earvin "Magic" Johnson, who burst onto the scene during the 1970s.

Earvin "Magic" Johnson. Courtesy of Michigan State University Archives and Historical Collections.

By the spring of 1976, sportswriters remarked that Johnson was the "city's most publicized high school athlete." In March 1974, when approximately 80 percent of the basketball team was Black, the *Lansing State Journal* introduced Johnson to Mid-Michigan. Under the headline "Dwight Rich Cager Rewrites Record Books," an open-mouthed staff writer recounted Johnson's amazing, record-setting play. The then six foot five forward for Dwight Rich Junior High set three city junior high school basketball records. In ten games, he scored 227 points and grabbed 138 rebounds. In one game, he scored 48 points. The legend of Johnson began. From December 1974, his sophomore year at Everett High School, until May 1976, Johnson was a household name in Michigan newspapers. While Johnson was praised for his basketball skills like Davis was for his talent on the gridiron, Johnson, like his predecessor, was also recognized for his off-the-court activities. As a high school student, Johnson worked closely with youth in Lansing's South Side Club. "He has an earnest desire to serve others and, on top of it all, he seems to have the maturity to handle the success he's enjoying in basketball," remarked the club's executive director in 1976.

"It's just unusual to find a young man who is having so much success who is willing to give so much of his time to others."[14] Though not as extensive as the coverage of Johnson, *State Journal* writers raved about Davis several decades later.

An accomplished sprinter and broad jumper as well as a talented basketball player who honed his skills at the Lincoln Community Center and made more than a few clutch baskets for the Big Reds, Davis was first noticed on the gridiron when, as a backup halfback sophomore in November 1937, he scored two touchdowns in a 13-6 victory over Eastern High School "before a wildly enthusiastic crowd of 7,500 at Pattengill field." The "little negro halfback," as he was called by a White journalist, carried the load "thrust on his shoulders like a true soldier." The enthusiastic looker-on added, "Davis was the Messiah of the Central team." His stoic performance against Eastern was ritualistically summoned up by Big Reds' fans, further etching Davis's name into the Lansing high school football history books. During the 1939 season in his senior year, he continued in this tradition. "Hugh Davis became a Central high school immortal last night," a *Lansing State Journal* sportswriter declared in November 1939 following Central's 21-6 victory over Eastern in which Davis scored "three times on runs of 48, 22, and 16 yards." The spectator added that Davis, "a climax runner, a 'flash' runner," was just what MSC needed in its backfield for the 1940 season. Davis also seemed to have impressed White admirers with his composure and humble disposition. "He is a modest, clean-living boy and one of this department's favorites," observed the *State Journal*'s Tom O'Brien. Drawing upon their experiences in the Jim Crow South, Joe and Nellie raised their children to be respectable and practice social awareness. At the end of the 1939 season, Davis was one of five Lansing Central players named to the Coach's All-Five-A League team. To the chagrin of his fans, he made the *Detroit Free Press*'s third all-state high school football team. O'Brien, who had covered Davis's career closely, was not alone in questioning why the elusive halfback didn't make the first team of this mythical squad.[15]

Davis's prowess on the gridiron and his upright character were celebrated by his high school and Lansing's Black community. In late November 1939, the Colored Women's Co-operative and Business Club sponsored a banquet, open to the public, held in Davis's honor. Among the notables in attendance at the Lincoln School auditorium were Michigan's governor, Lansing's mayor and school superintendent, and a group of Lansing Central's "officials." More than four hundred people attended the celebration to collectively sing Davis's praises. In 1940, shortly after graduating in January, Davis was awarded the Michigan Honor Trophy, an award sponsored by the University of Michigan "based on merits of leadership, athletic ability, and scholarship." This esteemed prize offered Davis something that his parents could have only dreamed of—a scholarship to attend the prestigious University of Michigan. Bypassing the opportunity to venture to Ann Arbor, as reported in the *State Journal* in February 1940, Davis decided to enroll in Michigan State in the spring 1940 term, focusing on track "to the exclusion of other sports."[16]

Davis could have played basketball at MSC. He led his 1939 high school team to nineteen wins and in 1940 was a leading scorer in the 5-A League. He probably would not have been welcomed on the MSC team. It wasn't until 1951 when the first African American, five-foot-six guard Rickey Ayala, integrated the college's varsity basketball team. The next several African Americans to play varsity basketball at MSC were forward Julius "Hooks" McCoy (1953–1956) and Marine veteran, superstar power forward, and future NBA All-Star "Jumpin'" Johnny Green (1957–1959). Davis didn't turn his back on hoops. He fulfilled his basketball fix by playing high point man on the Lincoln Community Center team in the early 1940s while attending MSC. Davis was impressed by MSC track coach Karl A. Schladerman who was openly supportive of talented African American runners as revealed by his appointment of Walter Arrington, '41, as captain. In the fall of 1940, Davis played on the MSC freshman football team. The transition from high school to college football was quite challenging for the undersized and tough as nails Davis. At five foot eight, 160 pounds, Davis was smaller than most of his teammates and opponents. He could no longer rely on his speed. During his freshman year, he had an outstanding game against the Central State Yearlings in early November.

Even though Davis, in one Lansing's sportswriter's assessment, didn't necessarily impress the varsity football coaches on account of his weak tackling and blocking skills, in the spring of 1941, other sportswriters were eager to see how "Lil Hughie" would play on the varsity squad. In August 1941, Davis was one of the forty-nine players, and one of nine halfbacks, to report to coach Charles W. Bachman's first practice on September 10. Davis made the 1941 varsity squad and was featured in an issue of the *State Journal* with five of his new teammates from Lansing whom he once competed against and got the best of. He was a living legend in Lansing high school football lore. He scored thirty-three touchdowns during his career, played historic games against Eastern, and in a game against Battle Creek High School averaged 17.1 yards on ten carries. Davis's football career at Michigan State was short-lived. He played only during the 1941 season. He impressed his pundits as a substitute against Michigan on September 7 at Michigan Stadium in front of sixty-seven thousand, and on October 18, he played an outstanding game against the Santa Clara University Broncos in a tight 0-7 loss. As recounted by a sportswriter for the *San Francisco Examiner*, in the fourth quarter the Spartans mounted a valiant comeback with "a little colored youth named Hughie Davis" who "stole the show" with several large gains on two variations of the "Statue of Liberty" trick play. Davis accounted for 30 percent of the Spartans' total running yards. He finished the game with four carries and forty-nine yards, behind starting halfback Dick Kieppe who had twenty-two carries for sixty-one yards.[17]

For whatever reason, Davis was not in the 1941 varsity team photo, but appeared in the 1942 *Wolverine* "Athletic" section that profiled the 5-3-1 squad. In addition to a headshot, a peculiar photo appears of Davis in this yearbook. He was given the jersey number 13, traditionally considered an unlucky number for football players. Davis once told a local sportswriter he was a bit superstitious about this. Under the title "Hughie Unhappy over His No. 13," on September 11, 1941, the Associated Press reported: "Sophomore Hugh Davis, 160-pound negro halfback from Lansing, sat on the sidelines dejectedly as the Michigan State college football team opened practice yesterday. 'Anything wrong, Hughie?' his mates asked. 'Nothing much,' he smiled wanly, slowing [*sic*] arising to display a large No. 13 on his Jersey. 'I'm not superstitious, but that isn't exactly a rabbit's foot.'" The large photo of Davis in the 1942 yearbook is of Davis's back. He posed in a non-football stance, scratching his head and seemingly grinning. Perhaps egged on by his teammates or part of his jovial demeanor, it appears as if Davis contorted his body to resemble one of entertainer and civil rights activist Josephine Baker's trademark vaudeville poses. Echoing the piece from the Associated Press, the caption reads: "a tense moment in the Temple game. Hughie looking for a rabbit's foot." The game against Temple was anything but tense. The Spartans, who were underdogs, won 46-0, and Davis probably saw Macklin Field that day. As noted by scholar Bill Ellis, in the early twentieth century, companies advertised rabbit's feet, claiming African Americans believed that it brought good luck.[18] These ads poked fun at African Americans for supposedly being superstitious and simple-minded. Were the references to Davis and "a rabbit's foot" rooted in this stereotype?

It's unclear why Davis stopped playing football. As a small halfback who was accustomed to sweeping around the ends and juking out defenders, he was not built for the Spartans' more traditional style of offense and pounding running game. Pundits remained skeptical of his defensive and blocking abilities. He was not to be intimidated by the roughness of college football. Toward the end of the 1941 football season, he told a Lansing sportswriter that college football was, in his estimation, cleaner than what he experienced in high school. While playing at Central, he believed that his opponents tried more dirty tactics against him. "They don't pile-on or twist your knees like they did to me in high school," observed Davis.[19] Perhaps he felt alienated being the only African American on the gridiron. He was, after all, the first African American to play on the varsity football team since 1934 when James McCrary, William H. Smith, and Albert Baker rocked the Green and White. After Davis's brief time on the squad, the next African American to play varsity football at MSC would be Jackson, Michigan, native Horace Smith who played in 1946 and 1947. The fleet-footed Davis decided to focus on track, realizing it was his best opportunity to pursue his academic commitments and love of sports. Davis was a talented sprinter. At Central, he ran the one-hundred-yard dash in 10.1 seconds.

In the 1942 preseason track trials under Coach Schlademan, Davis was impressive, winning the sixty-yard dash. He performed admirably on the track squad. In May 1942, he set a new varsity broad jump record at 23 feet 8 3/8 inches. He was a consistent contributor and high-spirited asset to the track team. In February 1943, he was the team's only double winner in a meet against the Wolverines, winning the sixty-yard dash and the broad jump. He was also a member of a record-setting relay team and during his junior year defeated many nationally ranked sprinters. But athletics did not define Davis. While attending MSC, he lived at home with his parents and remained active in the Lincoln Community Center that helped nurture him as a youth. He served as the adviser of the Junior Hi-Y club and coached the Hi-Y basketball team who were champions during the early 1940s. He played on the center's basketball team that competed

Hugh Davis as a member of the varsity track team. Courtesy of Michigan State University Archives and Historical Collections.

against other Black teams throughout the state and nation. In the early 1940s, Davis was also a counselor for Mystic Lake Camp's "negro camping period" when forty-three disadvantaged Black male youths enjoyed the opportunity of their lifetimes.

On February 16, 1942, Davis registered for World War II and about a year later began his military service. In mid-April 1943, a *Lansing State Journal* sportswriter lamented, "Gone are such dependables as Hughie Davis, sprinter." The Black press also praised his skills. In 1944, the *Chicago Defender* dubbed him "one of the five best sprinters in the middle west." Davis didn't lose his competitive edge in the army, playing in an informal basketball league. In January 1944, he returned to Lansing on furlough and two years later reenrolled in Michigan State. He earned a bachelor of science in physical education, health, and recreation for men on March 18, 1948. Between the late 1940s and the mid-1950s, he worked various manual labor jobs in Lansing. Even as a college-educated Black man who had brought fame to Lansing Central High School, his job prospects in the city were limited. He didn't have the connections that some of his White male contemporaries did. Limited job opportunities in Lansing led him to venture to New York City. In the late 1940s and early 1950s, Davis worked at the Harlem's Boys Club as "physical director," a basketball and track coach, and a boxing trainer. In 1949, the *New York Age* announced that Davis was "lining up scholarships for deserving athletes with all-around ability at Michigan State College." Several years later, the *New York Age* and the *New York Amsterdam News* reported that Davis had a "run-in with the law" in Harlem that inspired him to return to his home city.

According to Lansing city directories, he worked at Atlas Forge and Christman Company and in construction. By the late 1950s, he headed South to work at two historically Black colleges, coaching basketball at Talladega College in Mobile, Alabama, and then, in the early 1960s, at Florida Normal and Technical Institute in Opa-locka North, Miami Gardens, Florida.[20]

Davis died at age forty-three in Battle Creek, Michigan. His brief obituary from the *Lansing State Journal* on April 2, 1963, which contains a few inaccuracies, suggests that after earning his degree from MSC at age twenty-eight, he lived a full life. Under the title, "Ex-Football Star Hugh Davis Dies," reads: "Hugh Davis, 43, of 2109 W. Main St., former Michigan State University football star, died Monday at Veterans Hospital, Battle Creek. Mr. Davis was graduated from Central High School in 1939, attended Michigan State College and was a graduate of Columbia University. He taught at the Boys Harlem Center, New York City, Talladego [*sic*] institute and Florida Normal of St. Augustine, Fla., and was a veteran of World War II."[21]

One of the few African Americans from Lansing to enroll in the college before the era of World War II, Hugh "Hughie" Davis lived a short but remarkable life. Celebrated for his graceful ball-carrying on the gridiron, overall athleticism, and humble disposition, like countless other Americans, he put his allegiance to his country before his pursuit of his own dreams and aspirations. A multitalented athlete, he could have certainly made more history on MSC's track team. He bested Walter Arrington's personal broad jump record. One must take solace in the fact that Davis gave back to the small and tight-knit Black Lansing community that supported him so much and to historically Black institutions. Like Gideon Smith and Harry C. Graves before him and Earvin "Magic" Johnson after him, Davis passed along his deep knowledge and tricks of the trade about sports to African American youth. It's also admirable that he remained committed to his convictions and earned his degree from Michigan State about eight years after he first enrolled.

Several of Davis's and Franklyn V. Duffy's elder classmates stood out for their extracurricular achievements, especially Walter Alan Arrington, '41, and Julia Cloteele Rosemond, '41. Born in Madison, Virginia, on September 18, 1918, Arrington was a star on the Michigan State varsity track team from 1939 until 1941. "Arrington, only a sophomore, cracked the varsity jumping records and stamped himself as one of the country's leading jumpers for the next two years," the *Wolverine* commented on Arrington's performance during the 1939 season. He began the 1939 season very strong. In February, he performed exceptionally well at the Illinois Indoor Carnival in Champaign. "Negro Grabs Honors," the *Lansing State Journal* announced. Arrington placed second in the overall competition, winning the seventy-five-yard dash and the high jump and placing second in the shot put and third in the seventy-five-yard high hurdles. In his team's first outdoor meet against Purdue in April 1939, he made Michigan State history. He jumped 6 feet 1 ¾ inches in the high jump, breaking the college's "oldest existing" varsity track record dating back to 1912. The *M.S.C. Record* praised Arrington's talent, and in early May 1939, the *Lansing State Journal* featured a large picture of "the best jumper Michigan State has ever had." George

Walter Arrington broad-jumping. Courtesy of Michigan State University Archives and Historical Collections.

S. Alderton praised Arrington, using similar descriptions he applied to Gideon Smith decades earlier. "Walter Arrington, the New York colored boy," he wrote, "is the No. 1 handy man, of course. He can do just about everything, although he is a high jump specialist." In April 1940, a photo of Arrington, with his teammates, appeared in the *Record*, and his coach told Michigan State alumni that he was "the best all-around track athlete he has coached."[22] Arrington proved this by winning the all-around title of the Illinois Indoor Carnival with 5,577.5 points. Despite his achievements, Arrington could not escape discrimination. While traveling with his team for competitions, on more than a few occasions he was not allowed to stay overnight with his teammates in local hotels.

Arrington did not undertake the type of work Butler, '40, did, but assumed a similar leadership position. In 1941, Arrington was named captain of the track team, becoming the second African American to serve in this capacity for a Michigan State varsity sport. In January 1941, the *Lansing State Journal* published a large photo of Arrington with coach Karl A. Schlademan under the headline, "New Coach and Spartan Track Captain." This is one of the few articles that doesn't highlight Arrington's race. The photo tells it all. Arrington was also the first African American to appear in *Beside the Winding River*, a promotional pamphlet founded during Jonathan L. Snyder's presidency used to recruit prospective students. From 1941 until 1943, the iconic photo of Arrington's record-breaking high jump appeared in the catalog's "Physical Education and Athletics" section. Through the 1940s, Arrington was the only African American to appear in this promotional publication.

Though he was injured with a sprained ankle during his senior year and missed much of the indoor winter season, he performed well in his last home meet in May 1941. He "won 19 ½ points out of a possible 20," Alderton noted. "He captured the broad jump, shot put, discus throw and shared first place in the high jump." Arrington being named captain of the varsity track team was no small feat. His teammates and coaches respected his leadership abilities. Like Butler, he was among the first African Americans to serve as captain of any varsity sports at a Big Ten university. Julian Ware's service as captain of the University of Wisconsin's baseball team in 1902 was truly pathbreaking, and in 1924 low hurdles world record setter Charles Brookins captained the University of Iowa's varsity track team. During Arrington's first season at Michigan State, track phenom Bill Watson became the first African American to be chosen as a captain of any varsity team at the University of Michigan. Like Willis Ward before him, Watson had Olympics caliber talent.

Arrington's classmate Rosemond also broke ground for Black students at Michigan State, demonstrating to her White classmates African American students' and Black women's capacity to compete in intellectual spheres. "Cloteele Rosemond does not hesitate to tackle dilemmas affecting her sex, her youth, or her race," the *Detroit Tribune* recounted in the summer of 1940. "What she desires, loves and believes becomes part of her life." Rosemond was born on May 25, 1920, and grew up in Detroit. She was talented as a young girl. At age three, she began taking piano lessons and by age fifteen was an accomplished singer with a "soothing contralto voice." She drew great inspiration from renowned contralto Marian Anderson who made history with her 1939 Easter Sunday performance in the nation's capital. Rosemond's parents invested much into helping her pursue her goals. In 1937, she graduated from Miller High School and then enrolled in Bennett College, a historically Black school in North Carolina. In 1939, she transferred to Michigan State, majoring in hotel administration. She soon became "deeply interested in the problems of delinquency" and switched her major to "social administration." In 1940, she explained she wanted to be an educator. "I realize that few of these positions have been secured by Negroes but see no reason why there shouldn't be more."[23]

Julia Cloteele Rosemond. Courtesy of Michigan State University Archives and Historical Collections.

Rosemond was a first-rate orator at Michigan State. In late April 1940 during her junior year, she was a member of the Student Speakers Bureau and won first place in the women's division of the oratorical contest at Augustana College. Her oration, "Exiled by Prejudice," was described by the Illinois press as being "a plea" for the equal treatment of African Americans in U.S. society. She knew what racial prejudice entailed and effectively communicated this to her mainly White audiences. She was prohibited from participating in the 1940 national Pi Kappa Delta tournament in Nashville, Tennessee, but this didn't seem to distract Rosemond. She ended up topping the performance of the winner of this segregated event in a later competition. Michigan State took great pride in Rosemond's accomplishments. Her achievement made the front page of the *State News*, and Michigan State alumni even praised her. "Cloteele Rosemond, liberal arts sophomore from Detroit, was first place in the National Interstate Oratorical Association contest by the unanimous vote of seven judges," the *M.S.C. Record* boasted in July 1940. "After winning the Michigan Oratorical contest with 'Exiled by Prejudice,' a plea for recognition of the negro, Miss Rosemond entered the three-round elimination contest at Rock Island, Illinois, to win the unanimous vote again for first place. This is unprecedented in the association's history." As late as 1957, Rosemond remained the only Michigander to win the Interstate Oratorical contest. As a member of the Michigan State Student Speakers Bureau, founded in 1938, she was one of the forty students to address over fifty thousand people in 1941. Along with Black students Butler, who lectured on "The Great American Outdoors," and G. B. (Gladnil/Gladwin Bernell) Williams, who spoke on the topic of "The American Negro Faces the Dawn" (one of his Negro History Week orations), Rosemond shared her "Exiled by Prejudice" oration with numerous audiences in Michigan. The bureau's director, Paul D. Bagwell, saw the value in diversifying this organization, allowing outspoken African American students to hone their "practical speaking" while also representing the college in this vital "service to the community."[24]

After graduating in the summer of 1941 with a bachelor of arts degree from the Division of Liberal Arts, Rosemond attended graduate school at Wayne State University and became a public school teacher in Detroit. Other Black women followed in Rosemond's footsteps as talented public speakers. In 1945, first-year student Sally Margerette Cornwell won a major oratorical contest at Michigan State that was open to all undergraduate women at the college and represented the college at the state forensics contest with her oration, "The Racial Problem." Cornwell honed her skills at Lansing's Sexton High School. In the early 1940s, she won several city-wide essay contests. In a 1943 competition sponsored by the Veterans of Foreign Wars, she was recognized for her first-rate and objective interpretation of racial subject matter. Other Black women high school students made their mark on the podium. In 1932, Lansing Central High School sophomore Louise Brown won a district oratory contest for her tribute to Toussaint L'Ouverture that dazzled a University of Michigan professor who judged her performance.

Between the late nineteenth century and the end of the Great Depression, there were nontraditional African American students, or adult learners, at M.A.C. and Michigan State. Frances Langford, who graduated in 1937 at age thirty-four, is one example. Another example is Williams. In December 1941 at age forty-eight, Williams earned a bachelor of arts degree from Michigan State. His notable accomplishment was celebrated by more than two hundred members of Lansing's Black community at the Lincoln Community Center, including friends and admirers from Union Baptist church and Friendship Baptist church. Though old enough to be their parents, he befriended Rosemond and Butler who were also active in the Student Speakers Bureau. Born in Bedford, Michigan in October 1895, Williams's childhood was difficult.

His young mother died when he was four months old and "Gladdie" was raised by his grandmother, aunt, and father. When he was four years old, his father married a German immigrant and they moved to Racine, Wisconsin, where he attended a German Lutheran school. At age eight, Williams moved to Cleveland with his father and stepmother and attended another German school where he became proficient in German. As a child, he heard stories about slavery from his paternal grandfather who in 1862 migrated to Battle Creek from Kentucky. Williams and his family then moved to Battle Creek, and he attended school through the ninth grade. In 1910 as a freshman in high school in Battle Creek, Williams heard Booker T. Washington speak. He recounted at age fifty that he never forgot Booker T.'s message. His father became ill when he was seventeen, and Williams had to, in his words, start hustling. He dropped out of high school and moved to Bloomington, Indiana, plugging away at a variety of jobs to help himself and his family. His father died in 1912, and after returning to Battle Creek, Williams moved to Lansing in the summer of 1913 and worked at F. N. Arbaugh Department Store for several years. Several years later, he got a job at the Hotel Olds where he worked for many years.

Williams was active in Lansing's Black community, assuming leadership positions in the George R. Collins AME Church. In the late 1920s, he was "chairman of the troop committee" for the city's first "colored Boy Scouts" sponsored by the Hillsdale Baptist Church and the George R. Collins AME Church. In the 1930s, he served as president of the Lansing Colored Business, Professional and Civic League, working with Charles A. Warren, among others. In 1933, determined to earn his high school diploma, he enrolled in Central High School. "If you want to get anywhere nowadays," he told a reporter for the *Lansing State Journal* in 1935, "you've got to have an education."[25]

Williams entered Michigan State after earning his high school diploma from Lansing High School in 1935 at age forty. While an MSC student, he worked in the "washroom concession and shoe-shining parlor" in the Hotel Olds. Like Rosemond, Williams spoke throughout Lansing on the status of African Americans, including at Negro History Week events at the Lincoln Community Center. "I was very popular on campus," Williams recalled. He also found great joy in being a member of the Sociology Club and the Student Speakers Bureau. At MSC, one of his favorite teachers was his instructor of German. After graduating from MSC, Williams held a variety of jobs relevant to education. He began his career as a health educator for the Michigan Tuberculosis Association, an outreach position he held for seven years. Known formally as the director of the association's "Negro field service," he played a key role in informing Lansing's Black community about "the need for education in fighting tuberculosis." He worked regularly with the Lansing Negro Citizens' Health Committee and the Ingham County Tuberculosis and Health Society and was a regular speaker at the Lincoln Community Center and the George R. Collins AME Church. After a brief stint in the insurance business in Detroit during the early 1950s, he returned to Lansing. He was also a longtime mason and Grand Patron of the Prince Hall Grand Chapter, Order of the Eastern Star, of Michigan and in 1960 was elected to the "office of the international grand sentinel." For eleven years, he served as a supervisor at the Boys Training School and then as a substitute teacher at Eastern, Everett, and Sexton High Schools where he "taught almost every subject." He was a strong advocate of education. "I think education is the key to solving most of our problems." He viewed himself as a role model. "I like to think that the example I've set in showing how a person, Negroes included, can get ahead in this country will help young people to do the same," Williams noted while publicizing his self-published autobiography, *Look Not Upon Me Because I Am Black* (1970) that he sold for $2.75. In his later years after retiring in 1972, he became an advocate for the elderly. The first senior couple to live in Lansing's Oliver

Towers, Williams and his wife, Allene, were active in this Lansing Housing Commission project. Williams was elected the first president of the complex's resident council.[26]

Franklyn V. Duffy was not the only Black man to graduate from MSC in 1943. He was joined by James Albert Peal. Born in Chicago in 1922, as a toddler James lived in the Windy City and Kansas City. He came of age in Columbus, Ohio. His father, Allen S. Peal (born in 1874), was a veteran of the Spanish American War and World War I and following his service worked as a public school teacher and mail clerk. In 1933, when James was eleven, his father died and received a dignified soldier's burial. Born in 1895, James's mother, Helen, moved to New York City sometime after her husband died. In 1937, she studied dressmaking at Pratt Institute and in 1940 worked as a secretary at the Colored YWCA at Ashland Place. A graduate of West Virginia State College, she held many other jobs while in New York City, and in 1949 she became the executive housekeeper at the famous Hotel Theresa. While his mother was in New York City, James lived with his aunt Clara E. Christopher in Cleveland, Ohio.

In the late 1930s, James enrolled in MSC to study agriculture. He was active in several student organizations, especially during his senior year. A member of the YMCA, Peal also participated in the Agronomy Club, a group of like-minded students who met in Ag Hall on a biweekly basis, invited outside speakers to campus, held student-faculty picnics, and participated in Farmers' Week and 4-H Week. James was perhaps the first African American involved in the college's co-op movement, living with more than twenty of his White classmates in an East Lansing home. During the early years of World War II, students created the Michigan State Cooperative Federation to help "many students of limited financial resources to remain in college." Peal lived in the Hedrick House at 903 E. Grand River Avenue and is pictured with his housemates in the 1943 *Wolverine*. "Today the cry is unity; unity of effort and unity in the sincerity of purpose," the *Wolverine* described Peal's co-op, "for whenever great deeds are done, men must work together. The men of the fraternal cooperatives know the value of this fact. It is their axiom." After graduating from Michigan State in 1943, Peal moved to Washington, D.C., to pursue his education in a field much different from his major. In 1948, he graduated from Howard University's Medical School. From 1953 until 1955, he served in the U.S. Navy, and in the mid-1950s he worked as a psychiatrist at Napa State Hospital in Napa, California, and at the Clinical Psychology Service of the 820th Hospital Center, U.S. Army Reserve. In the late 1950s, he became an assistant superintendent in the Stockton State Hospital and then at the California Medical Facility at Vacaville and Agnew State Hospital. A fellow of the American Psychiatric Association, in 1964, he was appointed assistant director of the Michigan State Department of Mental Health.[27]

Back in the Lansing area, Peal was an advocate for those facing mental health challenges. In 1965, for instance, he penned an op-ed, "For the Patients," in which he championed the rights of mental health patients. "Let us never forget that patients are people," Peal proclaimed; "the most effective psychiatric treatment of patients capitalizes on the patients' assets, rather than focusing on their liabilities."[28] Peal became active in the East Lansing community in ways that weren't possible for him several decades earlier when he was a student. In 1966, Dr. Peal, who helped integrate East Lansing by residing on Cedarhill Drive, was appointed by the East Lansing City Council to the Human Relations Commission. Peal's wife, Puerto Rico–born Edithie V. Figueroa, taught Spanish at MSU. Peal's return to East Lansing was brief, lasting only about two and a half years. In 1967, he was named director of the Fresno County Mental Health Department. The White East Lansing community respected Dr. Peal. In early March 1967, the *Lansing State Journal* announced, "Dr. and Mrs. Peal Feted at Buffet Supper." After leaving East Lansing, Peal continued to excel at his job, further solidifying his national reputation in his field of expertise. In 1969, he secured an internship at Harlem Hospital in a city where twenty years earlier the widely read *New York Age* dubbed him "the son of popular Helen Peal." In the 1960s and 1970s, Peal was called upon to testify in various cases dealing with defendants' mental capacities.[29]

A year after Peal and Duffy graduated, another Black man, William Winans Bowie, '44, graduated from Michigan State. Like his predecessors, he applied what he learned in East Lansing to his future career. The son of Mississippi natives, William Sr. and Emily, Bowie was born in Detroit on August 25, 1918. Like countless Black men during the Great Migration, Bowie's father migrated to Detroit to work in the city's booming auto industry, drawn by the prospects of making five dollars a day. After graduating from high school, Bowie moved to Lansing, enrolling in Michigan State several years later. In 1938, he lived on W. Main Street and worked as a janitor at the State Board Tax Administration. He worked to support himself through college and in 1940, during his freshman year, married twenty-year-old Elsie Violet Thompson, the daughter of the first known African American to graduate from M.A.C., William O. Thompson, '04. About four years after marrying Elsie, Bowie was one of the fifty-three Michigan State seniors and former senior servicemen to be awarded degrees at the end of the winter quarter in mid-March 1944. Lieutenant Bowie earned a bachelor of music in public school music and enjoyed studying with baritone horn virtuoso and longtime Spartan Marching Band director Leonard Falcone. A World War II veteran who earned the rank of second lieutenant, Bowie earned a master's degree in music from his alma mater. While attending MSC, Bowie also served as director of the George R. Collins AME Church choir.[30]

Following World War II, Bowie settled down in Delaware, working as a teacher. In the late 1940s, he supervised "the playground program at the Booker T. Washington School" and oversaw a popular summer recreation program for youth of the Dover area. "He is well equipped to carry on a diversified program of activities," wrote the *Morning News* (Wilmington, Delaware) in June 1949, "and is launching an all-out effort to serve many of the young people as the area will permit." During the 1950s, while teaching music and directing the orchestras and string and brass ensembles at junior high schools, he directed several adult church choirs and the fellowship choirs of Wilmington and the YMCA Fellowship Choir. During the 1960s, he developed into a civil rights activist, participating in demonstrations and mobilizing Black youth. In 1964, he was awarded an Alpha Phi Alpha citizenship award for his outstanding civil rights activism, particularly for his "distinguished service as an organizer of youth to combat discriminatory practices of local businesses purporting to serve the general public." He was also active in the Concerned Citizens, an organization that fought for the rights of poor African Americans in Wilmington and advocated for fair housing. A talented trumpet player, Bowie taught music to countless youth until he retired in the early 1990s. According to those affiliated with the James Hillhouse High School community who dedicated a music room to him in 2004, "So many musicians who came out of New Haven Public Schools are doing well as a result of Bowie."[31]

Between 1940 and 1949, the total MSC student enrollment increased by 150 percent. Bowie and his Black classmates did not contribute to this massive growth. In total, there were probably no more than several dozen African Americans who attended MSC during the decade. A small subset of this population were graduate students. Following in the footsteps of Herschel Irons (MS, '38), during the early to mid-1940s, several African Americans earned graduate degrees from MSC to bolster their teaching careers at HBCUs. In the summer of 1940, thirty-three-year-old Southern University (Baton Rouge, Louisiana) instructor Dallas Benjamin Matthews earned a master of arts in education. In 1948, he informed his alma mater about his progress, letting the *M.S.C. Record* know he had just accepted a position as superintendent of the State Industrial School for Colored Youths in Baton Rouge, Louisiana. What he didn't spell out for his former classmates was that this was the first of its kind juvenile school for 120 so-called wayward African American youths in the state. In 1944, while serving as the head of the agricultural department at Fort Valley State College, a public land-grant historically Black university in Georgia founded in 1895, Hampton Institute alumnus Robert Louis Wynn earned a master of science degree in animal husbandry. Delaware State instructor William A. Wynder received a master's degree in agriculture in 1945, and a year later Frederick Leven Jr. earned a master's degree in economics and joined the faculty at Tuskegee Institute.[32] In 1952, one of the first sub-Saharan African students to attend Michigan State, Lincoln University (Jefferson City, Missouri) graduate Benjamin Yao Owusu from Ghana, earned a master of science degree in agriculture. About a decade later, Benjamin Gumbu Dennis from Liberia began pursuing a PhD in sociology and anthropology. Under the leadership of educator and MSU alumna Jacqueline "Jackie" Warr, Dennis was active in Lansing's Negro History Week movement in the mid-1960s. One of the first Africans to earn a doctorate in the social sciences at MSU, Dennis found a sense of belonging with African Americans in the capital city, the subject of his dissertation, and most likely with MSU's Association of African Students.

African Americans began pursuing advanced degrees at Michigan State more than a few decades after graduate programs were established in East Lansing. According to the *Michigan Agricultural College Catalog of Officers and Graduates, 1857–1916*, between 1861 and 1878, master of science degrees were conferred upon those graduates of three years' standing who had made what was termed as proper proficiency in their scientific studies and endeavors. During the Progressive Era, graduate degree programs were offered in agriculture, forestry, civil engineering, and mechanical engineering, and by 1916, at least one hundred students earned master of science degrees from M.A.C. In 1913, six women earned the first master's degrees in home economics. In 1909, several faculty members urged President Snyder to initiate doctoral programs in a few departments. M.A.C. awarded the first doctor of veterinary medicine in 1913, and it would take another decade for doctoral studies to formally emerge at the college. It wasn't until the mid-1920s when graduate studies, as exemplified by the launching of the college's first doctoral program, moved beyond being a marginal component of the college's curriculum and mission. This shift soon resulted in the creation of the doctor of philosophy degree in seven scientific disciplines. In the 1922–1923 academic year college catalog, under David L. Friday's brief presidency, doctoral study was available in bacteriology, botany, chemistry, farm crops, soil, entomology, and horticulture. The college awarded its first doctoral degree in 1925 to a student specializing in botany.

In the mid-twentieth century, Frederick A. Williams, who earned a master's degree in agricultural economics at MSC in the late 1930s, was celebrated by the *New Journal and Guide* as being "the first Negro to serve as a graduate assistant" at MSC.[33] During the 1930s, advanced degree recipients Williams and Herschel Irons charted new terrain for their people in East Lansing. The first African American to earn a doctorate in agricultural economics from the University of Wisconsin, Williams was a longtime administrator at his undergraduate alma mater North Carolina A&T, serving as the dean of the graduate school and the director of planning and development. Why didn't he pursue his doctorate in East Lansing? Perhaps it was because of MSC's uninspiring record of recruiting and graduating African Americans with graduate degrees. A pint-sized group of African Americans, probably less than a dozen, earned masters and doctorate degrees at Michigan State from the 1930s through the 1950s. By contrast, by the early 1940s, fifteen African Americans had earned advanced degrees from the University of Wisconsin (five master's degrees and ten doctorates). About two decades after the M.A.C. doctoral program in chemistry was inaugurated (the first doctorate in this field was conferred in 1926), the first-known African American earned a doctorate from Michigan State College of Agriculture and Applied Science. While chairing the science department at State Teacher's College in Montgomery, Alabama, Henry Lewis Van Dyke obtained a PhD in chemistry in 1944. A few Black chemists like Norbert Rilleux, George Washington Carver, Alice Ball, and Percy J. Julian made important discoveries and contributions before Van Dyke earned his doctorate.

The first African American to earn a doctorate in chemistry, St. Elmo Brady, did so in 1916 from the University of Illinois. Four years after Van Dyke made history at Michigan State, Marie Maynard Daly became the first Black woman to earn a doctorate in chemistry from Columbia University. By 1943, thirty-six African Americans had earned doctorates in this field, representing approximately 35 percent of all doctorates earned by African Americans in the physical sciences. Between 1930 and 1943 (a year before Van Dyke earned his PhD), about thirty-five thousand doctorates were awarded in the United States, approximately 315, or 1 percent, of which were granted to Black students. Through the early 1940s, Ivy League colleges and Big Ten universities far outpaced Michigan State in granting doctorate degrees to African Americans: University of Chicago (40), Columbia (35), University of Pennsylvania (28), Cornell and Harvard (25 each) Ohio State (22), University of Michigan (20), State University of Iowa (13), Illinois (10), Wisconsin (10), Northwestern and Indiana (6 each), Penn State (5), and Minnesota (3).

Michigan State's first-known Black PhD recipient was born on June 7, 1903, in Michigan and grew up in Penn Township (Vandalia Village) in Cass County. Native Michiganders, Van Dyke's father, Julius, was a farm laborer and his mother, Mary, a laundress. In 1920, Henry lived in the city of Three Rivers in St. Joseph County. He attended high school in Three Rivers and enrolled in Western State Normal School (now Western Michigan University) in the early 1920s, majoring in chemistry. He was encouraged to attend graduate school by two of his supportive White professors. There were few African American students at Western at the time, including Merze Tate who would go on to become the first Black woman to earn a PhD in political science from Radcliffe College, which later merged with Harvard University. The first Black woman hired by Howard University's history department, Tate remained friends with Henry and his wife. In August 1927, Henry married fellow Michigander Bessie Charlotte Chandler. On the eve of the Great Depression, he began teaching chemistry at State Teachers College in Montgomery, Alabama, and Van Dyke and Bessie's first child, Henry L. Van Dyke Jr., was born. Raised in Montgomery, Henry Jr. became an award-winning novelist and creative writing professor at Kent State University.

During his son's childhood, Van Dyke attended the University of Michigan and earned a master's degree in chemistry. In 1934, Henry Sr. became chair of the State Teachers College's science department. He also founded the Alabama Association of Science Teachers and was a member of several organizations, including the American Chemistry Society and the American Association for the Advancement of Science. In the early 1940s, he enrolled in the PhD program in chemistry at Michigan State. He probably crossed paths with at least one other student of color in the department, Nelson Ging from Foochow City, China, who earned a doctorate in the early 1940s. In 1944, Van Dyke successfully defended and submitted his dissertation, "A Study of the Fragmentation of Some Tertiary Carbinols of Aluminum Chloride." "To Doctor Ralph Chase Huston the writer wishes to express his appreciation for the very helpful counsel and guidance given to him in this work," Van Dyke wrote in his brief acknowledgements. Van Dyke's mentor joined M.A.C. in 1922 and retired in 1950. During his long career, the accomplished chemist and teacher served as dean of the Division of Applied Science and the college's small-scale Graduate School, mentored and advised countless graduate students, and was recognized as a national leader in the realm of graduate education. In 1949, Huston served as president of the Midwest Conference on Graduate Studies and Research. A member of the progressive Peoples Church, he believed in racial equality and actively mentored Van Dyke.[34]

While the Michigan State community did not celebrate Van Dyke's accomplishments, the national Black press certainly did. The *New Journal and Guide* and *Chicago Defender* proudly announced Michigan State's first Black PhD recipient. After earning his doctorate, Van Dyke remained at Alabama State College and worked as a consultant overseas for the United States and Indonesian governments. After he retired, in 1968 Western Michigan University honored him with the Distinguished Alumnus Award in recognition of his long commitment of working with youth, leadership, service to his profession, and presidency of the National Institute of Science.[35] In December 1968, the MSU *Alumni Association Magazine* announced his accomplishments without acknowledging his history-making in East Lansing two and a half decades earlier. In the late 1960s, Van Dyke resided in Lansing and was a member of the NAACP, the West Side Neighborhood Association, and the mayor's Model Cities Policy Board. He lived a long life. In July 1993, Van Dyke died in Los Angeles, California. His doctorate from Michigan State opened many doors and made him stand out. The same could be said of Burleigh C. Webb.

Born in Greensboro, North Carolina, at age twenty this experienced farmer's son graduated from North Carolina A&T College in 1943. A talented Central Intercollegiate Athletic Association conference boxer and skilled calf handler, Burleigh then joined the U.S. Armed Forces and saw action in Normandy. A year after being honorably discharged, he earned a master's degree in crop and soil science from the University of Illinois and embarked upon a teaching career at Tuskegee Institute. In the late 1940s, Burleigh and his wife Alfreda relocated to Mid-Michigan to pursue advanced degrees. "We went together to graduate school at Michigan State," Alfreda fondly recalled in 1971. "That was our honeymoon. It was hard, studying and keeping house, but I enjoyed it so much that when it came time to leave, I got physically ill." Alfreda earned a master of science degree in anatomy and physiology. Burleigh earned a doctorate in farm crops in 1952. Inspired by the trailblazing research of M.A.C. legend Robert C. Kedzie, he specialized in new methods for growing sugar beets with green manures. The Webbs became the power couple at North Carolina A&T. Alfreda taught biology, and her husband taught chemistry and agriculture. In 1962, Burleigh was appointed dean of the School of Agriculture, serving his alma mater for more than three decades in this position. Meanwhile, in 1972, Alfreda, a mother of three, became the first Black woman to serve in the North Carolina House of Representatives.[36]

From the mid-1940s until the late 1950s, Michigan State PhD recipients Burleigh Carl Webb, Van Dyke, Fred C. Westbrooks, Monticello Jefferson Howell, and Bernard R. Woodson Jr. as well as a small group of African American doctoral candidates took temporary leaves from their teaching careers at HBCUs to bolster their academic credentials, engage in rigorous research, and increase their knowledge. They were in a league of their own. The same could be said of their progeny in the 1960s. During the peak years of the Black Campus Movement, MSU's assistant provost for equal opportunity and director of the Center for Urban Affairs Ronald Lee brought to the fore that of the more than 2,200 doctorates earned at MSU from about 1960 until 1969, only twenty-one were awarded to African Americans. Two of these PhD recipients, Robert L. Green and Charles Scarborough, were hired as professors at MSU.

In the spring of 1968, in line the Committee of Sixteen's recommendations to President Hannah, the MSU Graduate School began its efforts at recruiting Black graduate students. Created in the fall of that year, the Equal Opportunity Program offered fellowships to several hundred minorities by 1970. In the fall semesters of 1968 and 1969, respectively, there were ninety-nine and 104 full-time Black students enrolled in MSU graduate programs. A few Black graduate students attained leadership positions in the university. In the late 1960s, Morris Kinsey, a graduate student in physical education, was hired as an assistant football coach. In 1970, graduate student Don E. Ensley served as the assistant ombudsman for minority affairs, and doctoral student Nolen Ellison was appointed assistant to President Clifton R. Wharton Jr. By the mid-1970s, the number of Black graduate students increased. During the 1973–1974 academic year, there were about 440 Black graduate students enrolled, and in the 1974–1975 academic year there were 485.[37] In 1976, about five years after the Association of Black Graduate Students in Sociology and Black graduate students in psychology mobilized to create community and tutor Black undergraduates, a group of Black graduate students established the Organization of Black Graduate and Professional Students. By the late 1970s, the university sought to increase the number of Black graduate students by launching the Competitive Doctoral Fellowship for Minority Students.

Chapter 22

Virtually Segregated, Strength in (Small) Numbers

O n December 10, 1999, the MSU Board of Trustees approved the appointment of Clarence Underwood as director of athletics. It had been a long road for the sixty-six-year-old Alabama native who was overlooked for this high post several times before. Christmas may have arrived a few weeks early for Underwood, but this promotion was by no means at all a gift. By the late 1990s, he had lived a compelling life, full of ups and downs. He was a longtime and devout Spartan for more than forty years. A recipient of the university's Distinguished Alumni Award in 2003 and inducted into the MSU Athletics Hall of Fame in September 2017, as an undergraduate from his early to late twenties Underwood attended Michigan State University of Agriculture and Applied Science. Along with soon-to-be legendary John M. "Jumpin' Johnny" Green and a small group of other Black men, he enrolled in the fall of 1955, shortly after the ever so popular William A. Reid—a consummate "race representative" who at the time served as president of "more organizations than any student in the history of the organization"—graduated.[1] Born in the same year as Underwood, Green joined Julius McCoy on the basketball team and developed into a star center particularly known for his dominating rebounding skills. Named the 1958–1959 Big Ten MVP, Green arguably became Michigan State's most famous basketball player of his times during his senior year. Underwood graduated with a bachelor of science degree in physical education two years after his friend Green made MSU history by becoming the fifth overall pick in the 1959 NBA draft.

Beginning in the late 1960s—when he was hired as an assistant ticket manager and an assistant for student-athlete academic counseling—until three decades later, when he became the university's second African American athletics director, Underwood wore many hats with different job titles in the MSU Athletics Department. He had gained invaluable experience outside the at times cloistered MSU community. Shortly after earning his doctorate from MSU in higher educational administration and serving as the associate director for the MSU Alumni Association, from November 1983 until 1990 he served as the assistant commissioner of the Big Ten Conference. In August 1990, George Perles recruited Underwood back to his alma mater to serve as assistant athletics director for compliance and student services. At the time, Perles, the former assistant coach of the Pittsburgh Steelers and 1988 Rose Bowl–winning MSU coach, occupied a unique and unconventional position. He served as the university's athletic director and head football coach. In June 1991, Underwood was promoted to associate director, a new position created by Perles. By early 1994, Underwood was then elevated to senior associate director of athletics, working side-by-side with Merritt Norvell Jr., the university's first Black athletic director and staunch advocate for minority college coaches.

After Norvell abruptly resigned in mid-April 1999 to embark on a career as a search firm executive, Underwood was named interim athletics director. He was elated. For a moment, he uncharacteristically abandoned his humble disposition, in part a carryover from his upbringing in the Jim Crow South. "I'm not here just to sit in a chair until they hire someone," he declared. "I'm a director of athletics. And I'm going to make decisions to move our department forward." Seven months later, after he was appointed permanent director of athletics, he told reporters, "When I first decided to come to Michigan State, I never would have thought this could happen. I never dreamed I could have this long association with the university." Building upon Norvell's philosophy, Underwood vowed to "build upon our stability" and "academic and rules compliance."[2]

The consistently virtuous Underwood candidly shares valuable snippets of his early years and life as a student at Michigan State in his fascinating 2005 autobiography, *Greener Pastures: A Pioneer Athletics Administrator Climbs from Spartan Beginnings to the Top at Michigan State*. Born on October 10, 1933, in Marion, Alabama, he grew up in the small industrial city of Gadsden in an all-Black neighborhood called Black Creek. He belonged to a large family; he had twelve siblings. Once a sharecropper, his father held a variety of jobs during Clarence's childhood, often plugging away at "two consecutive eight-hour shifts" earning a meager one dollar per hour. Clarence's mother kept the home, a home full of "love, fun, and discipline." She taught her children valuable lessons about surviving while being Black and poor in the Jim Crow South. Like many of his classmates, Clarence learned the meaning of hard work at a young age. He began "adulting" early in his life. By age thirteen, he worked in a lumberyard performing arduous manual labor with other African Americans under the constant gaze of White supervisors who often berated him and his coworkers with racial epithets. Though he received support and learned many valuable lessons in his parallel Black universe, he also witnessed great despair. "Black folks were segregated, powerless, frustrated, angry, and insecure," he recalled in his autobiography. "They were confined to areas that didn't provide for constructive social outlets and they had no legal protections in their own neighborhoods."[3]

A talented baseball and football player, Underwood would become the first in his family to graduate from high school and attend college. He attended Carver High School, the first of numerous high schools in Alabama named in honor of famous botanist George Washington Carver. Opened in the late 1930s serving about a thousand students grades 1 through 12, when Underwood traversed the school's ebony halls, the student population was approximately 1,500. After graduating in 1953, the talented athlete with a Herculean work ethic and evolving self-confidence had dreams of attending Tuskegee Institute. He didn't have enough money to cover his tuition, so he decided to join the U.S. Army. Like millions of veterans, he saw the G.I. Bill—signed into law by President Franklin D. Roosevelt in 1944—as a practical way to pay for college. Like "Jumpin' Johnny" Green and the other estimated six hundred thousand African Americans who served in the U.S. Armed Forces during the Korean War, Underwood enlisted when the U.S. Armed Forces was theoretically desegregated by President Harry S. Truman's 1948 Executive Order 9981 and hoped his voluntary service would help him fulfill his educational dreams while proving his loyalty to a country that still denied many African Americans their most basic civil rights. He served for about two years, training as a paratrooper.

Several months before marrying his high school sweetheart, Noreese, Clarence—as he repeatedly recounted decades later—spontaneously decided to change his college preference from Tuskegee to Michigan State. On New Year's Day in 1954, he watched the Spartans compete against, and defeat, the UCLA Bruins in the Rose Bowl. It was the first time this native southerner had ever seen African Americans and Whites playing together on the same team. His curiosity was piqued. There were almost a dozen Blacks on Biggie Munn's talented team. This public display of athletic integration at Michigan State was enough to persuade Underwood to believe the university, located more than seven hundred miles north of his hometown in the Lower South, was racially progressive, if not completely integrated. He enthusiastically applied and was admitted. Underwood's utopian vision would soon be called into question. With Noreese and their three-week-old daughter, he ventured to East Lansing just in time for the 1955 fall orientation. There were approximately 4,700 incoming freshmen, and the most popular majors were business and public service and engineering. Underwood and his classmates could look forward to three terms (fall, winter, and spring) and a summer session. The total student enrollment for the 1955–1956 academic year was approximately twenty-three thousand. Approximately 80 percent of the students hailed from Michigan, and there were two dozen undergraduates from Underwood's home state. Perhaps overly optimistic and even a bit naïve, Clarence had not secured living arrangements prior to his arrival. The small towner was a courageous risktaker.

After being denied housing in East Lansing on account of his race, he was demoralized and wondered if he had made a mistake by coming to Michigan State. "It occurred to me after making numerous telephone calls without success that maybe I should have gone to

Tuskegee. . . . I started to feel the same insecurity I had experienced in the South—feelings of discrimination, restrictions and no protection. I couldn't help but wonder how the black football players were coping in the East Lansing community." Robert G. Clark Jr., who earned his master's degree in education from MSU in 1959 and in 1968 became the first African American to serve in the Mississippi House of Representatives since the late nineteenth century, shared Underwood's reservations about relocating to Mid-Michigan from the segregated Deep South. A Mississippi native and graduate of Jackson State University, Clark was drawn to MSU because of its highly ranked College of Education and, like Underwood, was enamored with its integrated football program. He soon learned that life for some Blacks in Michigan resembled Black life in the segregated South, observing that the state was just like Mississippi without the blatant segregation signs. Perhaps this helped radicalize Clark who, after being elected to the Mississippi Legislature, told listeners at the National Democratic Congress in Chicago that Black people needed real political power. "It's high time for us to win our self-respect and dignity. The only way this is to be done so it appears to me, is through political power."[4] Refusing to give in to the Jim Crow North system that Clark described, the determined and resourceful Underwood, as was the case with Clark, soon found several places to rent in Lansing's Black community. In the spirit of racial solidarity, several Black Lansingites Underwood stumbled across were sympathetic to his predicament. They looked out for him. He then finally secured an apartment in Spartan Village and embarked upon his goal of earning a bachelor's degree in physical education. During his freshman year, seasoned civil rights activist Rosa Parks refused to comply with the racial segregation of public buses in Montgomery, Alabama, 150 miles from his hometown of Gadsden. In early December 1955, the Women's Political Council and the Montgomery Improvement Association launched what would become a yearlong campaign against dehumanizing segregation practices in the city's public transportation known as the Montgomery Bus Boycott. On the first day of the boycott, approximately forty thousand Blacks refused to ride the buses.

Lansing's Black community was puny compared to Montgomery's during the 1950s. In 1950, there were 2,951 Blacks in Lansing (3.3 percent of the city's total population). In Underwood's hometown of Gadsden, in 1950 there were approximately 10,000 African Americans (19.4 percent of the city's total population). By 1960, Lansing's Black population increased dramatically to nearly 3,800. Led by activists like attorney and NAACP branch president Stuart J. Dunnings Jr., during Underwood's undergraduate years, Lansing's small Black community continued to be active around civil rights issues. Underwood rolled up to East Lansing two weeks after the horrific lynching of fourteen-year-old Emmett Till in the Mississippi Delta. In early October 1955, the Lansing NAACP branch held a protest at the Lincoln Community Center in response to the acquittal of Till's cold-blooded murderers. In the spring 1956 term, following the lead of civil rights activist and New York (Harlem) congressman Adam Clayton Powell Jr., there was a

15-hour observance of World Day of Prayer at Lansing's Union Baptist Church. Thousands of Lansingites attended services from 9:00 a.m. until midnight to take a stance against segregation across the nation and in support of the Montgomery Bus Boycott.

In mid-February 1957 during Underwood's sophomore year, twenty-eight-year-old Martin Luther King Jr., who had recently graced the cover of *Time* magazine, spoke at the Lansing Civic Center. The Dexter Avenue Baptist Church pastor had meaningful connections with the city. This was not his first visit to Mid-Michigan. His uncle, Rev. Joel L. King, was the pastor of Lansing's Union Baptist Missionary Church. In 1951, he relocated to Lansing from Spartanburg, South Carolina, where he was president of the NAACP chapter. He was active in the Lansing branch and during his nephew's visit was campaigning for city council. Underwood became a member of the George R. Collins African Methodist Episcopal Church, a popular place of worship for Black students since the days of Charles A. Warren, William O. Thompson, and Myrtle Bessie Craig. By the 1940s and 1950s, some Michigan State Black students attended Union Baptist, and the university's small Black student population, especially those in Joel's congregation, was aware of King's visit to the capital city. The *State News* advertised that rides would be made available to students who wanted to attend King's talk at the YMCA house at 314 Evergreen. Michigan State students were among the three thousand eager onlookers in the Civic Center's Veterans Memorial Auditorium.[5]

Like the thousands of Black women, men, and children who boycotted Montgomery's racist public transit system and those who courageously challenged segregation and discrimination throughout the nation, the road was not easy for Underwood. But he was accustomed to struggle, dating back to his days on the rough streets of Black Creek that taught him so much. He reminisced about life as a Black student at Michigan State during the early years of the modern Civil Rights Movement:

> I found that Michigan State wasn't a very accommodating institution for Blacks. In 1955 there were about 100 Black students on campus out of a total student population of about 18,000. Many of the Blacks were student-athletes. The campus was virtually segregated. The only thing different from the conservative South was that Blacks and whites could attend classes together, live in the same on-campus residence halls, live in on-campus married housing apartments, and play some sports together. It wasn't popular for Blacks and whites to socialize together. . . . Several black football players told me they got in some of the assistant coaches' doghouses after being seen walking across campus with some white female students. . . . Frequently I was the only Black student in my academic classes, the exception being physical education classes. Black students usually would assemble between classes at the grill in the Union Building. They had to travel to Lansing to have their hair done, attend parties, and for other entertainment. . . . The few Black students who lived in East Lansing rented rooms over the Smoke Shop on Grand River across from the Union Building. Several students roomed together in the unkempt housing unit with a communal bathroom.[6]

Not only was Underwood routinely the only Black student in many of his classes, but he didn't know of any African American employees in his academic area of interest and never had a Black professor at MSU and wasn't aware of any on campus. Except for David D. W. Dickson and, by the late 1950s, William Harrsion Pipes, Underwood and his Black classmates didn't have any mentors at the university who looked like them, who understood their personal histories and experiences. Like the majority of African American students at predominantly White institutions (PWIs) throughout the country, Underwood worked a variety of jobs while going to school. He had to, especially because he had a family to support while scraping together money for his tuition. He was a young and unexperienced father but a consummate family man. By the time he graduated, he and Noreese had three young children. "I didn't perform as well academically as I was capable," he said in retrospect. "It was tough becoming accustomed to working all night and then having to go to classes at least half of the morning."[7]

Facing mounting financial pressures, in the late 1950s Underwood briefly withdrew from the university to save money for tuition. He and his family hastily moved out of Spartan Village. He secured a job working for James Russell Riley Sr., Lansing's first Black funeral home owner. Born in Memphis, Tennessee, in 1922, Riley migrated to Detroit at the beginning of World War II to work at the Ford Plant in River Rouge. After graduating from Wayne State University, in 1950 Riley secured his license for the practice of mortuary science and worked for different funeral homes in Detroit. In the summer of 1957, he opened the Riley Funeral Home at 326 W. Main Street and advertised his services in cutting-edge mortuary science in the pages of the *Lansing State Journal*. While working for Riley for about a year, Underwood lived rent-free in a cramped apartment over the funeral home. The funeral home's motto was "Service with Sincerity." During its early years, Riley's business faced roadblocks. He had difficulty convincing members of Lansing's small Black community (that grew from 2,971 in 1950 to 6,745 in 1960) of the importance of supporting Black-owned businesses, especially funeral homes. In his mid-twenties, Underwood witnessed a Black man visionary ten years his senior establish a long-term blueprint for success in the Jim Crow North. This approach was rooted in perseverance and hard work.

Underwood pursued his undergraduate studies at Michigan State at an interesting phase in the history of African Americans and higher education. In the several decades before *Brown v. Board of Education of Topeka*, most northern PWIs continued their early patterns of excluding African Americans from their campuses. Even by the mid-1960s, White administrators at the so-called progressive institutions did not do much of anything to welcome Black students to their campuses or to fight against racial discrimination. During the first half of the twentieth century, it's safe to say that many PWIs outside the Jim Crow South permitted and in some cases promoted residential segregation on their campuses and did not publicize antidiscrimination policies. Around the time Underwood enrolled in MSU, only about 3 percent of students enrolled at PWIs were African American. No PWIs launched major strategic efforts to actively recruit African American students (apart from some standout football players) until decades into the

Clarence Underwood. Courtesy of Michigan State University Archives and Historical Collections.

second half of the twentieth century, particularly beginning after the passage of the Voting Rights Act of 1965, the Higher Education Act of 1965, and the Black Campus Movement of the late 1960s and early 1970s.

On these alienating PWI campuses, Black students like Underwood and his contemporaries faced what Allen B. Ballard dubbed in his classic 1973 *The Education of Black Folk: The Afro-American Struggle for Knowledge in America* "psychic and social trauma." They were not, however, as Ballard stressed, "'whitewashed' intellectually." In his estimation, many African American students who were "plunged into a white environment" before and during the decade after *Brown v. Board of Education* were not "content to enter the mainstream of American life." On the other hand, he believed they became more "aware of the contrast between the ideals of America and the conditions of the Black masses." He knew this from firsthand experience. Raised in a nurturing Black community in Philadelphia, he "had the misfortune" of attending Kenyon College in rural central Ohio in the late 1940s and early 1950s. With another male classmate, he integrated the college. In 1950, the closest city, Mt. Vernon, had a Black population of less than 2 percent. Unlike Ballard and Underwood and his Black contemporaries at MSU and other Big Ten universities, during the 1950s most African American students attended HBCUs.[8] As late as 1960, 65 percent of Black college students were enrolled in HBCUs. In 1964, 51 percent were, and by 1970 34 percent were. By 1973, approximately three-fourths of Black college students were enrolled in PWIs and more than 50 percent of the student protests on these campuses during the late 1960s and early 1970s were set in motion by Black students. African American scholars have argued that before and several decades after *Brown v. Board of Education*, Black students who attended HBCUs often possessed positive self-images, heightened notions of racial pride and cultural awareness, and high levels of academic achievement. This may have been one of the reasons Underwood wanted to initially attend Tuskegee Institute.

In their 1963 study *The Negro Student at Integrated Colleges*, Kenneth B. Clark and Lawrence Plotkin found that a primary reason for some Blacks not persisting at PWIs between 1952 and 1956 was financial need. They also discovered that Black students they surveyed (who were profoundly driven to succeed for their families, communities, and themselves) dropped out of PWIs at lower rates than their White counterparts. Seventy-five percent of Clark and Plotkin's respondents were regularly employed in some manner during the academic year, most often working in jobs unassociated with their studies.[9] This was the case with Underwood who habitually worked during his undergraduate years, so much so that he had to take a brief hiatus from coursework. When Underwood arrived in East Lansing in 1955, there had been some marked advancements made by African Americans at Michigan State beginning late in the previous decade. By the late 1940s, there were several Black firsts whose presence and efforts represented key milestones for the miniscule African American college community. In 1948, the first African American faculty member, David Walton Daly Dickson, was hired, and on May 1, 1948, the Gamma Tau chapter of Alpha Phi Alpha was founded. On the eve of Underwood's enrollment in MSC, the Delta Zeta chapter of Alpha Kappa Alpha Sorority, Inc. was founded on campus.

In 1946, a group of twelve African American men attending Michigan State created a social club called the Gentlemen of State. According to one of these men, William Thompson, the son of the first known Black to graduate from M.A.C. (William Ora Thompson, '04), this group met in late 1946 to decide which Black fraternity they wanted to join. After deliberating and several rounds of voting, they decided to pursue membership in Alpha Phi Alpha fraternity, the oldest Black fraternity founded four decades earlier at Cornell University on December 4, 1906. In the summer of 1947, nine of the Gentlemen of State were initiated into the Sphinx Club. "The first meeting of the Michigan State College Sphinx Club was held on campus at the start of the fall term in October 1947," and "officers of the pledge club were elected and a committee was formed to create a constitution." After the Epsilon chapter "initiated nine brothers from MSC and four from the University of Michigan," the nine Michigan State students established the Gamma Tau chapter in the dawning of May 1948.[10]

Several months after the chapter's founding, the editor of the *Pittsburgh Courier*'s Detroit edition lamented that Blacks in Lansing were not as aggressive as other African American Michiganders in demanding citizenship rights. In contrast, during the late 1940s, Alpha men across the nation continued to be active in the long Civil Rights Movement. Leading the way, Charles Hamilton Houston, "The Man Who Killed Jim Crow," and his protégé Thurgood Marshall worked with the NAACP in countless test cases for *Brown v. Board of Education*.

Those who joined the fraternity at Michigan State were aware of this historical legacy of activism. The "closed installation ceremony" for the MSC chapter took place in the Union Building on May 1, 1948, and the "formal founding banquet" was held in Lansing's Olds Hotel. William H. Haithco was the toastmaster, and President John A. Hannah was the featured speaker at the banquet. Several other MSU representatives were there including the college registrar, the dean of students, and the chapter's faculty advisor, John N. Moore, professor of natural science. For Hannah, the speaker of the hour, this was another opportunity for him to demonstrate his support of Black excellence. The chapter was officially presented its charter by the fraternity's national vice president and was, according to a reporter for the *Lansing State Journal*, "recognized" by the Spartan interfraternity council.[11] In addition to first corresponding secretary Thompson, the group included Carl Armstrong, President Herbert H. Burnett, Clarence Gray, Vice-President Haithco, Treasurer Frederick D. Johnson, William D. Richardson, Secretary Calvin Sharpe, and Thomas Walker. Many in this group were quite accomplished in distinct ways during and after their days in East Lansing.

Born in Saginaw, Michigan, in 1923, Haithco took great pride in his fraternity. He dedicated his 2007 self-published autobiography *From the Farm to the Pharmacist and Beyond* to his brothers and credited the organization with providing him with "an understanding of and appreciation of our place in domestic affairs, both as a fraternity and as a people." After graduating from Arthur Hill High School at age seventeen in 1940, Haithco enrolled in Bay City Junior College to study mathematics. During his second year in junior college, he was inducted into the U.S. Armed Forces (the air force) and was stationed in several southern states. In 1946, he was honorably discharged and returned to Saginaw. He wanted to go to the College of Pharmacy at U of M, but "was told that the school was 'filled.'" With about two years of junior college education and several years of military experience, he enrolled in Michigan State and found Alpha Phi Alpha to be a godsend. As he concluded in a Founder's Day speech, "there is not a man who is strong enough to break the bond of Gamma Tau." Haithco earned a bachelor of science degree in physiology and pharmacology from MSC in 1950 and then enrolled in U of M where he earned a bachelor of science degree in pharmacy in 1952. In Ann Arbor, he befriended members of the Epsilon chapter of Alpha Phi Alpha founded in 1909. In 1953, he received his license to practice pharmacy in Michigan and then in 1957 opened Haithco Prescription Pharmacy. He became, in his words, "the first black Registered Pharmacist in the history of Saginaw, Michigan." In 1969, he founded the Saginaw County Parks and Recreation Commission, served as its chair for more than twenty-five years, and was active in community service. Today, there is a seventy-six-acre public park and man-made lake in Saginaw Charter Township named in Haithco's honor. Shortly before his death, he authored an autobiography.[12]

Haithco's classmate and Alpha brother Fred Daniel Johnson, '50, was also a Michigander. Born in Carthage, Arkansas, in 1924 to a working-class family and raised in the Grand Rapids metropolitan area, he was standout athlete at Grandville High School. Track and field was his thing. As a senior, he was the state champion in the one-hundred-yard dash and the broad jump. In June 1941, President Roosevelt issued Executive Order 8802, prohibiting discrimination in the defense industry. Several years later, after graduating from high school, Johnson was among the first flock of one thousand African American men to join the U.S. Marine Corps and train at the segregated Montford Point, North Carolina. By 1949, approximately twenty thousand had trained there. As noted by an endearing sportswriter for the *Norfolk Journal and Guide*, Johnson "topped all competition" in "all-camp track meets" while stationed in North Carolina. On a crude, makeshift track, it's said he ran a 9.9 second one-hundred-yard dash.[13]

Veteran Johnson enrolled in Michigan State in the 1946–1947 academic year and was immediately noticed. In his first competition at home indoors against Ohio State University on January 25, 1947, in front of more than 1,500 onlookers, Johnson became "a triple winner," besting his competitors in the seventy-five-yard dash, the seventy-five-yard low hurdles, and the broad jump (he leapt an impressive 24 feet, 4 3/8 inches, immediately making him "one of the best in the nation in the event"). His performances were necessary to eke out the victory over the Buckeyes. "A new track and field star in the person of Fred Johnson, Grandville, Mich., colored freshman, blazed across the skies for Michigan State college at East Lansing last night," a sportswriter for the *Lansing State Journal* waxed on under the headlines, "Freshman Triple Winner as MSC Beats Ohio" and "Colored Boy Leaps over 24 Feet, Wins Twice More." The next several freshman track stars to make such a splash were Willie Atterberry who broke the world record for six hundred yards in the spring of 1957 and Marshall Dill who joined the Spartans about twenty-five years later and in 1972 held the world record for the three-hundred-yard dash. Their predecessor Johnson did not disappoint during the remainder of his time in East Lansing. In 1949, many concurred with one enthusiastic Black sportswriter who crowned him the "Most Outstanding Track Performer" of the year. In one of his last performances in the spring of 1950 at the Purdue Relays, he had "one of the most outstanding individual performances of the year," recording a 6.3 second sixty-yard dash (for context, in 1972 Herb Washington ran a 5.8 second) and 6.8 second time in the sixty-yard low hurdles.[14] In January 1952, along with Don E. Coleman, the first Spartan football player to have his jersey retired, Johnson was named to Michigan State's 10 Most Distinguished Athletes. Inducted into the MSU Athletics Hall of Fame in 1993, the 1949 All-American in the broad jump and low hurdles shared a world record in the sixty-yard dash low hurdles and holds the MSU indoor long jump record (7.74 m, 25 feet 4 ¾ inches) set on March 6, 1948, at the Central Collegiate Conference meet in the Jenison Fieldhouse.

Coach Karl A. Schlademan had nothing but high praise for the humble Grand Rapids speedster. "Fred is one of the finest young men I have ever coached," he remarked in early April 1950 after Johnson sustained a career-ending injury. "We all admired Fred very much. He was the heart and soul of our winning team, in spirit as well as in body. He's as game as they come." Johnson and the other "Timber Twin" Horace Smith were so talented that another Black Spartan sprinter had to wait his turn. In early June 1951, Schlademan hailed Flint native Jesse Thomas, who also

Members of the Gamma Tau chapter of Alpha Phi Alpha at Michigan State, circa 1948. Courtesy of Michigan State University Archives and Historical Collections.

played halfback and defensive back for Biggie Munn, "one of the best all-around track men since Jesse Owens." In the late spring of 1951, he scored twenty points with four first places in a meet against the "powerful Illini," making him "the biggest point producer for a single year in Spartan Track history." He was also the top individual scorer in the Big Ten indoor meet. A year before Thomas made history, in 1950 Johnson completed ROTC training and earned a bachelor's degree in adult and continuing education. Johnson was not solely defined by his athletic prowess; he was also a service-oriented community activist. In 1949 and 1950, representing his fraternity, he was a member of executive director Morrison Ryder's "regular staff" at Lincoln Community Center, in charge of "recreation work" for the younger boys. Dorothy A. Strothers was his counterpart for the girls. When not going to class, studying, or practicing in Jenison, Johnson worked shifts at the center sometime between 3:30 p.m. and 9:00 p.m. during the weekdays and on the weekends.[15] The center was busy during his undergraduate years. In 1949, the total attendance was more than eighty-four thousand, a significant increase from the previous year. While MSC students were among the center's most active volunteer workers, Johnson, as revealed in coverage in the *Lansing State Journal*, appears to have been more active than his fellow classmates. Education was important to him. He eventually earned a master's degree in education from MSU and later worked for the State Department of Education for more than twenty years.

The recognition Johnson and his fraternity brothers received from the college had its parameters. When the MSC chapter of Alpha Phi Alpha (Gamma Tau) was founded, discriminatory clauses in White fraternities' and sororities' constitutions were common. In response to a bill sponsored by Representative Gerald Graves (R-Alpena) that sought to ban discrimination in fraternities on state-sponsored college and university campuses, in late January 1951, the MSC student council, interfraternity council (IFC), and Pan-Hellenic council began to rethink the discriminatory policies embraced by campus organizations, especially by fraternities and sororities. By 1951, the IFC had not yet admitted a representative from Alpha Phi Alpha. In fact,

Members of Alpha Phi Alpha (*far right*) take off for the "Junior 500" in the mid-1950s. Courtesy of Michigan State University Archives and Historical Collections.

the fraternity had been deliberately denied membership. The excuse provided for this blatant unjust treatment by the council's adviser, a campus counselor, was that new fraternities, across the board, were not being admitted because of the so-called present war situation.[16]

After finally gaining membership in the IFC, amid accelerated Black student protests during the Black Power era, Alpha Phi Alpha withdrew from the IFC and called upon other "Black Greeks" to do the same. On October 9, 1969, the president of MSU's first Black fraternity, whose group at the time did not have a "seat on the council," announced its withdrawal from the IFC because its policies were "overtly racist" and the Alphas' main goal, unlike their White counterparts, was to work more closely with the Black community. "Black Greeks do not want to be isolated in a purely social-academic environment," pronounced Detroit native Charles Dillard. "We want to work in the Black community to improve the plight of Black people, and the IFC was dysfunctional to this goal." In response to Alpha Phi Alpha's decision, the vice-president of the IFC admitted that White fraternities failed to understand Black students' problems and were "not too relevant to their needs." The IFC spokesperson offered excuses for past and present customs, remarking, "it was almost impossible to do much more until they took part in the organization."[17]

Although African American students had been members of White student organizations before World War I, Alpha Phi Alpha was the first authentically Black organization in the college's history. At the time of the chapter's founding in the late 1940s, there were, according to William Thompson, "only about forty or fifty" Black students at the college out of a total population of more than eighteen thousand (i.e., less than 0.3 percent). Because of the de facto racial housing covenants in East Lansing at the time, the brothers faced challenges finding a home. For six years, they were the only Michigan State fraternity, out of a total of twenty-six, that did not have a home. In the summer of 1954, Alpha Phi Alpha finally found a place in East Lansing at 318 Elm Place, a spacious home about one block from campus that had fourteen rooms and could accommodate between twenty and twenty-four people. With support from "Alpha men of Detroit, Flint, and Chicago," the national fraternity presented the Gamma Tau chapter with $5,000 toward the purchase of the home.[18] In late February 1955, the fraternity held one of its first major events at their new home, a celebration of their housemother, Mrs. Pearl Jeffries. Among the more than one hundred guests were the housemothers and presidents of other fraternities and sororities, the Michigan State dean of students, and members of the newly founded campus chapter of Alpha Kappa Alpha Sorority, Inc.[19] During their early years, the brothers of Alpha Phi Alpha not only participated in on-campus events but, following Johnson's example, volunteered at the Lincoln Community Center. Their other early activities included fund-raising efforts for polio treatment in Ingham County. In 1949, the chapter was recognized at a national level when junior and Lansing native Howard Brockington—who during the 1950s earned bachelor's and master's degrees in music from Michigan State, taught music at Florida A&M, and worked on a doctorate degree in music at the University of

Iowa—was selected, beginning on January 1, 1950, as the editor of the fraternity's publication, *The Sphinx*.[20]

Perhaps the racial discrimination the men of Alpha Phi Alpha fraternity faced provided them with the fuel for their stellar performance in the popular fifth annual mile-long pushcart "Little 500" or "Junior 500" race around Circle Drive. On May 17, 1952, "with its black and gold racer," Alpha Phi Alpha won the final heat of a competition that included twenty-three other racers from a variety of campus organizations. In May 1953, the "fleet-footed runners" were victorious again and set a record, completing the course in three minutes and three seconds. While of course not comparable to a Spartan football or basketball game, this was a popular ritual that took place during the last three weeks of classes. The 1953 competition attracted an estimated five thousand students and East Lansing and Lansing residents. The Alpha Phi Alpha "pushers" continued to have success later in the decade. In 1956, the five-member team, composed of student-athletes, "rolled-up an easy victory" and set another record. The next year, navigating a modified course, they won again.[21]

According to Clarence Underwood, in 1955 "there weren't many" Black women students at Michigan State.[22] In the 1954–1955 academic year, the total enrollment of women in the university was approximately 7,635, and Black women accounted for significantly less than 1 percent of this population. The interest of Romulus, Michigan, resident Roy Lee Davis—the first Black to win a General Motors college scholarship "based upon outstanding achievement in high school," to attend MSU in the mid-1950s—was certainly not based upon the presence of other students like her.[23] A large number of Black women would not be on campus until the Black Power era. In 1964, the same year sophomore and pre-med student Scherrie Payne became the first Black woman elected Queen of Case Hall and Detroit senior and Alpha Kappa Alpha Gloria J. Davis was named "Outstanding Business Education Student," an individual photo of a Black woman student appeared on the cover of the *State News* for the first time.[24] Three years later when the total Black student population was about seven hundred, junior Patty Burnette was crowned Miss MSU and represented the university in the Miss Michigan Pageant. By the late 1970s, a group of Black women founded Noveau Noir Productions, and in November 1975, there were enough Black women on campus to launch the Ms. Black MSU contest, an event sponsored by OBA and supported by Ebony Productions, who brought entertainers like the Spinners and the Pointer Sisters to campus as a part of the year's inaugural Black homecoming festivities. The winner of the 1975 contest was Flint junior Danielle Render.

While Underwood's observation two decades before the founding of Noveau Noir was accurate, Black women built community during the early years of the modern Civil Rights Movement. In the mid-1950s, a teenage amateur columnist for the *Michigan Chronicle*, Southeastern High School 1954 graduate Barbara Bullitt, penned several pieces about her trips to East Lansing. During the fall of her senior year, she recounted "galivanting around Michigan State's beautiful campus" in her commentary titled "Scribe Escapes Typewriter Jungle to Visit College

Campus Cuties." During her visit, she stayed with Connie Chapman, a Cass Tech graduate who loved MSC and made "oodles of friends," and her Black roommates, Betty Carnegie and Yvonne Brown. With a small group of other Black women, Barbara attended the October 17, 1953, MSC homecoming football game against Indiana where, during halftime, Gideon Smith and his teammates from Johnny Macklin's 1913 squad were honored. Barbara felt totally comfortable hanging out on MSC's campus. She noted the "lovely manner" in which they were "received by everyone" they met. After the game, Barbara and her crew went to a party hosted by the Alpha Phi Alphas in Lansing where they met "scads" of Black students "from all over the U.S." In the late spring of 1954, she returned for the college's "Annual Open House" and the "Women's Inter-Dorm Council formal affair." With her friends, she attended the "Inter-Dorm formal" and a party in a dorm. In her column detailing this visit, she dropped the names of more than two dozen Black MSC students she met who made up approximately 25 percent of the Black student population.[25]

As Bullitt's experiences revealed, there were enough Black women on campus to create community and establish the first organization that explicitly validated and supported Black women's unique experiences in East Lansing. In January 1953, a group of Michigan State Black women came together and formed an Ivyette interest club to become intimately acquainted with the sorority. The Ivy Leaf Club was mentored by members of the Delta Tau Omega Alpha Kappa Alpha graduate chapter founded in mid-December 1947. The bright-eyed MSC students demonstrated their commitment to community service by, among other activities, reading to blind students and providing visitors with tours of the campus. After a year of such undertakings, they demonstrated that they were committed to the sorority's mission, and the graduate chapter announced their plans to initiate seventeen young women who would form the nucleus of the newly organized group. The first Black sorority on MSC's campus was founded on February 3, 1954, nearly fifty years after the founding of the sorority at Howard University on January 15, 1908. The chapter was set up in the Union Building with the help of the sorority's regional director who traveled from West Virginia State College. On February 6, there was a delightful follow-up event in the Union with two hundred guests, many donned in beautiful all-white dresses, to honor the founding of the new organization. The charter members included Yvonne Cofer, Winifred Covington, Barbara Cross, Mary Edison, Lou Jean Evans, Yvonne Jackson, Elizabeth Kennedy, Vernelis Kinsey (who was also a member of Delta Gamma Mu, the national fencing honor society), Inez Lawson, Janice McKinney, Jacqueline Martin, Sylvia Moyer, Gloria Richardson, Beatrice Ringgold, Ruth Thayer, Jesse Thomas, Jacquelyn Van Dyke, and Barbara House. In 1955, Lou Jean Evans served as president. Lansing native and J. W. Sexton High School graduate Yvonne Jackson—a talented soprano singer who by 1954 had her own disc jockey show and won a major local talent show in May 1955—was vice-president. Janice McKinney was secretary, and Barbara Cross served as treasurer. Given the small number of Black women on campus, it's not an exaggeration to conjecture that at least 30 to 50 percent of the Black women on campus joined the sorority.[26]

The organization initially served as a much-needed social club. One of its earliest events in the spring of 1955 was a variety show, "East Side, West Side," a collaborative program at the Lincoln Community Center with the Delta Tau Omega chapter who wanted it to be known they were an inclusive, democratic, and interracial group committed to racial harmony. In a letter to the editor of the *Lansing State Journal* in 1956, one member of the sorority reminded the newspaper that the organization was not a "Negro sorority" as the paper had noted. "To clarify that statement," Dorothy Wilson wrote, "Alpha Kappa Alpha is not a Negro sorority. We have members of other races all over the country. As educated people we are trying to refrain from such detailed unimportant factors and live as democratic as we can." Wilson's observations echoed a *Lansing State Journal* staff writer who several years earlier labeled the on-campus organization "M.S.C.'s first national, inter-racial and predominantly Negro sorority" that sought to "promote unity and friendship among college women" and purportedly had one white member on campus in February 1954.[27] The chapter at Michigan State may have been more freethinking than the Lansing graduate chapter, but they did not explicitly share Wilson's sentiments. For them the sorority was created by and for Black women who were and had been marginalized on and off college and university campuses throughout the nation.

While they were expected to act locally, Michigan State Alpha Kappa Alphas believed in the sorority's national efforts, including health projects, job training, scholarship programs, housing reform on college campuses, and civil rights initiatives. In the mid-1940s, Alpha Kappa Alpha Sorority, Inc. created the American Council on Human Rights (ACHR), an advisory group that called upon the U.S. government to enact civil rights legislation. When the Michigan State chapter was founded, the ACHR actively supported key antidiscrimination court cases like *Brown v. Board of Education*. On their own and in collaboration with Alpha Phi Alpha, the members of Alpha Kappa Alpha participated in and sponsored events at Lansing's Lincoln Community Center. In the mid-1950s, for instance, they invited the president of the Detroit chapter to speak at the popular Black movement center about the Supreme Court's dealings with segregation and the need for continual and vigilant challenges to racial discrimination. During their first year, they also joined the Lansing Association of Women's Clubs, an umbrella organization that brought together Lansing's "Colored Women's clubs" to serve "all colored residents of Lansing" and to "cultivate peace, harmony and happiness among all citizens." Members of Alpha Kappa Alpha made their presence known in Greek life on campus. In 1957 and 1958, they won the annual "coed spring Olympics and the junior pushcart derby." In 1961, teaming up with football players Sherman Lewis, Herman Johnson, and Dewey Lincoln, they made history by breaking "the course record twice at the 14th annual running of the Junior 500 pushcart derby."[28] The first Black sorority at MSU paved the way for future Black sororities. Approximately seven years after the founding of the MSU Alpha Kappa Alpha chapter, the Epsilon Epsilon chapter of Delta Sigma Theta, well known for their annual fall "Ice Breaker" fundraiser for Black causes that began in 1963, was chartered in late April 1961.

Members of the Delta Zeta chapter of Alpha Kappa Alpha at Michigan State, circa 1954. Courtesy of Michigan State University Archives and Historical Collections.

When President Truman signed the monumental Executive Order 9981 into law, there were probably no more than fifty African American students at Michigan State. In the fall of 1949, the executive director of the Lincoln Community Center was delighted to report that twenty-two African Americans from the Mid-Michigan area—five women and seventeen men—were enrolled at Michigan State. When Underwood enrolled six years later in 1955, there were no more than one hundred Black students on campus. By this time, Michigan State seems to have developed a reputation as an ideal destination for young African American Michiganders, especially Black Detroiters. In 1955, more than a few young Black scholars in the making featured in the *Michigan Chronicle*'s "Boy of the Week" column expressed aspirations of attending MSU. By 1960, there were approximately 130 minority students at MSU, the vast majority of whom were Black. As a result of concerted recruitment efforts, in the fall of 1967, the Black student population increased to about 690, and by the end of the decade, the Black student population reached 1,500. During World War II, the Cold War era, and the first decade of the modern Civil Rights Movement, the number of Black students on Michigan State's sprawling campus was noticeably microscopic. Member of the Student Speakers Bureau Julia Cloteele Rosemond stood out as she dazzled spellbound audiences with her intellect and oratory skills, winning the annual National Interstate Oratorical Association contest during her sophomore year. The Detroit native's accomplishments were remarkable, even more so because of her identity as an outspoken "race woman" during the era of World War II. A decade later, Dick Lord certainly stood out.

Voted the "best athlete" of his high school in Westmount, Quebec, the Canadian-born Lord could have played competitive collegiate hockey in Canada. MSC head hockey coach Harold Paulsen wisely decided to cross the color line, recruiting him in 1949, nearly a decade before Willie O'Ree became the first African American to integrate the NHL. Lord was the second African American to play varsity collegiate hockey in the United States. The first was forward Lloyd Robinson who played his first varsity game for Boston University in December 1947. During his first year, Lord saw the ice and excelled on the varsity squad coached by former AHL player and Michigan Tech coach Amo Bessone, affectionately known as the Father of Spartan Hockey. Lord was a highly skilled all-around player and exceptional academic, majoring in chemical engineering. Co-captain of the 1953 Michigan State hockey team, vice-president of the Canadian Club, and president of the Varsity Club, the first Black icer at the university was, like Gideon Smith and other Black athletes through the early years of the Civil Rights Movement, racialized by White sportswriters. He was referred to as the "aggressive Negro defenseman," "the flashy Negro," "the scrappy Negro center," the "Montreal Negro," and the "swashbuckling Negro center from Montreal."

Lord took his position as president of the Varsity Club very seriously. In mid-February 1953, he told a reporter for the *Lansing State Journal* that "any student caught wearing a varsity 'S' sweater who has not earned a varsity letter will be thrown in the Red Cedar river." He also publicly spoke out against the Big Ten commissioner who charged MSC with using a "Spartan Fund" to aid student-athletes. Known for his defense, scoring ability, and toughness, Lord was often targeted by opponents and had to defend himself from racially motivated attacks. This was the case in a January 1952 game against Michigan Tech when he knocked a challenger "out cold on the ice" with "a bad cut on his lip" after a "five-minute brawl." It's not surprising that during his junior and senior years, he led the team in penalty minutes. His pugilistic talents and his teammates' watchful eyes were not enough to keep him safe in early January 1953 when the Spartans played Michigan. In a blowout 0-6 loss to their rivals at home, Lord found himself at the bottom of a "pile up." He suffered an "injured back nerve" and was taken out of Demonstration Hall "on a stretcher to the college hospital for a checkup." A similar thing happened to Boston University's Lloyd Robinson who was taken off the ice on a stretcher in late January 1949 after sustaining a violent check into the boards. Neither Robinson's nor Lord's injuries were career-ending. Bruised up a bit, Lord finished the remainder of the season, playing his final games against the University of Minnesota in early March 1953. Years after graduating when he was the "only Negro in politics in Quebec," Lord explained the philosophy that helped him persevere at MSU: "The black man has a duty to himself to advance. He must be proud of his own heritage, his people, build his own businesses."[29]

While Lord was toiling away as an engineer for the City of Montreal's Public Works Department, in the spring of 1960 many White MSU students and East Lansing residents were surprised and in some cases outraged to see sophomore Ernest Green and other members of the campus NAACP picketing in front of S. S. Kresge on Grand River Avenue. This was the first major civil rights demonstration near or on campus sparked by Black students. African American students in East Lansing were by no means passive before this historic protest, during the undergraduate years of Rosemond, Johnson, Haithco, Dick Lord, and Clarence Underwood. With their heads held high, generations of Black students integrated Michigan State and made community on campus. Members of W. E. B. Du Bois's "Talented Tenth," they represented and vindicated Black people in East Lansing. They found fellowship and their sense of purpose in Lansing's Black community, especially in the Lincoln Community Center. Despite their small population, Black students at Michigan State made their presence known before, during, and nearly a decade after Underwood's undergraduate years. They integrated White spaces, excelled on the gridiron, represented the race by excelling academically, performed outreach, created organizations, built community and supported each other, and participated in civil rights activities. They were "virtually segregated," but valiantly and enterprisingly demonstrated strength in small numbers. In the process, they expanded the notion of what it meant to be Michigan State students and alumni.

Chapter 23

Belated Welcome

Buried deep in the countless pages of the September 1964 "Welcome Week" edition of the *State News*, the campus chapter of the NAACP invited those interested in their cause, "the fight against prejudice," to join them Thursday of every other week at 8:30 p.m. in the MSU Union Building. Though most of their members were Black, including their past leaders and current president, in their short column, "NAACP Seeks to Combat Prejudice," they emphasized they were "not an exclusively Negro organization." A Black-marshaled interracial civil rights group, they embraced diversity and inclusion, welcoming with open arms those "from a wide range of races, religions, educational levels, ethnic backgrounds, and age groups." As described in their *State News* column, the purpose of the campus NAACP in the early fall of 1964 was straightforward: "to combat prejudice and bigotry, whether it was racial or religious, and to inform the public about the evidence and implications of prejudice in society." Providing potential members insight into their recent activities, they recounted what they did during the 1963–1964 academic year. They had much of which to be proud. They told of how they conducted fund drives for civil rights struggles in the Deep South, invited speakers to campus, participated in civil rights "summer projects" in Mississippi, presented "test cases" to the Michigan Civil Rights Commission, and, most importantly, worked with the East Lansing Human Relations Commission and the East Lansing City Council to, in their words, "vigorously get legislation that would create effective housing ordinances prohibiting discrimination." They underscored, "the struggle continues."[1]

What the campus NAACP curiously didn't mention in overviewing their recent activities was that on June 2, 1964, a day after the East Lansing City Council voted 3-2 against an open housing ordinance, they picketed outside of the university's Administration Building, President John A. Hannah's office, and the East Lansing City Hall. They also didn't overview many of their vibrant and impactful activities during and before the summer of 1964. They clearly sought to enhance their legitimacy and historical provenance but were modest.

In the early 1960s, the NAACP launched their struggle against housing discrimination by calling upon the university to enforce their policy of not including prejudice renters on the university list of approved housing. According to the regulation, off-campus renters authorized by the university could not discriminate based upon race, color, creed, or national origin. With their early activities, strategic use of the *State News*, and resolute struggle to dismantle housing discrimination in East Lansing and urge Hannah and his coworkers to back their campaign, the NAACP became the first major Black student-led activist group on campus. They also did not mention that they were a Black first in their 1964 column. Perhaps they showed deference to Black Greeks, more than a few of whom were active in their organization. In the early 1960s, the Gamma Tau chapter of Alpha Phi Alpha fraternity held events like the "freedom hootenanny" to raise the university community's awareness of the injustices endured by Blacks in the South and were involved in various self-help programs in Lansing's Black community. Founded six years after MSU's Alpha Phi Alpha chapter, the university's Delta Zeta chapter of Alpha Kappa Alpha was heralded as being very active by a writer for the *Michigan Chronicle*. During the early 1960s, the sorority co-organized with the campus NAACP a Career Conference on Negro Opportunities and sponsored events like a fund raiser for underprivileged Black families in Lansing. Several sorors, like Patricia Cawthon and Sandra Sims, were active members of the campus NAACP.[2] In 1964, the MSU Omega Psi Phi chapter had twenty-five members, two of whom had been presidents of the NAACP. In the early 1960s, they began helping underprivileged and at-risk children in an effort to serve the Lansing community.[3] Though before the rise of the campus NAACP, Black Greeks advocated for Black excellence, supported civil rights activities on campus, and performed community service in Lansing's Black neighborhoods, they were relatively small and exclusive organizations and did not primarily focus on civil rights activities during their formative years.

The campus NAACP's decision to march in protest of housing discrimination in East Lansing during the warmest season of 1964—coinciding with the grassroots Freedom Summer voter-registration movement in Mississippi—was not, as some onlookers might have conjectured, spontaneously organized. In late 1961, under the leadership of Ernest Green and President Joseph S. Syfax Jr., the MSU NAACP was instrumental in holding the university accountable for its anti-discrimination off-campus housing-listing policy. During their formative years, the campus NAACP began urging the university to take a firmer stance against East Lansing landlords who discriminated against Blacks. On March 17, 1960, the Board of Trustees instituted a policy stating, "It was voted to reaffirm the Board's policy that there be no discrimination for race, creed or national origin condoned in University housing or approved off-campus housing."[4] In February 1964, the campus NAACP called upon the recently formed East Lansing Human Relations Commission to explicitly endorse an open housing ordinance. From February until the city council's vote against an open housing ordinance on June 1, the campus NAACP ceaselessly fought for African American students' civil rights. Building upon a tradition of radicalism and protest, a significant number of African Americans attending MSU in the early 1960s, including members of the NAACP, were from the South and had firsthand experiences with segregation.

Their fall 1964 coming out in the "Welcome Week" edition of the *State News* had been building up since early 1963. They were impacted by the wave of mass Civil Rights Movement demonstrations, as well as key turning points during the twelve months prior to their 1964 protests against housing discrimination, including the March on Washington Movement, the bombing of the 16th Street Baptist Church in Birmingham, Alabama, the murder of Medgar Evers, the founding of the Mississippi Freedom Democratic Party, and riots in Cambridge, Maryland. Though their most prevailing endeavor, the fight for housing rights did not define the campus NAACP. Agile and vocal, they were an effective consciousness-raising group. They tested the limits of integration at MSU, making sure Black people were seen and heard in East Lansing. More than a few incidents stand out. The twenty months before the fall of 1964 were intense for the campus NAACP, preparing them for the pivotal 1964–1965 academic year. Less than two weeks after the MSU Socialist Club invited leftist historian of the Black past Herbert Aptheker to campus, in late January 1963, the campus NAACP brought arguably the most outspoken and radical Black leader to campus. Still the leading minister under Elijah Muhammad's Nation of Islam, Malcolm X addressed one thousand students in the Erickson Kiva, encouraging the Black students to be "field Negroes" and reject the implications of integration. Questioning the protests to integrate East Lansing, Malcolm called for "complete separation" between the races. Despite their reluctance to embrace everything Malcolm preached, such as his belief that the federal government should set aside land for Blacks to create a separate nation within a nation, the members of the campus NAACP were energized by his plain speaking and deep love of Black people. They were starstruck when they huddled with this hero of the Black Freedom Struggle in the Union Sun Parlor for about an hour before his talk.

An incident in the late spring of 1963 helped set the tone of some Black student-activists' strategy of picketing. In late May, a group of young African Americans, including the president of the Lansing Youth Council of the NAACP, were denied entry into Alward Lake Park, located a few miles north of Dewitt, Michigan. Members of the campus NAACP heard of this, and a group of about twenty Black and White student-activists returned several days after the incident and picketed. They succeeded in persuading the Clinton County prosecutor to examine the case to determine if "legal actions" could be taken against the owners who believed that they "had a right to refuse them admittance to their privately owned park."[5] During the summer of 1963, members of the NAACP continued to be active. In mid-August, along with members of MSU Students for a Democratic Society (SDS), local Student Nonviolent Coordinating Committee (SNCC) comrades, other Mid-Michigan civil rights activists, and a sprinkling of MSU faculty and staff, they joined a protest in front of Lansing's City Hall, challenging the ineffectiveness of the recently passed Human Relations Ordinance establishing a special committee to critically examine racial discrimination in employment and housing in Lansing jobs.[6]

During the first several weeks of classes in the fall of 1963, graduate student Green returned to the issue of housing discrimination, reminding *State News* readers that "open and flagrant discrimination in housing" flourished in East Lansing. He criticized the university. By its "reluctance to speak out," he argued, MSU "is underhandedly sanctioning the housing discrimination in East Lansing." The liberal editors of the student newspaper agreed with Green, soon thereafter publishing an editorial on "East Lansing Discrimination." Green called upon White students to get involved by joining SDS, SNCC, and the NAACP.[7] During the fall 1963 semester, the NAACP held regular meetings in the Union Building and participated in civil rights events like the Michigan College Workshop on Human Relations in Battle Creek, Michigan, in late October and the first of its kind National Student Leadership Conference in Washington, D.C. in late November. To their surprise, historian and civil rights activist Vincent Harding told the five MSU students, including the campus NAACP president, and more than three hundred other attendees that East Lansing was "one of those northern communities having problems with segregation." Harding heard this from the vocal MSU students.[8] While the MSU students were in the nation's capital, Herbert Hill, labor secretary of the NAACP, spoke on campus.

In mid-January 1964, the campus NAACP amped up their investigations of cases involving discrimination against Black students when attempting to secure apartments for rent in East Lansing. The organization's president at the time was senior and well-traveled (by age twelve, he had been to eighteen countries and three continents) Columbia, South Carolina, native Maxie S. Gordon Jr. He earned three degrees from MSU (bachelors '64, MA '66, PhD '79) and participated in the university's Nigeria Exchange Program in 1964. In response to the housing discrimination faced by African Americans in East Lansing, he lamented that not enough students reported to the university landlords who refused to rent to Black students. It was common for landlords not to rent to African Americans, and Gordon expected that White students who were aware of this would boycott living in such racist establishments. Though editors for the *State News* during the early 1960s consistently supported open housing, as late as 1963, the paper still published advertisements for "whites only" homes and apartments. When Black students called them out for this, they apologized and ended the practice. By the end of January 1964, the campus NAACP publicized to the MSU community their stance on housing discrimination. Sampling from Malcolm X, they framed their cause as a human rights matter. In a letter to the *State News* editors, "Human Rights Rules," the organization defined the freedom to live where one wanted to as being a fundamental human right and called out the university for not doing enough to challenge housing discrimination in East Lansing. Given Hannah's position as chair of the CRC, the indictment was also leveled directly at him. For them, the Michigan State housing regulation of not patronizing landlords who practiced discrimination was "totally inadequate." The campus NAACP went a step further, arguing that the university was more concerned with policies pertaining to "the use of intoxicating beverages." These young Black student-activists concluded their statement by calling for broader meaningful climate restyling at the university, observing, "at this point, we are more concerned about a change in behavior which will prevent such landlords from discriminating against all segments of the student population."[9]

Shortly after the NAACP's letter was published, a move by the editors of the student newspaper ignited Black student-activists who used the pen as their sword. From February 16 to 22, the Lansing Negro Heritage Week Committee, a group cofounded by former MSU students, sponsored a Black history celebration. MSU's Black students took advantage of the week's activities. On the fourth day of the celebration, many Black students were shocked by what they read about Alabama governor George Wallace in the *State News*. While traveling in Chicago, six staff writers for the *State News* ran into Wallace, interviewed him, and then published an editorial, "Lesson from a Governor," as well as a supplemental article, "Wallace Doesn't Fit 'Devil' Image." The student journalists argued that Wallace was a "friendly person," "a personable gentleman" whose segregationist ideas were normal given his background. They essentially opined that he, like all people, was a product of his environment and upbringing. They surmised he was "sincere" in his "convictions," finding "no fault" with his segregationist and racist thought and behavior. On top of this, the student paper featured a large photo of Wallace smiling. The *State News* rolled out the red carpet for the man who defied Hannah and the CRC and, a year earlier during his inaugural speech, shouted, "I say segregation now, segregation tomorrow, segregation forever."[10] Given the recent protests against discrimination waged by the campus NAACP, one wonders what motivated the six White students in the college's national journalism honor society to celebrate such a racist. They ignored the well-being of their Black classmates.

The campus NAACP wasted no time in responding to this affront. On Wednesday February 19, 1964, they were among the sixty students who picketed the *State News* office in the Student Services Building. President of the campus NAACP Maxie S. Gordon Jr. asked the *State News* if its staff had "forgotten the bombings, the killings, the treating of people like animals." He resented that his White classmates could not see beyond their own privilege. Gordon came from Columbia, South Carolina, and he knew, all too well, segregation. "In the South you know where you stand. There is no contact between Negroes and whites. There are few phonies. You soon learn that the white man is not your friend." Gordon continued, "One reason I left South Carolina was to leave segregation and get to know people from all walks of life. When I came to MSU I was disappointed. Here students are brought together. There is integration but not interaction."[11] Green also voiced his disappointment with the positive portrayal of Wallace.[12] The controversy continued for about a week. The student newspaper apologized while underscoring that no group would censor or control them. The Student Congress passed a resolution chastising the segregationist actions of Wallace, and Gordon wrote a letter to the editor insisting that Wallace's actions against human dignity needed to be reprimanded. History professor James R. Hooker, who later spoke to the campus NAACP on the "Dilemma of the White Liberal When He Associates Himself with Negro Movements" and had plans to open a center for the study of African American history on campus, closed ranks with the campus NAACP and indicted the author of the article on Wallace. Discussions about the Wallace article continued for more than a week with various points of view being expressed in letters to the editor. Most White student commentators did not understand the campus NAACP's dismay. Nina Simone's visit to campus on February 25, 1964, helped present a counternarrative to the flattery of Wallace. She fittingly ended her performance in the MSU Auditorium with her famous civil rights anthem, "Mississippi Goddam." "You don't have to live next to me," she chanted. "Just give me my equality."

In early March 1964, the campus NAACP embraced a new cause. From 10:00 a.m. until 2:00 p.m. on March 4, they sponsored "all-university protests" as part of a fund drive for voter registration in Hattiesburg, Mississippi. Among other students involved in the "fast for freedom" movement were chair of the drive sophomore Sandra Jenkins, Gordon, campus NAACP president-elect Melvin Moore, MSU Friends of SNCC president Michael Davis, and freedom singer and junior Gloria Gibson. Robert L. Green and campus pastor Rev. John Duley were among the featured speakers. The "fast for freedom" organizers set up collection booths across campus and raised $450 to send to Mississippi to help with voter registration. Alabama native Jenkins schooled *State News* readers about the challenges faced by Blacks in the South who sought to exercise their right to vote. "Negroes are forcibly and systematically withheld from the right to vote in Mississippi," she declared. From March 3 until March 6, the *State News* published a four-part series on "racial problems" in the United States featuring the voices of Black undergraduate students. The editorial writer interviewed several Black students, introducing them as "your classmates" and "the story of the American Negro living in the United States today." Gordon shared his experiences with southern racism. He pointed out that racism in the North could be harder to decipher than in the South. "In the South you know where you stand," he observed; "in the North a smile and a word don't mean much." Other African American students shared their personal experiences growing up in the Jim Crow South. A freshman from Georgia affirmed, "Slavery is not a thing of the past. . . . There is no justice for the Negro. . . . It hasn't been 100 years since the killing and the brutality. For the Negro the war has never ended. He is still fighting for his freedom."[13]

In mid-April, the campus NAACP invited twenty-nine-year-old Robert Moses, SNCC activist, codirector of the Council of Federated Organizations, and skipper of the Freedom Summer Project, to MSU. Guest lecturing in a sociology class, Moses reminded MSU students of the intimate connections between racial discrimination and poverty and sought to inspire MSU students to participate in the freedom schools and the voter registration movement in

Mississippi. His overarching message of fighting discrimination resonated with Moore and his fellow activists' concerns with housing bias in East Lansing. In late April, accompanied by the "Freedom Singers," civil rights activist and comedian Dick Gregory performed at MSU as part of his month-long fund-raising tour for SNCC at northern colleges and universities. Gregory's much anticipated visit was cosponsored by the All-University Student Government, the MSU chapter of the NAACP, and Alpha Phi Alpha fraternity. Henry Hagood, the fraternity's president, commented that Gregory was going to "shake Michigan State out of its indifference toward the racial situation in the U.S." He proclaimed, "Gregory is here to let all know that the Negro is ready, not in part, but totally." African American students and members of the campus NAACP were among the two thousand students who packed into the MSU Auditorium. Mixing comedy with real talk, Gregory said much to rouse African American students to act.[14]

Prophetically warning his listeners that the summer was going to be "frightening" and full of demonstrations, Gregory energized Hagood, Moore, and their fellow student-activists. "This is a revolution and in a revolution there is no room for compromise," he declared. Challenging White students in the audience, he asserted that "northern whites aren't the great friends of the Negroes they once thought they were." Pertaining to East Lansing's controversy over open housing, Gregory observed, "the North's the worst. You have more problems integrating a neighborhood in Lansing than Jackson, Mississippi." He also critiqued Big Ten football programs for not having any Black coaches. "If I was a Negro athlete, I wouldn't play for them," he trumpeted.[15] The event was a smashing success. In the days after his visit, the *State News* reprinted some of his most memorable jokes and observations, and the event raised $1,300 for SNCC's civil rights activities.

Gregory's speech and performance provided more motivation than NAACP executive secretary Roy Wilkins's keynote address did before a crowd of seven hundred at MSU's Fairchild Theater. In commemoration of the tenth anniversary of *Brown v. Board of Education*, on May 8 and 9, MSU hosted a symposium on the impact of segregation and integration on education in the United States. Joining Wilkins at this event were Black leaders and scholars James Narbit, Kenneth Clark, and Wilson Record. Following the event, the *State News* featured an image of Wilkins with Hannah, further promoting Hannah's image as a strong advocate of civil rights. Wilkins opened his much anticipated oration by praising President Lyndon B. Johnson's and Hannah's approaches to civil rights, neglecting to speak directly to MSU's Black students who attended his talk on "Education and the Racial Crisis." He stressed the obvious, that he thought the racial unrest of the 1960s was one of the most challenging domestic issues since the Civil War. This was something that Black students knew. Psychologist Kenneth Clark spoke more directly to the sentiments of Black student-activists frustrated with East Lansing's discriminatory housing practices.[16]

In the spring 1964 term, a first-year student from Detroit told *State News* readers, "Perfect equality will never occur in this generation. Everything still depends on what happens within the white man." This young Black woman recognized that racial discrimination and "racial problems" were not created by Black people and, therefore, could not be extinguished by them alone. Her classmates might have shared her pessimism. They may have believed that racial equality on campus hinged on "what happens within" Hannah.[17] Many who were active in the Long Black Student Movement thought otherwise. They believed they could alter the course of history and, more importantly and realistically, change Michigan State culture for the better. The explosion of activism during 1963 and 1964 built upon campaigns and struggles sparked in the 1950s. The campus NAACP was the heart and soul of the early Black student movement at Michigan State University of Agriculture and Applied Science.

Chapter 24

Early Black Student Movement

I n their column in the 1964 "Welcome Week" edition of the *State News*, "NAACP Seeks to Combat Prejudice," the organization's spokespersons recounted they had been "active at MSU for over ten years." This claim was a bit of an exaggeration. The organization was not founded until late in the 1957–1958 academic year. Through the mid-1960s, the campus NAACP branch provided reformist students the opportunity to directly participate in organized civil rights struggles on and near campus. It served as a small Civil Rights Movement center, offering African American students leadership opportunities and invaluable experience. Martha Mallard (later known as Martha "Bunny" Mitchell), who studied journalism at MSU, recalled that she used the "political organizations" such as the campus NAACP as "stepping-stones" for her future career as a special assistant to President Jimmy Carter. In the late 1950s when there were, in her estimation, "only a few hundred" Black students on campus, she helped in the "revitalizing of the campus NAACP and raising money for the sit-ins in the South." She recalled, "I pursued things I wanted to do without stopping to think a black man or a black woman should be doing this. I worked to change the school's rules because they didn't make sense."[1]

In the spring of 1960, under the leadership of eighteen-year-old Ernest Green, members of the newly founded and small but bold campus NAACP launched the first major Black student–led civil rights campaign in East Lansing that garnered significant local media attention. The Lansing chapter had been launched in the spring of 1919 with about one hundred members and was active in Ingham County. More than a few M.A.C. and MSC students and graduates either joined the organization or participated in their programs during the first half of the twentieth century. During the 1930s and 1940s, representatives of the spirited Detroit chapter closed ranks with several courageous Black students to challenge discrimination on Michigan State's campus.

The campus NAACP's activism laid the foundations for the explosion of Black student activism at MSU during the late 1960s and early 1970s when Black students throughout the nation began attending predominantly White institutions (PWIs) in larger numbers than ever before. This generation directly and unapologetically demanded that institutions of higher learning change to accommodate them. During what Ibram X. Kendi calls the Black Campus Movement, "hundreds of thousands of black campus activists" and their diverse group of allies "requested, demanded, and protested for a relevant learning experience." They ultimately sought to "reconstitute higher education."[2] Kendi also posits an important argument relevant to interpretations of Black student activism at MSU. He introduces the notion of a "Long Black Student Movement," highlighting that the peak years of the Black Campus Movement, approximately 1968 until 1972, belonged to a longer historical tradition, a sustained struggle to democratize higher education waged by generations of conscientious Black students. Conventional written and oral history accounts of Black student activism on MSU's campus largely ignore the existence of a "Long Black Student Movement" and the contributions of the campus NAACP. At the expense of pre–Black Power era student-activists' accomplishments and the NAACP's historical legacy, there has been a tendency to highlight the undeniable eruption of Black student activism "on the banks of the Red Cedar," focusing on the last two years of the 1960s when Black student enrollment and a corresponding militancy was on the rise. Such a narrow, shallow, and ahistorical depiction of the Black Campus Movement at MSU neglects to acknowledge the organized efforts of Black student-activists before the late 1960s as well as the consequential Black student movements during the early 1970s.

Don E. Coleman's assertion in his dissertation, "The Status of the Black Student Aide Program and the Black Student Movement at Michigan State University," that the Black Students' Alliance (BSA), founded in January 1968, was the first *major* Black student organization at MSU is not totally spurious or misleading. BSA definitely was the first on-campus Black activist organization with a large and diversified following to develop an intricate infrastructure.[3] By February they claimed to have about three hundred members and soon gained university-wide recognition and an appreciable seat at university bargaining tables. BSA was the first Black student organization to directly influence the university to institute sweeping and long-lasting changes. But beginning a decade before BSA came on the scene, the small group of Black students in the campus NAACP launched and sustained a powerful movement. They challenged the university and the city of East Lansing to treat African Americans as first-class citizens, paving the way for those Black student-activists who later adopted different rhetorical and strategic approaches. The Black Campus Movement at MSU is best viewed as a struggle that began in earnest with the campus NAACP's activism during the late 1950s and early 1960s. After the mid-1960s, the organization seems to have faded into the background as a new generation of Black students came to campus with different visions of activism and Black consciousness.

About four years after the founding of the Delta Zeta chapter of Alpha Kappa Alpha, in mid-January 1958, a day after President John A. Hannah told members of the Spartan Roundtable that "the most important problem the United States faces in 1958 is the race conflict," Stuart J. Dunnings Jr., president of Lansing's chapter of the NAACP, spoke to students in the MSU Union Building about developing a different type of organization that would serve the Black community. Approximately fifty students attended the meeting, about a half dozen of whom were White. Dunnings encouraged Black students to launch a Youth Council campus chapter of his organization to help them integrate more into campus life. As Detroit junior Vivian A. Chillis, one of the first African Americans to serve as the president of a residence hall, told Hannah in the fall of 1958, the dormitories were not yet "fully integrated." Dunnings suggested the main purpose of the campus NAACP be to "reach some agreement with East Lansing householders in regard to Negro off-campus housing." By the end of the productive meeting, they agreed the goals would be "Better understanding of the discrimination situation; Encouragement of social integration of this university; Formulation of a central group to aid in cases of discriminatory practices in the area."[4] Sometime shortly after Dunnings's visit, a chapter of the organization was founded at MSU as a registered student group by Samuel Harris, the organization's first president, and his committed workmates. While Dunnings helped inspire the mobilization of the campus NAACP, a small group of MSU students had already submitted an application "for official recognition" from the national branch of the organization in December 1957. Through the mid- to late 1960s, many Black student activists honed their leadership skills through their membership in the NAACP. In 1965, for instance, Muskegon, Michigan, native Alfred P. Williams III served as the chairman of the NAACP's National Youth Work Committee and after graduating developed into a respected Black community leader in South Bend, Indiana.[5] In the early 1960s, the campus NAACP was transformed by a young African American student celebrity who had made history shortly before arriving in East Lansing.

In late May 1958, Green, the first African American to graduate from Central High School in Little Rock, Arkansas, applied to Michigan State with the intention of studying law. An energized university official told local reporters the MSU community would be "eager" to have him join the Spartan community, that "he could make a valuable contribution here." On June 19, the front page of *Lansing State Journal* carried the story, "Negro Grad Is Admitted: Alumnus of Little Rock's High School Formally Accepted at MSU." Shortly thereafter, Green accepted the offer of admission. His decision made national headlines, placing East Lansing and Hannah further into the civil rights limelight. The dean of students erroneously claimed that Green was joining "hundreds" of other Black students. Green shared with reporters that MSU was attractive to him because of its reputation as being a "progressive" school when it came to the issue of civil rights, as symbolized by Hannah's role as chair of the U.S. Civil Rights Commission (CRC). In a

President of the campus NAACP Ernest Green leads the picketing of Kresge in East Lansing to protest segregation practices at lunch counters in dime stores located in southern states. Courtesy of Getty Images.

January 2003 interview with the History Makers, "the Nation's Largest African American Video Oral History Collection," Green disclosed he was also attracted to MSU because Black faculty member William Harrison Pipes was there and he had family in Detroit, Mr. and Mrs. Lewis L. Davis. He received several scholarships to support his educational pursuits in East Lansing, including a full tuition scholarship from an anonymous donor. This benefactor, as Green later discovered, was President Hannah. In the fall of 1958, Green was welcomed to campus; his arrival was widely covered in the local press. He was assigned to a room in Shaw Hall with a White roommate from Grand Rapids. Reflecting upon this arrangement, he was surprised to be paired with him because of university housing's penchant for placing "all black students together." Throughout his four years as an undergraduate student living in the dorms, Green had White roommates. According to him, he stood out on campus not only because he was a member of "the Little Rock Nine," but because he was a Black student on an academic scholarship. Green recalled an interaction he had with his one of his Black classmates:

> And in fact there were very few black students, black male students there on academic scholarship. I always tell the story I, I got stopped by a fellow. . . . And he said, he stopped me kind of the, the first or second day I was on campus. He said what do you do? I said what do you mean what do I do? I'm a student here. No, no, he said what do you do? He said you're too small to play football, you're too short to play basketball, you look too slow to be on the track team. You must be here on a soccer scholarship. 'Cause his view was that, that anybody at Michigan State, a black male, was there on some athletic scholarship. And the fact that you were there on an academic scholarship was just unheard of. So it, it, it began to click in my head that I would—if I was going to achieve the goals that I had set down for myself, that I needed to finish out that undergraduate degree and try to concentrate.[6]

The unpretentious Hannah did not want to "make a big deal" about Green's decision to attend his university. But the fanfare was unavoidable. Shortly after his arrival, on October 9, 1958, Green made "his first public appearance" on campus, speaking at the campus NAACP's first meeting of the year at 8:30 p.m. in the Union. The next day, on the front page of the *State News* was a brief summary of his talk, "Little Rock Negro Tells His Story." Seeking to reinforce amicable relations between Black and White students on campus, he remarked that most of his fellow White students at Little Rock were "friendly," that the hate came from "a small minority of radicals" and "students with lower scholastic averages." He embraced Martin Luther King Jr.'s strategy of nonviolent direct action. "When you are spit on," he said, "it is easier to walk away. This makes the person feel inferior." He also shared his story with Lansing's Black community. In January 1959, he sermonized to members of the Lansing Youth Council of the NAACP at Friendship Baptist Church. In June, the *Lansing State Journal* acknowledged Green's completion of his first year in a short editorial under the large and bold header, "Negro Little Rock Pupil

Completes MSU Exams." Green recounted that he thoroughly enjoyed his first year, and it proved his "theory that people can get along together without strife if they forget questions about race and color." For him, the racial atmosphere at MSU was "harmonious." Eight months earlier when asked about his plans for the academic year, he told a reporter he wanted to "become a normal student" and participate in "YMCA work and other extra-curricular activities." By his second year at MSU, such activities were decidedly in the realm of civil rights.[7]

On Saturday, March 5, 1960, amid heated campus debates about compulsory ROTC, eighteen-year-old Green, a prelaw major who was president of the newly established interracial MSU NAACP branch, organized picket-line protests outside of S. S. Kresge and F. W. Woolworth stores in East Lansing. Between forty and fifty student-activists joined the Arkansas native. Green stressed that the protests were inspired by the Greensboro sit-ins and not specifically targeted against the East Lansing dime stores. Instead, the demonstrations sought to castigate the national offices that permitted discrimination against African Americans in the South. The vice-president of the campus NAACP was more forthright with the significance of their protest. "The national office has not done what it is capable of through the legal process," Jerome McFarland pronounced; "the younger generation wants to use the same processes, but it wants to take action on the problems of removing the obstacles which prohibit the Negro to vote in the South."[8] Waged by Black and White students, the peaceful protests on busy Grand River Avenue lasted for about three hours and received a significant amount of local media attention, scrutiny that Hannah hoped to avoid. A small group of Whites, including a few East Lansing High School students, heckled them, and on the Monday following the protest, the *State News* published an editorial, "Inviting Trouble," chiding them for their tactics. The NAACP clapped back with a long letter to the editor, and former president Samuel Harris, in a concise and satirical commentary, reminded his White classmates that the days of "Uncle Tom" were long gone. Several days after the boycott, members of the group joined about four hundred other orderly NAACP demonstrators from across the state at the Capitol Building in the cause of creating stronger civil rights legislation.[9]

By his sophomore year, Green was the leading Black student-activist on campus. As president of the MSU NAACP chapter, he organized events, invited speakers to campus and, along with members of the MSU student government, raised funds to help Black students in the South who were arrested and expelled from school for directly confronting segregation.[10] He was also astute enough to persuade President Hannah to support the group's efforts. On April 11, 1960, Hannah spoke at an event on campus featuring an NAACP leader from New York City. Several months after their initial picketing campaign, on May 17, 1960, the campus NAACP picketed the East Lansing Kresge store again from about noon until 2:00 p.m. Green told reporters that the demonstration marked the sixth anniversary of *Brown v. Board of Education* (1954). MSU professor Charles P. Larrowe, who served as the group's adviser, led the march for the first hour. Along with five other faculty members—Carl Brehm, Andrew F. Brimmer, John P. Henderson,

Roger Wescott, and Robert Repas—Larrowe voiced their displeasure to the provost about the presence of a plainclothes police officer who was spotting taking pictures at the protest. They demanded to know how the photos were going to be used. Hannah responded, indicating that two plainclothes officers from the East Lansing Police Department were asked to be on the scene because of "potential retaliatory activity" by a local white supremacist group. Larrowe and his colleagues were adamant that the photos be destroyed and not placed within students' and faculty's "political files." Such surveillance practices, he reasoned, discouraged "students from engaging in activities that will help achieve the university's major goal."[11]

In late 1960 and early 1961, Green and other members of the campus NAACP (approximately 12 percent of whom were White in late January 1961) wrote and produced a play on the Black experience "from Africa to the present" in celebration of Negro History Week. Perhaps sampling from L. M. Collins's 1960 poem, the play was titled *A Man Called Nigger*. "It takes a more mature outlook than anything thus far on the subject," the campus NAACP's public relations and research director and founder and first president Samuel Harris commented; "the title is startling, but so is the play." In mid-February 1961, about a month after the assassination of the first prime minister of the Democratic Republic of the Congo, Patrice Lumumba, which rattled Green and other Black Michigan State students, radical NAACP member Ivanhoe Donaldson advertised the play—directed by St. Louis, Illinois, sophomore Janet Ross and choreographed by Detroit junior Gerry Adams—as constituting a combination of "song, dance, and drama . . . to pose the problem and elicit a desire to a solution."[12] On February 16, after many rehearsals, the play was performed in the Union Building Ballroom to a capacity crowd of more than six hundred. The cast was interracial and included more than forty students. It was the first performance of its kind on campus. After the showing, one of President Hannah's aide's, James Benison, accepted an award for his work as the chair of the U.S. Civil Rights Commission.

The play and Green's leadership of the MSU NAACP branch made national headlines in the Black community. In May 1961, around the time a resolution was passed stating that fraternities and sororities had to remove discriminatory clauses from their charters by January 1, 1962, the popular African American magazine *Ebony* featured an article on Green, "Little Rock Hero Makes Good Up North: Ernest Green and the NAACP Chapter at MSU." Praising *A Man Named Nigger*, *Ebony* portrayed Green as a transformational and humble young leader who avoided the limelight. "It was not a role that he had sought, but one which was thrust upon him by despairing fellow students, who had cast about for strong leadership capable of giving new life to a limp and faction-torn organization." Based upon their conversations with other Black students, the *Ebony* writer observed, "Perhaps his greatest asset is his quiet, personable and unassuming air of efficiency with which he moves about." A classmate added, "He goes about things quietly, but he gets things done." Included in the article are more than five photos of Green as well as photos of scenes from the play and members of the NAACP, Black and White. *Ebony* portrayed MSU as a racially progressive PWI, showing Whites and Blacks congregating together and even claiming MSU had six hundred Black students (approximately 2.7 percent of the total East Lansing campus student population). One wonders how *Ebony* came to this conclusion. In 1960, there were only approximately 130 total "minority students" enrolled in Michigan State, the majority of whom were African American.[13]

In May 1961 as his presidency of the campus NAACP came to an end, Green reiterated to *State News* readers the goals of the organization: to "eradicate the misconception of the Black man," highlight the contributions of Blacks to American history, challenge the notion that Blacks possessed "innate racial traits," and "provide means by which persons of the university have closer social contact with Negroes if they so desire." He was proud of the progress his coworkers had made, calling attention to their demonstrations against dime-store chains whose national offices permitted segregation in the South and challenges to the university's off-campus housing policies. He was proud of an interracial dance they sponsored, "A New Twist to Integration," that attracted five hundred students, and their 1961 play.[14] No doubt, the coverage he received in *Ebony* further contributed to his enduring celebrity-like status. In early June 1961, Green was among the spotlighted speakers for a Freedom Sunday program at the Friendship Baptist Church sponsored by the Lansing branch of the NAACP. More than 450 people listened to him reflect upon his experiences in Little Rock and work with the MSU NAACP.

In the early 1960s, a small group of White students at MSU actively supported African Americans' struggle for civil rights, and the *State News* regularly kept its readership aware of Civil Rights Movement episodes and developments throughout the nation. During Green's presidency, the membership and influence of the campus NAACP noticeably increased. In the dawning of the decade, one White student seems to have stood out in the MSU community for his civil rights activities. In chronicling the history of radicalism at MSU during the 1960s, a writer for the *State News* even intimated that this student was the most important on-campus civil rights activist during a period of student apathy. "1961: in this year, as through the rest of the Kennedy era, semi-complacency rather than supposed involvement of concerned youth was the rule. . . . The big radical event of 1961 was the arrest of student Woollcott Smith in Mississippi for freedom-riding."[15] In late July 1961, Smith, a senior from East Lansing whose father was an MSU psychology professor, was arrested in the Magnolia State "on a charge of provoking a breach of peace when he rode into town as a freedom rider." After spending four weeks in the Mississippi State Penitentiary, he was released on $500 bond and was scheduled to appear in court in late March 1962. Formed in February 1962, the Student Committee for Woollcott Smith launched a fund-raising campaign, the Woollcott Smith Fund, to raise $2,000 for his retrial legal expenses. In the process of publicizing Smith's case, they sought to "create widespread concern over the racial problem." The students on the committee, including Green, were backed by MSU faculty members including Walter Adams, Russel B. Nye, and Charles Larrowe and trustee Don Stevens. In the retrial, which Smith appealed, he was found guilty and given four months and a $200 fine.[16]

In 1961, Woollcott was not the most "radical" MSU student civil rights activist, nor was Green the only Black student-activist who made a name for himself on and off campus. One of Green's friends, Ivanhoe Donaldson, was among the most committed and militant MSU Black student-activists in the early 1960s. If Green was considered the soft-spoken leader, Donaldson was the boisterous one. Like Woollcott Smith, Donaldson was arrested in Mississippi for his risky civil rights activities. Unlike Woollcott's case, which was covered locally and mobilized a small group of White MSU students and faculty members, Donaldson's predicament was addressed by major civil rights leaders and organizations. His actions served as a rallying cry while laying the foundations for his future participation in the Student Nonviolent Coordinating Committee (SNCC).

Born in Harlem in 1941 and raised in the Bronx, Donaldson, "a very independent youngster," graduated from Andrew Jackson High School in Queens in 1959. He then enrolled in MSU as an engineering major and to run track. "I went to State, and State was a way of radicalizing you fast, if you are open to that," Donaldson recalled in a September 2003 interview. "But the interesting thing was there weren't that many African-American students at State," Donaldson added. "There were more Nigerians than African-Americans from Detroit." He noticed the impact of the student exchange program with the University of Nigeria founded by MSU in the fall of 1960. By the early 1960s, there were more than forty international students from sub-Saharan Africa enrolled in the university, a large enough group to create an African Students Association. Donaldson remembered East Lansing as a segregated college town where African American male students stood out, especially if they were not scholarship athletes. Deliberately seeking to defy this stereotype, several years after he arrived on campus Donaldson decided to become a staff writer for the *State News*. "They didn't think black people could write; that's why I went over there to work on the State newspaper," he reminisced. "You found that you wanted to break out of anybody's perception of your stereotype, you know, which people did a lot of back then."[17]

During Negro History Week in 1961, Donaldson became one of the first African Americans to publish a series of articles in the MSU student newspaper. On the second day of this commemoration, he penned an editorial outlining the history and purpose of this celebration founded in 1926 by historian and scholar-activist Carter G. Woodson. Citing quite liberally from Woodson, Donaldson boasted of African Americans' distinctive contributions to American culture. Echoing Frederick Douglass, he proclaimed, "a great part of America was built by the sweat and toil of the Negro slaves and their descendants." Like Woodson, he believed Whites' knowledge of Blacks' accomplishments could help eliminate racial prejudice and create "understanding" between Blacks and Whites. The next article authored by an MSU student to feature Woodson's Black history movement appeared more than a decade later in *Counterpoint: A Monthly Supplement to the State News* (February 1973). Jimmy Barfield detailed Woodson's life and work, highlighting how he popularized Black history. In a piece titled "Negroes Demand Complete Equality," Donaldson adopted an even more radical tone than Barfield would later. Celebrating the "rise of

(*Left to right*) James Forman, Ivanhoe Donaldson, Willie Ricks, Stokely Carmichael, and Charlie Cobb at SNCC sit-in at Toddle House restaurant in Atlanta, Georgia, December 1963. Photo by Danny Lyon. Courtesy of Magnum Photos, Inc.

Negro nationalism," Donaldson reiterated the "Black man's ingenuity" in "practically all fields." He also indicted Whites' treatment of Blacks. "The treatment of the Negro is America's greatest and most conspicuous scandal. . . . The Negro is the test case of America. He cannot be held down and kept in his place if democracy is to exist, or if Black and White are to live in peace." During the 1930s and 1940s, the *Lansing State Journal* reported on a few Negro History Week events in which Black Michigan State students participated. Even so, Donaldson's essays probably offered the majority of the university's White students their first introduction to this observance commonplace in Black communities throughout the nation. For some, it was a bitter pill to swallow. One White student was particularly enraged. "On Monday you printed two disgusting 'pro-negro' pieces," he complained in a letter to the editor. In reference to Donaldson's article on Negro History Week, he wrote, "It is this sort of chauvinism that make some negroes I know disgusted at being negroes and moreover, is a strong force in creating bigotry and intolerance. . . . Indeed, if you substituted Aryan for Negro in the article, you would have a typical example of the thinking of Nazi racists."[18]

Ivanhoe was not at all intimidated by such reactions to his unapologetic proclamations of Black pride and bold critiques of white supremacy. The campus NAACP's president Sam Harris introduced him to Malcolm X's brother, Philbert X, and a member of the Nation of Islam from Lansing who introduced him to Malcolm. Donaldson was enamored by Malcolm X. He was especially drawn to his political message, critiques of white supremacy, and beliefs in Black self-reliance and Black pride. Donaldson claimed to have invited him to speak at MSU. On May 29, 1961, Malcolm spoke in Lansing during the afternoon and, according to the *Lansing State Journal*, was "scheduled to speak at the Contemporary Issues Forum club in the Union Building at Michigan State university Monday evening." Given his role as the national representative for Elijah Muhammad, if Malcolm did speak at MSU, one wonders why the *State News* ignored it. Perhaps his visit was an informal one Donaldson helped arrange. It's still widely accepted that Malcolm's first visit to MSU was in late January 1963 when he delivered his "The Race Problem in America" speech in the Erickson Kiva.[19]

During the summers of his first two years at MSU, Donaldson volunteered for SNCC's voter-registration drives in the South. In October 1962, he was among the one hundred students who attended the presentation by several Detroit-based SNCC members in the Union Building sponsored by the newly created Campus Club Conference. This event was in direct violation of the new university policies pertaining to inviting speakers to campus. Like other civil rights activists, Ivanhoe regularly put his life on the line. "So how did you overcome fear," an interviewer asked him in 2003. "You never overcome fear," he retorted. "You just learn how to manage it." In the fall of his junior year in 1961, Donaldson dropped out of MSU to join SNCC full-time. He left one university for another. "SNCC became not only a place where social change was fomenting. It became a university because you met all of these people who know all of these things."[20]

In late December 1962, Donaldson and Benjamin J. Taylor, a social science junior from Camden, New Jersey, were arrested in Clarksdale, Mississippi, for the possession and transportation of narcotics. They had collected food, medicine, and clothing to help poor and suffering Black families in Mississippi who were not receiving state or federal aid. This was their second trip. Their arrest made national news and galvanized civil rights activists, attracting the attention of major civil rights organizations, including SNCC, the Southern Conference Educational Fund, Congress of Racial Equality, and the NAACP. "Free 2 Students Who Took Food to Miss. Needy," the *Chicago Defender* pleaded. In one of the most detailed accounts of their efforts, a writer for the *Gazette and Daily* of York, Pennsylvania, praised these students' self-sacrificing commitment to the cause. "It is worth recounting, not because of its intrinsic importance as a case, but as an illustration of what can be done when a few people care." Donaldson and Taylor's bond was set at $15,000 each and later cut down to $1,500. In early January 1963, an NAACP attorney from Jackson, Mississippi, posted their bonds. Taylor returned to MSU, and Donaldson remained in the Deep South. Donaldson's activism was memorialized when at age twenty-one he served as an SNCC field secretary. In 1964, filmmaker Harold Becker produced a film on Ivanhoe's activities in the late summer and early fall of 1963. In the end, Taylor and Donaldson spent about two weeks in jail in late 1962. In late January 1963, the Coahoma County grand jury refused to indict them with violation of the State Narcotic Act. The county officials, police, and grand jury felt the pressure from SNCC activists, local NAACP members, and other civil rights spokespersons and organizations. The U.S. Justice Department even got involved, and Hannah's Civil Rights Commission investigated the case. Many local Whites were even sympathetic toward Donaldson and Taylor, realizing "the magnitude of need among" poor Black agricultural workers in Mississippi. The president of the Mississippi NAACP Aaron Henry declared, "This is a victory for all the people in all parts of this nation who raised their voices against this injustice."[21] Perhaps in part inspired by Donaldson and Taylor, MSU students, including Whites and Blacks and members of the Alpha Phi Alpha fraternity, engaged in fund-raising for SNCC's voter registration drives during the early to mid-1960s.

Following his presidency of the campus NAACP, Donaldson's friend Green continued to be active. In November and December 1961 while serving as the group's public relations director, Green heeded Stuart Dunnings Jr.'s call and led a movement with the Michigan State chapter's president Joe Syfax to encourage the college to strengthen its off-campus housing policy. Syfax was well prepared for this leadership post. Born and raised in Greenwood, Mississippi, several years after his large family migrated to Detroit, Syfax graduated from Northern High School in 1954. After serving in the U.S. Navy for four years, in the late 1950s he enrolled in MSU. By the time he became president of the campus NAACP, he had worldly experience, which influenced his leadership of the annual international festival at MSU in the spring of 1961, and he was in no way intimidated by White racism. In 1962, he joined the Detroit Police Department reaching the rank of sergeant before his sudden death in 1975 at age forty. According to Green, Syfax, and other Black students, off-campus housing that was approved by the college often discriminated against Black students. Green himself recounted how he had attempted several times to rent a place in East Lansing that was identified by the university as approved housing. What Green and the campus NAACP wanted was for the university to ask landlords to sign waivers, when listing their properties with the university, indicating that they would accept any student who submits an application for a room or apartment. Based upon their test cases in which Black students were denied opportunities to live in certain homes and apartments, Green and Syfax accused the MSU housing department of not enforcing their rule, Housing Rule 8, that prohibited discrimination in off-campus housing. The campus NAACP also called out the *State News* for publishing advertisements from renters who discriminated against Blacks.[22]

Hannah was defensive in responding to Green and the campus NAACP chapter. "University approved off-campus housing must be offered on a no-discrimination basis," Hannah claimed in a rebuttal to Green's charges. "If the discrimination rule is violated by off-campus householders, the housing will lose its approved status." Suffering from historical amnesia, the college's housing director went a step further, contending that they had not received formal complaints and that they were striving for democratic ideals.[23] The housing director also refused to investigate complaints from Black students who didn't go through the proper channels for submitting a formal complaint and who weren't actually looking for housing. He wasn't willing to pursue cases that were test cases. Black students like those in the campus NAACP were perplexed by President Hannah's ambivalence toward East Lansing's largely uncontested racist housing practices. They knew the twelfth president of MSU was chair of the CRC who regularly identified racial integration the number one domestic problem and in the early 1960s opined that Detroit had serious racial problems that the city's officials needed to address. From time to time in the early to mid-1960s, Hannah validated Black student-activists' sentiments, mentioning in several of his speeches on civil rights issues that African Americans suffered discrimination more than other minority groups and had the right to fair housing and employment. In late January 1964, as reported on the front page of the *State News*, he declared, "Discrimination on the basis of race, creed, color or national origin is both morally and legally wrong." He also encouraged White MSU students not to rent apartments from landlords who discriminated against African Americans.[24] Hannah was disturbed by the blatant housing discrimination in East Lansing and regretted that the vast majority of the university's small Black faculty community had to live in Lansing. One month before the June 2 protests, he welcomed African American scholars and leaders, including executive secretary of the NAACP Roy Wilkins, with open arms to his campus to commemorate the tenth anniversary of *Brown v. Board of Education*. Though he was less reserved on campus with his civil rights speech toward the end of his leadership of the CRC, Hannah's approach to open housing in East Lansing was still ambivalent.

In 1963 and 1964, the campus NAACP became increasingly frustrated by their president's tactful approach to civil rights and the Black Freedom Struggle. In his September 1963 "Welcome Week" address, Hannah told students, "Each of you will exert some influence on Michigan State in your years on the campus, be a part to changing it, so the university I might describe to you today is not the same as the university of which you will be a part. The point of all of this is to invite you to work with the faculty and other students in helping to make our university an even better and greater one." The campus NAACP took Hannah up on his offer. They did so by stepping up their fight against housing discrimination.[25]

Chapter 25

Fair Housing Is a Must

At a historic meeting of the East Lansing City Council in mid-June 1963, Judith T. Kohls submitted a petition signed by sixteen perturbed East Lansing residents calling for the creation of a "Non-Partisan Commission on Human Relations." Civil rights activist Truman Morrison, the pastor of Edgewood United Church who "lived a life of social justice," created the East Lansing Citizens for Human Rights that strongly backed the request for this new group.[1] Among others also enthusiastically supporting this proposal was prolific social psychologist, scholar-activist, and longtime Michigan State professor Wilbur Brookover. Those present realized his endorsement carried weight. It could not be easily brushed aside. Armed with expertise about how schools' social environments impacted students' academic success and race relations in the Midwest, he had served as an expert witness in *Brown v. Board of Education of Topeka* (1954). He was steadfast in his belief that segregated schools were unequal, negatively impacting Black children's learning. Brookover was an outspoken advocate of racial equity in the Michigan State community. In the 1950s, Hannah appointed him chair of a college commission on discrimination. In 1958, Brookover hired the college's first African American woman secretary, civil and women's rights activist Josephine Ferguson Wharton.[2] She served as president of the Lansing Branch of the NAACP from 1959 until 1963, was well-known in East Lansing and Lansing for her forthright approach, and led the Black Women's Employees Association at MSU during the early 1970s.

Swayed by Brookover's and other civil rights–minded East Lansing residents' sentiments, at the June 17, 1963, city council meeting the motion to create a Human Relations Commission passed, the specific details of which would be "worked out at a later date."[3] It ended up taking four months to establish the commission's scope of work.

In mid-September, the city council unanimously supported the detailed five-section description of the duties, responsibilities, and capacity of the Human Relations Commission of the City of East Lansing. Soon thereafter referred to by the local media as the "Racial Commission" and the "Racial Unit," the commission was the city's first official civil rights advisory board. Appointed for one- to three-year terms by Michigan State communications professor and mayor Gordon L. Thomas, the nine members of the commission were expected to represent "the various racial, religious, professional, and cultural groups of the City." The "duty" of the commission was broad and multifaceted: "to promote amicable relations among the racial and cultural groups within the community; to take appropriate steps to deal with conditions which strain relationships; to aid in the coordination of the activities of private organizations concerned with these relationships; to assemble, analyze and disseminate authentic and factual data related to interracial and other group relationships." The commission was asked to "publish and distribute" their findings and engage in research "as are necessary for the performance of its duties." Most importantly, the commission was given the green light to offer recommendations "as it deems necessary to the City Council when adopted by an affirmative vote of five members of the Commission."[4]

The commission soon focused their attention on systematically addressing "problems of segregation, housing and job discrimination."[5] They sought to make it illegal for realtors to blindly follow their clients' wishes not to sell or rent properties to African Americans. By February 1964, the commission had established a subcommittee to collect and analyze data on housing and how it was related to racial discrimination. Assistant professor Robert L. Green—the only African American appointed to the commission and one of very few Black professors at the time—was among the most vocal members of the group, providing a much needed insider's perspective about the dehumanizing effects of racism. Throughout his service on the commission, he served as advisor for the campus NAACP, shared with his colleagues firsthand accounts of Black students who suffered from discrimination while searching for housing and employment, and warned his coworkers that when more Black faculty were hired by the university, the university would face greater challenges in navigating East Lansing's prejudiced housing patterns. He himself filed a formal complaint with the Federal Housing Administration, alleging discrimination when he attempted to purchase a home on Southlawn Avenue in East Lansing. During the 1960s, he publicized the city's discriminatory housing practices in speeches on-campus, in East Lansing, and elsewhere.

That this cause the outspoken Green and others embraced came to a head during the first half of the 1960s isn't surprising. For more than the city's first fifty years, issues revolving around open housing and race relations in East Lansing unquestionably existed, but they were too rare and isolated to have warranted much attention. Debates about open housing in East Lansing during the early 1960s were a direct consequence of the gradual increase in the Black presence on campus and, as a result, in East Lansing. Prior to the milestone Supreme Court case *Shelley v. Kraemer* (1948), racially restrictive housing covenants were commonplace in East Lansing and the surrounding areas. When William O. Thompson, '04, lived at "Elderkins" in Collegeville during the 1903–1904 academic year, he was most likely the city's only Black resident and was allowed to reside in the city because a White property owner permitted him to do so. From the 1890s through the Great Depression, most Black M.A.C. and MSC students lived in Lansing's predominantly Black neighborhoods. In 1930, the population of East Lansing was 4,380 and only one African American lived in city, most likely one of the several Black MSC students. Ten years later, there were three Black men and six women, probably students, living in the city that had grown to 5,839. The few African American men who lived in the dormitories between the days of Gideon E. Smith, '16, and Franklyn V. Duffy, '43, were permitted by the college to do so under a specific set of restrictions. They roomed with each other in designated areas. Such practices were in direct violation of Michigan law. From the early 1940s through the early 1960s, the small Black student population didn't cause much angst to those in charge of on-campus residential services. By the early 1940s, when Hannah informally desegregated the dormitories, MSU had an open, theoretically nondiscriminatory housing policy while East Lansing did not.

There were also limits to integration in the dormitories. Audrey Crowe, who attended Michigan State from 1948 until 1952, recalled that the university required applicants to submit photos and that racial segregation in the dormitories was commonplace. When Black students arrived on campus in large numbers during the late 1960s and early 1970s, distinct on-campus racial housing trends emerged. Fee Hall, Holden Hall, and Brody Complex became hotspots for social activities such as lively bid whist and pinochle games. By the mid-1970s, popular dorms for Blacks included Holmes, Hubbard, Case, Holden, and Wilson Halls, and Black students tended to have Black roommates. Racial incidents in the dormitories were not uncommon. In early March 1970, Enora Brown, who lived in Phillips Hall, was harassed. Revolting anti-Black notes were slipped underneath her door and the n-word was scrawled in plain sight on the walls near her room. She filed a police report and consulted with Black faculty like Ruth Simms Hamilton.[6]

During the long Civil Rights Movement, different racial customs governed MSU and the city to which it belonged, shaped, and, by and large, established. Without the college, East Lansing (once appropriately called Collegeville) would have been a small, rural town without much infrastructure and cultural diversity. It would not have been a destination for thousands of young people from various backgrounds. There is some irony to the fact that members of the college's chapter of Alpha Phi Alpha fraternity could live on campus in the integrated dormitories but were not permitted to rent a spacious home in East Lansing until more than five years after the fraternity was founded. In the summer of 1954 when they moved into the fourteen-room home at 318 Elm Place, they represented the largest off-campus concentration of African Americans living in any area of the city. After arriving on campus in the late 1940s, Michigan State's first African American faculty member, David W. D. Dickson, faced challenges purchasing a home in

East Lansing. Unsuccessful in his initial attempts during his early years in East Lansing, he lived in on-campus housing for faculty. Hannah then helped Dickson and his wife purchase a house owned by an MSU faculty member. Dickson recalled, "East Lansing was by no means ready for a Negro homeowner. Even some of my liberal departmental colleagues urged me not to buy a home in their neighborhood and, therefore, depreciate the only considerable capital investment."[7]

African American faculty who followed in Dickson's footsteps during the 1960s faced similar discrimination. More often than not, African Americans who integrated East Lansing in the 1960s had to do so with the help of their White allies. In July 1961, John W. and Lois Helen Porter purchased a house at 1551 Snyder Road for $10,400 with a mortgage from the East Lansing Savings and Loan Association. Porter, a Fort Wayne, Indiana, native who earned a doctorate from MSU in higher education in 1962, was supported by fellow members of Edgewood United Church.[8] In 1961 after becoming the first African American teacher in the East Lansing public school system, Clarence Underwood and his wife Noreese began searching for a home to accommodate their family. The two-bedroom apartment in Spartan Village was not sufficient for their three children. When he attempted to secure an apartment in East Lansing, he was turned down because of his race, Underwood recalled, he "was turned down on the basis of my skin color." In the summer of 1962, his friend attorney John Brattin sold him a three-bedroom home at 1403 Beech Street for $14,500. In his autobiography, Underwood recollected that his family was welcomed with open arms by the community who were used to having a Black neighbor. In the several years before the Underwood family moved in, Andrew Brimmer, a professor in MSU's Department of Economics from 1958 until 1961, rented the home.[9]

During the 1950s and much of the 1960s, African Americans' rights as tax-paying citizens and property owners in East Lansing had barefaced limitations, often determined by Whites' approval and support. Being Black in East Lansing during the Civil Rights Movement was eye-catching. In 1950, there were eighty-one African Americans residing in East Lansing, representing 0.4 percent of the city's population. Between 1940 and 1960, the Black population in East Lansing increased by more than 4,500 percent, from 9 to 422. In 1950 and 1960, the majority of the African Americans who lived in East Lansing were students and others affiliated with the university. Of the nearly seven thousand households identified in the U.S. census of 1960, 133 of them were "non-White." How many of these were African American households is unknown. In January 1965, Green contended there were only five Black homeowners in East Lansing. By 1970, significant transformations had occurred. Of a total population of 30,198 in East Lansing, 1,538 were Black (5.1 percent), and 36 percent of East Lansing's Black residents were in their twenties. This trend was similar to MSU's 1970 enrollment. In the fall of 1970, there were 40,511 total students enrolled and 1,954 Black students (4.8 percent). As the Black student population increased during the later years of the Civil Rights Movement, East Lansing was finally forced to reckon with its normalized and widely accepted discriminatory housing practices. Before the middle years of the Civil Rights Movement, a critical mass of Black people didn't traverse public spaces in East Lansing. When the campus NAACP marched on June 2, 1964, there were only a handful of Black faculty and academic staff members and probably no more than several hundred Black students on campus, a recognizable fifteen of whom were members of the football team.

During the 1963–1964 academic year, there was a recognizable increase in the Black student population. In the fall of 1963, approximately twenty disadvantaged African American male high school graduates from Detroit were admitted to MSU through a program called "Operation Ethyl." About six months after the program was launched, a writer for the *Detroit Free Press* as well as the university's director of admissions and scholarships described these young men in highly racialized and demeaning manners, claiming they came from slums and "culturally arid homes." Though part of a university program, these students had much to navigate on their own, including making sense of an unfamiliar academic and social environment. One MSU administrator commented that once they were in the program, they deserved "a chance to fail just like any other student."[10] Though there were only twenty-three young men in this educational welfare-like program, their presence was noticed in East Lansing. The gradual increase of Black students in the city during the late 1950s and the early 1960s sparked and influenced debates about open housing, which became a key issue in 1963 and led to the creation of the East Lansing Human Relations Commission.

Catapulted by the campus NAACP's consciousness-raising efforts, by early April 1964, momentum had built up on campus over the issue of discrimination in housing. Like Green, several Black students publicized their experiences with racism in the city. Two juniors from Detroit, Gerald Bray and William Smith, told the *State News* how they arranged to rent an apartment over the phone, but when they went to see the place the realtor representing the Claucherty Realty Company told them "they could not rent the apartment to Negroes because 'a family was living upstairs.'" One of the students reflected, "I cannot tell you how I felt when I was told that I could not rent the apartment because there was a family living upstairs. It hurt me, as if I would do something that would contaminate or be unhealthy for a family."[11] Moved by such testimonies, reporters for the *State News* attempted to investigate how East Lansing residents viewed fair housing policies. They were surprised when 35 percent of East Lansing residents they surveyed remained silent on the issue. In a piece aptly titled "The Shame of Silence," the editors of the student paper chastised the city's White residents for their apathy. In the spring of 1964, a research subcommittee of the Human Relations Commission, with Green and Mahlon Sharp taking the lead, submitted its report to the commission suggesting the group should counsel the city council to adopt an open occupancy housing ordinance. The meeting when the report was discussed was heated. The commission was not a unified front. The vote was 5-3 in opposition of recommending an open housing ordinance. Green was exasperated. Sharing their advisor's outrage and inspired by a visit to campus from Student Nonviolent Coordinating Committee (SNCC) activist Robert Moses, by mid-April 1964, president-elect of the campus NAACP Melvin Moore announced that his organization was going to be more active in persistently and aggressively confronting housing discrimination in East Lansing because of the university administration's reluctance to do so. He encouraged those in his group to "become a more integral part of the University system." Moore, a popular student named "Bachelor of the Year" by the MSU's Alpha Kappa Alphas, was well-prepared for leadership. Active in many organizations, including the Washington Conference, the Social Work Club, and Alpha Phi Alpha fraternity, he served on Green's research team in Prince Edward County, Virginia, in the summer of 1963 and participated in the sit-in movement, for which he was arrested.[12]

In early May 1964, about two hundred people—mainly East Lansing residents and student-activists including members of the campus NAACP—showed up at the City of East Lansing Offices, eager to hear the commission's deliberations on the fair housing ordinance. Many in this predominantly White crowd began congregating outside the offices nearly an hour before the meeting was scheduled to begin at 8:00 p.m. Black student-activists were scattered among the "orderly" crowd. About one in five of the 150 people in the standing-room-only crowd were African Americans. Flanked by Mahlon Sharp and James R. Ehinger, his fellow commission members who supported the open housing ordinance, Green was the only African American seated at the table. He was accustomed to this. Dressed like Malcolm X and evoking his classic no-nonsense mannerisms, Green was especially outspoken this time. "I've never known any broker who has offered to assist a Negro to buy a home in East Lansing," Green bellowed. "As a matter of fact I was recently told by a broker that he would never think of selling property to a Negro in East Lansing."[13]

Persuaded by Green's and others' testimonies, unlike the vote at the early April meeting, in a 5-0 vote (four members of the commission abstained, signaling their opposition without voting "no"), the commission recommended the city council "adopt, with punitive powers, a fair housing ordinance in order to protect and preserve and aid in the enforcement of every citizen's right to live in the city of East Lansing." The commission suggested language to the council that sent a strong message to the city's residents. "That it is the policy of the City Council," wrote the commission, "that all persons financially able to purchase or rent housing or residential property in the city . . . shall have the freedom of choice in housing and shall not be denied the right to purchase or rent housing or residential property because of race, color, religion, or national origin." Other recommendations included creating a "an open occupancy resolution" and processes for assessing discrimination complaints, acknowledging the existence of racial discrimination in the city and developing practical efforts to eliminate "racial differences" as well as "criminal penalties" for those who harass those who "are selling, buying or renting property in the city." The debates about the open housing ordinance were polarizing and extremely divisive following this meeting. The opposition from those siding with the Lansing Board of Realtors was quite straightforward. For them, it was within the rights of property owners "to dispose of their property as their consciences and convictions might dictate," even if that meant deciding not to rent or sell homes to African Americans. It was, they reasoned, within their "treasured right" to decide the fate of their property. They also opposed "any law" that compelled brokers to sell or rent property "on an open occupancy basis." Some White liberals who opposed the proposed ordinance believed it was premature. Several of those who abstained believed benevolent White city reformers could help Blacks seeking to buy or rent homes by chaperoning them during their searches, serving as character witnesses, and winning over their potential neighbors. Others were convinced the ordinance would "create animosity" between Blacks and Whites.[14]

In the early afternoon on Tuesday, June 2, 1964, thirty-five to sixty MSU students congregated and picketed outside of the university's Administration Building, today known as Robert S. Linton Hall. Located in the oldest part of campus and a stone's throw away from Beaumont Tower, "Old Administration" is the second oldest surviving building on campus and housed the Office of the President until 1969. Passersby were not necessarily surprised by what they saw outside of this historic building that faced the campus's "sacred space."[15] During the 1960s, picketing was common at colleges and universities throughout the nation, including "on the banks of the Red Cedar." This particular protest was organized by the MSU chapter of the NAACP in direct response to the East Lansing City Council's controversial 3-2 vote on Monday June 1, 1964, against the open housing ordinance that was recommended in May by the city's Human Relations Commission. The small and determined group of protesters was soon joined by more students and a few sympathetic faculty members and local clergymen. Interested and empathetic onlookers joined the picket line while other bystanders looked on with curiosity. The marchers communicated their outspoken disapproval of the three city council members who voted against a motion to forward a proposed open occupancy ordinance to the city's attorney for a legal opinion and deliberately began their picketing directly in front of the Office of the President.

The campus NAACP and their allies were particularly appalled by the opposition of councilman Max T. Strother, assistant to the director of purchasing at MSU. Several protestors marched with placards that read, "Is Strother Policy University Policy?" and "Why Is Strother Working Here?" In the protesters' minds, as a representative of MSU, Strother signaled to MSU's Black students and greater Lansing area residents that they did not have the right to reside in East Lansing if White real estate brokers, home sellers, renters, and neighborhood communities did not want them to. Strother insisted that housing discrimination didn't exist in the city and that if a case did surface, it could be considered by the city council. Maintaining that not enough "facts" pertaining to allegations of discrimination had been amassed and analyzed and that there was "no rush" with this matter, he argued that the ordinance was a violation of people's "personal freedom" and would "create more problems than already existed." He claimed his position was representative of East Lansing's (White) residents. "I was put on the council by the people of East Lansing, and they have expressed a definite opposition to this proposal." The "they" to whom Strother referred excluded MSU's and East Lansing's small Black community and progressive White city residents, many of whom were MSU faculty members and student-activists.[16]

Following in the footsteps of past outspoken campus NAACP presidents Ernest Green and Joe Syfax, Melvin M. Moore, junior and Inkster, Michigan, native, told reporters that their protests were sparked by Black students' valid concerns and represented just the beginning of more to come in the near future. When African American students "rent in the city," he told a *State News* reporter, "they are also residents. They want to feel free to go anywhere to rent an apartment." Moore and other Black students simply wanted to freely and unapologetically be *Black in East Lansing*. Proud that his organization mobilized enough students to publicize their cause on the eve of summer vacation, he also strategically used his interview with the student paper to announce that the struggle would be revitalized in the fall. He promised he would soon reach out to "national leaders" of the NAACP, the Congress of Racial Equality (CORE), and SNCC for guidance and support.[17]

After posting up and protesting in front of the Administration Building for about an hour on the noticeably cool summer day on June 2, 1964, during the last week of classes, the peaceful and convicted group that had grown to about one hundred people marched on to the East Lansing City Hall. They picketed there until about 4:00 p.m. Accompanied by about thirty students, Moore also picketed outside of the East Lansing Savings and Loan Company on Abbott Road where one of the city councilmen who disapproved of open housing worked. These events were conflict-free. Neither the campus police nor the East Lansing Police Department were called upon to intervene or monitor the demonstrations.

On Friday June 5, accompanied by about thirty student-activists, Moore returned to East Lansing Savings and Loan and closed the campus NAACP's account. Largely symbolic, this act was part of the African American boycotting tradition. The students let the bank know their unwillingness to patronize a company that had someone among its leadership who, in their minds, supported discrimination. After several hours, the group swelled to about 250 protesters, and they marched "in pairs down Grand River Avenue from Abbott Road to Division Street, then back up Grand River to the Union." Moore reiterated that he would calling upon "national civil rights leaders" to help publicize their cause and that "more picketing would result when students return to school in the fall, unless the City Council adopts fair housing legislation."[18]

Moore knew that discrimination in housing was a key battleground of the Civil Rights Movement. He and his coworkers knew they were part of a national Black Freedom Struggle. They deliberately linked their campaign to the countless sit-ins, protests, and demonstrations led by young African Americans throughout the nation. The small-scale protests in early June 1964 in East Lansing were incomparable to the unrest and ensuing anti-Black violence that took place in St. Augustine, Florida, during the summer as the U.S. Senate debated the Civil Rights Act of 1964, which it passed on June 19 and President Lyndon B. Johnson signed into law two weeks later. Yet the protests in East Lansing were unmistakably part of a historic moment, what comedian and civil rights activist Dick Gregory in April told two thousand students packed into the MSU Auditorium promised to be a "frightening" summer. Gregory was spot on with his

The MSU NAACP. President Melvin Moore (*center*), circa 1965. Courtesy of Michigan State University Archives and Historical Collections.

prognosis. Challenges to systemic racism and segregation were widespread during the summer of 1964, and Black students like the members of the campus NAACP were at the forefront.

The campus NAACP-led protests in 1964 were noticeable enough to garner the attention of the local press. Though *State News* staff writers were generally supportive of full Black citizenship rights, their coverage of the student rights movement and the campus NAACP was at times ambivalent, often revealing more about them than the struggles for social justice. The several photos published in the *Lansing State Journal* and the *State News* covering the early June demonstrations reveal the interracial flavor of the movement.[19] A *State News* reporter investigating the tense times emphasized that there were more Whites than Blacks in the picket lines, intimating that Whites directed things. The obvious was ignored. Black students on campus comprised less than 2 percent of the thirty-six thousand total students enrolled during the 1964 spring term. One photo in the *State Journal* features a preppy White male student sporting a crew cut, a button-down oxford, and dark khakis holding a sign that reads: "East Lansing City Council or White Citizens Council?" Another in the *State Journal* shows about twenty well-dressed and disciplined protesters marching in front the "temporary East Lansing City Offices at the Campus Press Building." The majority of those pictured appear to be White students. The photo on the front page of the *State News* on June 4, 1964, was similar to those in the *State Journal.* Two White marchers, a man and woman, are pictured picketing outside of the Administration Building. The woman is holding a sign reading "Jim Crow Must *Go*" that looks exactly like those commonly used in marches in the South. The man is holding a posterboard with a crudely drawn picture of two Klansmen and a burning cross. Underneath the drawing reads: "City Council."

The *State Journal* and the *State News* did acknowledge that the protests were orchestrated by the MSU NAACP branch. But the photos in these widely read local newspapers suggested the opposite, implying that the campus NAACP chapter was a predominantly White student organization. This portrayal was a trend in the *State News*. Beginning in the early 1960s, the student paper sporadically covered the campus NAACP's activities. With few exceptions, the photos they published showcasing student activism tended to flaunt individual White students taking moral stands. In March 1964, for instance, the *State News* featured two photos of the NAACP. One revealed six members of the largely Black leadership team accompanied by adviser Green. Gracing the cover of an earlier issue is a White woman, seemingly posed, holding a sign in support of the organization's fund drive for voter registration in Mississippi. This pattern of foregrounding White students' participation in civil rights activities continued in the following months when the student paper reported on East Lansing's open housing ordinance controversy. About a week after the June 2 protests, the *State News* featured an article reflecting upon the major events that transpired during the 1963–1964 academic year, in passing referring to it as a year filled with civil rights demonstrations. Further giving the impression that typical White MSU students embraced the cause of civil rights, the only photo included in this article dealing with civil rights is of a White student marching in front of the Administration Building holding a poster reading "Michigan . . . Or Miss.?" During the early to mid-1960s, the *State News* often featured photos of White students engaged in civil rights picketing with disillusioned protest placards.[20]

From *Brown v. Board of Education of Topeka* through the mid-1960s, the student paper tended to sympathetically cover civil rights activities in the South, featured a handful of articles about on-campus race relations and Black leaders' visits to the university, and generally supported the cause of open housing, calling the June 1, 1964, city council vote against the proposed housing ordinance a major setback for human relations. But the editors of the *State News* appeared to have had some sort of vendetta against the campus NAACP and felt uncomfortable with making East Lansing's problems the university's responsibility. In mid-May 1964 in an editorial titled "Where Are Rights Backers?," *State News* editors chastised members of the group for supposedly not showing up to a campus civil rights conference. "Members of the MSU community who consider themselves leaders in the cause of civil rights should be ashamed of their non-attendance at a human rights conference at the Kiva Saturday." The self-righteous student journalists continued, "Surely some NAACP members have been out of bed by noon. . . . Aren't the campus NAACP and the Human Relations Commission members interested in these problems too?" About two weeks later, the *State News* announced that the group's president, Melvin Moore, "unexpectedly cancelled" an important meeting between him, the Faculty Committee on Student Affairs, and dean of students John A. Fuzak to discuss "racial discrimination in off-campus housing."

The student reporters tapped into enduring anti-Black stereotypes. Characterizing the Black students as being lazy, unorganized, and unconcerned, the *State News* remarked, "Moore had cancelled his scheduled appearance because of difficulties in getting other NAACP officials to appear before the committee at its scheduled meeting time Monday morning." Several days after the June 2 demonstrations under the header "NAACP Off Target," *State News* editors opined that the campus NAACP's protests on campus were directed toward "the wrong target." These students were offended that Black students brought issues relevant to their day-to-day lives in East Lansing to campus. "The City Council, not the University," the *State News* editors insisted, "is responsible for placing property rights above human rights by its defeat of the proposed open housing ordinance."[21] The White student-journalists' paternalistic scolding of the campus NAACP reveals their unwillingness to empathize with their Black classmates' beliefs that Michigan State should take a bolder stance on this basic civil rights issue. They could not relate to the experience of being Black in East Lansing.

The editors of the *State News* also published letters to the editors and "points of view" that denigrated and trivialized the Civil Rights Movement and Black students' fundamental rights to express their views. Several weeks before the June 2, 1964, protests, the *State News* published a long, anti-Black "point of view" from a White male senior. A self-proclaimed racist, the student wrote: "What, in their long history on earth, have the Negroes as the racial ethnic group from Africa developed by themselves? The answer, to my way of thinking, is nothing or at least very little. . . . Why then, have Negroes not developed things the way Caucasoids and Mongoloids have, thus making real contributions to civilization. Well, you might say that they were off, separated from other peoples and cultures . . . The Negro group was separated, hemmed in the jungle, and stepped on. . . . So the reason for the Negro inferiority complex might possibly be that they are inferior."[22] The editors were well aware of what they were doing. Protected by notions of freedom of speech and their ability to say that such letters didn't reflect their beliefs, they sought to elicit reactions and generate controversy. And their strategy worked. For more than a week, students and even a few faculty responded to this white supremacist jibber-jabber, both endorsing and condemning the racist commentary. This was a classic case of race-baiting. Unsurprised by such opinions and the paper's decision to feature them, members of the campus NAACP remained silent. They refused to acknowledge such foolishness by responding. Black student-activists had more pressing concerns. They diverted their anger and frustration to their on-campus initiatives while connecting their efforts to the global Black Freedom Struggle.

During the summer of 1964, Black student-activists contributed to off-campus, out-of-state movements by participating in Freedom Summer, voter registration drives, and freedom schools. The MSU Student Congress allocated $300 to support several students in SNCC's Mississippi Summer Project. Among the student selection committee for this program were Melvin Moore and Detroit native and SNCC student-activist Gerald Bray. Participants were warned that the "project is not without its hazards," that there was "a possibility of jail sentences."[23] Student-activists made national concerns about civil rights focused in the South their own on campus. The Black student-activists, in particular, demanded to be seen and heard. When they demonstrated, they boldly claimed traditionally White spaces as their own. The campus NAACP was convinced that open and fair housing was the university's most important civil rights issue. Following the lead of their spokesperson Melvin Moore, members of the campus NAACP believed that Hannah and other university administrators could have done much more to influence policies and culture in East Lansing and to make sure that all MSU students were treated equally. Moore and other Black students had become impatient and frustrated with the city of East Lansing's Jim Crow North housing policies and the university administration's reluctance to support this basic civil rights effort. It was now time for them to act. They agreed with their predecessors, including Ernest Green, who confidently marched up and down Grand River four years earlier with signs proclaiming, "Not Yesterday Not Tomorrow but 'Now.'"

The winter and spring terms of 1965 witnessed a surge of on-campus civil rights activism, and liberal-minded *State News* staff writers evolved in their thinking toward the university's role in the fair housing controversy in East Lansing. In a January 27 editorial, they called out President Hannah. "As president of Michigan State, Hannah appears to be reluctant to take as strong a stand on civil rights as the commission must necessarily take." The editors continued, "with a national leader of the civil rights fight as its president, MSU remains relatively silent on what appears to be discrimination in its own community." They echoed the sentiments of a Black student from the South who in a letter to the editors commented, "He [Hannah] has worked all over the country to help find a solution to this problem. Yet he disclaims any responsibility to work for alleviation of the same problems in his own community." At the same time, some were most comfortable with a certain type of civil rights activism. *State News* editors reprinted Associated Press articles about the murder of Malcolm X on February 21, 1965, in Harlem's Audubon Ballroom but showed no sympathy for the slain martyr. "The violent Black Nationalist sect founded by Malcolm," they wrote claiming to speak for Black people, "is the antithesis of the kind of movement to which most Negro Americans subscribe." The most thoughtful piece published in the student newspaper after Malcolm's death was a letter to the editor from a senior from Liberia who stressed the importance of Malcolm to those adhering to the nonviolent direct action orthodoxy of the Civil Rights Movement. Perhaps at the end of February, members of the campus NAACP eulogized Malcolm at their Union Ballroom performances of the play *A Man Called Nigger*" a reboot of the 1961 performances this time to raise funds for the All-University Student Tutorial Education Project.[24]

As many students debated issues pertaining to student government and off-campus housing, the intensification of the social justice advocacy on campus was bolstered by President Lyndon B. Johnson's notion of the Great Society and War on Poverty, Bloody Sunday in Selma, Alabama, the passage of the Voting Rights Act, and, most importantly, overt protests against the Vietnam War. Several weeks after Martin Luther King Jr. spoke to thousands in the MSU Auditorium in early February, the MSU Committee for Peace in Vietnam organized a major on-campus demonstration against the war. In early March, more than one hundred students marched on campus in support of freedom fighters who were the victims of Bloody Sunday in Selma, Alabama. They linked their grievances to this movement, demanding that Hannah ask the federal government to intervene.

In late April 1965, members of the NAACP took their struggle directly into the secluded suburbs. Joined by members of the Committee for Student Rights, MSU Friends of SNCC, and other concerned students and faculty, they picketed the home of an East Lansing resident at 217 Beech Street who refused to allow Sandra Jenkins—an African American junior from Birmingham, Alabama—to rent a room from her after discovering she was Black. Their signs sent a clear and familiar message to the homeowner and curious onlookers. "Open Housing Now," "Is This the American Way?," and "Jim Crow Must Go!" Taken aback by the commotion outside her property, the homeowner explained that she reneged on the arrangement because she believed it was her right and responsibility to get her tenants' approval before letting a "Negro" move in. Her supporters conjured up common lines of defense, namely that property owners had the right to choose their renters and the NAACP's tactics were unwarranted.[25] Spokesperson for the protest Byron Peterson declared that what happened to Jenkins was "not an isolated incident." It was part of a tradition that "continues to exist now." Peterson continued, "Meanwhile the City Council and the Human Relations Commission of East Lansing either pretend that no problems exist or that those problems which do exist are not serious enough to warrant action. We feel that the problems are serious and warrant immediate and significant action with regard to an open housing ordinance for East Lansing." Peterson also warned East Lansing officials that, if necessary, he would be seeking outside support for this cause from Martin Luther King Jr., "who already knows our situation here."[26] This humiliating incident represented a significant moment in Jenkins's evolution as an activist. A member of the campus NAACP who was active in the March 1964 "fast for freedom" protest in support of Black Mississippians' voting rights, by 1966 Jenkins was president of the MSU chapter of SNCC and piloted a clothes drive for poor Black communities in the Mississippi Delta.

On May 13, 1965, CORE national director James Farmer visited East Lansing and spoke at an MSU teach-in in support of the student-led movement to end housing discrimination in the city. Calling the housing situation "a very great tragedy" and "a horrible blot on your fair city" and maintaining that residential segregation "is greater in northern cities than in the south," Farmer told a crowd of about 250 students he would return, if necessary, to help in their civil rights struggle. Other speakers included Robert L. Green, East Lansing councilwoman Mary Sharp, and state Democratic chairman Zolten Ferency. The day after the teach-in, Farmer, who was hosted by Green, met with members of the East Lansing City Council and the Human Relations Commission, encouraging them to remain active in the campaign for open housing. On the night of Monday, May 17, 1965, approximately three hundred students congregated near

Beaumont Tower, the original location of the first building on campus, College Hall. With the president of the campus NAACP Byron Peterson at the front of the diverse group, they marched to East Lansing city hall where council members debated the open housing ordinance. The majority gathered outside. They wanted the city council to adopt proposals for open housing and employ legal means to enforce ordinances. Dissatisfied with the symbolic verbal disavowals of racial prejudice, at about 9:10 p.m., about seventy-five of these protesters waged a sit-in in city hall. The protesters, who were removed from city hall "one by one by police," were cheered on by hundreds of their supporters who were posted outside of the building for more than five hours, "carrying torches and singing freedom songs." According to the editors of the *State News*, this event was the city's "first major sit-in."[27]

"The city has the power to insure equal opportunity in housing for all its citizens," the MSU NAACP chapter, the MSU Friends of SNCC, and members of the Canterbury Club declared a day after the sit-in. "It must act now to eliminate discrimination or face continued pressure from all those interested in civil rights and human dignity." The student-activists viewed their cause as being important and worthy of immediate attention. "The council's position that change must be gradual and not antagonize certain white residents of the city may be fine for those white residents, but not for the minorities who suffer from discrimination," they continued. "East Lansing must act to protect the rights of the minorities as well as of the majority." The student-activists also situated their struggle within the "national movement" and garnered support from SNCC leaders John Lewis and James Farmer who were scheduled to come to campus. "We want action now," declared Peterson. "We've waited for two years, and we don't want to wait two more years, two more months, or even two weeks." A day after the sit-in, the MSU NAACP chapter and its allies issued a Civil Rights Report, calling upon students to meet on the second floor of the Union Building at 1:00 p.m. for a March on City Hall for Open Housing. Peterson and his fellow student-activists' cause was endorsed by the Faculty Advisory Committee to the MSU NAACP and more than one hundred faculty members who issued a statement of support in the *State News*. Hannah also offered to meet with city officials to discuss its handling of civil rights issues.[28] On May 19, 1965, more than one hundred MSU faculty submitted a pro–open occupancy ordinance petition to the East Lansing City Council, and in the next week seventy-five student-activists gathered outside the Cowles House, demanding that Hannah intervene. He responded that he could not dictate to East Lansing officials what to do or how to act and wouldn't under any conditions sign on to their cause. He shared that he morally supported their concerns, but as he had practiced in the past, he wouldn't publicly endorse or demand the enforcement an open occupancy policy for the city. In late May following a spirited, standing-room-only meeting in the Union Building organized by the campus NAACP, about seventy student-activists, the vast majority of whom were White, blocked traffic on Abbot Road near city hall. East Lansing and state police arrived on the scene and arrested about sixty protesters. MSU buses were used to transport the demonstrators to the Ingham County Jail. Hannah showed no sympathy for the students, commenting the city had demonstrated patience, putting up with more than he would have. Disassociating the campus NAACP from these activists, Byron Peterson publicly stated they were not involved in this particular campaign. He knew that Black students who were arrested could face repercussions their White counterparts would not.[29]

During the remainder of 1965 and 1966, the campus NAACP, MSU student-activists, the Human Relations Commission, concerned East Lansing residents (such as the East Lansing Democratic Club and League of Women Voters), and even Governor George Romney continued to press for open housing in East Lansing. In early March 1966, the East Lansing Human Relations Commission produced a set of recommendations, but they didn't directly recommend that the city adopt a distinct open-occupancy policy. In their minds, this was not necessary because they believed discrimination in housing was "relatively infrequent and diminishing." They maintained that "equal opportunity can be best achieved without legal measures," that the citizens of East Lansing could themselves, without legal measures, achieve integration. They claimed an official ordinance "would polarize feelings of the community." In June 1966, the East Lansing City Council voted, 3-2, against an antidiscrimination ordinance (proposed Ordinance No. 174) that would have outlawed discrimination in housing, employment, and public accommodations. James A. Harrison, chairman of the East Lansing Democratic Club, called upon President Lyndon B. Johnson to remove Hannah from his post as the chairman of the U.S. Civil Rights Commission. In his mind, Hannah deliberately refused to speak out against the anti-Black housing discrimination that ran rampant in East Lansing throughout his long presidency. In his defense, Hannah reiterated to a *Lansing State Journal* reporter, "I'm not going to tell them how to run their community." He also urged students not to get involved. On the Fourth of July, a group of student-activists identifying with SNCC gathered outside East Lansing city hall to protest the defeat of the open housing ordinance. As 1966 drew to a close, members of the city's Human Relations Commission began thinking about how to strategically adjust the failed Ordinance No. 174 to be more palatable to its critics.[30]

In the next year, the debates about housing discrimination continued at a snail's pace. In early February 1967, the commission approved an ordinance to be sent to the city council for consideration. The ordinance essentially provided definitions of civil rights as they pertained to the three main areas of employment, housing, and public accommodations, and outlined the processes for addressing violations of the ordinance. They deliberately sought to make discrimination in housing a moral issue that would help them galvanize support from liberal Whites. In the realm of housing, the commission stressed that if persons believed they had been discriminated against based upon race, color, religion, or national origin, they could file a complaint with them and it would then be passed along to the Michigan Civil Rights Commission that was founded in 1963 and by 1965 became the Michigan Department of Civil Rights. While many East Lansing residents and even members of the East Lansing Human Rights Commission believed housing discrimination was not the pressing issue it once was, cases of prejudice against African Americans continued. In April 1967, for instance, the chairman of the MSU SNCC filed a complaint against a property owner who allegedly refused to rent to him because of his race. Toward the end of the year, developments in the capital city sent a message to their neighbors. On October 2, 1967, the city of Lansing passed the five-section Ordinance No. 139 that despite its limitations, prohibited discrimination in housing. They joined ten other Michigan cities. Based upon recommendations from the Human Relations Commission, in early November the East Lansing City Council went on record, in a 4-1 vote, supporting "statewide fair housing legislation."[31]

The assassination of Martin Luther King Jr. electrified the movement for fair housing practices in East Lansing and throughout the state and country. From April 4 through late May 1968, there were more than one hundred riots throughout U.S. cities. Recognizing the significance of this turning point in the Black Freedom Struggle, some historians have argued that the murder of King brought about the most consequential social unrest since the era of the Civil War and emancipation. Like leaders throughout the nation, Hannah had to take a stance. In the immediate aftermath of the murder of King, Hannah acknowledged that Michigan State had not been doing all that it could have been in challenging racial injustice. Though he excused MSU's past practices as belonging to broader patterns of apathy, this critical introspection was somewhat of a first for Hannah. He had no choice. He also didn't have to worry as much about being criticized for not challenging East Lansing's leadership about civil rights issues. Like him, they were thrust into action by King's death. On Monday April 8, 1968, at a special city council meeting, Mayor Thomas said that King's death compelled him and Councilman Wilbur B. Brookover to get their city to pass civil rights legislation before the federal and state governments. Thomas wanted to go beyond notions of conciliation by deleting from the code "a sentence citing conciliation as the only remedy for fighting discrimination." At the same time, the proposed ordinance sought to add a new section to the code, "making attempts to obtain housing as a 'test case' illegal."[32]

"As of Monday night, discrimination in East Lansing is not only against public policy—it is also illegal," a staff writer for the *Lansing State Journal* announced on Tuesday, April 16, 1968. The East Lansing City Council finally voted to make housing discrimination illegal. The newly approved ordinance eliminated a sentence "citing conciliation as the only remedy for fighting discrimination," adding a "penalty clause" for those violating the ordinance (up to a $500 fine and/or a ninety-day jail term). Among those who wrote letters in support of the historic ordinance were the East Lansing Human Relations Commission, the East Lansing Education Association, and a student Ad Hoc Committee for Open Housing at Michigan State University. Several months later, on June 11, 1968, Governor Romney signed the historic state fair housing bill into law. Effective ninety days after adjournment of the legislature, this law, subdivided into seven sections, prohibited "all types of discrimination in housing and rentals," and Romney claimed it was "stronger" than the federal act passed by Congress.[33] By the close of 1968, at least thirty-five Michigan communities had open housing ordinances. In the end, countless East Lansing residents—many of whom supported the Human Relation Commission's popular Good

Neighbor Policy—contributed to the long struggle that led to passage of the city's anti–discrimination in housing ordinance. East Lansing's new ordinance didn't put an end to discriminatory practices from landlords. About a year and a half after the East Lansing City Council finally made discrimination in housing illegal, a White landlord in the city denied two Black graduate students the opportunity to rent an apartment after he discovered their race. He told them he had just rented the unit they were interested in. The savvy students reached out to a White friend who agreed to see if she could rent the unit. She was allowed to rent the apartment. The Black students reportedly filed a complaint with the MSU Equal Opportunity Programs Office and the East Lansing Human Relations Commission. In his report, Joe McMillan, the director of Equal Opportunity Programs, indicated that he wanted the landlord in this case to lose his license. "In the city of East Lansing," he said, "there is no room for discrimination in housing."[34]

Though largely absent from the scene when these students stood up for their rights in early October 1969, the campus NAACP undeniably helped spark and sustain this civil and human rights struggle from the early to mid-1960s. Five years before East Lansing officials mandated that African Americans could freely reside where they wanted in the city, the campus NAACP was at the forefront of the struggle to unapologetically be Black in Ingham County.

Chapter 26

Apex of the Struggle

The day after Martin Luther King Jr. was assassinated, shortly before the city of East Lansing prohibited discrimination in housing with an enforceable penalty clause, Robert L. Green spoke to a group of at least eight hundred people in the MSU Union Building ballroom, the majority of whom were Black students, including about two hundred Black high school students from Lansing who were getting ready to march through the campus. Green used this moment and platform to call for much-needed reforms at the university. After those in attendance standing "two and three deep all around the ballroom" listened to a recording of one of King's speeches, Green shared with his grieving and agitated listeners tidbits of his personal relationship with the slain freedom fighter. He also chastised John A. Hannah for not taking an active stand against discriminatory housing practices in East Lansing, pointed out that there were no Black coaches at MSU despite Black athletes' contributions to the school, and lambasted the East Lansing mayor and city administrators for not proactively supporting an open housing ordinance.[1]

As public intellectual Michael Eric Dyson underscored, the death and martyrdom of King was one of the most important turning points in modern American history. From April 4 until late May 1968, riots spread throughout more than one hundred U.S. cities. Black students at colleges and universities throughout the nation marched, protested, and boldly made their concerns known to administrators. King's death sparked monumental changes at MSU, transformations that directly impacted race relations on campus and particularly the lives of Black students, faculty, and staff. His death became a call to arms for MSU's Black community. King, who visited MSU in 1965, was much more than a spokesperson or symbol for Black social justice in many Black Spartans' minds. On the morning after King was murdered, a group of over one thousand marchers congregated in front of Hannah's home, and members of the Black Students' Alliance (BSA) called upon the president to join them in commemorating their spiritual leader. "Informed of the assassination of Dr. King, I was more heartsick than ever before in my life," Hannah shared with MSU's Black community in particular. "What would please him most," he added, "would be the knowledge that all of us will honor him by taking a searching look at his unfinished work." He also used King's assassination to reflect critically upon MSU and the civil rights struggle. Wrapping up the "unfinished work" that Hannah mentioned immediately became the focus of African Americans on campus.[2]

John A. Hannah's leadership spanned from the uncertain era of World War II through the turbulent 1960s when scores of student-activists challenged the university's stance toward a range of issues, including civil rights. "One of Hannah's strongest characteristics had always been his consistency," remarked David A. Thomas, "but in his few final years as Michigan State's president, that consistency became a liability: the student body was changing, but the president was operating in much the same way as he had during the 1940s, the 1950s, and the early 1960s."[3] On April 1, 1969, the longest-serving president of MSU resigned when the campus was embroiled with anti-Vietnam protests and Black student unrest. Following his resignation, he became the head of the U.S. Agency for International Development and, as John Ernst argued in *Forging a Fateful Alliance: Michigan State University and the Vietnam War* (1998), the university's involvement in South Vietnam and U.S. Cold War foreign policy was under increased scrutiny. During the last decade of Hannah's long presidency, African Americans' enduring struggle for civil rights was the nation's most pressing domestic issue. This cause was discussed and debated at MSU, and African American students and some faculty were at the center of this on-campus movement. Black student activism exploded following the assassination of Martin Luther King Jr. when there were one thousand Black students on campus. Founded in January 1968, the BSA became the leading voice for the campus's Black student community. In the spring of 1969, the office of admissions amped up their recruitment efforts in Black communities. By May, more than one thousand Black students were "admitted, offered admission or offered testing for admission." These efforts, however, were not without their critics.[4] Nevertheless, in 1970, the Black student population reached 2,000 and during the remainder of the decade averaged about 2,400.

What happened at MSU was not isolated. The 1960s witnessed monumental changes in the composition of the student bodies at many predominantly White institutions (PWIs) including MSU. Before *Brown v. Board of Education* (1954), over 90 percent of Black college-goers were enrolled at HBCUs. After the U.S. Supreme Court declared the practice of "separate but equal" unconstitutional and called for the integration of U.S. public educational systems, African American student enrollments at traditionally White institutions of higher education began gradually increasing. A decade later, the Civil Rights Act of 1964 mandated universities like MSU, which were public and received state funding, to desegregate. It was illegal for institutions that were receiving federal aid to discriminate against students on the basis of race, color, or national origin. Some African Americans benefited especially from the financial assistance programs offered by the Higher Education Act of 1965. Between 1964 and 1969, Black student enrollment doubled, and by 1975 the majority of Black college-goers, approximately three-quarters, attended traditionally White institutions. Black students made their presence known at PWIs, demanding change. As educational historian Joy Ann Williamson points out, during the late 1960s, Black students accounted for less than 6 percent of the college and university population in the United States but were actively involved in more than 50 percent of campus protests. "Despite their modest numbers overall and the fact that many campuses had only a small number of activist Black students, many African American college students fought institutionalized racism on campus and carved a niche for themselves at PWIs."[5] These national trends played out at MSU, and its Black students were key drivers of institutional reform and change. It is no surprise that Black students were at the forefront of campus activism during the Black Power era. They pressured the university's power brokers to acknowledge their presence and needs. Following the murder of King, a new generation of Black student-activists emerged. They belonged to the same tradition of resistance as those who paved the way for them. They hailed from the same bloodline but were in many ways distinctly different from their campus NAACP predecessors.

In the late 1960s, countless Black student-activists mounted major protests at more than one hundred colleges and universities throughout the nation. Forty years later, two historians judiciously sought to unravel the intricacies of this pivotal moment in the Black Freedom Struggle that was widely covered in the mainstream press as it unfolded. In *The Black Revolution on Campus*, Martha Biondi argues that during the late 1960s and early 1970s, diverse groups of Black student-activists across the nation "moved to the forefront of the Black freedom struggle and transformed higher education." She uncloaks how they demanded Black Studies and "forced a permanent change in American life, transforming overwhelmingly white campuses into multiracial learning environments."[6] In Biondi's estimation, these "revolutionary" activists generated "greater campus change" than their White activist contemporaries. In *The Black Campus Movement: Black Students and the Racial Reconstitution of Higher Education, 1965–1972*, Ibram X. Kendi identifies 1969 as a turning point in Black student-activists' battle to transform higher education and demarcates the period from 1965 until 1972 as the "Black Campus Movement." Equally important, he meticulously unpacks how this particular movement owed a debt to previous Black student struggles, what he dubs "the Long Black Student Movement." Though scholars before them had threshed out episodes in the widespread Black Campus Movement at specific colleges and universities, Biondi's and Kendi's books, both published in 2012, are the first major explorations of the far-reaching nature of Black student activism during the late 1960s and early 1970s, including sustained movements at both HBCUs and PWIs.[7] Given the massive scope of the Black Campus Movement, it's understandable that neither Biondi's nor Kendi's accounts discuss in any detail the Black student unrest and substantive racial and social justice reform at MSU.[8] Black Spartan activists and America's first agricultural college were certainly part of this larger movement that swept across the nation.

During the early years of Clifton R. Wharton Jr.'s presidency, MSU Black students' strength in numbers was one of their greatest assets. Among Michigan public universities, only Wayne State University had a noticeably larger Black student population. By the 1972–1973 academic year, when slightly more than thirty PWIs had more than one thousand Black students, Wayne State had more than six thousand. During the Black Campus Movement, Black students at Michigan public universities demanded change. Black students at Eastern Michigan University were able to get a Black studies department opened, and Black students at U of M persuaded the university to build a Black student cultural center. Other Black students in Michigan were not as fortunate. In May 1970, members of the Northern Michigan University's Black Students Association appealed to Lansing legislators in the state capitol. Their concern was safety. Out of a total enrollment of more than 7,500, there were only 140 African Americans enrolled in NMU. They felt threatened by violent anti-Black rhetoric symbolized by an advertisement from a Marquette gun shop spotted on campus that purportedly announced, as shared with *State News* readers on May 20, 1970, it was "open season on n——s."[9]

Black student activism at MSU during the late 1960s and early 1970s was multifaceted. It contributed to the university's complexity and fluidity during this unique time. Many Black student leaders and Black student–led organizations were active during the Black Power era. In 1969, there were less than fifteen Black student organizations. By the mid-1970s, there were more than fifty.[10] During the mid-1970s, some Black student leaders were critical of the many Black organizations that had come and gone and, in their minds, didn't have the impact they perhaps could have had. While such student leaders' frustrations are understandable and were inevitably by-products of them being present in the moment without the advantage of a fuller historical perspective, the many Black student organizations founded during the Black Campus Movement were important, representing how Black students collectively responded to their experiences in White campus spaces.

The Black Campus Movement at MSU from 1968 until 1972, a fascinating and chaotic period during MSU's history, was unquestionably newfangled, dynamic, unpredictable, and fast-paced. Decentralized in nature, it is a complicated and bewildering movement for historians to demythologize and disentangle, involving a large cast of colorful characters. There were many heated debates and controversies. Black students from different walks of life expressed their discontent and desire for change through day-to-day activities, practical initiatives on and off campus, and major demonstrations. Confrontations between Black students and university officials and administrators were common. Engineered by typical African American students and outspoken leaders who created many organizations, the Black Campus Movement at MSU has the ingredients for an engrossing story that could be treated in its own book and within the broader context of student activism writ large. Instead of attempting to be encyclopedic or compendious, the following accounts historicize the Black Campus Movement at MSU and offer selective snapshots into the experiences and activities of diverse groups of Black student-activists by revisiting many of the movement's key organizations and leaders, episodes, and turning points from the founding of the BSA in 1968 until 1972—dubbed "a year of black activism" by *Grapevine Journal* senior editor George White—and a bit beyond.[11]

The responses of university presidents, spokespersons, and administrators to the explosion of Black student activism are of course germane to the story and cannot be nonchalantly brushed aside. Central to the following representation of this chronicle is how Black student-activists—as individuals and members of organizations—perceived their struggle and the vacillating race relations on campus while striving to transform MSU during a volatile and uncertain period in the institution's eventful history, a past shaped by students from diverse backgrounds. As "insider-outsiders," like their predecessors from bygone days, Black student-activists' paths during the late 1960s and early 1970s were not easy ones. As Amos Johnson, assistant director of financial aid, knew all too well, a noticeable number of Black students needed financial aid support during the late 1960s and 1970s.[12] Racial solidarity and their common experiences as marginalized and "othered" students united them. But they also often debated each other and implemented non-identical strategies and approaches. They encountered an assortment of obstacles and setbacks, and the White university community often scoffed at and pushed back against their demands and world views. These determined Black student-activists persevered in significant ways. They ultimately helped change the course of MSU's history that still reverberates today.

Black students' contributions and struggles are often marginalized in MSU's curious civil rights history. According to conventional portrayals and legends, two of the institution's most famous icons are often credited with most profoundly shaping the university's early civil rights legacy. President John A. Hannah, who served as the chair of the U.S. Civil Rights Commission for more than a decade, has been memorialized for his support of Blacks' civil rights. He initiated symbolic antidiscrimination initiatives on campus, was sympathetic toward individual Black students, and routinely declared civil rights the nation's most pressing domestic concern. On the gridiron, head football coach Duffy Daugherty's pathbreaking recruitment of African American players from the South during the zenith of the modern Civil Rights Movement has been deemed a twentieth-century Underground Railroad. He was crowned the Branch Rickey of college football. For many casual observers, the opportunistic integration of MSU football during Hannah's and Daugherty's days represents one of the most consequential expressions of civil rights activism at the university. The brief Black student-athlete boycott of 1968 and the demands of the Coalition of Black Athletes have been largely forgotten.

Sometime during the years after Hannah's presidency, the audacious and widespread Black student activism that began in the late 1960s sparked another prevailing narrative. In popular memory at MSU, the Black Campus Movement has been reduced to an often-recounted tale that centers several major episodes between 1968 and 1970. The abridged version of the familiar story is that following the assassination of Martin Luther King Jr. on April 4, 1968, a critical mass of Black students in the BSA mobilized, protested, and issued a laundry list of demands, some of which were shrewdly addressed by President Hannah and his dedicated brain trust. Then, a year later, militant Black student-activists staged a swift, controversial, and racially polarizing takeover of the Wilson Hall cafeteria that triggered acting president Walter Adams to give in to many of their demands, setting the stage for significant transformations in the university. In the late 1970s, one misinformed commentator at MSU even surmised that "Adams took the wind out of MSU's black movement by giving more than was demanded and giving with a sense of righteous indignation toward the conditions of MSU's blacks, coupled with a self-effacing sort of humility."[13]

After Adams's brief and contentious tenure, monumental restyling took place at MSU. "Wharton has done it again. As the newly appointed president of Michigan State University, Dr. Wharton will be the first Negro President of a major, predominantly white college in the country," the *New York Times* announced in mid-October 1969, "but he [Wharton] admits that in the decision to call him to Michigan State, which has a long history of promoting Negro enrollment, his race 'may have been an added attraction.'"[14] When Wharton took office, the story goes, the racial glass ceiling at MSU had supposedly been broken and the university's commitment to racial equity, diversity, and inclusion had been achieved. Black students' anxieties, demonstrations, and struggles were suddenly no longer perceived as being warranted. Some even believed that Wharton's appointment satisfied Black student-activists' concerns about representation in the university community and that it brought the Black student movement to an abrupt end. "When Adams turned over the reins to Clifton R. Wharton Jr. in 1970," an amateur historian claimed, "the black movement at MSU was over."[15] Though grossly oversimplistic, this myopic rendition of the pinnacle of Black student activism and racial reform at MSU is unsurprising. As was the case at colleges and universities throughout the nation, Black student activism at MSU in the late 1960s was conspicuous. It was unmistakably distinct and explosive, resulting in noticeable adjustments and reordering on campus, from token gestures to unparalleled transformations in the university's day-to-day operations and culture. The *State News* and the *Lansing State Journal* extensively covered the various protests waged by Black students, some of which made national news.

One of these protests, the 1969 Wilson Hall cafeteria "take-over," remained in the university's collective memory many years later. In the late 1970s, a *State News* staff writer juxtaposed the noticeable decline of Black student activism on campus by commemorating the importance of the occupation of Wilson Hall Cafeteria by a generation of Black students who were supposedly more committed to the protest tradition.[16] Approximately six months after the occupation, effective January 2, 1970, the appointment of Wharton as president of MSU was unquestionably pathbreaking and extraordinary. Several years earlier, Black students had demanded more Black administrators, and now, unlike any of their contemporaries at other major PWIs, they actually had a Black president. Wharton's appointment did not reconcile Black student-activists' wide-ranging demands or resolve volatile race relations at MSU, but it was historic and symbolically powerful. No matter how much Wharton sought to downplay his history-making achievement, he could not.

The prevailing folkloric perspective of several crucial years in MSU's history not only lacks historical causation, ignores the university's "Long Black Campus Movement," and downplays the teetering state of race relations on campus during Wharton's presidency, but it disregards the nuances and dynamism of the Black Campus Movement at MSU. It snubs the unique contributions of numerous Black student-activists during the late 1960s movement as well as the consequential Black student activism of the early 1970s.

The heightened Black Campus Movement at MSU lasted in earnest from 1968 until 1972 and was shaped by many Black student organizations and Black student leaders. After Wharton took office, the Black student movement continued. His appointment didn't by any means pacify Black student-activists. Black students held varying opinions about Wharton's presidency. During several racial incidents, some radical Black student-activists abandoned a blind commitment to racial solidarity and openly questioned his empathy with their plight and cause. They sometimes confronted their Black president as they did Hannah and Adams. In the early 1970s, Black students and leaders affiliated with an assortment of political, social, cultural, and academic organizations continued to mobilize. In 1973, there were at least fifty Black student organizations active on campus. Embracing self-determination and a new sense of Black consciousness, Black student-activists carved out autonomous spaces for themselves, voiced their angst, and orchestrated several major protests. Distinct as it was, the Black Campus Movement at MSU built upon a longer Black student-activist tradition dating back to the protests launched by the campus NAACP.

The kaleidoscopic movement that Black students established during the Black Power era was distinguishable from earlier Black student civil rights undertakings. Though their respective struggles were only separated by about four to five years, the campus NAACP's civil rights campaigns (namely their steadfast fight against housing discrimination) and the explosion of Black student mobilization and protest from 1968 until 1972 were strikingly different.

Chapter 27

Radical Departures

Often dressed in their respectable Sunday best, during the early to mid-1960s the campus NAACP made use of civil disobedience, marches, and picketing strategies. They embraced Martin Luther King Jr.'s philosophy of nonviolent direct action. They took on test cases and employed legal channels to fight for integration and equal access. As a group, they didn't directly participate in the southern Black student sit-in movement of the early 1960s but did publicize the widescale oppression of Black southerners following *Brown v. Board of Education* (1954). They actively supported the struggles waged by their brothers and sisters in the Deep South, raising funds to support voter registration drives and recruiting MSU students to work in the freedom schools in Mississippi.

While the assassination of King served as a rallying cry for Black students at MSU and throughout the nation, the murder of Malcolm X on February 21, 1965, did not lead to Black student protest at MSU. Instead, in the week after his death, the campus NAACP sponsored a student-produced play to raise funds for the Student Tutorial Education Project and "inform the campus public of the aims and history of the American Negro." MSU Black students memorialized Malcolm X Day during the Black Power era. In 1969, the Black Students' Alliance (BSA) called upon Black students not to attend classes on Friday, February 21, 1969, in commemoration of Malcolm's legacy. They viewed themselves as being heirs of his "spiritual legacy" and unwavering commitment to the Black Freedom Struggle. "Malcolm is loved more and more because we understand him more," BSA wrote. "We cherish the sacrifice—the ultimate sacrifices—he made that assured us of his supreme sincerity. We wish to honor him—in death—as we failed to do in his lifetime." In 1970, the event took on a more international flavor. For two days in late February, a group of African-descended students, led by Kenyan graduate student Kamuyu Kangethe, organized a series of events and activities, including the showing of the film *The Battle of Algiers*. Their goal was to highlight the importance of Pan-African unity, one of Malcolm's many legacies. These Black students must have been perturbed by Muhammad Ali's attack on Malcolm during his visit to MSU in late February as a part of the Associated Students of MSU's Great Issues series. After speaking before a crowd of more than 2,500 in the MSU Auditorium, Ali met with Black students. Wholeheartedly committed to Elijah Muhammad, on the eve of Malcolm X Day, he blazoned, "Malcolm X was no leader of blacks. . . . He was simply a pimp and did not have any power or support."[1] The Pan-African Students Organization in the Americas and other Blacks student organizations continued to celebrate Malcolm X Day through the mid-1970s and beyond. In 1975, one staff writer for the *Grapevine Journal* shared several of Malcolm's sayings with his readers, reminding his classmates that Malcolm's message was "still important."[2]

The campus NAACP put confidence in their strategy of consciousness-raising and moral suasion. Shortly after its founding, the organization's director of research and public relations, Samuel E. Harris, announced to *State News* readers that a primary purpose of the campus NAACP was to function as an "information dissemination agency." At the beginning of the 1964 fall semester, they reiterated to the MSU community that their ultimate goal was fighting against prejudice and bigotry, "whether it was racial or religious," and consciousness raising. In their words, they were committed to informing "the public about the evidence and implications of prejudice in society."[3] Their movement was also deliberately interracial. They welcomed White allies to join their cause, so much so that the local media often portrayed the campus NAACP as being a White-led organization. The organization was in reality a Black organization. In the early 1960s, approximately 10 percent of the members were White. Though they invited Nation of Islam leader and separatist Malcolm X to campus in 1963, the campus NAACP's struggle for open housing centered on achieving integration. They had dreams of radically transforming the university, but the time was not yet ripe for such change. They didn't have the numbers, the collective voice, or a widespread national Black student movement behind them to seriously get the university's undivided attention. Unlike their successors, members of the early campus NAACP and their Black classmates lacked the support of an organized group of Black faculty, administrators, and staff.

The struggles of countless Black student-activists at MSU and throughout the country in late 1960s—epitomized on February 13, 1969, by the massive Black student protests at University of Wisconsin–Madison, San Francisco State, the City College of New York, and Mississippi Valley State—"represented a profound ideological, tactical, and spatial shift from early 1960s off campus civil rights student confrontations."[4] Like their predecessors but with a larger presence, the Black student-activists of the late 1960s and early 1970s confronted practices and policies at MSU they considered to be racist. The radicals of the Black Campus Movement's peak years were disruptive in their challenge to day-to-day racism and openly rejected the implications of integration. They may not have appreciated his attack on Malcolm X, but many Black students gravitated toward Muhammad Ali's call for racial separation during his 1970 visit to campus.

Dressed in their soulful outfits, often sporting Afros, and believing "Black Is Beautiful," Black students during the late 1960s and early 1970s championed the new call for "Black Power" and the radical rhetoric of Black nationalist leaders who visited their campus such as Stokely Carmichael, the national chairman of the Student Nonviolent Coordinating Committee, Black Panther Party cofounder Huey P. Newton, and Black Arts Movement poet and playwright LeRoi Jones (Amiri Baraka). In mid-May 1969, seventy MSU Black student-activists shocked Republican officeholders when at a Michigan Senate session they raised their clenched Black Power fists. Still cognizant of the Black Freedom Struggle in the South, this generation of Black student-activists shifted their attention to the problems faced in Black urban communities after the hot summer of 1967 when more than 150 race riots broke out across the nation. Beginning on July 23, about ninety miles east of Lansing, the Detroit Rebellion was one of the most dreadful and perilous riots in American history. Acting locally, during the late 1960s and early 1970s, MSU Black student-activists initiated a variety of practical self-help programs in Lansing's Black community. By 1969, after the founding of the Black Liberation Front, International (BLFI), many Black students also adopted Pan-African and internationalist world views. Following the assassination of Patrice Lumumba on January 17, 1961, MSU NAACP members marched and voiced their despair.[5] But before the late 1960s, Black student-activists at MSU were focused on the Black Freedom Struggle in the United States.

The Black Campus Movement of the late 1960s and early 1970s was explicitly not an interracial one. Guided by self-determination and Marcus Garvey's dictum "Race First," during the Black Power era, radical MSU Black student-activists avoided alliances with their classmates in groups like the Students for White Community Action which was founded in mid-April 1968, had over five hundred members weeks after it was chartered, and endorsed many of BSA's demands. Large numbers of Black students didn't join White-led student organizations active during the 1960s like ASMSU, the Young Socialists, the Young Democrats, the Student Mobilization Committee to End the War in Vietnam Now, the Committee for Student Rights, Students for a Democratic Society, United Students, the MSU Student Liberation Alliance, the Action Group Against Racism, the MSU Committee Against ROTC, among others. In the early 1970s, Katherine Elizabeth White generalized that Black student-activists weren't highly concerned with causes unrelated to the Black Freedom struggle. Similarly, Jeanne Saddler, when referring to 1970, remarked that "most blacks were less than enthusiastic about the strike."[6] With few exceptions, this seems to have been the case.

The largescale protests in the spring of 1970 prompted Black students to evaluate their place in the broader "student power" movement. On May 5, 1970, the day following the Kent State

University shooting, thousands of students gathered in front of the Hannah Administration Building in support of a student strike. MSU students were among the more than one million students who participated in a wide-reaching antiwar movement by engaging in strikes and walkouts on countless college and university campuses throughout the United States. The MSU Student Strike Committee (SSC) initially demanded that the United States withdraw from the Indochinese Federation and free Bobby Seale, and that MSU abolish ROTC and support Kent State student-activists. SSC leaders soon called upon the university to enroll an additional two thousand minority students, namely Black students, by the fall of 1970 and revise its Eurocentric curriculum. Black students at MSU were not the major flagbearers in the mainstream student strike movement. Some Black student leaders questioned Whites' widespread apathy toward their struggles, and BLFI cautioned Black students to avoid being co-opted. On May 19, while the BLFI called for a meeting in Wells Hall to commemorate Malcolm X's birthday, White students in the Action Group to Combat Racism summoned students to the Union Building to rally for a university shut down. By the end of May, a group of Black students called for a temporary boycott of classes for different reasons than their White contemporaries. Under the leadership of Ron Johnson and Gerald Evelyn, the Akers Black Caucus urged Black students to skip classes and participate in their teach-ins from May 25 through May 29 in protest of eight African Americans who were killed Mississippi and Georgia. Other Black students were active earlier in the month. In the evening on Wednesday, May 6, after more than six thousand students marched from Beaumont Tower to the Alumni Chapel for a memorial service in honor of the four slain Kent State University students, President Wharton cancelled classes on May 8 so that students could participate in a variety of teach-in sessions. Black students, staff, and faculty organized a forum in the MSU Veterinary Clinic to discuss pressing issues facing the Black community. More than twenty presenters passionately spoke on a range of topics, and the intergenerational group issued a far-reaching position paper. Most MSU students did not participate in the strikes, boycotts, or protests. Nevertheless, May 1970 propelled some Black students into more organized action in the cause of Black liberation, however it might have been conceptualized.[7]

Injecting themselves into the larger "student power" movement, Black student-activists agreed with their radical White counterparts that the university needed to be democratized. Unlike their radical White counterparts, Black student-activists wanted and unapologetically called for more Black students, faculty, administrators, staff, and coaches; the creation of Black on-campus organizations; autonomous spaces (i.e., Black cultural rooms in the residence halls); Black dormitory residential assistants and aides; representation in student governance and on university committees; courses in Black Studies taught by Black professors; student services and programs designed with them in mind; and an end to racism on campus. Deploying confrontational tactics, this new generation of Black student-activists demanded and expected Michigan State to make meaningful and long-lasting changes to accommodate their presence and to serve them and their progeny's needs. Because of their bold ambitions, dedication, and political savviness, they were—to borrow from Martha Biondi's depiction of Black student-activists across the nation in the late 1960s—"revolutionary" in their approaches. As BSA president Barry D. Amis said in June 1968, "we demand a total revision of the educational system as it pertains to black people."[8]

The different approaches adopted by the campus NAACP and the radical Black student-activists of the late 1960s and early 1970s at MSU had much to do with the historical contexts in which they existed. Like Black students throughout the nation, they were shaped by the broader trends in the Black Freedom Struggle during their respective days on campus. Generally speaking, the members of the campus NAACP came of age during the modern Civil Rights Movement that ended with the passage of the Voting Rights Act of 1965. Nonviolent direct action and civil disobedience wasn't the only viable approach but was popular, oftentimes viewed as being pragmatic by its adherents and passed off by the mainstream media as being orthodox. Notwithstanding the debates about the "Long Civil Rights Movement" and the deeply rooted Black self-defense tradition, during the modern Civil Rights Movement from the mid-1950s until the mid-1960s, there was a widescale movement, largely through nonviolent direct action and mass civil disobedience, to directly challenge segregation in U.S. institutions, endorse integration, confront racial discrimination, and support legislative and constitutional reform.[9] The original goal of the "Big Four"—Martin Luther King Jr., James Farmer, Whitney Young, and Roy Wilkins—was integration. By 1964, when the campus NAACP embarked on a new phase of their fight against housing discrimination in East Lansing, leading civil rights activists called upon their followers to test the limits of the Civil Rights Act of 1964. African Americans struggled for their rights as guaranteed by Section 1 of the Fourteenth Amendment of the Constitution of the United States. When he spoke to a crowd of four thousand in the MSU Auditorium on February 11, 1965, King stressed the necessity of combating and eliminating racism and segregation. This message resonated with members of the campus NAACP more than what Malcolm X preached.

Conversely, the Black student-activists at MSU during the late 1960s and early 1970s were profoundly impacted by the Black Power Movement that spanned from 1966 until approximately 1975. A decentralized crusade during which young African Americans began rejecting integration as a fundamental solution, this new movement selectively sampled from the past but represented a distinguishable shift in the Black Freedom Struggle. Black students were often on the frontlines in this battle for liberation. As an MSU junior social work major from Detroit declared in early April 1968, "Young blacks are re-defining their blackness and their humanity. The white society no longer awes them and paternalistic attempts at integration won't work. There will be no more head-hanging by blacks." This conscious young Black woman added, "Black college students are expected to be innovators in the black movement and not laggers behind it." Many young African Americans wanted power, not integration. As declared by Stokely Carmichael, Black Power was a direct call to Black people to determine their own goals and to create their own independent organizations.[10] A new generation of Black activists, including Black students at MSU, insisted on having a seat at the table. They clamored for social justice and participatory democracy.

Aptly articulated in James Brown's 1968 classic anthem "Say It Loud—I'm Black and I'm Proud," Black Power activists, eloquently writes historian Peniel E. Joseph, "openly questioned American democracy's willingness to expand its boundaries to include African Americans. Even as civil rights activists attempted to pursue legal and legislative measures to pursue racial equality, Black Power militants aggressively confronted political, cultural, and economic institutions with a slogan that simultaneously demanded cultural autonomy, racial pride, and equal citizenship." With a renewed sense of swagger and self-determination, young African Americans engaged in what psychologist William Cross identified as a "Nigrescence."[11] In June 1968, a Black student leader announced this new attitude to *State News* readers: "Black students now adopt the militant stance of the Black Power philosophy."[12]

When contemplating the differences between the campus NAACP's activism in the early to mid-1960s and that of Black student-activists during the late 1960s and early 1970s, it is also important to acknowledge the differences in being a Black student at MSU during these respective times. It is difficult to determine with precision the Black student population at MSU before and during the early to mid-1960s. Early in his presidency, John A. Hannah mandated that the university remove all racial designations from student records. During the 1967–1968 academic year, efforts to convince students to indicate their race (with the options of "White," "Negro," or "Other"), in order to prove the university's compliance with the Civil Rights Act of 1964, largely fell flat. Black student-activists were particularly offended by this appeal, and several even protested it. In the spring of 1961, *Ebony* magazine publicized that there were some six hundred Black students enrolled in Michigan State, comprising approximately three percent of the total student population. Three years later in 1964 while the campus NAACP engaged in its campaign for open housing in East Lansing, a *Michigan Chronicle* reporter claimed that there were eight hundred Black students on campus.[13] This was a gross exaggeration. In all likelihood, during the 1963–1964 academic year, there were probably no more than several hundred Black students on campus who made up approximately 1 percent of the total campus student population.

In late October 1970 while directing the Center for Urban Affairs, which focused on urban-related problems and racial issues through research projects, curriculum development, speaker series, and practical on-campus and outreach programs, associate professor Robert L. Green and his team of researchers completed a report for the Presidential Commission on Admissions and Student Body Composition titled "The Admission of Minority Students: A Framework for Action." The Center for Urban Affairs' report was the first detailed study of its kind. It went far beyond the scope of the seven-page document "Admission of High Risk Students at MSU," submitted to the MSU Faculty Senate and the U.S. Department of Health, Education and Welfare, Office of Education in November 1968. The Center for Urban Affairs' meticulous, data-informed report directly critiqued the University Educational Policies Committee's report submitted to the provost on June 1, 1960, that totally neglected to explore the recruitment of Black students. The center's report also debunked the *New York Times*'s cursory claim in October 1969 that MSU had "a long history of promoting Negro enrollment."[14]

Green and his research team discovered that in 1960, the "minority student population" at MSU "numbered about 130," the majority of whom were Black. For the next five years, they determined that the Black student enrollment "remained relatively constant." In 1966, they noted a discernable increase in the Black student population, and in April 1968, when BSA issued its first set of demands to the university, Green and his team found that there were approximately seven hundred Black students enrolled. In the fall of 1967, 157 Black students entered MSU, and in the fall of 1968, the Black entering class was 357.[15] In the fall of 1968, the Black student population rose to 1,007, and by 1969, there were 1,523 Blacks enrolled in the university, representing about 3.8 percent of the total student population. In 1969, 234 of the 1,523 enrolled Black students were in various graduate programs. Between the 1967–1968 academic year (when there were sixty-four Black graduate students) and the fall of 1969, the Black graduate student population drastically increased.[16]

African American administrator Lloyd Cofer announced with pride that 610 Blacks were admitted to the fall 1970 incoming class. For the fall of 1970, Green estimated that the total Black student enrollment was between 1,800 and 2,000, somewhere between 4 and 5 percent of the total student body. He was not too far off. According to the MSU Office of Planning and Budgets' "Minority Enrollment: East Lansing Campus" (1994) covering the years from 1970 until 1994, in 1970 the Black student enrollment was 1,954, representing 4.82 percent of the total student campus population of 40,511. Early during his tenure, President Clifton R. Wharton Jr. was pleased by the growth of the Black student population and described MSU as being an ideal destination for Black college-goers. Though he was certainly measured when speaking on campus about increasing the Black student enrollment, he didn't mince his words at a press conference in the spring of 1970 in Detroit: "We at MSU have been increasing the number of black students at a rate such that, today, we have more black students enrolled at MSU than at any other non-urban, predominantly white university in the United States." Between 1967 and 1970, the MSU Black student population increased by 183 percent. Coinciding with Wharton's presidency, from 1971 until 1978, Black student enrollment consistently hovered around 2,500, peaking in the fall of 1972 when 2,678 Black students were enrolled. As was the case throughout the nation, the Black student population declined a little bit by the mid-1970s. The "minority" student enrollment also increased drastically early during Wharton's presidency. Between the 1970–1971 and 1971–1972 academic years, the "minority student enrollment" increased by nearly 1,000, from approximately 2,064 to 3,024. In the early 1970s, Wharton was also proud of the increase in the number of minority employees since the mid-1960s.[17] Many Black students were pleased with these changes, yet as *Grapevine Journal* staff writer Denise Outram observed in

May 1972, believed "the university must take immediate steps toward increasing also the services which are black oriented and to which black students can relate sufficiently."[18]

As Ibram X. Kendi suggests, on university campuses with large and diverse Black populations, it's difficult to determine with any precision the number of students actively involved in the Black Campus Movement. His general estimation that about a quarter were moderates or radical black nationalists seems reasonable for describing the situation at MSU, especially since the large Black student population in East Lansing often came from cities with significant African American populations, including Detroit, Flint, Grand Rapids, and Inkster. As was the case with Ernest Green a decade earlier, those from the South may have been radicalized by their direct experiences with Jim Crow segregation. The larger, more diverse, and increasingly radicalized Black student population at MSU in the late 1960s and early 1970s was more of a force to reckon with than their predecessors who numbered in the several hundreds in the mid-1960s.

Even though the outspoken and astute civil rights activist Robert L. Green advised the campus NAACP, Black students in the mid-1960s did not have many Black faculty to counsel, validate, and support them. In the mid-1960s, there were no active Black administrators on campus and only a handful of Black tenure-system faculty who could serve as mediators between Black student-activists and the executive administration. During this time, Green was among the few Black faculty members who translated and endorsed Black students' demands to the university's power brokers. During the 1968–1969 academic year, there were between nine and twelve Black faculty members, and by the fall of 1969 there were purportedly between twenty-one and thirty-two who formed the Black Faculty Committee, later renamed the Black Faculty and Administrators Association.[19] They worked closely with Black student-activists, publicly supporting many of the concerns held by vocal Black students. "The Black faculty and staff can and must play an integral role in the Black student movement on campus," declared BSA in an open letter in late February of 1969. In particular, BSA implored Black faculty to offer more courses relevant to the Black experience and to mentor Black students more intentionally.[20] As a result of Black student activism and the university's response to federally mandated affirmative action directives, by 1971 there were forty-four Black tenure-system faculty members on MSU's campus.

In the early to mid-1960s, Black students didn't benefit from a curriculum that reflected their cultural backgrounds. With very few exceptions—such as courses taught by Africanist James Hooker or expert on the Black preaching tradition William Harrison Pipes—they had no Black Studies courses to help shape their consciousness. By the fall semester of 1968, as reported in the "Welcome Week" edition of the *State News*, Black students influenced changes in how social science and humanities courses were organized and taught. Because of calls for widespread curricular reform, some professors attempted to integrate the Black experience into their syllabi, seeking to ideally "reflect the Afro-American's contributions to every facet of American life." The Department of English also purportedly began working toward creating a "M.A. and Ph.D. in Afro-American Literature and Culture."[21] While a *State News* staff writer exaggerated the pedagogical transformations that were actually taking place, for the first time, as a result of Black student protest, a collection of courses on African American life and culture were offered at MSU, including Negro Writers in America, The Negro in America: Varieties of Slavery, a 400-level seminar on Black politics, and a Black history course offered on closed-circuit television at MSU's continuing education centers in Grand Rapids and Rochester. In the early 1970s, there was even a course in the Evening College designed for Black women students, African Hairdos for Women, taught by a Nigerian woman whose husband was a professor of anatomy.

Black students were not completely satisfied with the measured curricular reform during the early and middle years of the Black Power era. In the fall of 1968, BSA complained that the descriptions of the courses in the schedule book lacked detail and were inadequately advertised. In mid-February 1970, a racially conscious first-year student from Baltimore, Maryland, Clarissa Brown, charged professors in the honors American Thought and Language (ATL) program with ignoring Black subject matter, marginalizing Black students with culturally insensitive assignments, and not having any Black professors among their ranks. "Need I say more? If so, I will," Brown concluded after convincingly making her case in a letter to the editors of the *State News*.[22] Similarly, in mid-March 1970, several Black students shared with the *State News* that many of the required courses in the University College for liberal arts majors marginalized Blacks' contributions. Detroit junior Lovell Summey criticized the required humanities course. "It starts with the Greeks and Romans and covers all European culture, omitting developments in Africa and other contributions by blacks throughout history." Detroit sophomore Estrella Lambert shared her classmate's concerns. "In courses such as ATL and Sociology the black man is only presented as he contributed to white America, not as he relates to black America. Often the material only deals with the obvious without deeper meaning given." Black students were quick to celebrate the courses they found relevant. In the first issue of the *Grapevine Journal* in September 1971, a student reporter praised the sections of the Philosophy 294 taught by Chui Karega. Advertised as a class that "takes an objective look at the condition of the Black man—past and present," Karega assured Black students that the course would provide them opportunities to express themselves about themselves while weeding out "the truth from the rhetoric through the study of history in particular."[23]

Shortly after the MSU Board of Trustees approved the creation of a Committee Against Discrimination, an Anti-Discrimination Judicial Board, and a new anti-discrimination policy expanding upon the 1935 version, in the fall of 1970, the university initiated its first "Affirmative Action Plan" that addressed the recruitment of Black students, faculty, and staff and laid the foundations for other future areas of concern within the realm of diversifying the large MSU community and moving toward a more inclusive culture. Black students during the late 1960s and early 1970s benefited in meaningful ways from these reactionary initiatives the university implemented to address their demands and satisfy affirmative action policies, including the creation of the Equal Opportunity Programs, the Center for Urban Affairs, the Black Minority

Aide Program, policies that increased Black student representation in university affairs, and a range of other student services.

The apex of the Black Campus Movement at MSU, from 1968 until 1972, simultaneously represented an extension of and departure from the struggles that began in earnest with the campus NAACP's activism during the early to mid-1960s. The movement reached a crescendo in the late 1960s with the Black student takeover of the Wilson Hall cafeteria in late April 1969. As the Black student population increased exponentially between 1969 and the early 1970s, namely during the first several years of Wharton's presidency, Black students formed scores of organizations to advocate for themselves. They often used off-campus events and took on causes on campus that didn't directly pertain to their academic experiences to fight for their rights as students. In no uncertain terms, they demanded the university undergo a makeover by acknowledging their presence and providing resources for them to genuinely feel affirmed and valued.

The Black enrollment at MSU fell from 2,678 in 1972 to 2,252 by the end of Wharton's presidency. Was there perhaps some sort of backlash against the heightened Black activism progress on campus? Whatever the case may have been, Ibram X. Kendi argues that the Black Campus Movement across the nation began declining in about 1972. This was also the case at MSU. In the late 1970s, Carl Taylor, then director of minority student affairs and assistant to the vice-president of student affairs, remarked that collective Black student activism at MSU noticeably tapered off after 1972, a year that was filled with student activism. The year started off with Black student mobilization. In January, in response to racial incidents in Brody Hall, about three hundred Black students from a variety of organizations—the OBA, the BUF, the BLFI, and fraternities and sororities—gathered in the hall to call for unity. Supportive of Black student-athletes, in 1972 MSU faculty members Green, Thomas Gunnings, and Joseph McMillan charged the Big Ten Conference with engaging in segregationist practices, the Coalition of Black Athletes—led by Allen Smith, Billy Joe Dupree, Herb Washington, and Nigel Goodison—demanded reforms for Black student-athletes, and approximately one hundred Black students affiliated with the Black Coalition Council and mobilized by their spokesperson Flint native Sam Riddle marched on the court before the MSU–Iowa basketball game at Jenison Fieldhouse, issuing a host of demands.

Following the killing of two Black students at Southern University in Baton Rouge, Louisiana, on November 16, 1972, after the governor called in the National Guard to quell students protesting inhumane living conditions on campus, MSU students organized and responded. The Multiracial Council of Progressive Organizations held meetings and issued statements, and the Black Brothers and Sisters of Brody protested by blocking a staircase into the Brody Hall cafeteria the day after twenty-year-old juniors Denver Smith and Leonard Douglas were murdered in front of Southern's administration building. On November 18, Nigel Goodison, with his first clenched above his head, marched on the court in Jenison Fieldhouse right before the annual Green and White basketball game. In the meantime, his comrades held protest banners. These were acts of solidarity with traumatized Southern University students. Goodison eventually left the court so the game could start. He returned to the court at halftime, demanding to address the crowd of two thousand for a few minutes over the public address system. He refused to leave in a timely fashion and was arrested and later released. In the meantime, Gus Ganakas's squad went back to the locker room, changed into their street clothes, and left Jenison. Throughout 1972 university administrators believed that the mounting racial tension on campus could have led to violence if preventative measures weren't instituted. In the spring, top University officials met privately and purportedly concluded that they discerned "a black–white polarization among students, faculty and staff that could lead to violence if currently emotionalism is not cooled."[24]

During the ever-evolving, brief, and eventful Black Campus Movement from 1968 until 1972 and a bit beyond, Black student-activists were the catalysts for some of the most far-reaching transformations at Michigan State. They did not totally succeed in transforming higher education in revolutionary manners. They did, however, compel the university to change in ways it had never done so before. The legacy of MSU Black students' activism during the Black Campus Movement extends far past their times.

Chapter 28

Black Power Arrives in East Lansing

On October 30, 1967, Floyd B. McKissick, the national director of the Congress of Racial Equality (CORE), visited East Lansing. The Associated Students of MSU booked McKissick as the inaugural speaker of the "Great Issues" series for the 1967–1968 academic year. In the MSU Auditorium, forty-five-year-old still fiery McKissick spoke before a crowd of approximately 300–350 people, mainly students, about the controversial and widely debated philosophy of Black Power that was popularized by civil rights organizer extraordinaire Stokely Carmichael during the summer of 1966. McKissick was unaware his visit and talk would help spark a Black student movement at MSU.

Under the leadership of McKissick, who in early January 1966 replaced the organization's cofounder and 1961 Freedom Ride organizer James Farmer, CORE abandoned Martin Luther King Jr.'s philosophy of nonviolent direct action and embraced Black Power. Given how the mainstream White media had misrepresented the bold concept, the focus of McKissick's oration wasn't surprising. MSU's student body was aware of the growing militancy among young African Americans. The slogan "Black Power" wasn't totally foreign to them. In February 1967, Stokely Carmichael spoke at MSU, and throughout the year the national media and the *State News* regularly covered the activities of "Black Powerists." In August 1967 at its convention in College Park, Maryland, the National Student Association, a confederation of college and university student government organizations founded in 1947, enthusiastically supported "student power" and more hesitantly endorsed Black Power. They agreed that Black Power entailed the unification of African Americans in the cause of Black liberation. To no avail, Blacks at the convention wanted to include Malcolm X's "by any means necessary" dictum to this statement (i.e., "liberation by any means necessary.") Heeding Carmichael's proclamation, the Black delegates advocated that Whites take a backseat in this struggle, that Blacks themselves lead their own struggles and determine their own destinies. One of the Black delegates from California State College in Los Angeles put it bluntly: "Stokely Carmichael says that the black man has to define his own identity. . . . We are not going to let those whites define our political movement for us."[1]

A week before McKissick's 1967 visit to MSU's campus, the prominent New York City book publisher Random House released Carmichael's and political scientist Charles V. Hamilton's *Black Power: The Politics of Liberation*. Highly anticipated, the book clarified the intricacies of what many considered a politically charged slogan. The book soon became a blueprint for a new approach to Black politics and liberation, especially for younger African American activists. Carmichael and Hamilton offered a road map for exploring the potential scope and content of "Black Power." By posing the appropriate questions and insightfully analyzing the problems encountered by Blacks, they aimed to help college-aged African Americans develop a new sense of Black consciousness in order to make sense of their collective reality and generate solutions to inescapable problems.[2]

In his talk at MSU in the early fall of 1967, McKissick, a lawyer, maintained that civil rights legislation, all too often in the "hands of racists," was not the solution to Black Americans' enduring struggle for equality; that even following *Brown v. Board of Education* in 1954 and the Civil Rights Act of 1964, African Americans remained segregated in "white-owned buildings" in the "ghetto." This represented a significant shift from his earlier approach as a civil rights lawyer in Durham, North Carolina. McKissick now insisted that Black people reject the implications of integration and instead create a "parallel society" in which they "control themselves in their own separate communities." In essence, he espoused Black self-determination and a version of Black economic nationalism similar to the pillars of Marcus Garvey's Universal Negro Improvement Association and Elijah Muhammad's Nation of Islam. His approach also dovetailed in some measure with what Robert L. Green told MSU Black students in September 1966. "The reason why whites feel threatened by black power is that they know what has been done with 'white power.' White power is not being able to get a house in East Lansing," Green professed. "What Negroes need today is not black power, but green power—economic power. This the Negroes must have."[3]

McKissick offered many suggestions to the small number of Black students in the audience. He encouraged them to follow the tenets of Black Power, cast off the racial designation "Negro" and instead self-identify as "Black" or "Afro-American," become "boat-rockers" by joining CORE and the Student Nonviolent Coordinating Committee (SNCC), and ultimately "make decisions for themselves." He had a different message for MSU's White leadership, chastising them for what he perceived as their mistreatment of Black students. "There ain't no meltin' pot in the meltin' pot of the world. We have been forced to be separate and apart even at MSU, where you have a whole lot of black football players, you still don't have a black coach," McKissick declared. "They know how to go recruit black men to play on their teams and make a name for the University, but you don't see one black coach out there training them." He also reprimanded the university for not offering courses in Black Studies, what he called a "Black Power curriculum."[4] With this critique, McKissick urged MSU's Black students to follow in the footsteps of Black students at several HBCUs and San Francisco State College who had been demanding Black Studies units, programs, and departments beginning in 1965 and 1966.

In the press conference following his impassioned speech, in response to a question about the rise in Black militancy symbolized by the founding of the Black Panther Party for Self-Defense in 1966, he remarked, "This is a violent country. To ask black people to be non-violent would be discrimination. Violence is pure American. We are the victims of violence. There can be change if the white man will change, but he won't face the truth of what he has done to the black man."[5] He also closed ranks with younger "militant" freedom fighters Carmichael and H. Rap Brown, saying they represented the sentiments of a new generation of Black freedom fighters. Following the press conference, McKissick met with Green and Black student-activists, counseling the ambitious youngsters about how to operationalize the concept of Black Power on campus.

Other "militant" Black civil rights leaders visited "the banks of the Red Cedar" and sparked the budding consciousnesses of young Black Spartans before McKissick. "Many of the liveliest and most controversial personalities in the nation speak on the MSU campus each year," boasted a student in the 1964 "Welcome Week" edition of the *State News*; "in recent years, campus speakers have included Negro leader Malcolm X, now the head of a controversial sect which advocates militant black supremacy." Four years after Malcolm's historic speech in the Erickson Kiva and nine months before McKissick's visit to MSU, on February 9, 1967, Carmichael, the celebrity-like national chairman of the SNCC, came to campus. He and McKissick knew each other well. With Martin Luther King Jr., Green, and others, in June 1966 they marched arm in arm during the continuation of James Meredith's March Against Fear. Carmichael delivered a talk to a "near-capacity crowd" of four thousand at the MSU Auditorium. Like McKissick's visit, this event was also part of ASMSU's Great Issues series. The small MSU chapter of SNCC, headed by Pat Smith, cosponsored this widely anticipated event, and members of MSU's Alpha Kappa Alpha and Delta Sigma Theta sororities and Alpha Phi Alpha fraternity served as ushers and helped arrange the logistics for Carmichael's visit.[6]

In a calm, measured, and scholarly manner, peppered with a bit of comedy, Carmichael defined Black Power, critiqued the media's portrayal of the Black Freedom Struggle, and offered a brief history of the modern Civil Rights Movement highlighting SNCC's role therein. He indicted white supremacy while drawing clear distinctions between "individual racism" and "institutionalized racism." Carmichael scoffed at the premise of integration and Bayard Rustin's "coalition theory" and cited extensively from the 1966 position statement in support of Black

Power by the National Committee of Negro Churchmen published in the *New York Times*. During the brief question and answer session, he underscored that the Black Freedom Struggle was to be led by African Americans. Without any hesitation, he told MSU's sympathetic and progressive White students that their role in the movement was to "work within their own race to civilize it." Unlike McKissick, Carmichael didn't talk about MSU's record of dealing with race relations, nor did he address the pressing issues facing Black students. The closest that he came to speaking directly to Black students was his comment, in response to a question posed by a Black student, that the college-educated "black bourgeoisie" had been "brainwashed" and needed to recommit themselves to the cause of Black liberation.[7]

Black students certainly attended McKissick's and Carmichael's speeches, but Whites were undoubtedly the majority of those in the MSU Auditorium on both occasions. There were at least ten times more people at Carmichael's talk than McKissick's. Given Carmichael's stardom, this isn't surprising. Many of those who attended Stokely's talk probably traveled from nearby Black communities to listen to the smooth-talking orator. The debonair twenty-six-year-old SNCC chairman probably also appealed to the students more than his elder McKissick who was born in 1922. Though young, Carmichael spoke as if he could have been one of their political science, history, or philosophy professors. Unlike their response to Malcolm X four years earlier, the White students laughed and applauded throughout Carmichael's carefully constructed talk. When Carmichael and McKissick visited campus, student activism in general was on the rise, especially the fervent anti–Vietnam War campaign. The loosely defined notion of "student power" had become a rallying cry at colleges and universities throughout the nation. A month after McKissick came to campus, MSU students in the left-wing Students for a Democratic Society (SDS) held a rally to protest the war at the Student Services Building. This was one of the largest on-campus antiwar demonstrations since the Orange Horse incident that took place in the fall of 1966, when several hundred students orchestrated a sit-in at Bessey Hall in protest of the firing of three American Thought and Language instructors who opposed the Vietnam War.

Though they were cognizant that Black casualties were proportionally higher than those of their White counterparts, Black students on campus were not noticeably active in SDS, an organization whose notion of "participatory democracy" didn't necessarily speak to their most pressing concerns. In the late 1960s, some Black students and staff at MSU seemed a bit ambivalent toward the national moratorium against the war. While Josephine Ferguson Wharton observed that young Blacks protested against the war alongside their White counterparts but received no attention from the mainstream for doing so, in 1969, two outspoken antiwar Black student-activists, Detroit senior Michele Lacey and Romulus senior Jason Lovette, similarly pointed out the differences between Blacks' and Whites' antiwar sentiments, echoing Muhammad Ali's beliefs about Blacks' serving in a war for a country that denied them their most basic civil rights.[8]

Six months before McKissick visited MSU, Ali famously refused to serve in Vietnam. "Why should they ask me to put on a uniform and go ten thousand miles from home and drop bombs and bullets on brown people in Vietnam while so-called Negro people in Louisville are treated like dogs and denied simple human rights? No, I am not going ten thousand miles from home to help murder and burn another poor nation simply to continue the domination of white slave masters of the darker people the world over," Ali announced; "the real enemy of my people is right here." In August 1971, Kimathi Mohammed (formerly known as Stanley John McClinton), chairman general of the Black Liberation Front, International, was placed on two years of probation for refusing conscription into the U.S. military. "I want to make it clear that the basis of my objection to racist and inhuman practices of the United States is ethical as well as socio-political and legal. We, Black people, descendants of Africans, stand for peace, whereas the United States military stand for war." Mohammed continued, "We stand for brotherhood of mankind within the context of the right of all peoples to self-determination, whereas the United States military stand for white supremacy."[9]

There were not as many Black students on campus in February 1967 when Carmichael spoke at MSU as there were in the fall of 1967 when McKissick visited. In the summer and fall of 1967, MSU initiated more deliberate efforts to recruit Black students. It's plausible that as many, perhaps even more, Black students attended McKissick's speech than Carmichael's based upon the increase in the Black student population between the 1966–1967 and 1967–1968 academic years. By the time that McKissick came to campus, the Black student population was becoming a bit more radicalized as a result of recent episodes following Carmichael's visit, including Martin Luther King Jr.'s denunciation of the Vietnam War, Muhammad Ali's refusal to serve in the military, the Black Panthers' armed protest at the California state capital, and the urban rebellions that swept the country during the summer of 1967. The devastating riots in Detroit in late July hit close to home for many of MSU's Black students. Their interpretations of what went down differed drastically from those offered by the *State News* reporters' extensive coverage through August. The mock slave auction held in Holden Hall several days after Carmichael's visit to campus to raise funds for "an orphan overseas"—as covered by the *State News* under the headers "Dorm Holds Slave Auction" and "Two Fine White Slaves with Rhythm" with an accompanying photo of a Black student dressed like a slave driver—would not have gone uncontested by up-and-coming Black student-activists in the days following McKissick's visit when they had begun contemplating the creation of a campus-wide Black student organization.[10]

In late October 1967 when McKissick lit up the MSU Auditorium stage, the estimated 690 Black students on campus represented about 2 percent of the total student campus enrollment of more than 38,000. Though diverse, the Black students on campus in the fall of 1967 and the late 1960s were often stereotyped as coming from so-called educationally and economically disadvantaged backgrounds, primarily from "inner-city" Detroit. Challenging this, in describing the incoming Black student population in 1969, Green pointed out that approximately 25 percent "did not qualify for financial assistance of any kind."[11] The labeling of Black students at MSU as being intellectually inferior and unprepared for the rigors at the university developed earlier in the 1960s when the university made some small-scale targeted efforts at recruiting Black students. The increase in MSU's Black student population beginning in 1967 as well as the prevalent derogatory stereotypes about Black students during the later 1960s can be traced back to university initiatives earlier in the decade, beginning in 1963, to recruit more severely disadvantaged students, most of whom were Black. Students in the campus NAACP were no doubt aware of this program.

Under the direction of William A. Finni, MSU director of admissions and scholarships, and Gwendolyn Norrell, assistant director of the MSU Counseling Center, the Office of Admissions and Scholarships established connections with five Michigan high schools who "served the most disadvantaged audiences" and invited their principals to nominate five graduating male seniors who demonstrated the "drive" and "motivation" to succeed. Clinging to the notion of Black male criminality and cultural deprivation and denying Black agency, Finni described the purpose of the program as "a chance to pull students away from a situation where they are destined to become public charges, on the welfare or unemployment rolls or in our criminal institutions." Finni added that once the students were on campus, they would have to figure out the new and foreign environment on their own. With a limited amount of funding from professors who donated the proceeds from their speaking engagements, MSU offered scholarships to these students—described disparagingly by the *Detroit Free Press* as youths "from slum areas and broken homes" who "never expected to go to college"—and secured them loans so they would only be responsible for coming up with one-third of their total university expenses. Twenty-two young men entered this program called "Project Ethyl" and "Operation Ethyl." They were advised by Norrell "who literally met with every member of the Project Ethyl for an average of more than once every week for that entire first year."[12]

This program was viewed as somewhat successful. Though many of the students understandably faced a range of challenges, 41 percent of the students graduated on time in 1967. At the time, the national average for the four-year graduation rate was about 40 percent. In part inspired by the results and potential of Project Ethyl, in the summer of 1967, the MSU admissions team established a new program called Project Detroit, interchangeably referred to as the Detroit Project. As it was described by the Department of Health, Education and Welfare, Office of Education based upon a report submitted by MSU administrators, the purpose of this program was "to increase black enrollment and raise the level of skills in non-whites in the Detroit community."[13] This time with support from the university and small grants from the Kellogg Foundation and the Ford Foundation and under the leadership of Lloyd Cofer, a contemporary of President John A. Hannah who migrated to Detroit in the mid-1930s and became the first Black counselor in the city's public school system and whose daughter attended MSC in the later 1940s, MSU admissions staff members worked with public school officials and African American community activists in Detroit, including a group that became known as the Volunteer Placement Corps, who helped recruit incoming Black freshman from the city. Sixty-six of the seventy students recruited into this program, students who "did not meet traditional admissions criteria," were admitted from thirteen of Detroit's public high schools. On campus, they were provided with support services, counseling, tutoring, and financial aid, when necessary. The coordinators of the program were encouraged by the results. Twenty-seven of the sixty-six Black students, 41 percent, returned in the fall of 1968, and the program was revised a bit for the 1968–1969 academic year.

In November 1968, the report on the program, "Admission of High Risk Students at Michigan State University," pointed out: "for 1969, we have been more vigorous than ever before in seeking to attract the nation's most able black youngsters to take an interest in Michigan State." The authors of the report admitted they faced challenges in recruiting "well-prepared black high school students," securing potential Black students with financial aid, and figuring out how to best predict which students would be successful.[14] Still, the coordinators of the program seemed optimistic, declaring that they were "in the business to stay." Of utmost importance to them was getting buy-in from faculty who would believed in this cause. Several years after the debut of Detroit Project, Green and his colleagues posed a handful of suggestions for increasing MSU's Black student population, such as the creation of a special admissions committee for "minority" (code word for "Black") students, improved support services, new nontraditional recruiting strategies, better financial aid packages, and a system for evaluating the strengths and weaknesses of such efforts. Unlike the authors of the November 1968 report, Green and his coworkers believed it was "incumbent upon the university administration, and no one else, to assume the leadership in mobilizing the total university community in developing the necessary strategies to initiate and put into action an immediate, strong and positive framework for action related to expanding higher educational opportunities for minority students at MSU."[15]

When described by the media, including the *State News*, those admitted through the Detroit Project were portrayed as being "needy," "disadvantaged," and academically deficient students who did not meet "the normal MSU admission standards." As the riots were taking place in Detroit, under the title "Detroit Project: 'U' Gives Deprived Youths a Better Chance at College," a staff writer for the student paper announced the arrival of "70 disadvantaged Detroit high school students" to East Lansing. She revealed they had test scores and school records that "would not normally qualify them for college admission," and they needed more "financial help" and "counseling and tutoring than most students." MSU, in her mind, took on the responsibility "for seeking out needy students, specifically needy Negroes, and helping them to come to college, stay and graduate." Although Gwendolyn Norrell of the Counseling Center, a long supporter of Black students at MSU who created one of the first surveys for first-year Black students in the fall of 1969, said that "they're fairly typical students," the student journalist stressed they were "special freshmen," requiring "special" treatment, including "special orientation tests" that would "be interpreted for them." Citing the director of admissions, the student shared, "They've already gotten a bad break—they're at an educational disadvantage, weaker in verbal skills—but they're willing to work. We don't want them to get another bad break in the form of flunking out." In mid-August, the *State News* reported on these incoming Spartans' separate "two-and-a-half day orientation session to glimpse college life, arrange a class schedule and register." The staff writers for the *State News* didn't have malicious intent when they penned their short exposés. Yet in the process of parroting and editorializing the university's description of the program, they promoted the stereotype of the poor, educationally disadvantaged Black student in need of remedial courses, hand-holding, and social refinement.[16]

Many Black readers were offended by how their soon-to-be classmates were portrayed. One student's response to a White professor's initiative called "Operation Get Acquainted"—a program that matched twenty "Negro children [who came] from fatherless homes" with middle-class white families in Lansing, Okemos, and Haslett for a week in August 1967—offers some insight into how some Blacks might have viewed the language employed in the articles on the Detroit Project. In a letter to the editors of the *State News* in late July 1967 entitled "Now It's Whitey's Turn," a Black student challenged how the "Negro youth" were portrayed in the article about "Operation Get Acquainted" as well as the entire premise of the program. "It seems to me that if you really wish to know the 'other race' it is up to you to humble yourself to enter his home, not he yours. Why not send your son or daughter to spend two weeks in the home of a Negro, regardless of class?" The student continued, "Your program gives the middle class white the same opportunity he has always had. That is to sit back and be the recipient of honor for having been so open-minded." In the summer of 1968, another Black student specifically commented that the Detroit Project, though highly touted by the university, "failed miserably as an attempt to placate the black community."[17]

Despite the pride the university took in the Detroit Project, considering it one of their "special projects" to increase Black enrollment, it was not the reason why the Black student population drastically increased during the late 1960s and the early 1970s. By the fall of 1970, President Wharton reported that 227 total Black students had been recruited to MSU through the Detroit Project and seventy more had been admitted for the fall of 1970.[18] For the fall of 1970, of the approximately six hundred Black students admitted to MSU, less than 10 percent of these students were admitted through the Detroit Project. In 1971, the initiative was discontinued and replaced with a new "Developmental Program" that spanned the entire state of Michigan. The impetus for the increase in the Black student population at MSU was the result of Black student activism following the assassination of Martin Luther King Jr. and the university's ensuing affirmative action initiatives. One of the Black student-activists to critique the Detroit Project as a mechanism to recruit a more diverse student body was outspoken graduate student-activist Barry D. Amis. In late October 1967, he heard McKissick's passionate appeals in the MSU Auditorium and met with him privately, along with other Black student-activists in the making. McKissick's timely visit and message inspired Black students in attendance like Amis.

In the several weeks following McKissick's visit, Black students began deliberately laying the foundations for what would soon become the first radical MSU Black student organization. In the early 1970s, BSA cofounder Richard W. Thomas reflected on the organization's inception, "It was 1967, and a group of us met in Robert Green's basement with Floyd McKissick afterwards. And McKissick said, 'You should have a Black student movement on this campus.'" In mid-November 1967, Amis, along with undergraduate students Charles Thorton, Phil Hart, and Richard Thomas, convened a Black student meeting in Owen Hall. More than one hundred students were there. The topic of the moment was "Getting Ourselves Together to Take Care of Business." Two weeks later, an organizational meeting was held in the MSU Union Building. The purpose of the consequential gathering was clear-cut: a call for unity and the selection a name for a new-fashioned organization and its officers. Among the suggested names included the Black Student Union, Soul, Inc., Afro-American Student Conference, and Us. After a high-spirited discussion, a consensus was reached. The new Black student organization became known as Black Students' Alliance (BSA). The BSA spent its first several months on practical initiatives such as battles for new ATL courses, tutorial projects for African American undergraduate students, cultural events, and meetings with MSU Black faculty and leaders like SCLC project director Stoney Cooks and comedian Dick Gregory. Led by Amis, early BSA steering committee members included Thomas, Jill Weatherspoon, Jason Lovette, Richard Allen, and Bob Robinson. Toni Eubanks and Billye Suttles served as the organization's first secretaries.[19]

Chapter 29

McKissick's and King's Progeny

When Floyd McKissick spoke on campus in the fall of 1967, Black students were not necessarily perceived as being leading outspoken activists by some of their White classmates. In late November 1967, editors of the *State News* excluded them among the radical student-activists in their overview of the "the many shades of student power" on campus. About a year later by the fall of 1968, the *State News* had a small change of heart. In overviewing the recent awakening of "student protest" at MSU, "sometimes referred to as a center of intense apathy," a staff writer commented on the activities of anti–drug prosecution protesters, Students for a Democratic Society (SDS) (whose national convention was held at MSU in June), the antiwar MSU Resistance, and the Student Liberation Alliance. The student journalist also fleetingly acknowledged Black student activism: "Another part of the student protest revival has been the growing demand for racial justice on campus as epitomized by the formation of the Black Students' Alliance (BSA) and a two day sports boycott on April 25 and 26 by 38 black athletes."[1] This lack of full recognition from the (White) student paper continued into the next year. In the spring of 1969, the author of a lengthy essay, "Historical Outline of Radicalism at MSU," totally ignored the campus NAACP and only mentioned BSA in passing, focusing instead on radical White student organizations.[2]

Between January and September 1968, BSA became the leading Black student organization challenging the university to deal with fraught on-campus race relations and the needs of Black students. Employing the philosophy of Black Power and new approaches to activism,

Barry Amis teaching a class as a doctoral candidate. Courtesy of Michigan State University Archives and Historical Collections.

they replaced the campus NAACP whose tactics of interracial collaboration and peaceful, respectable protest were no longer relevant to a new generation of Black students. Whether or not they realized it, BSA employed some of the same tactics as their predecessors, such as consciousness-raising, marches, and mass civil disobedience. But their rhetoric was more radical and their methods more confrontational.

About two months after McKissick's visit, on January 9, 1968, Barry D. Amis, a doctoral candidate in romance languages from Philadelphia, Pennsylvania, who was personally inspired by McKissick, authored a blistering editorial in the *State News*, "Educational Tokenism at MSU." This was his coming-out as the leading Black student spokesperson for the 1967–1968 academic year. Though his leadership of BSA lasted for less than a year, he did much to articulate the concerns of his Black classmates and help organize Black students into collective action. Given his mature sense of Black consciousness, educational background, and eloquent prose, he was a perfect spokesperson for the movement. In a 2022 interview with the MSU College of Arts and Letters, Amis reminisced, "I view my activities at MSU as a continuation of the struggle for worker's rights and racial justice of my father and the civil rights activities of my sisters in the South." Amis's father, B. D. Amis, was active in the NAACP, the Communist Party USA, and the League of Struggle for Negro Rights, and when Barry was a child, radical Black activists, including Paul Robeson, visited his family.[3]

In his January 9, 1968, editorial, Amis lambasted the student paper for celebrating the Detroit Project as being a part of the university's civil rights mission by simply admitting twenty-five Black students per term. "Even twenty-five hundred black students per term would not be sufficient to break down the de facto segregation at MSU," Amis rebutted. He told the mainly White *State News* readership that Black students would not be "appeased by token gestures." He asserted, "If Michigan State is to serve society, if it is to desegregate its component parts, if it is to be more than a white middle-class institution, then it must open its doors to black students."[4]

Echoing McKissick, Amis chastised MSU for investing too much energy and resources in recruiting star Black athletes. "Why can't a similar effort be made to bring in just plain students? Must we all be football players or basketball players?" Asking MSU administrators to be "sincere and honest," Amis declared, "Gestures are no longer sufficient. If MSU is going to recognize its responsibility then we welcome and support its action. If it only hopes to divert public attention from the true nature of this institution then we must expose it and condemn its officers as bigots and hypocrites." Amis's bold critique was as much leveled against the broader MSU community as it was an attack on President John A. Hannah whom he called the "amphibious head of the U.S. Civil Rights Commission."[5] That neither the *State News* nor any White readers publicly responded to Amis's well-written rant is somewhat surprising, especially considering White students' responses to Black-authored editorials about civil rights topics earlier in the decade and the *State News* editorial board's self-proclaimed liberalism. Hannah paid attention to Amis's editorial. Several days later, he invited the outspoken graduate student to talk about his concerns, concluding that his view of tokenism at MSU was a result of the university's poor communications strategy.

Less than two weeks after Amis penned his critical editorial, on January 18, 1968, the *State News* announced the creation of the BSA. Amis, who served with accomplished undergraduate poet, playwright and Detroit native Richard W. Thomas as cochair of the new organization, credited McKissick, whom he met with privately during his visit, for encouraging him and other Black student-activists to create the new organization. At an informal press conference in the days before the *State News* announced the group's formation, Amis explicitly and strategically defined the group as not being "anti-white" or "militant," but instead as constituting a "positive, contributive type organization." He reasoned the group needed to get formal approval to be an official on-campus student organization from ASMSU and didn't want it to be oversimplified as constituting a haphazardly organized reactionary group of disgruntled Black students without a serious vision and mission. He claimed he and other Black students, as many as three hundred, had been meeting earlier in the term.

Reiterating what he expressed in his January 9 broadside, Amis stressed that BSA was needed because Black students were excluded from "any major participation in University life other than athletics." He announced that the group sought to work with the Lansing chapter of the NAACP and similar Black student organizations at other universities in the state. That he didn't mention collaborating with the campus NAACP suggests they were no longer active or Amis and his followers didn't view them as being part of their newborn movement. According to Amis, BSA's chief concerns focused on contesting the university's request for students to indicate their race during registration, the "integration of the coaching staff and the University police," and, building upon the campus NAACP's efforts, getting the university to support open housing in East Lansing. "We hope that the university would assert itself as vigorously for civil rights as it does for intercollegiate athletics," Amis trumpeted.[6] The January 18 announcement of BSA's founding in the *State News* and the descriptions of what Amis said at the group's first press conference represent BSA's first documented public statements.

The emergence of BSA at MSU and their ensuing demands and activities were part of a larger Black student movement at predominantly White institutions (PWIs) throughout the nation. Amis, who became the go-to person for Black history–centered programs at the university during the late 1960s, was correct in the summer of 1968 when he observed, "on almost every college campus which has ten or more black students a Black Student Union or an Afro-American Society of one style or another has risen. At MSU we have the Black Students' Union."[7] Under such organizations, Black student-activists publicized and challenged racist incidents on their campuses and called for Black student unity and on-campus activism; the recruitment of Black students, faculty, administrators, and staff; African American and African cultural pride; student services for Black students; and the introduction of Black Studies entities. From its founding in mid-January 1968 until the summer of 1969 when it faded to the background and gave rise to the

Black Liberation Front, International, BSA was the primary movement center for Black student activism at Michigan State. BSA took the lead in galvanizing Black students on campus, and its leaders assumed the role of speaking with a collective voice for Black students, whether or not they agreed with their actions, approaches, and ideologies.

Reflecting the mood of Black college and university students across the nation, BSA introduced an experimental and new-fashioned approach to Black student activism. In the process, they inspired the creation of many other Black student organizations and the development of a cadre of Black leaders. Beginning in the spring of 1968, the Black Campus Movement that BSA helped launch spread rapidly. April 1968 was a particularly important month in the history of BSA and the burgeoning Black Campus Movement in East Lansing. On the eve of the assassination of Martin Luther King Jr., Black students were beginning to show signs that they were poised to act. Coincidentally, on the day that King was assassinated, before the news of his death was broadcasted throughout the world's airwaves, the *State News'* bi-weekly magazine, *Collage*, released a special issue, "The Black Revolution, through the Eyes of Students." Several Black students, including Amis, shared their views about the Black Freedom Struggle.

Detroit junior Jill Witherspoon lamented that Black students, from her perspective, still believed they could "'make it' in the white system" at MSU and "still be militants." She called upon her classmates to "be socially relevant to the black movement." Black athletes, she contended, "must understand that a call for black militancy includes them too." "Being one of Duffy's boys," Witherspoon aired, "can't be that rewarding." Echoing McKissick and Amis, she observed, "Why does this university go all over the United States in search of black athletes but not potential black physicists and mathematicians?" After lambasting MSU for not supporting open housing in East Lansing, she concluded, "Our identification with the black masses necessarily means that we see the relevancy of this university only in terms of its usefulness to our goals." In his brief commentary in the *Collage*, Amis critically overviewed the Kerner Commission Report, drawing connections between Black unrest throughout the nation and the status of Blacks at MSU. "This white, middle-class University," Amis opined citing several recent examples, "is a bastion of racism and apathy." For him, the university needed to demonstrate an unambiguous commitment to social justice.[8]

Thursday, April 4, 1968, was a major turning point in the Black Campus Movement at MSU and colleges and universities throughout the nation. "As a result of the death of Dr. Martin Luther King, Jr., the Black Student Alliance sought to resolve the discriminatory practices of the university through a series of demands," Don E. Coleman ascertained. In his 1973 dissertation on MSU's responses to Black student activism at MSU from 1967 until 1972, College for Urban Affairs administrative assistant Eric V. A. Winston echoed Coleman, concluding, "the events surrounding the assassination of Dr. Martin Luther King, Jr. was the incident which prompted the university to begin meaningful response to student concerns."[9] Several hours after King was assassinated, at about 6:00 p.m. eastern time, Black students at Holden Hall organized a solemn march across campus that lasted from about 9:30 p.m. until 11:30 p.m. The march ended at McDonel Hall where Amis briefly addressed the more than 150 marchers and requested that sympathetic White student marchers leave, allowing Blacks the necessary space to mourn and strategize. Following Stokely Carmichael's lead, Amis insisted that Blacks themselves organize to confront institutional racism.

The next day at about 9:00 a.m., approximately nine hundred people, "both black and white, student and faculty," assembled at the Union Building and proceeded to the ballroom for an "hour-long convocation for Dr. King" that would be followed by a march across campus. The gathering and march was organized by Robert L. Green, Amis, and BSA. In the ballroom, Amis told the crowd that the initial purpose of the demonstration was for Black students to "do some soul searching" and "do something *on our own*." After the playing of King's famous 1963 "I Have a Dream" oration, Green took to the podium and chastised the MSU White community and President Hannah, who was in attendance, for contributing to the conditions that led to King's death. He highlighted the university's weak stance on open housing in East Lansing. Following Green's solemn remarks, members of BSA asked the Whites in the audience to leave the ballroom and wait for them outside the Union Building for the march. At about 10:00 a.m., the march through campus began. Some of the enraged marchers reportedly chanted "We shall burn it down," wordplay on the gospel song and civil rights anthem "We Shall Overcome." There was no violence or destruction of property during the march. Aware of BSA's plans, the MSU police enabled for an orderly demonstration. By the time the group reached Berkey Hall, they were about 1,500 strong. The march ended at the Administration Building with hundreds of Black students cramming into the first floor of this historic structure located in the sacred part of campus. The gathering in Linton Hall became a sit-in. At the Administration Building, Amis, several other BSA officers, and Green met with President Hannah in his office while the other marchers headed back to the Union Building. Beginning in the early 1960s, members of the campus NAACP organized smaller scale marches and demonstrations. But Amis drew a clear distinction between BSA's approach and that of earlier Black student civil rights activists. "We black students have taken a moderate, responsible course, believing that whites at the University will be moderate and reasonable," Amis announced, "but the time for vague agreement in the principle and sympathy is over. The time for action is now."[10]

On behalf of BSA, on Friday, April 5, 1968, Amis presented a lengthy list of demands to President Hannah and the Board of Trustees. The demands were wide-reaching and prefaced by BSA's observation that there were "not enough" Black students, faculty, administrators, and employees ("including campus police, bus drivers, etc."). They called for the creation of several initiatives in honor of Dr. King: the "immediate upgrading of all black personnel at the university in all areas"; the "recruitment of more Negro students, faculty, and administrators"; the hiring of Black "coaches, doctors, professional counselors, residence hall staff, personnel, campus police, and bus drivers"; Black Studies courses; more scholarships designed for Black students; revised admissions procedures; support from the university for open housing in East Lansing; projects that linked MSU to Lansing's Black community; and an end to awarding "building contracts to companies known to discriminate in their hiring practices." BSA ended its list with a warning of some sort. "These are only a few of the demands that we express at this time." They continued, "We hope that this very sad occasion will be the start of long overdue changes."[11]

Hannah was purportedly pleased with his meeting with BSA representatives and claimed the university was already in the process of addressing some of their pressing demands with his specially appointed Committee of Sixteen, a group he assembled in late March to deal with issues surrounding race relations on campus. "In principle and in their objectives the list the alliance gave me are ones the University is presently working on," Hannah observed. "I believe the time has come for this University to really get moving in this area. But all of this has been in the mill before today and we don't need to have the assassination to have this come about." In

Led by Robert L. Green and Richard W. Thomas, Black students march after the assassination of Martin Luther King Jr. Courtesy of Michigan State University Archives and Historical Collections.

response to one of BSA's demands, Hannah explained how he instructed athletic director Biggie Munn and John Fuzak, chairman of the athletic council, to hire two Black coaches by the fall of 1968. Replying to the demand to recruit more Black students, Hannah echoed presidents of PWIs throughout the country, claiming it was difficult to find "qualified" Black students. To this unsubstantiated assertion, Amis sarcastically responded, "then just take black students." On Tuesday, April 9, Hannah canceled classes, allowing students to watch the full coverage of King's funeral on television, and addressed the campus community on a closed-circuit television system. He promised to make Black students' demands "a matter of high priority" and conjured up notions of MSU's admirable record of race relations. "Let us not dissipate our strength by abandoning the ground in which our strength is rooted," Hannah spouted; "the University must be faithful to its own traditions and its own ways of getting things done if it is to be truly effective."[12] BSA requested that Robert L. Green, his wife, and four Black student leaders be sponsored to attend King's funeral as personal emissaries of the university. Hannah, who called King a prophet, responded immediately to BSA's solicitation by designating Green as the official MSU representative to attend the slain leader's funeral. The MSU president gifted Green a personal check for one hundred dollars to cover the travel expenses for his wife and secured four hundred dollars from Howard J. Stoddard, the founder of the Michigan National Bank, to cover the travel costs of the four Black students.[13]

Several days later, in "An Open Letter to Black Students of Michigan State University," the steering committee of the BSA assumed the mantle of Black student leadership, dubbing themselves "the most powerful student group on campus." They warned, "We are now in a position to effect radical changes in university policies. We shall move this university into the area of social relevance or close it down by massive civil disobedience." They genuinely viewed what they were doing as being historic. "We are on our way toward relevant *Black* student power. We are rapidly developing a posture of organized strength from which to bargain. Never before on this campus has any Black group reached this stage. We intend to stay a relevant and powerful organization. We cannot afford to be too trustful of tactics conceived in the face of confrontation to placate us. We intend to make this university relevant to all people."[14]

In several pieces he penned for the *State News* between April and July, Amis, speaking on behalf of Black students, shared his views on the university's slow, reactionary approach to BSA's demands and Hannah's "ways of getting things done." Embracing Black Power as an approach and analytical framework, on April 24, in an essay "Fate of a Nation in Black and White," Amis articulated his and BSA's impatience with the university's conventional expressions of grief following the murder of King. Amis summoned the university community to "stop playing games" and commit to recruiting more Black students. Arguing that many Black students from major Michigan cities had been "miseducated in ghetto schools," Amis maintained, "MSU must commit itself to bringing in significant numbers of black students (four or five thousand) and providing them with the necessary tutorial, remedial and counseling services to make their experience here a successful one." He assured that BSA was not going to let things slide. "If the university truly believes that the plight of minority groups must be bettered then it must begin by admitting more students from those groups." Amis concluded, "the time for dilly-dallying is past. I say to Hannah and to the white students on this campus—do something!"[15]

The day after Amis's call to action was printed, on April 25, twenty-four Black football players skipped spring practice. A group of thirty-eight Black athletes, mainly football players whose names were printed in the April 26 issue of the *State News*, then called for a boycott of "all spring sports events and practices." Led by BSA member and halfback LaMarr Thomas, the group submitted a detailed list of grievances and demands to Hannah and athletic director Biggie Munn. The athletes were disgruntled by Munn's unwillingness to support an earlier statement asking Hannah to look into their concerns. Black athletes' concerns surfaced before April 1968. At the end of the 1967 football season, before the late November contest with the Northwestern Wildcats, a group of Black athletes representing different sports—Lee Lafayette, Don Crawford, Tony Keyes, and LaMarr Thomas—publicized what they described as mistreatment. By the early months of 1968, they were ready for action. On the eve of the boycott, Jack Pitts and Don Crawford consulted with Green and then sent a letter to Hannah and Munn on April 22. The response from MSU administrators was slow, and Munn claimed there was no discrimination in athletics at MSU. The boycott was successful in that it resulted in the hiring of several coaches including Jim Bibbs and, in the fall of 1969, Matthew Aitch, assistant freshman basketball coach, and Jerry Kimborugh, trainer.[16]

After Coleman was hired as MSU's first African American assistant football coach in mid-April 1968, Black football players Charles Bailey, Frank Taylor, and LaMarr Thomas presented a list of demands to an unsympathetic Munn. According to one Black football player, Munn glanced at the list, "then smiled and said, 'Ho, ho, I guess that you want a black ticket manager or something.'" Historian Johnny Smith suggests that "Munn's refusal to take the athletes' demands seriously precipitated the boycott." By late April, they were fed up and made it clear their actions were not spontaneous. Their maneuvers had been brewing for some time and were supported by other Black athletes. "We got together last fall and talked about this," Thomas divulged when describing the nature of the boycott. "We have the support of all black athletes, students, and from black athletes from State from 1964 on."[17]

The Black student-athletes, who collectively identified themselves as "the black athletes of Michigan State University," insisted that the university hire Black coaches, trainers, athletic counselors, and nonprofessional workers in the university athletic facilities. They were dismayed that MSU had never had a Black woman cheerleader. For the 1969–1970 academic year, two Black women, Flint senior Lynn Weaver and Detroit junior Celeste Moy, were invited to be on the MSU cheerleading squad. Not only did they face what they considered racial prejudice when they tried out, but while they were on the team they alleged being discriminated against. Supported by Black athletes, Coleman, the BLFI's Investigative Task Force, and others, Weaver and Moy charged the cheerleader coach with racism in 1970.[18] The Black student-athletes were also upset that African American student-athletes were discouraged from playing sports other than football and basketball, especially baseball. From 1950 until 1974, only eight Blacks lettered in baseball.[19] They critiqued those who advised them for routinely enrolling them in nonacademic courses so they could easily maintain their eligibility. The Black student-athletes viewed such courses as insults to their intellectual capabilities. Echoing concerns raised by Amis who most likely consulted with them, the Black athletes explicitly situated their concerns within the broader context of what scholar-activist Harry Edwards discussed in his pathbreaking 1968 book, *The Revolt of the Black Athlete*. They endorsed Edwards and the Olympic Project for Human Rights' call for a boycott of the 1968 Summer Olympic Games in Mexico City. "This is a racist university, much like the system of the world," MSU's Black athletes deduced. "It's a question of being black or used." They made it known they would boycott until their grievances were addressed. Reiterating his response to BSA in the immediate aftermath of the assassination of King, Hannah ensured the university would "move fast as it can in this area." Munn was more defensive than Hannah in his response. Claiming the university was "not just paying lip-service," the former head football coach rebutted that MSU had a stellar track record of recruiting Black athletes and that if the boycott continued, those participating would risk losing their scholarships.[20]

The boycott received a great deal of local media coverage, something Hannah and Munn sought to prevent. During the summer of 1968, a correspondent for *Newsweek* discussed the implications of the boycott, expressing his surprise that Black athletes in one of the most progressive football programs were disgruntled. Black football players' discontent served as a corrective counternarrative to one of the university's points of pride, directly questioning MSU's claim to fame as being a civil rights trailblazer on the gridiron under head coach Duffy Daugherty who never did totally grasp the deeper meaning of the boycott. Despite the hours he spent with his Black players, he had difficulty empathizing with them. In his autobiography, he celebrated the benevolence of his football program. Maintaining discrimination was "never a problem" in the program and that he was the first coach to "actively" recruit Black players from the South, he upheld, "There was a problem on campus as there was all across the country but it had nothing whatsoever to do with football." He belittled the Black Campus Movement, referring to BSA, of which his star halfback LaMarr Thomas was an active member, as the "so-called Black Student Alliance." He also portrayed the boycott as something very minor, recollecting, "The problems were aired and solved, and that was the extent of our so-called 'black problem.'"[21]

To Daugherty, Munn, and Hannah's delight, the boycott ended shortly after it began. A day after a rally in the MSU Union Building where a crowd of about two hundred listened to Thomas and Green, among others, on Friday, April 27, the group's representatives met privately with MSU's Big Ten faculty representative, John A. Fuzak, and an agreement was reached. The university agreed to work toward hiring more Black coaches, physicians, trainers, and employees in the Jenison Fieldhouse, the Intramural Building, and the Ice Arena; recruiting more Black baseball players and swimmers; and having Black cheerleaders by the fall. University officials also agreed to further discuss the prospects of hiring a Black counselor and meet with the Black athletes and members of BSA in the summer to discuss the "progress made toward fulfilling these commitments." In response, LaMarr Thomas remarked, "We did not start this for publicity. We wanted change, and that there has been change is proved by our return to practice."[22]

Several days after the short-lived boycott ended, on May 1, 1968, the Black athletes and BSA issued statements in the *State News* further clarifying their position in the midst of rumors and misinterpretations. BSA's steering committee stressed that the university's portrayal of the boycott as a minor "misunderstanding" about "alleged" grievances was patently false. They underscored that their classmates only returned because the university "agreed to act immediately on the demands." The Black athletes sought to correct the "distortions" of the case in the "mass media" and the *State News*. They reiterated that their demands had deep roots, they returned to practice only because the university's response was quick and appropriate, and they had no regrets for their actions. They explicitly situated their demands within the broader context of the Black Freedom Struggle. "We, as students, athletes, but most important as black people, want it known that our problems are just a segment of the problems which face all our people in this country." They continued, "the black students' problems are the black athletes' problems and the black athletes' problems are the black students' problems. We as black people share in this common fight against a society that will not allow black people to meaningfully participate in it. We hope that our efforts will encourage our brothers throughout the nation to search their souls and ask what might be done to insure a proper place for us in it."[23]

Largely as a response to BSA's demands, in late April 1968, the Committee of Sixteen offered its recommendations, encompassing increased recruitment of Black students, faculty, administrators, and staff and the creation of a Center of Race and Urban Affairs. Hannah welcomed and endorsed these suggestions. Taken together with the success of the Black athletes' momentary boycott, BSA had a full head of steam moving into the 1968–1969 academic year. Late in the spring of 1968, under the leadership of BSA officeholder Ronald (Ron) Bailey, the organization initiated a fund and clothing drive supporting the Poor People's Campaign in Washington, D.C., and during the summer of 1968, the BSA steering committee, composed of Amis, Bailey, Richard Thomas, Jason Lovette, LaMarr Thomas, and others "maintained a close-knit relationship," and stayed busy organizing programs and strategies for the upcoming academic year, namely consciousness-raising activities in the dormitories and workshops on the challenges faced by Black students and how to enhance their experiences at a large PWI.[24]

During the summer of 1968, Amis continued to publicize Black students' demands in the pages of the *State News*. In a late June commentary "MSU, the Do Nothing 'U,'" Amis outlined BSA's goals, explicitly calling for Black Power and defining their mission as being a departure from past approaches. "Black students now adopt the militant stance of the Black Power philosophy," he blazoned; "when forced by the intransigence of the university to demonstrate their earnestness, black students are now willing to confront both the university and the society." "The Black student organization at MSU has been characterized by its 'moderation' and its willingness to 'work with the University.' Yet, there arrives a point where moderation becomes acquiescence and cooperation becomes a sell-out." Amis added, "Black students will no longer tolerate such inequalities." For Amis and BSA, the university had not made notable progress "in the area" of racial equality since they issued their first set of demands in early April. "MSU could be a force for major social change; yet it is reluctant even to be a follower." In late June of 1968, Bailey echoed Amis, sharing BSA's philosophy with a group of college deans. "Black students are shaking up the ivory towers on college campuses," Bailey asserted. "Hopefully, they will shake them upside down."[25]

During the summer of 1968, Bailey—who served as president of MSU's chapter of the Blue Key Honor Society and as a member of the MSU Student-Faculty Judiciary—demonstrated his skills as a refined and still militant spokesperson for BSA. A native of Claxton, Georgia, where he attended all-Black schools growing up, Bailey worked for several months as an intern for the Joint Economics Committee in the nation's capitol. Such an opportunity matched ideally with Bailey's interests. A liberal arts major and Honors College student, he had a concentration in economics and had plans of attending law school. In late July, Bailey provided a statement to the U.S. Senate Committee on Appropriations in strong support of S. 2979, a bill "to establish a Commission on Negro History and Culture; to conduct a study of all proposals to research, document, compile, preserve, and disseminate data on Negro history and culture." In his brief testimony, Bailey celebrated past struggles to popularize Black history dating back to the days of "The Father of Black History" Carter G. Woodson, highlighted the influence of Black college and university students' demands for humanities and social science curricula reform, stressed that the commission should respect and support "the ongoing efforts in the black community to correct the hiatus of its treatment in American history," and asked the commission to envision Black history as integral to American history writ large. "The facts cannot be fully appreciated unless they are viewed in the entire framework of American history and their great impact on this history is carefully assessed." He added, "The contributions of Afro-Americans to this country were, in the final analysis, made as Americans, thus making black history not a thing apart, but rather an integral portion of America's history." In addition to his eloquent and partially measured statement, he submitted, as supplemental evidence, three zealous editorials he penned for the *State News* during Negro History Week in 1968 and a thoughtful essay, "Functional Implications of Black History," in which he explored the psychological role of history during the Black Power era, the concept of Black history as American history, the role of Black history in world history and the African diaspora, and African American history as a porthole for understanding contemporary race relations.[26]

While Bailey was interning and representing BSA and the cause of Black history in Washington, D.C., Amis wrote one of his last op-eds in the *State News*, "Racism in the Social Structure." Citing directly from Carmichael and Hamilton's *Black Power*, he charged MSU with practicing institutional racism, the type of racism that kept Black students "out of MSU" and East Lansing a non-diverse community. In his mind, no significant "racial progress" had been made and the university's prized "Detroit Project" was nothing compared to the "Summer Test Admits" program that admitted 350 White students who were academically unprepared. Taking a cue from African American intellectual icon W. E. B. Du Bois, Amis centered the role of Blacks in generating cultural change while, like later Afrocentric thinkers, downgrading European-American culture. "Yet what cultural contribution has white America given the world? The black American has a moral force which makes his white compatriot look like an uncouth boor. You can't even come close to matching Negro spirituals or the blues not to mention jazz or 'soul' music. Take pride in your mechanical achievements and buy your culture from Europe while your moral fiber decays like so much garbage." The solution for Amis was White America's recognition of what Blacks had to offer. "Racism pervades this society and it pervades MSU. The only hope is that white America will accept the spiritual regeneration which only black America can give it."[27]

At the beginning of the 1968–1969 academic year, BSA was excited to build upon the momentum they established following the assassination of King. Buried deep in the pages of the 132-page September 1968 "Welcome Week" edition of the *State News*, BSA extended a "warm bond of welcome to all new Afro-American students for the school year 1968–1969" and provided incoming Black students a general overview of their purpose. Emphasizing how they were "part of a much broader movement in society and the world at large," the BSA steering committee described their "primary purpose" as being "with our own people—Afro-Americans." They were no longer "Negroes." They added, "We, the members of the alliance, feel that ours is the ultimate problem of survival. And we refuse to be entertained by delusions of grandeur instead of what we perceive to be real trends in American society." They warned incoming Black students about what awaited them. "Racism here, you yourselves will very quickly find out, is quite subtle. MSU, because of its size, is able to divide and spread racism among the many offices and agencies of its bureaucracy. It only becomes evident when we start tallying up all the statistics and we note that all of the black students, black faculty, yeah, even the black janitors and maids can be counted in the hundreds while the white students alone have to be counted in the tens of thousands." BSA gave incoming Black students notice about the Eurocentric curriculum. "We note that out of the so-many thousand courses that our 'great' University offers, there was not one as of last year" that focused on the African American experience. "We the Black Students' Alliance," they continued, "simply feel that this must end: that priorities must be placed on courses in our educational institutions which accord with the problems in society at large. And no traditional contradictions in morality will keep us from obtaining our goals—in the words of Malcolm X, 'Life, liberty, and justice,' for all people."[28]

The BSA steering committee's vision statement differed drastically from how a staff writer for the *State News* portrayed the organization in a jesting commentary in the same special edition of the paper. It serves as a window into how some Whites on campus viewed Black students' militant self-determination. In a satirical rundown of five of the countless on-campus student organizations, clubs, and cliques, a White student journalist wrote specifically to his White readers: "What do you suppose B.S.A. stands for? No, no. It does not stand for Boy Scouts of America. It stands for Black Students Alliance. What is the typical average student doing? Right. He is demonstrating." The wisecracker continued, "If you have Soul you can join B.S.A. If you like Soul you can march with B.S.A. If you don't like Soul you are a racist. You wouldn't want to be a racist, would you? Nobody likes a racist. At least, not if he lives next door." Underneath this caricature is a cartoon of a stereotypical Black man deferentially pleading with President Hannah. While the artist's impression of members of SDS is unflattering to say the least, the depiction of the Black male BSA member is noticeably racist. His eyes are bulging, his lips are grossly oversized, he has a Stepin Fetchit facial expression, and he is sporting what appears to be a gold chain or some sort of African necklace.[29]

BSA's no-nonsense activism during the 1968–1969 academic year countered such belittling caricatures, and in the 1969 "Welcome Week" edition of the *State News*, a student journalist sang a different tune. MSU has been "'blessed' with a black student group of a high academic nature. Contributions from the Black Students' Alliance have ranged from confrontation to curriculum and culture," the executive editor of the student paper noted. "No doubt the most controversial move of MSU during its entire existence was the spring 1969 shutdown of the Wilson Hall cafeteria."[30] By the fall semester of 1968, BSA had succeeded in getting departments throughout the university to offer a range of courses dealing with the African American experience, and in late September 1968, Ronald B. Lee, a Black administrator, was hired to lead the Center for Racial and Urban Affairs and Equal Opportunity Programs and help implement the recommendations of the Committee of Sixteen that focused on improving the status of African Americans on campus. Meanwhile, BSA continued to mobilize Black students and pressure the university to address their demands from the previous spring.

In late October 1968, BSA, who issued a statement in support of Olympic athletes Tommie Smith and John Carlos, returned to these demands, informing John Fuzak they were prepared to protest during the October 25 MSU–Notre Dame football game if their demands were not met. "With the campus psyching itself up for the big Notre Dame game approaching, the time is right to focus attention on issues of much greater impact," BSA maintained. They didn't protest at the big game. Instead, BSA representatives met with Fuzak and Jack Breslin on the day before the game to discuss "racial problems" in the athletic department and the university as a whole. They agreed to a proposal to create an all-university equal opportunity committee that would include Black students in future decision-making processes about race relations.[31] The timing of the meeting was unsurprising. It was called by Hannah to prevent BSA from disrupting the long-anticipated matchup on the gridiron. Considered a staunch advocate of civil rights, the chairman of the U.S. Civil Rights Commission could not stomach such negative national publicity.

During the remainder of the fall 1968 semester, BSA pushed on, and soon "each residence hall complex developed a BSA organization with its own elected officials." As BSA grew and became more diverse, different groups of students developed distinct concerns. In mid-November 1969, for instance, some of the organization's Black women challenged BSA's masculinist orientation. Phyllis Lovett, Gail Williams, Anita Bayliss, and Sandra Adams created the Sisterhood of BSA to develop programs related to Black women's unique experiences.[32] Early in the winter 1969 term, BSA was seeking to establish branches in dorm complexes and reached out more to Black faculty, expressing their desire to collaborate on publicizing their classes, creating innovative community projects, establishing "a liberation school and black radical institute," and helping raise funds for financially stressed Black students.[33] During the term, BSA met regularly with Black faculty to strategize about persuading the university to hire more Black faculty, administrators, and staff. They agreed with Ronald Lee, assistant provost and director of the Center for Urban Affairs, who in early February 1969 told the MSU chapter of the American Association of University Professors that the university needed to "commit itself to changing its total approach to education" and recruit more minority students. Hired late in the fall of 1968, Lee was militant in his criticism of MSU's treatment of African Americans. In an article in the *State News* during Black History Week in 1969, "Black Week Should Stress Future, Not History," Lee explained his "disalliance" with the commemoration and argued for "Black Present Week" and "Black Future Week." Citing specific examples, he dug into MSU's past and contemporary treatment of African Americans. "Michigan State has not escaped the pervasive racism manifest in society as a whole," he explained; "in my opinion, MSU is a slightly imperfect microcosm of America 10 years ago. Why 10 years ago and not today? Well, an answer that would satisfy thoroughly all of the academics who might read this would require the entire space of this publication, not just the 150 typewritten lines I was told I could have."[34]

Shortly before Hannah's resignation, on March 27, 1969, BSA submitted a statement to university officials highlighting their concerns about the future of the Center for Urban Affairs. Following Ronald Lee's resignation from the position of assistant provost for Equal Opportunity Programs and the center's director in the late spring of 1969, BSA spokespersons began publicly campaigning for Green to be his logical successor. Like Lee, who made it known to the local press that he would like to see Green appointed to this position, BSA leaders argued that the outspoken civil rights activist was totally, "on all fronts," qualified for the position.[35] They also insisted that the Center for Urban Affairs and the Equal Opportunity Programs needed to be adequately supported with additional significant funding and more personnel. While demanding Green be promoted, BSA also prepared for the year anniversary of King's assassination. On April 1, 1969, with their newly designed logo of the letters *B*, *S*, and *A* on a bolded three-dimensional cube, they circulated to "Brothers and Sisters" on campus an announcement of what they planned to do in commemoration of the year anniversary of the death of "Brother King." Beginning at 9:00 a.m. in the Union Building, they would be holding a series of panel discussions led by Mike Tripp, Shirley Echols, Sam Riddle, Bailey, Thomas, and Peter S. Kamulu. The range of the topics reveals the breadth of BSA's interests. The subjects under exploration included Black cultural nationalism, "the Black Revolution," race relations, "Black Students and the Black Community," "Black Economic Development," "Tactics and Strategies in the Movement," and "African Liberation and Black Power." BSA implored their Black classmates to attend the panels, the all-university memorial service in the auditorium, and an open discussion in Bessey Hall. "Dr. King sacrificed his life for the liberation of the oppressed," BSA concluded their letter to Black students. "It is not asking too much if Black people are asked to devote one day in honor of his sacrifice."[36]

On April 2, BSA delivered a statement to acting president Walter Adams and the Board of Trustees urging them to honor King's legacy and the "ideals of love, peace, and understanding for which he sacrificed his life." BSA introduced their demands, some of which they made a year earlier, in a straightforward manner, holding university officials accountable for their past rhetorical commitment to honoring King's legacy and instituting reforms. "In light of Rev. King's ultimate sacrifice, the University's expressed concern over his death, the supposed dedication of Michigan State and the world to the principles he advocated, and our intentions of seeing that actions begin to conform more with expressions, we urge the following." BSA proceeded to list three demands they believed "should be initiated without delay," including naming a "major University structure" in honor of King, the establishment of a memorial scholarship fund, "of substantial amount," named in his honor, and the creation of an endowed Martin Luther King professorship in social philosophy. On April 4, acting president Adams excused students from attending classes in memory of King, and the *State News* published BSA's tribute to King and an editorial. These passionate student-activists used this as an opportunity to express their anger, growing militancy, and vision of the future. They described the assassination of King as being a by-product of Whites' "collective conscious(less)ness" and Blacks' "collective weaknesses" and called upon Black students to act. "Wake up, black people, take heed. Only until America is convinced that each atrocity against black people will be met with black uncontrollable power will it move forcefully to alleviate the racism-based cases of such acts." BSA told MSU administrators to "put up" or "shut up," warning them that "whatever comes you will have asked for."[37]

On Friday, April 18, a day before Smokey Robinson and the Miracles performed before a crowd of nine thousand at Jenison Fieldhouse, seventy-five Black students, many of whom were members of BSA, attended a historic Board of Trustees meeting. The board approved the allocation of $1.5 million to the Center for Urban Affairs and the Equal Opportunity Programs, a motion proposed by trustee Blanche Martin. The board also committed to recruiting "up to 1,000 additional disadvantaged students" and passed a resolution requiring all contractors hired by the university to provide proof of nondiscriminatory employment practices. Two outspoken

BSA members, Flint freshman Samuel L. Riddle and East Lansing junior Jason Lovette, spoke to the trustees. Riddle, who would later call upon the university to increase the Black student population to 16 percent, observed that BSA's demands from April 5, 1968, had not yet been adequately addressed, insisting they "must be resolved." Speaking on behalf of BSA in a calmer tone, Lovette presented seven "matters for consideration" that he specified were not demands per se, including an endorsement of Green, who was at the meeting, to be the next director of the Center for Urban Affairs, a call for an increase in the number of Blacks "in various areas of the University community," and a request for a "black student observer" on the board. He also charged the university with exploiting Black athletes, critiqued work-study programs, and declared ROTC had "no relevance to the academic community."[38]

About a week later, BSA released a public statement, parts of which were published in the *State News*, chastising Gordon A. Sabine, vice-president for special projects, for his comment at the April 18 Board of Trustees meeting that there were not one thousand "qualified" Black students who could be recruited to MSU. BSA considered Sabine's flippant response inappropriate and "a personal affront." Convinced that Black administrators were better suited to oversee programs designed for Black students, BSA contended all programs related to minority and Black students be moved to the Center for Urban Affairs. They resented how the university segregated its recruitment of Black students in "special" programs and projects. "It is time that Michigan State realized that the recruitment of all segments of society to this University is not a special project—but its most important responsibility. This realization could be next manifested by assigning an established, on-going, relevant and receptive structure the responsibility for its execution." BSA concluded its statement, "the Black Students' Alliance will leave no stone unturned as we work to guarantee that this thrust toward greater relevancy pervades the entire University. Michigan State deserves no less."[39]

Beginning with the one-year anniversary of the death of Martin Luther King Jr., April 1969 was an intense month for BSA and the MSU Black student community. At the end of the month, BSA's discontent with the university's formulaic response to their demands reached a crescendo. Black students initiated the first major on-campus sit-in, a protest that temporarily made BSA the leading on-campus student-activist group, rocked different segments of the university community, and provided the impetus for a whirlwind of local media coverage. Shortly after armed Black students in Cornell University's Afro-American Society occupied the university's student center in late April 1969, BSA orchestrated a controversial and racially polarizing takeover of the Wilson Hall cafeteria protesting against the alleged racist harassment of three Black women employees. For them, the everyday racism cafeteria workers and Black students faced was one and the same. The student-activists strategically used incidents such as this, which didn't necessarily directly pertain to their daily academic and social lives, to take a collective stance against on-campus racism, reintroduce some of the demands they made a year earlier, challenge the university to acknowledge their strength, and catapult their struggle to another level. For them, the days of amicable meetings behind closed doors with seemingly sympathetic university administrators had passed. It was now time for direct, widespread, and confrontational action.

The Wilson Hall cafeteria sit-in represented the peak of BSA's handiwork and a major turning point in the history of Black student activism at MSU. In the weeks following the takeover, numerous members of the university community debated the sit-in's purpose and ramifications. Most agreed it was a consequential event in the history of unrest on the campus. Eleven days after the takeover, an executive reporter for the *State News* considered the disturbance monumental within the context of the university's long history, remarking, "In a word, Wilson Hall cafeteria is institutional—and hardly the place one would think of as the scene of one of the most important confrontations in MSU's 114-year history." At the beginning of the fall 1969 term, a *State News* reporter commented, "the Wilson Hall 'Incident,' probably a foreign phrase to anyone who wasn't on campus last spring, bears significant implications on the University's past and even greater meaning on its future." Black students recognized the importance of this event as well. A sophomore from Colorado Springs, Colorado, reflected the sentiments of many of his Black classmates. Three years after the takeover he concluded, "If we examine the history of the black student movement at Michigan State University we will find that the tactics of heightening contradictions and interrupting 'business-as-usual' has produced most of today's programs instituted for the black student body." He added, "a cursory examination of the student activism finds that the Wilson Hall and Holden Hall cafeteria take-overs by radicals changed the residence hall and university structure."[40]

Chapter 30

Takeover

Deciphering what actually transpired from the early evening of April 28 until April 30, 1969, during the Wilson Hall cafeteria sit-in is a bit challenging for historians. To begin with, there are very few existing photographs of the occupation, also known as the "Wilson Hall cafeteria takeover," the "Wilson Hall Affair," and by many Black student-activists, "the occupation of Wilson's cafeteria." The Black Students' Alliance (BSA) didn't allow members of the mainstream media to enter the space. The most revealing images—"*exclusive* photographs of activity inside the student-occupied MSU cafeteria"—were snapped by undergraduate student-activist Gerald Bray and appeared in the *Detroit Free Press* on April 30. The four images are powerful: Barry D. Amis and President Walter Adams squaring off like boxers before a match, Richard Thomas attentively seeking counsel from Robert L. Green, sophomore Michael Moore taking a nap before his "tour of duty in the round-the-clock occupation," and several Black women students cleaning the cafeteria's kitchen following an evening meal.[1] While the testimonies provided at the unprecedented and controversial public hearing in Wilson Hall on April 29, are invaluable to historians, the outspoken Black student leaders in BSA and several Black faculty and administrators like Don E. Coleman and Green also offered valuable insight into what transpired.[2] The *State News* provided the most accurate and detailed media coverage of the demonstration from the day after the occupation began through its immediate aftermath. The *Lansing State Journal*, on the other hand, was lambasted for its misleading portrayal of the protest.

Approximately one month after the sit-in drew to a close, the Greater Lansing Community Organization (GLCO) and the Lansing branch of the NAACP released a meticulous twelve-page report prepared for the Michigan Civil Rights Commission and the Michigan Press Association. Citing specific examples, they asserted that the paper's coverage of the sit-in was "biased and inflammatory," that Lansing journalists didn't "self-consciously apply their efforts to telling the true story of race relations in our community." According to the GLCO and the NAACP, the *Journal* staff writers' renditions of what transpired went counter to the 1968 Kerner Commission Report's discussion about responsible media practices by presenting a "distorted picture of the activities and their meaning," which "resulted in furthering community mistrust and anxiety." The GLCO and the NAACP demanded objectivity and the "kind of reporting that helps people live together." *State News* editorial board members closed ranks with these organizations in condemning one of Mid-Michigan's leading newspapers for its irresponsible and "sensational" coverage of the "black student take-over of the Wilson Hall cafeteria." According to the MSU student journalists, the *Lansing State Journal* increased racial hostility, ignored a "delicate situation," and failed to understand "the actions and underlying motivations and attitudes involved in our current conflict."[3]

In addition to Charles A. Dillard's "Report on the Wilson Hall Incident," one of the most detailed accounts of the initial stages of the occupation of the Wilson Hall cafeteria was outlined in a widely circulated memo written by Coleman on either April 28 or April 29. "The Black Students at Michigan State University would like to inform White students at Michigan State University that the occupation of Wilson's cafeteria was a necessary move," Coleman opened the announcement he crafted in consultation with the BSA.

> Black Students cannot tolerate racists action any longer. Therefore read the issues involved before you make any value judgements. Then give us your support in what ever manner you deem necessary. Do not let individuals lead you to believe that Black Students are attacking white students. Although many white students will have to eat in other halls, Black students must remain in Wilson Hall until the University resolves this situation. It is the white ruling class who must be held responsible by both Black and white students. The Black students at Michigan State University will occupy Wilson Cafeteria until an open session can be structured for 3:00 Thursday, May 1, 1969. The occupation of Wilson cafeteria took place after the BSA was contacted about the harassment of five Black Employees in Wilson's Food Service Department by the managers at Wilson.

In the remainder of the four-page account, Coleman described the "case at hand," highlighting the "tendencies of racism" characterizing each of the employees' cases. "White administrators in Wilson evidently are operating under an old stereotype that Negroes (Black) [*sic*] are lazy, happy-go-lucky people," he concluded.

Coleman's sentiments resonated with those of BSA. "Black students have felt it necessary to occupy the Wilson cafeteria since they learned of the overt and covert acts of racism that have occurred in Wilson. Several black employees have been harassed to the point that some have voluntarily left their jobs," BSA announced in a Spartan green flyer. "This is an issue that concerns all people at MSU who are committed to equal opportunity and an end to racism at this University and in society."[4]

About a year after the assassination of Martin Luther King Jr., on Monday, April 28, 1969, at about 5:00 p.m., approximately one hundred Black students, marshalled by BSA, initiated a takeover of Wilson Hall's cafeteria to protest the alleged racist mistreatment and harassment of four Black women cafeteria workers and one Black male freight elevator operator—Carolyn J. Hatcher, Joleen Shane, Roxie Tripplett, Wilma Phelps, and John Williams—by White coworkers and White supervisory personnel, Joseph Trantham, Jennie Mishler, and Jim Starkley. Collectively, these Black employees alleged they were the victims of verbal abuse from their White coworkers, were overlooked for promotions, and were discriminated against during their routine evaluations by their supervisors. The main plaintiffs included Hatcher, Shane, and Tripplett who complained about how they were treated by Trantham and Mishler.

Fed up with the hostile work environment, Hatcher quit her job several weeks before the end of her six-month probationary period. This mother of six who was known as the "Salad woman" told BSA that her supervisor, Trantham, threatened to fire her and transfer her to the custodial staff because she was, he claimed, "working below standards." She also indicated that unlike other employees, she was not afforded consistent days off. According to Coleman's investigation into Hatcher's case, her White coworkers' poor performance was overlooked. "I see this clearly as a racist thing and something is going to be done about it," he promised. Perhaps in an act of solidarity, Shane and Tripplett followed Hatcher's lead. A mother of two who was employed by the university for three years, Shane accused another manager of the cafeteria, Mishler, of refusing to "hear staff members out," denying her "self-expression," and "being prejudiced against blacks and she acknowledged it." Tripplett, who had been employed at MSU for seven years, testified she was "the target for much abuse" and that the cook supervisor "caused friction among the black staff and is always critical of their output." In one instance, she said she took a pregnancy leave and upon her return was forced to "start at the lowest pay rate."[5] The three Black women's actions were not totally spontaneous. Before walking off their jobs, an African American male worker quit, and Hatcher, Shane, and Tripplett had voiced their particular grievances to Trantham and supervisors in the South Complex.

Cognizant of BSA's growing reputation, Hatcher reached out to the organization for help. She deliberately bypassed seeking help from the Local 1585 union of the AFL-CIO to which she and other university employees belonged. Before contacting BSA, Hatcher indicated she had reached out to the union who, she recounted, ignored her complaints. Her decision to sidestep attempting to work further with Local 1585 was strategic. As Hubert C. Hill, president of Local 1585, observed more than a month after the sit-in, by working with BSA, Hatcher and her colleagues got results in three short days. If Hatcher and her coworkers had pursued their case through the union, its processing of their grievances would have taken thirty days or more.[6] Reflecting upon how things panned out after BSA called a halt to the sit-in, Hatcher expressed she was grateful to BSA, Coleman, Green, Joel Ferguson (who initially helped her secure the job at MSU), and President Adams for their support. She stressed that "BSA didn't speak for me. I speak for myself," adding, "I'm a proud woman."[7] Backed by Coleman, BSA strategically used Hatcher and her coworkers' plight as a rallying cry for their broader concerns about their own experiences at the university. Coleman called upon the university to "cease and desist from these practices," hire Black supervisors in the kitchen and dining rooms and receptionists in the dorms, and "open job opportunities" for Black students. BSA issued a new set of demands that given the circumstances, carried more weight than those they put forward after King's death. Their occupation of the Wilson Hall cafeteria was intense and short. It ended two days after it began.

However brief, the protest represented a monumental event in the Black Campus Movement at MSU. It galvanized Black student-activists. They learned that with unity, organized action, self-determination, and proper timing, they could succeed in impacting university policy-making processes. For the first time on a mass scale, the sit-in exposed members of the White campus community to Black student-activists' rage and discontent, widespread unity around a common cause, and unwillingness to accept racial discrimination wherever it reared its head on campus. Three weeks after the sit-in ended, the editors of the *State News*, who had bought into MSU's romantic history as a civil rights institution of higher learning, portrayed BSA's campaign as a pivotal turning point in the university's history. "Once regarded as a liberal haven and noted for harmonious race relations, the University is now the scene of almost continuous racial confrontation."[8] The approximately seventy-two-hour occupation of Wilson Hall cafeteria publicized BSA's activism, gave rise to a new generation of Black student leaders, and resulted in concrete changes in the university's handling of racial incidents and the demands of Black students.

Hannah resigned effective April 1, 1969, and the "Wilson Hall Affair" fittingly marked an end to his "ways of getting things done." Acting president Adams's management of the incident, which was unquestionably sympathetic to the Black student-activists, was highly controversial and divisive. He approached the situation much differently than Hannah most likely would have. Adams himself served as "the main communication link between the administration and BSA." He met with the group for many hours during and after the protest, joked and debated with them as professors would with their star students, and listened attentively and respectfully to their grievances. In characterizing Adams's approach, BSA spokesperson Sam Riddle commented, "Talk among some faculty and others who lean towards 'fairness' seems to be that black students are lucky that Walter Adams is president, however, I feel it's the University that better be glad that Walter Adams is president."[9] Many Whites believed Adams too easily and nonchalantly caved in to their demands. The stakes were high, and while other presidents of major predominantly White institutions (PWIs) might have handled such an incident differently, Adams worked his charm to appease the resolute students in order to avoid further unrest and negative national publicity for the university. He was keenly aware of what happened at other universities, such as Cornell. His handling of the situation endeared him to MSU's small Black community, while sparking an uproar among many Whites on campus and in the state's political circles. Though the university community was ready for change provided by a leader from outside the Spartan nation after Hannah's resignation, Adams's empathy toward BSA probably adversely impacted the possibilities of him becoming MSU's next president.

While unique at MSU, the Wilson Hall cafeteria takeover was one of countless similar Black student protests at PWIs of the late 1960s during which droves of Black students occupied buildings on their campuses. Unlike some of these other occupations, the Wilson Hall sit-in was fairly tame. There was no violence, and no force was used to end it, something Adams took pride in. How it was handled was somewhat unconventional. BSA's brief and effective occupation of the Wilson Hall cafeteria was part of a larger movement that was bound to happen in East Lansing. Green and others were correct in observing that what transpired in Wilson Hall was a byproduct of the recent past. "This is the culmination of a series of incidents," Green pointed out. "In the future—and this is a warning—when racism exists in a component of this institution, we will close that component down."[10] Momentum had been building up in the Black Campus Movement at MSU since the founding of the BSA in January 1968 and the assassination of Martin Luther King Jr. several months later.

In a statement released on April 28, BSA declared: "If those who rule or govern the operations of the University cannot control their racist employees who are in positions of management, black students will do their job for them." In a meeting in the Wilson Hall Kiva on the first night of the sit-in before a crowd of approximately two hundred White students, one BSA spokesperson, Sam Riddle, declared, "There have been overt and rather blatant actions on this campus against blacks. Wilson cafeteria is the place where we thought it would have to be stopped." Wilson Hall's White residents were caught off guard by the occupation. They were initially torn about how to respond. Many were angered by the inconvenience of not being able to grab their dinners. During the meeting in the Wilson Hall Kiva, Riddle boldly asked for a show of hands from those who supported BSA's cause, and nearly half of the White students reportedly raised their hands.[11] Though they couldn't relate to the Black experience on campus, many were aware of their Black classmates' pent-up frustrations. BSA didn't enlist their White classmates in their campaign. As Stokely Carmichael had instructed, they believed Whites could best serve the cause by working to end racism in the White community.

In an act of racial solidarity, members of BSA and other Black student-activists themselves—with the support of some sympathetic Black faculty and staff like Coleman and Green—were determined to challenge the "dehumanization" suffered by those who could have been their sisters, cousins, aunts, or mothers. They were dedicated to exposing what they perceived as racism at MSU. The "black students at MSU," BSA continued in their statement, "consider the harassment of black employees a direct insult. Undoubtedly this University is only trying to buy black students

Sam Riddle addresses a diverse crowd of students on campus. Courtesy of Michigan State University Archives and Historical Collections.

off. The University gives us $1.5 million which shows their commitment. However, this does not tell black students anything as long as blacks are still being de-humanized." BSA spokespersons told reporters that on April 30, they would be holding a special "open session" during which they would outline their grievances and further explain the sit-in. BSA announced they intended to remain in Wilson Hall holding teach-ins until Thursday when they would be demanding a meeting with acting president Adams whom they expected would provide an effective process through which to address the employees' concerns. BSA's initial demands included firing the two food service managers, hiring more full-time Black employees, and rehiring Carolyn Hatcher to a higher position. BSA also used this incident as a way to address the general mistreatment of Blacks on campus and return to their demands that more African Americans be hired in various capacities throughout the university.[12]

On Tuesday, April 29, less than twenty-four hours after the occupation started, acting president Adams participated in a heated open forum with members of BSA and others for more than three hours during which BSA demanded the allegations from the three Black women be dealt with immediately. Adams decided to act swiftly. He feared if he didn't, the situation could have escalated. In haste, he established an adjudicating committee—also described as a "specially appointed review board" and "special biracial review board"—to investigate the allegations, allow the workers and employers to tell their stories, and then deliberate to make some decisions. The committee was composed of four Blacks and four Whites, including two students. There were three Black students on the Adjudicating Committee for the Wilson Hall Affair: Stan McClinton, Mike Hudson, and Maina Kinyatti. Vice-president of student affairs Milton B. Dickerson and mathematics professor and chair of the Black Faculty Committee Irvin E. Vance served as cochairs of the committee. On the same day in a mock court trail, Lansing attorney Stuart Dunnings and BSA members Ron Bailey and Sam Riddle served as the spokespersons for the prosecution, and the accused were defended by Lansing attorney Duane Hildebrandt. The announcement described and advertised to the public hearing as follows: "BLACK WORKERS AND STUDENTS SHALL HOLD A PUBLIC HEARING IN WILSON CAFETERIA AT 3 P.M., APRIL 29, 1969 TO PRESENT CASES OF RACISM IN MANAGEMENT." BSA's opening statement in support of the Shane, Hatcher, and Triplett was unambiguous. "It is abundantly evident to us that several black employees in the food Service division of Wilson Hall have been constantly abused by administrators in the division. That these acts were purposeful is obvious. That these acts were, in great measure, rooted in motivations of racist nature is just as obvious," BSA continued, "Black students, faculty, and staff of Michigan State University have already made known its intent to leave no stone unturned as we work to make this University responsive to the needs of society and force from inequality of treatment stemming from consideration of racial origins." Adams's review board listened to hours of testimony from the workers, their employers, and BSA. Hatcher, in particular, recounted many examples of being mistreated because of her race. "Atmosphere at the meeting was pro-black," commented a reporter from the *Lansing State Journal*, "most of the hundreds there were black. Statements and charges from blacks were greeted with cheers and handclapping."[13]

After deliberating for more than thirteen hours, on Wednesday, April 30, Adams's "special committee" came up with nine recommendations leading to the end of the occupation. Late in the afternoon, Adams convened a meeting in the Wilson Hall cafeteria and told a crowd of more than four hundred, "I find the recommendations perfectly reasonable and justifiable and I intend to act in accordance with them." The nine recommendations were precise and detailed. The special committee concluded: (1) "that a position be established for a black person in the central personnel office" whose job it would be to recruit Black personnel throughout the university, (2) Blacks be immediately upgraded in jobs in the residence halls, (3) "a black college graduate" be hired in a management position in Wilson Hall, (4) MSU issue a statement against discriminatory practices, (5) and (6) those accused of racial harassment by Hatcher be transferred out of Wilson Hall, (7) the university create a "plan for an arbitration system to adjudicate" the type of "controversy" that occurred in Wilson Hall, (8) the president request that the students who participated in the sit-in not be penalized for missing classes and assignments, and (9) a progress report on these plans be sent to Black faculty and BSA between June 1 and October 1, 1969.[14]

Black students leave the Wilson Hall cafeteria in late April 1969 following the end of the well-orchestrated takeover. Courtesy of Michigan State University Archives and Historical Collections.

In the immediate aftermath of the speedy, unconventional hearings, Adams was pleased with how things turned out, highlighting that nobody was injured, the academic operations of the university were not adversely impacted, and no property was destroyed. Months later, in September 1969, he stood by his initial assessment, underscoring that the incident helped move the university toward developing policies and procedures for dealing with allegations of on-campus discrimination and racism. He established the Brookover Committee to explore these issues and announced plans to act on the Committee of Sixteen's year-old recommendations. He also expressed his relief that force was not used to end the sit-in. This would have been disastrous in his estimation. In *The Test* (1970), a chronicle of his momentary yet action-packed presidency, Adams forthrightly described how he, in his estimation, contributed to Blacks' struggles on campus and reflected upon his cautious, student-centered response to the controversial Wilson Hall Affair, deducing it was a byproduct of legitimate past grievances.[15]

Some rejected Adams's rosy perception of the successful handling of the "Wilson Hall Affair." His leadership in this case was widely debated, dividing members of the MSU community and making waves in the greater Lansing–East Lansing area. The *State News* wasn't alone in calling the hearings a "Kangaroo Court." Debates about how Adams handled the "Wilson Hall Affair" continued in the pages of the student newspaper through the month of May. Duane Hildebrandt, the lawyer for the two White MSU employees charged with discrimination and racial harassment, immediately pointed out that the makeshift hearings Adams allowed to take place were miscarriages of justice, violating his clients' basic civil rights and neglecting due process. His clients, he argued, were denied a fair trial in a "proper judicial process." He claimed he was personally intimidated by the students before and during the hearings. He was particularly upset with Coleman. "I am surprised and shocked that a person in a position such as Coleman would destroy his relation between the University and students by siding with the militants," Hildebrandt charged. He added that Black students had already been given so much by MSU. "People are offering money and assistance galore. The community is stunned that this could happen in the United States of America."[16] Several MSU faculty closed ranks with Hildebrandt. The chair of the Department of Economics and friend of Adams, agreed with the accused's lawyer, calling the process Kangaroo proceedings, charging Adams with violating the rules of due process, and expressing great dismay with the "bizarre proceedings."[17]

An Ad Hoc Committee on the Residence Halls publicized its disapproval of Adams's approach and, in an open letter, the East Wilson Hall council called upon Adams and the adjudicating committee to provide the factual findings and evidence that informed their decisions and recommendations. Their requests were reasonable and their tone was respectful. Lead by economics professor Charles P. Larrowe, ninety-four faculty members and graduate students signed their names to an open letter supporting Adams's quick response and respect for students' grievances, wisdom, and leadership. About a week later, more than two hundred MSU staff members and employees signed two petitions condemning BSA, dubbing the actions of Adams, trustees Don Stevens and Blanche Martin, Green, and Coleman as irresponsible, and clamoring for due process procedures for the two managers who were placed on temporary leaves based upon the hastily organized hearings.[18]

Nearly all the letters from Michiganders the *Lansing State Journal* published beginning in early May 1969 chastised BSA's tactics. "Why do these students even need to be given the time of day? Since when do intelligent educated men need to bow down to the demands of ignorant, immature persons claiming to be adults yet act worse than children, all considered minors?," opined one of the first Michigan residents whose letter to the editor of the *Journal* was published days after the sit-in ended. "If this country is so bad, why don't they leave it instead of trying to ruin it?" Such letters were not uncommon and were in part influenced by the paper's biased coverage. Adams received loads of hate mail, calling him all sorts of names. In one letter printed by the *State News*, an anonymous racist told Adams, "You surrendered to the black murder boys instead of calling in the National Guard. That is the only way of dealing with these armed bandits. God bless America: damn the niggers." On May 3, a group of forty East Lansing businessmen demonstrated their opposition to the sit-in and Adams's response to it by marching to Beaumont

Tower and laying a wreath symbolizing for them the "death of the MSU administration." The group's leader said to his followers that he was most concerned with "the destruction of civil rights of a silent majority by a vocal minority in all aspects of American life." Adams's actions made waves in Michigan's political circles. More than thirty Republican members of the House of Representatives signed a resolution seeking to withhold funds from MSU. Among the most outspoken was a Lansing Republican senator who declared: "in my opinion, any concession to any student or students using tactics which are contrary to law or the rules of the university should be met in kind. I think militants disrupting the academic harmony of the school should be expelled regardless of who they are. If I had been the president of the university, I would have moved the students out, using whatever means necessary."[19] BSA leader Amis received hate mail that was more repulsive than the vile letters sent to Adams. After spewing racist hatred, the author of a letter postmarked from Detroit in early May 1969 wrote, "in a few years, my generation will smother *all* of you in plastic tents. To allow you to live is to kill the white race, therefore *you* will die." Another xenophobe predictably added, "If you hate this country so much, why don't *you* go over to Africa to help your black brothers? You blacks want everything *handed* to you—without working to get ahead."[20]

Adams did have his devout cheerleaders. Chairman of the Board of Trustees, Don Stevens, and the only Black board member, Blanche Martin, issued a statement in support of his willingness to come up with an "equitable and honorable solution" while demonstrating his compassion to upset Black students. "His indefatigable efforts were exceeded only by his inspired and courageous leadership," they pronounced.[21] Despite his position as cochair of the adjudicating committee, Milton B. Dickerson, vice-president of student affairs, challenged those who believed BSA and their Black faculty supporters had gotten over on the system. "Black faculty and students would be the last to inflict injustice on others, of this I am certain," he said on record. The Lansing branch of the NAACP and the Interim Committee of the GLCO echoed Stevens and Martin's sentiments. The NAACP met with representatives from BSA on May 4 and passed three resolutions in support of the sit-in. One spokesperson for the Lansing branch of the NAACP declared to BSA, "We're behind you and if the people of Lansing don't get out and support you, don't blame it on the NAACP." The GLCO issued a statement commending Adams's actions in the cause of social justice and calling for the end of institutional racism at the university. The editorial staff of the short-lived *Inner City Times* announced their support of BSA's "cry for help" in support of the Black Wilson hall cafeteria workers "whose humanity had allegedly been violated."[22]

In early May, African American state representative Jackie Vaughn III, who met with BSA during the sit-in, wrote a personal letter to the student-activists. Addressing the students as his "Brothers and Sisters," he applauded them for closing ranks with the Black women employees and carrying themselves in a respectable manner. He was impressed they "could exercise so great an influence upon the University administration." Vaughn commented, "All of you are to be congratulated on your success, and I personally want you to know that I am grateful to have been able to share some moments at your protest; I learned much from you." He closed his thoughtful letter assuring them he was there if they needed his services in the future. Following Vaughn's lead, in mid-May, eleven Black legislators presented a letter at a session of the Michigan Senate in which they closed ranks with BSA and called for an end to racism on college campuses in the state. For them, what transpired in Wilson Hall was a result of "unchanging conditions of discrimination."[23]

Of the several faculty who submitted individual statements to the *State News*, associate professor of Justin Morrill College Dhirendra Sharma's stands out. In her lengthy editorial "White Majority Distorts Justice for Black Minority" published two weeks after the sit-in ended, Sharma congratulated BSA "for such a tremendous awakening caused by them." Sharma criticized the White faculty members who attacked BSA's intentions and methods, asking one of them to "paint himself black and move into the society for a few days, and he shall have an insight of the black's perception of reality." Sharma, who visited the sit-in one evening, challenged the *Lansing State Journal*'s portrayal of BSA as a "violent group of hoodlums," testifying that the students were organized, "quite orderly and courteous." "To me," Sharma remarked, "it appeared to be the most ideal non-violent expression of steamed up black frustration."[24]

Black faculty were largely supportive of BSA's actions. From the beginning of the sit-in, Coleman and Green wholeheartedly backed BSA. On the first day of the sit-in, Green proclaimed, "I wholeheartedly support the shut down." Since the organization's founding, Green served as their unofficial adviser and adamantly defended them when others in the university condemned their actions. He met for hours with members of BSA in the Wilson Hall cafeteria. Despite his status as a respected professor, the students viewed him as being one of them. When the Academic Council criticized BSA and the hearing process, Green spoke out. "Gross hypocrisy exists on this campus," he argued. "When blacks were treated in an unjust manner, Mandlstamm and Lanzillotti, faculty who have criticized the proceedings, sat quietly in their offices. These people are recent civil libertarians." In his mind, many Whites on campus had never been concerned with "the violation of the rights of blacks."[25] Though he may have been less vocal than Green, Coleman was in full support of the students' protest from its inception, investigated the case, spoke with the plaintiffs, and wrote one of the most complete overviews of what prompted the occupation. Deeming the sit-in "necessary" and underscoring that "no one should have to live in fear of a job," in late April 1969 he wrote, "Black Students cannot tolerate racists' action any longer."[26] While he maintained objectivity as cochair of the special adjudicating committee, Irvin E. Vance defended BSA's approach, and when questioned after the hearing by the mainstream media, his silence was an affirmation of the committee's work and recommendations. A week after the sit-in ended and on the same day that coauthor of *Black Power: The Politics of Liberation* Charles V. Hamilton spoke on campus in Fairchild Theatre as a part of the "Provost Lectures" series, the Black Faculty Committee, which Vance chaired, submitted "an Open Letter to the

University community regarding the Wilson Hall incident." The committee endorsed Adams's approach as "fair and courageous" and in the "best interests of the total University Community." With specific examples, they argued the "Wilson Hall Affair" was best viewed within the context of the prevalent "racism against blacks at MSU."[27]

Those opposed to the procedures Adams quickly established to resolve the "Wilson Hall Affair" were somewhat vindicated. Backed by a group of respected faculty members, on May 7, the Academic Council passed a resolution recommending the two temporarily suspended managers be granted a new hearing. Adams didn't have a problem with this suggestion and authorized the university attorney to reach out to the two employees and their attorneys.[28] The sit-in and rushed judgments certainly impacted the accused, and they were probably shocked by how Adams and the university dealt with their alleged behavior. Their reputations were called into question, but they were not fired by the university. Instead, after the hearings and their temporary suspensions were lifted, they were reassigned to "special projects" without any reduction in their salaries, but in nonsupervisory capacities. Trantham maintained his innocence, remarking in early May to a *Lansing State Journal* reporter, "I feel the outcome of the committee's report has been slanted to indicate a degree of guilt which I know I am not guilty of, and I believe that subsequent investigation will prove that I was a scapegoat."[29]

As pointed out by a former Wilson Hall food services manager, the treatment Hatcher, Tripplett, and Shane said they endured was not new. Before the late 1960s when the on-campus Black student population was small, Black employees became somewhat accustomed to belittling and traumatizing acts of day-to-day racism, what people in higher education now call "microaggressions." Those working in the Wilson Hall cafeteria shortly after the incident were instructed not to speak to the media. Most seemed to adhere to this order. But Hatcher and Tripplett refused to remain silent. While Hatcher commented that her White colleagues resented her role in the hearings and she was pleased with the final outcome, Tripplett reportedly said that what happened to her was not racially motivated, the hearing was "unfair," and she had received harassing phone calls. She felt like an "outcast." Tripplett was adamant in her willingness to stand up for her rights. Joleen Shane, on the other hand, preferred not to talk about what transpired and the complaints she leveled against Mishler in particular. She wanted to move on with her life. Some African Americans voiced their support of the three Black women. "I have just read Friday's *State News* and I'm happy and sad at the same time. Mrs. Hatcher, you are wonderful. Your strength and courage typifies that which has made black women the backbone of America," a Black woman from Lansing wrote in "an Open Letter" in the *Westside News* on May 17, 1969, "to Mrs. Roxie Tripplett. Like the children say, keep on pushing. We are winners.... Remember, you are not alone in this thing, your whole race is with you. We are all Rosa Parks. We are all tired."[30]

In assessing the impact of the Wilson Hall incident, Coleman surmised it "raised the question of how the university should deal with a sit-in to deal with the question of allegations of discrimination and racism on campus."[31] Many of the MSU department chairs, college deans, and administrators who responded to Eric V. A. Winston's 1972 questionnaire on the origins and expressions of Black student activism at MSU opined that the Wilson Hall cafeteria sit-in was one of the most significant incidents that "prompted response from the university."[32] As was the case with the assassination of Martin Luther King Jr., with the "Wilson Hall Affair," Black student-activists rallied around nonacademic issues. They viewed these incidents as direct assaults against their humanity and used them as vehicles to fight for improving their academic, social, and cultural well-being on campus. The crux of their demands revolved around recruiting and retaining Black students, faculty, administrators, and staff; obtaining equal rights and representation; and getting the university to provide them with more culturally relevant services and to institute antiracist policies. With slight modifications, these are the very same issues Black student-activists at MSU have rallied around ever since.

The leading Black student journalist during the late 1960s and early 1970s, Jeanne Saddler, eloquently captured the importance of the Wilson Hall incident. In Lansing's short-lived Black newspaper, the *Westside News*, she trumpeted:

> It was a Court of Black Indignation, and the procedure was more fair than those traditionally shown to blacks. The brothers and sisters were just sticking together, displaying power, co-operation and determination. Evidently, this mild display of Black Power caused some officials to fear the end of white control, domination, and victory at MSU. The thought was obviously equivalent to death for some East Lansing businessmen, who laid a wreath at Beaumont Tower. . . . We now see effects of unity, and moving, protesting, and voting in a block. We are no longer appealing to the morals of conscience of America. Black people are ready to deal, and Black Power is commanding respect. . . . If black people keep their thing together, we can see that they are never disappointed. We can make [the] American system of justice a lot more black, and a lot more beautiful.[33]

The success of BSA's occupation of the Wilson Hall cafeteria, like countless turning points in history, had much to do with timing. Black student unrest throughout the nation was commonplace, and Black activists at MSU were poised to take more consequential actions. As Sam Riddle noted, they decided this was the right case to spark a movement. If BSA had not used the incidents in Wilson Hall to mobilize around, they would have certainly found other suitable cases through which to air their grievances to an institution struggling with how to create a more inclusive culture.

The polarizing "Wilson Hall Affair" impacted MSU administrators' responses to diversifying their campus. In late May 1969, weeks after the takeover, the university engaged in "its most intensive statewide efforts to recruit able black freshmen." The MSU director of admissions and scholarships commented, "We have admitted, or offered admission to or offered testing leading to admission, plus all needed financial aid to a total of 1,244 black students for the class starting this September."[34] It also marked the end of BSA during the Black Campus Movement. A new group of student leaders would reconstitute the organization. During the summer of 1969, BSA temporarily dissolved, giving rise to the Black Liberation Front, International (BLFI). A new generation of Black student leaders emerged, many of whom were active during the Wilson Hall cafeteria campaign. In the September 1969 "Welcome Week" issue of the *State News*, Inkster sophomore and BLFI member Mike Hudson explained the transition. "Wilson Hall more or less marked a change in the whole organization. We're at a point where we no longer feel we have to react to issues and react to problems. Now we can act. We're not on the defensive anymore. We're constantly on the offensive." In 1971, Richard W. Thomas, a cofounder of BSA who in 1969 was dubbed "one of the finest black poets of his generation," stressed the importance of the organization. "The first Black Student Political Force on campus was the Black Student Alliance in 1967, although its original members are all over the country, it provided the first Black political thrust on campus in many years, all other groups after, . . . i.e. BUF, BLFI, . . . etc. were affected by some of the political thrust on campus in many years."[35]

Chapter 31

Golden Age of Organizing

Jeanne Saddler, one of the first African American associate campus editors of the *State News*, enrolled in MSU about six months after Martin Luther King Jr. was assassinated and the recently created Black Students' Alliance (BSA) issued their first set of major demands to university leaders. In the fall of 1970, during her junior year when approximately two thousand Blacks were enrolled in the university, Saddler wrote a radical open letter to incoming Black students in the widely read "Welcome Week" edition of the *State News*.

Boldly titled "Blacks: Prepare for Revolution," her commentary tells us something about how some Black students who had been at MSU since the fall of 1968 might have perceived the Black experience at MSU. "Black students of the freshman class of 1970—welcome to the struggle of black people in East Lansing," Saddler casually opened her brief piece. She advised the recent high school graduates to be cognizant of the "hell of an age" they were living in and to be conscious of the Black revolution and the history of repression they and their ancestors endured, including "the assassinations and lynchings of 300 years" followed by "more overt forms of legalized murder and execution." "As a black nation we cannot afford to lie in the sun and forget about our people," she declared. "Let's not sleep through the storm." The stakes were high in Saddler's mind, "liberation" on the one hand, "genocide" on the other. "Many of us will die, without doubt," she prophesized, "but we must at least try to prevent a mass tragedy." Saddler called upon Black students to "get your soul together" and to view their time at MSU as a training ground for activism and consciousness-building. "Go inside yourself and come out a black man or woman. Develop a philosophy and learn self-discipline. Investigate everything but don't be led away by fools." Sampling from multitalented Black Panther leader Elaine Brown's 1969 album *Seize the Time*, she ended her revolutionary plea, "Seize the time . . . to get ready."[1]

Saddler's years at MSU helped radicalize her. There were others like her. She arrived on campus when BSA was leading an unwavering Black Campus Movement and inspiring the formation of other similar organizations. The late 1960s and the dawning of the 1970s represented an apex of Black student activism at MSU. It was a time of cultural and political awakening for Black students on campus who more often than not had noticeably different world views, cultures, experiences in East Lansing, and expectations of what education should be from their White counterparts. During the late 1960s and early 1970s as the Black student population grew, they constituted a distinct student body within a larger White student population. They had the numbers to constitute a small HBCU. Reflecting their ideological diversity and building upon the foundations laid by the campus NAACP and BSA, they created a collection of their own organizations and initiated protests to express their discontent and fight for their rights. As noted by an administrator who worked closely with student groups in 1977, during the late 1960s and early 1970s, Black "political and educational reform groups were dominant."[2]

On September 18, 1973, the Black Faculty and Administrators Association (BFAA) sponsored the Black Student Orientation Program in 108 B Wells Hall. Fifty Black student organizations—including all the fraternities and sororities, more than a dozen dormitory caucuses, and numerous other social, cultural, and academic groups—set up registration tables to welcome their new classmates, spread their messages, and recruit potential members.[3] Four years earlier, there were about a dozen registered Black organizations on campus, only a few of which were dormitory Black caucuses. Between the summer of 1969 and 1972, the most active Black student organizations included the Black Liberation Front, International, who often worked closely with the Pan-African Students Organization in the Americas, the Black United Front, the Office of Black Affairs (OBA), the Black Coalition Council, and Project Grapevine, a Black-run communications organization who launched a newspaper, the *Grapevine Journal*. Following BSA's short heyday, a new generation of student-activists continued MSU's Black Campus Movement.

Founded in April 1969 as a branch of ASMSU, the OBA was arguably the longest lasting Black student organization established during the Black Campus Movement. Twenty years after its creation, one of OBA's active members, Jeffrey Robinson, helped launch Black students' occupation of the Hannah Administration Building. Originally founded as the ASMSU Office of the Vice President of Black Affairs, OBA was created because Black students demanded formal representation in MSU student government. Occupying a small office in the Student Services Building, in the spring of 1970, the OBA board included Claire McClinton, Ervin Armstrong, Bernard Carver, John Deacon Jones, and June Manning. They were known for their programs, such as their "Getting Together on Blackness" workshop that included discussions from twenty-four Black faculty and students. In September 1975, OBA leaders, who declared

Program for the 1970
Black student orientation.
Courtesy of Michigan
State University Archives
and Historical Collections.

their organization to be the official voice of Black students at MSU and a force against Black apathy, published a "Black Survival Guide" booklet that included a summary of their past, present, and future activities; advice on how to make it in an inhospitable environment; a list of more than twenty Black faculty, staff, administrators, and organizations; and numerous suggestions for resources. OBA originally sought to help Black students succeed by providing a range of resources and services. They had overarching ambitions, striving to ensure Black students' holistic survival, "academically, financially, politically and socially." This approach was embodied in the organization's mantra for the 1973–1974 academic year, "To Work and Study Towards Survival." Working closely with the Black United Front (BUF), early on they published a leaflet that let students know the ratings of professors. The officers were elected annually in campus-wide elections, and the director was approved by ASMSU. Stan McClinton was among the office's key early leaders, and he was revered by some younger comrades. One up-and-coming Black

E.Head, A.Karega, J.Jones and T.Woodland

Office of Black Affairs. Courtesy of Michigan State University Archives and Historical Collections.

student-activist remarked that McClinton "was regarded as the most astute black leader and political brain on campus."[4] He was clear in his belief that this position wasn't going to amount to tokenism. "I don't see this position as a forum to solicit symbolic rewards and gifts from the board of the university. I will not act to contact black students in this position. My primary goal is meaningful change," McClinton proclaimed.[5] During its first year, OBA had a budget of about $3,000 and sponsored a Black freshman orientation program and other initiatives.

By February 1970, OBA severed their ties with ASMSU, despite their ability to still obtain funding from student government for their activities. In the fall, they developed the Black Political Theater to promote cultural awareness. By 1972, the OBA director, James Weathers, remarked, "the office is trying to make black students more sensitive to community needs. We must help black students understand their specific place in the black struggle."[6] During the early 1970s, OBA engaged in a range of practical activities seeking to improve the Black experience at MSU. They represented Black students' interests "through proper university channels." In order to develop programs and strategies, they studied the conditions of Black students. Beginning in the fall of 1970, they helped coordinate the Black Freshman Orientation Program and created a Black Student Handbook. Don E. Coleman created the orientation program to help prepare Black students for what awaited them at MSU. These orientations featured OBA leadership as well as Black faculty and administrators—including Robert L. Green, Joseph McMillan, Gloria Smith, Thomas Gunnings, Carl Taylor, Charles Scarborough, Amos Johnson, and others—who welcomed Black students to campus, imparted practical advice, warned them of the possible challenges they faced, and shared information about vital support services upon which they could draw. "You can't just survive," assistant provost James Hamilton told those who attended the orientation in September 1973. "You got to be more than average." Gloria Smith reminded students, "the education gotten today will determine tomorrow's success."[7]

During the Black Campus Movement, OBA was the center of controversy on one particular occasion. In mid-November 1972, the group sponsored the visit of Stokely Carmichael to campus. Before Carmichael took to the podium in the jam-packed Conrad Hall Auditorium, the fifty to one hundred White students in attendance were asked by OBA members to move to the back and then asked to leave the event. OBA representatives allegedly told them that the event was only for members of the organization. The next day, a disgruntled White student filed a complaint with the Office of Equal Opportunity and the Office of Human Relations contending that his rights as a student were violated because the event was sponsored by ASMSU and was, therefore, open to the public. ASMSU got word of the situation and immediately got into the mix, demanding a response from OBA leadership. ASMSU contributed $900 to bring Carmichael to campus and provided OBA with a budget of $4,500 for the 1971–1972 academic year. In their minds, OBA, technically an agency of ASMSU, had violated university policies by kicking out White students from the university-sponsored event. At an impromptu press conference, OBA leader James Weathers justified what they did, doubling down on their conviction that Carmichael came to campus this time to directly speak to members of the OBA office as a form of professional development. Weathers and his coworkers, however, found themselves in a bit of a pickle. OBA didn't advertise Carmichael's talk as being for members only, so they were in violation of university policies. The situation was referred to as a "racial incident" ("the Conrad incident") and was widely discussed and debated in the pages of the *Lansing State Journal* and *State News*.[8]

The student community was divided along racial lines. Many White students were appalled, considering OBA's actions a form of anti-White racism, or reverse discrimination. Black students who submitted editorials to the *State News* advocated for Black separatism based upon how they were marginalized on campus. Student journalist Jane Seaberry penned a brilliant, satirical essay. With cynicism and also respect for OBA, she penned that the Conrad Hall incident would reverberate and "echo through the generations." As a result of OBA's actions, she wrote, "Conrad Hall became a landmark for blacks at MSU." Perhaps like many other Black students, including members of the *Grapevine Journal* editorial team, she believed the incident "was a lesson for many whites." The BFAA, who in the early and mid-1970s called upon the Board of Trustees and the Human Relations Department to hire more Black faculty, stood behind OBA. After much controversy, in mid-February 1973, around the time African American Oscar Butler was named assistant vice president of student affairs and dean of students, the Student-Faculty Judiciary ruled that OBA didn't violate the university's policies. They concluded that Carmichael's visit, though not advertised as being an all-Black affair, was indeed foremost for members of the organization. While the members of OBA were pleased with the outcome, Weathers insisted, "There should never have been a hearing in the first place."⁹ The incident revealed to MSU's White community that some Black students on campus believed the Black struggle was of the province of Blacks and, as Carmichael underscored in *Black Power* (1968), Whites could best contribute to Black liberation through their own organizations. The incident also challenged Black student leaders to articulate their vision. OBA survived this controversy and remained active on campus through the late 1980s.

Following OBA's lead, a new organization, BLFI, convinced ASMSU they could not determine how they secured additional funding or how they used the funds they received from them. In January 1970, Sam Riddle, at the time a member of BLFI's executive council, became a general member-at-large of ASMSU and, like McClinton, refused to be tokenized in this position. He communicated many of BLFI's demands directly to ASMSU. He called for better treatment of African American students and veterans and more community outreach programs. Several months after their takeover of the Wilson Hall cafeteria, a faction of students active in BSA created the Black Liberation Front, International (BLFI), often simply referred to as the Black Liberation Front or BLF. They were very similar in structure and function to BSA, and BLFI's movers and shakers cut their teeth in BSA's activities. They thought it was time to restructure themselves, symbolized by their new name. In the several years after the founding of BLFI, other organizations emerged. BSA had not seen its last day. The organization was resurrected in the years following the end of the Black Campus Movement.¹⁰

The exact circumstances leading to the disappearance of BSA as the vanguard of Black student protest at MSU are challenging to reconstruct. According to Coleman, during the summer of 1969, Black student-activists grew increasingly frustrated with the university's laissez-faire approach toward their demands and the tenuous nature of on-campus race relations. In Coleman's chronicling, BSA leaders—namely Sam Riddle, Stan McClinton, and Mike Hudson—spent the summer traveling around the country "attending various 'Black Power' conferences." Upon returning to East Lansing in the fall, they called for the creation of a more "militant" organization focused on Black separatism, liberation, Pan-Africanism, and internationalism. "The leadership of BSA (Richard Thomas, Jason Lovette, Barry Amis, LaMarr Thomas, and Ron Bailey)," Coleman ascertained, "did not contest the new organization, although they were not consulted in advance that a change was to take place. Black students were not consulted about the change, and it was basically viewed as a coup."¹¹ The members of BSA who were not involved in the formation of the BLFI apparently decided BSA had run its due course. They didn't aggressively oppose the world views of a new generation of their classmates who had strong opinions about how the movement should proceed.

The first public announcement of BLFI appeared in an editorial in the September 1969 "Welcome Week" issue of the *State News*, "Nightmarish Trace of the Black Experience." The author, former BSA member Mike Hudson, praised what BSA had done for the cause, observing "the Alliance has been the most effective instrument of change on the MSU campus." Speaking as if the organization was still active, Hudson declared, "Our organization strives to meet the need for human dignity, pride, strength and freedom. . . . Our purpose is liberation." Then, implying that BSA had recently been co-opted and "bogged down in rhetoric," "pettiness," confusion, indecisiveness, and "self-imprisoning," he assured that as of the summer of 1969, "BSA had become the Black Liberation Front." Without providing any specific detail about the new group's philosophy or agenda, Hudson promised they would "get all things done which must be done" and, like Malcolm X advised, do so "by any means necessary." In another overview of Black student activism in the 1969 "Welcome Week" *State News* issue, Hudson declared the Wilson Hall cafeteria sit-in revealed to him and his comrades that new, less reactionary approaches were needed to solve the pressing problems faced by MSU's Black students and those encountered by local Black communities and African descendants throughout the vast African diaspora. Their motto reflected their broad inclusive vision: "to insure justice for all black and oppressed peoples worldwide."[12]

In late September 1969, Jeanne Saddler, who regularly covered topics pertaining to African American culture and current events for the *State News*, added more context to BLFI's origin story. Echoing Coleman and Hudson, Saddler explained that BSA "ceased to exist" and "gave birth to" the BLFI, which had a "different philosophy" and new set of programs distinguishing it from "the old BSA." One of the main differences between the two organizations, observed Saddler, was that BLFI would be concerned with "the problems of *all black people*," not simply the predicaments identified by MSU Black students.[13] Such a transition in Black student activism was common. At colleges and universities throughout the nation, Black students debated the course of their movement, formed new organizations when they saw it necessary to do so, and embraced internationalist world views.

Led by executive committee heads Sam Riddle, Stan McClinton, Mike Tripp, and Mike Hudson, BLFI sought to "work for the liberation of all black and oppressed peoples" using Lansing's Black community as a focus. McClinton stressed, "We are very interested in relating to our brothers and sisters at home, in our urban communities, because the black student no longer wants to be cut off from his people from a dubious success in white institutions."[14] BLFI advocated a broad and Pan-African philosophy, exemplified in the leadership offered by Maina Kinyatti and Kumunyu Kangethe. In their purpose statement, they outlined how they sought to "facilitate the development of Pan-African Unity, to politicize and radicalize students, to protect the interest of people of African descent in Western educational institutions, and to assist black communities in their struggle against racism, colonialism, and imperialism." Like the Black Panther Party's Ten-Point program but replacing "We want" with "We believe," the BLFI outlined their beliefs, all of which hinged upon self-determination. Echoing Malcolm X, they believed "that all black people have the right to utilize any/or all means necessary to insure . . . the security and perpetuation of our race and heritage." Their major goals were to develop

Black Liberation Front, International headquarters in Lansing. Courtesy of Michigan State University Archives and Historical Collections.

educational models for Black communities, produce "relevant educational materials for African people," unite Black people, coach "committed personnel" for the struggle (as they did with their Cadre Training Program), and develop a "communication organ" to share their ideas with the community. BLFI had an executive board, four complex chairmen, and dorm organizers.[15]

From the fall of 1969 through the early 1970s, BLFI initiated many programs and protests on and off campus. They also helped raise students' awareness by inviting to campus radicals like members of the League of Revolutionary Black Workers and the Black Panthers. They played a key role in representing Black students in the university. BLFI became the first Black student organization at MSU "to control a university-sponsored program." As part of one of their first major activities on campus, BLFI sought to shape the Black Student Aide Program that resulted from BSA's demands during the 1969 spring term. During the summer, South Complex director Gary North, Detroit senior Richard W. Thomas, and Shirley Echols evaluated the residence halls system in order to determine how a Black student–centered residence hall support system would best work. In essence, the purpose of this program was to "provide a black resource person in residence halls who was sensitive to the problems and needs of black students." These aides would "work to foster a good racial climate in the hall and be knowledgeable of all resources which enable black students to survive." Coleman described their roles as being ambitious: "a Black Aide does not just have one section to handle, he must be wherever he is needed," he told the *State News* in late January 1970.[16]

Provided with room and board funding by the Center for Urban Affairs and the Equal Opportunity Program, Black student aides would, theoretically, be like resident assistants, but for African American students. In exchange for room and board, Black aides were required to participate in orientation programs and take Education 416, Leadership Training Program—Black Student Aide, maintain a 2.0 GPA, submit weekly reports, and work a minimum of twenty hours per week. Members of the BLFI convinced the Black Student Aide Program coordinator to allow them to play a role in selecting the aides. In choosing the twenty-four aides, twelve men and twelve women, BLFI sought to recruit student-activists. A coordinating committee for the program was created including the dean of students, the director of the Equal Opportunities Program, a residence hall manager and complex director, the program's coordinator, and two students from BLFI. According to Coleman, BLFI viewed the Black Student Aide Program as a way to endear themselves to Black students beginning in the fall of 1969. BLFI and other Black student-activists were frustrated that under Coleman the program was becoming "nothing more than a scaled down version of a resident assistant." Shortly after Coleman helped get the program started, Carl Taylor, as student journalist George White emphasized, became the director of the minority aide program, making him "MSU's youngest administrator." Named an inaugural MSU presidential fellow in 1970 during his junior year and elevated to assistant coordinator for residential life and assistant director for minority affairs, Taylor could relate to young Black students making the transition to East Lansing from Detroit. "Remembering my roots, I try to keep on a close personal level with my aides and the minority students they serve," Taylor told the *Grapevine Journal* in the early 1970s. "It's the only way I can accurately gauge the jobs that the aides are doing." In the 1970s, Taylor mentored Black students to become reformers. In 1974, he founded With A Child's Heart, a charitable non-profit organization that brought together Black faculty and students, namely Black aides, Black caucuses, and Black Greeks, to provide basic human needs services to struggling Lansing residents.[17]

Differentiating themselves from BSA, BLFI engaged in practical programs with Lansing's Black community, many of which were covered in the *Westside News*, a weekly newspaper produced by members of the city's Black community to afford "opportunities for young Black people" to develop journalism skills and learn "the other facets of the mass media." BLFI established a Cadre Training Program for Lansing high school students.[18] On campus, they advocated for empowering Black students. They were in part responsible for getting the *State News* to hire the paper's first Black associate editor. In order to raise the consciousness of their classmates, they sponsored workshops and events and brought speakers to campus like Trinidadian scholar-activist C. L. R. James. They supported programs with students in residence halls, the OBA, and other Black student organizations and helped African American fraternities and sororities, who formed their own interfraternity council, get involved in Lansing's Black community. Though they were often cliquish, Black Greeks related to the racism endured by the masses of Black students. White fraternities and sororities historically discriminated against them, and during the 1960s this subject was often debated in the pages of the *State News*.

Despite their outreach efforts, as early as the spring of 1970, BLFI admitted they were facing significant setbacks as an underdog organization. They had some clear internal strife leading a faction of the organization to create a Committee for Change that accused other members of the BLFI of not representing the masses of Black students. In April of 1970, the Committee for Change held a mass movement in the Wonders Kiva to discuss the future of the Black student movement.[19] By the spring of 1970 as their influence continued to grow, BLFI was challenged to reorganize in order to allow more Black students in the dormitories to elect a representative council who would serve as representatives to the organization's executive council. This led to the creation of the Black United Front that was founded in the summer of 1970. Within a relatively brief period of time, BLFI made their presence known, initiated a range of activities on and off campus, and fought for Black students' rights in significant ways.

Early in the fall 1969 term, BLFI began its efforts at fighting for Blacks' rights on campus and beyond the campus walls. In a statement released in early October, BLFI called upon the Lansing Board of Education to address several racial incidents at Eastern High School. In particular, they wanted the board to suspend Eastern's principal for allegedly physically assaulting a Black student, sophomore Roy Williams, on October 2. According to Williams, the principal threw him to the ground and restrained him with knees to his groin and head because he was about to fight with another student. Williams later reportedly checked into the hospital. "As a concerned Black organization that has committed itself to the Black community, we want an explanation," BLFI wrote. "We want to see the Lansing Board of Education act to alleviate the injustices within the school system." BLFI organized its own "fact-finding team" composed of Mike Hudson, Diana Rhodes, Mickey Haskiens, and Robert Demps to investigate what went down. On October 6, BLFI organized a demonstration with about two hundred high school students outside of Eastern High School, calling for the suspension of the school's principal. Sam Riddle argued they had evidence of the principal's "strong-arm tactics." Although no charges were issued against the school's principal, BLFI used this case to build its reputation and endear itself to some in Lansing's Black community. The Lansing Board of Education and the superintendent had to deal with BLFI as equals and as a result of BLFI's activism could not sweep the controversial incident under the rug.[20]

Around the same time BLFI members challenged the Lansing Board of Education's investigation into the case of Roy Williams, BLFI began its deliberate Pan-African struggle on campus using the African Studies Center as its target. In the morning in early October 1969, members of BLFI staged a protest in front of the International Center beginning its prolonged attack on the African Studies Center's White leadership. As expressed by Riddle, they demanded the African Studies Center be "expanded" so Black students could "take full participation" in its day-to-day operations. They were particularly offended that Ruth Simms Hamilton was the only African American faculty member working in the center. BLFI occupied the International Center for about four hours. They met with administrators Milton Dickerson, Green, and McMillan who were called to the scene. Green was especially supportive of the students, remarking, "This is as ludicrous as having a center on east European culture staffed and manned by a group of brothers from Detroit, who managed to get a Ph.D. somehow."[21] BLFI had allies in their opposition of Whites' control over the study of African life and culture at MSU. The MSU branch of the Pan-African Students Organization in the Americas, Inc. (PASOA), founded in April 1969 by African students Maina Kinyatti, who also served as the national secretary of PASOA, and Kumunyu Kangethe, released a statement after the African Studies Center takeover stating they too believed the center should be under "black control." PASOA accused the center of being unconcerned with the challenges faced by African nations since decolonization as well as the conditions faced by Blacks in the Americas and Caribbean. PASOA embraced the radical rhetoric of BLFI. "Both PASOA and BLF are waiting and watching carefully for an immediate response regarding the African Studies Center and its program," PASOA declared on October 19, 1969; "the black students want to make it clear that they can destroy the center, but the center cannot destroy them."[22]

Though BLFI underscored they were going to adopt different strategies than BSA, several weeks after the protest at the African Studies Center, on Tuesday, October 21, 1969, about one hundred members of the organization forced a short shutdown of the Holden Hall cafeteria. There were various versions of the events leading up to the demonstration. Many seem to concur that on Monday, October 20, BLFI leader Sam Riddle was prevented by a White employee from entering Holden's cafeteria despite the fact that he had a meal pass permitting him dining privileges in different residential halls on campus. Riddle and other BLFI members often visited different cafeterias to recruit and politicize students. A scuffle ensued between Riddle and a residence hall cafeteria employee. Riddle and his friends then left and met later that evening to discuss how they would handle the situation. They decided to return to Holden the next day with a larger contingency. Approximately one hundred BLFI members ate at Holden in protest of what happened to Riddle. After eating, they told the White students to leave the cafeteria. Though some White students willingly departed, others refused to do so and a handful of minor fights broke out between members of BLFI and some White students. The MSU police and the dean of students were called to the scene. The management temporarily closed the cafeteria, telling the students to dine in Wilson Hall. BLFI then met in the Wilson Hall auditorium to deliberate and made it known that if a Black student on campus was assaulted, they would "take aggressive action."[23]

In the end, BLFI didn't occupy Holden Hall's cafeteria as BSA did Wilson Hall's cafeteria six months earlier. The incident was minor in comparison. But it caused some controversy. Senator John T. Bowman (D-Michigan) sought to pass an outlandish resolution to prosecute Riddle and members of BLFI who occupied the cafeteria for less than an hour. The senator called them "thugs" and "a group of black hoodlums and black bums" to the chagrin of his colleagues Coleman Young and Basil Brown who deemed Bowman's resolution racist. The resolution had little support and went nowhere. Seeking to decrease the tension and avoid another Wilson Hall affair, residence hall management provided certain members of BLFI with special passes so they could "enter dining rooms to recruit students, not to dine."[24] This was nothing out of the ordinary as other student leaders were afforded this privilege. The incident at Holden Hall sparked some activism among the hall's Black and White students and Black students in other residence halls. About a week after the incident, Holden's Committee for Racial Understanding released a statement arguing the brief demonstration was the by-product of racial tensions that had been building up on campus. For them, the solution was to create a Black culture room where White students could learn more about Black culture by opening new lines of communication. The group's announcement gained traction. Shortly after the incident in Holden Hall, Donald Means and Amos Johnson led the Black Culture Committee. The Holden Hall Black Consciousness organization of the late 1970s was a descendant of the Holden Hall Black Caucus and the Black Culture Committee.[25]

Other Black students sought to make spaces on MSU's campus more appealing to their classmates in other ways. In February 1970, Roy D. Sigh, who entered MSU in 1968 through the Detroit Project, developed plans to remodel Fee Hall's grill "with black artifacts and pictures depicting black history." Sigh's envisioned "Walls of Dignity" would celebrate the Black historical experience and motivate Black students. He reached out to Coleman for support and met with art professor Bob Weil and historian Harry A. Reed to help him with the exhibit and historical interpretation. Several years later, Sigh gave back to Black students by publishing a thirty-five-page pamphlet of advice for "minority students with limited educational background" called "Hit De Books Baby."[26] In early November 1970, the Black People of Shaw established the first fully operating Black culture room, with a small library with Detroit senior Laurie Davis as its coordinator. The Shaw Hall Black culture room soon became a popular place for students to study, read books about Black history, and hold meetings. Students in other residence halls followed the examples of Holden's Committee for Racial Understanding and the Black People of Shaw. Black culture rooms and Black caucuses soon became common fixtures on campus.

At the end of Black History Month in 1970, Black students welcomed and saluted the opening of Holden Hall's Black culture room in the lower east lounge of the building. Supported by the Committee for Racial Understanding in Holden Hall and created in response to the Holden Hall sit-in, this space symbolized much to Black students. President Clifton R. Wharton Jr. and his wife, Delores, attended the historic event. "The first step in reducing polarization between black and whites must come through greater understanding of each other especially through understanding black culture, black history, and black psychology," Wharton told those gathered in Holden Hall cafeteria on Sunday, February 22, 1970, in celebration of the new Black space.

Students meet in a Black Culture Room in the early 1970s. Courtesy of Michigan State University Archives and Historical Collections.

Thomas Gunnings also spoke at the gathering, highlighting how the center would play a major role in bringing Black and Whites together, "moving toward a united front." Riddle added that the creation of the culture room revealed how Black and White students could promote racial understanding.[27]

Late in October 1969 after the hasty Holden Hall takeover, BLFI in collaboration with PASOA returned to their beef with the African Studies Center and its director, Charles Hughes, issuing a statement that labeled the center "a nursery-school for neo-colonialist academic scholars." This time, they were upset that Black students were not recruited to attend an African studies conference in Montreal. Ruth Simms Hamilton, the only African American faculty member employed by the center, supported the students' critique. Supported by Green and McMillan, in mid-November, BLFI and PASOA crafted a seven part manifesto calling for a total restructuring of the center to include a "special African Studies program" for Black students to help them become better equipped to solve the problems facing African people. They insisted on the promotion of Hamilton to acting codirector of the center, the recruitment of Black students to study Africa, summer programs in Africa for Black students, and a graduate program in African studies. In response, Hughes established an ad hoc committee to review the BLFI–PASOA manifesto. He was understandably defensive, rejecting many of the students' claims.[28]

On Friday, November 21, about fifty members of BLFI and PASOA picketed outside of the International Center, blocking traffic for a few minutes on Shaw Lane. After about an hour of marching and chanting, they moved into the International Center where Riddle, McClinton (Kimathi Mohammed), and PASOA leaders called for Hughes's resignation. By early December, BLFI and PASOA became increasingly dissatisfied with Hughes's lack of response to their manifesto and continued to clamor for his resignation. As a result of BLFI and PASOA's protests, Hughes resigned and a steering committee was created to revisit the students' demands. Emboldened by their success, BLFI and PASOA issued another manifesto, insisting they be represented on the steering committee. They maintained they were more qualified than White Africanists to interpret African history and culture. "All peoples have the right to self-determination," they wrote; "in that respect, we reserve the right to be the only legitimate authorities on matters that concern us as African people."[29] The protests waged by BLFI and PASOA paid off. By early June 1970 under the leadership of acting director Victor Low, the African Studies Center made notable changes and openly acknowledged their work needed to be more relevant to people of African descent throughout the world.

BLFI and PASOA were ultimately concerned with how African history and culture was portrayed. They believed African cultural awareness was central to Black students' identity. BLFI, for instance, established an Umoja Committee that organized African cultural events. Along with PASOA, which created the quarterly journal *Mazungumzo* in the early 1970s, they took great offense to negative and stereotypical portrayals of African history and culture. On February 27, 1970, the same day that Muhammad Ali spoke before a crowd of about 2,500 in the MSU Auditorium, members of the groups attended the Beal Film Group's showing of the controversial film *Africa Addio* and, twenty minutes into the film, demanded it be stopped. Days before, BLFI and PASOA warned the organization not to show the film because of its racist representations of Africa. Directed and written by two Italian filmmakers in 1966, the raw, gory, and sensationalized so-called documentary focused on episodes of violence in Africa during the transition from colonialism to decolonization. Early in his career, famous film critic Roger Ebert called it a "brutal, dishonest, racist film" that "slanders a continent and at the same time diminishes the human spirit." BLFI and PASOA joined the ranks of the film's staunch critics while members of the Beal Film Group defended showing the film in the name of freedom of speech and noncensorship. The editors of the *State News* closed ranks with the film group, with the exception of the only African American editor, Saddler. MSU administrators were aware of the discontent about the showing of *Africa Addio*. Police were present. After the incident, Wharton met with the Black student protesters.[30]

BLFI seems to have faded away on campus about a year after its founding. "The political leadership on campus changed again at the end of 1970 from the BLFI to the Black United Front with the BLF making the decision to move off campus," W. Kim Heron observed in mid-September 1973. At one level, BLFI became Black United Front (BUF) in late May 1970. The BUF was founded in the spring of 1970, around the time sophomore Harold M. Buckner became the first African American elected chairman of ASMSU. By the fall of 1972, the group was considered the largest Black student organization. The new organization was created to be a more representative organization whose leaders were elected by Black students across campus. By the fall of 1970, among the early executive board members were George Flemming, Tony Martin, Bill Powers, LaMarr Thomas, and Walter Thomas. They sought to unite Black students and raise the levels of Black consciousness across campus with programs such as their political workshops. Among its first campaigns was campaigning and fundraising for the creation of a Black Culture Center. Several days after the police killings of two Black students protesting at Jackson State College in Jackson, Mississippi, on May 15, 1970, Wharton cancelled classes, ordered flags be flown at half mast, and called for the creation of a new off-campus Black Cultural Center. The center, however, never came to fruition. BUF turned its attention to more practical, grassroots efforts. In the summer of 1970, under the directorship of George Flemming, the group launched its free breakfast program for African American children at Lansing's West Side Drop-in Center. While they didn't explicitly claim membership in the Black Panther Party, their program was clearly modeled after the party's Free Breakfast for Children Program established in January 1969 in West Oakland, California. With OBA, BUF challenged Wharton to follow through with his proposal to create a Black Cultural Center with their input in late April 1971.[31]

Working with several of the city's Black organizations, BUF received a food permit from the Ingham County Health Department and began serving breakfast to between fifty and seventy-five

A member of BUF teaches children how to cook. Courtesy of Michigan State University Archives and Historical Collections.

youngsters, ages two to eighteen, Monday through Saturday from 7:45 a.m. until 8:45 a.m. One participant observed, "It was Black students making a real contribution to the community." Another noted, "the breakfast program is the first step of a long hard struggle to achieve total brotherhood." Though the program faced challenges, students respected such service. In the early 1970s, the United Blacks of Wonders launched their annual Ujamaa Award for community service. In 1973, the award went to Detroit senior Ralph Hanson, who was "at the head of the Black United Front at its onset" and had worked with the breakfast program for three years. Five others who received honorable mention certificates were also involved in the community including the breakfast program. Black students participated in other programs aimed at helping Lansing's Black youth. In the early 1970s, a group of Black students volunteered for the Teach a Brother program. Initiated by the MSU Volunteer Bureau, this program provided after-school tutoring for kids ages six to eighteen in the city's west side.[32]

BUF also called for political action on campus. In solidarity with persecuted Black Panther Party members and in protest of the mistreatment of Blacks by law enforcement across the nation, BUF called for a boycott of classes on November 18, 1970, and scheduled a range of activities from 8:00 a.m. until 8:00 p.m. The main event was Black Panther Party chairman Huey P. Newton's speech. By 10:00 a.m., at least two thousand students and community members gathered at the MSU Auditorium to hear Newton speak. Members of the BUF's Committee for a Black

One of the numerous teams in the BUF Basketball League. Courtesy of Michigan State University Archives and Historical Collections.

Moratorium provided security. After a long delay, Newton took to the podium for two hours delivering one of his standard orations, assuring his impressionable audience, "the only culture worth holding on to is a revolutionary culture and that is a culture of constant change." In the summer of 1971, BUF executive board member Leon Grant explained in the *Grapevine Journal* that the purpose of the organization had expanded, seeking to "raise the political consciousness of the general populace," contribute to the "academic survival" of Black students, close ranks with Black Greeks, sponsor and host a variety of workshops, and promote "cultural nationalist" approaches. BUF worked closely with other organizations, such as Project Grapevine. First released in early June 1970 and maintained by a communications committee, the *BUF News-letter* included the voices of radical Black students and updated the Black student community about current events and future programming. They embraced what they called "revolutionary democracy."[33] They had an executive board of nine elected members and an elected representative council. BUF also provided social functions for Black students, many of whom felt alienated in

East Lansing, such as a Revolutionary Film Series. The Black Basketball League and the BUF Basketball League were among BUF's most popular initiatives.

Founded by Detroit native Ervin Armstrong in 1970, the BUF Basketball League took place during the winter term and brought many Black students together. "If you are in the Men's Intramural Building at about 7 p.m., Monday through Friday, and you happen to pass by the West Gym on the second floor, you'll probably hear the roars of excitement and the rhythmic chanting of, 'to the hoops . . . to the hoops,'" a staff writer for the *Grapevine Journal* recounted in November 1972; "at that point you have discovered the fun-filled pass-time of hundreds of black students . . . BASKETBALL, . . . bringing together more brothers and sisters than any other sports or social activity at MSU." The popular teams included Valentine and the Superflies. Though mostly Black and dubbed "the only all-Black affair of its kind," one of the league's coordinators, Ocie Albert, noted that Whites participated in the league and in 1972 several women's teams were formed. By 1973, there were approximately thirty teams of ten players each who belonged to the league's three divisions. The on-campus league was composed of teams from many of the residence halls, showcasing more than a few talented basketball players. In 1973, a BUF team played the MSU freshman team and lost by only two points. At the end of the season, the league's coordinators organized an awards banquet. For several years, the BUF Basketball League provided entertainment and a sense of belonging to hundreds of Black students. As its organizers claimed, it provided a "meeting place for Blacks to unite." Though short-lived, by adopting an approach that blended together grassroots activism, Black consciousness, and popular social activities, BUF successfully attracted a diverse cross-section of the Black student population.[34]

Chapter 32

I Heard It through the *Grapevine*

Many minority students attending colleges and universities have many conflicts other than those of their white counterparts. Many of these conflicts are due to no information or misinformation pertaining to areas vital to their survival as *students* . . . i.e. jobs, housing, and etc. Thus, many minority students become disenchanted because they don't have the *means* to obtain and utilize information necessary to survival."[1] This was the rationale that St. Louis, Missouri native, U.S. Air Force veteran, and MSU social science major James Ballard gave for the creation of Project Grapevine, a registered student organization he founded in September 1969 and secured office space for in the Student Services Building a year later.

Project Grapevine was arguably the most resilient MSU Black student organization during the Black Power era. It was also the most well-documented Black student organization during this tumultuous and transformative period in MSU's history. Housed in the Michigan State University Archives and Historical Collections, the impressive *Grapevine Journal* Collection—the largest single archive on Black student organizing at MSU before and during the Black Campus Movement—includes six cubic feet of materials covering a wide range of subjects, personalities, and events. The scope and depth of its contents suggests that Project Grapevine's leadership realized their history-making efforts in real time. The assortment of materials is even more appreciable because they were perhaps almost destroyed. "I must inform your office and interested parties that thirty days after our official closing date," Ballard wrote to the president of ASMSU in late July 1975, "all records for Project Grapevine and *Grapevine Journal* will be destroyed. Please make this an official public notice." What prompted Ballard to announce his momentary plans to destroy the records of Project Grapevine is unknown. Given the contentious relationship he and his organization had with the *State News* and some of the university's power brokers, perhaps he didn't want his foes to have any access to Project Grapevine's inner workings. He could have also been upset with the end of a long and courageous run at "providing the way for minority students to develop their ideas through their own initiative and energies."[2] Whatever the case may have been, the *Grapevine Journal* Collection is a documentary trove, providing an illuminating porthole into the day-to-day operations of one of the most important Black student movements in the history of MSU.

In late January 1971, a writer for the *Lansing State Journal* announced the group's existence. He mislabeled Project Grapevine "Operation Grapevine" and in passing commented that it "functions as an information center for minority groups about job opportunities and housing." While Ballard welcomed the publicity, he was a bit miffed with the misnaming of his movement and the sketchy description of its objectives. In his application for an account with the MSU Controller's Office, he jotted down the purpose of the group: "to create an avenue of communication essential for existence at MSU." In a subsequent memo, he further described the primary aim of Project Grapevine as providing African American and minority students with information about jobs, housing, tutoring, counseling and other relevant "basic information" through a handy, grassroots newsletter. In Ballard's words, the organization initially extended "a service which adds strength and sensitivity of communicating what and where services are available."[3]

Building upon a research project he completed in a Department of Education class taught by Professor Louis Hekhuis, whom the *Lansing State Journal* reporter curiously interviewed about Project Grapevine's raison d'être, during the spring of 1969 and the fall of 1970 Ballard regularly printed and distributed a brief "help sheet" called "Info," which was soon published in both English and Spanish. On Mondays, he passed along copies of the newsletter to Black dormitory aides to distribute to Black students. The Black United Front also occasionally produced a newsletter espousing their ideologies. Ballard viewed his newsletter as being a "service *of* Blacks *for* Blacks" to "help guide Black students on the tough college road." The enterprising Ballard soon cobbled together enough resources to hire the organization's first staff worker, Gloria Black. Eventually referred to as the "Grapevine," a nod to Motown songwriter Norman Whitfield's 1966 "I Heard It through the Grapevine" that Gladys Knight and Marvin Gaye popularized, the simple newsletter began gaining popularity. Overburdened with the strenuous workload, Ballard realized he needed to expand his largely one-man operation. He had spread himself too thin. While plugging away at his bachelor's degree, which he earned in 1972, he worked on the assembly line as a conveyor attendant at Oldsmobile. In April 1970, he determined his newsletter would require a staff of at least four, equipment (most importantly a typewriter and a mimeograph machine), and an operational budget of approximately $6,000 per year.[4] During the 1970–1971 academic year, Project Grapevine was housed in room 25 of the Student Services

Building, and Ballard worked out the logistics for transforming the simple "Info" handout into a newspaper. He envisioned a biweekly newspaper that would include "the BUF newsletter, dorm publications, the Grapevine newsletter and newssheet and 'all' publications adhering to the needs of minority students."[5]

"We, the Black Student population of MSU, need a viable instrument to voice our opinions," Ballard and his coworkers declared. During the peak years of the Black Campus Movement, groups of Black students at predominantly White institutions throughout the nation founded their own newspapers. As noted by Ibram X. Kendi, among these newspapers were "*Nommo* at UCLA, *Watusi* at U-Montana, *The Black Exposition* at West Carolina, *Harambee* at New Mexico State and Duke (after the U.S. organization's publication title), *Black Explosion* at U-Maryland, *Pamoja* at U-Georgia, *Black Fire* at SF State, *Uhuru* at CSU Fresno."[6] Whether conscious of it or not, these Black student-activists built upon a deep Black Press historical tradition dating back to creation of the first African American newspaper, *Freedom's Journal*, founded in 1827.

Like their predecessors from the antebellum era through the modern Civil Rights Movement, Black students during the Black Power era recognized the power of the media and the necessity of representing themselves and challenging anti-Black images in the mainstream White media. Collectively, they reasoned their institutions' White-run student papers didn't adequately or accurately cover local and national race relations as well as current events in the vast African diaspora. For MSU Black students like Detroiter Arnold N. Reid Jr. who attended the university during the Black Power era and authored an essay "SN Articles Display Bias," many commentaries published in the student newspaper represented "overtly racist journalism." They knew their campuses' widely distributed newspapers, which were often supported through fees imposed by their universities, largely ignored Black culture in the United States, Africa, and the vast African diaspora, sidelined Black students' unique perspectives and world views, and put forward subtly and overtly biased interpretations of race relations. Heeding Stokely Carmichael's advice, Black students believed a media network under their control was a powerful tool in their struggle in White spaces. In October of 1967, managing editor of the storied *Michigan Chronicle* (Detroit, MI) Albert Dunmore spoke at MSU, underscoring that the mainstream White media's coverage of Black America needed to be drastically improved. Ballard believed this wholeheartedly. "Neither the *State News* nor the *State Journal* is adequately covering the minority communities and there is a real need for a paper that operates on truth and honesty," he maintained.[7]

Ballard's idea for a Black newspaper in the Greater Lansing area wasn't entirely new. There were several short-lived Black newspapers in Lansing during the 1960s. In mid-May 1963, the first issue of *Lansing Post*, founded by Robert R. Chapman, appeared. From November 1968 until the late spring of 1969, Ralph R. Barnett Jr. served as editor of the *Inner City Times*, a community newspaper whose primary concerns were issues facing Lansing's Black community. Barnett and his team covered issues related to the Black community and regularly reprinted Black history cartoons originally published by historian J. A. Rogers in the *Pittsburgh Courier* as part of "Your

History" and "Facts about the Negro." In the spring of 1969 under the editorship of Detroit native Ernie Boone, a group of Black activists launched Lansing's *Westside News*. Boone was much more experienced than Ballard and his coworkers. He graduated from MSU in 1964 with a bachelor's degree in journalism and then secured a position as a sportswriter for the *Lansing State Journal*. While at MSU, Boone wrote several articles for the *Michigan Chronicle*, the state's leading Black newspaper at the time. Settling down in Lansing after graduating, Boone became an outspoken civil and human rights activist, assuming leadership roles in the Michigan Welfare League, Lansing's Model Cities program, and the Westside Action Center. "The *Westside News* is the product of the West Side Action Center's Journalism Class," Boone announced in May 1969. "It is the outgrowth of the Westside Advisor—the culmination of our year's efforts on the part of a group of youngsters and Michigan State University students to learn to write, report, and publish news. It grew out of the need for black youngsters to learn to communicate writing, look realistically at their community and to take pride in something of their own." Boone underscored that the paper was "our paper" and strove to "provide an outlet for black literary and journalistic talent and to write about events of interest and importance to Lansing's black community."[8] Fizzling out when the *Grapevine Journal* was taking off, the *Westside News* offered MSU Black student journalists and writers an ideal space to share their ideas and hone their craft. In line with MSU's outreach and engagement tradition, these wordsmiths, like Richard W. Thomas and Michael Hudson, sought to keep Lansing's Black community informed about the Black experience on campus.

The *State News* did not provide a welcoming space for Black students. In 1963, the talented George Junne served as the chief photographer of the *State News*. He was probably the first African American to work in such a leadership capacity for the paper. Only a few were on staff with the paper during the early to mid-1960s, and in the late 1960s prior to the founding of the *Grapevine Journal*, only a small number of Black students aired their opinions in the *State News*. Their pieces were rarely feature stories. The *State News*'s spring 1968 issue of its biweekly magazine *Collage*, "The Black Revolution, through the Eyes of Students," was certainly an exception. Black student columnists' pieces for the *State News* tended to focus on issues pertaining to race relations and Black student life. They were more often than not buried within the campus daily. During the late 1960s and early 1970s, very few Black students were regular contributors to the paper. Though BSA leader Richard W. Thomas was listed as being a *State News* staff writer during the summer of 1968 and authored several pieces on African American urban life and the Poor People's Campaign, Jeanne Saddler, a regular staff writer for Boone's *Westside News*, was one of the only Black *State News* staff writers during the peak years of the Black Campus Movement.[9] In 1969 and 1970, she penned a collection of well-written essays on issues relevant to the Black community, highlighting the activities of Black student-activists. Her *State News* essays provided the most detailed overviews of Black organizations, and several of her writings were front page stories. During the early 1970s, a few other Black student journalists regularly penned articles for the student newspaper, including staff writer Wanda Herndon, future leader in the communications industry, and eventual "*State News* Hall of Famers" Karen Brown Dunlap (staff writer, 1970–1971) and Charles B. "Chuck" Johnson (sports writer, 1971–1975). Upon more than a few occasions, African American students submitted editorials to the student paper, sharing their thoughts about what a group of students in 1972 called "the bias inherent in the *State News* coverage and lack of coverage of issues important to black people on this campus."[10]

In late January 1970, the *State News* editor-in-chief appointed Saddler associate editor for Black affairs in charge of covering the Center for Urban Affairs, the Equal Opportunities Program, minority student groups, and issues facing African Americans off campus. She didn't let this position soften her militancy. Several days after she was promoted, she expressed her dissent over the editorial team's coverage of President Wharton, arguing that their critiques had "racial implications" reminiscent of the "Old South" and days of slavery. She was the only woman on the seven-member editorial team, holding this position through mid-January 1971. In 1972, she graduated with honors in journalism, was "one of the 50 most outstanding graduating women in campus," and was listed in the 1972 "list of 'Who's Who in American Universities.'"[11] While a student, she worked as a staff writer for the *Detroit Free Press*. Saddler's experience with the *Free Press* and *State News* helped lay the foundation for her future career. After earning an MS degree in journalism from Columbia University, she worked as a correspondent for *Time* magazine and the *Wall Street Journal*. Most Black students seeking a career in journalism at MSU didn't get the opportunities the gifted Saddler carved out for herself. With few exceptions, those Black students with radical ideas about the Black condition didn't view the *State News* as being a viable outlet.

Project Grapevine, on the other hand, provided many students from traditionally un-derrepresented backgrounds, especially African Americans, hands-on training in the media industry. In 1972, then Project Grapevine director and Detroit native and sophomore George White defined the organization as being an "academically oriented," "educational unit" that was "open to all students in all majors." "We offer a product and a process with the training for minority journalists and communications specialists through practical experience," the project's leadership team summed up in 1974. " We introduced a new set of voices into the lopsided field of communications." Shortly after it was decided to create the *Grapevine Journal*, the purpose of Project Grapevine, the "parent organization" of the newspaper, was straightforward: "to give minority students a communication channel to express themselves, and to learn and practice arts of good journalism." Their mantra was imparting "communicative skills to those who have been deprived of those skills."[12]

Eight pages in length and formatted like an amateur newsletter, the first issue of the "new" *Grapevine: A Project Grapevine Publication* was released in early June 1971. Approximately 2,500 copies of the issue were distributed to residence halls with Black and minority student populations, the Office of Black Affairs, and the African Studies Center. A large Black Power fist holding the scales of justice appears centered on the cover with "Power to the People" and

"Fraternity Equality Liberty" written in bubble letters. Revealing Project Grapevine's concern with minority populations, surrounding the imposing fist are images of an armed member of the Black Panther Party, a Native American elder, and a group of Chicano/a activists. Ballard dubbed the paper "a tabloid" composed "on a manual typewriter and pasted together on a makeshift light table."[13]

Ballard forecasted that the paper's success depended upon student participation. "I can hustle the money to keep it going financially," he commented in the June 3, 1971, debut issue, "but if the minority students on campus do not contribute their articles, ideas, poems, or news, it cannot function properly or efficiently." The editor added, "the step has been made, now it is necessary for the minority students to keep the *Grapevine* going. We need your ideas, articles, news, and any other information that will be of importance to our becoming a more dynamic publication. HARAMBEE!!"[14] In addition to Ballard (the paper's first director and editor), the initial staff included five students: four young women, three Blacks and one Chicana (A. Brown, L. Medina, D. Gant, and A. Hicks), and one young African American man (F. Lewis). Supported by ASMSU, the Black United Front, the Office of Black Affairs, the Center for Urban Affairs, and Student Activities, the first issue covered a range of topics, featuring articles on Black Greek life and the MSU branch of the Pan African Students Organization in the Americas, the Office of Black Affairs, the Black Student Aide Program, the Black United Front, and the Center for Urban Affairs. Student reporters also showcased the contributions of MSU staff members Don E. Coleman, Maxie Jackson, Larry Redd, and "Sister" Joanne Collins, assistant financial aid director and counselor. A section entitled "Gallery of Poems" included a collection of ten poems focusing on the Black Freedom Struggle. In the tradition of the "Info" newsletter, the editors shared with readers job opportunities and available housing near campus.

Though the first issue of the "new" *Grapevine* focused on Black students, several pieces did speak to the experiences of other students of color. As Ballard underscored, "Blacks, Chicanos, and Indians must submit articles because they are minority students. Grapevine is designed to help out all minorities in as many ways as possible." In a "letter of Interest" addressed to "the Indian people," Cherokee-Shoshoni Roland L. Blevins lambasted the Bureau of Indian Affairs' acculturation efforts and called upon Indigenous peoples, "the tribal cultures of our race," to maintain the "Indian way" of living and knowing. In "The 'Ah So!' Syndrome," Ying Li creatively satirized the denigrating stereotyping of "Amerasians in the U.S.," dubbing the mimicking of Asian peoples, especially Chinese culture, a rampant "disease" that "merits closer scientific attention." Li chastised "Amerasians" who played into these caricatures and suggested that the root cause of the "affliction" of the "'Ah So!' Syndrome" was jealousy.[15] The next issue featured an article on Movimiento Esfuerzos Chicanos de Azlan, the first major Chicano/a student organization at MSU, originally founded as the Mass-Mexican American Students at State.

Volume 1, number 1 of the rebranded *Grapevine Journal* appeared on September 20, 1971, and was strikingly different from the make-do, pathbreaking, initial issue. The circulation had miraculously increased to ten thousand. Advertised as being "operated by black students at Michigan State University to provide a medium of communication for all black students, faculty, other minorities and interested parties," this edition set the tone for future issues. The topics explored ran the gamut: local and national issues impacting African Americans and communities of color, national politics, Black liberation movements in the United States, Africa, and the African diaspora, updates on the activities of African American leaders, and happenings on campus relevant to Black students. Most subsequent issues included an editorial page with a "Point of View" section; "News in Brief" with articles reprinted from Washington, D.C.'s National Black News Service and the Liberation New Service (New York City); various articles authored by student journalists; photos of Black leaders and historical icons and MSU students, faculty, administrators, and staff members; poetry featured in the "Poet's Corner"; and a range of announcements and advertisements, including shout-outs to local barbers such as Joe Barkley in the Union Barber Shop, Robert's Barber Shop in Lansing, and the Minority Books International Inc. located at 210½ Grand River Avenue. Cofounded by MSU graduate students Eric Winston and Patricia Duignan and Lansing surgeon Thomas Robinson, the bookstore, later renamed New Visions Community Shop, was as much a bookstore as it was a small Black consciousness movement center. The covers of the *Grapevine Journal* often featured images of famous Black leaders, everyday Black children, and the newspaper's logo, an outline of the African continent with a globe in the center.

Throughout *Grapevine Journal*'s existence, support from Black faculty, staff, and administrators was vital. The College for Urban Affairs was one of its staunchest backers. The student journalists paid homage to their elders. In several issues of the *Journal*, occasionally in a "Faculty Focus" section, appreciative Black student writers profiled the activities and contributions of Black faculty, administrators, and staff, including Robert L. Green, Coleman, Joseph McMillan, Thomas Gunnings, Jimmy Raye, Gloria Smith, Payton Fuller, Pat Barnes-McConnell, Clifford Pollard, James Hamilton, Jim Bibbs, L. Eudora Pettigrew, and President Clifton R. Wharton Jr. This was part of their mission of furnishing their Black readers with basic information about what the university had to offer them. As it is today, MSU was a large and difficult-to-navigate university. There were literally thousands of faculty members, only a handful of whom were Black. The majority of Black students might not have been aware of the presence of Black faculty on campus beyond those affiliated with the Center for Urban Affairs. The *Journal* introduced their readers to these scholars who looked like them. Engaging in cross-generational dialogues, a few faculty members also published in the newspaper like Richard W. Thomas, cofounder of the Black Students' Alliance (BSA) who was appointed instructor and research director for media projects in the Center for Urban Affairs in the summer of 1972. Shortly before his official appointment, he wrote an essay in the first issue of the paper calling for a "Black Summit Conference" bringing Black students, faculty, and administrators together to coordinate their politics. Several years later, in an essay titled "Black Students Mistake Priorities," he summoned

Grapevine Journal staff. Courtesy of Michigan State University Archives and Historical Collections.

educated African Americans, including students, to use their expertise and knowledge to help improve the Black community.

As the newspaper evolved, so did its organizational structure and job-task descriptions. Ballard served as the executive director of Project Grapevine's Advisory Board and chair of the *Grapevine Journal*'s Board of Directors. Other positions included a director, an editor-in-chief, a managing editor, several managers, a photographic editor, reporters, and copy and rewrite desk editors. During its formative years, Project Grapevine's staff, budget, and reach expanded by leaps and bounds. From its inception as a single-sheet newsletter in the fall of 1969 until the early spring of 1972, the *Journal* existed on what Ballard called "a subsistence level." They received minimal support from units and individuals within the university, and their advertising campaign proved to be challenging. Ballard recalled, "During this early period, the paper was printed through the strenuous efforts of a volunteer staff." Despite these obstacles, from the publication of the initial eight-page tabloid in early June 1971 until early March 1972, seven issues of the *Journal* appeared. After the March 1972 issue, two more issues were released in 1972, one in early May and the other in late October.[16]

Less than a year after the first issue appeared, the *Journal* faced some significant financial woes. "THE GRAPEVINE JOURNAL IS DYING," the editorial staff announced in their March 1972 issue. "We began building a foundation for the GRAPEVINE JOURNAL in the summer of 1971. But because of inappropriate funds during the fall terms, the GRAPEVINE JOURNAL had to operate under extremely sporadic conditions." Though Project Grapevine had acquired office space and "essential equipment," increased their staff, expanded their advertising clients, and produced "better, more functional newspapers," they needed more funding to continue their "high quality newspaper." Speaking directly to Black students, the newspaper's staff concluded their plea, "Help give to us life. It's up to you!" Overcoming the odds, in May 1972, the *Journal*'s eight key staff members released a twenty-four-page issue, the largest in the paper's history. It featured an insightful and lengthy essay by Ron Johnson, "The Struggle of the Black Athlete," overviewing the Black athlete's movement at MSU within a broader historical context. Celebrating the Black Athletes Coalition and Green's activism, Johnson spoke critically of MSU's famed integrationist football tradition and argued that Black gridders were often placed in remedial courses and stacked in "foreign" positions so that MSU could satisfy a racial quota.[17]

In the summer of 1972, the journal expanded its advertising efforts, W. Kim Heron became the editor, George White took over "major administrative duties," and the staff worked hard on the 1972 "Welcome Week" issue (September 18–23). Heron, who worked hard on this issue with Madelyn Bridget, expressed discontent with the issue and commented that the staff "was in shambles" at the time. The final product was impressive. Thirty-two pages in length, the "full color tabloid drew 1,700 dollars in advertising, combining for the first time editorial quality with revenue making potential." The *Journal*'s circulation had reached forty thousand, offering, in Heron's estimation, "the total student body an alternative voice and community awareness" and "bridging the gap between Black and White by providing important information and news not otherwise covered at Michigan State."[18] It had, hands-down, become the nation's largest Black student newspaper. Up-and-coming student journalists were inspired by the paper. In 1972, a freshman from Jackson, Michigan, and his friends in the Brody Complex launched the "Ghetto Speaks," a newsletter aimed at keeping Black students updated about events on campus relevant to their success and the Black community.

With the "Welcome Week" issue, the newspaper announced its new publishing schedule, the second week of the fall, winter, and spring terms. In the fall of 1972, George White used his position as a staff writer and columnist for the *State News* to promote the *Journal* while taking direct jabs at the mainstream student paper and university administrators. In the 1972 "Welcome Week" issue of the *State News*, he chastised the university for not supporting the *Journal*. "The imbalance is revenue. The *State News* gets $33,000 in student fees without a referendum. The *Grapevine Journal* gets $0. If the *Journal* dies, the University can take credit." White also scoffed at administrators' suggestion that "minority students" be taxed for the *Journal* when "all" students were being taxed for the *State News*.[19] The issue of lack of support given to the *Journal* from the university would soon become a rallying cry for Black student activism.

In mid-January 1973, the *Lansing State Journal* took notice of the *Grapevine Journal*'s success. This was the first major publicity the newspaper received from the local mainstream media. A large photo of Ballard, White, and Heron in Project Grapevine's office accompanied the celebratory article. With swag resembling that of chairman of the Illinois chapter of the Black Panther Party Fred Hampton, the imposing and stern Ballard seems to be speaking while looking directly into the eyes of the reporter. Under the headline "'Grapevine' Flourishes," the *State Journal* staff writer portrayed the newspaper as a true rags to riches story. "What began in 1969 as a single-sheet newsletter providing black students with information about housing and jobs has grown into a professional-looking news publication with a circulation of 20,000. In the 1971–72 academic year, the Associated Collegiate Press (ACP) gave the *Grapevine Journal* a 'first class merit award.'" Ballard and senior editor George White were interviewed and emphasized that the *Journal* served as "an 'alternative' to the *State News*." Written from an explicitly "black perspective" that avoided a "leftist approach," the *Journal*, Ballard added, served as a "medium of communication among blacks" as well as "a place where students can learn skills." Neither Ballard nor his colleagues implied the paper was in any type of financial predicament. Instead, Ballard intimated their advertising revenue was beginning to pay for printing and staff members' salaries.[20]

Protecting the public reputation of their enterprise, Ballard didn't reveal the pressing financial challenges Project Grapevine encountered. The nonprofit organization wasn't making enough money through advertising and allocations from different units in the university to support its daily operations. By the spring of 1973, things took a turn for the worse for Project Grapevine. "Our staff is not paid in accordance to the amount of work that they do, we can't afford to pay them that way. Most of the hours they put in go unrewarded financially. They are just good people who feel that they are performing a service to the community," Ballard shared with *Grapevine Journal* readers in the spring of 1973.[21] By May 1973, the paper had a staff of thirty-five and an advertising revenue of $1,350. But it was on the brink of closure.

In the spring and summer, the *Journal* leadership sent a letter to President Wharton and the Board of Trustees requesting financial support and calling for the university to suspend the one dollar student tax used to subsidize the *State News*. They found it preposterous that the *State News* received such high levels of support while their enterprise struggled to exist. In mid-May, Ballard told a *Lansing State Journal* reporter, "All we want is free access. As it is, the *State News* had a monopoly the University supports. Other student publications can't grow. And they won't be taken seriously as long as we have that monopoly." With their backs against the wall, on May 18, Project Grapevine hosted Rev. Jesse Jackson, director of People United to Save Humanity (PUSH), who spoke in the MSU Auditorium for a Project Grapevine fund-raising event. The fee for admission was one dollar, symbolically the same cost as the student tax for the *State News*. The roughly three hundred people who attended Jackson's speech were treated to his captivating rhetoric as well as a performance from the PUSH gospel singers. The funds raised by this program did little to solve the *Grapevine Journal*'s mounting financial woes.[22] But the outspokenness of the Project Grapevine's leadership wasn't totally in vain. They did effect change and gained a seat, however marginal, at the table.

In early May 1973 in response to Project Grapevine's persuasion, the *State News* Board of Directors—which included one African American, premed student Roland Williams—charged the newly created Committee for Alternative Publications with distributing about $21,000 of the paper's total profits to "other segments of the printed media" on campus. In late May, director of Project Grapevine and senior editor of the *Journal* George White and other members of the newspaper's staff met with President Wharton and the Board of Trustees. White shared with Wharton and the board a brief history of the newspaper entitled "Successes on a Rough Road." He insisted they deserved the same level of support the university offered their White counterparts. The *State News*, White pointed out, "through the cooperation of the university annually receives over 100,000 dollars in student taxes." Calling the funds the *State News* agreed to turnover to the *Journal* "welfare," White believed the campus's Black newspaper should receive systemic financial support. He ended his plea taking pride in his team's ability to persevere: "With few resources but a will to work, achieve, learn and teach, the *Grapevine Journal*, to this point—has survived."[23]

Following White's impassioned plea, President Wharton and the Board of Trustees agreed to establish the Ad Hoc Committee on *Grapevine Journal*, chaired by African American trustee Aubrey Radcliffe (the second African American elected to the MSU Board of Trustees) to explore the issues raised by White and his coworkers. In June 1973, the committee concluded that the newspaper made notable contributions to the campus culture and deserved to be continued if possible. A month later, the committee added that the paper could not continue unless it was guaranteed a regular source of income beyond what was generated through advertising. Following the committee's recommendations, the Board of Trustees loaned Project Grapevine $15,000 to cover expenses through the summer of 1973. The *Journal* received additional support from the Alternative Voices Fund, a funding source established with surplus revenues from the *State News*. The financial support the *Journal* received in the summer of 1973 wasn't sufficient for the paper's future survival. Nearly half was used to cover an overdue printing bill. For the 1973–1974 academic year, Heron indicated the total funding required to run the journal was $88,775, half of which would pay for personnel and production costs.[24]

As the *Journal* faced mounting financial problems, many came to their defense. Administrators Green, Coleman, Thomas Gunnings, McMillan, Amos Johnson, Kullervo Louhi, and C. L. Wender offered the newspaper some minimal financial and moral support. In early June 1973 under the leadership of George Logan, the Black Faculty and Administrators Association (BFAA) urged President Wharton to support young Black journalists' professional development. Characterizing the newspaper as "an attempt to provide a valid academic-training experience for Black students" and "a meaningful organ of communication in the University community, reflecting a Black perspective," BFAA recommended "immediate assistance" with the newspaper's financial problems and "the development and implementation of long range strategies" to help the newspaper persist and flourish. "We, the Black Faculty and Administrators Association, are concerned about the monopoly of the campus and University community by one campus based newspaper," Logan wrote, echoing Ballard's and White's concerns. "As such, we strongly recommend your immediate assistance in the development of a mechanism to support *The Grapevine Journal*'s financial and academic program needs."[25]

Democratic Michigan Congressmen John Conyers and Charles Diggs Jr., whose father had helped desegregate Michigan State's men's dormitories more than three decades earlier, publicly expressed their support of the *Journal*. In late June 1973, Conyers wrote to editor-in-chief Heron, telling him he was "a strong supporter." In Conyers's estimation, the paper was an "excellent example of Black journalism" worthy of backing. "I am sorry to hear that you are experiencing some reticence as to the degree and term of support by the University." Conyers added, "I believe the University should give every consideration to your request for on-going and long-term support. If there is anything I can do to help assure the survival and growth of the *Grapevine Journal*, please don't hesitate to contact me." A month later, Diggs sent letters to the Democratic members of the MSU Board of Trustees. He wrote, "I should like to add my voice to those appealing to your continued financial support for the Black student paper on the MSU campus, *The Grapevine Journal*. It is extremely important for those voices that were silent for so long be given an opportunity to come to the fore."[26]

During the summer of 1973, the *Journal* staff waited anxiously for further recommendations from trustee Radcliffe's ad hoc committee and support from the Board of Trustees. In mid-July, Heron wrote a three-page letter to President Wharton and the board reiterating the *Journal*'s request for funding for the 1973–1974 academic year to cover the costs of staff members' salaries, equipment, and printing. The ad hoc committee, in his estimation, failed to comprehensively address this. "Our long-term problem needs attention at this time if the paper is not to face closing with the exhaustion of summer staff funds." Wharton's response to Heron was brief and to the point. He underscored that the ad hoc committee determined "the $15,000 advance," essentially a loan that needed to be paid back in full, was as much as the *Journal* was going to get from the university.[27] This was a death blow.

In the first issue of the *Grapevine Journal*'s third volume released in mid-September 1973, the paper's staff announced, "the distribution of this issue of the *Grapevine Journal* marks the possible end of the paper as well as its current high point." Under the title "Journal Expands Faces Closing," staff members reminisced on the challenges they faced in sustaining the paper. Looking back at the paper's evolution during troubling times, Heron remarked, "the journal was on the verge of becoming the country's most important training ground for minority students in journalism and advertising." Managing editor Madelyn Bridget was more optimistic, vowing, "It looks bleak. But we haven't given up by any means. We're going to work until we have no choice.

I'm looking for something to work out. I think they'll have the *Grapevine* around longer than they imagined."[28] Bridget's optimism didn't pan out.

In the fall of 1973, approximately two years after the first volume appeared, the *Journal*—what journalism major and staff writer Angela Martin called the "print sector of Project Grapevine"— was forced to discontinue publication. In early 1974, the journal's board of directors dissolved its operations, and the director of Project Grapevine George White announced new plans. "In the absence of the *Grapevine Journal*," he promised, "Project Grapevine, the paper's funding organization, will strive to initiate and continue projects aimed at meeting the needs of Michigan State University's community. With the community's support, we will succeed."[29]

Sensing the precarious status of the *Journal*, beginning during the summer of 1973, Project Grapevine began engaging in other activities, including focused outreach work. From July 8 until July 21, 1973, the organization collaborated with the *State News* on an Urban (Summer) Journalism Workshop. The Panax Corporation, founded by an MSU alumnus, contributed $1,000 toward the cause. The original idea for this workshop was proposed by Roland Williams, a biochemistry

Michigan high school students who participated in the *Grapevine Journal*'s summer workshop. Courtesy of Michigan State University Archives and Historical Collections.

major and member of the *State News* Board of Directors, who served as the program's coordinator. "It's my idea that the greater exposure of young Blacks to the mass media and its power, the more probability of good black news media." He added, "There should be a black voice in every community—a voice for positive suggestion and a directing type or organ which would reflect the day by day condition of the black community."[30] A selection committee including Williams and four members of the *Grapevine Journal* team (Ballard, Floresta Jones, Heron, and White) selected twenty high school students from Detroit, Westland, Flint, Benton Harbor, Battle Creek, South Haven, Jackson, Muskegon Heights, and Lansing to participate in this program. The students, whose names were included in the late May 1973 issue of the *Journal*, stayed in Mason and Abbot Halls with several MSU student counselors and participated in workshops led by *Journal* and *State News* staff, diverse groups of newspaper reporters, and MSU faculty.

Described by a Flint newspaper as "two weeks of hard labor," the workshop was intensive. Most days began at 8:00 a.m. and ended between 7:00 p.m. and 9:30 p.m. The program was directed by MSU alumna and former *State News* superstar Saddler, who at the time worked as a reporter for the *Detroit Free Press*. The topics of the workshop ran the gamut, including copy editing, typography, editorial writing, interviewing, advertising, photography, the history of the Black press, and television and radio journalism. The students took field trips to the *Lansing State Journal*, the Detroit Press Club, and the Printco Corporation in Greenville, Michigan. The two-week program was very hands-on. Not only did the students practice interviewing and writing, but they put together their own draft of a simple newspaper, *Third World Genesis*. While Heron reflected that several of the lectures were over the students' heads, the program exposed them to the fundamentals of journalism and dimensions of the MSU campus experience. Toward the end of the program, a professor from the MSU School of Journalism offered the students tips about majoring in journalism. Most of these bright youngsters had probably never visited a college campus nor interacted with university professors and Black college students. The workshop was capped off with a reception for the students' parents and a graduation ceremony in the Union Building. The six "most outstanding" students received $500 scholarships toward their college education.[31]

Shortly after the Urban (Summer) Journalism Workshop, in September 1973, Project Grapevine began cosponsoring a Black radio news talk show called *Black Insights*, which by January 1974 they completely produced under the directorship of Heron. A variety of topics were addressed on the show, such as African and Afro-diasporic history and culture, Black women's liberation, and pressing issues facing Black students. *Black Insights* built upon work started by Larry Redd. In 1970, Redd, who later became a professor of communications at MSU, started Lansing's only news and public information radio program for the Black community, *Taking Care of Business*. Redd served as the producer-director on this program aired on MSU's WKAR-AM (870) until the fall of 1972. Airing Monday through Friday from 2:00 p.m. until 5:00 p.m., Redd's show was cosponsored by WKAR and the CUA. He brilliantly mixed Black history with varieties of Black music. A year later, supported by MSU students Jason Lovette and Thomas Hardy, he began hosting *Perspectives in Black* on channel 10 at 7:00 p.m. This program was unique in offering a crew of about a dozen students with hands-on experience in the television industry.

Project Grapevine's movers and shakers were not totally fulfilled with incorporating radio and television into their cause. In 1973, several contributors to the *Grapevine* including George White, Angela C. Martin, Heron, and Irene Davis contributed essays to the first-of-its kind Black History Week issue of *Counterpoint: A Monthly Supplement to the State News*. *Grapevine Journal*'s former staff decided to return to the publishing world. In early April 1974, Project Grapevine released "its first publication since the *Grapevine Journal*." Funded by the organization and produced in collaboration with local artists, *Obatala: New Arts Magazine* sought to introduce readers to the "full spectrum of the arts including fiction, poetry, essays on art, graphic art, artistic photography." During its formative stages, George White was excited about the short-lived magazine's potential. Featuring the work of local artists, he promised the publication would "mark the first time that Black college students edited an Arts magazine." In the fall of 1974, Project Grapevine published another magazine, *Good Times Magazine*. Managing editor Tom Whitfield claimed ten thousand copies would be distributed on campus each week. Organized as a six-page weekly focusing on MSU sports and local entertainment, with a TV guide, the magazine differed significantly from the *Grapevine Journal*. Its content and focus gives credence to the theory that the spirit of Black student activism was significantly changing forms by the mid-1970s. Though it was underneath the Project Grapevine umbrella, *Good Times Magazine* was registered as a student organization in October 1974 and had a short existence.[32]

The Project Grapevine team took pride in *Good Times Magazine* and appreciated what they considered to be the university's positive reaction. But deep down, James Ballard, George White, and others longed to have their award-winning, flagship newspaper back. By the spring of 1974, they had a reason to be optimistic. As a result of Project Grapevine's challenge to the student tax system supporting the *State News*, ASMSU proposed a constitutional amendment that was approved by students to create the Student Media Appropriations Board (SMAB). This group was charged with collecting a refundable tax from students that would be distributed to various on-campus publications. In approving the creation of this new board, MSU students, the vast majority of whom were White, collectively voted to tax themselves to support the *Grapevine Journal* and other publications. This reform was catapulted by consistent pressure from Black student-activists. Beginning in the early 1970s, Project Grapevine supporters sustained and publicized their argument that the university laid the grounds for a monopoly of the student press. A short time after Project Grapevine learned of their new funding source, which was enough to support the basic publication of the paper, in mid-February 1975 George White announced that the paper would resume in March as a monthly magazine with an innovative and refreshing layout.[33]

The reboot of the *Grapevine Journal* was released in early March 1975, followed by several other issues in April and May. The last known issue appeared in May 1975 (volume 5, number 3). In late May, weeks before his much anticipated graduation, White asked MSU trustee Warren Huff for some help. The funding from SMAB was crucial, helping resuscitate the paper. White indicated the funds were limited in scope. They could not be used to pay wages or salaries. White stressed to Huff that acquiring funding to compensate student workers was essential, especially since he and other key personnel, who had been making great sacrifices since the early 1970s, were moving on. Without further financial support, he concluded, "the *Journal* may not continue beyond June 1975." White's assessment was spot on. In late July 1975 after six years of struggle and stick-to-itiveness, James Ballard informed the president of ASMSU that "Project Grapevine plans to close on October 1, 1975." He expressed appreciation for ASMSU's support over the years in helping make his beloved organization "a lasting memory to many students at this university."[34] By the time Ballard decided to close Project Grapevine's doors, he and his dedicated coworkers had much of which to be proud. Like their predecessors in the BSA and other Black activist student groups of the late 1960s and early 1970s, they forced the university and student governance to rethink how they conducted business. Their measured agitation resulted in meaningful reform and the creation of more inclusive practices benefiting diverse groups of students. They created a Black student–run social movement serving countless people on and off MSU's campus. The legacy and impact of Project Grapevine/*Grapevine Journal* can be deciphered and conceptualized in various ways.

The *Journal* offered practical, down-to-earth opportunities for numerous African American students interested in journalism. Many of the paper's staff members were first- and second-year students, some of whom aspired to become professional news correspondents. Ballard and the editors recruited and welcomed those interested to join their cause and maintained high expectations for excellence. Ballard supported their professional development. In February 1972, he raised funds to send five of his staff members to the National Conference for Black Communications at Howard University in Washington, D.C. Ballard and his colleagues like George White and Heron often expressed their low tolerance for subpar performance. Like professors, they challenged their staff to improve their skills. Ballard didn't hesitate to fire those who failed to fulfill their responsibilities. He admonished the editorial staff when they produced issues he viewed as being second-rate. He believed they were "race representatives," that their work reflected Black intellect and an opportunity to dispel prevalent anti-Black stereotypes. In his mind, the stakes were high. He was particularly upset with the October 10, 1972, issue. "If we as a community intend to grow and prosper, then we must be totally aware and well versed about what is going on around us. The *Grapevine Journal*'s primary purpose is to achieve that end," he told the editorial staff, "SO DO NOT HAVE ANOTHER FUNKY ISSUE DONE! PLEASE!"[35] The high turnover rate of employees suggests that many students were able to test the journalistic waters. Many benefited from the experience.

By the mid-1970s, former *Grapevine Journal* staff members secured positions with the *Lansing State Journal*, the *New York Times*, the *Detroit Free Press*, and the *St. Petersburg Herald*, among other newspapers. *Journal* team members were not alone in benefiting from professional development opportunities. Project Grapevine sponsored special seminars, training sessions, workshops and programs that extended beyond their own ranks. In addition to the Urban (Summer) Journalism Workshop they conducted in 1973, they sponsored lunches that brought together students, faculty, administrators, and professionals to discuss the communications field and profession. Among the featured guests were President Wharton, *New York Times* photographer and Federal Communication Commission counsel Chester Higgins Jr., and executive editor of *Jet* magazine Robert E. Johnson, "a giant in the Black publishing industry." In advertising Johnson's late April visit, the *Grapevine Journal* staff declared, "Discover the inner-workings of Johnson Publications, the Black-owned industry." The aspiring student journalists learned a great deal from such luminaries.[36]

Project Grapevine sought to reward and financially help Black students on campus. During its existence, many Black students were employed by the organization. As revealed by correspondences in the *Grapevine Journal* Collection, some relied upon this income to get by, even at the rate of approximately one to two dollars per hour. In the 1973–1974 academic year, after the *Grapevine Journal* closed for the first time, Project Grapevine developed its Media Achievements Grant program. In order to qualify for this one-time grant of three hundred dollars, students had to be a junior or senior majoring in journalism, television, radio, advertising, or communications. Most importantly, viable candidates were required to demonstrate their "outstanding media work in the community" while maintaining "good grades." George White described the motivation behind the grant. "This is an organized attempt to stimulate young people both in high school and college to become actively involved in communications and we have set up this media grant as an incentive and reward." Many students applied for the grant. In the fall of 1974, a selection committee composed of MSU faculty members, Project Grapevine staff members, community leaders, and representatives from the local media selected three winners who were treated to an award dinner at the Kellogg Center.[37] They initially planned on only selecting one recipient, but the applications were so impressive they decided to support three outstanding student practitioners.

The *Grapevine Journal* had thousands of readers, especially from the fall of 1971 until the fall of 1973. Students from diverse backgrounds as well as African Americans in the Greater Lansing area and across the country subscribed to and read the paper. During its peak years, the *Journal* had a circulation of tens of thousands and was the most widely circulated Black student newspaper. Libraries and Black Studies programs throughout the nation requested copies of the paper. African Americans from various walks of life wrote the editor-in-chief requesting subscriptions.

In mid-October 1973, an inmate in the maximum security section in the Virginia State Penitentiary in Richmond, Virginia, asked Heron for a "gratis" subscription. "I am very much interested in Black current events and would very much like to be in receipt of a subscription to your publication, however though, because of my current political status here as well as my lack of financial resources, I am unable to afford a paying subscription." Bro. Larry X. Davis followed up, asking if Heron could send copies of the paper to his eighteen-year-old brother who was serving a life sentence in Fort Leavenworth, Kansas. "I'm sure that you realize how important all of this is to us," the eager reader concluded. "THANK YOU VERY MUCH!!!" Heron maintained communications with such incarcerated Black men. One inmate in the Michigan State Prison in Jackson asked for support and advice, and Heron offered it. "I will be sending more material shortly on the areas you suggested. Please reserve your right to make any suggestions you wish," the aspiring writer commented, "as I have very little knowledge of writing, and I will appreciate it very much whenever your advice is offered."[38] Heron's engagement with incarcerated Black bodies fell in line with the *Journal*'s commitment to report on the criminalization and incarceration of African Americans. The *Journal* carried stories on George Jackson, Angela Davis, and the Attica State Prison Uprising of 1971 and called upon Black students to be more sympathetic toward their imprisoned brothers and sisters. In the rebranded debut September 1971 issue, Omari M. Asifa beseeched Black students to contribute to Lansing's Black Political Prisoners Library Fund. "The Black student population of Michigan State University," he declared, "has an obligation to African people." In 1973 in an article "Women in Prison Work," staff writer Angela Martin publicized the efforts of two Black women MSU graduate students, "the first female counselors in an all-male penal institution in Michigan."[39]

In 1972, George White remarked, "minorities make up about 95 percent of the *Journal*'s staff." While the paper was written from a "Black perspective" and its main targeted audiences were African Americans and other "people of color," Whites also read the *Grapevine Journal*. As James Ballard told a reporter for the *Lansing State Journal* in January 1973, "Most of our readers are white, simply because there are more whites than blacks on campus. So, we're trying to bridge the communication gap there." A letter to the editors in the early 1970s reveals how some open-minded White students were impacted by the paper. "I just read your newspaper and it was excellently done. The articles were very informative and enlightening because they offered facts that otherwise would not be known," a freshman living in North Wonders Hall wrote. "My problem is this. I want very desperately to become active in some radical organization that is doing something. I would most like to work in connection with a black group. Only I am white so I can understandably see why I would not be wanted. But I would really appreciate it if you could possibly recommend some type of action that I could take or some groups I could become involved with. Thanks a lot and keep on writing a great paper."[40]

During its existence from September 1969 until October 1975, Project Grapevine defied the odds and accomplished much. A prideful George White remarked that their work was "the first time in history that a small group of Black students got together to build a Black press at a predominantly white university and have it gain success." While White's claim was not necessarily accurate, during the early 1970s the *Grapevine Journal* was the most widely circulated Black student newspaper in the nation. It had a board of directors, an explicit charter, and a detailed set of bylaws. It was the most durable activist and academic leaning registered Black student organization at MSU during the Black Campus Movement. During the late 1970s, editor Charlene G. Gray, and the more than one hundred Black students who contributed their one dollar refund from the *State News* to the cause, might have perceived the *People's Choice* magazine as a replacement for the *Grapevine Journal*, but it only lasted for several years.[41]

Project Grapevine and its various initiatives, especially the *Grapevine Journal*, provided crucial opportunities for Black students to develop their skills in the broad field of communications. The organization served as a movement center and training grounds, in James Ballard's words, "a starting place for people who want to get involved in communications skills." The student journalists learned from MSU professors and giants in the Black publishing industry like executive editor of *Jet* magazine Robert E. Johnson who conducted a workshop for the *Journal* staff on April 28, 1973. His visit was more interactive than award-winning senior editor of *Ebony* magazine Alex Poinsett's 1969 stopover during Black History Week. Though not a daily and published somewhat erratically between 1971 and 1973 and in 1975, the lively issues of the *Journal* were effective, functioning as an alternative publication to the *State News*. Off-campus editor Madelyn Bridget kept her assessment of the paper's role simple, observing, "for those who see Blacks in merely stereotyped roles of house cleaners and garbagemen, the *Grapevine Journal* acts as an eyeopener. Blacks and other minority peoples become real, with the same desires and hopes as whites. They also love and hate and have educational and professional aspirations." Campus editor Jacci Bates added, "the *Grapevine Journal* offers a positive means for expressing dissenting opinions."[42] Produced by full-time students who balanced their jobs as amateur journalists with their academic pursuits and personal lives, the *Journal* had its flaws, imperfections that its directors and editors acknowledged and strove to get rid of. It cannot be denied that it offered the MSU campus community and others outside of East Lansing with refreshing perspectives on an assortment of issues relevant to Black life on campus, in the United States, and throughout the sprawling African diaspora.

Project Grapevine/*Grapevine Journal* afforded a group of African American students a space to grow as thinkers, scholars, and planners as well as opportunities to shape the minds of their diverse readership. Black students who read the *Grapevine Journal* appreciated the opportunity to learn more about their community from a source they could trust, and according to a survey conducted by Project Grapevine, Black students "wanted the Journal to publish more often because they felt the paper was relevant to blacks."[43] The staff drafted hundreds of pages of proposals, strategic planning documents, correspondences, meeting minutes, interviews and notes, cover designs and advertisement layouts, and, of course, drafts of articles. They were inquisitive researchers and bona fide, albeit novice in many cases, investigative journalists. They kept up with current events, subscribed to numerous Black and minority newspapers, and reprinted articles from major media outlets. With their ears to the ground, they paid attention to their primary audience and clientele. They wanted their mission to be in alignment with the needs of the Black student community. Cognizant of their history-making efforts, they periodically chronicled their own inspiring past, situating this brief history within the context of the enduring Black Freedom Struggle. Working hard at honing their technical skills, they strove for continual improvement and endeavored to fend off their skeptics. Project Grapevine's leadership consistently sought to expand their activities. As early as the summer of 1972, they announced their plans to get involved in the television and radio industries, and several years later they did so. In line with MSU's values, they were committed to outreach and engagement at various levels, from mentoring high school students to sponsoring events for the broader public to advocating for and communicating with incarcerated African American men.

The Grapevine Project staff members were not as confrontational as the BSA or the Black Liberation Front, International. Using the pen as their sword and demanding a seat at the table with President Wharton, the Board of Trustees, and ASMSU, Project Grapevine's leaders clamored for equal treatment. They refused to be silent or to accept the status quo. They forced the university to change. In the spring of 1974, George White fittingly summarized the scope and impact of the *Grapevine Journal* and "its parent organization" Project Grapevine. He reflected:

> In our five years of struggle we have threatened court action, called meetings, written letters, written articles, pleaded on television, gone before the MSU Board of Trustees and in the fall of 1973 we turned to student government with the proposal on which the present Student Media Appropriations Board is based. We are proud that this body is now making the new level of student press freedom possible on the MSU campus. . . . We offer a product and a process with the training for minority journalists and communications specialists through practical experience. We introduced a new set of voices into the lopsided field of communications, thus we have given minority students a greater awareness with the *Grapevine Journal*. . . . We also have conducted special seminars and training sessions that reach beyond our workers. . . . Our product, the *Grapevine Journal*, is a needed communications vehicle for the minority student severed from his community and news of relevance to his life. The information is sorely needed too by the white student groping for an understanding of a society faced with the options of understanding its own pluralism or disintegrating.[44]

Chapter 33

Rise and Fall

I n 1969, ASMSU and the Honors College sponsored the Provost Lecture Series on the theme "The Black Experience in America" and invited playwright, poet, and activist LeRoi Jones to be the first speaker. "Nationalism describes us as a nation of people, a race of people, an aggregate of African peoples—despite sociologists' attempts to classify us as faceless Americans," Jones told the Black students in the MSU Auditorium on May 5. "We are searching for the physical, mental and spiritual space to become a self-determining people."[1] Jones's message resonated with Black student-activists. By the early 1970s, there were numerous Black organizations on MSU's campus. In the 1972 "Welcome Week" issue of the *State News*, Black students advertised a sampling of the organizations for "minority" students under the catchy caption, "Getting Down Is the Bomb! But It Won't Get You Over. GET INVOLVED with the minority organization of your choice!" "We have reached a point where we have many isolated political entities on campus but no unified political strategy," Black Students' Alliance (BSA) cofounder Richard W. Thomas told *Grapevine Journal* readers in 1971. "We perceive white power differently and organized around these perceptions instead of around the 'real power politics.' Therefore, we need to call a Black Summit Conference to discuss and co-ordinate our politics."[2]

During the 1970s, the creation of Black caucuses in many of the dormitories contributed to the proliferation of Black student organizations. Like the Black Liberation Front, International (BLFI) and the Black United Front, the Akers Black Caucus provided breakfast for underprivileged Black children in Lansing. Fee Hall's Black Student Association was considered among the most dynamic groups when it was directed by Art Webb. The United Blacks of Wilson was quite active. Members paid dues of between six and ten dollars annually and embraced the organization's overarching goals as spelled out in their constitution: "to promote black unity, to aid other blacks in resisting racism, oppression, and exploitation, to provide social activities for blacks residing in Wilson Hall, and to create the presence of black culture in Wilson." By November 1972, *Grapevine Journal* staff writer Angela Martin identified at least twenty-two "Black dorm organizations" speaking "to the needs of black students." They included the United Blacks of Wonders, Black Students of Case, McDonel African Caucus, the Bad Brothers of Bailey, the Black Organization of Holden Hall, the Holmes Black Action Committee, the Kamara of Campbell, the Black Brothers of Armstrong and Bryan, the Black People of Shaw, the Emmons Black Caucus, and the Black Students of Hubbard.[3]

Founded in the fall of 1969, the nearly forty Black Brothers of Shaw were quite active. Under the leadership of Irving Armstrong, among others, they promoted positive relationships between the BLFI and Black Greeks, organized cultural events and dances, travelled across the nation to hear Black leaders speak, responded to racial incidents in the dorms, participated in free breakfast for children programs in Lansing, created a library with hundreds of books, and launched a newsletter, *The Deal*, in January 1970. In 1974, Black students organized an umbrella organization, the Black Student Dorm Coalition. Black women also created their own organizations in the dormitories like the Sisters of Rather, the Black Sisters of Butterfield, Black Women in Yakeley Coalition, and the Black Sisters of Gilchrest. By the early 1970s, Black women benefitted from some staff members looking out for their interests. Toni Eubanks—who attended MSU as an undergraduate from 1965 until 1969, was very active in the Black student community, and worked with Professor Alex Cade's Upward Bound Program—was hired as a graduate assistant for minority students in the dean of students office in 1970. Her charge was to counsel and develop programs for Black women who largely outnumbered their male counterparts at the time. Of particular importance to Eubanks was instilling within young Black women a sense of pride, self-care, and self-affirming beauty.[4]

Cultural groups affirmed Black students as they coped with daily life in East Lansing. Founded in 1971, the Black Arts Company (BAC), the university's first Black theater company, provided a valuable space for Black students interested in the dramatic arts. Unlike the Performing Arts Company, the BAC was not supported by the university's Department of Theatre. Starting with forty committed members, they sponsored Black cultural festivals and put on dramatic and musical productions. In the spring 1972 term, they held a weeklong program with performances and lectures, "Dimensions in Black Theater." In early April 1972, Yolanda King visited campus with her mother Coretta Scott King for the third annual Dr. Martin Luther King Jr. Lecture on Social Change. Coretta had another connection with MSU. Her sister Edythe Scott Bagley worked in the Center for Urban Affairs. During her visit, Yolanda, who was considering MSU, talked to several Black theater majors and was impressed with the space the company provided for young Black actresses like herself.[5]

Established in the fall of 1971 by Amy Boyce, Mickey Assata, and Wanda Lindsey, the Black Orpheus Gospel Choir began with about seven members and had at least twenty-five members by 1974 when they practiced twice a week, including from 3:00 p.m. to 6:00 p.m. on Sundays, on the third floor of Case Hall. They first performed on campus in the Erickson Hall Kiva in April 1972 and performed at other colleges and universities in the state. Reflecting upon the significance of the group, one of its founders remarked, "for many black students up here Black Orpheus is the only contact they have with a religious atmosphere." Assistant director Hiawatha Lewis added that the choir "offers an outlet for people who like to sing and perpetuate the music of Black ancestors."[6] This gospel choir wasn't the first of its kind at MSU. Directed by Wyhomme J. Sellers, the MSU All-Student Ebonite Choir performed on campus at least one year prior to Black Orpheus. One of their first major performances was in early April 1970 at a commemorative program in honor of Martin Luther King Jr. featuring President Clifton R. Wharton Jr. and Benjamin Mays. At the same time, on April 4, led by Mike Hudson and other BLFI leaders, about two hundred Black students picketed three banks in East Lansing that didn't acknowledge the anniversary of Martin Luther King Jr.'s death by closing their doors for the day. Black Orpheus was also active in the Lansing community, performing at the fifty-second anniversary of the Trinity African Methodist Episcopal Church. Another Black arts group active during the 1972–1973 academic year was the Black Modern Dance Workshop.

During the Black Power era, many young African Americans across the nation embraced the philosophy of self-defense. Jim Kelly, the first major Black martial arts film star who won

Members of the Black Arts Company perform at the Black Arts Festival in the Arena Theatre of Fairchild Auditorium. Courtesy of Michigan State University Archives and Historical Collections.

karate titles in the early 1970s, opened a dojo in California, and costarred in Bruce Lee's *Enter the Dragon* (1973), inspired young Black men to take up martial arts. As historian Maryan Aziz argues, during the mid- and late 1960s, Black activists like Mfundishi Maasi, Balozi Zayd Muhammad, and members of the Black Panther Party advocated hand-to-hand combat, stressing the connections "between the mind and body."[7] A small group of African American students at MSU gravitated toward an Afrocentric form of martial arts. Led by brown belt and former president of the campus NAACP Maxie Gordon and Clifford Price, the largely Black Third World Karate Club was formed in October 1971 and provided students a space to meditate and learn martial arts. According to Gordon, the club was an alternative to the "too large and impersonal" MSU Karate Club, a space where "third world people" could "learn and work and enjoy themselves at the same time." In the fall of 1972, several former members of the club founded the Umoja-wa Karate Club. Gordon commented about the group's focus, "we're teaching people lethal skills along with the beauty and grace of these skills. Each individual person has to decide how much he's willing to invest."[8]

The Black Pathseekers, founded in the winter term of 1972, dispelled the myth that Black northerners didn't enjoy the outdoors. Under the leadership of Irving Armstrong, their purpose was to focus on a recreational programs that emphasized physical activities, especially outdoors. In the early 1970s, the Black Veterans Association was founded in order to serve the interests of Black student veterans. The group publicized they were open to all Black veterans in the area. Among their early initiatives was the sponsorship of forums on prison reform and expressions of racism in the antiwar movement. In May 1972, Black students created the Robert F. Williams Legal Defense Committee to raise funds to support Williams, the president of the NAACP in Monroe, North Carolina, who advocated armed self-defense. In 1961, he faced extradition to North Carolina where he faced trumped-up charges of kidnapping. Reflecting the sizeable number of Black Spartans from the Motor City, there was even a group called Black Students from Detroit whose purpose, under the leadership of Gerald Hayes, was to develop programs that would address issues faced by Blacks in Lansing and Detroit. Beginning in 1970, Earle Robinson began hosting of *Taking Care of Business* on WKAR-AM 870, a show featuring a wide-array of contemporary Black music mixed with discussions of issues facing Black life on campus. "The program content is designed and geared toward the black community," Robinson noted; "However, it helps everyone."[9]

There were more than a few academic-focused Black student organizations founded during the Black Campus Movement. Under the leadership of the Office of Black Affairs (OBA), in the late spring of 1973, three other Black student organizations—the Minority Pre-Law Association, the Black Pre-Medical Student Association, and the Concerned Students for Human Survival—came together. While the university established the Office of Minority Programs in 1973 to "insure non-discriminatory access" to MSU, increase "the number of minority personnel" and students, and support the retention of minority students, these Black organizations remained committed to practical, student-led self-help endeavors. "Minority students, particularly Blacks, at Michigan State University are in a precarious situation," the four organizations' leaders announced. "We have increasingly become the victims of: legal suppression, decreasing financial aid awards and institutional racism 'via' academic negligence on the part of this society to prepare minority people for higher education and professional careers." They continued, "As a result of the nature of these problems, certain minority organizations at Michigan State University have come together to initiate a 'multi-faceted' approach to deal with the said troubles." These four organizations created what they called a "1973-Summer-Fall-Winter-Spring Program Proposal."[10] In this lengthy proposal, each organization outlined what they had done to help Black students survive at MSU and contribute to the Black Freedom Struggle as well as their future plans to collectively help Black and minority students.

Founded in the spring of 1971, the Minority Pre-Law Association was "concerned with the necessity of politicizing minority students to the role of the minority lawyer." Following NAACP lawyer and Howard University dean and professor Charles Hamilton Houston's notion of "social engineering," they encouraged minority law students to use their training "as a vehicle to change the social condition of oppressed people." They maintained that Black lawyers had an obligation to their "minority clientele." They had ambitious goals for the 1973–1974 academic year. Recognizing the challenges faced by Black and minority students, they sought to have a "hired attorney" available to minority students and organizations and sought to better publicize bondsmen services for minority students facing legal challenges. They mapped out plans to sponsor LSAT classes and workshops, establish a "Legal Defense Fund" for minority students encountering legal mishaps and a "Legal Scholarship Program" for minority students planning to attend law school, and create a "Legal Newsletter" aimed at informing Black students about current legal events.[11]

Composed primarily of students from the College of Natural Science and Lyman Briggs College, the Black Pre-Medical Student Association (WAGANGA) met on a weekly basis, Saturdays at 3:00 p.m. in room 330 of the Student Services Building, and focused on professional development activities for African American students interested in the medical field. In their words, they attempted to "deal with real problems that black pre-medical students face" and to "protect and lead the students who are here now and the younger ones which are pre-destined to arrive." They were a precursor to the Black Student Nurses Association that by the mid-1970s under the leadership of junior nursing major Cassandra Edmonson challenged the marginalization and mistreatment of African Americans, primarily Black women, in the School of Nursing's curriculum and program. Critical of the lack of Black faculty and staff, they were particularly upset with a section in an introductory course called "The Black Patient" that promoted harmful stereotypes about Black men and women. Distrusting of the school's federally funded Minority Nursing Project established in 1972, Black women nursing students like Evelyn Shields, who filed an official complaint in January 1975 with the Office of Human Relations alleging she "experienced constant discrimination in classes," took their stories to the local media beginning in early February 1975. A group of Black women recounted being disparaged and abandoned, racially profiled, and disproportionately labeled "academically deficient" students. One Black woman in the school said, "It's the instructors who treat us like hell." Of her professors' disposition, another recounted to *Grapevine* staff writer Delilah Nichols, "Always the negative things, never the positive ones or things I might do well." Seeking to counter such alienation, among WAGANGA's most popular activities were trips to hospitals and tutorial programs. Under the leadership of one their early presidents and member of the *State News* Board of Directors, Roland Williams, they functioned as "an advising body for students in pre-med." One of their mantras was "Motivation harnessed into action." By 1973, they mentored local high school students. "We plan to increase interest and the number of Blacks who are entering the medical field," they underscored. WAGANGA also initiated a film and speaker series, programs to help raise health awareness in Black communities, a health "survival pamphlet" for Black people, and MCAT classes and workshops. During its existence, the organization provided Black students interested in the medical field with a sense of belonging, exemplified in their idea to make lab shirts with the club's emblem.[12]

Founded in the fall of 1972 under the leadership of William Sparks, the Concerned Students for Human Survival (SHS) was "concerned about black and other minority students' survival, both mentally and physically." While student teaching in the Detroit public school system, Sparks collaborated with a teacher at Campbell Community School to establish a "Health Week" program. On campus, SHS engaged in a range of other collaborative activities. They sponsored social activities such as a "Cultural Extravaganza" in mid-April 1973 that attracted nearly two thousand Black students and a performance from Dick Gregory in May. They joined forces with OBA, the Minority Pre-Law Association, the Black Student Aide Program, and Project Grapevine to help improve the social and cultural well-being of Black students. As foreshadowed by their early work in Detroit, their activism spread beyond East Lansing. In the spring of 1973, they worked with Black students at the University of Michigan to help "ex-addicts" and "welfare mothers."[13]

Though not part of the coalition that drafted the ambitious "1973-Summer-Fall-Winter-Spring Program Proposal," the Black Students of Engineering (BSE), also known as Minority Students of Engineering, was among the most active academic-centered Black student organizations. In 1969, when there were about forty-three Black and minority students majoring in engineering, the university's College of Engineering created the Engineering Equal Opportunity Program (EEOP), an effective initiative funded by Ford, Dow Chemical, IBM, Burlington, and Exxon. Graduate student Jack Pitts directed the program, and soon the number of Black and minority students in the college doubled. Working closely with the EEOP and concerned with promoting the academic survival and success of Black students majoring in engineering, BSE had about eighty members by 1972. Like the Black Pre-Medical Student Association, they

The Minority Students of Engineering, one of the only Black organizations to appear in the *Wolverine* yearbook during the early 1970s. Courtesy of Michigan State University Archives and Historical Collections.

developed a tutorial program and academic counseling initiatives and secured jobs for dozens of Black engineering majors in the Department of Engineering. One of their trademark programs was their annual Black seminar on engineering.[14]

During the Black Power era, Black fraternities also joined the fray. In mid-October 1969, under the presidency of Detroit junior Charles Dillard, MSU's Alpha Phi Alpha fraternity declared its withdrawal from the interfraternity council (IFC) and urged other Black Greek organizations to follow suit. "We were involved in a group that is dysfunctional to our interests and that includes fraternities in its membership whose policies and practices are overtly racist," Dillard blazoned; "our intention is to establish a Black Greek fraternity organization which will be relevant to our needs and to our role in the black community."[15] Dillard's sentiments and actions had concrete historical antecedents. Throughout the 1960s, discrimination in MSU's fraternity system was a hot topic of conversation. The routine excuse Whites in the IFC offered for the countless White fraternities was that Blacks had no desire to join them. This was in part true. The vast majority of Black students at MSU during the 1960s felt unwelcome and out of place in White fraternities, especially ones that had historically adhered to Whites-only policies.

The first issue of *Grapevine Journal* (June 3, 1971) included several articles on Black fraternities authored by Fred Lewis. "Black Greeks have come under fire from many Black organizations, nationally as well as locally, for not being relevant to the Black cause," Lewis asserted. "Many people have misconceptions as to what these fraternities are actually doing." In brief essays entitled "Black Greeks on Campus" and "Relevancy thru Brotherhood," Lewis challenged these "misconceptions." He detailed the activities of Omega Psi Phi (Sigma chapter), Kappa Alpha Psi (Delta Pi chapter), and Phi Beta Sigma (Delta Kappa chapter), highlighting their work with the local Black community, social functions, and collaborations with other political and cultural Black student organizations. By 1972, there were four Black fraternities and four sororities on campus. Their collective purpose as articulated in the "Welcome Week" edition of the 1972 *State News* was to provide "a complete mix of social, financial, and cultural activities designed to be relevant to the surrounding black community." By the mid-1970s, there was what Carl Taylor described as an escalation of community service programs initiated by Black fraternities and sororities in Lansing's Black community.[16] The MSU National Pan-Hellenic Council was established on May 11, 1977.

In 1972, racial tension on MSU's campus reached a fever-pitch. The number of reported confrontations between Black and White students in the residence halls was on the rise, and by late February, university officials believed the racial climate even had the potential to turn violent. The university was on high alert. What were the causes of this rise in Black student activism and ensuing Black/White polarization on campus? During the first five months of the year, there were a series of Black student protests that made Whites on campus feel very uncomfortable. Unfamiliar with the Black experience on campus, they could not understand what was going on.

On February 11, 1972, MSU professors and administrators Robert L. Green, Joseph McMillan, and Thomas Gunnings charged the Big Ten Conference with promoting segregationist practices adversely impacting the lives of Black athletes. They called for a host of changes, including the hiring of Black officials and one Black official at each Big Ten sanctioned contest at all levels for the remainder of the season no later than fall 1972. They wanted a public hearing at the next Big Ten Conference meeting where they and Black athletes could make more specific recommendations. As the spokesperson for the group, Green warned they would work with the NAACP and take the necessary steps to remedy the situation. Green, Gunnings, and McMillan garnered support from MSU trustees Blanche Martin, Patricia Carrigan, and Don Stevens, while a more understandably cautious President Wharton endorsed introducing this subject at the Big Ten Conference meeting in early March 1972.

Some Black athletes supported Green, McMillan, and Gunnings's arguments. "Their concerns highlight many of the problems faced by black athletes not only in the Big Ten but the nationwide athletic community," a group identified by the *State News* as "the black athletes of MSU" contended. "Ultimately a Big Ten Conference for all black athletes to be held at MSU might prove a viable means for determining more specific concerns and more specific ways to deal with the problems of black athletes." They discussed the high financial stakes of the game. "It will be the end to black athletes being used simply to fill the arenas or stadiums to bring money into this university. Black athletes are used for four years, then dumped to pasture, at age 21." During the remainder of the month, Black student-activists worked closely with Green, McMillan, and Gunnings, but also took matters into their own hands. On February 22, a group of MSU athletes calling themselves the Coalition of Black Athletes held a press conference at Jenison Fieldhouse. Positioned like Bill Russell, Muhammad Ali, Jim Brown, and Kareem Abdul Jabbar had been at the meeting of the Negro Industrial and Economic Union in Cleveland, Ohio, five years earlier, MSU athletes Billy Joe Dupree, Herb Washington, Allen Smith, and Nigel Goodison issued a list of seven demands to the university's Athletics Department.[17]

The demands read by Smith were (1) the hiring of a Black academic adviser in the athletics department, (2) financial aid to Black athletes after their eligibility expired, (3) the immediate creation of a grievance board comprised of Black athletes, coaches, and faculty, (4) the elimination of what Goodison called "slave contracts" for Black players, (5) a comprehensive year-round health plan for athletes, (6) the inclusion of at least two Black athletes on the search committee for the new athletic director, and (7) an increase in the number of Black officials at MSU sporting events, coaches, and trainers. Comparing his early 1970s descendants to his generation, Don E. Coleman noted, "Our scope was not that big. It was just for survival. The black athlete today is concerned about his fellow black citizen. He is much more aware of social issues. The black athlete today will not tolerate derogatory behavior." The members of the coalition, who expressed appreciation for the support they received from Green, Gunnings, and McMillan, were impatient and unwilling to be "pacified" with token gestures. In their statement, they insightfully held MSU accountable for its recent history of recruiting Black students. "Michigan State occupies the leadership position in terms of black enrollment in the Big Ten, and as such the central administration should pioneer the quest for desegregation in the athletic arena."[18] Perhaps having a flashback to late April 1968, university administrators were concerned. But, at this point, they didn't consider the situation a state of emergency. This would soon change.

Three years after members of the BSA stood up and raised their fists during the playing of the national anthem at the Michigan State–Ohio State basketball game like Tommie Smith and John Carlos at the 1968 Summer Olympics, on February 26, 1972, approximately one hundred Black MSU students calmly marched to the center of the court in Jenison Fieldhouse before MSU's basketball game against the Iowa Hawkeyes, delaying the start of the contest by nearly an hour. The protesters were members of the Black Coalition Council, an umbrella organization founded earlier in the term comprised of a wide array of Black student organizations: Black fraternities and sororities, the Coalition of Black Athletes, the Black Veterans Association, BLFI, Black dormitory caucuses, and other Black student activists. The spokesperson for the protest was well-known activist, Flint senior, U.S. Army veteran, and Honors College student Sam Riddle. He was a member of the BLFI, and though he had been active on campus before, including in antiwar demonstrations, this was one of his most radical activities on campus. Riddle, who "could hardly be heard over the boos, jeers, catcalls and threats from the predominantly white audience," read a prepared statement in which he defended two University of Minnesota basketball players suspended for fighting in the Minnesota–Ohio State game in January, called for better usage of funding for "minority programs" at MSU, an increase in the recruitment of "minority" students, and the reinstatement of an assistant professor of natural science, Eileen Van Tassell. He also explicitly backed the demands of the Coalition of Black Athletes and Green, Gunnings, and McMillan.[19]

President Wharton arrived on the scene after Riddle finished speaking. MSU vice-president Jack Breslin, who supposedly granted Riddle permission to read his statement, wasn't initially present at the game but made it to Jenison shortly after he was summoned. In interviews after the incident, Riddle remarked that the Black Coalition Council decided to protest because they were denied permission to do so at a January 29 contest against Indiana and that the council was exploring a larger collaboration with Black student-activists at other Big Ten institutions. He threatened that if the two Black players from Minnesota were not reinstated, the MSU–Michigan game would be interrupted by his foot soldiers and other Big Ten games would also be in jeopardy. His justification of the Black Coalition Council's actions was rooted in Black Power ideologies. "Our existence in America has been radical," Riddle proclaimed, "therefore we must employ what may seem as radical methodology to bring about a solution." In early March as the Coalition of Black Athletes worked with Jack Breslin toward a solution to their demands, Riddle asserted that the Black Coalition Council was considering shutting down the MSU–Michigan game and was going to reserve some seats together as an act of solidarity. Echoing the Black Panther Party, he also added some militant rhetoric. "If the MSU Police is not disarmed by April 1—that's April Fool's Day—we will arm ourselves." Riddle and his followers showed support to Green, Gunnings, and McMillan. In early March, the Board of Trustees, in a 5-3 vote, issued "censures" against the three, ruling that they did not and could not speak for or on behalf of the university. The concerns of one plainspoken social commentator in early March 1972 fell on deaf ears. "The Board of Trustees should rescind its censure of Green, McMillan and Gunnings. The point has been made that they do not speak for the total university on this issue. I don't think they ever purported to do so," continued this concerned critic; "the Board should, at the same time, highly commend these men for the work they have been doing on this campus in relation to the Black community and for equal opportunities." It would not be until five years later that the board revisited this decision and finally voted to rescind this decree that brought pressing issues of free speech to the forefront.[20] The university did, however, make some concessions. In early April 1972, Breslin and Allen Smith issued a joint statement indicating that the seven demands of the Coalition of Black Athletes from late February were being addressed, including having a Black athlete on the search committee for the new athletic director.

Shortly after the MSU–Iowa incident that he chastised, President Wharton warned that such actions in the name of freedom of speech would not be tolerated and those engaged in such activities "must be prepared to accept the consequences which the university will vigorously apply." In preparation for possible protest, the university moved the game to 2:00 p.m. Wharton's threats didn't prevent Black students from protesting at the MSU–Michigan game. At halftime, members of the Black Coalition Council unveiled two banners at the north end of Jenison Fieldhouse that read: "Big Ten: Open Up or We'll Shut It Down" and "MSU: Uncle Cliff's Cabin." The signs remained up for the remainder of the game.[21]

Several Black student-activists believed they were targeted as a result of their convictions. Riddle, whose antiestablishment ideas were featured in an article in the *Lansing State Journal* in late March 1972 titled "Sam Riddle Fights Society's Contradictions," had run-ins with the law. In early April 1972, he was arrested by the MSU police for allegedly assaulting an officer after he was pulled over for a minor traffic infraction. Riddle, who had been arrested before in East Lansing, charged the university police with profiling him. "In the three years I've been here at the University," he told the *State News* several days after his arrest, "I've been subjected to undue harassment from the police." In mid-April, Riddle filed a complaint with the MSU Office of Equal Opportunity Programs headed by Joseph McMillan, charging the university with supporting an "emerging policy of harassment of black students." The charges against Riddle were not new. Several years earlier, the BSA voiced concerns about how Black students were racially profiled and treated by police authorities on and off campus. Among other things, they called upon the university to have the on-campus police work closely with a faculty-student committee."[22] The director of MSU Public Safety vehemently denied Riddle had been systematically profiled. Riddle decided to defend himself (retaining the right to call upon counsel if needed) and had a very credible witness who suggested otherwise. Clifford Ashe, a former MSU police officer, testified that his former colleagues dealt with Riddle using "unnecessary precautions," that he was the subject of routine harassment. Ashe recalled the MSU police kept track of the cars Riddle drove, observing, "when Riddle was seen driving down the street, it was common practice to run a warrant check on him to see if he had any outstanding parking tickets or arrest warrants."[23]

Five years after student journalist Jeanne Saddler's militant message to incoming Black students in the 1970 "Welcome Week" edition of the *State News* titled "Blacks: Prepare for Revolution," another Black woman wordsmith, Cassandra Spratling, who would go on to have a long career as a feature writer for the *Detroit Free Press*, offered a noticeably different message to her brothers and sisters arriving in East Lansing in the 1975 "Welcome Week" edition of the *State News*. Spratling declared, "I tried to imagine how I would feel if I were a black student beginning college life now with everyone assuming that black students no longer care about anything outside of their own individual thing and amid reports that the so-called 'commitment' to black students is over." She then paid homage to her predecessors, "alliances of black students" in the 1960s who paved the way, reminding her soon-to-be classmates "it was all because of the demands of those students that over 2,000 black students are here today." She issued a different warning than Saddler, pointing to a "reversal in the trend to help black students" at MSU and nationally. Black students, she surmised, were losing ground as revealed in the decreasing financial aid opportunities for "minority students," the failure of MSU's affirmative action goals to be realized, the shutting down of the *Grapevine Journal*, and the inability of Black Greek organizations to hold their functions in the residence halls. Spratling ended her message by encouraging incoming Black students to become active. "Even though black students have made significant gains in the past we will have a way to go, and more importantly, we must see that the gains we made in the past are maintained and promises are kept," she concluded, "but needed even more now is a commitment on the part of each to get all we can out this university. . . . We owe much to the brothers and sisters of the '60s but even more importantly, we owe it to ourselves."[24]

Spratling's observations that by mid-1970s, Black student activism at MSU began to decline significantly are not surprising. This seems to have been the case at other colleges and universities throughout the nation, and as several historians have argued, the Black Power era began to decline by about 1975, symbolized by the death of Elijah Muhammad, the longtime leader of the Nation of Islam. Pessimism toward Black student activism at MSU began several years before Spratling's 1975 "Welcome Week" message to her classmates. Beginning in the early 1970s, Black students accused their peers of being apathetic and detached from the Black Freedom Struggle.

"The Black student population at M.S.U. is suffering from a paralytic state known as chronic inactivity," Omari M. Asifa blazoned in 1971. In this case, he chastised Black students for not supporting Black political prisoners or protesting the murder of George Jackson and the incarceration of "our brothers and sisters."[25] Similarly, in a "Point of View" column on the first page of the November 18, 1971, issue of the *Grapevine Journal*, the editorial staff accused Black MSU students of being self-centered, pessimistically surmising the Black Campus Movement had seen its last days. "Black Students in 1971 do not congregate or physically identify with any movement of political activism or show any progressive activity in trying to bring about a viable social lifestyle for all Black people in America."[26] In Project Grapevine activists' estimation, less than one hundred Black students were active in political struggles on campus, and the majority of the Black student population didn't fight for fair housing, turned their backs on grassroots Black arts or media movements, and underappreciated the Center for Urban Affairs. A year later, Denise A. Outram, a junior from New York City, penned a letter to the editors of the *Grapevine Journal*, "Black Apathy," in which she called upon her classmates to act. Upset with her peers' lack of concern about the publicized mistreatment of a Black parolee from Jackson State Prison, she questioned their commitment. "Too many of us are ready to shout 'right on' at the drop of a feather but how many of us are ready to shout even louder by backing our words with constructive and meaningful action?"[27]

In the fall of 1973, the editorial staff of the *Grapevine Journal* returned to its plea for increased Black student activism, offering a brief and critical synopsis of the Black Campus Movement at

MSU. "If the 1960s was the decade of Black activism, the 1970s may be considered the period of Black deactivism. If present trends continue, the 70s will be seen as a period when Blacks shifted from progression to regression," they continued; "the Black student activism has given way to the Black student apathist." From their vantage point, while the BLFI continued the Black student-activist tradition, the solution to reenergizing the movement at MSU was in the hands of Black organizations like the Black United Front, the OBA, Black "pre-professional organizations," and Black Greeks. Writing for the *State News* in 1974, student journalist and *Counterpart: A Bi-weekly Supplement to the State News* editor Jane Seaberry observed, "the black movement has not died, but seems to have faded away. Black History Week, Feb. 10–16, passed with hardly a ripple of activity." Not everyone was as pessimistic. "I think the average Black student is more politically aware now just in terms of having seen the limits of integration and that sort of thing," Sharon Peters opined in the fall of 1973. "I think there is more Black awareness and less Black unity. Even as there stopped being one Black leader, people were talking more in their little groups. There are groups popping up in dorms and liberation flags flying." Outspoken activist Jason Lovette was not as optimistic, but still believed Black students during the early 1970s were making progress. "I don't think the unity will decrease. But I don't think it will show itself, in a student movement," he continued; "the revolution is still coming about. But I don't think it's going to be the way we thought it would be."28

In 1977, there were more than thirty registered Black student organizations, but more than half of them were dormitory caucuses and social groups. During the late 1960s and early 1970s, Black History Week and Black History Month activities, especially those sponsored by the BSA, were widely publicized and popular. After about 1974, however, such commemorations tapered off. By 1978, events for Black History Month (still referred to as Black History Week in the *State News*) seem to have been film showings, soul dinners, roller and ice skating parties, gatherings, bowling, and performances from the Black Orpheus Gospel Choir. In explaining the decline in Black student activism during the 1970s, in 1977, Carl Taylor, director of minority student affairs and assistant to the vice-president of study affairs, observed, "It's not so much that the (black) movement has died, as the times have changed. Black students, as all students at this University, are concerned with what they are going to do when they get out of here." A year later, Taylor was more critical in his assessment when interviewed by *State News* staff writer Reginald Thomas who believed Black activism "has all come and gone." Taylor accurately identified the period from 1969 until 1972 as representing the peak of "black awareness" and suggested the OBA had been on the decline since 1974. "We can't seem to hit a median. Maybe we went to the extreme in '68–'69. And now in the late 1970s we have been to apathetic," Taylor put forward. "We've got to question people on campus because we are the leaders of tomorrow. We have progressed and regressed at the same time."29

Chapter 34

Black and Green and White

A report accusing Michigan State University of racial discrimination in some hiring practices is on file with the Office for Civil Rights Department of Health, Education and Welfare," the nonprofit cooperative Associated Press divulged in mid-March 1968. The twenty-page report included "recommendations for correcting the situation," encouraging the university to create an office of equal opportunity and "seek Negro faculty members from Negro colleges."[1] At the time, there were purportedly between eight and twelve Black faculty at MSU. In July, one university administrator offered an all-too-familiar explanation, remarking: "One of the greatest problems in attracting Negro professors is that there are not enough of them."[2] Despite the *State News* editors' claim that there were twenty Black faculty in early 1969, during the 1968–1969 academic year, the scarcity of Black faculty at MSU persisted.[3] During Black History Week in 1969, associate professor Robert L. Green warned Black students not to be fooled by the presence of a few token Black professors on campus. In June 1969, the newly established MSU Equal Opportunity Programs and the Center for Urban Affairs released a report on the employment of racial minorities at MSU, concluding that the university was seriously deficient in this area. After several months of formulating plans for affirmative action and equal opportunity programming, the university filed its first official affirmative action plan with the Chicago Regional Office of the U.S. Department of Health, Education and Welfare in September 1970. A primary purpose of this plan was to increase the employment opportunities for women and racial minorities.

For the first time in its history, the university thus began deliberately documenting the number of tenure-system faculty by race and ethnicity, using the broad and somewhat imprecise designations "Black," "Oriental," "American Indian," "Spanish Surnamed," and "Caucasian & Other." As was the case at other large universities, the data lacked comprehensiveness, largely because it was "supplied by administrative units on visual survey." According to the university's affirmative action reporting, in 1970, approximately 95.5 percent of the tenure-system faculty were "Caucasian & Other" and there were ninety-six "minority" tenure-system faculty (which included "foreign nationals"), at least 30 percent of whom were probably "Black." Of the university's 8,431 "total employees" (4,732 men, 3,699 women), 632 (235 men, 397 women) were identified as "Black."[4]

Six years prior, in early June 1964, several days after the East Lansing City Council voted 3-2 against a proposed open occupancy ordinance, President John A. Hannah casually and misleadingly insinuated the university had recently recruited a sizeable number of Black faculty members. He remarked to a *Lansing State Journal* staff writer, "I feel it's important that East Lansing take whatever action necessary to make it possible for faculty and employes [*sic*] of the university to buy or rent the kind of property they want." He continued, "*There are many Negro members on the faculty now* and there will continue to be other minority group members here."[5]

This wasn't the first time that Hannah gave the impression that Michigan State boasted an admirable record of recruiting Black faculty. In late August 1962, former MSU professor, author, and heretical columnist Russell Kirk publicly attacked Hannah's leadership in an op-ed in the conservative *National Review* magazine. The editor of the University of Michigan's *The Daily* decided to reprint it because of their supposed "great interest in MSU." He asked Hannah to offer his reactions in about 750 words. Hannah was promised his piece would be featured in U of M's newspaper at the end of September along with Kirk's article. Hannah agreed to this peculiar request, and the *State News* also reprinted *The Daily* editor's letter, Kirk's article, and Hannah's counterarguments.[6]

Kirk's characterization of MSU and Hannah was harsh, demanding a reaction. He nicknamed MSU an "empire-building," "waist-high university" and insulted its longest-serving president, calling him an "energumen." He scoffed at Hannah's leadership of the U.S. Civil Rights Commission and "desire to be known as a champion of the rights of colored people." Maintaining that MSU had only one Black faculty member, David W. D. Dickson, Kirk queried, "Why has President Hannah never appointed another scholar of color? Does he want only a prize exhibit?"[7] Five years earlier, a broadside of this nature would not have bothered Hannah as much. In 1957, he purportedly "refused to submit to demands" to "hire a specific quota" of Black faculty "just for the sake of employing members of the race." His explanation to the *New York Times* was wishy-washy and neutral enough to fend off potential detractors from various political schools of thought, especially African American integrationists. "It is not the policy of the university to examine the color of a man's skin for the purpose of either qualifying or disqualifying him for employment," declared Hannah.[8]

In the fall of 1962, the chair of the U.S. Civil Rights Commission sang a different tune. Understandably ruffled by Kirk's flippant personal attack and egged on by his antagonists in Ann Arbor, Hannah pointed out the errors of his foe's claims. (One also wonders how Hannah felt about Kirk's visit to campus in May 1963 sponsored by the Campus Conservative Club.) The prideful eleventh Michigan State president retorted, "the truth is that M.S.U. has *several* Negro faculty members, and I suspect as many or more non-white faculty members as other comparable universities." In attempting to rationalize the small number of Black faculty at MSU, Hannah postulated that young African Americans' overall lack of educational opportunities "discouraged" them from pursuing degrees "that would fit them to compete for academic appointments." He surmised, "the result is that even at a university as dedicated to fair treatment as M.S.U. is, there are too few Negro faculty members" to choose from.[9] Hannah's perfunctory and defensive response to Kirk was nebulous. While Kirk's assertion that MSU had "just one" Black faculty member in 1962 was factually incorrect, Hannah's decision to use the imprecise descriptor *several* in characterizing the number of Black faculty was deliberate and intentionally vague. He was also being truthful. In late September 1962, there were indeed *more than two but not many* African American faculty members employed by MSU. But Hannah missed an ideal opportunity to celebrate Black scholarly excellence. He didn't mention by name MSU's several very accomplished Black faculty members. This lack of acknowledgement was particularly curious because Kirk singled-out and praised the university's first Black tenure-system professor, noting "everyone agrees that he is very good indeed."

Two years later, Hannah's declaration in the June 3, 1964, issue of the *Lansing State Journal* that there were "many" Black faculty members at MSU was a gross exaggeration. At the time, all of the predominantly White institutions (PWIs) across the nation combined didn't even employ a large number of African American faculty. According to a *New York Times* study, in 1963 eleven of the seventeen "major universities" surveyed had at least one African American professor. Supposedly leading the way in the Big Ten was Indiana University with four Black assistant professors and the University of Iowa, whose officials claimed to have twenty-three Black "academic staff members of all ranks, including technicians." In 1964, when the University of Texas hired its first Black faculty member (twenty-eight-year-old engineer Ervin Sewell Perry), six African Americans were appointed to the faculty at the University of Illinois at Urbana, allegedly bringing the total number of Black faculty "on the assistant and associate level to some 20 persons, in addition to the two full professors in the medical and dental colleges."[10]

Among the major colleges and universities in the state of Michigan, Wayne State University decidedly led the way. By the mid-1940s, Wayne University, as it was called from 1934 until 1956, had several African Americans on its staff, including bacteriologist Charles Wesley Buggs (PhD, University of Minnesota, 1934). In 1943, Buggs, a specialist in the treatment of wound infections and burns, became the first African American to hold a full-time faculty position at Wayne and in the entire state of Michigan.[11] In April 1961, this major research institution in

Detroit employed at least nine Black scholars leading one writer for the *Michigan Chronicle* to forecast a brighter future. "Times have really changed, we're happy to report. Negro educators are sprinkled throughout Michigan's major colleges. And in the next 25 years, it can reasonably be predicted that it will be a rarity to find a college in the state without at least two or three Negro professors on its staff."[12]

Hannah had his own predictions in 1964. His confident assertion that other minority scholars would soon be joining MSU's faculty played out during the final and contentious years of his long presidency and during the 1970s when MSU developed and executed its intentional affirmative action initiatives under President Clifton R. Wharton Jr. In 1973, the seventeen colleges in the university were required to establish informed and aspirational three-year goals for hiring women and minority tenure-system faculty. Hannah's 1964 pitch about a recognizable presence of Black faculty in East Lansing would have been more convincing in the spring or summer of 1969 after the Board of Trustees, in a 6-0 vote, appropriated up to $1.5 million to the Center for Urban Affairs to help recruit Black faculty members, during the transformative Wharton years (1970–1978), or during the early years of President M. Cecil Mackey's tenure when in 1980 MSU employed sixty-one Black tenure-system faculty (forty-seven men and fourteen women) and twenty-two Black fixed-term faculty (nine men and thirteen women). Beginning early during Wharton's historic presidency, the number of Black faculty and administrators at MSU grew conspicuously. In the 1968–1969 academic year, there were possibly as few as nine Black tenure-system faculty and four administrators.[13] In January 1971 and November 1972, there were forty-four tenure-system Black faculty (thirty-eight men and six women), and in April 1973 there were fifty (forty-three men and seven women). Significant change had indeed taken place within a relatively brief period of time. The number of Black faculty increased dramatically between the early 1960s and the early 1970s.[14]

In late September 1962, when Hannah clapped back at the disgruntled and mean-spirited Kirk's public roasting in the *National Review*, MSU had five African American tenure-system professors. Four were on campus: associate professor of English David W. D. Dickson, who was hired in 1948 as an instructor and promoted with tenure a decade later; assistant professor of speech William Harrison Pipes who arrived at MSU in 1957; Alfred L. Edwards who was hired as an assistant professor of economics in 1958; and Clifford J. Pollard who had just been hired, effective September 1, 1962, as an assistant professor of botany and plant pathology.

On the eve of Kirk's editorial, MSU lost one of the most promising and talented Black faculty members in the university's history. Andrew F. Brimmer, "the Jackie Robinson of economics," joined the Department of Economics a year after Pipes's appointment but left in August 1961 for a position at the prestigious University of Pennsylvania's Wharton School of Business. Born in Louisiana in 1926 to a family who survived by sharecropping, Brimmer earned a PhD in economics from Harvard in 1957. Before arriving in East Lansing, he gained valuable, hands-on experience working for the Federal Reserve Bank of New York. During his brief pitstop at MSU, he and his wife Doris, despite all the difficulties, rented a home from a liberal White attorney in East Lansing at 1403 Beech Street. Doris was a leader in Lansing's League of Women Voters, and Andrew was active as a prolific scholar, public intellectual, and activist. He served on the Lansing Civil Liberties Union and, as a member of the board of the Lansing Branch of the NAACP, advocated for African Americans' civil rights. He produced one book while at MSU, *Life Insurance Companies in the Capital Market.* Adopting a proto–Black Studies perspective, he meticulously researched the causes and impact of segregated housing in Lansing, concluding that African Americans were relegated to residing in west Lansing because of financial institutions' and real estate agents' racist practices. Brimmer participated in several major on-campus conferences, including a symposium on housing and civil rights in late November 1959 and the third annual conference on labor relations in 1960. While at MSU, he was often interviewed by the local press and widely respected as a "monetary expert." In 1963, President John F. Kennedy appointed the thirty-seven-year-old star economist deputy assistant secretary of commerce for economic policy and soon thereafter assistant secretary of economic affairs, the first African American to hold these posts. In 1966, President Lyndon B. Johnson named Brimmer to the Board of Governors for the Federal Reserve Bank, the "principal shaper of the nation's monetary policy." Eight years later, he resigned and opened up his own economic forecasting firm. Brimmer returned to speak at MSU in 1974 and 1989.[15]

Brimmer was only one of the exceptional African American economists and Black firsts hired by Michigan State in the late 1950s. In 1957, a year before he earned a PhD from the University of Iowa while he was teaching at Southern University in Baton Rouge, Alfred L. Edwards (1920–2007) joined the university as an instructor of economics. The *Michigan Chronicle* was elated, declaring "Negro Added to Economics Staff at MSU." A year later, the Key West, Florida, native was promoted to the rank of assistant professor. A member of the American Economics Association, the Southern Economics Association, and the National Tax Association, Edwards was a prolific scholar and hit the road running in East Lansing. In the late 1950s and early 1960s, he reviewed books in journals such as the *Journal of Negro Education* and *American Economy* and published a major article on an alternative approach to compensatory property taxation in the *National Tax Journal* and another article in *Land Economics* on land reform in Iraq. His expertise was acknowledged in Michigan. In the fall of 1959, the *Lansing State Journal* covered his important research on Michigan's economic state and potential future that highlighted "the rate at which its citizens are taxed by the state and communities." Edwards actively participated in functions within Lansing's Black community. In the spring of 1960, he delivered the keynote address at the annual Men's Day Rally at the George R. Collins Memorial African Methodist Episcopal Church and participated in a voter registration clinic sponsored by the Lansing chapter of the NAACP at the Lincoln Community Center. In the fall of 1960, Edwards was appointed to Michigan State's "nine-man team" for the recently created university in Nigeria. In 1963, while residing at 820 Knoll Road in East Lansing, Edwards received a Ford Foundation fellowship in business administration and economics for his research on public finance and economic development in Nigeria.[16]

On November 5, 1963, newspapers across the nation announced that Edwards became the first African American to be appointed to the position of deputy assistant secretary of agriculture. African American newspapers were especially delighted with the forty-three-year-old's history-making. The *Afro-American* shared with its readers a brief biography of Edwards, stressing that seven major agencies reported directly to him. Early on in his new position, Edwards advocated for oppressed African Americans. In December 1963, he lamented that 84 percent of Black farmers were "boxed in" and "locked in" the "hard core of the pockets of poverty," making up "the largest number of deprived of any group in the Nation." He added, "We are concerned because these farmers are truly the most distressed economic groups in America."[17] Though not on campus beginning in 1963, Edwards held onto his position at Michigan State until he officially resigned on August 31, 1966. He remained deputy assistant secretary of agriculture until 1973, earning the Distinguished Service Award from the Department of Agriculture in 1969. In 1974, he became a faculty member in the Ross School of Business at the University of Michigan where he remained until he retired. Longtime faculty advisor of the Black Business Students Association, he was known for his mentoring of traditionally underrepresented students. He was well respected in his field, serving as president of the National Economic Association in 1976. Beginning in 1981, he served on the Western Michigan University Board of Trustees for sixteen years. His obituary captured the essence of his character. "He had many wonderful qualities; intellect, humor, strong moral values based on his Christian faith. He believed in education, independence, fairness and a belief that successful people used their influence, wealth or knowledge to help others. He was a truly wonderful father in so many ways."[18]

A year before Brimmer left MSU and while Edwards was settling into his new position, in the fall of 1960 Hannah recruited George M. Johnson, appointing him professor in the College of Education. Johnson's appointment was strikingly different from his four Black colleagues' positions. Though technically considered faculty, Johnson's primary responsibility was serving as acting principal of the University of Nigeria.[19] That MSU appointed him at the rank of full professor speaks to his exemplary qualifications and national reputation. In 1938, Johnson earned a doctorate in law degree from the University of California, Berkeley, and during World War II he served as the acting general council for President Franklin D. Roosevelt's Fair Employment Practices Committee. From 1946 until 1958, he served as dean of Howard University's Law School, founded the *Howard Law Review Journal*, and worked closely with NAACP lawyer Charles Hamilton Houston, "the Man Who Killed Jim Crow," on several monumental civil rights briefs that laid the foundations for *Brown v. Board of Education* (1954). A key member of the U.S. Civil Rights Commission, Johnson worked closely with Hannah, knew him well, and won his favor.

In 1963, two African American men who earned their doctorates from MSU were hired as full-time faculty members. Shortly after earning his PhD in psychology from MSU, about eighteen weeks after Kirk's attack on Hannah, in January 1963, scholar-activist Green became the sixth African American tenure-system faculty member hired by MSU and one of the handful of African American scholars in his field working at a PWI. He began his long and eventful career in East Lansing as an assistant professor in the College of Education. Effective September 1, 1963, Alex J. Cade (PhD, psychology, MSU, 1963) was hired as an assistant professor of social science. In 1966, he began directing MSU's Upward Bound Program. In the summer of 1963, the MSU Board of Trustees also approved the appointments of accomplished sculptor Robert L. Weil and doctoral candidate in zoology Charles S. Scarborough as instructors on a ten-month basis. In the same month, David W. D. Dickson accepted the position of chair of the Department of Language and Literature at Northern Michigan University, becoming that university's first Black faculty member. Though Dickson was well known and respected at MSU and in the East Lansing community, and the university had in previous years lost its fair share of productive scholars and excellent teachers to its competitors, including Andrew F. Brimmer in 1961, the university didn't go to great lengths to retain the trailblazing English professor. After fifteen years of service at MSU, forty-four-year-old Dickson could not turn down this golden opportunity unavailable to him in East Lansing.

In 1964 when Hannah remarked that any faculty member, including Black scholars, should be able to secure housing in East Lansing and put forward his bold proclamation about the so-called diversity of his faculty, there were only three familiar Black tenure-system faculty members and two full-time instructors "on the banks of the Red Cedar." Pipes, Pollard, Green, Weil, and Scarborough assumed the burden of representing Black intellectuals and scholars on campus. They represented less than 0.2 percent of the MSU faculty population when approximately 9 percent of Michigan's residents were African American. The MSU Black faculty population reached 3 percent two decades later. Perhaps in 1964, the ambitious Hannah was optimistic because of hires and plans in the making. In the fall of 1965, the number of tenure-system Black faculty members doubled with the hiring of assistant professor of psychology Dozier W. Thornton and Theodore R. Chavis, assistant professor of social work.[20] Historian and former Danforth and Woodrow Wilson fellow DeWitt S. Dykes Jr. was also hired as an instructor of American Thought and Language. In 1967, mathematician Irvin E. Vance was hired and Leslie B. Rout Jr. joined the Department of History. In mid-December 1967, MSU recruited Lloyd Cofer—formerly principal of Mackenzie High School in Detroit and chairman of the Board of Trustees at Central Michigan University—as professor of education and the director of the Detroit Project, the university's first major Black student recruitment program.[21]

In response to Black student-athletes' demands following the assassination of Martin Luther King Jr., in mid-April 1968, the MSU Board of Trustees approved the hiring of former MSU football All-American Don E. Coleman, one of two MSU gridders at the time whose jersey had been retired, as "assistant professor and assistant football coach, intercollegiate athletics." Coleman was initially reluctant to accept the position, letting it be known that the offer from athletic director Biggie Munn was "less than I (Coleman) make right now." At the time, Coleman, who earned a master's degree from MSU in health and physical education in 1954, had established a teaching career in his hometown of Flint, Michigan. He was well known at his alma mater Flint Central High School and was a respected community activist. Nine months later, Coleman voluntarily vacated his coaching position. "Frankly, I found that football coaching was not for me," Coleman explained. "During the years that I had been out of football the game had changed so drastically that I felt lost." The man who, in Duffy Daugherty's estimation, "revolutionized football," particularly the offensive tackle position, had been away from football culture for a long time. Coleman's career on the gridiron essentially ended in the early 1950s when he served in the U.S. Army for two years. The MSU football legend then became an assistant director of student affairs in the office of the dean of students with a dual appointment in the Center for Urban Affairs and the College of Osteopathic Medicine as director of the Minority Comprehensive Support Program. While working on his doctorate, Coleman oversaw the Black Student Aide Program launched in the fall of 1969. In 1970, he was appointed to the position of director of minority students.

All-American Don Coleman (#78) during his playing days. Also in the photo, Willie Thrower (#27), Arthur Ingram (#16), and Leroy Bolden (#39). Courtesy of Michigan State University Archives and Historical Collections.

Coleman wasn't the only ex-Spartan gridder to return to his alma mater. Beginning in 1968 during several of his off-seasons while playing with the Minnesota Vikings, Gene Washington worked as an assistant placement counselor at MSU.[22]

In the spring of 1950, an optimistic sportswriter for the *Detroit Tribune* called upon President Hannah and athletic director Ralph Young to hire Detroit high school hoops coach and legend Will Robinson as the next head basketball coach. Two decades later, the first Black head coach was hired at Michigan State. Effective July 1970, the MSU Board of Trustees also approved the hiring of another former MSU star Black student-athlete. Jamaican-born former All-American soccer player Payton Fuller succeeded founding and legendary head soccer coach Gene Kenney, becoming the first Black head coach of a Big Ten sports program. Neither the *State News* nor the *Lansing State Journal* pointed out the historic nature of Fuller's accomplishment. Fuller, who was working on his PhD in mechanical engineering at the time, coached for three seasons before he was unceremoniously and disrespectfully relieved of his duties. Fuller refused to accept his firing without a fight. Backed by Joseph McMillan, former elementary school teacher and assistant vice-president of MSU's human relations, in October 1974, he boldly charged the university with discrimination. "I didn't like the way I was treated in four years of coaching, I didn't like the way I was fired and I think that it was all a matter of racism," Fuller expressed to the MSU Human Relations Board; "it is the principle I am contesting. I was fired because I am black and was coaching a mostly white team." Athletic director Burt Smith, who fired Fuller without directly notifying him, "vehemently" rejected the charge of racism, and Fuller's complaint seems to have fallen upon deaf ears.[23]

With the Board of Trustees' approval, in May 1968, Hannah appointed George M. Johnson "to head an Equal Opportunity program," a position McMillan assumed a year later. Hannah also named Johnson assistant to the president, making the experienced sixty-seven-year-old civil rights lawyer the first African American to serve in this capacity at MSU. Johnson's specific charge was to chair a "special MSU committee on Civil Rights," also known as the Committee of Sixteen. "'We need a black man heading this up," Hannah said of Johnson, a long-time friend. "It's the most effective way to show we really mean what we say." After accepting his new appointment, Johnson was quite frank about the MSU landscape: "It is simply impossible for a white person to imagine what it is like to be a Negro in the year of our Lord, 1968. There are inconsistencies, incongruities. Not a day passes, but one is reminded of being an American Negro. It's more baffling to the young Negro. One of our hopes is to appreciate how they think and close the generation gap."[24] In July 1968, Hannah recommended the appointment of Benjamin E. Mays, longtime president of Morehouse College, as a part-time visiting professor and adviser to the President for the 1968–1969 academic year. Per the agreement, Mays was expected to be on campus for about fifty days throughout the academic year and was supposed to be available to Hannah for consultation.

On September 20, 1968, in response to recent Black student unrest and at Hannah's urging, the MSU Board of Trustees approved the appointment of Robert B. Lee as assistant provost, full professor, and director of Equal Opportunity Programs and the Center for Urban Affairs effective immediately. Hannah worked his magic to recruit Lee, for a salary of $31,000 per year, from his position as director of the Office of Planning and Systems Analysis in the U.S. Post Office Department in Washington, D.C. With the hope of reaching a consensus with the Black Students' Alliance (BSA), Lee arrived on campus in November 1968 and began holding a series of weekly "brainstorming" and listening sessions with Black students to help inform his "five year plan." Lee didn't remain in East Lansing long enough to execute this plan. In late March 1969, rumors circulated about his departure to become assistant postmaster general in Richard M. Nixon's administration. By mid-April, the scuttlebutt was confirmed. In explaining his decision to leave MSU, Lee was candid about his frustration with decision-making processes in higher education. He disliked the slowness of the faculty governance process that, in his estimation, lead to delayed decision making. Lee officially resigned on May 15, 1969, a month and a half after Hannah left East Lansing for a position in the U.S. Agency for International Development.

"Michigan State University's governing board fits the national pattern racially (predominantly white)," announced the *Lansing State Journal* in early February 1969. History had been made in East Lansing. "One of the newest members represents a variance in several respects—Dr. Blanche Martin is a 32-year-old Negro dentist and Democrat." Though he wasn't hired as a faculty member, in November 1968 when he was elected the first African American to the MSU Board of Trustees, Blanche Martin taught classes at the University of Detroit School of Dentistry while operating his own dental office in East Lansing, the city's first known Black-owned business. With a doctor of dental surgery, the youngest member of the board was a scholar-practitioner and held the highest academic degree of any board member. A former MSU football star who earned All-American and Big Ten academic honors in the late 1950s and briefly played in the NFL, this River Rouge, Michigan, native arguably held the most visible public position for an African American in the university prior to Wharton's presidency. In the 1968 election, Ingham County and East Lansing voters backed Republican candidates. Statewide Martin (Democrat) received 1,330,635 votes, the most of any candidate. He accomplished this without downplaying his support of the Black Campus Movement. An active member of the NAACP, while running for office, Martin sympathized with the struggles of Black students and "said he was willing to participate in the recruitment of black students if asked as a board member." In 1968, he critiqued the Equal Opportunity Program Johnson led, declaring it be called a "more opportunity" program. Reflecting upon his days as a student-athlete, he maintained that the university's star Black athletes "are often given courses they can be sure to pass and are not given credit for having any brains." Closing ranks with faculty members Green and Irvin Vance, and BSA representatives Sam Riddle and Jason P. Lovette, in mid-April 1969, Martin proposed the action to appropriate $1.5 million to support the university's Center for Urban Affairs and the recruitment of Black students and faculty. Later in the month, he supported Black students' controversial occupation of the Wilson Hall cafeteria.[25]

Blanche Martin, MSU's first Black
Board of Trustees member. Courtesy of
Michigan State University Archives and
Historical Collections.

Forty years after Martin was elected, in 2008, longtime educator, executive vice-president of the American Federation of School Administrators, and MSU alumna Diann Woodard, '73, became the first African American woman elected to the MSU Board of Trustees. The first Black woman to seek a seat on the board was Nancy Waters who began her campaign in the spring of 1972. She wasn't nominated at the Democratic state convention in late August. Her stance toward race might have won over many African Americans in the state but didn't endear her with White voters. "My main concern is that there seems to be a void on the board as it relates to blacks," she told a *State News* reporter in April 1972. Thirty-year-old Waters respected her elder trustee Blanche Martin but believed his full-time dental practice "prevented him from giving necessary attention to black student concerns."[26]

Black women scholars joined the ranks of MSU employees much earlier than Diann Woodard broke the glass ceiling. Overcoming racism and sexism, Black women faculty members faced a more complicated set of obstacles than their male counterparts. Twenty-one years after David W. D. Dickson was hired, during the late 1960s and early 1970s, the first group of Black women joined

MSU as tenure-system faculty members. MSU was not a Big Ten groundbreaker in this regard. In 1960, the Ohio State University hired its first Black woman faculty member, Alvia Bozeman. Nearly a decade later, sociologist and Africanist Ruth Simms Hamilton (PhD, Northwestern University, 1966), who began her career at MSU as an assistant instructor in 1968, was promoted to an assistant professor with a joint appointment in MSU's Department of Sociology and the African Studies Center. Four years after the University of Mississippi's Medical School in Jackson reluctantly hired Marion Myles as assistant professor of pharmacology, in August 1969 Georgia A. Johnson (MD, University of Michigan, 1955) joined Hamilton in East Lansing, becoming the first Black woman physician on the faculty of Michigan State University's medical college. In July 1970, MSU then hired educational psychologist L. Eudora Pettigrew, the first Black woman appointed at the rank of associate professor at MSU, in the Center for Urban Affairs and the College of Education. A year later, Governor William Milliken appointed her to the Michigan Women's Commission. In the summer of 1971, the MSU Board of Trustees approved the hiring of the fourth Black woman tenure-system faculty member, Gloria Stephens Smith, assistant professor, Counseling Center and Special Programs, Provost's Office, and developmental psychologist Patricia Barnes-McConnell as an instructor in the Center for Urban Affairs.

In the fall of 1969, when African Americans made up less than 1 percent of all students enrolled in doctoral programs nationwide, there were enough African Americans teaching courses on campus to create the first organization for Black faculty, the Black Faculty Committee, also referred to as the Black Faculty Caucus and Black Faculty and Staff. This group began mobilizing following the assassination of Martin Luther King Jr. By the early 1970s, they rebranded themselves the Black Faculty and Administrators Association and during the decade urged the university's leadership to hire more minority and Black faculty. In 1976, they publicly pressured President Wharton and the Board of Trustees to aggressively hire more faculty: "Blacks who comprise 12–15% of the national population should have 12–15% of the faculty positions at MSU. . . . Today, MSU is retrogressing—going back on a commitment made during the Civil Rights Movement. We are witnessing one of the most acute retrenchment programs in the history of MSU." Years earlier in May 1969, several months after alleged "cases of racial discrimination involving black faculty and staff had come to light," the Black Faculty Committee issued one of its first public statements in the *State News*. In what they called "an open letter" and "statement of position," the committee supported Black students who orchestrated the polarizing Wilson Hall sit-in, called out the university for being investigated by "Federal officials" concerning "discrimination against" Black employees, and summarized the "facts," in their minds, about "racism against blacks at MSU." "The black faculty at MSU is committed to a sense of fairness and justice [for] the total university."[27]

In late September 1969, a *Lansing State Journal* staff writer claimed there were twenty-one Black MSU faculty members, all of whom reportedly supported acting president Walter Adams for the permanent position on account of his dynamism and "concern" for "poor and dispossessed minorities in communities."[28] These twenty-one African Americans identified as faculty were most likely a mix of tenure-system and "temporary faculty" members, instructors, and perhaps even postdoctoral fellows. In his 1973 dissertation on Black student activism at MSU, Center for Urban Affairs administrative assistant Eric V. A. Winston identified twenty Black "faculty" and nine "administrators" for the 1969–1970 academic year. In the summer of 1968, instructor Dewitt Dykes created one of the first lists of Black faculty that included fifteen tenure system faculty. It's possible that the number of full-time tenure-system Black faculty jumped from about fifteen in July 1968 to twenty by September 1969. The number of Blacks identified as faculty by college deans, department chairs, and administrators conspicuously increased between the falls of 1968 and 1969.[29]

What is more certain is that the years between Hannah's June 1964 proclamation in support of open housing in East Lansing for MSU's Black employees and the end of the decade witnessed noticeable and unprecedented growth in the number of Black faculty. There were a few White faculty members like associate professor of political science Caroll Hawkins, who in an op-ed in the *State News* in early April 1968 opined the university prioritize the hiring of professionally capable Black scholars. It appears most White faculty members didn't believe or publicly proclaim that racially diversifying their ranks constituted an urgent concern. In the late 1960s, movers and shakers in the miniscule group of Black faculty, administrators, and staff worked closely with Black students and consistently called upon the university's executive leadership to recognize their presence, improve campus race relations, hire more Black faculty, administrators, and staff, recruit more Black students, and ameliorate the overall treatment of Black people in the MSU community.

Beyond what transpired "on the banks of the Red Cedar," the impetus for the hiring surge of Black faculty, administrative personnel, and staff beginning in the late 1960s and peaking during the early to mid-1970s was a direct result of student activism and the broader transformations characterizing PWIs throughout the nation following the urban rebellions of 1967 and the assassination of Martin Luther King Jr. Like their determined counterparts at northern PWIs, in the late 1960s, MSU's Black students abruptly began vocalizing their demands for more faculty who looked like them. The increase of African American faculty and employees went hand in hand with the Black student population's sudden growth during the turbulent Black Power era. By the end of the Black Power era in 1975, there were 2,500 Black students and fifty Black tenure-system faculty members at MSU. By the late 1970s, however, a report issued by the U.S. Department of Labor concluded that Black scholars had "trouble gaining entry to the MSU tenure stream," and MSU had to improve its approach to and monitoring of affirmative action.[30] President Edgar L. Harden responded by agreeing to develop a plan to recruit more women and minority faculty.

On Friday, April 5, 1968, the day after King was assassinated, hundreds of Black students congregated on the first floor of the Administration Building. Barry Amis, president of the recently created BSA, presented a list of grievances and ultimatums to President Hannah.

Printed by the *State News* on the following Monday, these wide-ranging demands included BSA's pressing concerns about the lack of Black faculty, administrators, and employees. They wanted and expected Hannah to address this immediately. "There are not enough black faculty in the University," BSA declared. "There are no black administrators in this University. There are not enough black employees in this University." A week later, BSA presented their eleven demands to the Board of Trustees, calling for, among other actions, the recruitment of more Black faculty, students, and staff. In late April, under the leadership of football player LaMarr Thomas, thirty-eight Black student-athletes—who identified themselves as the Black athletes of Michigan State University—clamored for the hiring of more Black coaches who would, for them, be the equivalent of professors. In their minds, they spent as much if not more time with their coaches than other undergraduates did directly engaging with their professors.[31]

Also, in late April, the "Committee of Sixteen," a special committee founded by President Hannah to "study and develop Civil Rights guidelines" on campus, issued its report and recommendations for reforming the university. Calling for "fundamental changes of attitude and behavior of white Americans toward the Negro in American society," among the committee's seven main recommendations was "a search for Negro faculty members" in all colleges and departments in the university and a "conscious and continuous effort" to "increase … the number of Negroes in administration." The committee also suggested the creation of a Race and Urban Affairs Center (later known as the Center for Urban Affairs) that would theoretically employ a significant number of Black faculty, administrators, and staff.[32] Like other PWIs who scrambled to launch Black Studies departments, programs, and centers during the late 1960s and early 1970s, MSU's leadership sought to attract and recruit Black scholars through a new Black-centered unit as opposed to hiring them in traditional departments. Unlike the countless other PWIs, MSU didn't label their program a Black Studies entity by name. "Urban" was code for Black.

When viewed within the broader context of the snail-paced hiring of Black faculty at major research institutions throughout the nation, the situation at MSU is not surprising or remarkably distinctive. With very few exceptions, PWIs did not begin hiring their first Black faculty members in significant numbers until the later years of the modern Civil Rights Movement and during the Black Power era. Such efforts in diversifying higher education resulted in noticeable change, but several decades later the number of Black faculty at PWIs remained dismally low. In the late 1990s, the managing editor of the *Journal of Blacks in Higher Education*, Robert Bruce Slater, lamented, "by the year 1992 blacks had broken through the racial barrier at all of the nation's 25 highest-ranked universities." Pessimistically, he added, "if the nation's highest-ranked universities continue to hire black faculty members at the same rate as has been the case in recent years, it will be several centuries before the level of black faculty reaches even the current percentage of black college and university professors nationwide."[33]

Despite the proliferation of numerous faculty diversity recruitment and retention initiatives at colleges and universities throughout the nation in response to the Black Lives Matter

Movement, especially following the police killing of George Floyd in late May 2020, Black faculty continue to face challenges reminiscent of earlier times. According to the National Center for Education, in the fall of 2018, approximately 6 percent of full-time faculty in degree-granting postsecondary institutions were Black, and there were seven thousand Black full professors—4 percent of the total population of full professors. (In the fall of 2018, African Americans made up 4.4 percent of MSU's faculty, the same percentage as in 1991.) "There has never been a golden age for Black faculty in the United States," a Black professor and administrator at the University of California, Irvine, pessimistically observed in the fall of 2020. "Too often people assume that there was after the Civil Rights Act, that the door was opened, that there was no more resistance. On the contrary, there has been and will likely continue to be resistance." Another professor despondently added, "the absence of Black faculty in institutions of higher learning is a national crisis."[34]

African American academics and scholars faced even greater challenges during the era of Jim Crow segregation. In 1876, Edward Alexander Bouchet earned a PhD in physics from Yale, making him the first African American to earn a doctorate and the sixth person in the Western hemisphere to earn a PhD in physics. (Nearly one century later, Willie Hobbs Moore became the first African American woman to earn a PhD—University of Michigan, 1972—in physics.) Despite his impressive credentials, Bouchet could not secure a position teaching at a PWI. From Reconstruction through World War I, there were approximately twenty African American doctorate holders, none of whom held full-time professorships at major PWIs. The prolific W. E. B. Du Bois, the first African American to earn a PhD in history (Harvard, 1895), was temporarily given the title "assistant in sociology" at the University of Pennsylvania while he conducted research in the city for his pathbreaking *The Philadelphia Negro* (1899).[35] This position was in no way a traditional professorship. He didn't teach any courses. "His title was symbolic of the rather shoddy treatment Du Bois felt he received at Penn."[36]

In his exhaustive *Holders of Doctorates among American Negroes* (1946), the director of Teacher Education at West Virginia State College, Harry Washington Greene, documented that between 1876 and 1943, 381 African Americans earned doctorates, representing less than 1 percent of the total number of American doctorate recipients. Put another way, between 1926 and 1942, 335 of the total 38,765 doctorates in the United States were awarded to African Americans. The first Black women to earn doctorates did so in 1921, Georgiana Rose Simpson (German, University of Chicago), Sadie Tanner Mossell (economics, University of Pennsylvania), and Eva B. Dykes (English language, Radcliffe College). During the interwar period, African American scholars made some notable progress. In the 1930s, 189 African Americans earned doctorates, from 1940 until 1943, 128 did, and from 1944 until 1951, about 292 did. In 1946, of the approximately seventy-eight African Americans teaching at forty-three PWIs, only twenty-nine had "continuing appointments." By the late 1950s, approximately 673 African Americans had earned doctorates. By the end of the decade, "not more than 200" African Americans were teaching in "continuing capacities" at approximately seventy-two PWIs, roughly 40 percent of whom were teaching in New York. From the days of Edward Alexander Bouchet through the modern Civil Rights Movement, nearly all PhD-holding Black scholars who taught at postsecondary institutions did so at HBCUs.[37]

There were a few history-makers who defied the odds. During the mid- to late 1940s, the Black press was optimistic about measurable progress made by Black scholars in the mainstream White academy. "In recent years qualified Negroes have been added to the faculties of white colleges and universities," observed a writer for the *Detroit Tribune* in 1945. In 1947, under the headline "60 Negro Professors Teach at White Colleges," the *Chicago Defender* blazoned, "the steady growth in the number of Negroes who have been placed upon faculties of white colleges throughout the north, and even as far south as Black Mountain college in North Carolina, has come about with a swiftness which has caught many of us unaware." A year later, literary scholar Arthur P. Davis told *New Journal and Guide* (Norfolk, Virginia) readers, "Negro professors are yearly increasing in our best white schools." Citing from a study conducted by the Cornell University NAACP chapter, in 1948, the *Associated Negro Press* seemed somewhat sanguine about the prospects of Black faculty in Ithaca, New York. The university's White faculty members "were not wholly against hiring or working with Negro instructors."[38]

The majority of Black scholars teaching at PWIs from the 1940s through the early 1960s were hired as non-tenure-system instructors. In 1942, when he was hired by the University of Chicago, W. Allison Davis became the first Black tenure-system faculty member at a traditionally White major research university. Five years later, he became the first African American to earn tenure at a major PWI. The next two African Americans to earn tenure at prestigious PWIs were Ralph J. Bunche and J. Saunders Redding, who were promoted with tenure in 1950 at Harvard University and Brown University, respectively. In 1956, historian John Hope Franklin was appointed chair of the Department of History at Brooklyn College, possibly making him the first African American to serve as a department head at a public PWI.[39] Not including units in the College for Urban Affairs, one of the first African American chairs of a traditional department at MSU was Ernest J. Moore, chair of the Department of Audiology in the early 1980s. All told, between the late 1940s and the early 1960s, about a dozen African American scholars were hired as tenure-system faculty by the nation's most prestigious research universities.[40]

Before David W. D. Dickson was hired, the Michigan State community had minimal exposure to and contact with Black professors and scholars. Hale Woodruff's visit to campus in January 1944 was unique, a first-of-its-kind arrangement. A renowned painter and muralist, Woodruff was a leading African American artist of the Harlem Renaissance and Great Depression era and beyond. He attended prestigious art schools, studied in Paris, and rubbed shoulders with art world legends such as Pablo Picasso, Henry O. Tanner, Diego Rivera, Romare Bearden, and many others. At the time of his stop-off in East Lansing, Woodruff was a seasoned art professor at Atlanta University who founded its art department that became known as the "'École des

Beaux Arts' of the Black South." At Michigan State he participated in "a three-day lecture and demonstration series." The featured event was a lecture he delivered in the music auditorium, "Art in a Changing World."[41] Though the former expatriate's work appeared in government-sponsored, World War II propaganda, his most famous pieces were Black history centered, such as his depictions of lynching, linoleum cuts of everyday southern Black life, and famous Amistad murals commissioned by Talladega College in the late 1930s. Several months after Woodruff's presentations, President Hannah invited Mordecai Johnson, the first Black president of Howard University, to speak at the student convocation and address the faculty at a general staff meeting. By the end of the decade, Hannah hired the first Black Michigan State faculty member.

Chapter 35

Trailblazing Educators

W hen David W. D. Dickson arrived at Michigan State in 1948, he was a member of a microscopic and exclusive club of tenure-system African American professors employed by northern predominantly White institutions (PWIs).[1] In 1950, MSU joined the Big Ten and was one of the few conference members with a tenure-system Black faculty member. Founded nearly four decades before MSU, the University of Michigan hired its first Black faculty member in 1952, Albert Wheeler, an assistant professor of microbiology and dermatology. A contemporary of Dickson, Wheeler earned his doctorate from the University of Michigan School of Public Health five years before Dickson earned his doctorate from Harvard. With his wife Emma, who "chose to stay at home and raise their three daughters rather than pursue a professional career," Wheeler, after earning his doctorate, developed into an outspoken civil rights activist in Ann Arbor.[2]

Like Dickson, but navigating more potential pitfalls given his disposition, Wheeler walked a tightrope while a professor at U of M where he worked, with a series of leaves, from 1952 until 1981. Cofounders of the Ann Arbor Civic Forum (a group that challenged racial discrimination in housing, education, and employment), the Wheelers helped create the Ann Arbor NAACP chapter in the late 1950s. For a long time, Emma served as the organization's president. During the early 1960s, this husband and wife team led a movement to establish a fair housing ordinance in the city. Albert was active in many local civil rights initiatives, including Ann Arbor's Coordinating Council on Civil Rights and Human Relations Council. In 1963, "he drafted a proposal that led to a provision in the Michigan Constitution establishing the state's Civil Rights Commission," and in 1966 he was head of the state chapter of the NAACP. In 1970, he led a group called Blacks United for Liberation and Justice that called out the city's racial profiling and criminalization of Black male youths. In 1975, he became "Ann Arbor's first and only Black mayor." Dubbed a "relentless warrior" who "fought racial barriers with tenacity" by the *Ann Arbor News*, Wheeler died in 1994 at age seventy-eight.[3]

Dickson and Wheeler approached the Black Freedom Struggle in different manners. Dickson took pride in his racial heritage, advised Black students, participated in Black community events, integrated East Lansing, and, like Wheeler, was active in the NAACP. He was, however, first and foremost a scholar and a teacher. Working as an interracial mediator of some sort, Dickson was an effective race representative on campus and in and around East Lansing. A first-rate biblical scholar whose most popular class was The Bible as English Literature, in his speeches and popular scholarship, such as essays published in the *Lansing State Journal*'s "The Book Shelf" in the early 1960s, he strove to make the Old and New Testaments relevant to the here-and-now without focusing explicitly on African Americans' struggle for civil rights. The only tenure-system Black faculty member at MSU for nearly a decade, Dickson was highly visible and exuded Black excellence. In his own way, he helped diversify the faculty and the classroom. He was countless White students' only Black professor and many of his White colleagues' only Black friend and acquaintance. He bore the burdens of being "the only one" and representing the race, a charge consistently lingering in his conscious and subconscious mind. Surrounded by those who could not relate to the Black Freedom Struggle and his experiences, he understood W. E. B. Du Bois's timeless musings in "Of Our Spiritual Strivings" in *The Souls of Black Folk* (1903): "It is a peculiar sensation, this double consciousness, this sense of always looking at one's self through the eyes of others." Despite the alienation and microaggressions he endured as well as his commitment to service beyond the proverbial call of duty, Dickson benefited from his experiences at MSU. It served as training grounds for his future career, culminating with his presidency of Montclair State University from 1973 until 1984.[4]

In the late 1970s, psychologist, assistant director of the MSU Counseling Center and president of the Black Faculty and Administrators Association (BFAA) Lee N. June told a *Lansing State Journal* reporter, "with 2.5 percent of the faculty, students can go through four years of college and never have a black instructor—we know that one of the things that affects career development is role models." In the decade before June's observations, Black students had far fewer potential Black role models on campus. The small group of pioneering Black faculty whose stories are featured in this book served as living object lessons, mentors, and advocates for Black students while finding and creating community for themselves, leading by example, and developing innovative programs, initiatives, and research trajectories. Shaped by the Civil Rights Movement and the Black Power era, they tended to embrace opportunities to support Black students. Three decades before the first annual African American Celebratory

Commencement was fittingly held in the Wharton Center's Pasant Theatre, in 1975 the BFAA inaugurated Black Senior Recognition Day to honor three hundred graduating Black students. Instructor and member of the event's planning committee Larry Redd, who as a graduate student produced and directed WKAR's first major Black show, *Takin' Care of Business*, explained that this program sought to "reinforce the sense of achievement by black students and to give some encouragement to others to enter the university."[5] This program continued into the 1980s and represented a precursor to the African American Celebratory Commencement started in 2002. As "insider-outsiders," the first major cohort of Black faculty members at America's first agricultural college embraced Redd's vision. Joining the MSU community between the long Civil Rights Movement and the Black Power era, they often served as a moral conscience for the university and helped change and transform the ever-evolving campus culture with their presence and different world views, academic perspectives, approaches to leadership, praxis and pedagogy, and conceptions of service, outreach, and engagement.

A World War II veteran, exceptional scholar and teacher, public intellectual, and interracial mediator, David Watson Daly Dickson was the only Black faculty member at Michigan State for about a decade until William H. Pipes was hired in 1957. As a writer for the *New York Times* noted in Dickson's obituary, "He spent more than 40 years in academia as a teacher and administrator before he retired in 1989." Born on February 16, 1919, in Portland, Maine, Dickson learned a great deal from his working-class parents who immigrated from Jamaica in search of the American Dream. His parents educated their children "to a high degree by dint of their own foresight and industry with the great help of American philanthropy," the Black New Englander stated. "Though Negroes, we were never permitted by our parents to be embittered or enervated by infrequent difficult rebuffs; we were taught to turn shoves into forward pushes, to lament America's limitation in the interracial area but to appreciate the many people who were especially kind to us of the minority."[6]

In 1943, under the title "Dickson Bros.' Record Unique at Bowdoin," the widely read *Pittsburgh Courier* shared with its readers the monumental achievements of Dickson, his brothers, and other "race students." Dickson's four siblings excelled in college, but he was especially brilliant. After graduating from Portland High School, in 1941 he became the second man in Bowdoin College's history to earn all A's "with various prizes and awards including summa cum laude and Phi Beta Kappa." A year later, he earned a master's degree from Harvard. He then enrolled in the doctoral program at Harvard but was "called to the army in June." During World War II, from 1943 until 1946, he served in the U.S. Army and distinguished himself by rising from the rank of private to "first lieutenant as the adjutant of the commanding officer of the medical unit of the Army Air Forces base in Tuskegee, Ala.," the training grounds for the famous Tuskegee Airmen.[7] After serving his country, Dickson returned to Harvard, served as a teaching fellow for one year, studied Greek, Hebrew, and biblical studies, and earned a PhD in English literature in 1949.

David W. D. Dickson, the first Black faculty member hired at Michigan State. Courtesy of Michigan State University Archives and Historical Collections.

Dickson was an adept multitasker. In 1948, while completing his dissertation, he was hired by MSC as an instructor with the expectation he would be promoted to assistant professor once he defended and officially submitted his dissertation. According to Dickson's son, "There were perhaps only a half dozen white institutions nationally that would consider employing a Black man as a professor, and Harvard was not among them. My dad was undaunted and applied to Michigan State."[8] Pulitzer Prize–winning author and pioneer of cultural studies Russel B. Nye, who taught at MSU from 1941 until 1979, was chair of the Department of English when Dickson was hired and wholeheartedly supported him. Dickson's area of expertise included John Milton, biblical studies, and seventeenth-century lyric poetry. Upon his arrival in East Lansing, twenty-nine-year-old Dickson lived in an apartment on campus in Cherry Lane. Several years after Dickson married Vera Mae Allen in 1951 in Dowagiac, Michigan, the Dicksons, thanks to John A. Hannah's interventions and connections, became the first known African American family to own a home in East Lansing.[9] For more than ten years, the Dickson family lived at 224 Elizabeth Street.

Dickson soon gained a reputation for his exemplary teaching. In 1952, he was voted "best instructor" at the college and was awarded the first annual MSC Alumni Distinguished Teacher Award. The competition was stiff: he was selected from a list of "60 candidates submitted by college departments," and the selection criteria included "nine qualities deemed most desirable for a college professor." A picture of Dickson receiving a congratulatory handshake from Hannah was featured in the *Lansing State Journal* and several major national African American newspapers. African Americans across the nation took pride in Dickson's achievement. In the Kansas City *Plaindealer*, under the headline "Negro Teacher Voted Best at Michigan State," there's a large photo of Dickson, $500 cash prize in hand, receiving a congratulatory kiss on the cheek from his wife Vera Mae.[10] Several decades after leaving MSU, Dickson recalled his success in the classroom. "Very soon, my classes in Biblical Literature, required for majors in journalism, became very popular. Students no longer force-fed the Bible at home found the Old Testament especially a treasure trove of full-blooded biography, exciting narrative, and lyric and prophetic poetry of surpassing beauty and power." Dickson continued, "My own enthusiasm for the work was contagious. . . . My reputation as a teacher was readily recognized." Though Dickson reminisced that he "quickly gained promotion to Associate Professor," he was promoted a decade after arriving in East Lansing.[11]

Shortly after arriving at Michigan State, Dickson became a well-known figure in the East Lansing and Lansing communities. Dickson recalled, "I spent too much of my time and talent in giving speeches in the community. As the only Black professor at a major college and university, I was soon on too many church and social agency boards. On campus, I was asked to advise the only Black fraternity and expected to help solve any 'color problems.'"[12] Recognized as one of the "resource leaders" of the sixth annual youth conference at the Lincoln Community Center in 1950, he often spoke at this recreation center as well as at other events sponsored by a myriad of groups including local churches and the Greater Lansing Council of Churches, the Lansing–East Lansing Phi Beta Kappa, the Kiwanis Club of East Lansing, the Lansing Women's Club, and the YMCA. The senior warden of East Lansing's All Saints Episcopal Parish in 1962, Dickson regularly delivered lectures about the Bible, events open to the public often advertised and summarized in the *Lansing State Journal*. Handsome headshots of him often accompanied this coverage. Dickson believed the scripture could help guide Americans in the cause of social justice. "Less reliance on the might of arms and alliances and more attention to man's craving for bread and dignity in keeping with God's demand for social justice is the real key to international harmony we crave so much," he told an audience at a luncheon at the Lansing YMCA in October 1957.[13]

Apart from talks like the one he delivered at Central Methodist Church's "Race Relations Sunday" program in 1960, most of his speeches before White and interracial audiences didn't focus on race or African Americans' civil rights. In some cases, when addressing Whites, he presented watered-down renditions of U.S. history. "With considerable literary power," Dickson recounted at the 1962 Thanksgiving program sponsored by the Zonta Club of Lansing held at the Jack Tar Hotel, "the germ of our Declaration of Independence was grown in the soil of Nazareth and our national joys and blessings which we talk about should rightly be attributed to God, if we are to view things in the proper stance." He told his listeners that they, as privileged Americans, had inherited "rich blessings" and they should be reverent and humble. Celebrating a mythic American past as aspirational, he suggested they should strive to renew "the spirit of the early settlers in America" that stemmed from their "deep faith borne of dedication to God" and belief that "all men are brothers."[14]

On campus, he was committed to service, mentoring and advising student groups. Early in his career, he was the inaugural adviser for the MSC Literary Club, the chairman of the honors committee in the college of arts and sciences, the adviser of the Canterbury Club (a student organization open to those interested in the Episcopal Church, religious study, service, and fellowship), and the adviser for the Michigan State chapter of Alpha Phi Alpha fraternity. He also helped organize major on-campus events. In late December 1952, he served as host for a conference held at the Kellogg Center for more than one hundred international students from across the country. Though he was understandably not necessarily outspoken about civil rights in manners his successors during the Black Power era were, he and his wife, Vera, were active members of the Lansing branch of the NAACP. Vera served as cochair of the branch's general membership committee, and David served as chairman of the education committee. David spoke at events sponsored by the branch and co-organized the branch's "Careers Unlimited," an informal vocational fair held in mid-October 1960 at the Friendship Baptist Church for more than two hundred young African American Lansingites. A year later, he served as the master of ceremonies for the NAACP's installation of new officers and a program concentrating on the implications and limitations of desegregation and integration. Under the presidency of Josephine Ferguson

Wharton, the branch was most concerned about discrimination in housing and employment, something Dickson knew firsthand.[15]

In 1962, Dickson's stature in the Lansing area increased when he was elected president of the Lansing Family Service Agency. The next year, in celebration of National Family Service Week, the *Lansing State Journal* featured a story on four admirable fathers and board members of the agency and their exemplary families. "Dr. and Mrs. Dickson of Elizabeth in East Lansing enjoy many things with their three children, David, Debra and Deirdre, besides the books and music one expects to find in the home of a university professor." Women's editor for the *Journal* Virginia Redfern continued, "Most of all they like people."[16] The full-page article featured a photo of Dickson, his wife Vera, and their three children that resembled photos of middle-class families in *Jet* or *Ebony* magazines. In her piece celebrating this exceptional East Lansing Black family, Redfern also announced Dickson was leaving MSU to become chair of the English Department at Northern Michigan University in Marquette, Michigan. A testimony to his contributions to the East Lansing community, the city's Interracial Fellowship Society, founded about twenty years earlier by an interracial and interdenominational group of church women of the Greater Lansing area, held a reception in his honor in early May 1963.

During Dickson's first year at Northern, Governor George Romney appointed him to the Michigan State Council for the Arts. While at Northern from 1963 until 1968, he moved up the administrative ladder, becoming dean of arts and sciences and academic vice-president. After holding the position of provost for a year at Federal City College in Washington, D.C., from 1969 until 1973 he served as a professor of English, assistant to the president, and dean of continuing education at the State University of New York at Stony Brook. Three years after Wharton was appointed president of MSU, in 1973 Dickson became the president of Montclair State University in New Jersey, serving in this role until 1984. For the next five years, he returned to his passion of teaching as a distinguished service professor until he retired in 1989. Considering his success at Dartmouth and later Harvard, Dickson was destined for greatness in the academy. His career at MSU as a teacher, researcher, mentor, and publicly engaged scholar helped pave the way for not only his future success as an academic thought leader, but for those Black faculty who joined the MSU community after him.

During and shortly after Dickson's time in East Lansing, very few Black scholars were hired by PWIs. Though American Dietetic Association member Jacquelyn Van Dyke Williams held an instructorship in the Michigan State's Department of Nutrition and Roy L. Hill was a fellow teacher in the Department of Communication Skills in 1956, the university hired its second full-time Black faculty member a decade after Dickson's appointment.[17] In the spring of 1957, the State Board of Michigan State College approved the appointment of Dr. William H. Pipes as a professor of English and speech, effective September 1, 1957. An exceptional student during his undergraduate and graduate years, Pipes's pre–Michigan State life and career was much different than his younger New England colleague's. Dickson grew up in Maine and attended two of the nation's most prestigious and elite PWIs. Pipes was born and socialized in the Jim Crow South and attended, and later taught at, several HBCUs. Both were humanities scholars and shared an interest in biblical studies. Pipes focused on dimensions of African American religious thought. He was more outspoken than Dickson on issues pertaining to African American history and culture and Blacks' enduring struggle for civil rights. His upbringing and previous experiences at HBCUs inevitably shaped his career at Michigan State.

William Harrison Pipes was born in Inverness, Mississippi, on January 3, 1912. His parents, Hez (or Hessie) Pipes and Ada L. Pipes, were born in Mississippi and labored to make ends meet as sharecroppers on a cotton plantation. Pipes credited his mother for instilling within him the value of education. "Through the influence of Booker T. Washington, the famous founder of Tuskegee Institute, my poor but devout mother had resolved when I was a baby to help me obtain an education. And from my childhood reading of the struggle of the success of the little engine that 'thought it could' reach the top of the hill despite its heavy load of coal, I had believed that if I worked and prayed and 'thought I could' get an education, then I could."[18]

From the late 1920s until graduating in 1934, he attended Tuskegee, working to cover his tuition and living expenses. His humble upbringing profoundly informed his later years as an academic. "I was born in poverty and grew up picking cotton and plowing," Pipes remarked in the late 1940s; "This background is important for an understanding of my philosophy of education for the masses of my people in the South." He was well known at Tuskegee. He won "the best drilled Tuskegee cadet" at the annual competition in 1929 and earned straight A's. He was a member of the varsity debate team, editor of the *Campus Digest*, orchestra leader, and the president of the student executive organization. He was also a bit iconoclastic. In the fall of 1934, he and one of his classmates were disciplined for publishing and selling more than five hundred copies of a sixty-four-page pamphlet, *Collegiana, the Crab's Bible*. This booklet, called by his colleagues a "fine piece of literature," provided overviews of the college's traditions while poking fun at several faculty members, Tuskegee president R. R. Moton, and even his son. Tuskegee officials were outraged and banned the *Collegiana*. A graduating senior at this time, his stellar performance saved him from being more harshly reprimanded.[19]

After graduating from Tuskegee, in 1937 Pipes completed his MA thesis in the Department of English at Atlanta University. With this thoughtful piece of densely footnoted scholarship, "Sources of Booker T. Washington's Effectiveness as a Public Speaker," a twenty-five-year-old Pipes committed himself to rigorously studying African American history and culture and participated in the proto–Black Studies movement. Though not trained as a historian, Pipes dug into the archives for this project, getting vital assistance from Tuskegee Institute archivist Monroe Work and Washington's son, E. Davidson. Filling a void in the existing historical scholarship, Pipes's primary goal was to unpack the roots and expressions of Washington's success as an orator and his impeccable communication skills. He demonstrated a keen understanding of the historical context that shaped Washington's rhetorical style, the ideas of historians like Carter G. Woodson,

Washington's speeches and writings, especially *Up from Slavery*, and theoretical scholarship on speech. Unlike many of his contemporaries, Pipes was a fan of Washington, believing he was one of the most impressive speakers of his era. In Pipes's estimation, to win over his various audiences, Washington used language that resonated with his different audiences and creatively employed specific, finite verbs, vivid compound adjectives, parallel phrases, repetition, figures of speech, similes, metaphors, biblical references, and anecdotes. For Pipes, Washington mastered the craft of the literary artist.[20]

Shortly after studying at Atlanta University, Pipes left the South for Ann Arbor, Michigan, to pursue his doctoral studies. In 1943, Pipes earned a PhD from the University of Michigan, becoming the first African American to earn a doctorate in speech. His meticulously researched dissertation, "An Interpretative Study of Old-Time Negro Preaching," laid the foundations for his future scholarship, culminating in his first book, the pathbreaking *Say Amen, Brother! Old-Time Negro Preaching: A Study in American Frustration* (1951). While working on his doctorate and shortly thereafter, he taught at Fort Valley State College in Georgia, Southern University in Louisiana, West Kentucky State College, and Langston University in Oklahoma. From 1945 until 1949, Pipes served as president of Alcorn A&M College, a public historically Black land-grant university in Lorman, Mississippi. He was the only African American with a doctorate in the state when he was hired. Like his role model Booker T. Washington, Pipes was shrewd and tactful when sharing his philosophy of education with White segregationists. As he told members of the Mississippi Chamber of Commerce in 1946,

> My background has taught me one thing: that the Negro's Number One Problem is an economic one ... the South will remain mostly agricultural. Therefore, the special type of education best suited for the masses of the South—black and white—seems to be that which prepares students for agriculture and for industry. . . . Once we can get a broad base of Negroes who are economically secure, then these people will be able to send their children to law schools and to medical schools and will be able to support our professional men. But this will take time, as it has taken for the development of every other people in the history of mankind. [21]

His appointment was initially questioned by some Black activists in Jackson, Mississippi, but he managed to make an immediate impact. In the late 1940s, the Black press reported that under the youthful and progressive Pipes, the college witnessed great improvements. He oversaw more than one-half a million dollars in rebuilding and won over Mississippi governor Fielding L. Wright and his Building Commission. This good favor soon faded. Effective June 30, 1949, the Baltimore *Afro-American* announced, Pipes was forced to resign from his position at Alcorn "allegedly because he would not commit himself to the announced segregation program of Dixiecrat Governor Fielding Wright." The Black press praised Pipes for his "refusal to play ball with the segregationists," even in the face of "threats of physical violence." Pipes, who took

William Harrison Pipes. Courtesy of Michigan State University Archives and Historical Collections.

great pride knowing one of his former students was freedom fighter Medgar Evers, wasn't accommodating enough for White Mississippian power brokers. Pipes left Alcorn for Philander Smith College in Little Rock, Arkansas, where he served as a dean and professor of speech until 1956. Before arriving at MSC, he spent his sabbatical year at Wayne State University in Detroit as a visiting professor.[22]

In 1957, when Michigan State hired him, effective September 1, as assistant professor of communication skills, Pipes, a former college president, was an accomplished teacher, administrator, and scholar. He was happy to leave the South (in *Death of an "Uncle Tom"*, he recounted an instance in July 1945 when he feared he might have been lynched). Still, the transition from the South to the North took some adjustment on his part. In the South, outside the walls of Alcorn and other HBCUs, he was accustomed to following segregationist etiquette. In Mississippi, he reminisced, he "learned not to look too closely at white people—really not at all to look at white women." At Michigan State, he learned, in his words, how to overcome being "white-people-blind." Pipes was cognizant of the challenges encountered by African Americans in Michigan and throughout the North. As he noted in a commencement address at Fort Valley State College, Georgia, in 1963, "I left the South seven years ago—but I did not leave the Negro's plight for freedom. The problems of the Negro, North or South, are basically the same." Pipes was disrespected as a scholar when he was hired by MSU.[23]

"With a PhD degree from the University of Michigan (1943), after some twenty years as College Professor, Academic Dean and President, and having published two books and more than a score of articles," he reflected a decade after arriving in East Lansing, "I was surprised when Michigan State University offered me an academic rank less than full professor." When he questioned why he wasn't hired at the rank of full professor, the chair of his department told him he should feel grateful to be the second Black professor in the institution's history. When Pipes's promotion to full professor was approved by the Board of Trustees in the spring of 1968, a freshman from Hazel Park, who must have known Pipes and clearly admired him, celebrated the former college president's achievement. After chronicling Pipes's many administrative and scholarly accomplishments, this conscientious student chastised MSU for offering Pipes "no more than an assistant professorship" when he was first hired. The student wrote, "In my opinion, this illustrates that racial prejudice and white racism are wide spread on this campus. My only hope is that the actions of the Board in awarding Pipes his much deserved professorship and President Hannah's ad hoc committee on race relations are indicative of a changing attitude and a step toward ending discrimination at MSU. To Pipes again I extend congratulations." Like Dickson, Pipes faced prejudice in moving up the ranks. Despite being one of the most popular and accomplished teacher-scholars on campus, he was promoted to full professor more than a decade after he arrived on campus. Unlike Dickson, Pipes spoke out publicly about the racism he faced at MSU. In a speech he delivered before the Lansing YMCA in early November 1963, Pipes boldly called out, by name, a colleague who addressed him with the derogatory name

"George" as if he was a pullman porter. Pipes, as he recalled, put his colleague in check when he insulted him with this pejorative.[24]

Pipes remained at Michigan State from 1957 until 1976 in the Department of American Thought and Language. He was promoted to associate professor in 1962 and then more than five years later became the first African American to reach the rank of full professor within the university's system.[25] He was the first Black professor at Michigan State to promote a Black Studies agenda through his teaching, research, and service and participated in mainstream academic as well as interracial organizations. On campus, he served as a board member of the University Faculty Club and a member of Hannah's Committee of Sixteen. In April 1969, he was selected as one of five alternates for the presidential search committee for Hannah's successor. For a decade, he edited *The Crescent*, Phi Beta Sigma's national magazine, and helped the fraternity grow. In the late 1950s, he purchased a home in Lansing at 519 West Street. He was an active member of Lansing's NAACP Urban League branches, the Greater Lansing Coordinating Council on Human Rights, and the city's Torch Club.

Pipes's scholarship was centered on the African American experience. Before arriving at Michigan State, he published his first book, *Say Amen, Brother!*, a cultural and historical exploration of the "old-time" or "old fashioned" Black preaching tradition and its practitioners using Macon County, Georgia, as a case study. With the help of his students at Fort Valley State College and his wife, Anna Howard Russell, Pipes collected much data and engaged in interviews and observation. He was a self-proclaimed participant-observer. Contemporary reviewers in the leading African American scholarly journals of the time, including the *Journal of Negro History*, tended to be critical of his approach as a social scientist and were bothered by his iconoclastic polemics. In 1992, when *Say Amen, Brother!* was reprinted, renowned public intellectual Cornel West hailed it a "neglected classic in an overlooked field of American cultural studies" that was among the pioneering works on the Black preaching tradition. West credited Pipes for situating this tradition within "social, political, and cultural contexts," providing a nuanced analysis of "the form of style" of the Black sermonic tradition, and, in the spirit of Black Studies, discovering "a usable past for the present Black struggle for democratic citizenship." Like Carter G. Woodson did in his classic *The Mis-Education of the Negro* (1933), Pipes called for highly-educated Black leaders and ministers to dedicate themselves to the masses of their people. Pipes described his book as being revisionist in nature. In his estimation, "old-time" Black preachers had all too often been portrayed as being semi-comic figures. Pipes made this clear when highlighting that he, who was raised in a home wherein the old-time religion existed, approached his subject matter with great care and compassion. Prescriptive in nature, Pipes's *Say Amen, Brother!* was an impassioned plea for African Americans fundamental civil, human, and citizenship rights. Pipes concluded, "Long-range first-class citizenship will come to the Negro mainly through the unity of effort on the part of Negroes themselves; this unity of effort must be used to prepare the race to exercise wisely his rights as a citizen.… Undoubtedly, the old-time Negro preacher is *the* Negro leader today; it is to him that the great majority of Negroes in this country look for guidance."[26]

Pipes's next well-known book, published in 1967 and favorably reviewed in the *Lansing State Journal*, was atypical for a Black professor of his generation employed by a major PWI.[27] In *Death of an "Uncle Tom"*—a compilation of excerpts from essays, speeches, book reviews, and radio plays that he produced between the early 1930s when he was an undergraduate student at Tuskegee until the early 1960s—Pipes candidly chronicles and comments on the evolution of his thinking "from the acceptance of racial segregation" to "a burning demand for integration and, finally, to simply a desire that the Negro be granted his constitutional rights as a man." Reflecting upon what he said and wrote from his early twenties until his early fifties, he critically deciphered his own thoughts. In this sense, *Death of an "Uncle Tom"* is part of the African American autobiographical tradition. While writing this book, Pipes was also working on an unpublished autobiography, *Hezekiah*. In the end, he reveals the disappearance of what he called his "'Uncle Tom' thinking." When Pipes wrote his book, as he notes, the term "Uncle Tom" was commonly used as an insult directed toward Black men.[28] The character and persona Uncle Tom was first introduced by abolitionist Harriet Beecher Stowe in her popular 1852 novel *Uncle Tom's Cabin*, the best-selling novel in the United States during the nineteenth century. Based upon the life of Josiah Henson, Stowe's Uncle Tom character was an enslaved African American who made great sacrifices for his people. He was a martyr. During the early years of the Great Migration, writers for the *Chicago Defender* began using Uncle Tom as an insult for subservient Black men. Novelist Richard Wright further popularized the moniker as a diss with his 1938 collection of novellas, *Uncle Tom's Children*. In the years before Pipes published his book, Malcolm X popularized using the term as an insult to American male leaders who avoided directly confronting white supremacy.

Pipes embraced Malcolm's and Herbert Hill's and Wyatt T. Walker's 1965 definitions of the term. "'Uncle Tom,'" wrote Hill, "is a term used to identify Negroes who behave without self-respect and dignity and without racial pride in relation to white persons and to white-controlled institutions." For Wyatt, an "Uncle Tom" was "an American Negro who survives (and even sometimes thrives) by accommodation." Dissecting his previous ideas, Pipes is candid in his self-analysis, describing his transformations from what he calls the "'Uncle Tom' in the first degree" when he was an undergraduate student to a prideful Black man by the late 1950s and early 1960s. His early ideas about Blacks' supposed inferiority, he underscored, were a by-product of his upbringing "on a Mississippi cotton plantation."[29] That Pipes released his book in 1967 isn't surprising. It was the Black Power era, and Stokely Carmichael and Charles V. Hamilton's book *Black Power: The Politics of Liberation* had just been released. At fifty-five, Pipes closed ranks with his militant younger counterparts and made sense of how the Black Freedom Struggle shaped him.

Pipes died in 1981, five years after retiring from MSU. His legacy lived on. William and his wife Anna, who in 1967 was one of the first Black women appointed assistant professor at Lansing Community College, had three children, all of whom attended MSU. Born in 1940,

Harriette Pipes McAdoo earned a PhD in educational psychology and child development from the University of Michigan in 1970. After a long career at Howard University's School of Social Work from 1970 until 1991, her alma mater MSU hired her at the rank of full professor in the Department of Family and Child Ecology. In 1996, Harriette became the second Black woman to earn the title of University Distinguished Professor. She is recognized as a leading authority on Black children and African American families. Originally published in 1981, McAdoo's edited volume *Black Families* has undergone numerous revised editions and remains a classic. Like her parents, she lived a life of service, mentoring and teaching multiple generations of students. A founding member of MSU's African American and African Studies PhD Program, McAdoo embraced the mantra of the National Council of Black Studies, "Academic Excellence, Social Responsibility." While William Harrison Pipes didn't achieve the scholarly fame his daughter did, in 2003 he was named one of "MSU's iconic professors" for his contributions that "were so significant they need to be remembered by future generations." Sharing the company of a select group of the institution's most influential professors, including William J. Beal, Robert C. Kedzie, Linda Landon, and Russel Blaine Nye, he was most fondly remembered "for his strong and interesting lectures and interest in his students."[30]

Chapter 36

Anything but Silent Generationers

O n a somewhat remote part of campus, in the Plant Biology Laboratory, you'll find a very accomplished, black plant biologist," a writer for the *Grapevine Journal* reported in April 1973. "His name is Clifford Pollard and if you're interested in knowing about the vapor phase oxidation of picolines on the biological function of vitamin E, he's the man to see." Born in Henderson, Texas, in 1930, Pollard, who served in the U.S. Army from 1953 until 1955, earned his bachelor's and master's degrees from Prairie View A&M College, an HBCU in Texas. In 1959, he earned his doctorate in biochemistry from Georgetown University. In the summer of 1962, he was hired as an assistant professor of botany and plant biology at MSU. Described by one MSU student as being "nice, personable, candid," Pollard was a productive researcher, adviser to graduate students, and active university citizen.[1]

Funded by the American Cancer Society, in the late 1960s MSU was engaged in "fascinating research projects" on cancer treatment. With his expertise on ribosomal RNA, Pollard contributed to the university's fight against cancer and moved through the academic ranks quite swiftly. He was promoted to the rank of full professor in 1971, approximately nine years after he arrived in East Lansing. President Clifton R. Wharton Jr. viewed him as having leadership potential, appointing him to serve on several important university committees. In 1971, he served on the Presidential Commission on Admissions and Student Body Composition, and from 1970 until 1972, he served as chair of the Anti-Discrimination Judicial Board. The first major case the board considered under Pollard's leadership took place in the fall of 1970 and revolved around a racial issue. A Black woman cheerleader alleged she was discriminated against by the cheerleading coach and a specialist in the Department of Health, Physical Education and Recreation. In January and February 1970, Celeste Moy, one of two Black cheerleaders (the other was Lynn Weaver), recounted to members of the student-led Black Liberation Front, International's (BLFI) leadership how she had been mistreated because of her race, which included being excluded from participating in various activities. The BLFI established a "task force" to investigate the allegations and demanded justice for Moy. In his role as assistant director of the Dean of Students Office, Don E. Coleman sided with Moy. "The Black cheerleader," he observed, "should be able to feel a sense of belonging and loyalty." In the end, the Anti-Discrimination Judicial Board, led by Pollard, recommended dismissing the case because of "lack of probable cause to credit the allegations." Pollard and his colleagues concluded that the situation involved poor communications. This experience remained with Moy decades after she earned her bachelor's degree from Justin Morrill College, MSU. In 2019, she returned to her alma mater to receive the inaugural Justin Morrill College Distinguished Alumni Award. During her acceptance speech, she shared how her struggles impacted her and her decision to become a lawyer.[2]

"A retirement party is planned to celebrate Charles Scarborough's 39 years of service to Michigan State University," the *Lansing State Journal* announced in early September 1998. "Charles began his employment as a teaching assistant in zoology in 1959, when he was accepted in a doctoral program at MSU. He eventually became a full professor and the dean of Lyman Briggs College. . . . A scholarship in Charles' name has been established for students in Lyman Briggs."[3] While Scarborough was working on his PhD, in the summer of 1963, the MSU Board of Trustees appointed him an instructor of natural science. Six years later, after he earned his doctorate in zoology, he was promoted to the rank of assistant professor, and in 1972 he became an associate professor with tenure. A former basketball player at his alma mater, Rust College, an HBCU in Holly Springs, Mississippi, Scarborough was involved in MSU athletics. In 1972, he served on the search committee for the new athletic director, and during the spring and summer of 1975, he was a member of the small committee established by President Wharton to investigate the football program's recruiting practices involving "two of the nation's most sought-after players." It was rumored that legendary Ohio State coach Woody Hayes tipped off the National Collegiate Athletic Association and Big Ten about what he claimed were MSU's questionable tactics. Under the leadership of assistant athletic director Clarence Underwood, who was sitting in for the hospitalized athletic director, Scarborough and the other four members of the committee were enlisted to prepare a "full study" of the allegations.[4]

Scarborough was active in the Black Faculty and Administrators Association (BFAA) and didn't let his appointments to predominately White university-wide committees impact his commitment to the struggle faced by the on-campus Black community. In 1976 and 1977, he represented BFAA before the Board of Trustees when they called for the removal of the vice-president for university and federal relations from the handling of MSU's affirmative action processes and pushed for the hiring of more Black faculty. Representing his colleagues, he expressed dismay with the limited progress made since 1971. "The figures don't really tell the story," he surmised. "We're not doing that well in minority hiring."[5] Scarborough's legacy as a leader went beyond serving as a spokesperson for BFAA. He was also an outspoken administrator. In the early 1980s as acting dean of Lyman Briggs College, one of two African American deans on campus, he took a strong stance against President M. Cecil Mackey's failed attempt to close the residential colleges as part of a set of comprehensive budget reductions. He and his colleagues' politicking paid off. In early April 1981 amid controversy, the Board of Trustees considered Scarborough's endorsement and voted on whether or not to retain Lyman Briggs College with significant reductions in its budget. In a close vote, the motion failed. Then, a trustee moved to retain the college with reductions and as a school with a director instead of a dean in the College of Natural Science, a proposal Scarborough supported as a last resort. This motion also failed by a roll call vote 4-4. Martin then changed his vote from "no" to "yes," and the motion carried to retain Scarborough's unit. Though he undoubtedly wanted more for his coworkers, Scarborough was spirited in his defense of Lyman Briggs, and his efforts were vital to the college's future.[6]

While Scarborough was plugging away as a doctoral candidate, a $1.5 million gift from the Kresge Foundation of Detroit in the spring of 1956 laid the foundations for significant changes in the study and appreciation of the visual arts at Michigan State. The Kresge Art Center was completed in the fall of 1958 and was officially dedicated in early May 1959 as the headquarters for the new art department. Following World War II, the Art Department had limited and temporary offices on south campus. Located in between the MSU Auditorium and the Alumni Memorial Chapel, the four-story Kresge Art Center overlooking the beautiful Red Cedar River revealed, in President John A. Hannah's estimation, the university's renewal of its commitment to the arts and humanities. Designed to pair well with existing architectural patterns on campus and equipped with nearly twenty classroom studios, the center included a library, workrooms and lounges for faculty and students alike, a photo lab, and a seventy-by-thirty-eight-foot windowless gallery with convenient moveable partitions. This space was particularly designed for showing nationally circulating exhibitions and housing works from the university's permanent collection. The first major exhibit at Kresge took place on May 9–10, 1959, attracting nearly 2,500 visitors.[7]

In the fall of 1963, Robert L. Weil (1932–1997), a talented and up-and-coming artist in Detroit's burgeoning Black Arts Movement, made his presence known in this state-of-the-art building. The fiercely independent and outspoken artist was among the ten new faculty members recruited into the MSU Department of Art in the fall of 1962 to help teach the growing number of students enrolling in art classes. A decade later, a writer for the *Detroit Free Press* heralded him a "New MSU Legend."[8]

Weil was the first African American art professor at the university as well as the first prominent Black sculptor to settle down in the Lansing–East Lansing metropolitan area. Weil, who took a liking to drawing as a youth, was recognized for his talents during his teenage years.

"Robert Weil, 12B student, is one of Miller's most promising artists. His paintings have won him many awards, including a scholarship," the *Detroit Tribune* announced in 1949. "Robert hopes after graduating to go to the University of Michigan and continue his art education." Weil attributed part of his artistic success to the encouragement he received from one of his teachers, Ruth Spencer, who "believed in Black art and Black artists."[9] Weil came of age in Detroit during the Civil Rights Movement when African Americans using different artistic mediums launched a Black arts renaissance. Shortly after he arrived in East Lansing, the popular *Negro Digest* magazine published a lengthy article on this Black cultural and artistic renaissance that was "transforming the image of the Motor City." Building upon the earlier efforts of painter and Wayne State University graduate Hughie Lee-Smith, sculptor Oliver LaGron (the first African American to attend Cranbrook Academy of Art), painter, ceramicist, and model Myrtle Hall, the Pen and Paulette Art Club, and "an uncommon number of brilliant and talented young people," in 1956 a group of artists known as the Arts Extended Groupe, opened the first Black art gallery in Detroit near the bustling university center. Several years later, Henri Umbaji King and Harold Neal launched the Contemporary Studio on the second floor of a five-room flat off of the John C. Lodge Expressway. A member of the Arts Extended Groupe who frequented the studio, Weil was among the many young artists who showcased his talents throughout the city. "Of the two current sculptors, perhaps the most prominent are Robert Weil and Oscar Graves," Alma Forrest Parks noted. "Weil, a member of the Arts Extended Groupe, is a former John Hay Whitney fellow and winner of the Albert Kahn Prize in the annual Michigan Artists Exhibition. He is a sculpture instructor at Michigan State University."[10] Weil maintained his connection with Detroit's Black Arts Movement into the next decade, working with the Detroit Metropolitan Black Arts organization.

Initially joining Michigan State as an instructor of "direct metal sculpture," Weil earned a master of fine arts degree in sculpture from Wayne State University. His graduate work was supported by the prestigious Whitney Foundation fellowship program established in 1949 to "further the careers of promising young Americans who, because of racial, cultural and other artificial barriers, might be prevented from realizing their full development and making their fullest contribution to society."[11] Soon after he arrived in East Lansing, he transformed how art was perceived and taught at the university. He hit the ground running. In the spring of 1963, Weil's sculptures and drawings were exhibited for the first time on campus at the Kresge Art Center. With great admiration, throughout the 1960s and 1970s, the *Lansing State Journal* spotlighted Weil's sculptures when describing exhibits at Kresge. A huge supporter of the arts who certainly convinced her husband to invest more in the arts on campus, MSU first lady Delores Wharton was a big fan of his. Named a council member of the National Endowment for Arts in 1971, Delores had good taste in art informed by her undergraduate study in art history, her scholarship, her travels, and her constant engagement in the art world. At her insistence and part of her tradition of displaying art "on a revolving basis," Weil's pieces were featured in the Whartons'

Robert Weil. Courtesy of Michigan State University Archives and Historical Collections.

home, including a life-sized "aluminum cast baby" on their porch. Delores maintained, "Arts and the home must exist in harmony, and since we have many people visiting us from all over, we thought we should expose the excellent works created by members of the MSU Art faculty."[12]

Weil was among the first group of African Americans to integrate East Lansing. Upon arriving in the city whose White residents largely accepted discriminatory housing practices through the 1960s, he initially resided at 801 Cherry Lane. With his wife Judith, he later purchased a home on Lilac Avenue in the secluded and historic "Flower Pot" district where the Weils raised their three children. Through the 1970s, this scenic neighborhood off of Harrison Road South within walking distance from campus had many unpaved roads and no sidewalks. It was an ideal location for an artist and local community activist like Weil to call home. A "street-corner philosopher" of some sort with "an endless stream of friends," he enjoyed making his way around the city on foot.[13]

He had some reservations about moving from Detroit to East Lansing. "I hated it when I first came here," he candidly reminisced in 1971 shortly after being promoted to the rank of associate professor with tenure. "I thought that when I got here I would be allowed to do anything I liked. John Hannah (MSU president at the time) nearly fired me because he couldn't stand the sight of my mess about the building. Then I built a foundry. The officials nearly went through the roof." Hannah's tiff with Weil was short-lived. The MSU president approved the construction of a custom, enclosed, outdoor studio for the eccentric artist where he could work and store his "huge piles of scrap iron, plaster and steel wire, figures, wood sculptures, assorted rusty tools, frames and other objects." One admirer commented that his outside studio space was "destined one day to become a replica of the New York Museum of Modern Art's famous inner court." Weil produced his early art with discarded items. He viewed his materials, "ex-junk," as representing "future pieces of art." "All of my stuff comes out of the junkyard. I take $3 per week to negotiate with."[14] Weil located his philosophy and approach within a broader context, emphasizing that what others viewed as being idiosyncratic was actually quite typical. "Almost all the 20th century sculptures have been created from scrap metal which has been resurrected," he told an admiring *Lansing State Journal* reporter in September 1969.[15]

Weil's philosophy of teaching—summed up by his mantra "Success builds good people"—was collaborative and empowering. For this former elementary school teacher who cut his teeth in the Detroit public school system, "art is a device of protest." But, he added, "you have to know what you are protesting about." One of the approximately two hundred faculty in the MSU Faculty Committee for Peace in Viet Nam (and one of two Blacks in the group), Weil viewed his own art as being, in the tradition of W. E. B. Du Bois's famous 1926 assertion that "all art is propaganda and ever must be," protest art or at least work that had "something to say." In an interview with the *Grapevine Journal* during the early 1970s, Weil commented that Black culture should be "celebrated and ritualized. "It can't be so simplistic as Black is beautiful," he added; "The next step is to lay it out." Whether or not he viewed his work as exclusively being "Black art," his identity as an African American man from Detroit signaled this to the public. His creations were displayed in venues such as one of Lansing's first Black art festivals during Black History Month in 1969 and an exhibit of Black artists' work sponsored by Those Interested in the Links at the Lansing Community Art Gallery in 1972.[16] One of his most explicit nods to Black historical revivalism was his bust of Martin Luther King Jr. that he completed in the early 1980s.

As he stressed nonchalantly, Weil balanced his career as an artist and professor with outreach and engagement. He wasn't driven by "success, prizes, money." Beginning in the late 1960s, he participated in "cultural enrichment" programs in Detroit middle and high schools, seeking to introduce art to African American youth. Through his "art achievers program," he helped recruit so-called disadvantaged students to pursue art at MSU. He rejected the notion that "inner-city" Black youth had unsurmountable academic deficiencies. For him, "academic handicaps were no barrier to enthusiasm and talent." "I see these so-called 'disadvantaged' students as advantaged,"

Weil remarked in 1969. "Like most people, they have a lot of skills that are related to art. Take the way they dress or talk or dance—that's their way of expressing their individuality. But these skills, which are all related to the body, are related to art. Most of them have a real gut-level bedrock feeling about life . . . And death." Black students seem to have been impressed with what Weil brought to the table. Fascinated by the iconoclastic Detroit native, a writer for the *Grapevine Journal* highlighted how Weil's art "always related somehow to the spontaneity of jazz, the solitude of rural life which he figures into the Black aesthetic." During the early 1970s, several young Black artists at MSU may have been inspired by the accomplishments of their elder, like Will Roberts, Art Sims, Michael Hurd, and Jeff Harris who, like Weil, believed "if you're an artist, you do what you feel."[17]

Weil's work with Black students from Detroit dovetailed with the philosophy of the university's Center for Urban Affairs. In 1971, he was one of the few senior scholars and humanists in this unit, and his salary reflected the discrepancies between compensation for faculty in the arts and humanities compared to those in the social sciences. Embracing the center's local extension work, in the early 1970s, he joined the Edgewood United Church and the planning committee for the low-income housing project, Edgewood Village. In 1974, he created a three-ton steel cube sculpture for the neighborhood's day care center. He had more ambitious plans for the center. Recognizing the impact environment had on children's social and intellectual development, he envisioned installing a fish pond and "sacred Japanese house" in the center's backyard. Such visions stemmed from his days in Detroit when he had dreams of converting some of the city's abandoned buildings into studios where artists could work with schoolchildren.[18]

A member of the East Lansing Aesthetics Committee and the city's Fine Arts and Cultural Heritage Commission, Weil encouraged artistically conservative East Lansing officials to be more deliberately involved in efforts to incorporate more sculptures on campus. It's not an exaggeration to conclude that the sculptures currently peppering the streets of East Lansing are the result of Weil's efforts five decades earlier. Just as he maintained earlier in his career, Weil believed the MSU campus could be an innovative university by showcasing provocative sculptures. With other artists, during the early 1970s, he tried to convince East Lansing officials to allow him and a group of his artist friends to adorn some of the city's alleys near businesses with air sculptures and paintings. In November 1974, he presented to the city council his idea to transform a one-hundred-square-foot abandoned gas station at the corner of M.A.C. Avenue and Albert Street into a sculpture garden and "headquarters of the arts."[19]

A year later, with support from the Michigan Council of the Arts, his proposal became somewhat of a reality when, in anticipation of the bicentennial celebration, the city council cautiously approved the placement of sculptures throughout the city. The codirector of the Fine Arts and Cultural Heritage Committee gave Weil his due props. "The idea is Bob Weil's, who is a well-known area sculptor." The project was eventually called "From the Bottom Up: 12 Contemporary Michigan Sculptures." Located on Grand River Avenue, Albert Street, the corners of M.A.C. and Albert and Oakhill and Evergreen, and in several alleyways downtown, the pieces received mixed reviews from community members. Weil accomplished his goal of challenging East Lansing's residents to grapple with the meaning of art in their daily lives. He was also active in Lansing. In 1976, he was one of the designers of Lansing's Riverfront Park and completed a mosaic under the Shiawassee Street Bridge.[20] Nearly three decades after he arrived in East Lansing, Weil was the progenitor of an art movement emanating from North Lansing on Turner Street, one of the oldest parts of the city. Frustrated with the MSU art scene, Weil grumbled several years after the last major exhibit of his work at the Kresge Gallery in the 1980s, "I want to live inside the art community and be alive. The university is not a real art community." In 1989, Weil opened a studio and gallery with a colleague, Kris Love.[21]

Weil's career at MSU coincided with that of fellow Detroit native Robert L. Green. Contemporaries separated in age by six months, they were different types of professors for sure. Despite the distinctly divergent ways they generated interpretations of the world around them and fulfilled the outreach vision of the Center for Urban Affairs, during the 1960s and 1970s, the two Robert L.s worked closely with Black communities and sought to transform East Lansing and the evolving mission of Michigan State.

In commemoration of Martin Luther King Jr. Day in 2017, I had the honor to participate on a panel in Case Hall, "Martin Luther King, Jr. and the Future of Black America," with Green. The still dynamic scholar was the ideal featured speaker for this program, an annual event organized by Professor Curtis Stokes and sponsored by James Madison College. After all, decades earlier, Green courageously accepted King's invitation to join the Southern Christian Leadership Conference's (SCLC) freedom struggle in the South. He considered King among his principal mentors and King, likewise, respected Green. In a 1967 speech before the American Psychological Association in Washington, D.C., "The Role of the Behavioral Scientist in the Civil Rights Movement," King proclaimed: "From its inception, the Southern Christian Leadership Conference, which I have the privilege of serving as president, has recognized the value of social scientists—and welcomed the vast support. It must be added, however, that in ten years only one social scientist left a university to engage in full-time activity with us. Dr. Robert Green of Michigan State University spent more than a year with us and is presently a part-time member of the staff."[22]

In 2017, I was aware of Green's pathbreaking scholarship on Prince Edward County (PEC) and his close relationship with King. While writing this book, I learned much more about Green's staunch and extensive civil rights activism during and beyond the Hannah years. His legacy as a civil rights activist was cemented in East Lansing in September 2021 when Pinecrest Elementary School was fittingly renamed Robert L. Green Elementary School and his former house at 207 Bessemaur Drive in East Lansing was designated with a state historic marker.

Green, who earned his PhD in educational psychology from MSU in December 1962, was hired as an assistant professor in the College of Education in January 1963. Six years later, he became the director of the Center for Urban Affairs and an assistant provost. In 1973, he became the first African American dean at MSU. From the mid-1960s until Wharton officially took office as MSU's fourteenth president, the local and national mainstream media routinely covered Green's activities more than those of any other African American affiliated with the university. In and around East Lansing, Green's name was synonymous with Blacks' struggle for civil rights. On and off campus, he was much more vociferous than his predecessors in his approach to the Black Freedom Struggle. Throughout his career at MSU during the 1960s and 1970s, Green deliberately didn't separate his role as an academic and researcher with his life as a community and civil rights activist. The *State News* and the *MSU Alumni Magazine* routinely covered his activities, especially following the assassination of Martin Luther King Jr., as well as his campaign against racial discrimination in Big Ten athletics in 1972. In the spring of 1978, the *MSU Alumni Magazine* published a tribute to the man who academia "failed to domesticate," aptly titled "Dean Robert Green: A Scholar-Activist." "So it has begun," the author forewarned; "the Greening of MSU."[23]

In the mid-1960s, the FBI monitored his dealings, planting an informant in one of his classes. Though wholeheartedly dedicated to King's strategy of nonviolent direct action, Green was militant, forthright, and outspoken in his critiques of racism and white supremacy. He refused to hold his tongue. Slightly younger than King, Green was older than the architects of the Black Power Movement and served as a mediator and consensus-builder between the old guard civil rights leadership and the younger militant generation, including MSU Black students. In his illuminating *At the Crossroads of Fear and Freedom: The Fight for Social and Educational Justice* (2016), Green details his civil rights endeavors through the Black Power era and beyond, showcasing his work with King and other key freedom fighters. Green was born on November 23, 1933, in Detroit. His parents, Thomas and Alberta Green, had nine children and, like many Black southerners during the interwar period, migrated to Detroit from Georgia because of the job boom in the city's auto industry. A World War I veteran, Thomas became a Pentecostal minister, opened a church, worked in the Fisher body plant, and "sold coal from a wagon" to support his large family. Green's parents were firm believers in education as a means to self-knowledge and upward mobility. They shared with their children their own encounters with expressions of white supremacy. Green's father told him about a friend of his who was lynched when he was fourteen years old in Jones County, Georgia.[24] All of Robert's siblings earned college degrees. After graduating from Northern High School, Green was drafted into the U.S. Army and then attended San Francisco State College, earning his bachelor of arts degree and master's degree in 1958 and 1960, respectively. He then enrolled in MSU and earned his doctorate in psychology in December 1962. His dissertation, "The Predictive Efficiency and Factored Dimensions of the Michigan M-Scales for Eleventh-Grade Negro Students—an Explanatory Study," laid the foundations for his future research trajectory.

While a doctoral candidate, he lived in Spartan Village and on Durand Street in East Lansing and in 1964 became one of the first African Americans to own a home in the city that actively practiced housing segregation. Later in his life, Green recounted how a friend, Jerry Wish, loaned him money for the down payment for a home on Bessemaur Drive. Hannah offered to help Green by buying a home and then selling it to him. Green appreciated his generous offer, but replied to the supportive president, "If you buy a home for me and sell it to me, the next person of color who comes around to buy a home will have the same experience, so thank you, but no."[25] In January 1963, the newly minted PhD was hired as an assistant professor in the College of Education and soon thereafter became a member of East Lansing's Human Relations Commission, an organization that advised the East Lansing City Council on civil rights and racial relations. Discouraged by the commission's gradualist approach, in January 1965 he resigned from the group. According to the *Lansing State Journal*, it was "the end of a long, stormy relationship." The last straw for Green was his colleagues' refusal to write a letter of support for a Michigan chain store that had recently decided to boycott goods produced in Mississippi because of their segregationist policies. In response to the commission's stance, Green proclaimed: "We can't divorce ourselves from what's going on in Mississippi." Green continued, "As long as this commission is overly concerned with its image, we will never make any real progress in this (civil rights) area." While leaving his final meeting, he reassured his former colleagues that he was by no means through with the struggle. "This does not mean I'm finished with civil rights by any means," he warned.[26]

As David A. Thomas correctly pointed out, it was instances like this that propelled Green to became "the area's most outspoken and perhaps most effective civil rights activist."[27] In the early 1980s, MSU president M. Cecil Mackey remarked that Green had often "served as a 'conscious for the university.'"[28] During the Civil Rights Movement and Black Power era, and beyond, Green, who was active in the NAACP and the Urban League, worked closely with civil rights icons including King, Malcolm X, Stokely Carmichael, Roy Wilkins, Floyd McKissick, James Meredith, his best friend Andrew Jackson Young, and Arthur Ashe, among others. Green's commitment to African Americans' civil rights began early in his scholarly career. As a doctoral student and assistant professor, he meticulously researched the desegregation movement in PEC, Virginia, for John F. Kennedy's administration. He was considered an expert on the impact of the 1954 U.S. Supreme Court decision in *Brown v. Board of Education of Topeka* and during his long scholarly career served as an expert witness for many of the NAACP cases. He was prolific. By 1983, he was a "widely recognized scholar and researcher" who had published "more than 100 articles, books and research papers" and had "many times been an expert witness in school desegregation cases."[29] The editorial director of the NAACP's *Crisis* magazine Chester A. Higgins Sr. aptly described Green's productivity. "The sheer volume of all this, accomplished by a man who is yet in his 40s, is an irritating reminder to some of the least enterprising of us of what can be accomplished given the talent and brains and stern discipline that abhors flittering away time."[30] In the mid-1980s, Higgins highlighted Green's duality, observing: "He's a first-rate scholar, and he has the tough inner core of a Detroit street dude."[31]

Green was outspoken concerning African Americans' human and civil rights, and his scholarship was intimately intertwined with his activism. During the 1960s, as a principal investigator for the U.S. Office of Education, much of his research focused on the education of Black children, especially the impact of four years of school deprivation on Black youth in PEC when officials closed public schools in protest of the Supreme Court's landmark decision. He worked closely with the local NAACP's PEC Freedom Schools Association to desegregate the PEC schools and was active in civil disobedience in Farmville, Virginia. In 1964 and 1966, he was the lead author on two cooperative research projects published by the U.S. Office of Education, Department of Health, Education and Welfare, and in 1967 and 1969, he published two vital articles in the *Journal of Negro Education*—"Some Effects of Deprivation on Intelligence, Achievement, and Cognitive Growth" and "The Effects of Resumed Schooling on the Measured Intelligence of Prince Edward County's Black Children"—that expanded upon his research on Black children's educational challenges because of segregationist thought and illegal practices. Green's research played a vital role in the "opening of the Prince Edward county Free Schools in the fall of 1963," helping guide the Free School in overcoming "the handicaps of being denied education."[32]

The expert on the impact of segregation on Black children's education was active in the creation of the Association of Black Psychologists (ABPsi) in 1968. In response to the racism of the American Psychological Association, the members of the ABPsi "pledged themselves to the realization that they are Black people first and psychologists second." Echoing Carter G. Woodson's *The Mis-Education of the Negro* (1933), they challenged doctorate-holding African American psychologists trained at predominantly White institutions (PWIs) for not focusing on the daily problems faced by their people. "In the final analysis," they asserted, "the Black psychologist must become sensitized to the needs of the Black community." Because of his past activism and scholarly achievement, Green was "unanimously elected" as one of the first cochairmen.[33]

While Hannah was the chair of the Civil Rights Commission, Green was arguably the most active civil rights activist in the history of MSU, a freedom fighter who added to the university's legitimacy in the Black Freedom Struggle outside of "the banks of the Red Cedar."

From 1965 until 1966, Green worked closely with King as the national education director of the SCLC, an umbrella civil rights organization founded in 1957 that collaborated with local, grassroots civil rights activists throughout the South and organized and participated in voter registration drives, mass marches, boycotts, and educational reform. While Green worked with SCLC, the organization was becoming less popular with young African Americans who embraced Carmichael's call for "Black Power." Green was with the organization when they initiated the Poor People's Campaign. He first met King in 1956 while the civil rights icon was visiting San Francisco to deliver the keynote address at the national NAACP convention. Though their meeting was spontaneous, Green remained in contact with King over the next decade. Two years after he helped organize Malcolm X's visit to campus, Green organized King's visit to

Robert Green, along with Floyd McKissick, Martin Luther King Jr., Stokely Carmichael, and others, leads a confrontational voter registration march in Mississippi in June 1966. Courtesy of Getty Images.

MSU in February 1965, picked him up from the airport, and served as his personal chaperon. He impressed King. Following his speech, King told the MSU professor, "Brother Green, you ought to join us in the struggle. . . . You ought to consider working with us in the South." King saw Green as being a unique asset. As Green recalled, one of King's favorite mantras was "Activism must be combined with education." King wrote Hannah requesting Green be granted a leave from September 1965 until the fall of 1966 to work with him, replacing Andrew Young. With little choice in the matter, Hannah agreed to the arrangement. This was a prudent decision. If he hadn't, the firebrand would have certainly publicly chastised the chairman of the U.S. Civil Rights Commission. To his credit, Hannah afforded Green carte blanche as he navigated his career as an activist-scholar. This was an opportunity of a lifetime for the thirty-two-year-old Detroit native and newly hired professor. In his position with SCLC, Green helped the organization develop its educational initiatives, aided in antidiscrimination campaigns, and participated in voter registration drives. Green was straightforward in his assessment of the challenges African Americans faced in the South. "From my observation," Green said in 1966, "it is apparent that the educational system in the South is deliberately and systematically designed to make certain that colored students will forever be second-class citizens."[34]

One of the pinnacles of Green's civil rights activities took place in the summer of 1966. In early June, James Meredith, who integrated the University of Mississippi four years prior, embarked upon his famous 270-mile solo March Against Fear, planning to walk from Memphis, Tennessee, to Jackson, Mississippi, as a protest against racism and voter suppression. The day after he began his trek, he was shot by a racist White sniper and was in critical condition. Green, along with King, McKissick, and Hosea Williams, met with Meredith in the hospital. A group of civil rights organizations, including SCLC, then decided to carry on the march with some modifications. Green was one of the march's organizers. In his autobiography, he provides a gripping day-by-day account of the march from Hernando, Mississippi, to Jackson, Mississippi, from June 7 until June 26. He played a leading role in the "largest civil rights march in Mississippi history," symbolized by his placing of an American flag on top of the Confederate monument in Grenada, Mississippi. Green forged a close relationship with Carmichael. On June 15, he helped get him released from jail in Greenwood, Mississippi. Immediately following his release, Carmichael began popularizing the "Black Power" slogan. Like King, Green urged younger freedom fighters to not use the term because he believed it conflicted with the movement's pragmatic strategy of measured civil disobedience and nonviolent direct action. After Green retuned to campus in the fall of 1966, faculty and students, he recalled, "clamored for stories" about his experiences. He continued to work with SCLC, participating in the integration of an elementary school in Grenada, Mississippi.[35]

Green's activism continued at MSU during the Black Power era, and beyond. A former adviser to the campus NAACP, in 1967, at a meeting in his East Lansing home, he counseled Black student leaders who officially founded the Black Students' Alliance (BSA) in January 1968. Green was a mentor and advocate for many Black students and community members. "If there was a Black at MSU or even in the city of East Lansing, that had a problem and they came to Bob Green, he dealt with it," recalled Green's first graduate assistant in the Center for Urban Affairs, Maxie Jackson. "It didn't matter if it was in his academic unit, if it was in the university or out of city, if you came and said I've got a problem, he dealt with it."[36] Shortly after the devastating riot in his hometown of Detroit, Green made news by admonishing Indiana senator Birch Bayh for calling for the prosecution of Carmichael who had recently returned to the United States after visiting France and Cuba. Still on leave from MSU working for SCLC, Green represented the university and sent a telegram to Bayh. Black people, he warned, will "use any means necessary to achieve total freedom and equality in America even if it means employing systematic and organized violence." He continued, "you choose to castigate Carmichael for mere 'statements' made outside the United States and you overlook what white Americans continue to do to Negroes. You and your fellow lawmakers have well demonstrated that you are more interested in oppressing the Negroes' movement for justice in America and less concerned with eradicating white racism."[37]

Following the assassination of his friend and mentor King, Green addressed members of the MSU community in the Union Building and led a march galvanizing the burgeoning Black student movement. With other Black faculty members, during the late 1960s and early 1970s, Green served as an advocate and mouthpiece for restless Black student-activists. During the Black Power era, Black students demanded that PWIs offer them a curriculum that reflected their interest in Black life, history, and culture. In response to their demands, by the mid-1970s, more than one hundred Black Studies degree programs and more than five hundred Black Studies centers, projects, and units had been launched at colleges and universities throughout the nation. In late 1968, MSU created the Center for Urban Affairs under the directorship of Ronald Lee, professor of administration, director of equal opportunity, and assistant provost. Hannah used his connections and negotiating skills to recruit Lee from his position in Washington, D.C., as the director of Planning and Systems Analysis for the U.S. Post Office Department in November 1968. In addition to community outreach, one of the center's main goals was to create courses and a curriculum that incorporated the experiences of African Americans and other racial minorities. Disgruntled with the lack of change at MSU, Lee resigned in the spring of 1969, and the BSA demanded the hiring of Green, then an associate professor with appointments in educational psychology, the counseling personal service, and James Madison College, as Lee's replacement.

Effective July 1, 1969, Green was appointed director of the Center for Urban Affairs. Supported by Wharton, Black faculty and students wanted to have a degree-granting college. A center, they reasoned, was insufficient. Initially proposed as the College of Race and Urban Affairs, in 1972, despite persistent pushback and opposition from four Board of Trustees members, the degree-granting College of Urban Development became MSU's seventeenth college. Wharton viewed this as one of the most important accomplishments of his early presidency and claimed the college was the first of its kind in the nation.[38] In May 1972, Green was named acting dean of the college that by 1973 included two departments, Racial and Ethnic Studies and Urban and Metropolitan Studies. With about three hundred students enrolled in ten different courses and twenty-two newly declared majors, the College of Urban Development began in earnest in the fall of 1973. For the first time in the university's history, students could take a collection of courses on urban life and culture such as Racism & Ethnocentrism, Urban Community Self-Development, and Black (African) Diaspora. With a supportive group of faculty guiding them, they could systematically examine the problems of inequality in American culture emanating from racial and ethnic discrimination. In late October 1973, the search committee unanimously recommended Green as the dean of the college, selecting him over the ninety applicants from across the nation.[39] Green hit the ground running by recruiting faculty, students, and staff, advocating for increased investment in the college, serving as an ambassador for the unit, and developing outreach initiatives.

As James B. Hamilton recalled, Green "pressed vigorously to increase the numbers of African Americans on the MSU faculty." Even though the BFAA was active, Hamilton maintained Green "was that leader ['the outspoken African American leader on campus'] during his tenure at MSU. He was widely respected among African American faculty and staff. Bob made frequent presentations before the Board of Trustees on issues affecting African Americans at MSU," adding, "Usually these were made independent of BFAA." He accepted his deanship without compromising his activist disposition. He used his connections to legitimize the college and kicked off the college's inaugural lecture series by inviting his good friend Representative Andrew Young, D-Georgia, to campus. Green's mission as MSU's first African American dean was clear. "We hope to prepare first-rate urban experts who can return to urban communities and dedicate themselves to their improvement," he declared during Black History Month in 1974. From 1973 until 1982, he served as the dean of the College of Urban Development. After briefly serving as the president of the University of the District of Columbia from 1983 until 1985, he returned to MSU. After retiring, he returned to campus on many occasions to share his life story with numerous audiences. In his 2016 autobiography, framed as a series of absorbing flashbacks, he wrote fondly of MSU presidents Hannah, Wharton, and Lou Anna Simon. "MSU has a tradition of engaging the world to help create positive outcomes," he ascertained.[40]

Green was one of two Black psychology PhD recipients to be hired by the university in 1963. In July, the Board of Trustees approved the appointment of Alex J. Cade as assistant professor of social science. Like Green, Cade was an exceptional faculty member. Both were promoted to the rank of full professor in the spring of 1969. In 1966, Cade's appointment was shifted to Justin Morrill College and he was named head of MSU's Upward Bound Program, a "pre-college program for high school seniors facing economic roadblocks in higher education" that was supported by the federal Office of Economic Opportunity and the university. Under Cade's guidance, the program began by offering sixty local high school rising seniors exposure to university life. For several months during the summer before their senior years, the students lived in Snyder and Phillips Halls and benefited from group counseling, introductory coursework, high levels of individual attention, cultural and recreational events, and part-time jobs. Cade employed sixteen MSU first-year students, "tutor-counselors," to help the students navigate the massive university. In the process, they earned credits and learned vital lessons in "intercultural living."[41]

"Hopefully," Cade commented in July 1966 to the *Lansing State Journal*, "participation in the Upward Bound Program will improve their grades, motivations, and understanding of the world enough to make them eligible for admission to college." By the program's second year, Cade saw the initiative's great potential. "We discovered the kids had abilities and talents neither they nor their teachers thought they had; and a lot of them are going on to college." In 1968, Cade, a recently appointed member of President Hannah's Committee of Sixteen, broadened the program by recruiting students from outside the greater Lansing area. Supported by university funds and donations, he selected an additional thirty-one students from Baldwin, Ecorse, and Highland Park, bringing the total number of participants in 1968 to nearly one hundred. In response to the growing number of Black students in the program, Cade supported the incorporation of Black history in the social science curriculum. As revealed in a lengthy essay appearing in the *State News* during Black History Week 1969, "Black Man, Black Man, Find the Individual," he showed no apprehension about broadcasting his philosophies of Black liberation. Cade was active in the broader community as well. An active member of the Michigan State Convention of Christian Churches, the Michigan Council of Churches, and the Church Vocational Committee of the United Christian Missionary Society, in late 1968 he was appointed director of the Board of Church Extension of Disciples of Christ. As revealed by a speech he delivered in June 1971, "A Proposal for a Church Center Coping with Alienation and Poverty," he was concerned with the less fortunate. In the early 1970s, his appointment was moved to "counseling, personal services and educational psychology." Cade retired from MSU in 1985.[42]

Two years after Green transitioned from being a PhD candidate to a tenure-system faculty member, MSU hired its third Black psychologist. In 1965, Dozier Thornton, who earned a PhD from the University of Pittsburg, was hired as an assistant professor in the Department of Psychology. Looking back at his early years on campus, he recalled, "I felt respected and highly regarded by my white colleagues." While Thornton wasn't involved in leading civil rights marches like Green, he was involved in a range of activities on and off campus during the Civil Rights Movement and Black Power era that served diverse communities. In 1968 at a meeting in the East Lansing city hall with the Community Chest and the East Lansing Human Relations Commission, he shared some of his thoughts about race relations, stressing that integration needed to involve both parents and children. "It fails if you have an integrated classroom where the white teacher is communicating her anti-Negro attitudes in subtle ways," Thornton observed with a sense of firsthand knowledge of this phenomenon. Recognized for his balanced, compassionate, and methodical approach as a psychologist, in the fall of 1968, he was appointed by the East Lansing mayor to the Human Relations Commission and encouraged the commission members to work to "identify racial issues and how racism is manifested in East Lansing."[43]

Early in 1969, Green issued a statement calling upon the Board of Trustees to allow Black students and faculty to select their own representatives to serve on the presidential search committee charged with finding Hannah's successor. While Green's suggestion was not taken up, Thornton, an assistant professor, was elected vice chairman of the committee that eventually recommended the appointment of Clifton R. Wharton Jr. Thornton was the only Black faculty member on the committee, and William Harrison Pipes was named an alternate. Outspoken Black student-athlete/activist LaMarr Thomas was also appointed to this important committee. Ten days after being elected to this honorific committee, on April 17, 1969, accompanied by Thomas, Thornton provided an update about the search to about fifty people at the Black Faculty, Staff and Students luncheon-meeting in Owen Graduate Hall. Thornton found himself the only Black face on other committees. The only African American on the university's Academic Council in 1970, Thornton supported "minority group student representation," especially on the nominating committee. Like many African Americans during the historically conscious Black Power era, he expressed interest in African American history. He and his wife, for instance, helped the MSU Museum curate one of their first Black history exhibits, *Our Black Settlers*.[44]

Four years after arriving at MSU, Thornton was promoted to associate professor and received a prestigious graduate student training grant of $220,000 from the National Institute of Health with which he supported nearly thirty graduate students. He was also engaged in the East Lansing and Lansing communities. Not only did he routinely speak at events in the cities, but he served as the coordinator of training for those working at Listening Ear, a crisis prevention center opened in East Lansing in mid-July 1969 that received about one thousand calls per month during its early years. People called with "all kinds of problems." Several years later, Thornton provided training for Lansing's Southside HELP Center that was patterned after Listening Ear. In the mid-1970s, he continued his outreach work by hosting, with June Jackson from MSU's Counseling Center, an eight-part series on WKAR-TV that focused on cultivating one's assertiveness. It was, in essence, a practical, self-help initiative. Like his colleague Thomas Gunnings, Thornton opened up a private practice to serve his community.[45] While an associate dean in the Graduate School later during his career, he administered the King-Chavez-Parks Future Faculty Fellowship program that helped numerous graduate students of color, particularly African Americans, make the transition to the professoriate.[46]

Chapter 37

Excellence in Mathematics, History, and Counseling

I n the summer of 1967, Michigan State University made a prudent decision to hire Irvin E. Vance as an assistant professor in the College of Natural Science. Vance, who earned his PhD in mathematics from the University of Michigan, was multitalented. As Johnny L. Houston recalled about coming of age as a budding mathematician during the late 1960s, pervasive academic racism excluded most African American mathematicians from participating in the mainstream U.S. mathematics profession. Like some of their counterparts in other disciplines, a notable number of African American mathematicians during and after the modern Civil Rights Movement decided to work at HBCUs and Minority Serving Institutions (MSIs).[1] Several African Americans integrated the Mathematical Association of America shortly after its founding in 1915, but only a pint-sized number of African Americans had earned doctorates in mathematics by the time Vance was hooded in Ann Arbor.

In 1925, World War I veteran and future longtime Howard University professor Elbert Frank Cox became the first African American to earn a PhD (Cornell University) in Vance's chosen field. Nearly two decades later, in 1943, Euphemia Rosalie Lofton Hayes became the first Black woman mathematics PhD holder, earning a doctorate from Catholic University in Washington, D.C. For about a half century, she taught in many of the leading public schools in the nation's capital. From 1925 until *Brown v. Board of Education* (1954), approximately eighteen African Americans earned doctorates in mathematics. From 1943 until 1972, approximately twenty Black women did. Several years before Vance arrived in East Lansing, game theorist, mathematical statistician extraordinaire, and former president of the Institute of Mathematical Statistics David Blackwell made history when he was elected to the National Academy of Sciences.[2]

During Vance's early years at MSU, the leading African American mathematician in Michigan was Albert Turner Bharucha-Reid, a professor at Wayne State University who from 1967 until 1981 served as the director of the university's Center for Research in Probability. In late January 1969, a group of seventeen Black and ethnic minority scholars under the name Black and Third World Mathematicians began organizing at the American Mathematical Society (AMS) meeting in New Orleans in order to discuss and seek to remedy the challenges faced by traditionally underrepresented mathematicians. At the next year's AMS meeting, members of this group and others created the National Association of Mathematicians (NAM), an organization devoted to promoting excellence in the development of mathematicians from underrepresented minority groups in the United States. By the mid-1970s, NAM began convening annual meetings. Vance was a member of this network of race-conscious Black and minority mathematicians.

In the late 1980s, mathematician Patricia Clark Kenschaft lamented, "a recent survey shows only .7% of the American doctorates in mathematics having been held by blacks, although they constitute over 12% of the population. The disparity is glaring."[3] Kenschaft's concerns continued on into the twenty-first century. According to the *Journal of Blacks in Higher Education* (*JBHE*), Blacks' progress in the field of mathematics at predominantly White institutions has been snail-paced since Vance began his career at MSU. "As late as 1999 there were only four blacks teaching mathematics among the more than 900 faculty members of the mathematics departments of the nation's 25 highest-ranked universities. In 2003," *JBHE* added, "only 16 of the 994 PhDs awarded in mathematics by American universities went to blacks." In 2005, they identified approximately one hundred Blacks who were "teaching mathematics or in a closely related field at American colleges and universities."[4] "Fewer than 1 percent of doctorates in math are awarded to African-Americans," a national correspondent of science and society for the *New York Times* wrote during Black History Month in 2019. In that year, there were about a dozen Black mathematicians "among nearly 2,000 tenured faculty members in the nation's top 50 math departments."[5] If Black mathematicians like Edray Herber Goins (PhD, Stanford University, 1999) felt discriminated against and isolated as a full professor at Purdue University during the twenty-first century, Black mathematicians of Vance's generation must have felt extreme alienation, constantly having to disprove the stereotype that African Americans could not excel in STEM fields.

While completing his doctorate in mathematics from the University of Michigan during the peak years of the Civil Rights Movement, Vance—the soon-to-be inaugural chair of the MSU Black Faculty Committee—taught math in the Detroit public school system and at U of M. He transitioned smoothly into his new job, finding his place in the East Lansing community. In 1968, the East Lansing Human Relations Commission appointed him to a special committee to explore the availability of low-cost housing for minority groups, and in April 1969, his wife was in charge

Irvin Vance. Courtesy of Michigan State University Archives and Historical Collections.

of publicity for the MSU Newcomer's Club. Irvin quickly established himself as a productive scholar, a leader among the small group of Black faculty, and a first-rate teacher with a deep commitment to the university's tradition of outreach and extension. He was a National Science Foundation fellow and a member of the mainstream scholarly associations in his field, such as the American Mathematical Society, the National Council of Teachers of Mathematics, and the Mathematical Association of America. He published his early research in journals such as *The Arithmetic Teacher*, the official journal of the National Council of Teachers of Mathematics, and coauthored the widely read *Algebra and Geometry for Teachers* (1970). Vance was wholeheartedly committed to strengthening Black youth's math and science skills.

In 1969, Vance, who supported Black students' controversial occupation of the Wilson Hall cafeteria, became the director of MSU's Inner City Mathematics Project (MSUIC-MP). With nearly $300,000 in grant funding from the National Science Foundation and the U.S. Office of Education as well as additional support from MSU's Center for Urban Affairs, Vance created this program to provide "efficient math skills to students and teachers at all levels." As a result of his successful grant applications and excellence in teaching, research, and service, three years after his initial appointment as an assistant professor, he was promoted to the rank of associate professor with tenure. While the MSUIC-MP targeted disadvantaged youth, particularly African Americans, he stressed his initiative was "by no means a remedial program."[6] In addition to providing training for math teachers in "inner-city" schools, Vance's initiative prepared undergraduate and graduate students to educate urban youth in math and science and established "a program which reaches inner-city students at an early age" as well as an undergraduate program that provided "mathematics and science teachers for inner-city students." Vance was convinced of his program's necessity. In his estimation, colleges, universities, and urban public schools miserably failed to "provide the educational experiences for many college capable children" that would provide them with opportunities "to attain the educational height commensurate of their abilities."[7]

Vance invited administrators and teachers from eleven school districts with large Black student populations to participate in summer workshops on campus. From late June until early August, students from eighth to twelfth grades were offered a range of six-week workshops devised to supplement their schools' curricula. All participants were required to take three forty-five- to fifty-minute classes between 8:15 a.m. and 2:30 p.m. Between 1969 and 1971, about five hundred students benefited from this program, affording them opportunities of independent research, field work, seminars, and lab work. Equally important, students' stay on campus exposed them to salient aspects of day-to-day life at a major Research I institution of higher learning, something they had never experienced before. The students lodged in dormitories, and many of the universities' facilities and resources were made available to them. Vance recruited nearly twenty members of the mathematics department to teach classes and had a staff of six graduate students who worked one day a week with administrators, faculty, and students in a particular school district. Vance's primary goal with MSUIC-MP was to help African American high school students from urban areas attend college and he had great faith in his program, an initiative he considered a reform project that addressed pressing challenges in underfunded, urban high schools while contributing to MSU's outreach and extension tradition.

His cutting-edge outreach work gained national recognition and brought acclaim to MSU. The university approved a post-tenure leave for Vance from September 1, 1971, until August 31, 1972, at New Mexico State University (NMSU). Impressed by his leadership skills and talents, NMSU wasted no time in poaching him from the Spartans. In August 1971, as it was reported in many local New Mexico newspapers, NMSU appointed him coordinator of ethnic programs and associate professor of mathematics. He was charged with starting what NMSU's president called an "ethnic program for Blacks." The president was delighted, commenting, "He is a very talented mathematician and should also be a big help in getting our ethnic program for blacks started."[8]

After laying the foundations for the Black Studies program for about a year, Vance returned to full-time teaching. In 1977, he received a major grant from the National Science Foundation to develop a program to increase math awareness and recruit minority faculty in the sciences. He ran the Summer Mathematics and Science Program for Minority Youth through the 1980s. By the late 1980s, Vance became increasingly frustrated in Las Cruces, New Mexico. At a Martin Luther King Jr. holiday "rally" in 1989, the university's sole Black full professor blazoned, "in the last 15 years, NMS has not hired one black faculty member, except for an athletics coach. Despair abounds in our world today. The dream has still been deferred."[9] Elected to the board of directors of the National Council of Teachers of Mathematics, Vance returned to MSU in the early 1990s. In 1994, twenty-five years after he launched the MSUIC-MP, he participated in the Summer Mathematics and Science Program for Minority Youth that brought eighty competitive kids "from all over Michigan to come learn about math and science for six weeks." In the next year, he directed the National Science Foundation–funded Michigan Mathematics-Science Camp and Saturday Academy at MSU. "We need to have more programs like this around the state," he observed in 1995. He remained committed to the cause of educating Black and minority youth in math and science after he retired. In 2001, he led a tutoring program for Lansing elementary schoolchildren with the Epsilon Tau Sigma chapter of Phi Beta Sigma Fraternity Inc., and in 2006, he was head of his fraternity's Educational Fund.[10]

After he died on December 31, 2017, many of those who participated in Vance's MSUIC-MP testified how he helped shape their future careers and adult lives. "The experience was rich and prepared me for success in college," recalled S. Cathy McCrary who participated in the program between her junior and senior years of high school and went on to earn a PhD in business administration. "I am grateful for the impact that Dr. Vance's efforts have made on my life and the lives of my students." Another student reflected, "Dr. Vance was my greatest inspiration. His never ending drive to educate youth throughout MI made him the greatest mentor I know." James (Jim) Boles testified, "the inner-city math and science program he directed, prepared me to attack these subjects with confidence throughout my high school, college and professional career years." Lansing native Byron F. Carter similarly reflected upon how the MSUIC-MP changed his life and inspired him to engage in youth programs. When Carter was reacquainted with Vance in 2015 at a Phi Beta Sigma Lansing graduate chapter event at Vance's home, he dropped to his knees "to shake his hand" and told him how much he meant to him "as a kid back in 1970."[11]

Born several years after Vance was hired, internationally renowned recording artist, jazz bassist, and professor of jazz double bass Rodney Whitaker has transformed jazz studies at MSU in the College of Music for more than two decades. One of the few African American University Distinguished Professors, Whitaker has established one of the most respected and successful jazz degree programs and performing faculty groups in the United States. A native of Detroit, Michigan, who attended Wayne State University and studied with trumpeter Marcus Belgrave and Robert Gladstone, former principal bassist for the Detroit Symphony Orchestra, among others, Whitaker began his illustrious career at MSU in 1994. "At 28, Whitaker is one of the most sought-after young bassists in Jazz, well-known for his bear-sized tone and deeply swinging pulse. A Detroit-native, he's the current generation's answer to a long line of important Motown-bred bass players," a writer for the *Detroit Free Press* remarked shortly after he arrived in East Lansing.[12]

Several decades before Whitaker joined the MSU educational community, there was another MSU African American faculty member who was an accomplished jazz musician, Leslie B. Rout Jr. This baritone saxophone player was a member of the award-winning Paul Winter Sextet who performed at the White House in November in the early 1960s and toured South America on a State Department cultural exchange program. While a doctoral student in the Department of History at the University of Minnesota, Rout played with the Lionel Hampton Orchestra, the Claude Thornhill Orchestra, and the Woody Herman Orchestra. He continued to perform after he earned his doctorate and was hired by MSU in 1967, playing the saxophone in Randy Gillespie's Band. He was foremost a historian by trade who published important scholarship and established a national and international reputation as a scholar. Equally important, he advocated for the teaching of Black history at MSU, the academic advancement of African American students, and university reforms commensurate with the changing times.[13]

Leslie Brennan Rout Jr. was born in Chicago on February 26, 1935. His early years were challenging, distinctively shaping his future thought and approach toward life. After his father abandoned his family when he was five years old, he and his mother and sister were deemed an ADC (Aid to Dependent Children) family, a designation carrying with it a range of stigmas. While in college with scholarships, he earned a living as a musician. He had originally planned to pursue a career as a scientist, declaring physics as his undergraduate major. To his dismay, his work schedule interfered with the time he was required to spend in the lab. He decided to major in European history and as a graduate student specialized in Latin American history.[14] After earning his bachelor's and master's degrees from Loyola University, he earned a PhD in Latin American history from the University of Minnesota in 1966. He then taught at Purdue University for a year and taught some music classes at Northwestern University. In 1967, he was hired as an assistant professor at MSU, becoming the first full-time tenure-system African American faculty member in the Department of History. Promoted to the rank of associate professor in merely two years (effective July 1, 1969), Rout was a hard worker and prolific scholar. Not only did he publish numerous articles, including scholarly pieces on jazz, but relatively early in his career he published three books: *Politics of the Chaco Peace Conference, 1935–1939* (1970), *Which Way Out? A Study of the Guyana-Venezuelan Boundary Dispute* (1971), and the expansive, first-of-its-kind *The African Experience in Spanish America, 1501 to the Present Day* (1976).

One of his colleagues observed that Rout was "tireless, often staying up half through the night writing and researching." The recipient of the Teacher-Scholar Award in the spring of 1969, Rout was an accomplished teacher. "In lectures, he was a showman, but even as students enjoyed his commentaries, they were being deluged with sophisticated concepts," recalled MSU professor John F. Bratzel in 1988. He was known for being a demanding teacher, maintaining high expectations of his students. Many of his students had similar admiration for him, dubbing him an entertaining professor and comedian who "greets his students as if he is a guest host on 'Saturday Night Live'" and "transforms his performance from the stage to the classroom, giving a jazzy version of American history." The history professor seemed to agree with such descriptions, commenting in the late 1960s, "As a musician, I find it very easy to go before a class and perform." Rout ventured outside of his field of specialization to teach African American history. In an April 1968 special issue of the *State News* on "the Black Revolution," Rout authored a brief and thoughtful essay on the history of jazz, "America's only indigenous musical form," from 1910 until the late 1960s. "Few have been as systematically victimized as the Negro jazzman," he deduced. Rout focused on how Black musicians, especially during the era of bebop and the "Free Jazz" movement, challenged cultural appropriation and transformed this art form into expressions of resistance. Though measured, he argued African Americans brought a feeling of "soul" that their White counterparts could only imitate "by living in a presumably" Black environment. He believed jazz would continue to be influenced by the "prevailing racial tensions in the nation."[15]

There were very few courses in African American history taught at MSU before Rout arrived there. Hired in 1961, James R. Hooker, an Africanist historian who was well-versed in the history of Pan-Africanism, touched upon elements of African American history in his courses. In the fall of 1966, a course called "Voices of the American Negro" was taught in MSU's Evening College. In February 1968, a group of Black students, led by Jill Witherspoon, conducted a study of the university's general education offerings and called upon the university to incorporate the study of African American history in the American Thought and Language curriculum. "We don't want an isolated Negro history course," Witherspoon told a *State News* reporter on the anniversary of the assassination of Malcolm X. "We want Negro history to be put where it belongs." The written statement submitted to President John A. Hannah and the vice-president for student affairs added, "Because Michigan State University is an institution of learning, we as black students demand the education that is due us. We are no longer willing to pay for ignorance."[16]

In the 1968–1969 academic year as he played saxophone at various events with other musicians and students like vocalist from Flint Dee Dee Garrett, Rout introduced the first coherent and popular courses in African American history taught at the university. His mission was, in part, personal. "When I was in school," he recalled, "the only Black face I saw in the history books was Booker T. Washington." By the 1969 winter term, three hundred students, many of whom were White, signed up for his course charting the history of Black people and their contributions to world civilization in North and South America. His course was about the African diaspora with a focus on African Americans. "In some respects, teaching this course is a rather touchy business," Rout said in 1969. He found himself having to interpret the Black past for multiple audiences simultaneously, including Black students who were being politicized by the Black Power era, leftists, and a group he called "white flaggelists." Rout wanted to recruit more Black students into his new classes. "Every Black student, by one means or another, should wind up taking a class like this," he professed. He ultimately believed courses such as his would help contextualize Blacks' present status, equip students to develop a fuller understanding of America's past and contemporary U.S. society, and help improve race relations. Black students were not universally appeased by Rout's new classes. On the front page of the October 14, 1970 *BUF Newsletter*, in an essay entitled "BUF Accuses Negro Professor," a member of the BUF communications committee alleged that Rout was distinctly hard on Black students. Shortly after Rout's class debuted, the Department of History introduced two enduring courses on the Black historical experience—The Negro in the Americas: Varieties of Slavery and The Negro in the United States: Since Emancipation.[17]

Unlike Black cultural nationalists during the Black Power era, he didn't necessarily believe that knowledge of Black history was a precursor or pivotal to African Americans' advancement. He encouraged young African Americans to know their history, but also championed that they improve their mathematical skills and enter the STEM and engineering fields as opposed to earning degrees in disciplines in the social sciences and humanities.[18] In large part as a result of Rout's efforts, the Department of History introduced courses in African American history that Harry A. Reed would further develop beginning in the mid-1970s. The sequential African American history courses currently offered at MSU stem from Rout's initial hard work. In 1970, history professor James R. Hooker broke new ground by introducing Pan-African Revolutionary Thought, which he taught with student-activists from the Black Liberation Front and the Pan-African Students Organization in the Americas. The Political Science Department also followed Rout's lead. During the 1969–1970 academic year, Black Canadian David Bell, who was hired in 1969, taught a "black political movements" course spanning from the era of slavery to the twentieth century. In January 1970, about 20 percent of his students were Black.

Rout's success as a scholar and teacher helped him be identified as a leader of some sort on campus. Appointed by President Clifton R. Wharton Jr. in May 1970 to the university's Committee Against Discrimination, in the summer of 1979 Rout was named "faculty intern and special assistant to MSU President M. Cecil Mackey in connection with minority faculty and student affairs" for the fall 1979 term. Following directives from the Board of Trustees who recognized the limitations of the "affirmative action program" that was introduced by President Edgar Harden, early in his presidency Mackey nominated and appointed several African Americans to administrative positions. In higher positions than Rout, Mackey nominated Moses Turner as vice-president for student affairs and services and appointed Lee June, at the time an associate professor and assistant director of the counseling center and an active member of the Black Faculty and Administrators Association, as acting assistant provost for special programs. June's responsibilities would increase by the early 1980s when he was appointed "special assistant to help the university assess minority student problems." Though not as engaged as June, in his part-time administrative role Rout attended the president's staff meetings and offered recommendations to Mackey. Among other initiatives, he launched a short-lived program to provide "special assistance in introductory computer science" to "minority students" in order to better prepare them for the future competitive job market. A self-proclaimed pragmatist, Rout focused on "a single problem at a time" and recognized how change occurred based upon his keen understanding of the historian's craft, historicism, and historical causation. "Only liberals believe in onward and upward. But human history shows that it's a lie," Rout deduced. "Historians know that events go back and forth, back and forth." Rout's intriguing two-decade career at MSU ended in 1987 when he died shortly after being awarded a Fulbright Fellowship to conduct research in Argentina.[19]

"Make sure that you include Tom Gunnings," I was instructed by MSU College of Education professor emeritus and former interim director of the African American and African Studies PhD Program Gloria S. Smith during one of our long conversations. She emphasized how he was an active member of the Black faculty community, mentored countless Black students, and did a lot of important things for many people, things he often didn't get credit for doing. "He thought the world of his daughter, Sonya," Smith added. "When she was young, he brought her to lectures with him. If you want to know who Tom was, just look at Sonya." Such sentiments were echoed by others. "That was the beauty of Tom," said Joel Ferguson, chair of the MSU Board of Trustees when Gunnings passed away in 2010. "Every time I'd get a phone call from him, it was always what can we do for someone else." Gunnings's daughter, Sonya Gunnings-Moton, PhD, who followed in her father's footsteps by mentoring African American students and traditionally underrepresented students at MSU as an associate dean in the College of Education, mused following her beloved father's passing: "He was just a good man about the right things and used his positions and influence to try to impact the lives of individuals who did not always have a voice."[20]

The first MSU African American counselor and first assistant dean in the College of Human Medicine, Gunnings was unmistakably one of those respected and outspoken Black faculty members hired during the Black Power era who was active in the Black Freedom Struggle on and off campus, advocating not only for his colleagues and community, but also for the Black students whose activism helped pressure the university power brokers to hire him and his colleagues in the aftermath of the assassination of Martin Luther King Jr. As a writer for the *Lansing State Journal* underscored, Gunnings was a mentor, confidant, and therapist for many Black students.

Thomas Sylvester Gunnings was born on February 8, 1935, in Gastonia, North Carolina. He grew up in the Jim Crow South and attended high school where he was an exceptional football player and student. According to Gunnings's daughter, one of his coaches, Robert O. Mason, mentored young Thomas, encouraging him "to leverage his football talents for his academic pursuits." After graduating from high school in the same year as the Supreme Court's historic decision in *Brown v. Board of Education of Topeka* (1954), Gunnings attended Winston-Salem State Teachers College, a historically Black public university founded in 1892 as Slater Industrial Academy. By the mid-1920s, Winston-Salem became the first HBCU to "grant degrees for teaching in the elementary grades." While Gunnings was enrolled, the college's curriculum expanded to include training in secondary education. In 1963, the school became known as Winston-Salem State College, and six years later it was renamed Winston-Salem State University. Gunnings took advantage of what Winston-Salem had to offer. A student-athlete who played football as a "two-way lineman," a background that later informed his mentoring of Black football players at MSU, twenty-three-year-old Gunnings graduated from Winston-Salem with a bachelor's degree in education in 1958. He then became a principal of an elementary school in the Charlotte-Mecklenburg school district. With hands-on experience in the classroom working with children, he earned an MEd degree in guidance and psychology from Oregon State University in 1967. Two years later, he earned a PhD in counseling psychology from the University of Oregon. Navigating being a Black man in Corvallis and Eugene, Oregon, unquestionably prepared him for the next stage in his career.[21]

As announced in the *Lansing State Journal* in late June 1969, effective August 1, Gunnings was hired as an assistant professor in the MSU Counseling Center. At the time, he held the position of visiting scientist for the American Psychiatric Association and was the only Black counselor on MSU's campus. Shortly after he arrived in East Lansing, Black students heard about him "through the grapevine" and began flocking to his office. In early 1970, he told a staff writer for the *Lansing State Journal* that most of his "clients" were Black, that they "seem to ask for me." During his first year on campus, Gunnings realized MSU's Black students often faced a range of challenges, including maintaining their identities in White spaces, dealing with financial pressures, adapting to life in East Lansing, and being taught from Eurocentric perspectives. In response to such issues, Gunnings pointed out that many Black students sought refuge on the fourth floor of the Union Building in the Center for Urban Affair's and the Equal Opportunity

Program's Urban Counseling Center. "This allows," stressed Gunnings, "a place for students to mix and find people who look, act, and behave like them." Under Gunnings, who identified "environmental problems" as being central to the perpetuation of racism in American society and on MSU's campus, African American and traditionally underrepresented graduate student counselors helped scores of students navigate MSU and life in general.[22]

Though he keenly understood the necessity of providing counseling for Black students, he stressed, "we must treat the cause, not the symptom." He called upon MSU to reform its counseling services to address the system that was "the basis" of the problems encountered by his Black "clients." As his daughter reminisced, Gunnings used his position at MSU—a position that very few Black men of his generation held—to unapologetically advocate for Black students. Along with Vance, Robert L. Green, and Nolen Ellison, Gunnings worked closely with the African American student group Black Liberation Front, International in support of President Wharton's proposal in May 1970 to establish an off-campus Black Cultural Center. He supported investing more in the Detroit Project and the Detroit Geographic Expedition and Institute (DGEI). Part of MSU's outreach and engagement tradition, the latter program was initiated by the Center for Urban Affairs to offer free college-level education in numerous fields to nontraditional students in the city. When the DGEI faced financial challenges in the fall of 1970, Gunnings joined his colleagues and Detroit sophomore Gwen Warren, the program's director who enrolled after participating in the institute, in urging the university to help support approximately four hundred students during three terms. In June 1972, with Gloria Smith and a planning committee, Gunnings, who was active in the Black Faculty Committee (by the early 1970s the Black Faculty and Administrators Association), co-organized a celebratory banquet in honor of twenty Black retirees, mostly women staff members.[23]

With Green and Joseph McMillan, in 1972 Gunnings called out the Big Ten Conference for what he and his colleagues perceived as being its racist tendencies, policies, and behaviors. With concrete evidence, they determined the conference practiced segregation. Gunnings and his colleagues, with Green often serving as the spokesperson, called for the desegregation of the Big Ten through the employment of Black officials for football and basketball games, the hiring of Black coaches, and the end of the exploitation of the Black athlete. "It will be the end to Black athletes being used simply to fill the arena or stadium to bring money into this university. Black athletes are used for four years, then dumped to pasture, at age 21," read their statement publicized in the *Lansing State Journal*. Green, Gunnings, and McMillan garnered support from MSU trustees Blanche Martin, Patricia Carrigan, and Don Stevens, while a more understandably cautious President Wharton endorsed introducing this subject at the Big Ten Conference meeting in early March 1972. Before the meeting, the Board of Trustees, in a 5-3 vote, issued "censures" against Gunnings, Green, and McMillan, ruling they didn't and couldn't speak for or on behalf of the university. The concerns of one plainspoken social commentator in early March 1972 fell on deaf ears. "The Board of Trustees should rescind its censure of Green,

McMillan and Gunnings. The point has been made that they do not speak for the total university on this issue. I don't think they ever purported to do so." Continued this concerned critic, "the Board should, at the same time, highly commend these men for the work they have been doing on this campus in relation to the Black community and for equal opportunities." Five years later, the board revisited this decision and finally voted to rescind this decree that brought pressing issues of free speech to the forefront.[24]

In 1972, Gunnings accepted a position in the MSU College of Human Medicine where he served as an associate dean for health programs for seven years (he would later attain full professorship in the Department of Psychiatry). He continued to place the counseling of Black students at the core of his mission. In the mid-1970s, with funding from the National Institute of Mental Health, Gunnings directed an institute at MSU seeking to "train 'central city counselors'" in what he dubbed the "systematic intervention approach." The innovative institute featured a cutting-edge curriculum that combined counseling methods, research methods, and field work in "community, school and prison settings." With Gloria Smith, director of MSU's Urban Counseling Mental Health Program in the College of Education, Gunnings organized a major conference at the Kellogg Center from October 12 to 15, 1975, to "define the problems of minority people and view current counseling strategies used in problem solution." A member of numerous scholarly associations, including serving as president of the Association for Multicultural Counseling and Development, Gunnings expanded the scope of his counseling activities by opening, in 1977, the "largest Black-owned private mental health and substance abuse treatment facility in the Greater Lansing area," Meridian Professional Psychological Consultants. He continued to organize and participate in conferences at MSU focusing on pressing issues in the Black community. In 1979, he delivered a keynote address at the Association of Black Psychologists' annual spring conference, "Black Youth: Crisis or Opportunity," that was held in the MSU Union Building.[25] During the remainder of the 1970s and 1980s, Gunnings continued to be active as a scholar and was often called upon as an expert consultant.

In May 1979, a Black woman in Lansing killed her husband in self-defense. It was a response to domestic abuse she repeatedly endured. Agreeing with his colleague and fellow MSU Black professor L. Eudora Pettigrew, Gunnings explained and rationalized this survivor's actions—as well as the similar acts of self-defense of many other Black women—as being the by-product of a culture of domestic abuse in the Black community and as a violent consequence of Black masculinist culture. While serving as president of the Association for Non-White Concerns in Personnel and Guidance, Gunnings was part of "a team of psychologists" who descended upon Atlanta in the early 1980s to help the city's horrified Black community cope with the infamous "Atlanta child murders" that terrorized Black Atlantans from July 1979 until May 1981. Gunnings argued that the city's underdeveloped health care system was inadequately prepared to deal with the impact of the murders. Recognizing that poor and working-class African Americans were not accustomed and socialized to seek professional therapy to deal with traumatic experiences,

Gunnings and his coworkers initiated a series of workshops to help train Atlanta's ministers and teachers to better help children, adolescents, and adults process and deal with stress and racial trauma.[26]

Gunnings was also active in politics. In 1980, he was president of the Ingham County Black Republicans and from 1990 until 1992 served on a committee in President George H. W. Bush's administration. Gunnings explained his support of the GOP when the vast majority of African Americans supported the Democratic Party. "Blacks can no longer be identified, and taken for granted, as a voting bloc in just a single party," he asserted in 1980. "Blacks have been stuck with the illusion that because they voted for one party, they had political power. When Democrats win, Blacks think they have power. But we don't have leverage."[27] Malcolm X made a similar charge against African Americans in his famous 1964 speech that he delivered in Detroit, "The Ballot or the Bullet." Several years before retiring, Gunnings joined other members of the Black Faculty and Staff Association to challenge the university's leadership for not living up to one of its then six guiding principles, "diversity." As Gunnings reflected, perhaps favorably reminiscing on the Wharton years, the 1980s, and even the early 1990s, "we had been making some progress years ago. The last few years, we've slipped."[28] One can only wonder what he would say about the massive decline in the number of Black faculty from 2006—when there were astoundingly 106 tenure-system Black faculty members—until 2020. From 2015 through the early 2020s there were, on average, fewer Black faculty members at MSU than there were during the 1990s. Throughout his career, Gunnings embodied the mantra that he ritualistically imparted to his daughter, "Stay strong of mind, body, and spirit."

Chapter 38

A Century of Combined Service

Lee N. June was among the recognizable cohort of Black faculty who joined MSU during the early to mid-1970s who benefited from Thomas Gunnings's plainspoken counsel. As a newly minted PhD at MSU and during his early years as an administrator, June attentively observed and bounced ideas off of Gunnings. Long before faculty mentoring became a common practice at the university, Gunnings and his contemporaries served as confidants, counselors, and cheerleaders for up-and-coming Black scholars on campus like June. James B. Hamilton, who arrived at MSU in 1968, had nothing but praise for Robert L. Green's impact on his life, remarking he was instrumental in his participation in the Black Campus Movement. At twenty-eight years old, Hamilton's contemporary June accepted an offer from MSU in part because of the support and sense of community he received from Green, Gunnings, Hamilton, Gloria S. Smith, James P. Howard, Joseph Patterson, and others. Considering his upbringing as the descendant of several generations of farmers who tilled the land for a living, June was perhaps destined to become an Aggie.[1]

June was born in Manning, South Carolina, in 1945. Manning was in "the heart of the cotton belt." During his formative years, this small predominantly Black city, the county seat of Clarendon County, was governed by the dehumanizing rules of de facto and de jure segregation. The schools for African Americans in Clarendon were not equal, by any stretch of the imagination, to those for Whites. Amid the Civil Rights Movement, activists staged sit-ins and protests in Manning, and the NAACP considered including a case from the city as one of the five combined cases in *Brown v. Board of Education* that was argued in December 1952, reargued a year later, and decided on May 17, 1954.[2] June grew up on his father's eighty-acre farm. From age six until graduating from high school, he worked on the family farm with his siblings, planting and harvesting cotton, tobacco, corn, and sweet potatoes. One of his primary tasks, assigned by his unflagging father, was picking cotton for processing and sale. For every pound he picked over his assignment of one hundred pounds from Monday through Friday of the harvesting season, his father rewarded him several cents per pound. Like the majority of students who attended Michigan Agricultural College and most Black men born and raised in the South during the first half of the twentieth century, as a child and young adult, June learned the value of hard work, self-sufficiency, and living off of the land. His parents, deacon Lawson June Sr. and deaconess Harriet Smith June, didn't complete high school, but instilled within their children a faith in God and sense of spirituality and supported their educational pursuits, especially Lee's. They noticed his studious disposition, and two of Lee's aunts who were schoolteachers identified his talents. With their support, he devoted his vacations and free time from working in the fields to his studies. His teachers at the all-Black Manning Training School recognized his intellectual aptitude and arranged for him to graduate from high school in three years at age sixteen.

After contemplating joining the U.S. Air Force (he soon discovered that he was too young to do so), he decided to attend Tuskegee Institute in Tuskegee, Alabama. A biology and premed major, June recalls that his experiences at Booker T. Washington's brainchild shaped his later developing Black consciousness as well as his career at MSU. At Tuskegee, he was enthralled by speeches delivered by nationally recognized Black leaders like Malcolm X, Benjamin Davis Jr., Whitney Young, and Martin Luther King Jr., as well as local movers and shakers like Lucius Amerson ("the first Black sheriff in the South since Reconstruction") and president of the Tuskegee Civic Association Charles G. Gomillion. June participated in several days of the 1965 Selma to Montgomery marches. In early January 1966 during his senior year, veteran and civil rights activist Sammy Younge Jr. was shot to death in Tuskegee by an elderly gas station attendant for attempting to use a "whites-only" restroom. Younge's murder horrified and enraged Tuskegee students. It was one of the first murders of a Black student during the modern Civil Rights Movement, and as historian Brian Jones highlights, "Younge's life and death were an inspiration to activists to redouble their efforts and commitments." June joined countless students and activists in protesting this brutal cold-blooded murder (Younge was shot in the face at close range).[3]

After graduating from Tuskegee, June's supportive Black professors encouraged him to pursue graduate studies. In 1966, he received a fellowship from the Rockefeller Foundation, a pipeline program created to increase the number of Blacks in higher education. With approximately sixteen other young African American scholars in the making, June took classes in psychology at Haverford College in Haverford, Pennsylvania. This was his first time living outside of the South and outside of a segregated, yet nurturing, Black community. In 1967, he enrolled as a graduate student in the University of Illinois, earning an MA in clinical psychology and an

MEd in rehabilitation counseling in 1969. Five years later, he became the first known African American to earn a PhD in clinical psychology from Illinois. While finishing his dissertation, June completed an internship at the University of Cincinnati and was then hired as an assistant professor in the Counseling Center at MSU in 1973. Although offered a tenure-system position at Florida State University, June recalls he jumped at the unique opportunity at MSU because of the sizeable number of seasoned Black faculty, the Counseling Center's deliberate initiatives for Black and other marginalized students, namely the Multi-Ethnic Counseling Center Alliance (MECCA), and the university's burgeoning commitment to diversity under the leadership of a Black president.

Promoted to the rank of associate professor in 1978 and full professor six years later, June developed his data-informed leadership skills early in his career as the assistant director for minority counseling programs and a coordinator in MECCA from 1975 until 1979. With Gunnings and Gloria S. Smith, June embraced what he calls an outreach-centered "seeking out model" of advising students that provided judgment-free counseling and mental health services to Black students and students of color in particular. June maintained an "open door policy" for students in need and attended countless Black student events, reasoning he needed to listen to those he sought to help. In the late 1970s, June served as the president of the Black Faculty and Administrators Association, and under his leadership, the group held press conferences, routinely met with the Board of Trustees, addressed the challenges facing Black students and faculty, and provided on-point critiques of the university's annual affirmative action reports. In the late 1970s, as a spokesperson for the Minority Coalition for Affirmative Action, June challenged the university's restructuring of affirmative action.[4] "We were bold back then," June reminisced in 2021.

President M. Cecil Mackey's team recognized June's leadership abilities and potential, skills he further cultivated during a sabbatical leave at Duke University's Divinity School where he worked with renowned scholar C. Eric Lincoln. In 1979, he was named acting assistant provost of special programs, and from 1981 until 1989, June served as director of the Counseling Center. In response to the 1989 study-in, President John DiBiaggio appointed June senior adviser to the provost for racial, ethnic, and multicultural issues. He then became assistant provost for academic support services and racial, ethnic, and multicultural issues. From 1996 until 2010, he served as vice-president for student affairs and services and associate provost for academic student services and multicultural issues. June strategically negotiated for this dual appointment so he could continue helping students of color while maintaining direct reporting lines to both the president and the provost. In 2010, he became a professor in the Honors College and the Department of Psychology. June would agree with the poet John Donne's notion that "no man is an island entire of itself." His life adds credence to the African proverb "it takes a village to raise a child." Dr. June is an institution in himself. This was highlighted in late April 2023 at the groundbreaking ceremony for the $38 million, 34,000-square-foot MSU Multicultural Center on the corner of North Shaw and Farm Lanes. Those who took to the podium on this brisk yet sunny day, like Interim President Teresa Woodruff, Senior Vice-President for Student Life and Engagement Vennie Gore, and Rema Vassar, the first Black woman chair of the Board of Trustees, gave June well-deserved shout-outs. On this day, June delivered his most passionate on-campus oration, reminiscing on the long struggle leading to the historic event. He was clearly touched by the progress, however gradual at times, his beloved university had made over half a century. Today Dr. June represents a living link between MSU's Black past and present.

The other longest-serving Black MSU faculty member, geographer Joe T. Darden, was hired a year before his friend Lee in September 1972. Darden's initial appointment was in the recently created Center for Urban Affairs with a minor appointment in the Department of Geography. A year later, he had a joint appointment in the Department of Geography and the Department of Urban and Metropolitan Studies in the newly established College of Urban Development. In 1980, a year before the center was closed and the year in which he was promoted to the rank of full professor, his appointment was fully transferred to the Department of Geography.

Born and raised in Pittsburgh, Pennsylvania, Darden (b. 1943) was, like June, a strong student beginning during his elementary school days. At the historic Schenely High School in Pittsburgh's North Oakland neighborhood, Darden, the son of a steel-mill worker, became interested in the social sciences and debating current events with his classmates and teachers. With a full-ride academic scholarship from 1961 until 1965, he attended Jackson State College in Jackson, Mississippi. The transition from day-to-day life in the Northeast to the still Jim Crow Southeast was not drastic for him. His paternal grandfather, Mose Darden, owned a lot of land near Meridian, and since his early childhood Joe had visited him during the summer months. At Jackson State, his Black professors supported him, advising him to pursue graduate studies in a field with little Black representation. This would, they reasoned, open more future opportunities for him. Heeding this counsel, he decided to major in geography, a discipline then unavailable at many HBCUs and with few African American PhD holders. At Jackson State, Darden excelled academically. He was, for instance, one of two Jackson State students to participate in the annual 1963 meeting of the Association of Social Science Teachers, the theme of which was "the Emancipation Proclamation, 100 Years After."[5] Darden's time in Mississippi coincided with brutal attacks on Black social justice seekers, including the riots at Ole Miss in 1962, the assassination of the state's NAACP field secretary Medgar Evers on June 12, 1963, and the murders of civil rights activists James Chaney, Andrew Goodman, and Michael Schwerner in June 1964.

After graduating in 1965, with a graduate assistantship, Darden pursued his graduate studies in geography at the University of Pittsburgh. He was one of the small handful of African Americans pursuing a PhD in his chosen discipline. Harold Rose (PhD, the Ohio State University, 1960), the first African American to earn a doctorate in geography, became one of Darden's scholarly role models. In the late 1960s under the guidance of geographer Donald R. Deskins Jr. (PhD,

University of Michigan, 1971) with a grant from the U.S. Office of Education, the Association of American Geographers launched the Commission on Geography and Afro-America (COMGA) to "prepare future geographers for college and university posts, to retrain black college faculty and secondary teachers, to improve the quantity and quality of course offerings at black institutions, and to develop a geographical framework for focusing on the problems of Black America." COMGA provided fellowships for African American graduates pursuing MA and PhD degrees.[6] Darden's 1967 MA thesis explored the historical geography of cemeteries in Pittsburgh. From 1967 until 1969, while completing his doctorate coursework at Pitt, he worked at the university's college of arts and science advising center, serving as assistant director in 1969. He also joined the Association of American Geographers, the leading scholarly organization in the field founded in 1904. At the annual conferences during the late 1960s and 1970s, he was one of the few Black faces.

As a researcher, Darden focused on urban social geography, specifically on the residential patterns of Pittsburgh's Black population. While completing his dissertation, he taught geography part-time at California State College in California, Pennsylvania. Darden put the finishing touches on his dissertation, "The Spatial Dynamics of Afro-Americans in Pittsburgh," while a fellow at the University of Chicago from 1971 until 1972. He enrolled in seminars taught by two leading Black scholars, sociologist William Julius Wilson and historian John Hope Franklin. "I would not have become the researcher I did had I not spent that time at Chicago," Darden reflected. John Hope Franklin—who, like clockwork, responded to Darden's routine greetings with "Still struggling!"—challenged him to be a historicist and shared with him the trials and tribulations he faced as a Black scholar during the era of Jim Crow segregation.

Months after he defended his dissertation in the spring of 1972, MSU hired the newly minted Pitt PhD. Darden recalls that he was "aggressively recruited" by Green and received a phone call from Wilbur B. Brookover with the job offer. Influenced by Harold Rose's *The Black Ghetto: A Spatial Behavioral Perspective* (1971), Darden developed the first class on race, residential segregation, and Black urban social geography in the Department of Geography, GEO 418: The Ghetto. He defined "the ghetto" at the outset of his classes in a straightforward manner. The ghetto, he explained, is "any area of a city where the majority population is African American and they are there because of past or present discrimination in housing and/or de jure or de facto segregation practices." Darden recalled how some of his White students perceived him at age twenty-nine. "When is the professor going to come to class?," some students enrolled in his course whispered on first day of class. Positioned near the front of the classroom, Darden, with some defiance and acerbity in his voice, announced, "I *am* the professor!" Like Green who was ten years his senior, Darden was prolific early in his career. In his words, he was driven by the mantra that he "had to be better than" his White male colleagues.

In 1976, he was promoted to the rank of associate professor with tenure. He became one of the sixteen Black associate professors who comprised 2.6 percent of the faculty members at this rank and one of the small group of geographers engaged in researching African Americans. In 1978, Harold Rose, the first and only Black president of the American Association of Geographers, used his prestigious position to deliver a controversial presidential address, "The Geography of Despair," calling upon geographers to explore "spatial patterns associated" with the "differential incidence of homicide" in "high-risk environments."[7] Like his ideological mentor Rose, Darden had an impressive publication record when he submitted his tenure and promotion materials, more than ten solo-authored articles and a book, *Afro-Americans in Pittsburgh: The Residential Segregation of a People* (1973). In 1977, he served as codirector for a research project on the impact of school desegregation in New Castle, Delaware, that was awarded $368,000 from the Rockefeller Foundation. Many newspapers throughout the nation covered his and his colleagues' findings with this project. In 1980, eight years after arriving at MSU as an assistant professor, thirty-seven-year-old Darden joined the small cohort of Black full professors. In the same year, he was a vital member of a research team in the College of Urban Development that produced a 250-page report, "Discrimination and the Welfare of Urban Minorities," for President Jimmy Carter's administration. The recipient of the university's Distinguished Faculty Award (1984), from 1984 until 1997, Darden served as the dean of the Urban Affairs Program (UAP).

While leading the UAP, Darden shifted much of his research focus to African Americans in Michigan, an interest he developed in the mid-1970s. This was a logical decision for him. As he told his students, in order to be a credible urban geographer, one needed to "intentionally observe" the community under investigation. "You got to be able to smell the place," he insists. In 1976, he produced a group of articles on residential segregation in Michigan, highlighting Detroit and Flint. A year later, Darden completed a study on segregation patterns in Michigan's ten largest cities and suburbs, putting forward timely suggestions to state policymakers. From 1984 until 1993, he teamed up with the Michigan Urban League to annually produce *The State of Black Michigan*. Modeled after the National Urban League's *State of Black America*, these volumes included analyses of the conditions faced by Michigan's Black population. After they completed each volume, Darden and his team held press conferences, sharing their findings with university officials, members of the state legislature, and the mayor. In the mid-1980s, newspapers throughout the state were eager to share the research team's findings as well as his warnings that politicians, educators, and community leaders needed to address the challenges faced by African Americans in Michigan. Darden, who published pieces in the *Journal of Black Studies* and the *Western Journal of Black Studies*, embraced the descriptive and prescriptive tradition of Black Studies. When describing the status of African Americans in Detroit during the late 1980s, he underscored that much more progress needed to be made. "The social and economic inequalities and discrimination are still present today," Darden told the Associated Press. "In many areas, the conditions facing blacks have worsened. Socially and economically, blacks in Michigan are moving backward, not forward."[8] Darden continued to study African Americans in Detroit, culminating in the edited volumes *Detroit: Race and Uneven Development* (1987) and *The State of Black America, 1967–2007* (2007), and the award-winning *Detroit: Race Riots, Racial Conflicts, and Efforts to Bridge the Racial Divide* (2013) that he coauthored with historian Richard W. Thomas. As a full professor, Darden published countless scholarly articles, book chapters, and essays and seven coauthored as well as coedited books from 1981 until 2013. "If you are a *true* scholar, you would be able to convert a conference paper into a journal article," Darden quipped at a meeting of the core African American and African Studies (AAAS) Program faculty members in 2017. Darden was responding to a few of his junior colleagues who had voiced reservations about being able to generate scholarly articles from presentations that would be delivered at a proposed on-campus AAAS symposium. Though they didn't offer direct rebuttals to Darden's passionate clapback, his younger colleagues' facial expressions revealed their bewilderment. "Did he really just say that?" they very well may have been thinking to themselves.[9] In retrospect, that Darden had such high expectations is unsurprising. One of the first ten African Americans to earn a PhD in geography in the United States, a member of the first group of African Americans to reach the rank of full professor at MSU, and a founding AAAS core faculty member, Darden had little patience for stepping down from a challenge.

Chapter 39

Shattering the Glass Ceiling

Between mid-November 1971 and the winter of 1972, the elected officers of the newly created Black Women's Employees Association of Michigan State University (BWEA)—Gloria S. Smith, Beverly Holman, Louise Taylor, and Josephine Wharton—produced the first historical overview of African American women's employment at MSU. Their history was deliberately linked to protest. As part of a bold presentation on February 25, 1972, calling upon the Board of Trustees to "rectify" the ill-treatment experienced by Black women "at all levels of employment," the fearless group offered a concise "*history* of inequities involving black women at this University since its foundation."[1]

Their "careful" analyses of historical documents and "many personal interviews" revealed interesting findings. Prior to their research, the university had been minimally concerned with the data they uncovered. Understandably overlooking the hiring of a Black woman named Mrs. Evans by President Jonathan L. Snyder in 1906 to manage the kitchen in the Women's Building, the BWEA determined the first Black woman employee was hired as a "housekeeper" in 1923. According to their research, in 1948 the university appointed the first Black woman, a technician, to an academic position. In the 1950s, they noted, the first Black women clerical workers and stenographers were hired. Though they didn't mention that alumna Jacquelyn Van Dyke Williams became in instructor in Michigan State's Department of Nutrition in the early years of the modern Civil Rights Movement, they were on point in underscoring that it took more than a century for a Black woman "to attain faculty or academic status as an assistant instructor" and

BUILDINGS AND UTILITIES CLEANING STAFF 1956

"Buildings and Utilities Cleaning Staff 1956." Members of the BWEA pointed out how Black women were disproportionately represented in certain types of employment at the university. Courtesy of Michigan State University Archives and Historical Collections.

to become an administrative-professional employee. "In September 1969, Black women began appearing in higher rank than instructor." These pathbreakers were sociologist Ruth Simms Hamilton and physician Georgia A. Johnson. In late February of 1972, the BWEA found that there were 329 Black women employees at the university, twenty-one of whom held positions above the "clerical-technical level," including seven faculty members (the highest ranking being associate professor L. Eudora Pettigrew).[2]

The history of Black women faculty at MSU resembles trends at predominantly White institutions (PWIs) throughout the country. While different generations of Black male PhD holders secured full-time positions at PWIs during World War II, the 1950s, and the 1960s, Black women from various disciplines didn't begin getting these opportunities in recognizable ways until the Black Power era, the late 1970s, and the 1980s. In the twenty-first century, we still hear of cases of the *first* Black women being hired, granted tenure, and promoted at PWIs throughout the nation. There have always been significantly more Black male than Black female tenure-system faculty at MSU and most PWIs. The slow growth of Black women faculty at MSU was mirrored in the low numbers of Black women undergraduate students. Of the approximately sixty African Americans who graduated from the institution between 1904 and 1950, less than 20 percent were women. Black women also understandably joined the ranks of graduate students at a noticeably slower pace than Black men. In 1944, Henry Lewis Van Dyke became the first known African American to earn a doctorate at MSU. About two decades later, the first known Black women earned doctorates from MSU, South Carolinians Mildred Beatty Smith and Rose Toomer Brunson.[3]

Born in Union, South Carolina, Smith—who went to elementary school in a one-room schoolhouse—earned her bachelor's degree from South Carolina State College and then pursued her master's and doctoral degrees at Michigan State. Her doctoral dissertation, "Interpersonal Influences on the Educational and Occupational Aspirations and Expectations of Sixth Grade Students" (1961), was based on data she collected while she taught in Flint, Michigan. A year after earning her doctorate, she worked as a general elementary school consultant for the Flint Community Schools and directed several programs aimed at helping "underachieving children." She then became the director of elementary education for Flint Community Schools and the director for coordinated parent involvement in the Flint Public School System. During the 1960s and 1970s, she was recognized throughout the state and nation for her expertise. Governor George Romney appointed her to the Social Welfare Commission and to the first board of control (what would become the Board of Regents) of Eastern Michigan University. In the early 1970s, she served as a visiting senior lecturer at MSU and was appointed by U.S. Department of Health, Education, and Welfare secretary Elliot Richardson to the Advising Committee on the Rights and Responsibilities of Women in the United States Department of Health, Education, and Welfare. As late as the 1980s, her scholarship on the role parents play in educating children and cultivating high-achieving young children was consulted across the country.[4]

Born in St. George Township, South Carolina, in the first decade of the twentieth century, Brunson, the daughter of a farmer who was bright enough to attend Allen University in Columbia, South Carolina, during her high school years, relocated to Lansing in about 1940 with her husband of about a decade, Robert Douglass Brunson. They met when they attended South Carolina State College. Several years after they graduated, in 1933, Robert earned a master of science degree in agricultural economics from Cornell University. In Ithaca, New York, Rose took classes at Cornell in social work, engaged in extension work, and plugged away as a teacher and recreational leader at the Southside Community Center. In 1937, she was among the charter members of Beta Xi chapter of Alpha Kappa Alpha Sorority, Inc., which included students from Cornell and Ithaca College. She appears to have placed her academic aspirations on the back burner to support her husband's career during the 1930s.[5]

Residing for some time at 1405 Olds Avenue and later at 1623 Main Street, Rose and Robert were active in Lansing's Black community that in 1940, at 1,638 residents, represented 2 percent of the city's population and less than 1 percent of the Black population in Michigan. "One of the first things" Rose did after settling down in Lansing "was to volunteer time to social service agencies in the area." She played active roles on the Mother's Club Organizing Committee for the Day Care Nursery School and the board of Lincoln Community Center. She cared deeply about the condition of Lansing's Black community, especially the welfare of children of poor and working-class migrants from the South. She helped Black families who migrated to adjust to the rhythms of the capital city. She became known to provide aid to Black children and young adults who, chaperoned by family friends and relatives, migrated to her newly adopted city to join their parents. She was horrified to discover Black children, once better acquainted with their new surroundings, fending for themselves while their parents worked. After helping a "frightened little girl about three years old" attempting to cross a street near R. E. Olds, according to Rose, she boldly requested a meeting with Ransom Eli Olds concerning childcare for his employees. "Something has got to be done about these children moving around with no one to look after them," she told him. Olds, Rose recounted several decades later, agreed to support her and her fellow community activists' cause with funding.[6]

In the mid-1940s, Rose served as the first president of the newly founded Lansing Association of Colored Women's Clubs, also known as the Lansing Association of Women's Clubs (LAWC). In the tradition of the National Association of Colored Women founded in 1896, the organization was explicitly founded "for the purpose of uniting and co-ordinating the activities of Negro women's clubs in the Greater Lansing area and to serve as representatives for state and national agencies doing similar work."[7] In 1945, the determined South Carolina native, along with cofounders Gertrude Lee and Ina Major, raised enough money to purchase a home, affectionately known as their "clubhouse," at 1024 William Street located across from the Lincoln Community Center. Among their initial priorities were establishing a community nursery for African Americans, prenatal care classes with professionally trained nurses, dinners for senior citizens, classes in homemaking, and other social and scholastic activities for children and young adults. Their fund-raising activities—namely benefit and rummage sales, fund drives, bazaars, teas, fashion shows, and holiday charity balls—were ceaseless. LAWC leaders were savvy. They knew the power of the mainstream press. During and after Brunson's presidency, the *Lansing State Journal* routinely advertised and promoted their projects and activities.

Within several years of its founding, the clubhouse was open seven days a week and offered children and young adults a wide range of educational and recreational opportunities. By the 1940s, the organization had more than one hundred members belonging to the city's small but popular Black women's organizations. Members of the LAWC publicized their cause: "to promote the social, cultural and economic welfare of residents of the vicinity. . . . To cultivate peace, harmony and happiness among citizens of all races, colors and creeds." They also celebrated

Black womanhood. Combating prevalent negative stereotypes about Black women during the Cold War, they inaugurated Lansing's Negro Mother of the Year award.[8] A highly educated Black woman, Rose strove to represent and uplift Lansing's Black women. In 1947, with five other sorors, she was a charter member of the Delta Tau Omega chapter of Alpha Kappa Alpha founded in Lansing in mid-December 1947. She served as chapter president from 1947 until 1950. Her round-the-clock civic activism and hands-on work with African American migrants from the South soon became more than simply a pastime or passion project. In the late 1940s, impressed by her commitment to "community work," the longtime director of the MSC School of Social Work, Ernest B. Harper, recruited Brunson and awarded her a scholarship to engage in graduate study. Her previous coursework at Cornell and bona fide, hands-on experience made her a perfect fit for the program. Her guidance committee included three supportive women faculty members. While completing her master's thesis, she assisted in the establishment of the Delta Zeta chapter of Alpha Kappa Alpha Sorority, Inc. at MSC (founded in early February 1954). Her sister-in-law Virginia native Dorothy Toomer (married to Cole Blease Toomer)—who worked as an assistant to the director of the Lincoln Community Center and advocated for increased educational opportunities for Black youth—served as the dean of pledges and the graduate advisor of the new chapter. The initiation of the new members took place at Rose's home in late May 1954, and she mentored these young women.

In 1955, she completed a master's thesis on Blacks mainly from the rural South who settled down in the West Side of Lansing (Tract Eighteen) from World War II through the mid-1950s. The majority of her subjects hailed from Arkansas, Georgia, Mississippi, Alabama, and North Carolina. By the mid-1950s, approximately 65 percent of African Americans resided in the West Side, and between the early 1940s and the mid-1950s, the once largely White area became 50 percent Black. For her thoughtful research project that was firmly rooted in the college's outreach and extension traditions, she interviewed at least 10 percent of the Black families living in Lansing. With her new scholarly credentials, she secured a position as a case worker for the Lansing Family Service Agency. She also served as a "graduate student supervisor" for students in MSC's School of Social Work, making her most likely the first Black woman to hold such a status at the college. Beginning in the late 1950s and early 1960s, she served on the Urbandale Community Committee, a group of social reformers who recommended improvement for the blighted Urbandale residential area, a collection of largely rundown rental homes on the east edge of the city in Lansing Township. Urbandale's residents endured substandard living conditions. At least seventy-five homes in the early 1960s lacked "either water or sewer connections or both." For Brunson, public policy, social welfare, economic reform, and self-help needed to work hand in hand to solve the web of problems faced by these destitute Mid-Michiganders.[9]

In 1962, she completed a fascinating PhD dissertation on the persistence of southern culture focusing on folk medical remedies and foods in Lansing among Black migrant communities. For this exhaustive ethnographic work, Brunson, a participant-observer who preferred using open-ended questioning methods, interviewed 150 "housewives" and discovered that Blacks in urban areas like Lansing retained a great deal of "their Southern folkways." She believed these cultural traditions were important to Black urban culture but argued that poor Blacks in Lansing needed to change their diets and healthcare practices. She connected with her subjects, observing in 1962, "I'm a southerner at heart." A staff writer for the *Lansing State Journal* acknowledged Brunson's place in Green and White history. "Her involvement with the migrants resulted in her earning the distinction of becoming the first black woman to receive a master's degree in social work and a Ph.D. degree in behavioral sciences from MSU." Shortly after earning her doctorate, she secured a position as a medical social worker for the Michigan Department of Public Health (MDPH). Widely respected by her peers, she traveled extensively in the United States and abroad, representing MSU and the state at the International Conference of Social Workers in 1966. By the time of her death in 1978, Brunson was still employed by the MDPH and belonged to numerous professional, civic, and social organizations. As the head of the Lansing Family Service Agency remarked about her, "She's always ready to fit into any spot when her help is needed. You can't tell where her casework ends and her compassionate service begins."[10] Though she never held a tenure-system faculty position in East Lansing, Brunson advised and mentored MSC students during and after her graduate career, collaborated with faculty and staff, and participated in many social and academic activities on campus.

As documented in 2012 by Marshanda Smith in "A History of Black Women Faculty at Michigan State University, 1968–2009," between 1968 and 2009, MSU hired ninety-two Black women faculty members (approximately 22 percent of whom were hired between 2001 and 2009). In the late 1960s, when White women comprised about 10 percent of the total tenure-system faculty population, there were two Black women scholars out of approximately two thousand MSU tenure-system faculty. The growth in the number of Black women faculty at MSU was slow and gradual. White women made noticeable gains during the Civil Rights Movement and the 1970s. They were the primary beneficiaries of MSU's early affirmative action initiatives. In 1972, the university completed a major report, "Women at Michigan State University: Positive Action for Equal Opportunity." Six years later, MSU's Department of Human Relations noted, "A measure of progress over the eight-year period can be taken by inspecting our data for women tenure-system faculty."[11]

Between January 1971 and February 1972, 1.6 percent of new hires were "minority women," 7.4 percent were "minority men," and 20.5 percent were "caucasian women." Between the 1962–1963 and 1972–1973 academic years, White women tenure-system faculty increased by about 80 percent, and White women at the rank of full professor increased by 225 percent, from twenty to sixty-five. They were most visible in the Colleges of Human Ecology, Education, and Arts and Letters. In April 1973, 20 percent of White women employed at MSU were in academic positions and .9 percent of Black women were, and "18.4 % of all women in the labor classification" were Black. During the 1970s, the university lumped many of its efforts at recruiting tenure-system White women faculty together with their attempts to attract Black and minority faculty to East Lansing. In February 1973, when minorities constituted about 5 percent of the tenure system faculty, the university created the Office of Minority Programs and the Office of Women's Programs. Working together, in June 1974 they produced a resource guide, "Women and Minority Recruitment," that failed to recognize the distinctly different challenges facing White women and traditionally underrepresented racial and ethnic PhD holders in U.S. higher education. They discovered that a one-size-fits-all approach wasn't viable. Black women didn't benefit from the university's Academic Administrative Program for Women established during the 1973–1974 academic year.[12]

In April 1973, there were seven tenure-system Black women faculty members. In June 1975, nine (3.2 percent) of the 284 women tenure-system faculty and seventeen (5 percent) of the 336 women "temporary faculty" were Black. Two of the sixty-eight women full professors were Black. At least one MSU Board of Trustees member saw this as being problematic. In 1975, Aubrey Radcliffe, the second African American to serve on the board (1973–1981), shared his frustration with the *Grapevine Journal*. "The hiring of Black women is what I really want to see, but I can't get the board or anyone to even discuss it." Radcliffe continued, "MSU is totally lacking in this area, it is thoroughly embarrassing. The area of recruiting black women to the faculty staff is one that has been neglected completely, no one can refute it; it is too obvious."[13]

Three years later, little had changed. Of the 313 women tenure-system faculty members in June 1978, 287 were White and fourteen (4.5 percent) were Black women—two professors, four associate professors, seven assistant professors, and one instructor. Forty-two percent of nonacademic Black women employees fell under the classification of "labor." In 1984, the number of Black women tenure-system faculty reached twenty and by the end of the decade reached thirty. During the 1990s, the number of Black women tenure-system faculty members peaked at thirty-seven in 1992, representing 38.5 percent of the total Black faculty population. The largest number of Black women tenure-system faculty employed at MSU was in 2005 when there were forty-five, a whopping increase of approximately 29 percent from the previous year. Between 2006 and 2016, the Black women faculty decreased by 20 percent, and between 2016 and 2020, they increased by 20 percent, from thirty-six to forty-five.[14]

The experiences and lives of the first identifiable group of Black women faculty at MSU hired between 1968 and 1971 is fascinating. These remarkable women—Ruth Simms Hamilton, Georgia A. Johnson, Patricia Barnes-McConnell, L. Eudora Pettigrew, and Gloria Stephens Smith—overcame various obstacles, barriers Black women routinely encountered in higher education. In their own ways and with their individualized interpretations of respectability politics, they represented Black women on and off campus and helped change MSU's culture. They contributed to the broader Black Freedom Struggle in higher education and to the university's deep tradition of service and outreach. Coming of age as scholars during the tail end of the modern Civil Rights Movement and during the turbulent Black Power era, they were keenly aware of the deeper implications and significance of their presence "on the banks of the Red Cedar."

The vibrant careers of the five notable Black women faculty whom MSU hired between 1968 and 1971 and the efforts of the short-lived Black Women's Employees Association are inspiring. Underappreciated today, these driven and unsparing groundbreakers paved the way for future generations of their sisters in arms who came up against similar roadblocks during their times. It would not be until 1976 when MSU hired the next Black women faculty members, June Manning Thomas and Margaret Aguwa. The university's 1976–1977 affirmative action report intimated that progress was being made, indicating that the number of Black and Spanish-surnamed women holding tenure-stream positions increased. In the remainder of the decade, Dorothy Harper Jones, Frankie J. Brown, Wanda Lipscomb (currently the longest-serving MSU Black woman faculty member followed by Eunice Foster who was hired in 1982), and Bonita Pope Curry joined the MSU faculty community. Revisiting the lives and careers of MSU's first cohort of Black women faculty members provides context for the contemporary status of Black women scholars at MSU and similar PWIs. This story starts with a remarkable scholar.

"Gone is MSU sociologist Ruth Simms Hamilton, who helped awaken the world to the contributions of the African race," the *Lansing State Journal* announced in mid-November 2003. "Hamilton left her students with much to work with" and "demanded much from them." Her former students revered her. "She was doing the work she was told not to do," her indebted advisee Raymond Familusi recalled based upon what his mentor shared with him about her experiences at Northwestern University as a doctoral candidate. Another grateful former student observed, "She wanted to empower people. She was almost a decade ahead of most other academics."[15] Former MSU President Clifton R. Wharton Jr. eulogized: "Trying to capture the spirit of Ruth is a daunting task. There are so many words to describe her approach to life. She was a rare human being whose life made a difference to us all. Her life was a priceless jewel that will always be remembered."[16]

An expert in the study of the vast African diaspora, Ruth Simms Hamilton—MSU's first full-time Black woman faculty member—came to East Lansing in June 1968 from Ames, Iowa, with her husband, Chicago native and Korean War veteran James (PhD, Iowa State University, 1968), who secured a postdoctoral appointment in the Department of Chemistry. With their infant son, they found an apartment at 941 Ann Street, within walking distance from campus. A year after their move from Ames, Ruth and James were appointed assistant professors. The first African American married scholar-couple hired by the university, Ruth and James both worked tirelessly in various capacities in the university, their respective disciplines, and the broader Lansing–East Lansing metropolitan area. In his autobiography, James recalled, "As a young African American family we were a curiosity but also of substantial interest to many African American students. This was doubly the case since we both had Ph.D.s—a rarity. Our home became a regular haven for many undergraduate and graduate African American and African students at Michigan State." Among those student-activists to frequent the Hamilton home were Richard Thomas, Barry Amis, and Ron Bailey.[17]

Early in his career, James had more leadership opportunities than his wife did. With the help of Barbara Gunnings, he directed Project TAC, a tutorial program for students, many of whom were African Americans, "with weak preparation in math or chemistry." He also worked with members of the Black Students in Engineering. Recognized for his dedication to working with diverse groups of traditionally underrepresented students, in 1971 he became an assistant provost of special programs in charge of supportive programming for "educationally disadvantaged" students and those with physical disabilities. Effective January 1, 1973, James was promoted to associate professor, and during the early 1970s, when MSU was piloting and debating the admission of "disadvantaged students" with low test scores, he openly responded to detractors who had little faith in these students. In 1976, he became an assistant dean in the Graduate School, and by the time that he became full professor in 1980, shortly after serving as the director of the Division of Educational Programs for the Argonne National Laboratory, he was named assistant provost for undergraduate education at MSU. Following his death, an award and scholarship were fittingly named in his honor.[18]

One of the nation's first Black women Africanist scholars, Ruth, who attended Talladega College as an undergraduate, earned her PhD in sociology from Northwestern University in 1966. For her dissertation, "Urban Social Differentiation and Membership Recruitment among Selected Voluntary Associations in Accra, Ghana," she conducted nine months of fieldwork in Ghana and interviewed more than five hundred respondents, including members of the National Council of Ghana Women. Hamilton boldly questioned White Africanists' assumptions, disparaging accounts of African urbanization, and closed system approach to characterizing voluntary associations in Africa. An unapologetic revisionist scholar, she stressed the complexity of African urbanization processes and the structures of contemporary African societies. She took pride in her African heritage but didn't root her analysis of modern African social structures in the past. After earning her PhD, she secured a tenure-system position as an assistant professor of sociology and anthropology at Iowa State University while James worked on completing the requirements for his doctorate.

A year after arriving in East Lansing, she was promoted to an assistant professor with a joint appointment in the university's Department of Sociology and the African Studies Center. Many of the African American and African student-activists thought very highly of her. Shortly after she arrived in East Lansing, members of the Black Liberation Front, International and the Pan-African Students Organization in the Americas demanded she be promoted to the position of acting codirector of the African Studies Center. Hamilton was Afrocentric in her orientation. Not only did she sport African clothing from time to time, but in the early 1970s she insisted her family visit Ghana. The trip had a profound impact on her husband who had never visited the motherland. She balanced the duties of motherhood with her career. She traveled to Africa and

Ruth Simms Hamilton. Courtesy of Michigan State University Archives and Historical Collections.

Europe with her children, enrolled them in music classes, and was active in the Brownies and Girl Scouts with her daughter. She and James stressed the value of education to their children.

Though it would be years later in the 1970s when she served in administrative roles as associate director of the African Studies Center and assistant director of the Center for Urban Affairs, the university's executive leadership recognized Hamilton's contributions in other ways. In 1971, she received the prestigious Teacher-Scholar Award. Quite soon thereafter, she was promoted to the rank of associate professor with tenure. In the early 1970s, Hamilton was appointed to a range of university committees. For instance, in June 1973, Wharton appointed Hamilton to the newly created Minority Advisory Council. In addition to her service on several other important university-wide selection committees, in 1980 M. Cecil Mackey appointed Hamilton to a special advisory committee, known as the green-ribbon committee. The eleven distinguished and widely respected faculty members on this committee were charged with the difficult task of helping him develop controversial proposed programmatic cuts. Hamilton and her coworkers understandably endured a fair share of criticism from their faculty colleagues. Hamilton didn't take this critical feedback personally; she was keenly aware of the arduous position she occupied, especially as the only Black woman on the committee. She was one of the university's fourteen Black women faculty members and one of the three Black women full professors. In 1987, she was the keynote speaker for the undergraduate graduation ceremony and six years later was among the many renowned scholars nominated to be the next MSU president, which included lawyer, political scientist, and former Texas senator Barbara Jordan.[19]

Hamilton was active during her long career that spanned thirty-five years, teaching courses in racial and ethnic studies and global dimensions of African-descended peoples. According to her husband, in the 1970s, she "proposed a college built around Black Diasporan Studies, but this idea was rejected by staff in the provost's office." She did successfully create the African Diaspora Research Program in the mid-1980s. By the 1970s, she had developed plans to produce a multivolume study "of the global dispersal and settlement, reaching far beyond the usually noted movement of Blacks in the era of slavery." Leading a group of researchers with similar interests at MSU, she was committed to unearthing what she called in 1979 "communities of consciousness" and "change and conflict" characterizing "the general historical development within a changing global system of political and economic relations." In 1979, she was appointed to an eleven-member Study Commission on U.S. Policy Toward Southern Africa sponsored by the Rockefeller Foundation and spoke out against apartheid. She further honed her skills in leadership and diplomacy, serving on the Board of Trustees for the Carnegie Corporation in New York in the 1980s and from 1989 until her sudden and tragic death in 2003 on the Board of Trustees for the Teachers Insurance and Annuity Association of America (TIAA).[20] Her legacy as a scholar is manifested in the generations of graduate students she mentored and the several volumes of her proposed eleven-volume comprehensive collection, *Routes of Passage: Rethinking the African Diaspora*, that were posthumously published. In 2005, TIAA established the Ruth

Georgia A. Johnson. Courtesy of Michigan State University Archives and Historical Collections.

Simms Hamilton Graduate Merit Fellowship to honor her legacy. The fellowship provides generous support for MSU doctoral students researching subjects pertaining to the expansive African diaspora.

While Hamilton attentively mentored graduate students in researching dimensions of the African diaspora, in 1997 at age sixty-six, retired MD Georgia A. Johnson accomplished another milestone in her action-packed life. The first Black woman hired by the MSU Medical School twenty-eight years prior, she had "raised three career-oriented daughters; two are physicians and the other is an attorney. Johnson then went on to win the 100 meters at the Senior Challenge in September 1996. . . . Johnson now has plenty to keep her busy. Besides training with her new starting blocks and spikes, she began piano lessons last year and will continue her career as a writer."[21] After retiring from MSU in 1985, Johnson, who was later inducted into the Michigan Women's Hall of Fame, welcomed new challenges. This was part of her personal history. Johnson, who had wanted to be a doctor since her early childhood, overcame great odds when she earned her MD degree from the University of Michigan in 1955. She was one of six women in a class of more than two hundred. The Michigan Senior Olympic Games multiwinning gold medalist came from a humble background. One of nine children, she grew up in Van Buren, Michigan, graduated from South Haven High School, and earned a bachelor's degree from Western Michigan University in Kalamazoo where she worked at Borgess Hospital. The university later gave her a Distinguished Alumna Award. In 1969, she reminisced that her success was the result of help she received from her family, Western professors, and others concerned about her wellbeing.

A year after Ruth Simms Hamilton was hired, thirty-nine-year-old Georgia A. Johnson became the first African American woman physician faculty member in the College of Human Medicine with a joint appointment in Olin Health Center. The chairperson of the Department of Medicine questioned her academic credentials and claimed to have been pressured to hire her. Acting president Walter Adams, Robert L. Green, and the dean of the College of Human Medicine actively recruited her. While Hamilton's arrival wasn't met with much fanfare, the *Lansing State Journal* featured a laudatory story on Johnson, announcing "Dr. Georgia A. Johnson, who worked her way from a humble background into the prestigious world of medicine moves now into academe as the first Negro woman physician on the faculty of Michigan State University medical college." Johnson had a wealth of experience. For a year after she graduated from U of M, she was the first Black woman intern and medical staff member at Evanston Hospital in Evanston, Illinois, and then worked at Detroit Receiving (General) Hospital, Wayne County General Hospital, Ypsilanti State Hospital, and the Ingham County Health Department. "As a physician, she moved toward the goal of equal access to medical care and the right of informed consent." A pro-choice advocate, she dedicated a significant amount of time to gynecological counseling.[22]

When she arrived at MSU, her three daughters were ages ten, nine, and seven. Johnson mindfully balanced the duties of motherhood, teaching, research, mentoring, and caring for her patients. She invested much time into cultivating her children's intellectual development. When they attended Post Oak Elementary School, she published a forty-seven-page book of their poetry and drawings. Like those active in Carter G. Woodson's early Black history movement, she firmly believed Black children needed access to books related to their lives. "Not too many books of this sort by black children are published," she observed. After retiring from MSU, Johnson returned to the publishing world, founding Georgia A. Johnson Publishing Co. in 1989 and writing a collection of fiction books during the 1990s, including a historical novel on the Underground Railroad, *Towpath to Freedom* (1990). The amateur historian spent years conducting historical research for this novel, visiting libraries, archives, and actual locations in Canada, Kentucky, and Ohio.[23]

Johnson's retirement in 1985 may have been influenced by her negative experiences at MSU. In 1976, a year after being denied tenure, she filed a suit against the university maintaining she "had been denied promotion and a grant of tenure because of her race, color and sex," that "she suffered administrative indignities and was not given tenure because she was a black female."[24] In her complaint, Johnson charged that the Medical School provided her with no guidelines, never evaluated her performance, retaliated against her for filling formal complaints with the U.S. Equal Opportunity Commission, and, in essence, "made her life miserable." In her mind, how she was treated went counter to the spirit of the university's affirmative action program that facilitated her employment. The first three years of her appointment went fairly smoothly. At her third-year review, the chair of the Department of Medicine recommended her reappointment, observing that she performed her job "faithfully and effectively." By the early 1970s, her relationship with the chair began deteriorating. She felt like an "outsider" and a casualty of discrimination. She refused to be silenced, registering complaints with the department as well as the Michigan Civil Rights Department and the U.S. Equal Opportunity Commission. In mid-April 1975, the chair informed Johnson her appointment would be terminated effective July 1 because she had purportedly not met the department's loosely defined expectations. Johnson appealed the decision, and the University Appeals Panel, of which Lee June was a member, sided with her, concluding she had not in fact been provided with annual evaluations nor afforded the protections of the "Statement of Non-Tenured Faculty." They ruled she be granted an additional three-year appointment as an assistant professor with detailed guidelines for tenure and promotion. Johnson refused to sign the revised memorandum of understanding. She resigned from her position as a tenure-system faculty member and worked full-time at the Olin Health Center for the next decade.

The case dragged on for more than five years, finally going to trial between late August and late December of 1981 in Lansing. Significant parts of the testimonies during the proceedings suggest Johnson's complaints were substantiated. Prepared for the character assassinations that awaited her, she kept meticulous records of her alleged mistreatment. During the trial, her White male colleagues, including the chair, reinforced the stereotype of the "angry Black woman," describing her as being "not receptive to constructive criticism," "unwilling to accept advice," "at odds" with others, and "abrasive, intimidating and authoritarian." The court determined plaintiff Johnson "failed to meet her burden of proof on her Title VII claim." In 1982, Judge Douglas Woodruff Hillman of the U.S. District Court for the Western District of Michigan upheld the decision, asserting that Johnson's termination had nothing to do with her sex or color and that Johnson's allegations that she, in particular, was kept in the dark about the tenure and promotion expectations and requirements were "without merit." Hillman did, however, acknowledge that the Department of Medicine failed to provide her with annual performance evaluations, conceding she established "a prima facie case of discrimination." He also accepted the university's explanation that the department had an overall laissez-faire attitude toward the tenure and promotion process and that Johnson was in no way singled out because of her sex or race.

The second MSU Black woman faculty member had a remarkable career despite the mistreatment she endured and her ensuing decision to resign from her tenure-system position five years after relocating to East Lansing. These experiences probably influenced Johnson to embark on a book project on the "problems of prejudice" faced by African American medical school graduates from the era of Reconstruction through 1960.[25] The challenges Johnson encountered at MSU were and are not unique. As scores of journal articles, scholarly monographs, op-eds, personal testimonies, and edited anthologies have revealed, Black women scholars have historically faced disproportionate discrimination and injustices in higher education when it comes to tenure and promotion. In May 2021, the well-publicized decision of the University of North Carolina at Chapel Hill to offer Pulitzer prize–winning journalist Nikole Hannah-Jones a five-year position without tenure sparked great debate and controversy. Black scholars, in particular, have expressed their outrage. Hannah-Jones's defenders mobilized, circulated petitions, and blasted the Twittersphere, accusing UNC of discriminating against her because of her *New York Times* "1619 Project," outspokenness, and race and gender. Unlike Hannah-Jones, Black women academics of Johnson's generation more often than not had very few publicly come to their defense. During the early 1970s, Johnson's Black women colleagues may not have endured the hardships she did in East Lansing, but they still had to put their White colleagues on notice about their legitimacy as scholars.

In January 1971, a heated discussion took place at an East Lansing School Board meeting about how the ninety-minute lunch hour should be coordinated. Parents of the elementary schoolchildren in the Bailey School district were required to pick up their kids during lunchtime. "At least a third of the parents" were in favor of having their children eat at school, "brown bag" style. By and large, the teachers, custodians, and principals opposed this proposal for a range of sensible reasons. They claimed it would be difficult to accommodate and supervise the children in the school's limited facilities, that children tended to be "more tired and unruly if they stay at school for lunch," and that teachers and custodians would be overworked. The members of the Bailey School Parent-Teacher Association, on the other hand, argued that working mothers and parents who "lived quite a distance" from the Bailey neighborhood would benefit from the new arrangement. One of the only African Americans at this meeting, Patricia Barnes-McConnell, "a newcomer to this community," made her presence and strong opinions known. "Baffled to learn that education is approached on such a piecemeal basis," she accused the school leaders who opposed the PTA's proposal of showing no concern for working mothers' and children's well-being. In her estimation, the lunch hour could serve as a useful "time for social development," filling "a need in youngsters' growth."[26] Barnes-McConnell was more knowledgeable than those in the room on the complex subject of early childhood development.

At the time, this developmental psychologist was completing her dissertation, "Studies of Cognitive Development in Early Infancy," at the Ohio State University. In 1971, about a year before she earned her PhD, the MSU Board of Trustees approved the hiring of Barnes-McConnell as an instructor in the Center for Urban Affairs. Several years later, her husband, David G. McConnell, was appointed professor of biomechanics and biochemistry with tenure and Patricia's appointment as an assistant professor was transferred to Urban and Metropolitan Studies. Two and a half decades later, she had produced an impressive body of scholarship and became a recognizable authority in her field, especially on issues pertaining to the causes and alleviation of poverty.

Her participation in the debates about the lunch hour in the Bailey School district fore-shadowed the tenor of her future community work. During the 1970s, Barnes-McConnell participated in various programs and initiatives in the East Lansing and Greater Lansing area communities. As member of the East Lansing Human Relations Commission, she took the lead in creating the Buddy Family program, an initiative seeking to help newcomers adjust to life in East Lansing. She often spoke to Mid-Michiganders about pressing issues, such as the challenges facing minority populations and equal access to health services. In 1975, she was appointed to the East Lansing School Board's Citizen's Advisory Committee on School Enrollments and the state of Michigan's Health Planning Advisory Council. In 1977, she served as the chairperson of the board of trustees for the Michigan Mid-South Health System Agency as well as an appointee to the state's newly created Juvenile Justice Services Commission. She was especially concerned with the conditions and well-being of African Americans and conducted extensive research on health disparities and race, attributing premature higher death rates in Black communities to environmental and stress factors. "It is amazing to me that there are any (nonwhite) old folks left at all," she remarked in 1977; "by continually helping in the socialization of children, by telling stories, passing along old sayings and putting today's stresses in a broader historical context, the old generation can do a lot to help the younger ones learn to survive."[27] Barnes-McConnell's analyses of the existing data revealed if Blacks in Michigan lived to be fifty, they had strong chances of outliving their White counterparts. Her findings were striking enough to receive coverage in an issue of the widely read *Jet* magazine.[28]

On campus, Barnes-McConnell was recognized as a leader. During the 1980s, she served as the coordinator of the Office of Women in International Development, and in 1984, the MSU Board of Trustees named her to the thirteen-person presidential search committee following the resignation of President Mackey. She was one of the two faculty members serving on this important and time-consuming committee. Beginning during the 1980s, Barnes-McConnell also worked in the university's International Institute of Agriculture and directed a $3 million project that involved other land grant universities and agricultural research institutions seeking to help developing countries increase the consumption of beans and black-eyed peas.[29] From 1983 until she retired in 2001 as professor in the Department of Resource Development in the College of Agriculture and Natural Resources, Barnes-McConnell served as the director of the Bean/Cowpea Collaborative Research Support Program.

An accomplished scholar like Barnes-McConnell, Pettigrew faced a different set of challenges navigating MSU. "I am reminded of another case of sexism and racism facing MSU's first black woman full professor, Eudora Pettigrew," reminisced professor of human ecology Verna Hildebrand in 1991. "She had to file a grievance to get promoted to full professor! Her

L. Eudora Pettigrew mentors a student. Courtesy of Michigan State University Archives and Historical Collections.

later candidacy for associate provost was rejected. Apparently, being a black woman at MSU, she had to be more than twice as good. However she soon became the president of a SUNY university."³⁰ Hildebrand's comment that Pettigrew had to be "twice as good" was something Black women scholars and faculty at MSU and other PWIs knew all too well before, during, and after Pettigrew's time in East Lansing. Pettigrew was keenly aware of this reality and often spoke about the adversity encountered by women in higher education. In 1973, several years after Pettigrew arrived in East Lansing, a journalism and public relations major and writer for the *Grapevine Journal*, Joyce Conway, celebrated Pettigrew, describing her as "an excellent example of what a woman who makes up her mind to be independent can do." Pettigrew shared with Conway and *Grapevine* readers her disappointment with the MSU administration's treatment of Black women faculty members. "I have learned to make it on my own. Like most other Black women, I would like to see strong Black men who could be leaned on, but not at the expense of her own individuality and independence." Pettigrew attested, "the contributions that Black women can make and have made are great and there is no reason why they should be pushed aside. To be Black is to be discriminated against, but to be Black and female is to be discriminated against with contempt."[31]

Born in Hopkinsville, Kentucky, in 1928, Pettigrew earned a bachelor of music degree from West Virginia State College in 1950, an MA degree in rehabilitation counseling from Southern Illinois University in 1963, and a PhD in educational psychology from Southern Illinois in 1966. With experience in teaching in public schools, she began her scholarly career as an assistant professor of psychology and education at the University of Bridgeport in Connecticut. She was a scholar-activist, consulting on a range of community-based projects. The local NAACP presented her an award for her civil rights pursuits. During her four years at Bridgeport, she was a productive scholar, accomplished enough that in 1970 MSU hired her as an associate professor in the Center for Urban Affairs and the College of Education. With the exception of the director and associate director, she was the college's highest paid faculty member. Immediately after arriving on campus, others appreciated her leadership abilities and potential. In June 1971, Governor William Milliken appointed her to the fifteen-member Michigan Women's Commission to replace a member who suddenly retired.[32] Pettigrew was an excellent choice. At the time, she counseled the Michigan Education Association and had just completed Teacher Corps, a program seeking to improve communication between parents and teachers. Much of her research centered on women's roles in U.S. society.

Pettigrew made it crystal clear she wasn't interested in being a token representative on the Michigan Women's Commission. "If the commission is window-dressing, I'll probably resign," Pettigrew proclaimed after her initial appointment. "If it's going to work for better living and working conditions for people, I'll be most happy to serve." Pettigrew believed women needed to be valued beyond their roles in the domestic sphere. "I've been a wife and I am a mother—but women can do much more." Months later, she accepted a full three-year term, but not without vocalizing her concern with the lack of resources given to the commission and her colleagues' apathy. "There are a lot of things that I don't like, but I am going to stay and fight," Pettigrew told a *Lansing State Journal* reporter. Her primary concerns included women's underrepresentation in the Department of Labor, feeble legislative reform, and issues surrounding no-fault divorce and maternity leaves. She called for diversifying the commission, which she labeled "pretty much upper middle class [White] professionals." Pettigrew expressed skepticism toward Equal Rights Amendment legislation and didn't believe legislation alone would change women's status in U.S. society. "It may be theoretically, but I can't see that (any amendment) has made change in people's values and actions." In May 1972, endorsed by the liberal Project City Hall who called her "a person of energy and credentials," Pettigrew ran for a four-year term on the East Lansing Board of Education. Conservatives swept the election. Pettigrew garnered 1,474 of the votes cast, coming in fourth.[33]

Troubled with the plight faced by women in U.S. society, Pettigrew was especially outspoken about Black women's status during the Women's Liberation Movement. In August 1974, she presented a paper on the topic, "Women's Liberation and Black Women," at the annual conference of the Association of Black Psychologists. Labeling this campaign a "counter force to the civil rights movement," Pettigrew maintained her sisters encountered more predicaments in the workplace and domestic sphere and called out Black leaders for ignoring this. Speaking about the mistreatment of Black domestic workers and the lack of protective laws for them, Pettigrew declared, "No civil rights leaders or black women rose to speak out against such legislation. . . . Yet these laws affect black women more than anyone." Employing an intersectional analysis, Pettigrew deduced that "sexism interacts with racism," that Black men undervalued Black women in the struggle against racism, and that White women marginalized Black women in the fight against sexism. "The increased assertion of the black male is often interpreted to mean liberating the black male at the expense of the black woman."[34]

Throughout the 1970s, Pettigrew balanced her career as a productive researcher and scholar with her civic undertakings in the Greater Lansing area. In the mid-1970s, she convened public hearings as chair of the Ingham County Equal Opportunity Program. She remained committed to working toward tangible reform, accepting nothing less. In 1977, the consistently skeptical Pettigrew, who had just been named the head of Urban and Metropolitan Studies in the College for Urban Affairs, refused to accept a certificate of appreciation from Ingham County officials for her three and a half years of commitment to the Equal Opportunity Program. She defiantly returned the certificate, calling the program a "farce." "It is my feeling that Ingham County has entertained no serious thought about equal opportunity for Ingham County residents," she charged. "I, personally, cannot allow my integrity to be denigrated in this manner and it is for this reason that I requested that I not be reappointed to the Ingham County Equal Opportunity Program Committee. My national reputation in equal opportunity is too important to me to allow it to be misused by actions which are not in support of equity for American citizens." This seems to have been one of the turning points in Pettigrew's discontent with being in Michigan. She was a transformational leader whose creativity and vision was too unconventional for many of her coworkers. Though she acknowledged "we know we have a ways to go in this area," her colleague Debbie Stabenow had a hard time understanding the disposition of her Black woman coworker.[35] Like others, she learned that Pettigrew wasn't the type of African American spokesperson willing to simply accept the honorific status as an exceptional Black race representative. Pettigrew continued to be active in local politics as a member of the Michigan Employment and Training Council. In 1978–1979, she also chaired the state of Michigan's legislative task force on spouse abuse.

As chair of the Department of Urban and Metropolitan Studies in the College of Urban Development, she spoke out about the challenges faced by African American students. In response to the drastic decline in the number of Black students pursuing graduate degrees at MSU during the mid- to late 1970s (in 1976, there were 151 Black doctorate students enrolled, and in 1979, there were 111), Pettigrew opined that Black women applying for graduate study in fields "not traditionally pursued by blacks" were often "put through admission procedures other than usual." Pettigrew was frustrated by the university's lack of specific recruitment and retention programs for talented Black graduate students. "It makes no sense," she maintained. "It's a travesty to admit foreign students who can't even speak the language to graduate school, and not help our own black and minority students." Pettigrew was not a nativist. She supported the recruitment of international graduate students while also believing domestic African American and traditionally underrepresented graduate students deserved to be afforded "the same rights."[36]

By the late 1970s, as a department chair with aspirations of being a provost, Pettigrew was ready to take her talents elsewhere. She cultivated skills that would serve her in future leadership roles. In late 1980, she was appointed full professor in the College of Urban Affairs and Public Policy and associate provost for instruction at the University of Delaware. Though she wasn't involved in agricultural work at America's first agricultural college, one of her first innovative plans in the mid-Atlantic was to introduce urban farming to create new jobs and help beautify the so-called inner city. In June 1986, Pettigrew made history again when the State University of New York at Old Westbury appointed her president. She became the "first black woman to be a college president in New York's 64-campus university system." Six months after arriving on campus, she began shaking things up. "Make Way for Minorities, Black SUNY President Says," read a headline in the *Press and Sun-Bulletin* (Binghamton, New York) in early December 1986. Speaking to a large crowd at a conference at SUNY at Binghamton, she argued that colleges and universities, including her own, need to "be more open and concerned about students we have traditionally ignored in the past." She critiqued the U.S. secretary of education for what she considered his elitist vision of education. Even as a college president, Pettigrew didn't shy away from "speaking truth to power." Her college and university president colleagues respected her. She held leadership positions in the International Association of University Presidents (IAUP) and strove to promote disarmament, conflict resolution, and peace throughout the world. As an IAUP spokesperson, she traveled to different corners of the globe. After retiring in 1998, she continued to share her opinions with the public. In the early 2000s, she penned several editorials for the *New Journal* (Wilmington, Delaware). In a 2001 piece about the deeper implications of Black History Month, she provided a methodical roadmap for how White Americans could benefit from this annual commemoration. "Do all you can to eliminate racism and prejudice and do it publicly," she declared. These were indeed words that guided how Pettigrew lived her own life.[37]

"Gloria Smith is the prime architect of the counseling-minority students conferences at Michigan State University. A contributing author to professional journals and periodicals, she is program director for the Urban Counseling Program in the College of Education, president of the Lansing Alumnae Chapter of Alpha Kappa Alpha Sorority, Inc. and chairwoman of the Education Committee for the Greater Lansing Urban League and the NAACP Freedom Fund Program Committee."[38] In 1977, when Pettigrew chaired a department at MSU, this is what a staff writer for the *Lansing State Journal* wrote about Gloria Stephens Smith who had recently received a prestigious local award. Smith had been honored before. Three years earlier, she had received an award and standing ovation at the second National Conference on Counseling Minorities for her distinctive contributions and steadfast commitment to the advancement of minorities through educational and counseling activities. The award she received in 1977 was different. In September, Smith was one of eleven Lansing area women to receive a resolution, certificate, and custom-made pendant for her noteworthy accomplishments as an industrious MSU professor and devout community activist. Established in 1975 and named after the Roman goddess who embodied dedication and strength, the Diana Award was sponsored by the Greater Lansing YWCA to honor the achievements and leadership of women from various walks of life. Smith was in good company at the second awards ceremony held at MSU's Kellogg Center. MSU alumna Debbie Stabenow, the first woman to head the Ingham County Commission, also received the honor. Though several Black women—self-sacrificing educator Eva Evans, and director of the Lansing Model Cities program, Jacqueline Warr—were presented with this award two years earlier, Smith was the first Black woman MSU professor Diana Award recipient.[39] Smith was certainly a woman who had made notable contributions to her field and was recognized as a leader in her community.

Born in Cleveland, Ohio, in mid-April 1937, Gloria Stephens developed an interest in music as a youngster. When she was in elementary school, her parents noticed her talents and enrolled her in music lessons with an organist from their church. For several years, she routinely made the trip to her strict instructor's home for private lessons. Her love of music gave her the courage to cope with the cockroaches that lined the ceiling of her tutor's humble home. Young Gloria excelled at the piano and viola and as a sixth grader began taking lessons from a member of the renowned Cleveland Orchestra. Like famous Harlem Renaissance poet Langston Hughes, she took classes, attended programs, and performed at the Karamu House, the oldest African American theater founded in 1915 on Cleveland's east side by two Oberlin College graduates as the Playhouse Settlement. Recognized as a historic site by the U.S. federal government, the theater was the epicenter of Cleveland's Black cultural renaissance. In the early 1950s, Smith participated in and was shaped by this movement, and while she was in high school, her musical accomplishments were covered in local newspapers.[40]

After graduating from John Adams High School, she was offered a full music scholarship from "one of the first colleges in the nation to admit students without regard to race or gender," Baldwin Wallace University in Berea, Ohio. Without visiting campus before moving into her comfortable dorm room suite, Smith decided to enroll in Miami University in Oxford, Ohio, the second oldest university in the state founded in 1809. She accepted a prestigious scholarship from the university's alumni association. She recalls that when she arrived on campus, university officials were surprised to discover the exceptional student and pianist they accepted was Black. At Miami, Smith continued her music career, performing throughout the state as the sole African

American member of the university's Women's Choral Society and Young Artists Guild. One of the very few Black students on campus, during her senior year she served as the president of the Women's Choral Society, further honing skills of interacting with White people that would later help her navigate MSU.

Music and the arts were not Smith's only calling. Minoring in music and mathematics, she majored in elementary education. She had heard stories about her maternal grandfather who was a Baptist minister and a teacher at an HBCU in South Carolina and felt compelled to carry on his tradition. Her decision had other influences as well. In 2021, she recalled she wanted to become an educator because she never had any Black teachers. After earning her MA degree from Miami University and working briefly as a teacher counselor and administrator in the Cleveland public school system, in 1971 she earned a PhD in education with a specialization in educational psychology from the University of Massachusetts at Amherst. Her dissertation, "An Integrated Sex Education Program for Urban Schools: Implications for Guidance and Counseling," revealed her early interests and expertise in educational reform in urban Black communities. She built upon this project when she chaired the National Conferences on Counseling Minorities at MSU during the 1970s. While completing her dissertation, Smith gained valuable experience teaching in White settings. She taught and served as the director of the Counseling Center and the Psychological Study Center at Mount Holyoke College, a private women's liberal arts college in South Hadley, Massachusetts. Though in 1960 educational psychologist Frances M. Kerr became the college's first Black professor, Smith was one of the very few African American instructors on campus during the Black Power era. She was on campus during a tense time in the college's history of race relations. In 1968, the recently founded Afro-American Society organized a sit-in, and a year later their meeting place mysteriously burned down and the college responded by launching a small Black Studies program.

In about 1970, Smith presented a paper based upon her dissertation project at a conference sponsored by the mainstream American Personnel and Guidance Association (renamed the American Association for Counseling and Development in 1983). A senior MSU faculty member in attendance was impressed by her research trajectory and recruited her as a part of the university's recently developed efforts to hire more Black faculty. Smith recalls that the on-campus interview process was unusually intense and long. She impressed her soon-to-be colleagues. In the summer of 1971, newly minted Dr. Smith accepted a position as assistant professor in the MSU Counseling Center and for special services for disadvantaged students in the provost's office. As she articulated in a 1974 presentation, "Counseling for a Lifetime," her philosophy was straightforward. "Counselors cannot be content to maintain a personality 'fix-it' shop but must work to improve society which inflicts injury to minority persons at an early age and aggravates the injury throughout life," Smith declared; "the counselor must prevent any minority person from being treated or feeling inferior in this society." She had other more demanding concerns while innovating counseling at MSU.[41]

Gloria Smith. Courtesy of Michigan State University Archives and Historical Collections.

"When I came to Michigan State," Smith recalled in 2021, "I was concerned about raising my sons." The fourth tenure-system Black woman faculty member, Smith, a determined single mother, balanced the daily grind of raising her twin sons, who were in kindergarten when she came to MSU, with the rigors of being a professor, counselor, and community activist. She found a supportive community among Black faculty and in the Friendship Baptist Church. She was an unpretentious mover and shaker. Like her Black women community activist predecessors during the modern Civil Rights Movement, Smith often humbly worked behind the scenes. With little fanfare and for close to four decades, she committed herself to serving generations of traditionally underrepresented and underserved students, Black women's humanity, and the community she considered home. In recognition of her achievements, she received the MSU All University Professor's Excellence Award for Teaching, Research, and Service. Beginning early in her career, she was active in the field of counseling at a national level. She was among the Black scholars who helped create the Association for Non-White Concerns in Personnel and Guidance (ANWC), a division of the American Personnel and Guidance Association (APGA) founded in 1972 with the purpose of representing "non-Whites" in the field while striving to eliminate prejudice and discrimination. Following the founding of ANWC, the minority membership of the APGA tripled. In October 1972, the ANWC launched its journal, the *Journal of Non-White Concerns* under Smith's editorship, and from 1974 until 1975, Smith served as the association's second president. Leadership development was central to the association's formative years, and Smith contributed to this tradition.[42]

A key component of Smith's teaching and service was mentoring students. Among those to benefit from her counsel and support was Wanda Lipscomb. Born Wanda Elizabeth Dean in Richmond, Virginia, in 1953, Lipscomb is one of the first dozen Black women faculty members hired by MSU. She earned a BA in mathematics from the oldest degree-granting HBCU in the United States, Lincoln University in Chester County, Pennsylvania. After earning her MA in psychology from the Minority Mental Health Program at Washington University in St. Louis, Missouri, she pursued a PhD in counseling psychology at MSU. She was recruited to MSU by Smith to join the PhD program in Urban Psychology, a joint program housed in the College of Education and the College of Urban Development. Smith oversaw this program that sought to "train specialists" in "the context of the relevant issues" facing African Americans in urban communities. The goal, Smith believed, "is to produce counselors who are able to effectively meld research and counseling techniques in order to rehabilitate people, systems, and problem situations." Central to the training of Lipscomb and her peers were "practical field experiences with urban residents and in a variety of urban settings." Lipscomb embraced her mentor's philosophy.[43]

As a doctoral student advised by the "super-organized" Smith, Lipscomb was active in the Association of Black Psychologists and the Black Student Psychological Association and published several articles promoting a Black-centered psychology. Calling upon Black psychologists to develop their own distinct approaches, she beseeched her colleagues to be committed to their communities. "We cannot expect the white institutions to solve our problems; we must take the initiative to solve our own problems," she asserted in a 1977 article. "As professionals we are challenged to free the minds of our people and to help them deal with the world in which we live. We must join forces—for the time to act is now!" In 1978, Lipscomb completed her dissertation, a study that embodied the Urban Counseling Program's vision, "The Effect of an in-Service Training Program in Systemic Management on the Decision Making Skills of Counselor Supervisors in the Detroit Public School System." Lipscomb followed in her adviser's footsteps by securing a position with MSU. She is currently the longest-serving Black woman tenure-system faculty member who for more than forty years has been committed to diversity, equity, and inclusion initiatives like her former adviser. Under the presidency of Samuel L. Stanley Jr., she gracefully cochaired the historic MSU Diversity, Equity, and Inclusion Steering Committee. Reflecting upon Smith, Lipscomb noted that she was the "only Black women faculty member she saw" and interacted with "all of the time." Setting high expectations and stressing that there were "no easy ways out," Smith routinely told Lipscomb to "never live without a grant," set goals and work hard, and create networks outside of MSU.[44]

Lipscomb's mentor Smith retired in 2007 as one of the longest-serving Black professors in the history of Michigan State. On the eve of her retirement, as interim director of the African American and African Studies (AAAS) PhD program, she resurrected an interdisciplinary unit by recruiting, retaining, and supporting cohorts of African American graduate students, mobilizing faculty and encouraging cross-generational dialogues, and operationalizing the National Council of Black Studies' mission of promoting "academic excellence and social responsibility." An elder statesperson with an unparalleled knowledge of MSU's complex inner workings, she mustered up resources to support AAAS and worked closely with graduate students. In March 2006, with Sankofa, the program's graduate student association, she organized a state-of-the-art conference, "The Black Scholar and the State of Black America." In the same year, she also launched her beloved annual Black Religion and Spirituality in the Twenty-First Century conference. Such activities were nothing new to Smith's vast portfolio. She embarked upon this type of organizing shortly after arriving in East Lansing. In the years before and shortly after receiving the Diana Award, Smith coordinated and presided over major conferences on campus, played a leading role in the graduate urban counseling program, and served as the founding editor of the scholarly journal in her field. She spoke out about issues from "Domestic Violence and Neglect" to "the plight of (Black) urban dwellers" to the rights of Black women and children, collaborated with her colleagues on a range of projects, ran for the East Lansing School Board, and held key leadership positions in several African American organizations—including the Association for Non-White Concerns in Personnel and Guidance (renamed the Association for Multicultural Counseling and Development), the Advisory Committee of the Cleveland Job Corps Center for Youth, the National Conference on Counseling Minorites, and the Delta Tau Omega chapter of Alpha Kappa Alpha Sorority, Inc.[45]

Several months after Smith arrived in East Lansing, she partnered with other Black women on campus to create the first-of-its-kind Black Women Employees Association of Michigan State University (BWEA). In less than no time at all after the organization's founding, on November 19, 1971, the BWEA, represented by Patricia Barnes-McConnell, met with President Wharton and the MSU Board of Trustees, presenting them with a "statement regarding the status of Black women employees, which included inequities in employment of faculty, administrative-professional and clerical technical personnel of Michigan State University." The association asked President Wharton and the board to "rectify these inequities" by (1) promoting Black women to "positions of authority," (2) recruiting Black women "in all colleges and units of the University, not limited to the traditional areas of female employment," (3) hiring more Black women into the tenure system, and (4) "conferring of tenure to Black women." Trustees Patricia Carrigan, Warren Huff, and Blanche Martin were sympathetic toward Barnes-McConnell's pleas. The only African American on the board, Martin urged "the University undertake a program similar to the successful one instituted a few years ago for the recruitment of Black faculty."[46] In early 1972, the BWEA elected officers. Gloria S. Smith was the coordinator, and Josephine Wharton (no relation to President Wharton) was the public relations director. Other officers included "Mrs. Beverly Holman, food services manager at Wonders Hall cafeteria, secretary; Mrs. Louise Taylor, food services supervisor at Landon Hall, budget officer." There were twelve members of the board—Barnes-McConnell, Margaret Gamble, Laura Henderson, Joanne Collins, Delores Reed, Ann Graves, Sandra Watts, Elsie Whitmire, Cynthia Garnett, Corean Scott, Vera White, and Verna Bradley. In anticipation of the letter they planned to send to President Wharton and the board in late February, on February 10, 1972, skilled leader, organizer, and publicist Josephine Wharton told a *Lansing State Journal* reporter that "about 330 women" belonged to the association.[47] In other words, she declared that all Black women employees were active in the organization.

Wharton was an ideal BWEA spokesperson. Born Josephine Henrietta Jeffries in the small city of Niles, Michigan, in 1915, "Jo"—as she was called by her friends during her teenage years—graduated from Niles High School in the early years of the Great Depression. At age twenty-one, she married Rollin Ferguson and lived in Lansing, working as a stenographer. Josephine became active in the Lansing branch of the NAACP in her twenties and in 1946 became the organization's secretary under the presidency of W. Rankin Lewis. Several years later, she began her career at Michigan State as secretary of the Christian Student Foundation, an interdenominational and interracial group supported by East Lansing's Peoples Church. She was also active in the Alpha Theta chapter of Iota Phi Lambda, the first Black business sorority founded in 1929, and during the 1940s and 1950s she was highly involved in the Lansing NAACP and the Lincoln Community Center.

A year after Wharton was hired as secretary in the College of Education, becoming the first Black woman to hold such a position at Michigan State, in 1959 Josephine became president of the Lansing NAACP and held the position for two terms. She had big shoes to fill, succeeding Stuart Dunnings Jr. Josephine was active during the civil rights era. Named "assistant leader" and secretary of Lansing's Human Relations Commission in 1963, Wharton was outspoken in her commitment to ending discrimination. In the early 1960s, she fought for equal employment and housing rights for African Americans. "Too long have our city fathers turned deaf ears to the requests of minorities," she wrote in a *Lansing State Journal* editorial in 1963. Following the bombing of the 16th Street Baptist Church in Birmingham, Alabama, she helped establish a restoration fund for her southern brothers and sisters. A supporter of the Black Arts Movement and member of the Ingham County Democratic Women, during the Black Power era she continued to call upon others to make Lansing, according to her one of the "troubled cities throughout the nation" in terms of race relations, "a city of peace and harmony." In 1972, the MSU Board of Trustees appointed her to serve as the coordinator for women and minority training programs, and President Wharton selected her to serve on the Presidential Women's Steering Committee as a representative for administrative and professional women. As celebrated in the *MSU News Bulletin*, she was an outspoken advocate for secretaries and women support staff. With fifteen other women, Josephine was charged with designing and recommending "a permanent structure which could advise Michigan State University on the status of women at the institution." Her service on this committee exposed her further to the deeply rooted inequities experienced by

Josephine Ferguson Wharton. Courtesy of Michigan State University Archives and Historical Collections.

Black women at the university, and she challenged White women on the committee to adopt intersectionality.[48]

With Josephine leading the organization's messaging, several months after their first meeting with the Board of Trustees, on February 25, 1972, the BWEA sent a detailed follow-up letter to President Wharton and the board. After reiterating their initial set of charges, they sketched out a brief history of Black women employees, emphasizing that it took the institution a very long time, more than a century, to hire a Black woman professor and "for a Black woman to attain faculty or academic status as an assistant instructor." They were lucid, critical, and bold in their summary. Highlighting that they faced "racial discrimination as well as sex discrimination," they declared:

> Our research has revealed some very questionable employment and promotional practices at this land-grant, state-sponsored institution. Why is it that a capable, qualified Black woman with a background in business training was hired in 1943 as a housekeeper in one of the dormitories and retired in 1970, 27 years later, still employed at the same level? . . . Black women are tired of being overqualified, underemployed, underpaid and excluded from positions with promotional opportunities. All forms of discrimination at this University against Black women must cease! . . . There is absolutely no reason for this University to maintain this status quo. The only alternative is to correct these inequities and effect progressive change for the benefit of the entire University. When the minority is benefited, the majority becomes a beneficiary. The creation of a system of inequities involves carefully-calculated, deliberate and contributory efforts on the part of those in positions of decision making and policy implementation. Therefore, the establishment of an effective and stable system to provide and maintain a climate of equity in employment throughout the University is the responsibility of you, the Governing Board of Michigan State University.[49]

Like the Black student-activists with which they collaborated, BWEA gave the board a long list of recommendations, including the creation of an administrative position to be filled by a Black woman in charge of recruiting, supporting, and promoting "Black personnel at all levels of employment"; the establishment of high-profile administrative positions for Black women, "in-service training opportunities" for Black women, and programs for (White) supervisors and managers to create "better human relations throughout the University as it particularly pertains to the employment of Black women"; and the representation of Black women in the Office of the Vice President for Student Affairs and the residence halls. They concluded with an overall directive: "At this time we again charge you, Members of the Board of Trustees of this State institution of higher learning to specifically designate the necessary percentile of new positions to Black women to effectively increase the overall percentage of Black women to a minimum of 12 percent at all levels of employment."[50]

BWEA's demands and recommendations were not taken very seriously by President Wharton or the board. Seven months after BWEA submitted its list of recommendations, the *Lansing State Journal* publicized their efforts in a fairly lengthy article, "MSU Black Women Refuse Token Status." They encouraged the Women's Steering Committee to include several of their demands in the report they completed on June 1, 1972.[51] The only two Black women on the committee, BWEA officers Wharton and Verna Bradley, directly challenged their White colleagues to highlight the plight of minority and Black women in the final report. In part because of the consciousness-raising efforts of BWEA as well as Black students' demands for more Black faculty after the assassination of King, the number of Black women faculty members at MSU gradually increased by 100 percent between 1972 and the end of the decade, from seven to fourteen. Between 1979 and 1982, the number of Black women faculty increased by 50 percent. During the 1980s, about a dozen Black women professors joined the MSU faculty—Carrie B. Jackson, Eunice F. Foster, Linda S. Beard, Ida J. Stockman, Denise Troutman, Lauren S. Young, Julia R. Miller, Darlene Clark Hine, Ruby Perry Felton, Georgia Padonu, Patricia Edwards, and Geneva Smitherman. In 1989, five Black women were hired, and by 1990, there were thirty-two Black women tenure-system faculty. A decade later, in 2000, there were thirty-four Black women faculty members.[52]

As a formal organization, BWEA faded away during the early 1970s. One of their last initiatives was a banquet they put together for twenty Black retirees, mainly women, with the Black Faculty and Administrators Association (BFAA) in the summer of 1972. Gloria S. Smith took the lead in organizing the event with Tom Gunnings, president of BFAA. "I didn't realize you would find what we were doing so important," Smith said to me, chuckling a bit, during one of our long conversations fifty years after BWEA's founding. Smith is what historian Lerone Bennett Jr. would have called "living history." Her and others' work with this avant-gardist on-campus Black women's organization, as short-lived as it was, represented and symbolized the power in Black women's deep tradition of mobilizing to address the double and triple oppression they faced, and still do, in higher education and American society. Though during the turbulent Black Power era they might not have recognized their history-making, the members of the Black Women's Employees Association pressured the university's leadership to live up to its democratic ideals, aspirations that President Wharton routinely evoked.

Chapter 40

A Historic Presidency

Amid substantiated rumors that President John A. Hannah was contemplating leaving his beloved MSU for a federal position in Washington, D.C., on February 7, 1969, vice chairman of the House Democratic caucus David S. Holmes Jr., D-Detroit, boldly called upon the MSU Board of Trustees to "name a black man" as the university's longest serving president's successor. In his letter to the board, parts of which the *Lansing State Journal* reprinted immediately under the attention-grabbing title "Negro Successor to Hannah Urged," he wrote: "I would like to express a concern on behalf of the black people and other minority groups of Michigan that the Board of Trustees give extremely careful consideration to the choosing of a successor and that the board choose a man who is equipped to respond to the demands of our revolutionary times." Holmes continued, "I submit that there are a number of blacks in this nation who meet these qualifications and that they should be given serious consideration."[1]

Three months later, others indirectly discussed the prospects of a Black president at MSU. "You must have a man who has enough insight to legitimate problems students raise and can understand them with enough courage to respond," Senator Coleman Young opined in May 1969; "on most campuses there is discrimination and legitimate grievances that demand an answer." Young added, "if the new president were black, he would have to be a man of great courage." Black student-activists were more direct in calling for Black leadership. LaMarr Thomas, the Black Students' Alliance representative on the presidential search committee, endorsed political scientist and coauthor of *Black Power: The Politics of Liberation* Charles Hamilton and Nathan Hare, the director of the Black Studies program at San Francisco State College. ASMSU cabinet vice-president for the Office of Black Affairs Stan McClinton believed Ron Lee, "a man of integrity," would have made an ideal president.[2]

A little less than a year later, Holmes's recommendation became a reality. On October 17, 1969, scores of newspapers throughout the nation eagerly announced the groundbreaking selection of Clifton R. Wharton Jr. as the fourteenth president of Michigan State University, and in early January 1970, the approximately two dozen Black faculty and 1,954 Black students were joined in East Lansing by a man who would become the most powerful and high-ranking African American in the history of the university.

Hannah resigned in late March 1969 and left campus six months later. Walter Adams, at one time a candidate for the permanent position who had garnered much student support as well as the endorsement of the Black Faculty Committee and African American student organizations, was appointed acting president; the "acting" designation was later symbolically removed from his title by the MSU Board of Trustees. After some controversial debates sparked by three dissenting board members, the first Black president of MSU was appointed effective January 2, 1970. Though he did not explicitly suggest his race had anything to do with the 5-3 vote or the "political wrangle" over his selection, he described it as unusual, to say the least. "My path to the presidency of Michigan State University led through a maze of politics and paranoia so Byzantine that writing about it even decades later leaves me in a state of near-disbelief," Wharton observed; "at the time, though, it was all too real."[3]

Wharton's identity as a Black man captured the attention and imaginations of onlookers. His racial identity was inevitably a popular topic of discussion in public and undoubtedly behind closed doors. The implicit racial bias present in higher education today was even more pervasive immediately following the Civil Rights Movement when there was a drastic increase in the Black presence on predominantly White institution (PWI) campuses throughout the nation. The catchy newspaper headlines—such as "MSU Names Negro to Head Michigan State," "Michigan State Appoints Negro," "First Negro Head of a Major University," "Negro to Head MSU; Board Splits on Issue," "Michigan State Will Get Negro Prexy in January," "Negro New President of Michigan State 'U,'" and "Negro Economist Is Named Head of Michigan State University"—rarely identified Wharton by name. Instead, as was the case with Gideon Edward Smith more than half a century earlier (who was routinely labeled "the Aggies' colored tackle," "the giant colored tackle," "the negro tackle," and "the big Negro star," among other racialized monikers), Wharton was instinctually othered by many in the mainstream White media. He was defined and pegged by his race and Blackness. Reporters repeatedly specified he was foremost the *Negro* president of MSU. All the press releases, write-ups, and accounts inescapably emphasized he was a historymaker. He became known as the *first* African American to be named president of a major public university.

The day after his selection, a writer for the *Detroit Free Press* shared with his readers a concise overview of Wharton's life, concluding: "Because of the unusual combination of his race and background, Wharton is used to being a 'first Negro.'"[4] If the majority of the jumpy journalists had deeply researched Wharton's background like this *Free Press* reporter, they would have learned not only that he was well acquainted with being a "Black first, but that he was undoubtedly ready to be the first Black president of MSU. He was destined for such a visible and consequential leadership position. He was used to this. His upbringing and previous experiences laid the groundwork for the politics of leading MSU as a racially conscious Black man. A contemporary of Malcolm X and Martin Luther King Jr., Wharton, given the duties of serving as president of a major PWI, embraced a nuanced approach, a strategy that responded to the Black Freedom Struggle Malcolm and King helped drive and shape.

The implications of Wharton being MSU's first Black president and his stance toward the Black presence on campus can be deciphered by exploring, among other sources, media coverage and his autobiography. The media coverage often tells us more about the journalists' ideas about Wharton than about his deeper thoughts. The *Lansing State Journal*, in particular, regularly reported on the challenges he faced and his responses to often unpreventable crises, his plans for the university, and his innovations. This local newspaper cited from a handful of Wharton's countless speeches, including publishing editorials. Like most public figures, Wharton was skeptical and distrustful of media coverage on him, especially the MSU student–run *State News*. In his lengthy autobiography, he reflects upon his long life, dedicating several chapters to his career at MSU. By nature, autobiographies are deliberately framed by their authors. They afford their creators opportunities to write their own personal histories and revise conventional narratives on them and their times. The African American autobiographical tradition is often characterized by their subjects using themselves as object lessons or inspirational testimonials for their readership, particularly their African American audiences. Using the overarching themes of *prejudice* and *privilege* as portholes into his life, when recounting his time at MSU Wharton does not center how race impacted his presidency. He does not focus on his attempts to address the issues revolving around the university's Black population. In the end, he portrays his role as MSU's first Black president as a challenging one, underscoring that he had to be hyperconscious of the various stakeholders in the large university community. His concern with the MSU Black community's plight was among a host of other high-priority situations, especially during his first tumultuous six months in East Lansing.

Wharton was accustomed to and comfortable with being a Black first in a variety of contexts. He was socialized to take on these responsibilities of race representation and breaking down barriers. From an early age, he recognized his father's position as a U.S. counsel "represented some sort of pioneering or breakthrough." His father, Clifton Reginald Wharton Sr. (1899–1990), was the first African American to enter the U.S. Foreign Service following the passage of the 1924 Rogers Act. In 1953, he then became the "first Black career diplomat to head a U.S. mission in a European country," and in 1961 he came to be known as the "first African American career Foreign Service officer to become an Ambassador."[5] Born in 1926 in Boston, beginning during his high school years at Boys Latin School, Wharton Jr. was a stand-out student. Unlike the vast majority of his African American contemporaries, he attended prestigious PWIs. After graduating with a bachelor's degree in history from Harvard University in 1947, he became the first African American admitted to the Johns Hopkins University School of Advanced International Studies in Washington, D.C., and the first African American to earn a master's from this competitive program in 1948. He was the first African American to earn a doctorate degree in economics from the University of Chicago in 1958. A decade later, when he was appointed director of Equitable Life Assurance Society, at the time one of the ten largest in the nation, he became one of the first African Americans to lead a major U.S. corporation. His work with a seemingly never-ending list of programs, initiatives, and agencies (the American International Association for Economic and Social Development, the National Planning Association, the Agricultural Development Council, the American Universities Research Program, the Agribusiness Council, the East Asian and Pacific Affairs of the State Department, and the Presidential Agriculture Mission to Vietnam, just to name handful) prepared this well-traveled scholar and multidimensional leader in the diplomacy required for leading a large educational institution with an international outreach component. His previous experiences prepared him for the intricacies of navigating overwhelmingly White male spaces as a high-achieving, exceptional, and opinionated Black man during the era of Jim Crow segregation, the Civil Rights Movement, and the early years of the Black Power era.

In his fascinating and candid 2015 autobiography aptly titled *Privilege and Prejudice: The Life of a Black Pioneer*, Wharton demonstrates not only his enduring memory, attention to detail, and skills as a historian, but also reveals how he was socialized, beginning at a young age by his parents, to understand the deeper implications of what it meant to be Black in American society and entailed to be a Black face in a high place. From his father, he learned how to have "stoic courage in the face of racism." Wharton's mother was the "dominant force" in his education. She schooled young Clifton Jr. about African American contributions to American history. "Thus, for me," Wharton deduced, "American Negroes were an unquestioned, important, long-standing part of the United States from its very beginning and had made tremendous contributions throughout its history." After he was called the n-word for the first time in Boston while in the third grade, his mother told him to take pride in his heritage. "Clifton," she counseled her son, "this is the way some people try to put you in a box and label you inferior. Don't let them do it. Be proud that you are a Negro, and never see yourself only as a Negro or as inferior because of it. Be proud of *everything* you are!" Wharton resolved "to hold fast to my pride in my heritage that my mother had done so much to nurture, but never to collude in anyone's attempt to define me by one thing alone."[6] He adopted a philosophy that many middle-class African Americans of his generation did: to prove, through his own actions, African Americans could achieve seemingly monumental feats regardless of their race and the pervasiveness of institutional racism. Other experiences during Wharton's childhood also influenced his views of his Blackness. At Camp Atwater in North Brookfield, Massachusetts, a summer camp for African American boys founded in 1921, he was surrounded by many youngsters like him. This helped him further develop his pride in being Black.

After graduating from Boys Latin School, at age sixteen Wharton entered Harvard University as one of three entering Black freshmen. While he didn't recount experiencing overt racism in Cambridge, he certainly knew what it meant to be a representative of the race. Enamored by the triumphs of the famous Tuskegee Airmen, during his junior year, Wharton volunteered his services to the U.S. World War II effort by applying for the ten-month air cadet training at Tuskegee Institute. As a flight cadet, he experienced a type of racial hazing and terrorism that profoundly impacted him and shaped his views of quotidian anti-Black discrimination. He was exposed to what countless of his southern contemporaries knew all too well. "I had never experienced such racial humiliation," he recalled. During his flight test in his primary course, a White flight instructor did his best to dehumanize him. Wharton refused to allow the racist antics shake him. Following the Japanese Instrument of Surrender, he opted for honorable discharge and continued his education at Harvard. At Tuskegee, Wharton learned an important lesson that would serve him well when he piloted MSU. "I discovered that I could deal with the most virulent manifestations of racism without losing self-control—and succeed." Echoing the eloquence of W. E. B. Du Bois, Wharton continued, "I learned that racial prejudice is an insidious fog which enters your pores to pierce your soul by destroying your self-worth and denying your humanity—but that succeeds only if you let it."[7]

After he returned to Harvard, he reckoned with how his experiences in the Jim Crow South heightened his awareness of subtle and overt racism, especially given his identity as a "high-achieving" Black man. During his time at the School of Advanced International Studies as its first Black student, he experienced firsthand how segregation existed in the nation's capital. According to Wharton, while working with various agencies as one of the few Black faces and while pursuing his PhD in economics at the University of Chicago as the only Black graduate student in the program, he didn't experience racism reminiscent of his experiences at Tuskegee. Amid the Civil Rights Movement, Wharton and his family lived abroad in Southeast Asia for a significant amount of time where, beyond a few run-ins with exported U.S. racism, he didn't regularly encounter racial prejudice. After spending six years in Southeast Asia removed from the day-to-day realities of Black life in the United States when issues of civil rights and "race relations" were among the country's most pressing domestic issues, Wharton began to question what he had, in his words, "done for the cause." He reasoned he had been a front runner for African Americans in the realm of philanthropy and higher education. He was, he maintained nearly five decades later, "clear and visible proof that a Black could succeed on innate talent and merit and in any area he or she chose" while having "a special impact in achieving racial progress and integration."[8] He evoked Du Bois's notion of the Talented Tenth.

As the newly selected president of MSU, Wharton's consciousness of the nuances of racial prejudice resurfaced. He often found himself responding to inquiries about how his race supposedly influenced his selection. He repeatedly told reporters what he shared with a writer for the *Herald-Press* of Saint Joseph, Michigan: that he had never "knowingly accepted a position or a job where race was the primary consideration." Wharton tripped up his White interviewers, and probably alienated many African American students, by emphasizing he "was a man first, an American second, and a Black man third." Challenging the notion he'd been hired because he was Black, he said his appointment was "an important symbolic occasion." In a few interviews, he "admitted to a little feeling of strain at representing the race" and the "extra pressure" of being a Black pioneer. He was humble in his feat, assuring the public he was not as unique as they portrayed him to be. He told a reporter for the United Press International that there were "many other qualified Blacks in the country and it may be very well only the luck of timing which put me into this position."[9] Looking back at his rocky start at MSU characterized by student unrest and demonstrations, Wharton obviously understood the deeper meanings of his achievement and viewed himself as being a "pioneer." Amid the negative reporting on African Americans in the late 1960s, Wharton deduced that his appointment "offered tentative proof that a Black could succeed at a high level based on merit." In doing so, he embraced the "racial uplift" philosophy of many elite African American spokespersons during the Progressive Era. Like other African Americans in high-profile public positions, as epitomized later by President Barack Obama, Wharton had to carefully strategize how he would address issues facing his constituencies—mainly Black students and faculty—and what was ambiguously dubbed "race relations."[10]

When he arrived on campus and was asked by leaders in the Black Liberation Front, International how he planned to address their concerns, he "gently but firmly," in his words, let them know he was going to be "president of the entire university, not a president of Blacks or a Black president." Wharton "assured" Black students he "would naturally be sensitive to Black issues." Yet he underscored his "major concern was fairness, regardless of a person's color." He accentuated his commitment to principles of equal opportunity "without appearing willing to sacrifice high standards of academic excellence." Unlike his White male counterparts in the Big Ten or elsewhere, Wharton reasoned: "How I handled 'Black issues' might well make or break my presidency." He was correct in this assessment and had an unusual burden to bear, often finding himself walking a tightrope. "From the moment I arrived in East Lansing," he recalled, "it was clear my success would depend in very large part on how I dealt with 'the race problem.'" He embraced a balanced, nuanced, and nonthreatening approach and let the MSU White community know that his agenda "was based upon 'integration,' not 'separation.'" He and his wife, Delores, made sure to not appear to openly display preferential treatment to African Americans. "While we often gave special attention to MSU's Black students and their needs," Wharton recounted, "we did not behave in an exclusive manner." As the first African American president of MSU and a major research university, he knew his "every word, action, and decision would be instantly seized upon, dissected, analyzed, and judged."[11] He and Delores went to great lengths to win over the

President Clifton R. Wharton Jr. and Delores Wharton. Courtesy of Michigan State University Archives and Historical Collections.

MSU community by opening up the historic Cowles House to visitors, engaging with students, faculty, and alumni, and serving as respectable ambassadors for the Spartans. The Whartons regularly visited dormitories, and Delores even spent a week in a women's dorm.

In a front-page story in the *Lansing State Journal* on October 17, 1969, a staff writer who routinely covered issues pertaining to MSU's Black students' protests and "race relations" highlighted Wharton's qualifications but dedicated much of the story to the so-called controversy behind his selection, insinuating Wharton was selected because Governor G. Mennen Williams lost in a 5-3 vote and former star M.A.C. athlete Jack Breslin "lost by a 4-4 vote when nominated for the presidential post" the day before. The journalist suggested Blanche Martin, the only Black trustee, was one of Wharton's main supporters by virtue of him introducing the motion to elect him. Wharton "was apparently agreed upon," the reporter delineated, by a group of bipartisan supporters "during an executive session Thursday night following a meeting with the All-University Search and Selection Committee." Trustee Frank Hartman, D-Flint, the *Lansing State Journal* and *State News* reported, was upset with what he called a nontransparent and "rigged" process allegedly used to elect Wharton. While he supported the nomination of Williams and Breslin, Hartman disagreed with the process by which Wharton was elected. "The vote was taken despite Hartman's request that it be delayed a month so that he could become better acquainted with Dr. Wharton," reported the *Lansing State Journal*. "Right after the motion to name Wharton, Hartman charged the five with 'ramrodding.'"[12] Wharton shared a different story of the "political wrangle" behind his appointment. He shared how the three trustees who voted against him let him know their disappointment in no uncertain terms; he knew he would have to continuously watch his back. He was attuned to what many others might have been thinking. "After two years of racial turmoil both close to home and throughout the county," recounted Wharton, "the MSU trustees had selected as Black president. *What could they be thinking*?"[13] Wharton's battles with several trustees continued during his presidency. This did not go unnoticed. His Black political allies, namely Detroit Democrats Senator Coleman A. Young and Representative Jackie Vaughn III, accused at least one trustee by name of racially harassing Wharton. Whatever transpired, Wharton's presidency sparked noticeable debates about racism.

Wharton being an "outsider" probably influenced his opposition's and skeptics' thinking, especially because the university had been run by the legendary Hannah for close to three decades. As intimated by the editors of the *State News*, there may have been concerns about how Wharton, having such big shoes to fill, would deal with "protesting students, particularly Blacks." Some Whites might have thought he would combat the "economics of poverty" and inequality by paying particular attention to the complex, widely publicized, and contentious status of Black students, faculty, and staff on campus. Oftentimes when African Americans step into influential positions in PWIs, such concerns, even if unspoken, materialize in the minds of those who have never been exposed to Black leadership. Why such a successful "pacesetter" would want this position in the first place probably also crossed peoples' minds.

In the end, in late October 1969, the student editors of the *State News* closed ranks and welcomed Wharton as a departure from the days of "the 28-year tenure for University presidents." Despite the fact that in their liberal broadside they had the nerve to conjure up stereotypes of "Uncle Tom" (which Wharton wasn't, in their estimation), they directly called upon the MSU White community to transcend presumptions about race. "Yes, our new president, a man with great capabilities as a human being and as a professional, happens to be Black. It is a sad reality that many will judge his every move with some reflection on his badge of color." The student editors continued, "If America is to exist as one nation, Black men must be allowed to remain Black and be judged solely by their accomplishments."[14]

Indeed, as Wharton himself testified, he possessed the impeccable credentials and skillset that would, with some careful fine-tuning, silence his critics and win over his diverse stakeholders and supporters. The MSU *Alumni Association Magazine* outlined his credentials, discussed the bipartisan vote leading to his election, and explained the "quiet firster's" notion of "positive militancy." The magazine didn't portray him as being a "radical" *Black* president with a *Black* agenda. "Wharton was not immediately endorsed by the black faculty or black students who were solidly in Walter Adams' corner." The magazine ultimately portrayed him as an exceptional African American of his generation who would not be an "activist president" but rather a "responsive" one committed to the university's "tradition of service to the people." They perceived him as being affable and unthreatening. "All who meet Dr. Wharton come away saying he is extremely personable and likeable," observed a writer for the *Alumni Association Magazine*; "a fairly big man, Dr. Wharton is still lean looking and youthful, especially in the face. He smiles often, and broadly (radiantly, say some). He has some modest nervous habits when he is fielding questions from the press—slight lip biting, brow furrowing. But he articulates his answers marvelously and in all respects comes across with dignity and good humor."[15]

The mainstream media coverage of Wharton's appointment recognized its historical significance, but often understated his qualifications and diversified career. The Black press, on the other hand, took great pride in his history-making. Large-sized photos of a debonair Wharton and his family appeared in major African American newspapers like the *Chicago Defender*. African American journalists saluted his accomplishment. Louis Martin of the *Defender* hailed Wharton's feat a "major breakthrough for Blacks in the field of education." He continued: "in these days when some racists are trying to revive the old bromide that the Black brother is born with inferior genes that put him in a second-class intellectual bracket, it is good to see some recognition of the abilities and capacity of an individual like Wharton." For this social commentator, Wharton's appointment represented "one of the few major openings in the field of education where one should have expected greater progress." Because of Wharton's and other's accomplishments and abilities, Martin concluded: "We believe that there is not a job in the nation for which a qualified Black man cannot be found and that includes the presidency of the United States. What the Black man needs is what democracy promises him—equal opportunity."[16]

"We know Dr. Wharton will make a good president at Michigan State," added a reporter for the Baltimore *Afro-American*, "His appointment enables a Black man to have a significant role at the decision-making level of higher education. It further enables him to be a part of the effort of education to be relevant in the inner city development, because Michigan State's democratic policies and teachings will be meaningless without some inner city involvement."[17] This reporter celebrated Wharton's selection as a collective victory for the Black community while charging him with the responsibility of encouraging "inner city development." This was a roundabout way of saying he could address issues of Black student enrollment and admissions. Wharton transcended different color-lines in his life and advocated for progressive changes for African Americans as early as his days in the National Student Organization. But his past experiences were not centered on Black community development. His expertise was in working with Southeast Asia and Latin America, cross-cultural engagements that broadened his world view. The challenges faced by these countries' poor populations were similar to those encountered by Blacks in major urban areas who, as argued by Black Power theorists, suffered from internal colonialism.

Months into his new position, in the spring and summer of 1970, Wharton's achievement was featured in the most popular Black magazines, *Jet* and *Ebony*. In late October 1969, *Jet* magazine proudly shared with its large readership that Wharton "was the first Black named president in the 114-year-old Michigan State University in East Lansing," highlighting this was but one of his "major breakthroughs."[18] About eleven months later, a photo of Wharton graced the cover of the May 21, 1970, issue of this popular, pocket-sized weekly magazine. Founded in 1951 by businessman, publisher, and founder of Johnson Publishing Company John H. Johnson, *Jet* featured stories on African American life, current events, history, and highbrow society. Seeking to counter the mainstream White media's misrepresentations and omissions of African American history and culture, "the Weekly Negro News Magazine" spotlighted the accomplishments of Black leaders, celebrities, and entertainers, success stories, and "Black firsts." Wharton was ideal subject matter.

Based upon an interview with Wharton, Valerie Jo Bradley assured her readers Wharton was making progress at MSU. Perhaps partially in jest while also demonstrating his Black historical consciousness, MSU's first Black president, "in his Boston-bred accent," began the interview by informing Bradley he wasn't the first Black president of a major PWI. This distinction, he clarified, adding to what he shared with members of the Lansing chapter of the NAACP in late January 1970, went to Patrick Francis Healy (1834–1910) who was president of Georgetown University from 1874 until 1882. Though Healy passed as a White Irish-American, he was born during the antebellum era to an enslaved Black mother in Macon, Georgia. Wharton let Bradley know the lack of acknowledgement of Healy was "a striking example of the need for Black studies," something Wharton supported at MSU with the Center for Urban Affairs. Wharton didn't totally skirt the issue of his "racial triumph," reiterating he had to be "particularly aware of what I can do and how I do it." He considered his new position "the most demanding and challenging" endeavor of his career. Rejecting the notion he was hired because of affirmative action, Bradley overviewed his "impressive list of credits." Wharton explained to his interviewer that he sought to be a president who didn't lead by decree or directives. Instead, he stressed his policies and decisions would be derived from "a reflection on the issues" concerning the students and the university as a whole.[19]

When asked about how he was going to approach issues related to Black students, he replied he was not going to strive "to prove to the white majority that I was the right choice." He praised MSU's efforts to recruit Black students during the previous decade and reiterated that his approach would be guided by "fairness and common sense." He was most concerned with enrolling quality Black students through his recently established Presidential Commission on Admissions. In order to help clarify the oftentimes misconstrued perceptions of the Black experience on campus, Wharton shared with *Jet* his plans to develop business workshops for African American students and "a series of Black journalism workshops." Perhaps in response to blinkered coverage in the *State News* and the *Lansing State Journal*, Wharton observed: "in listening to white students, they are not sensitized to and are not aware of the Black dimension, and my theory is to put it into an educational context whereby Black journalists can come and help to develop among the whites a greater awareness and sensitivity to this dimension."[20]

Several months after the *Jet* cover story, the ever popular *Ebony* magazine, founded by John H. Johnson in 1945, featured a story on Wharton, boldly titled "A New Boss Takes over at Michigan State." In this more detailed exploration of Wharton's first six months in office accompanied by more than ten photos of Wharton in various settings and often engaging with Black and White students, faculty, and administrators, including former president Hannah, Wharton surmised he was an appealing choice as MSU's president because of his academic background and his administrative acumen. Citing African American student Michael Hudson, *Ebony* positioned Wharton as a Black leader who had the potential to help African American students. "After talking to him," recounted Hudson, "I could tell that he would be sympathetic to the Black student movement and that he has an extensive knowledge of problems facing the Black community." Highlighting Wharton's firsthand run-ins with racism and his ability to sympathize with the Black Freedom Struggle, *Ebony* shared how he aced an Air Force pilot test at Tuskegee Institute. Based upon his handling of recent events, such as U.S. troops being deployed to Cambodia and Kent State University and the campus protests that followed, *Ebony* deduced Wharton possessed the diplomatic skill set to lead with compassion. "Wharton has demonstrated a gift for bringing together in amicable common effort persons who had never considered working with each other," concluded the author of this piece. "His proven expertise in cultivating support for projects, rather than trying to ram them down people's throats, will be valuable at MSU."[21]

In a handful of interviews, Wharton was quite candid about how he had to be judicious in framing his vision for MSU, particularly when dealing with the mounting concerns of Black students, faculty, and staff and the overall notion of "race relations" on campus. "I've been more deliberate and more cautious than I would normally be," he told a reporter for the United Press International in the summer of 1970. "This is not because I do not want to make a mistake, but because I know there is a tendency to examine everything that I say and do with a microscope. And, in fact, some of the reactions I get, especially the negative ones, are, I suspect, in part a reflection of this." He added, "There are a large number of people—though by no means a majority, I know—who would like nothing better than to see me not do so well. And therefore they are quick to find something they can point to and say, 'see. I knew it.'"[22] Wharton would have probably included several members of the MSU Board of Trustees in this group.

In a conscious effort to deflect the presumption existing in certain circles that he would be partial to MSU's Black community, Wharton assured Spartans, just as he told Black student-activists, he was a president for the entire university. "Let me assure each of you that my full allegiance is to Michigan State University—to the total university, not to any particular segment," he told hundreds of faculty members who belonged to the Faculty Club in the MSU Union Building on January 20, 1970, in his first major on-campus speech, "Presidential Credo." The "particular segment" to which Wharton referred might very well have been a veiled reference to Black people. He reiterated this inclusive approach through his concept of "universal higher education" and MSU as a "pluralistic university" that would ideally provide access to higher education for "everyone who has the desire and basic ability to do college work."[23] While Black students were most likely one of the main groups targeted in the "pluralistic university," Wharton didn't pitch the concept in such a manner. He prudently introduced diversity, equity, and inclusion initiatives.

Wharton was not afraid to put a spotlight on issues pertaining to race on campus. While Hannah routinely declared in the late 1950s and 1960s that the issue of civil rights was one of the most important domestic issues in U.S. life, he was guarded when addressing campus race relations, particularly before the assassination of Martin Luther King Jr. About a month after he took office, Wharton observed: "This (racial situation) is one of the most explosive situations we face at this university."[24] In response to this, expanding upon the efforts of President Walter Adams, Wharton created a Presidential Commission on Admissions to explore, among other issues, the admissions of "minority" students (the majority of whom were Black) and "disadvantaged whites." In rolling out his plans, Wharton indicated he was building upon a progressive tradition at MSU. "We at MSU have been increasing the number of Black students at a rate such that, today, we have more Black students enrolled at MSU than at any other non-urban, predominantly white university in the United States," wrote Wharton in March 1970.[25]

Working with Robert L. Green and Joseph McMillan, Wharton further empowered the Office of Equal Opportunity Programs by transferring it from the Center for Urban Affairs to the Office of Vice President for University Relations. Under his leadership, McMillan viewed the Office of Equal Opportunity Programs as being "an intra-university civil rights commission." Wharton's support for the Center for Urban Affairs was evident. He publicly declared that the problems faced by African Americans in the so-called urban ghetto should be addressed by the university as part of its outreach and land-grant legacy and supported the further growth of the center, proposing it be transformed into a college, tentatively called the College of Urban Development. "The social need for an effective university contribution to solutions [f]or the urban crisis is no longer debatable," he trumpeted. By 1973, the College of Urban Development was created.

Building upon Hannah's efforts, the Whartons were outspoken supporters of the arts. Delores went to great lengths to support the arts on campus. "She championed the university's commitment to the fine arts." In the mid-1970s, Wharton, who had donated his "appointive earnings" to art, pushed for the building of a Center for Performing Arts, an endeavor that required a fund-raising campaign to which the university was not accustomed. Completed about five years after Wharton left to become chancellor of the sixty-four-campus State University of New York system and named the Clifton and Delores Wharton Center for the Performing Arts, the center was the brainchild of MSU's first Black president. This wasn't the only cultural center Wharton proposed. Although it never formally came to fruition, in May 1970 following the tragic killings of students at Jackson State University in Mississippi and the riots following the suspicious death of teenager Charles Oatman in Augusta, Georgia, Wharton called for the creation of an off-campus Black Cultural Center, "a meeting place and cultural headquarters for members of the Black campus community." While Wharton's proposed Black Cultural Center was never built, he endorsed the creation of the Center for Urban Affairs' Urban Extension Center in Lansing. Dedicated in June 1970, the center provided a range of services mainly for Lansing's "Blacks, Mexican-Americans and disadvantaged whites."[26]

Beginning early in his tenure, Wharton addressed issues faced by African Americans on campus, promoted diversity, and addressed discrimination. He hired and promoted Black administrators, such as MSU doctoral candidate Nolen E. Ellison whom he promoted from associate director of the Center for Urban Affairs to his presidential assistant. He created the Committee Against Discrimination and an Anti-Discrimination Judicial Board and supported the university's Affirmative Action Plan. Such initiatives contributed to his vision of MSU as a "pluralistic university." During the first three years of his presidency, the Black student population increased by 37 percent, growing from 1,954 in 1970 (81 percent of the total minority student population) to a record high during the decade of 2,678 (6.47 percent of the total student enrollment). During Wharton's years, MSU "stood at the forefront among American colleges in recruiting black students." The year after his resignation, the number of Black students at MSU decreased by 7.5 percent and didn't begin significantly increasing again until the late 1980s. In 1969, there were 521 total Black employees at MSU. A year later, there were 632. The number of Black faculty increased noticeably during the Wharton years. When he took office, there were roughly a dozen Black faculty. Several months before the Associated Press announced in October 1977 that Wharton accepted the position of chancellor of SUNY ("the nation's largest university with 350,000 students"), there were fifty-seven tenure-system Black faculty (forty-four men and thirteen women), representing about 2.5 percent of the total tenure-system faculty. Another seventy faculty members were classified as "ethnic." The Black tenure-system faculty reached 3 percent in 1983 (forty-five men and nineteen women) and 4 percent in 1990 when there were eighty-five Black professors employed by MSU (fifty-three men and thirty-two women).[27]

From January 1970 until the end of December 1977, Wharton's presidency of America's first agricultural college was much more complex than this chapter has conjured up. His exhaustive autobiography, *Privilege and Prejudice*, provides great insight into how he navigated being the first African American president of a major predominantly White research university. While not as extensive as the exhaustive John A. Hannah Papers, the Clifton R. Wharton Papers in the MSU Archives and Historical Collections are far-reaching, providing future researchers with further insight into his career at MSU. "In contrast to John Hannah," the Associated Press commented in response to Wharton's resignation, "Wharton's style was generally considered low profile. He was once called 'a man happy to let everyone else make the waves.'"[28] Wharton was often shrewd and cautious when grappling with and making decisions about numerous challenges, from race relations and Black student unrest to major student protests in the early 1970s to fiscal problems and budget cuts to an National Collegiate Athletic Association investigation into MSU's football recruiting practices. To say that Wharton was "happy to let everyone else make the waves" is a blatant mischaracterization of his presidency, underappreciating the thorny path he navigated in East Lansing during the Black Power era. Green's assessment of Wharton's approach is more accurate. "When Wharton first arrived as president, many white faculty and staff members were apprehensive and unsure what to expect. They soon learned that he was a good leader. Although he was very confident, he was also self-effacing. In addition, he was a good listener and excellent consensus-builder."[29]

In strikingly different ways than President Hannah and acting president Adams, Wharton constantly reckoned with how his identity as a Black man impacted those he collaborated with, led, and served. Wharton had loads of practice code-switching and, as MSU University Distinguished Professor Emerita Geneva Smitherman would describe, style-shifting. He was often called upon to speak throughout the nation. During his first six months in office, for every speech he agreed to deliver, he declined ten to twenty invitations. Wharton carefully adjusted his speeches to align with his particular audience. The subject matter and tone of his speeches to Black audiences differed from those talks he delivered to White listeners. One of his first public appearances as MSU president took place about three weeks after he took office at the annual banquet of the Lansing chapter of the NAACP. In November 1970, he was the keynote speaker at the seventy-fifth anniversary commemoration for the National Medical Association, an organization for Black physicians and health professionals created because the American Medical Association barred African American participation. Wharton minced no words in telling an audience of more than three thousand highly educated African Americans they had

President Wharton with some children in the Hannah Administration Building. Courtesy of Michigan State University Archives and Historical Collections.

a responsibility to the masses of their people. Echoing messages from Carter G. Woodson's *The Mis-Education of the Negro* (1933), he pronounced: "Too long the Black intellectuals and professionals have effectively turned their backs on the plight of their brothers and sisters." He added, "We must recognize the relationship between poor health and poverty, and simultaneously endeavor to remove the social, political and economic shackles from inner-city residents."[30]

Periodically celebrated in the "Spartan Nation," epitomized by the cover story in the Spring 2019 issue of *Spartan Magazine: Michigan State University Alumni Magazine*, Wharton's legacy at MSU extends far beyond the Center for Performing Arts that bears his and his wife's name on East Shaw Lane across from the Veterinary Medical Center. Despite their limitations, symbolic victories for African Americans have time and again contributed to the Black Freedom Struggle. Whether they accepted it or not, Black firsts have inevitably borne the burdens of representing the race in traditionally White spaces. They have always been cognizant of this. Like Booker T. Washington, Wharton developed and mastered the arts of polyvocality and race representation. Unlike Black conservative leaders, he didn't downplay his Blackness or commitment to African Americans' civil rights to curry favor with his White constituents. He also didn't always see eye to eye with radical Black faculty, administrators, and students. Wharton envisioned his MSU as being an idealistic "pluralistic university." He purposefully promoted diversity and inclusion unlike any of his predecessors. He was one of MSU's most broad-minded leaders. African Americans on campus were among Wharton's chief beneficiaries. They could hold their heads high knowing that one of their own made history and represented them with such poise, eloquence, dignity, and excellence.

Chapter 41

1989, the Number

I n 2017, the incoming African American freshman class at MSU, 634, was reportedly the largest in the Big Ten. A year later, in May 2018, spokespersons for the university proudly announced that its incoming freshman class was the "largest and most diverse in the school's history." African American student enrollment was "up nearly 24 percent." In 2018, there were a total of 3,505 Black students enrolled in MSU, 2,930 of whom were undergraduates. University representatives and officials continued to celebrate what they perceived as constituting breakthroughs in the diversity of the student body into the second decade of the twenty-first century. By the fall of 2020, as announced by the MSU Office of Institutional Diversity and Inclusion, "students of color enrollment increased by 6.8% at MSU since fall 2019, a 49.4% increase since 2010." And in 2023, university spokespersons reported that "MSU's total enrollment includes more diverse students than any previous year."[1] When deciphering such milestones, it's worthwhile reflecting upon earlier periods, namely the mid- to late 1960s and the Wharton years. The growth of the Black student population in the second decade of the twenty-first century can be juxtaposed with its unprecedented expansion during the late 1960s and early 1970s. The first significant cohort of Black students was recruited to MSU during and immediately following the Civil Rights Movement through a series of programs and initiatives. During Clifton R. Wharton Jr.'s presidency, the university established the reputation of being a destination for young African Americans in and outside of the Great Lakes State. Reflecting on the late 1960s and early 1970s, in

1982, amid a decline in Black student enrollment, trustee Blanche Martin remarked to a *Lansing State Journal* reporter, "Michigan State was THE place to be."[2]

The Black student population grew from 1,000 in 1968 to 1,500 by 1969. By 1972, the Black student population had blossomed to over 2,500. MSU arguably "stood at the forefront among American colleges in recruiting black students."[3] By the mid-1980s, MSU experienced a noticeable decline in Black student enrollment. Between 1975 and 1981, the Black student population decreased by 8.7 percent. Black students noticed this decline during the mid-1970s. Celebrating MSU's past recruitment efforts, *Grapevine Journal* writers Angela Martin and Delilah Nichols believed that "Blacks are no longer being recruited as aggressively as they were four years ago."[4] It seems by the mid-1970s, following the end of the Black Power era and the creation of hundreds of Black Studies programs, centers, departments, and units at colleges and universities throughout the nation, the conditions of African Americans at major public universities like MSU fell off the radar. During the 1980s and 1990s, under various circumstances, MSU presidents were challenged to develop strategies for recruiting Black and traditionally underrepresented students.

The hiring of more Black faculty at MSU has been an issue Black students have raised since the late 1960s. With the creation of the Black Faculty Committee and later the Black Faculty and Staff Association—then renamed the Black Faculty, Staff and Administrators Association (BFSAA)—Black faculty called upon the university to increase the numbers of Black tenure-system faculty. All MSU presidents since John A. Hannah, Walter Adams, and Wharton have been pressed and urged to hire more Black tenure-system faculty. For five decades, MSU's faculty has not been as diverse as its student body, and the percentage of Black faculty has not matched the percentage of Black students. This is the case at major research universities throughout the nation. The status of tenure-system African American faculty at MSU has certainly undergone a host of transformations since the first major hiring surge during the late 1960s and early 1970s. In 1965, there were less than ten Black faculty at MSU. By the end of the decade, there were at least twenty. Between 1969 and 1977, the Black faculty population witnessed its largest growth in history, increasing by almost 200 percent. In 1977, there were sixty-one Black tenure-system faculty, about the same as in 1981. During the presidencies of M. Cecil Mackey Jr. and John DiBiaggio, the 1980s witnessed significant growth in the number of tenure-system African American faculty, increasing by nearly 52 percent between 1980 and 1990 (from sixty in 1981 to ninety-one in 1991).

During the 1990s, the number of African American tenure-system faculty averaged approximately ninety-one (in 1990, there was a low of eighty-five, and in 1992, there was a decade high of ninety-six). The initial growth in the number of Black faculty during the 1990s was directly linked to protests waged by Black students in May 1989. "We need to do better," admitted one MSU administrator during the spring 1989 semester when talking about recruiting Black faculty. "We as an institution need to be much more aggressive, particularly in hiring at the upper levels."[5] By the late 1990s several years after Merritt Norvell became MSU's first African American athletic director, Black faculty voiced concerns about the recent decline in their numbers. In 1997, when the number of tenure-system Black faculty dropped to eighty-nine, marking a steady decline from 1992 and 1995, the BFSAA expressed their anxieties to President Peter McPherson. "This has been building for years," president of the Black Faculty and Staff Association George Rowan observed; "the time has come to raise awareness of the issues." Thomas Gunnings added: "We had been making some progress years ago. The last few years, we've slipped."[6]

Between 2003 and 2006, the African American tenure-system faculty population grew significantly, from ninety-three to a record of 105. Between 2006—when Proposal 2 (the Michigan Civil Rights Initiative) was passed, prohibiting affirmative action at the University of Michigan, MSU, Wayne State University, and other public colleges and universities in the state—and 2018, the population of tenure-system African American faculty declined by approximately 18 percent. On average, between this span of about a dozen years, there were fewer Black tenure-system faculty at MSU than in the 1990s. During this same period, the number of Asian faculty increased by 67 percent, the number of Hispanic faculty increased by 85.7 percent, the consistently small number of American Indian faculty decreased by 12.5 percent, and the White faculty population decreased by 8.8 percent (from 1,587 to 1,447). When contemplating the drastic decline in the number of tenure-system African American faculty between 2006 and 2018, it would be useful to revisit past recruiting and retention efforts, conduct data-informed analyses, and shine a spotlight on past campus climate issues. Like African American students at predominantly White institutions (PWIs) throughout the nation, in the twenty-first century, African American students at MSU have spoken out about the importance of Black representation in the faculty ranks. They have cyclically reevaluated their own distinctive status as students and have actively sought to promote reform on campus. With vigilance, they have confronted racism—from what we now call microaggressions to more blatant expressions of racial prejudice and bias—and have called upon the university, through ongoing lists of "demands," to attend to the long-running problems they have ordinarily encountered. The demands of Black students from the late 1960s through the first two decades of the twenty-first century are strikingly similar, suggesting certain salient issues and concerns have remained somewhat constant, manifesting themselves in comparable manners in distinctly different time periods.

Though there are a handful of examples of Black student activism at MSU before the passage of the Voting Rights Act of 1965, like Albert H. Baker and James L. McCrary's challenge to the college's discriminatory "practice teaching" policies in 1935, Franklyn Duffy and his supporters' 1940 stand against the college's segregationist on-campus housing customs, or Ernest Green and the MSU NAACP chapter's activism during the early 1960s, expressions of Black student activism on campus expanded and multiplied after the assassination of Martin Luther King Jr., in large part because of the sudden increase in the university's Black student population. During an era of amplified student unrest and demonstrations, one of the first major Black student protests was the highly publicized and, for some, contentious occupation of the Wilson Hall cafeteria in 1969.

Usually in response to racial incidents that have served as rallying points, since the late 1960s and 1970s, Black MSU students have continued to advocate for change. In the several decades since the passage of the Voting Rights Act of 1965, one major Black student movement stands out, a campaign that resulted in heightened awareness about Black students' experiences and concrete policy changes that were reminiscent of those following King's assassination.

A reporter for the *Lansing State Journal* wrote on May 12, 1989, "a sit-in by black students has turned MSU's John A. Hannah Administration Building into an island of the 1960s on a 1980s campus."[7] For the duration of the well-publicized landmark 1989 takeover, the paper covered the daily activities of the Black student-activists and the responses of the university's administration. Many of its reporters seemed fascinated and surprised by the Black student-activists' commitment, discipline, and racial solidarity.

Echoing the demands of their predecessors, two decades after the Wilson Hall incident that helped solidify the Black Students' Alliance (BSA) as a vanguard for Black students' concerns, African American students orchestrated what the mainstream media labeled a "sit-in," and what they called a "study-in," in the Hannah Administration Building in May 1989 during the university's Cross-Cultural Week. Articulated by the movement's leaders and spokespersons, Darius Peyton of United Blacks of Wonders and MSU NAACP chapter president Jeffrey Robinson, the demands of these students echoed those put forward by their predecessors. On May 9, 1989, at approximately 4:30 p.m., a group of about seventy Black students entered the lobby of the MSU administration building with a mission: to launch what would become an eight-day occupation. "There's no alternative. That's why we're here now," Peyton told a *Lansing State Journal* reporter. "We have tried time after time—meeting after meeting after meeting, assembly after assembly and protest after protest—to raise the consciousness and awareness of the university and let them know the seriousness of the issues." Peyton continued, "We're willing to stick it out for the long haul."[8] Several days into the protest, Robinson added: "Days, weeks, however long it takes. We want a time table."[9]

Peyton, Robinson, and the other determined Black student-activists, who over the course of the historic occupation swelled to between two hundred and four hundred, were dissatisfied with what they viewed as MSU president DiBiaggio's inadequate response to the existing "racial tension" that had surfaced on campus since the beginning of the year, including what some Black students perceived as being discrimination against Black candidates who ran for MSU's student government in February 1989 and racial threats and harassment against Robinson and other Black students. Most likely in response to charges that Robinson and his classmates had leveled against ASMSU for "discriminatory practices" and the *State News* for publishing what they called "race-baiting" commentaries from students in mid-February, Robinson received a message on his answering machine from an anonymous caller "spewed with a tirade of racial insults," warning Robinson "to leave the university on the threat of burning his room." Days later, several other officers of the campus NAACP chapter received similar threatening phone calls.

Darius Peyton, middle, addresses Black students outside of the Hannah Administration Building. Courtesy of Michigan State University Archives and Historical Collections.

Robinson was no stranger to such cowardly racial intimidation. In December 1988, "a paper bag containing a dead rat" was nailed to the door of his room in Holmes Hall. The n-word was also "scrawled on the door."[10]

The May 1989 campaign represented a culmination of Black students' frustration throughout the decade. In late April 1980 at a Board of Trustees meeting, Black students lambasted President Mackey and the board, fearing the discontinuation of the Black Student Aide Program. In the dawning of the 1980s, the Office of Admissions launched "Minority Visitation Day" while the university closed its College of Urban Development, a college with a large number of Black students. In early 1982, more than 350 Black students, faculty, and alumni packed into the Kellogg Center Auditorium to voice their discontent with the decline in Black student enrollment since the mid-1970s. In response, the *Lansing State Journal* carried a series of articles on Black student life at MSU, stressing that the "transition to life at MSU can be traumatic for many students who come from predominantly black communities." Black students were also enraged about recent cuts in short-term loans and "racial incidents," including the n-word and other racist threats doodled on Black students' dorm room doors and "KKK" being scratched on the door of the Armstrong Hall Black Caucus room. In late May 1982 during Greek Week, the *State News* published an advertisement for a fraternity featuring a photograph of their members huddled around a "black minstrel statue identified as 'Willie,'" a longtime "fixture" in the fraternity home. A group of about three hundred students, the majority of whom were African Americans, responded by marching from Beaumont Tower to the Hannah Administration Building, posting up outside of President Mackey's fourth-floor office. Backed by the Greater Lansing Black Greek Alumni Association and the Black Coalition for Organizational Unity, they presented a list of demands to Mackey who responded by declaring: "Racism in any form is absolutely inconsistent with the principles and commitments of MSU."[11] In the mid-1980s and again in the late 1980s, MSU's vice-president of student affairs and services Moses Turner noted there was an increase in "expressions of racial hostility among Michigan State University students," something he chalked up to the rise in racial incidents in U.S. society during the Reagan years.[12] In 1987, while covering the racial incidents that rocked the University of Michigan, the *New York Times* reported there were "worsening racial tensions" at colleges and universities throughout the country. In response, DiBiaggio confidently remarked that such episodes had not significantly impacted the MSU community. "We don't have any blatant incidents such as with the U of M," he injected. "We've had a few incidents on campus, but not on a level that would get news coverage."[13] Despite DiBiaggio's confidence, in July 1987, the Black Alumni Association challenged him to address Black graduation and retention rates; the hiring of Black faculty, administrators, and coaches; and lingering campus climate issues.

DiBiaggio's optimistic characterization would soon be called into question. On March 2, 1989, in an editorial in the *State News*, "Slurs Have No Place at MSU," DiBiaggio found himself addressing "racial incidents" that took place on campus during Black History Month. "Recent threats on our campus, obviously directed at the race of those students, rightly deserved our immediate and forceful attention," he announced. "Some renowned observers of the American scene tell us that expressions of racial intolerance in 1989 are once again garnering unchallenged acceptance. In our society and at MSU such expressions are absolutely inappropriate. Racial discrimination at MSU—overt or covert, shouted or whispered—is deplorable and must be condemned."[14] As an East Lansing minister cryptically warned a day before the 1989 study-in began, the "university has the opportunity and responsibility to help shape the future generations of society. Take the task seriously, and don't foster, by your silence, the plague of racism."[15] By the late 1980s, inspired by the spirit of Malcolm X, frustrated with the university's handling of racial incidents, and supported by an outspoken group of Black parents whom the university could not risk ignoring, a generation of Black students was poised to embrace a newfangled approach, garner attention, and evoke change.

Shortly after Robinson was harassed in mid- to late February 1989, a group of African American students and the newly created Black Parents Association (BPA), led by Robinson's father and civil rights activist the Reverend Loyce Lester of the Original New Grace Missionary Baptist Church in Detroit, and Cloyzelle Jones, president of the Urban Education Association, made several trips to East Lansing to meet with university administrators. They initially connected with the vice-president for student affairs and services on February 23, several days after Robinson received the threatening message on his telephone answering machine. On February 28, "about 75 parents, students, and administrators packed the university's boardroom for two hours to air concerns around tensions on campus."[16] The purpose of this meeting, as Lester pointed out, was to encourage DiBiaggio to "take a hands-on approach to correct its [MSU's] problems in the racism area."[17] The BPA presented the president with a "Position Statement," "Agenda," and a list of "Problems That Must Immediately Be Corrected." Among BPA's more than a dozen demands were the establishment of forums on racism, the termination of employees who engaged in racist behavior and discrimination, the hiring of more Black faculty and employees, the incorporation of the Black Faculty and Administrators Association into "the MSU infra-structure," a commitment to affirmative action, investigations into "allegedly racist comments" made by an MSU professor during a class meeting, the end of "race-baiting" in the *State News*, and a reassessment of the MSU Department of Public Safety's interaction with Black students.[18] The mobilization efforts of Lester and the BPA received media attention and were clearly effective. After one of their visits in early March, the BPA attended a meeting sponsored by the Office of Black Affairs with approximately three hundred students in attendance.

DiBiaggio's initial response was to tell the BPA and the concerned Black students that MSU would "more forcefully inform the MSU community that we will not tolerate racial prejudice." He then issued a letter to members of the MSU community, and then a statement in the *State News* on March 2 reiterating this. Evoking Hannah's notion that as a land-grant university MSU should lead "an assault on inequality," DiBiaggio called upon his community to "meet this challenge." Dissatisfied with DiBiaggio's response, on March 2, Lester wrote a letter to him. He mailed an extended version to Governor James Blanchard, Black churches in the Detroit area, Congressmen John Conyers and George William Crockett Jr., Representative Morris Hood, Senators David Holmes and J. Vaughn, Representative and Chairperson of the Congressional Black Caucus Teola Hunter, and "Concerned Others." In his three-page letter to DiBiaggio, Lester didn't mince any words. He began by emphasizing that the BPA only wanted to deal directly with him and not provost David K. Scott whom they believed needed foundational training in the area of on-campus race relations. On behalf of the BPA, he called upon the MSU president to provide a straightforward one-page response with a "list of dates that Agenda/Statements demands will be satisfied." Lester underscored they were not interested in receiving "self-serving responses." They wanted responses with action items and a timeline by March 14. "We don't want a 'paper' Dr. DiBiaggio," Lester insisted. "We are prepared to directly assist you and MSU. But this involves a partnership that you may not be desirous of. Whatever the case, MSU is long overdue in effectively addressing its problem of campus racism." Lester concluded, "Please send us the one page of dates and nothing more. Then, let us move forward from this action, to make significant headway in strengthening a fine institution."[19] In his letter to Blanchard, Lester explained the BPA's involvement in the case, noting: "a key objective of our involvement with MSU, is to cause MSU to comprehend that significant numbers of Blacks from around the country are justifiably unhappy with MSU's product of institutional racism. MSU, unfortunately, may want to play the 'numbers' game; its leadership, if racist itself, would demonstrate this mindset by claiming that the *Black Parents Association* are not representative of the large whole of Black parents or students who attend MSU." Lester asked the governor to "come forward and provide leadership" to influence change at MSU. He concluded, "we want MSU, whom we support financially and politically to over-haul its product."[20]

One day before the BPA's deadline of March 14, DiBiaggio wrote a letter to the members of the organization, addressed "Dear Parent." He told them he thought a lot about their concerns, met with the "appropriate administrators," and categorically deplored "the racist incidents" on campus. He promised to punish, "according to due process," those responsible for the racial threats. "As MSU parents," he wrote, "you deserve my personal commitment to eradicating on this campus behavior and practices that are marked by racial intolerance." DiBiaggio then addressed, one by one, the "areas of concerns" BPA shared with him on February 28, highlighting the steps to be taken and explaining why certain actions could not be taken, as in the case of terminating employees accused of discriminatory behavior. He concluded by ensuring he was committed to generating "changes" so that "diversity thrives" and that he would not simply issue "reports" and "pronouncements."[21]

Several days after Civil Rights Movement veteran Rev. C. T. Vivian spoke on campus at the International Center and on the same day a newly formed organization called Coalition of Leaders Opposing Racism invited Martin Luther King III to speak on campus, on March 7, Lester and Jones surprised DiBiaggio by attending his annual budget meeting with the House Subcommittee on Higher Education. They spoke up. Jones was unambiguous in describing BPA's approach and determination. "They're going to do what we ask whether they want to or not. We're not interested in playing games," she declared, promising that Lester would "go to the state and the national level."[22] DiBiaggio faced the pressure President Robert S. Shaw did when Senator Charles C. Diggs Sr. vowed to publicize and politicize Franklyn Duffy's case against the college's de facto segregationist on-campus housing practices. DiBiaggio was ready in that he had prepared a statement (a version of which he shared with members of the MSU academic council on March 7) in which he condemned the "racial intolerance" that recently reared its head on MSU's campus. He voiced sympathy for the members of the BPA.

"Last week, the parents of Black students from Detroit visited our campus to express their concerns," DiBiaggio told the subcommittee. "I applaud their commitment to their children, and I commend their willingness to discuss matters of concern in a reasoned and reasonable fashion. They were hurting; and I felt it." He added that he was going to send members of the

BPA his "personal statement of commitment" and that he had already taken significant steps in addressing the problems. "As a steward of values as well as of funds, I can promise you that MSU will not only continue to lead that assault on inequality, we will step up our efforts. You have every right to expect results." DiBiaggio guaranteed, "I can assure you that our board, our administration, our faculty, our staff, and our students will not allow MSU to be complacent. We must not focus on how far we have come, but on how far we have to go."[23]

The parents and students were unimpressed with DiBiaggio's measured response. By late March, Lester and the BPA grew increasingly impatient. Lester, who personally received threats for speaking out, declared, "I'm not afraid. It's not going to stop us from fighting for what's right. And we're going to support these kids all the way to the end of the victory."[24] In early April, as DiBiaggio and his team worked out a plan to address the publicized on-campus racism, a longtime MSU professor with a record of civil rights activism allegedly made some disparaging comments about Black students' intellectual abilities in an interview on WDIV Channel 4. DiBiaggio was disappointed, commenting: "We've come so far. And now this." He added: "It makes our deliberations and discussions with parents more difficult because I think we had been making progress."[25] A day following this incident, on April 7, 1989, MSU leadership released its response to the on-campus "racial tension" and the BPA's and Black students' demands.

The product was the MSU IDEA (Institutional Diversity: Excellence in Action), a forty-three-page plan that identified fifty goals for increasing diversity and supporting affirmative action at the university. DiBiaggio and the university's spokespersons were judicious in how the plan was messaged to the public. Several days before officially releasing the plan, the assistant vice-president for university relations and director of public relations counseled DiBiaggio to highlight that it was part of a "long-standing effort," not a reactionary gesture responding to recent demands. He told the president to stress that diversity "is the reason FOR" the university's excellence and that the road map was "a plan for life in the next century" and a "call to action"—a "type of climate control." It should be pitched, DiBiaggio was counseled, as a collaborative plan that would be evaluated and that was not "set from on high."[26] Despite this mindful and calculated instruction, the MSU IDEA was by no means a strategic plan with an explicit vision or mission or detailed objectives, goals, strategies, or metrics. While its architects called for change and included a timeline for some of the initiatives, the aspirational fifty-point plan was wide-ranging and onerous, lacking descriptions of strategies or metrics. It was not a strategic plan. Without an exact comprehensive timeline or precise goals and deliverables, it broadly outlined how the university would attempt to—using at one point "will try" to explain the approach—address the complex problems raised by the BPA and African American students.

The MSU IDEA was an acknowledgement that efforts needed to be made by the university to change the campus climate and such a task required an all-embracing approach. President DiBiaggio rhetorically acknowledged the larger problem. Echoing Hannah's characterization of the struggle for civil rights during the late 1950s and 1960s, he said, "Racism lives in our society. Since we are a microcosm of society you should expect that it will be here as well as everywhere else."[27] To the dismay of Black student-activists, the MSU IDEA didn't aggressively address many of their demands. It did not focus on Blacks' conditions. Peyton was skeptical, to say the least, observing that it "was so broad" and "too vague."[28] Despite the fact that Black student-activists helped influence the creation of the fifty-point plan, the main subjects initiating change were identified as MSU, the university, the office of the provost, and the colleges. Yet, unlike in DiBiaggio's responses to the Black students' thirty-six demands crafted more than a month later, Black people as subjects were not singled out or the focus of any particular point in the MSU IDEA. MSU administrators identified "minority groups," "women," "handicappers," "underrepresented groups," and "veterans" as the target groups for their plan. Throughout the document, Blacks were interchangeably identified as "minorities" and "underrepresented groups." Such a deliberately inclusive plan failed to address the first major demand of the Black students: the increase in the number of *Black* faculty and staff. Blacks were mentioned specifically in points 19, 28, and 31, which, respectively, indicated that MSU would collaborate with faculty at HBCUs, increase its collaboration with the Black Family and Child Institute, and seek to increase the persistence of Black students, among other underrepresented student populations.

The decision that hundreds of Black MSU students made to occupy the Administration Building represented a response to local issues and their disappointment with the MSU IDEA. But it was also part of a broader movement and tradition. Not only were Black students engaged in similar activities throughout the country, but Black students in the state, namely at Wayne State University and Ferris State University, had occupied buildings on their respective campuses in the weeks and days before the study-in at MSU. During the eight days of the movement, the MSU student-activists were supported by their parents, Black faculty and staff, the Black Alumni Association, and local community activists. Student spokespersons Darius Peyton and Jeffrey Robinson met regularly with President DiBiaggio and other university administrators. Black students' demands mirrored those made by their counterparts during the Black Power era, including calls for more Black faculty, staff, and administrators; a condemnation of racism from the president of the university; the end of what they called harassment from the MSU Department of Public Safety; increased funding for African American–centered initiatives and curricular changes; more resources for minority student programs; and the adoption of affirmative action policies throughout the university. Throughout the week-long occupation, there were many deliberations and much back-and-forth.

After a final negotiation meeting that lasted from 3:30 p.m. on May 15 until 7:00 a.m. on May 16, the study-in ended on the evening of Tuesday, May 16, 1989. Bringing the eight-day-long campaign to a close, at about 6:00 p.m., DiBiaggio delivered a letter to "Students Protesting in the Hannah Administration Building" addressing in detail each of their thirty-six demands based upon their long and intense deliberations. Among the key highlighted issues were sponsoring

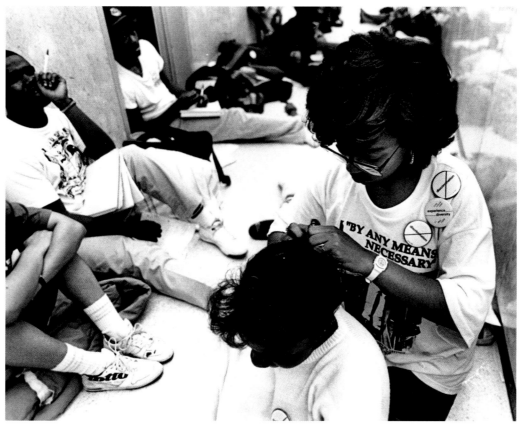

Rocking a Malcolm X "By Any Means Necessary" tee shirt and adjusting to a new, temporary living arrangement, a young woman does her classmate's hair. Courtesy of Michigan State University Archives and Historical Collections.

forums on "racism and diversity," acting against those who engage in "racist behavior," meeting periodically with students about issues of racism and campus diversity, and increasing efforts to recruit and retain Black and minority students, staff, faculty, and administrators (including the hiring of a senior advisor to the provost for minority affairs by the spring of 1991). DiBiaggio also promised that university leadership would consult regularly with BFAA, initiate "multi-cultural" training for the university's Department of Public Safety and "ethnic sensitivity training for appropriate groups" on campus, create a "scholarship pool" for recruiting Black and minority graduate students, and explore the "creation of a black studies thematic program." He said the university would launch an "all-University conference on diversity and pluralism" on Martin Luther King Jr. Day, encourage colleges to identify individuals "with specific responsibilities for minority affairs," further support the Office of Black Affairs, and entertain supporting the development of "a new, minority newspaper." The university also agreed to "forego prosecution of known (identified) participants" as long as they remained "peaceful" and vacated the premises by 8:00 p.m.[29] DiBiaggio's responses to the 1989 study-in arguably represent the most extensive reactions of the university's leadership to Black students' demands and "racial tension" in the history of the institution.

As was the case with the Black student occupation of the Wilson Hall cafeteria twenty years earlier, the 1989 study-in revealed to participants that with an organized, unified, and disciplined movement, Black students could influence change. While they might not have been keenly aware of previous campaigns for racial justice on campus, they recognized that noticeable interventions would not have taken place without struggle, unity, and consciousness-raising. During the 1989 study-in, Black student leaders emerged and matured. A determined group of Black students banded together in a common struggle. Like previous generations of Black activists involved in civil disobedience, they organized and developed strategies, locked arms in unity, and sang civil rights anthems and created slogans (e.g., "Too Black, Too Strong!," "Whose House? Our House!"). As one freshman participant said, "Everyone has to make a stand. If you know deep in your heart what's right you'll stick behind it. And that's what we did. It paid off. I don't have a moment's regret."[30] The student-activists' efforts produced tangible results. They realized that support from elders, especially the persistent BPA, was crucial in publicizing their cause. During the final negotiations at around midnight, another racial incident occurred that under a different set of circumstances would have probably led to wide-scale reactions from the Black community on campus. Police found "a 30-inch by 40-inch cross planted across from the administration building, topped with a gasoline-soaked rag and scorched at the bottom."[31] Black student-activists vowed to hold the university accountable to their plans and proposed actions. In the fall of 1989, Black students who participated in the historic study-in marched in front of the Hannah Administration Building to express their discontentment with the snail-paced progress.[32]

From the 1990s through the first decade of the twenty-first century and beyond, numerous episodes like those that helped spark the 1989 study-in resurfaced. Racial incidents on college and university campuses across the country are not uncommon. As DiBiaggio admitted in 1989, the campuses are microcosms of U.S. society. The *Journal of Blacks in Higher Education* has a link on its website (www.jbhe.com/incidents) devoted to describing more than one hundred "campus racial incidents" since the early 2010s. In the twenty-first century, a handful of racial incidents at MSU stand out. In 2003, Black students mobilized in response to racist fliers posted in Shaw Hall and racial slurs in Emmons Hall. In 2006, the Residence Halls Association initiated a "Not in Our Hall" effort to address racism in the dormitories. In October 2011, under the leadership of Mario Lemons, BSA lead a "silent march" in protest of several racial incidents, including the hanging of a Black doll by its neck in the Biomedical and Physical Science Building. Not too long after their Black History Month commemorative program for the 1989 study-in, on October 28, 2011, members of BSA met in Brody Hall with MSU administrators and President Lou Anna K. Simon. They asked for the creation of a multicultural center, cultural sensitivity training, and an increase in the numbers of Black students, staff, and faculty. "Because the administration has not spoken to us and heard our voices, (and) have not made a priority to have those discussions with us we are more aggressive today," Lemons asserted.[33]

Four years later, the Liberate MSU movement issued a set of well-publicized demands centered on Black students' presence. As Darius Peyton observed in 2016, "almost all of their demands are the same we had."[34] Just like those Peyton and his colleagues proposed echoed those from BSA in 1969, Liberate MSU's demands were part of a larger historical tradition. In 2015, the group organized a march and briefly occupied the Kellogg Center during President Bill Clinton's visit to campus. Though they didn't go to the extent of their 1989 predecessors, Liberate MSU, under the leadership of graduate student A. J. Rice, effectively mobilized followers, engaged in extensive social media consciousness-raising, and created a series of demands. Most importantly, they called for a new college with departments addressing the realities of more than a few traditionally underrepresented social identities (including a department of African American and African Studies), a freestanding multicultural center, an increase in African American tenure-system faculty, training in cultural competency for resident hall assistants, the hiring of staff members with expertise in issues facing minoritized students, and an increase in underrepresented students from urban cities in Michigan. Cognizant of past Black student activism, Liberate MSU called upon the university to return to BSA's 2011 demands.

In October 2019, BSA generated a list of eight demands focused on the university's attitude toward racist incidents in the residence halls. This was in direct response to what appeared to some as a noose made of toilet paper placed on the door of a Black student's room in Bryan Hall and a professor's Qualtrics research survey on a website including racist statements. Members of MSU's Council of Racial and Ethnic Students and Council of Progressive Students and other students posted up on the fourth floor of the Hannah Administration Building and issued a list of demands to newly appointed President Samuel Stanley Jr. To demonstrate such cases were not unusual, amid a controversial and racially divisive presidential election, BSA publicized a "timeline of racist incidents" that had occurred on campus since 2016. One of the most recent incidents that received national attention at MSU was a display in the Wharton Center gift shop during Black History Month in 2020 that "depicted current and historical African American figures hanging from trees," evoking imagery of lynching. While this incident didn't directly result in mass protests like the incidents that took place in 1969 and 1989, it signaled to the university administration the need to continue to ramp up its diversity, equity, and inclusion work. President Stanley responded immediately to this incident by issuing several statements to the MSU community, announcing a national search for vice-president and chief diversity officer, and creating the MSU Diversity, Equity, and Inclusion Steering Committee. In the summer of 2020, he also created the MSU Racial Equity Task Force. In 2021, the steering committee completed its lengthy and detailed "Report and Plan," the first major report of its kind since the *MSU IDEA II: Institutional Diversity, Excellence in Action* (1992).

The fall 2023 semester witnessed a noticeable spike in Gen-Zer Black student activism. In part sparked by their belief that the university mishandled a racial incident in early June, BSA, the campus NAACP, and other Black student activists began amping up their mobilization efforts, including a statement-releasing campaign; meetings with Board of Trustees members, administrators, faculty, and staff; a walkout; and townhalls. While these determined students turned to social media to publicize what had been happening to them on campus and how they didn't feel safe, a few staff writers for the *State News* also sporadically covered these topics during the fall semester in manners reminiscent of coverage in 2019.

The racial incidents that MSU Black students have experienced in the late 2010s and early 2020s are nothing new. They date back to when significant numbers of Black students began attending the university in the late 1960s and early 1970s and even earlier. Similar trends exists at other PWIs throughout the nation. Likewise, the historical pattern of responses to anti-Black racial incidents at MSU is by no means unique. It's a widespread approach adopted by countless PWIs throughout the nation, a modus operandi that began in earnest after the modern Civil Rights Movement. Ever since the late 1960s, African American student-activists and their allies at MSU have routinely spoken out for racial justice on campus and strategically used racial incidents—mainly on campus, and at times those in the national spotlight—as points of departure for challenging the administration to reevaluate its commitment to diversity, equity, and inclusion with a focus on African Americans' status in the community. This stratagem can be considered reactionary and perhaps unimaginative, but it's proven to be logical and prudent. It reveals how distinctly different generations of Black students find themselves routinely dealing with similar issues. They have recognized that when anti-Black racial incidents become publicized, controversial, or crises, they become important and unavoidable. For more than half a century, the Black presence on MSU's campus has functioned as part of the university's collective conscience. The status of MSU's Black community and racial climate can be used as a barometer to gauge the university's success and commitment to its often celebrated land-grant heritage, a mission and ethos that has significantly transformed since the first Morrill Act of 1862 was signed by President Abraham Lincoln and must be critically unpacked, especially as it relates to Native American land dispossession.

In the aftermath of the police killing of George Floyd on May 25, 2020, colleges and universities stood at an interesting crossroads. Like other sectors of U.S. society, institutions of higher learning responded to the murder of Floyd (and other African Americans) and the ensuing mass civil disobedience, protests, and unrest by scrambling to address racial injustice. They began with symbolic gestures, such as carefully crafted public statements on websites. Colleges and universities repackaged their commitment to the broadly conceived notions of diversity, equity, and inclusion and to improving their campus climate, particularly for "people of color" (now often called "BIPOC"). Some created university-wide committees tasked with examining racial inequity and developing recommendations and initiatives. This is nothing new.

The MSU 2020 Task Force on Racial Equity is a descendant of President Hannah's Committee of Sixteen. In moments such as the 2020 resurgence in national discourse about race with a focus on anti-Black racism, MSU leaders have tended to reflect upon their past commitments to racial justice. This is also a trend. Dating back to the Great Depression when the Michigan State Board of Agriculture (now the Board of Trustees) issued the institution's first major antidiscrimination pronouncement, MSU has had an intriguing past of attending to Black equity and civil rights. At some times more than others, the university's leadership has recognized the unique status of its Black population. Before and since the landmark 1989 study-in, Black students, faculty, and staff have consistently reminded the university of the democratic ideals the university claimed to espouse.

Afterword

I n an essay that appeared in a special twentieth volume issue of *Ebony* magazine (August 1965) entitled "The White Man's Guilt," James Baldwin observed, "History, as nearly no one seems to know, is not merely something to be read. And it does not refer merely, or even principally, to the past. On the contrary, the great force of history came from the fact that we carry it with us, are unconsciously controlled by it in many ways, and history is literally present in all we do. It could scarcely be otherwise since it is to history that we owe our frame of reference, our identities, and our aspirations." Baldwin's timeless musings underscore history's centrality to the human condition. All history is "living history." History is always with us, helping us untangle and make sense of the present. History defines us and profoundly shapes our world views.

That this artist-scholar-civil rights activist extraordinaire offered these reflections in 1965, when the historic Voting Rights Act was passed, isn't surprising. Born in 1924, he came of age during the World War II and Cold War eras and the modern Civil Rights Movement, publishing three novels between 1953 and 1962. Lecturing throughout the South for the Congress of Racial Equality (CORE), participating in the historic March on Washington for Jobs and Freedom, and unapologetically speaking out for African Americans' humanity, Baldwin keenly understood that the conditions faced by African Americans in 1965 were unambiguously linked to their everlasting struggles for civil and human rights in the United States. He understood that anti-Black thought in 1965 was a descendant of pro-slavery ideologies just as he was aware that the Civil Rights Movement was a decisive phase of a much older Black Freedom Struggle. Baldwin's observations are manifestly relevant to the subject of this book.

This book is part of my own personal history and deep connections with MSU. Beginning in the early 1990s when I worked in the African Studies Center's resource room and outreach division, I have been employed by the university for more than three decades. I made the transformative decision to be among some 1,700 undergraduate students who transferred to MSU in the fall 1990 term. During my undergraduate years, MSU had fall, winter, spring, and summer sessions. I'm old enough to have experienced the chaos and joys of "the pit" where students waited for hours—swapping classes, exchanging stories, making new friends, and hanging out. MSU was an ideal university to support my growing interest in African American history and Africana Studies. The Department of History had four full professors who specialized in African American history: Harry A. Reed, Richard W. Thomas, Wilma King, and John A. Hannah Distinguished Professor Darlene Clark Hine. Curtis Stokes regularly taught courses in Black political thought in James Madison College, and the Department of English had several specialists of African American language and literature including University Distinguished Professor Geneva Smitherman and Linda Beard. Ruth Simms Hamilton shepherded the African Diaspora Research Program, and the African Studies Center sustained grassroots outreach and extension programs. The decision to transfer to MSU transformed my life in consequential ways. One day in early February 1991, I met my late wife—who earned a BA and MA from the MSU College of Education—on the East Wing of the MSU Main Library (first floor) in front of where the rudimentary copy center used to be. (Our three sons, graduates of MSU, grew up with the campus as their extended backyard.)

During the 1990–1991 academic year, I lived in 509 East Wilson Hall and will never forget crossing "the Tundra" on many wintry days. I entered James Madison College majoring in this top-notch residential college's field of international relations. In the winter quarter of 1991, I enrolled in History 310A: Black American History, 1865–1945, taught by Harry A. Reed, the second African American professor in the Department of History who began teaching Black history in the early 1970s. After witnessing him lecture, I knew what I wanted to do. I longed to one day, like him, be able to gaze out a classroom window while dropping historical knowledge and, like a modern-day African American griot, recount fascinating tales from the African American past. I impulsively switched my major to history. I took every class I could from Dr. Reed: Black America Since 1945; America, the First 100 Years; The Black Experience in American Slavery; The History of Black Women in America; as well as several independent study courses. I ritualistically visited him during his office hours on the spooky fourth floor of Morrill Hall—a building constructed in 1900 as the Women's Building that much later housed, among other units, the Department of History until it was demolished in 2013. I tried to devour the countless books Dr. Reed assigned and recommended. In the summer of 1992 and 1993, he served as my mentor for the MSU Ronald E. McNair Postbaccalaureate Achievement Program and the Summer Research Opportunity Program and later the adviser of my PhD guidance committee. He retired from MSU in 2003 and passed away in May of 2019, at the age of eighty-four. Many generations of students benefited from his knowledge and sociability, whether through his engaging lectures, the fellowship that occurred at his house (he routinely invited his classes to his home near campus to sample his famous chili), and his generous office hours often held at his favorite coffee shop in East Lansing (Café Royale, which used to be on Abbott Road near Beggar's Banquet and Rick's American Cafe). Every year at the Department of History's annual awards banquet, he is evoked with the granting of the Harry Reed Endowed Scholarship in History, an award presented to undergraduate history juniors with either African American history or American history as their major area of emphasis.

The MSU Black community, especially the student body, provided me and my contemporaries with a vital sense of belonging. When I entered MSU about a year after the 1989 study-in, there was a total student population of about 42,800. At 2,944, the Black student body made up 6.9 percent of the total MSU student population. The early 1990s were similar to the early 1970s. It was like being at a small HBCU, a college within a university. During the 1990s, there were seemingly countless Black student organizations, such as the Black Students' Alliance (lead by Raymond Hearn, Bediaku Shapley, and others), AS ONE, the campus MSU NAACP branch, B-Black, B-More, Black Notes, Womyn of Colors, scores of residential Black caucuses, the MSU National Society of Black Engineers, and Ebony Productions. AS ONE was particularly outspoken. Under the presidency of the always dressed-to-the-nines Lawrence H. Tucker, aka "L. T.," AS ONE identified its "ultimate purpose" to be "the uplifting of Black people socially, educationally, economically, and politically" and embraced the motto "Just Watchin' Your Back." In early March 1991, AS ONE sponsored the first annual "Black Nation Rally." A month later, on April 2, 1991, during MSU's "Diversity Week," minority aide Clifton Divers, founder of the Revealers of Hidden Truths Bookstore Eric Ellison, and Black student-activists and aspiring writers initiated "Operation Common Sense."[1]

This was a practical campaign, encouraging Black students to get their $2.75 refund from the *State News* to donate to the *Focal Point*, MSU's second major Black student–run newspaper. Founded in the early 1980s, during the early 1990s, the paper was revived under the editorship of journalism major Trabian Shorters and psychology major Cazzy Jordan. Like the *Grapevine Journal*, the *Focal Point* relied on student support to thrive. I distinctly remember getting my refund and placing it in the jar outside of room 248 in the Student Services Building. Like their predecessors did in the early 1970s, Wilson Hall residents Divers and Shawn Williams also routinely distributed the newsletter *Blackwatch* to the residence halls' Black residents. During the 1990s, Black student-activists invited to campus many Black spokespersons, celebrities, and Afrocentric scholars. The roll call included Angela Davis, Yosef Ben-Jochannan (aka "Dr. Ben"), Jawanzaa Kunjufu, Imari Obadele, Dick Gregory, Bobby Seale, Oba T'Shaka, Leonard Jeffries Jr., Amiri Baraka, Frances Cress Welsing, Minister Louis Farrakhan, Robert Franklin Williams, Malauna Karenga, Molefi Kete Asante, Ossie Davis, and Ruby Dee, just to name a handful. During Black History Month in 1993, Kwame Ture, formerly Stokely Carmichael, spoke on campus and generously met with Black student leaders until the wee hours. As I listened to Ture in the Erickson Kiva describe his Pan-Africanist ideology and dissect the impact of Bill Clinton's administration on Black America, I had no idea he first came to campus twenty-five years earlier, helping to inspire a Black Campus Movement.

In the late 1990s and early 2000s, the Comparative Black History program, a one-of-a-kind program founded by renowned historian Darlene Clark Hine, hosted two major state-of-the-field conferences. Like the Office of Urban Affairs and College of Urban Development several decades earlier, it served as a vital learning community for numerous graduate students interested in Black life, history, and culture. While a graduate student, I served as the student chairperson of the Black History Committee (BHC). Mentored by Curtis Stokes, Murray Edwards, Rodney Patterson, and Fred Watson, other students in this organization included Muddasar Tawakkul, Charmagne Andrews, and Sydney Plant. Our motto was "Preserving a Proud Past, Redefining Our Future," and our mission was to highlight "African Americans' contributions to America and the world through a multidisciplinary forum." Giving a nod to Malcolm's Lansing roots and historic visit to MSU in 1963, the organization's signature event was "Malcolm X Week." We invited to campus speakers like Ivan Van Sertima, Ben Chavis, Sonya Sanchez, Wallace D. Muhammad, and Asa Hilliard. BHC sponsored events included a Black film series and the play *The Meeting* that depicted an imaginary 1965 encounter between King and Malcolm in Harlem. In the early 1990s with Marcus Shapley, Lisa Mechele Carpenter, and Nicole Tate, I cofounded an African drum and dance troupe, Amka Africa and the Sound Tribe, a cultural ensemble that performed at various events, from fraternity functions to "A Taste of Blackness" galas to BSA festivities to Black History Month celebrations to "Noontimes at the Union" to African American Student Welcome Receptions and beyond. In line with MSU's tradition of outreach and extension, we held workshops at secondary schools throughout the state, from Detroit to Flint to Grand Rapids to Harrison in Clare County. Shepherded by lead dancers Ayanna Smith, Khaleelah Jones, and Cassandra "Lil-Bit" Joseph and hyped up by Ronn-Vey Price and Jonathon Dungey in the late 1990s and early 2000s, the "Amka Sisters" (and few "Brothers") formed a sorority-like organization and shared with the MSU community an authentic Africa-inspired Black American culture. As I later learned, Amka was a descendant of the Black Arts Company of the 1970s.[2]

After earning a doctorate in history from MSU late in 1999 and teaching for several years at Wayne State University, I accepted a position as a tenure-stream assistant professor in the Department of History at MSU. Since then, I have routinely thought about how the road was paved for me and others by previous generations of African American students, faculty, and staff. My passionate curiosity in the African American experience at the university has been fueled by witnessing MSU's living Black history, a past that is unfixed and open to multiple interpretations and representations. For more than a century, the Black experience at MSU has been shaped by things said and done in the past. Its evolution and retellings have been influenced by the ever-changing and unpredictable present. Black life at America's first agricultural college from the late nineteenth century through the long and monumental Hannah years and beyond was inevitably impacted by the enduring Black Freedom Struggle. It was shaped by a range of local and national events and trends, by key transformations and turning points on campus and in U.S. society and culture, and by the actions and rhetoric of a diverse group of historical figures. The present circumstances of MSU's African American students, faculty, and staff have concrete historical antecedents. Likewise, the closer we look at them, past "racial issues" and "racial incidents" on campus are similar to, and even ideological precursors to, more contemporary expressions. To borrow again from Baldwin's rehashing of history philosophers' ideas, the constantly in-flux present is part of a larger historical context, and we can more fully comprehend the here and now by attentively exploring the past. By revisiting the recent and more distant past and acknowledging pivotal milestones, we can foster morale and pride, foreground moments of reform and progress, and use the past for inspiration, hope, and faith. Generations of MSU community members have realized this custom.

In addition to Baldwin's observations that open this afterword, words from historian Edward Hallett Carr's *What Is History?* resonated with me as I wrote this book. "The past which a historian studies is not a dead past, but a past which in some sense is still living in the present." Carr maintained that history is "a continuous process of interaction" between historians and their facts, "an unending dialogue between the present and the past." While writing this book, more than a few recent turns of events and milestones at MSU prompted me to reflect upon Blacks' historical experiences at the university within the context of Baldwin's and Carr's reasoning. What will transpire at MSU in the future cannot be predicted. One thing remains clear. We can learn a great deal about MSU's present, which changes with each passing day, by reflecting upon a rich, dynamic, and fascinating history. When centering African Americans, this history has been characterized by struggle, collaboration, perseverance, give and take, gradual change, and much more. The perception that "history repeats itself" is overly simplistic and unsophisticated. But "the great force of history comes from the fact that we carry it with us" and "history is literally present in all that we do." This book was not written with the ultimate intention of being historically prescriptive. If some readers find it to be, that would be an added plus. I hope this book's many stories, accounts, and renderings serve as revealing portholes into, and thought-provoking interpretations of, the intimately intertwined past and the present, eliciting a sense of measured optimism and enduring faith for a bright future.[3]

Go Green!

Acknowledgments

I began thinking about this book more than twenty years ago. I finally started seriously writing at a very strange time. It was during Michigan State University's spring 2020 semester, right after classes were abruptly shifted to remote learning amid the early stages of the COVID-19 epidemic. I converted my living room into a makeshift office. As a source of extra motivation, I placed a nicely curated collage of early African American Michigan Agricultural College students—namely, Charles Augustus Warren, William Ora Thompson, Myrtle Bessie Craig, and Gideon Edward Smith—above my living room table and new work space.

I'm indebted to these courageous souls for inspiring me, and to many others in the MSU community for support they offered as I researched and wrote. A conscientious, "old-school" historian and true sleuth who loves digging deep into the archives, LaShawn D. Harris helped track down more than a few students whose stories I recount and patiently listened as I anxiously shared my discoveries. She raised questions and offered feedback that improved this book. Thanks, LaShawn, for always having my back! Gabe Dotto, former director of Michigan State University Press, enthusiastically supported this project from its early stages, and current director Elizabeth Demers was very encouraging and helpful. I thoroughly enjoyed working with Caitlin Tyler-Richards, Kristine Blakeslee, Anastasia Wraight, Deborah Oosterhouse, and the MSU Press team. Thank you all for your patience and help. It was very challenging to conduct archival research with limited, remote access to the bewildering amount of materials in the MSU Archives and Historical Collections (UAHC). Ed Busch helped me maneuver MSU's exhaustive collections. I appreciate the willingness of the Special Collections Reading Room and UAHC teams to accommodate me, often on short notice. I thank Susan O'Brien for helping me navigate the fascinating *Grapevine Journal* Records. Jennie Rankin, who compiled the excellent "African Americans at MSU: A Guide to Resources in the Michigan State University Archives," helped me locate important documents and photos. Thanks, Jennie, for finding the awesome photo of Charles Augustus Warren with the class of 1900! Processing archivist Whitney Miller not only scanned numerous documents, but also offered me some important leads, including information about possibly one of the first African Americans who briefly attended M.A.C. in the early 1890s. Joseph Salem provided vital support. In January 2021 as dean of University Libraries, he approved having carefully packaged bound copies of the *Holcad* student newspaper sent directly to my home on loan. I can't thank him enough for this. Thanks also go to Kurt and Bob for the timely deliveries on those many Mid-Michigan cold and snowy days. Melissa Del Rio, Kate Metz, and the Graduate School team supported me in various key manners as I wrote this book and multitasked. Thomas Jeitschko and Teresa Woodruff's confidence in my leadership in the Graduate School—as well as their routine inquiries about the status of my book—was encouraging and motivating.

I thank my friends and colleagues for listening to me as I went off about MSU's past and my subjects' lives and contributions. I thank Nwando Achebe, Glenn and Terah Chambers, Walter Hawthorne, Sowande' Mustakeem, Tom Summerhill, Dean Rehberger, Daina Ramey Berry, Linda Greene, Jerlando Jackson, Tracy Washington, Alan Haller, John Ambrose, and Peter Alegi for listening to my tales and providing me spaces to think out loud about the historian's craft. Derrick P. Alridge's sage counsel has been a godsend, and his feedback on earlier incarnations of this book was on point. I thank Rashida Harrison for her friendship and allowing me to play a role, as "Uncle P," in Khamari's life. Longtime friend Marshanda Smith cheerfully shared with me her vast knowledge of the history of Black women faculty at MSU. As we worked together for countless hours on university initiatives, Wanda Lipscomb constantly validated my historical frame of analysis and mentored me. Dave Weatherspoon, who comes from a long line of M.A.C.–like Michigan farmers, has calmly and consistently served as steadfast sounding board and big brother. Terry Curry's mentorship over the years provided insight into a type of leadership that helped inform my understanding of past African American administrators, and multitasker extraordinaire Vennie Gore helped me further appreciate the work ethic involved in higher education stewardship. I'm blessed to have learned from a historian who knows more about MSU's early history than anyone. I agree with my former colleague, David T. Bailey, who predicted Keith R. Widder's first-rate history of MSU's formative years would "be the source of a raft of research projects," with many more stories to be recounted. This book includes some of these stories. Keith enduringly listened to me during our many meetings and upon numerous occasions when I, bursting with excitement, called him to share what I discovered and peppered him with a barrage of questions. I'm grateful for his gentle criticism, friendship, and constant encouragement. He is a humble master of the historian's craft.

I have learned a great deal about MSU's Black past from insightful memoirs, namely those authored by James B. Hamilton, Clarence Underwood, Robert L. Green, Clifton R. Wharton Jr., and Maya Washington. I thank Drs. Underwood, Green, Lipscomb, Sonya Gunnings-Moton, Carl Taylor, Lee June, Joe T. Darden, and Jeffrey Robinson for sharing their recollections of different eras, episodes, and personalities from MSU's rich past. Gloria Smith—who supported me beginning during her term as director of the African American and African Studies PhD Program—not only recounted stories about her experiences at MSU during the early 1970s, but also passed along to me precious documents from her own personal archives. I thank my friends and sports historians and aficionados Nate Colon (who always picked up when I called and answered my texts in real time), Derrick White, Lou Moore, and Johnny Smith for sharing their insights about the history and evolution of African American athletes in collegiate sports. Conversations with members of the MSU drum and dance troupe Amka Africa and the Sound Tribe helped jog my memories about aspects of the more contemporary MSU historical experience. About a decade ago, longtime members of the MSU community Murray Edwards, Lee June, and Curtis Stokes approached me with the idea of writing an accessible, oral history–based book canvassing the experiences of African American faculty and staff at MSU since the modern Civil Rights Movement. This book is part of this spirit. Thanks, Murray, for keeping it real since my undergraduate days. Passionate about the early African American presence on the MSU gridiron, Bryan Chapman knows much about the university's pathbreaking football players. After meeting him during the 2012–2013 academic year, whenever I spontaneously ran into him on campus, he would ceremoniously show me countless laminated images, newspaper clippings, and archival documents in his large and weathered binder, and our conversations were always uplifting.

I thank Eric Thomas (E.T.), Paulette Granberry-Russell, John Beck, Kris Renn, and Debra Johnson for providing me soapboxes from whence to share my research related to this book with various publics in the vast Spartan community. In the spring of 2021, Cindy Hunter Morgan previewed my project in the library's widely distributed *Insight* newsletter. Ashley Baker helped launch interest in my project by inviting me to deliver the keynote address for the MSU Department of Athletics' 2022 Spartan Summer Conversation, "History of Race, Sport, and Social Change," and it was my pleasure to address the team on the opening day of the 2022 fall camp. I thank the Council of Diversity Deans; the MSU Strategic Planning Committee; the Diversity, Equity, and Inclusion Steering Committee; and Jabbar Bennett and BAG for providing me spaces to draw connections between the university's past, present, and future. I thank graduate students in my History 808: Research in Early American and U.S. History course during the peculiar spring 2020 semester and those graduate students I advised while writing this book for listening to me habitually go off about my project and teaching me how to be a better professor and mentor. I thank Ajamu Dillahunt, Gloria Ashaolu, Taz Amin, and DuJour Johnson for their help as research assistants. Shondra Marshall, former national secretary and national president of the MSU Black Alumni Inc., graciously provided me with vital documents pertaining to the history of the MSU Black Alumni Inc.

I thank my parents, sister Sika, cousin Ron Combs, and sister-in-law Patricia McQueen for always being there. My mom attentively listened to me frantically babble about MSU's Black past for hours. To my three sons and fellow Spartans, Perovi, Kokou, and Agbelé, thanks for putting up with me over the years and as I wrote this book (and, yes, I am going to keep the photos of "old-school" Black Spartans on the wall above our dining room table, including the laminated cut-out one of Gideon!). Thanks, Perovi, for often asking me, "How's your book going, Dad?" and cosigning in our call-and-response tradition by uttering, in your monotone yet concerned voice, "Okay" after I proceeded to share with you more than you probably were interested in hearing about.

Finally, for inspiring me to write this book, I must give thanks and praises to those African American students, faculty, and staff who paved the way for me to be at MSU. Whenever I faced obstacles while writing this book, I found inspiration by reminiscing upon their lives, accomplishments, and determination.

Notes

INTRODUCTION

1. Since 1855, the institution has had six different names: Agricultural College of the State of Michigan (1855–1861), State Agricultural College (1861–1909), Michigan Agricultural College (1909–1925), Michigan State College of Agriculture and Applied Science (1925–1955), Michigan State University of Agriculture and Applied Science (1955–1964), and Michigan State University.

2. *M.A.C. Record* 8, no. 1 (September 16, 1902): 2; "New Students," *M.A.C. Record* 8, no. 4 (October 7, 1902): 1–2.

3. Enticing advertisements for the college routinely appeared in early issues of the *M.A.C. Record* from the late 1890s through the early twentieth century. See "Michigan State Agricultural College," *M.A.C. Record* 1, no. 20 (June 2, 1896): 8. Cindi Steinway, "Myrtle Mowbray, '07: MSU's First Black Graduate, Remembers M.A.C.," *MSU Alumni Magazine*, November 1972, 15.

4. Steinway, "Myrtle Mowbray, '07," 15.

5. W. Kim Heron, "Black Students at MSU," *Grapevine Journal*, September 18, 1973.

6. Steinway, "Myrtle Mowbray, '07," 15.

7. Before the city of East Lansing was chartered in 1907, the rural area was known as Collegeville. For the history of Collegeville and East Lansing, see Whitney Miller, *East Lansing: Collegeville Revisited* (Charleston, SC: Arcadia Publishing, 2002).

8. "What's Going on in Lansing," *LSJ*, November 10, 1917; Dave Hanson, "Efforts Made to Recognize Achievements of Black Citizens," *LSJ*, February 8, 1970.

9. Identifying people's race and ethnicity based upon photographs is rife with challenges. There are pictures of more than a few students in early issues of the *Wolverine* who appear to be of African descent. I didn't make assumptions about students' racial identity based upon yearbook pictures. An early example of a student who could appear to be of African descent can be found in a photograph of a group of students in about 1898 gathered around the college's first observatory (the man reading a book who is leaning against the window). See "MSU Unearths Observatory Foundation More Than a Century Old," *MSU Today*, August 2, 2023, https://msutoday.msu.edu/news/2023/msu-unearths-observatory-foundation-more-than-a-century-old.

10. Booker T. Washington to President, Michigan State Agricultural College, April 28, 1893, Oscar Clute Papers, UA 2.1.5, box 863, folder 92; Clute to Washington, May 2, 1893, Clute Papers, UA 2.1.5, box 863, folder 92; Washington to Lewis Gorton, May 12, 1894, and May 22, 1894, Lewis G. Gorton Papers, UA 2.1.6, box 873, folder 37, Michigan State University Archives and Historical Collections (hereafter UAHC), East Lansing, Michigan.

11. J. J. Pipkin, *The Negro in Revelation, in History, and in Citizenship* (St. Louis: N. D. Thompson Publishing, 1902), 413–417; Rossiter Johnson, ed., *The Twentieth Century Biographical Dictionary of Notable Americans* (Boston: Biographical Society, 1904); "Educator Dies," *Pittsburgh Courier*, September 11, 1926. According to the *Michigan State Agricultural College General Catalogue of Officers and Students, 1857–1900* (1900), "J. W. Hoffman" attended M.A.C. in 1894–1895.

12. Washington seemed excited to recruit Hoffman, but by 1896 he received negative teaching evaluation from his colleagues and Washington lost confidence in him. See Booker T. Washington to Nathan B. Young, March 26, 1896, in *The Booker T. Washington Papers, vol. 4: 1895–98*, ed. Louis R. Harlan (Urbana: University of Illinois Press, 1975), 145–149.

13. Jonathan L. Snyder to Hugh M. Browne, May 25, 1905, Jonathan L. Snyder Papers, UA 2.1.7, box 808, folder 122, UAHC.

14. "Annual Commencement Exercises of the Detroit High School—Full List of Promotions from the Lower Grades," *Evening News* (Detroit), June 22, 1894; W. S. Williams, "History of Lt. Frank Cheek Post," *Detroit Tribune*, July 11, 1942.

15. "Signal Honor," *Detroit Free Press*, October 8, 1899; "Lieut. Cheek Has Gone with His Colored Regiment," *Detroit News*, November 10, 1899; "The Fear of Death," *Detroit Free Press*, August 19, 1900; "Lieut. Cheek Grew Fat on Fun in the Philippines," *Detroit Free Press*, July 10, 1901.

16. "A Scene of Dazzling Splendor Painted by Our Social Elite," *Colored American*, September 27, 1902; "Oyster to Judson," *Washington Bee*, August 12, 1911; "Public Men and Things," *Washington Bee*, December 13, 1913; "The Week in Society," *Washington Bee*, January 17, 1914; "Died," *Evening Star*, April 11, 1914; "Foreign War Veterans to Meet," *Detroit News*, September 30, 1914; *Detroit News*, October 19, 1921; Williams, "History of Lt. Frank Cheek Post"; "Unique Meet Featured at Vets Bldg.," *Michigan Chronicle*, August 7, 1943.

17. Hattie Robinson, "Eight Negro Workers of Detroit Are Present," *Detroit Tribune* (*Tribune Independent*), July 28, 1934; "Milk Inspector," *Michigan Chronicle*, December 4, 1943; Beatrice Brown, "City-Reared Boy Scores Farming Honors with Sharpshooter Success," *Chicago Defender*, July 16, 1949. After it was founded in 1936, the *Chronicle* advertised educational opportunities at Michigan State such as 4-H programs, home economics

lessons (canning seminars were popular), and workshops for farmers.

18. In 1973, *Grapevine Journal* editor W. Kim Heron cited a source claiming there were about two hundred Black students on campus in the late 1950s. In 1970, Robert L. Green determined there were approximately 130 "minority" students on campus in 1960, the majority of whom were Black. See Robert L. Green, "The Admission of Minority Students: A Framework for Action," October 22, 1970, Robert L. Green Papers, UA 17.20, drawer F.D., folder 3, UAHC. It's difficult to determine the Black student population at the institution before the late 1960s. In 1973, Sharon Peters estimated that there were approximately 37 Blacks students enrolled in 1949, 200 by the end of the 1950s, 275 in 1962, and 500 in 1967. See Peters, "Black Students at Michigan State University: A Preliminary Research Report," Ruth Simms Hamilton Papers [hereafter RSH Papers] UA 17.269, box 2359, folder 14, UAHC. The data compiled by Green and his team in "The Admission of Minority Students" seems to be the most accurate.

19. Green, "The Admission of Minority Students"; Helen Clegg, "Qualified Negroes Studied," *LSJ*, July 24, 1968.

20. See Department of Human Relations, "Michigan State University Number of Black Enrolled by Year," in *Annual Report on Affirmative Action Prepared for the Michigan State University Board of Trustees* (East Lansing: Michigan State University, January 21, 1982). The Black student population was the largest population of students of color until the twenty-first century. In 2021, for the first time, the Asian student population was larger than the African American student population. In the fall of 2023, the total Asian student population was 4,002, and the total Black student population was 3,261. See *Michigan State University Enrollment Report* (East Lansing, Michigan State University, September 27, 2023), https://ir.msu.edu/-/media/assets/ir/docs/fall-enrollment/EnrollmentReportFall.pdf.

21. From 1970 until 1979, Blacks made up the vast majority of the minority student population, from a high of 83 percent in 1971 to a low of 74 percent in 1979. During the 1970s, the "Hispanic" student population was as follows: 299 in 1970, 237 in 1971, 288 in 1972, 297 in 1973, 305 in 1974, 328 in 1975, 307 in 1976, 335 in 1977, 324 in 1978, and 360 in 1979. See Department of Human Relations, "Michigan State University Number of Hispanic Students Enrolled by Year," in *Annual Report on Affirmative Action Prepared for the Michigan State University Board of Trustees* (East Lansing: Michigan State University, January 21, 1982).

22. Throughout this book, I use the abbreviation PWIs (predominantly White institutions) to refer to institutions of higher learning (i.e., colleges and universities) during various time periods. Unlike other designations characterizing colleges and universities in the Higher Education Act, PWI is not an official designation, and as Brian Bourke argues, it's often used nonchalantly. For Bourke, a PWI is not simply designated as such because of demographic trends. "Embedded institutional practices that are based in whiteness" must be considered. "Race and racism," Bourke adds, "are the cornerstones on which these institutions were built." My usage of PWI designation also draws from Eduardo Bonilla-Silva and Crystal E. Peoples's observation that "with a history, demography, curriculum, climate, and set of symbols and traditions" these institutions have embodied and reproduced whiteness. See Brian Bourke, "Meaning and Implications of Being Labelled a Predominantly White Institution," *College & University* 91, no. 3 (2016): 12–18, 20–21; Eduardo Bonilla-Silva and Crystal E. Peoples, "Historically White Colleges and Universities: The Unbearable Whiteness of (Most) Colleges and Universities in America," *American Behavioral Scientist* 66, no. 11 (2022): 1490–1504.

23. Data for MSU student enrollment dating back to the 1850s can be found at Office of the Registrar, "Historical Enrollment and Term End Reports," Michigan State University, https://reg.msu.edu/ROinfo/EnrollmentTermEnd.aspx.

24. Lynn Hunt, *History: Why It Matters* (Cambridge: Polity Press, 2018), 39.

25. Sarah Maza, *Thinking about History* (Chicago: University of Chicago Press, 2017), 4.

26. Sarah Haley, *No Mercy Here: Gender, Punishment, and the Making of Jim Crow Modernity* (Chapel Hill: University of North Carolina Press, 2016), 3–16, 46, 62–63.

27. Edward Hallett Carr, *What Is History?* (London: Penguin, 1967), 12, 24.

28. Arnold Rampersad, "Design and Truth in Biography," *South Central Modern Language Association* 9 (Summer 1992): 3, 6.

29. Between 1857 and 2025, Michigan State has had twenty-five presidents, including interim and acting presidents. Other Michigan State presidents whose dealings with African Americans are addressed to a lesser degree in this book include Frank S. Kedzie, Robert S. Shaw, Walter Adams, M. Cecil Mackey, and John DiBiaggio.

30. See, for example, Clarence G. Williams, *Technology and the Dream: Reflections on the Black Experience at MIT, 1941–1999* (Cambridge, MA: MIT Press, 2001), Lena M. Hill and Michael D. Hill, *Invisible Hawkeyes: African Americans at the University of Iowa during the Long Civil Rights Era* (Iowa City: University of Iowa Press, 2016), Don Wycliff and David Krashna, *Black Domers: African-American Students at Notre Dame in Their Own Words* (South Bend, IN: University of Notre Dame Press, 2017), Robert Greene II and Tyler D. Parry, eds., *Invisible No More: The African American Experience at the University of South Carolina* (Columbia: University of South Carolina Press, 2021), Geeta N. Kapur, *To Drink from the Well: The Struggle for Racial Equality at the Nation's Oldest Public University* (Durham, NC: Blair, 2021), and Theodore D. Segal, *Point of Reckoning: The Fight for Racial Justice at Duke University* (Durham, NC: Duke University Press, 2021). There has recently been a collection of books published on Black Power–era student activism by scholars Shirletta Kinchen, Kathryn Schumaker, Roderick A. Ferguson, Marilyn Allman Maye, Jelani M. Favors, Joshua M. Myers, Eddie R. Cole, and Brian Jones.

31. See Stefan Bradley, *Upending the Ivory Tower: Civil Rights, Black Power, and the Ivy League* (New York: New York University Press, 2018), 1–21; Bradley, *Harlem vs. Columbia University: Black Student Power in the Late 1960s* (Urbana: University of Illinois Press, 2009), 1–19.

CHAPTER 1. RECOGNIZABLY ABSENT

1. Jeanne Saddler, "Black Educator Influenced Founding of MSU," *State News*, August 13, 1970; Blanche B. Coggan, *Prior Foster, Pioneer Afro-American Educator: First Afro-American to Found and Incorporate an Educational Institution in the Northwest Territory* (Addison, MI: Woodstock Manual Labor Institute, 1969); "Prior Foster," *Working for Higher Education: Advancing Black Women's Rights in the 1850s*, Colored Conventions Project, https://coloredconventions.org/women-higher-education/biographies/prior-foster/.

2. *The Agricultural College of the State of Michigan* (Lansing, MI: Hosmer & Fitch Printers, 1857), 33.

3. According to Eduardo Bonilla-Silva and Crystal E. Peoples, "most colleges and universities in the United States are in fact historically white colleges and universities (HWCUs)" and, among other characteristics, "embody, signify, and reproduce whiteness." See Eduardo Bonilla-Silva and Crystal E. Peoples, "Historically White Colleges and Universities: The Unbearable Whiteness of (Most) Colleges and Universities in America," *American Behavioral Scientist* 66, no. 11 (2022): 1490.

4. *Catalogue of the Officers and Students of the State Agricultural College* (Lansing, MI: John A. Kerr & Co., Book and Job Printers, 1861), 11.

5. Eric Foner, *Forever Free: The Story of Emancipation and Reconstruction* (New York: Vintage, 2005), xxx, 42.

6. Robert Beasecker, ed., *"This Is a War for the Utter Extinction of Slavery": The Civil War Letters of James Benjamin Franklin Curtis, Hospital Steward, 1st Michigan Colored Infantry* (Allendale, MI: Grand Valley State University, 2020), 4, 60.

7. "Lt. Col. Strobel," *M.S.C. Record* 50, no. 1 (January 1945): 6. Founded in 1896 as the *M.A.C. Record*, the name of the paper was changed in 1925 to correspond with the college's new name, Michigan State College. See the *M.S.C. Record* 31, no 1. (September 21, 1925). In 1928, it began being interchangeably called the *M.S.C. Record* and the *Michigan State College Record*. In 1939, while still officially called the *Michigan State College Record*, on many of the cover pages through 1955, the paper was simply called *The Record*. When citing sources from the paper between 1925 and 1955, it will be hereafter in the notes referred to as the *M.S.C. Record* as opposed to the *M.A.C. Record* (1896–1924).

8. *The Agricultural College of the State of Michigan*, 25, 48, 49.

9. Paul Finkelman, "The Surprising History of Race and Law in Michigan," Michigan Supreme Court Historical Society, April 27, 2006, http://www.micourthistory.org/wp-content/uploads/speeches_vignettes_pdf/the_surprising_history_of_race_and_law_in_michigan.pdf.

10. Tiya Miles, *The Dawn of Detroit: A Chronicle of Slavery and Freedom in the City Straits* (New York: The New Press, 2017), 1–20.

11. Finkelman, "The Surprising History of Race and Law in Michigan"; "The Lynching of the Delhi Murderer," *Detroit Free Press*, August 13, 1866; "'Hogsback,' Scenically Beautiful, Reminder of Ingham's Only Hanging," *Lansing State Journal* [hereafter *LSJ*], September 4, 1916.

12. Finkelman, "The Surprising History of Race and Law in Michigan."

13. Historians have offered various explanations for the rise in anti-Black violence and racism during the early twentieth century, including competition for jobs, the increased migration of southern Whites to Detroit during the interwar period, and the rise of the Ku Klux Klan in the state.

14. Justin L. Kestenbaum, *Out of A Wilderness: An Illustrated History of Greater Lansing* (Woodland Hills, CA: Windsor Publications, 1981), 45.

15. See Tiya Miles, "'Shall Woman's Voice Be Hushed?': Laura Smith Haviland in Abolitionist Women's History," *Michigan Historical Review* 39 (Fall 2013): 3.

16. See Rashid Faisal, "A Touchdown for Equality, George Jewett," *Michigan History Magazine* 104, no. 2 (March–April 2020): 28.

17. John M. Green, ed., *Negroes in Michigan History* (Detroit: John M. Green, 1985), 106, 287, 288. This volume

includes *Michigan Manual of Freedmen's Progress*, compiled by Francis H. Warren and authorized by Act 47, Public Acts 1915 (Detroit, 1915).

18. W. E. Burghardt Du Bois and Augustus Granville Dill, eds., *The College-Bred Negro American* (Atlanta: Atlanta University Press, 1910), 45.

19. Margaret Lawrence, "Celebrating the Second Morrill Act of 1890," National Institute of Food and Agriculture, U.S. Department of Agriculture, August 30, 2022, https://www.nifa.usda.gov/about-nifa/blogs/celebrating-second-morrill-act-1890.

20. Steinway, "Myrtle Mowbray, '07," 15.

CHAPTER 2. BOOKER T. WASHINGTON AND M.A.C.

1. Barack Obama, "Remarks by the President at Signing of the Farm Bill—MI," (speech, Michigan State University, East Lansing, MI) The White House, President Barack Obama, February 7, 2014, https://obamawhitehouse.archives.gov/the-press-office/2014/02/07/remarks-president-signing-farm-bill-mi.

2. The audio for Malcolm X's speech was uploaded to YouTube numerous times between 2011 and 2020. The MSU University Archives and Historical Collections has an open reel audio tape recording of Malcolm speaking in the Erickson Kiva and at a press conference in the MSU Union Building.

3. Les Payne and Tamara Payne, *The Dead Are Rising: The Life of Malcolm X* (New York: Liveright Publishing, 2020).

4. In 1954, King spoke at Union Baptist Church where his uncle, Joel King, served as pastor, and he met with the Lansing branch of the NAACP. In 1957, he spoke at the Lansing Civic Center.

5. Martin Luther King Jr. and Malcolm X met for the first and only time in Washington, D.C., on March 26, 1964. See Peniel E. Joseph, *The Sword and the Shield: The Revolutionary Lives of Malcolm X and Martin Luther King Jr.* (New York: Basic Books, 2020), 1–13.

6. "North Breeds Watts Riots, Claims King," *LSJ*, March 10, 1966.

7. Keith R. Widder, *Michigan Agricultural College: The Evolution of a Land-Grant Philosophy, 1855–1925* (East Lansing: Michigan State University Press, 2005), 130; MSU Campus Archeology Program, "Field of Dreams: An Eclectic History of the Adams Field Area," November 2, 2017, http://campusarch.msu.edu/?p=5626.

8. Between 1951 and 1992, there were commencements held during the fall, winter, and spring terms. From 1992 until 1995, there were fall and spring commencements. Beginning in 1995, there were two ceremonies for fall semester baccalaureate degrees.

9. Washington authored several autobiographies during his lifetime. His most famous was *Up From Slavery*. For Washington's discussion of his mother and childhood, as well as the identity of his father referenced here, see Booker T. Washington, *Up from Slavery: An Autobiography* (Garden City, NY: Doubleday, 1900, 1901), 1–3.

10. Booker T. Washington, *My Larger Education: Being Chapters from My Experience* (Garden City, NY: Doubleday, Page, 1911), 6, 9, 11, 12.

11. Jonathan Snyder, "President's Address: The Higher Education of Famers' Children," *M.A.C. Record* 5, no. 39 (June 26, 1900): 2–3.

12. "President Emeritus, J. L. Snyder, Dies," *M.A.C. Record* 25, no. 5 (October 24, 1919): 4–5; "Doctor Snyder, Educator, Dead," *LSJ*, October 23, 1919.

13. Widder, *Michigan Agricultural College*, 78, 74. For more on Snyder, see Maurice Raymond Cullen Jr., "The Presidency of Jonathan LeMoyne Snyder at Michigan Agricultural College" (PhD diss., Michigan State University, 1966).

14. "President Emeritus, J. L. Snyder, Dies," 4–5.

15. State Board of Agriculture Minutes, Michigan Agricultural College, November 19, 1919, UAHC.

16. Roger Rosentreter, "Pomp and Presidents: TR and Bill Clinton Visit MSU," *Michigan History Magazine* 79, no. 5 (September/October 1995): 31.

17. Herbert W. Collingwood, "The Negro as a Farmer: What the Tuskegee Conference Shows," *Outlook*, March 20, 1897; "Tuskegee Farmers Meet in 35th Annual Get-Together," *Chicago Defender*, February 13, 1926.

18. Washington, *Up from Slavery*, 241.

19. "Personals," *Detroit Free Press*, March 2, 1902.

20. "This Year a Record Breaker," *M.A.C. Record*, 5, no. 2 (September 19, 1899): 2.

21. State Board of Agriculture Minutes, Michigan Agricultural College, June 30, 1900, UAHC.

22. Booker T. Washington, "Solving the Negro Problem in the Black Belt of the South," in *Thirty-Ninth Annual Report of the Secretary of the State Board of Agriculture and the Thirteenth Annual Report of the Experiment Station from July 1, 1899 to June 30, 1900* (Lansing: Wynkoop Hallenbeck Crawford Co. of Lansing, Mich. State Printers, 1900), 453.

23. Widder, *Michigan Agricultural College*, 278.

24. Washington, *Up from Slavery*, 246–247.

25. "Booker T. Washington–Commencement Orator," *M.A.C. Record* 4, no. 18 (January 17, 1899): 4.

26. "Booker T. Washington Will Not Address Us," *M.A.C. Record* 4, no. 31 (April 18, 1899): 1.

27. John W. Robinson to [Jonathan L. Snyder], June 7, 1899, and Snyder to Robinson, June 12, 1899, Jonathan L. Snyder Papers, UA 2.1.7, box 804, folder 94, UAHC.

28. Anne Hogenson, "Pilgrim, Hughes Uncover Forgotten History of Campus Diversity, Identify Prominent Africa-American Attendees in Early 20th Century," *Ferris Magazine* (2018) https://ferrismagazine.com/hidden-stories/.

CHAPTER 3. BLACK CULTURE IMAGINED IN COLLEGEVILLE

1. "Booker T. Washington Here in June," *M.A.C. Record* 5, no. 19 (January 23, 1900): 1.

2. Morris Wade, "Booker T. Washington and His Tuskegee Industrial School," *M.A.C. Record* 5, no. 35 (May 15, 1900): 1.

3. J. Brock Westover, "Our Colored Brothers," *M.A.C. Record* 5, no. 11 (November 21, 1899): 2. The first reference to Washington in the *M.A.C. Record* was in E. Dwight Sanderson, "A Danger and a Duty," *M.A.C. Record* 1, no. 44 (December 8, 1896): 4.

4. W. O. H., "History," *M.A.C. Record* 6, no. 3 (October 2, 1900): 3. Hedrick was a longtime professor at the

college. See Madison Kuhn, "Prof. W. O. Hedrick, Retired Ten Years Ago, Is Michigan State's Most Faithful Student," *M.S.C. Record* 53, no. 5 (July 1948): 10.

5. "Woman's Historical Club," *LSJ*, January 29, 1916; "Woman's Historical Club," *LSJ*, February 5, 1916. Professor W. W. Johnston was scheduled to discuss the drama with the club.

6. Carter G. Woodson, "Negro Life and History in Our Schools," *Journal of Negro History* 4 (July 1919): 275.

7. Sam Walter Foss, "Sambo's Prayer," *M.A.C. Record* 4, no. 31 (April 18, 1899): 4.

8. *College Speculum* 1, no. 2 (October 1, 1881): 21.

9. F. W. Yaple, "The Negro Voter in Southern Cities," *College Speculum* 13, no. 3 (October 15, 1894): 37–39.

10. Westover, "Our Colored Brothers," 2.

11. "The College Oratorical Contest," *M.A.C. Record* 3, no. 39 (June 14, 1898): 1. A horticulture professor mentioned that lynching was a crime. See "Prof. Smith's Lecture–Unsolved Problems," *M.A.C. Record* 2, no. 16 (April 27, 1897): 1. In 1899, Robert C. Kedzie made a passing reference to lynching. He wrote: "A mob has no conscience—and this is the central fact in lynchings." See Kedzie, "A Word to New Students," *M.A.C. Record* 5, no. 1 (September 12, 1899): 2.

12. "Emancipation Day in Washington," *M.A.C. Record* 1, no. 28 (July 28, 1896): 4–5.

13. "Annual Contest," *M.A.C. Record* 1, no. 44 (December 8, 1896): 1.

14. Sanderson, "A Danger and a Duty," 4.

15. T. B. Keogh to Gorton, July 18, 1895; Gorton to Keogh, July 25, 1895; Keogh to Gorton, July 29, 1895; Keogh to Gorton, August 10, 1895, Lewis G. Gorton Papers, UA 2.1.6, box 873, folder 47, UAHC.

16. Keogh to Gorton, August 10, 1895, Lewis G. Gorton Papers, UA 2.1.6, box 873, folder 47, UAHC.

17. Exactly how long Stevens taught at the Agricultural and Mechanical College for the Colored Race, Greensboro, North Carolina, is unknown. He arrived there for the start of the fall 1895 semester and began working at Connecticut Agricultural College on September 1, 1907.

18. *Biennial Report of the Trustees of the Connecticut State College at Storrs* (Hampton, CT, 1934), 25.

19. A. T. Stevens to Gorton, November 6, 1895, Gorton Papers, UA 2.1.6, box 873, folder 54, UAHC.

20. "Member of Storrs Faculty Investigated Markets of West Indies," *Hartford Courant*, January 19, 1930.

21. Ray Stannard Baker, "The Negro in a Democracy," *M.A.C. Record* 15, no. 8 (November 9, 1909): 2.

22. Booker T. Washington to Ray Stannard Baker, February 1, 1907, in *The Booker T. Washington Papers*, vol. 9: *1906–8*, ed. by Louis R. Harlan and Raymond W. Smock (Urbana: University of Illinois Press, 1980), 208.

23. Pero Gaglo Dagbovie, "Reflections on Conventional Portrayals of the African American Experience during the Progressive Era or 'the Nadir,'" *Journal of the Gilded Age and Progressive Era* 13 (January 2014): 4–27.

24. Robert Bruce Slater, "The First Black Graduates of the Nation's 50 Flagship State Universities," *Journal of Blacks in Higher Education*, no. 13 (Autumn 1996): 72.

25. Robert J. Norrell, *Up from History: The Life of Booker T. Washington* (Cambridge, MA: Belknap Press of Harvard University Press, 2009), 1.

26. "Booker T. Washington's Visit," *Morning Star* (Wilmington, NC), October 14, 1910.

27. "Wichita Hotels Barred Washington," *Detroit Free Press*, January 19, 1905.

28. "Joke on Booker T. Washington," *Diamond Drill* (Crystal Falls, MI), September 23, 1905.

29. Department of Commerce and Labor Bureau of Census, *Thirteenth Census of the United States Taken in the Year 1910: Statistics for Michigan Containing Statistics of Population, Agriculture, Manufactures, and Mining for the State, Counties, Cities, and Other Divisions*, Reprint of the Supplement for Michigan Published in Connection with the Abstract of the Census (Washington, D.C.: Government Printing Office, 1913), 595, 618, 619.

30. Bill Castanier, "A House Divided: The Movement in East Lansing to Open Housing for Blacks," City Pulse, February 25, 2015, https://www.lansingcitypulse.com/stories/a-house-divided,5505; Eric Lacy, "East Lansing Apologizes for Decades of Racism, Plans Annual Community Conversations," LSJ, March 1, 2018, https://www.lansingstatejournal.com/story/news/local/2018/03/01/east-lansing resolution/380710002/.

CHAPTER 4. PRAISE SONG FOR TUSKEGEE

1. "Industrial Education," *M.A.C. Record* 1, no. 41 (November 17, 1896): 4–6.

2. Booker T. Washington, "Solving the Negro Problem in the Black Belt of the South," in *Thirty-Ninth Annual Report of the Secretary of the State Board of Agriculture and the Thirteenth Annual Report of the Experiment Station from July 1, 1899 to June 30, 1900* (Lansing, MI: Wynkoop Hallenbeck Crawford Co. of Lansing, Mich. State Printers, 1900), 451–452.

3. Pres. J. L. Snyder, "To Prospective Students," *M.A.C. Record* 4, no. 41 (August 8, 1899): 2.

4. Washington, "Solving the Negro Problem in the Black Belt of the South," 452.

5. Morris Wade, "Booker T. Washington and His Tuskegee Industrial School," *M.A.C. Record* 5, no. 35 (May 15, 1900): 1.

6. Thomas Dixon Jr., "Booker T. Washington and the Negro: Some Dangerous Aspects of the Work of Tuskegee," *Saturday Evening Post* 178 (August 19, 1905): 1–2. For a summary of Dixon's speech at M.A.C. in 1902, see "Thomas Dixon, Jr.," M.A.C. Record 7, no. 25 (March 11, 1902): 1.

7. Washington, "Solving the Negro Problem in the Black Belt of the South," 452–454.

8. "Agricultural College: Two Benton Harbor Young Men Graduated–Booker T. Washington's Address," *Herald-Palladium* (Benton Harbor, MI), June 22, 1900.

9. During the early twentieth century, students received college calendars that included photos of campus buildings and students, facts about M.A.C., and mottos and sayings. For the Michigan Agricultural Calendar for 1900, see *On the Banks of the Red Cedar*, UAHC, https://projects.kora.matrix.msu.edu/files/162-565-62/S188_1900.pdf.

10. "An Account of a Speech in Columbus, Ohio," May 24, 1900, in *The Booker T. Washington Papers*, vol. 5: *1899–1900*, ed. by Louis R. Harlan and Raymond W. Smock (Urbana: University of Illinois Press, 1974), 542–543.

11. For Creelman's account, see chapter 15, "The Secret of Success in Public Speaking," in Booker T. Washington, *Up from Slavery: An Autobiography* (Garden City, NY: Doubleday, 1900, 1901).

12. Jonathan Snyder, "President's Address: The Higher Education of Farmers' Children," *M.A.C. Record* 5, no. 39 (June 26, 1900): 2.

13. "A Big Gathering: State School Teachers Meet in Grand Rapids," *Owosso Times*, December 20, 1901.

14. "Washington and His Mission," *Herald-Press* (Saint Joseph, MI), December 30, 1901.

15. "Gets $12,000: Booker T. Washington That Much Richer on Leaving Battle Creek," *Herald-Press* (Saint Joseph, MI), March 20, 1911.

16. "Negroes Taught Dignity of Labor: R. D. Taborn Tells of Tuskegee and Its Mission–Colored Race Helped," *LSJ*, May 6, 1912.

17. "Booker Washington Will Speak Here," *LSJ*, October 5, 1912; "Booker T. Washington, in His Tour of Michigan, Will Come to Lansing and Speak at Y.M.C.A.," *LSJ*, October 12, 1912.

18. "B. T. Washington's Lecture Is Free," *LSJ*, October 15, 1912; "Booker T. Won't Talk Politics: Noted Negro Educator Give an Address on Tuskegee Institute," *LSJ*, October 17, 1912.

19. "Booker T. Won't Talk Politics."

20. *LSJ*, October 31, 1912.

21. *M.A.C. Record* 18, no. 15 (October 15, 1912): 4.

CHAPTER 5. HISTORIC COMMENCEMENT CEREMONY

1. "Commencement," *M.A.C. Record* 12, no. 37 (June 4, 1907): 3.

2. The 1904 commencement activities took place from June 19 until June 22. Under the header "Commencement" in the June 21, 1904, *M.A.C. Record*, the following appears: "The exercises began with the baccalaureate sermon on Sunday, June 19, which was well attended, and ended with the conferring of degrees by Pres. Snyder on Wednesday, June 22."

3. "Commencement," *M.A.C. Record* 9, no. 39 (June 21, 1904): 3.

4. Thompson's name doesn't appear in the 1904 commencement program. This omission doesn't appear to have anything to do with Thompson's race. The June 21, 1904 issue of the *M.A.C. Record* included the names of fifty-seven graduates, and the 1904 program lists fifty-one graduates.

5. Thompson is currently considered the first known African American to graduate from the university. Craig remains the first known Black woman graduate. For "the heart of the academic program" being the agricultural course, see Keith R. Widder, *Michigan Agricultural College: The Evolution of a Land-Grant Philosophy, 1855–1925* (East Lansing: Michigan State University Press, 2005), 111–131.

6. W. E. Burghardt Du Bois and Augustus Granville Dill, eds., *The College-Bred Negro American* (Atlanta: Atlanta University Press, 1910), 45. In this study, Du Bois identifies the number of Blacks who graduated from American colleges from 1823 until 1909, pointing out "that mathematical accuracy in these studies is impossible."

7. Du Bois and Dill, *The College-Bred Negro American*, 26.

8. For a discussion of the first African Americans who graduated from PWIs, see Robert Bruce Slater, "The Blacks who First Entered the World of White Higher Education," *Journal of Blacks in Higher Education*, no. 4 (Summer 1994): 47–56.

9. H. C. stands for Henry Clay. He was identified as "H. C." in the 1904 commencement program and in the *M.A.C. Record*.

10. Dr. H. C. White, "Commencement Address," *M.A.C. Record* 9, no. 39 (June 21, 1904): 3–5.

11. Lester D. Stephens, "Darwin's Disciple in Georgia: Henry Clay White, 1875–1927," *Georgia Historical Review* 78 (Spring 1994): 68, 88.

12. "In Retrospect," *M.A.C. Record* 13, no. 38 (June 30, 1908): 2. The editors noted it was unfortunately "unable to give in full the address of Miss Jane Adams gave at commencement."

13. Widder, *Michigan Agricultural College*, 359.

14. Keith R. Widder, "White Privilege at Michigan Agricultural College, 1855–1925" (unpublished paper, in author's possession, 2005). Widder provides an example of how three Japanese students were "hazed (or attacked)" in the later 1880s. In response, they left M.A.C.

15. "'Tic' Minstrel," *M.A.C. Record* 9, no. 23 (March 1, 1904): 1.

16. "New Students," *M.A.C. Record* 5, no. 4 (October 3, 1899): 2.

17. "A Student from Puerto Rico," *M.A.C. Record* 5, no. 2 (September 19, 1899): 3.

CHAPTER 6. CLASS OF 1900 HONORABLE MENTION

1. "A Senior Goes to Tuskegee," *M.A.C. Record* 5, no. 8 (October 31, 1899): 1.

2. According to an obituary, Warren was born on December 25, 1871. See the *South Bend (IN) Tribune*, June 27, 1964. In several U.S. censuses, his birthdate is listed as 1872. It seems December 25, 1871, is most likely his birthdate.

3. "New Students," *M.A.C. Record* 1, no. 35 (October 6, 1896): 4.

4. According to Widder: "It is no surprise that the college's dormitories were apparently closed to black students." See Keith R. Widder, "White Privilege at Michigan Agricultural College, 1855–1925" (unpublished paper, in author's possession, 2005). For an example of the advertisements showcasing what M.A.C. had to offer prospective students from the 1890s and early 1900s, see "Michigan Agricultural College," *M.A.C. Record* 1, no 20 (June 2, 1896): 8.

5. *M.A.C. Record* 1, no. 1 (January 14, 1896): 2–4.

6. Keith R. Widder, *Michigan Agricultural College: The Evolution of a Land-Grant Philosophy, 1855–1925* (East Lansing: Michigan State University Press, 2005), 66.

7. W. J. Beal, *History of Michigan Agricultural College and Biographical Sketches of Trustees and Professors* (East Lansing, MI: Agricultural College, 1915), 134, 103.

8. Widder, *Michigan Agricultural College*, 70.

9. Widder, *Michigan Agricultural College*, 270–271.

10. "Cut Into Pieces, Then Burned," *Detroit News*, April 24, 1899; "Two More Killed," *Livingston County Daily Press and Argus* (*Livingston Republic*), April 26, 1899. The horrific story was often carried on the front page of countless papers with gory and attention-grabbing titles.

11. See Crystal R. Sanders, "'We Very Much Prefer to Have a Colored Man in Charge': Booker T. Washington and Tuskegee's All-Black Faculty," *Alabama Review* 74 (April 2021): 99–128.

12. *Tuskegee Student* 12 (May 5, 1900): 2.

13. George Washington Carver, "Some Ceresporae of Macon Co., Alabama," in *Bulletin No. 4, 1901* (Tuskegee: Tuskegee Institute Steam Print, 1901).

14. Lindo O. Hines, "George Washington Carver and the Agricultural Experiment Station," *Agricultural History* 35 (January 1979): 75.

15. Louis R. Harlan, *Booker T. Washington: The Making of a Black Leader, 1856–1901* (New York: Oxford University Press, 1972), 272.

16. "Old Students," *M.A.C. Record* 6, no. 37 (June 18, 1901): 8.

17. Charles A. Warren, "Some Remarks on Tuskegee," *M.A.C. Record* 6, no. 36 (June 11, 1901): 6.

18. "Grand Rapids M.A.C. Association," *M.A.C. Record* 7, no. 16 (January 7, 1902): 2–3.

19. John M. Green, ed., *Negroes in Michigan History* (Detroit: John M. Green, 1985), 23.

20. "Alumni," *M.A.C. Record* 18, no. 15 (January 7, 1913): 1.

21. Green, *Negroes in Michigan History*, 304–311.

22. Green, *Negroes in Michigan History*, 282–287, 304–311.

23. *LSJ*, May 15, 1915; "African Methodist Jubilee on Sunday," *LSJ*, May 19, 1917.

24. Green, *Negroes in Michigan History*, 32.

25. Green, *Negroes in Michigan History*, "Introduction," 6–27, 30–33, 37.

26. "What's Going on in Lansing," *LSJ*, October 12, 1917; "Prominent Negro Resident Is Dead: W. R. Roberts, State Employee, Engrossed Many Diplomas, Dies Here," *LSJ*, January 3, 1924.

27. "Card of Thanks," *LSJ*, November 28, 1914; *LSJ*, March 17, 1916; *LSJ*, October 12, 1917; "A. M. E. Church Will Dedicate Service Flag," *LSJ*, January 12, 1918; *LSJ*, October 18, 1919; "Ingham Workers Go to Interchurch Meeting," *LSJ*, December 18, 1919; "Kind o' Uppity is Official View," *LSJ*, March 2, 1920; "Colored Community House Expects Further Growth in Second Year," *LSJ*, October 31, 1921; "Plan Social Season at Community House," *LSJ*, November 21, 1921.

28. "Colored Group Hears Urban League Speaker," *LSJ*, May 15, 1930; "Michigan: Charles A. Warren," *South Bend (IN) Tribune*, June 27, 1964.

29. "Michigan: Charles A. Warren," *South Bend (IN) Tribune*, June 27, 1964.

CHAPTER 7. ALUMNUS EXTRAORDINAIRE

1. Emma Lou Thornbrough, *The Negro in Indiana before 1900: A Study of a Minority* (Indianapolis: Indiana Historical Bureau, 1957), 141, 206, 318, 361, 362–363.

2. See Hugh Leach, "Black MSU Grad Found in 1904 Class," *LSJ*, April 27, 2007.

3. W. J. Beal, *History of Michigan Agricultural College and Biographical Sketches of Trustees and Professors* (East Lansing, MI: Agricultural College, 1915), 142.

4. " A Reminiscence," *M.A.C. Record* 1, no. 22 (June 16, 1896): 1; "Three Civil War Veterans Want Clear Records," *LSJ*, February 1, 1912. When the term "Jim Crow North" appears in this book, I am drawing from the definitions offered by Brian Purnell and Jeanne Theoharis, "Introduction: Histories of Racism and Resistance, Seen and Unseen; How and Why to Think about the Jim Crow North," in *The Strange Career of the Jim Crow*

North: Segregation and Struggle Outside the South, ed. Purnell, Theoharis, and Komozi Woodard (New York: New York University Press, 2019), 1–42.

5. Keith R. Widder, *Michigan Agricultural College: The Evolution of a Land-Grant Philosophy, 1855–1925* (East Lansing: Michigan State University Press, 2005), 346.

6. "Alumni," *M.A.C. Record* 11, no. 14 (December 19, 1905): 2.

7. For Etta's cause of death, see Leach, "Black MSU Grad Found in 1904 Class."

8. *M.A.C. Record* 10, no. 28 (April 4, 1905): 3.

9. "Choate and Twain Plead for Tuskegee," *New York Times*, January 23, 1906.

10. See Rayford W. Logan, *The Betrayal of the Negro from Rutherford B. Hayes to Woodrow Wilson* (New York: Collier Books, 1965), 11–164. Logan originally published this book in 1954 as *The Negro in American Life and Thought: The Nadir, 1877–1901*. In the revised 1965 edition, Logan extended "the nadir" beyond 1901 into the first several decades of the twentieth century. For the referenced statistics on lynching for 1906, see National Association for the Advancement of Colored People, *Thirty Years of Lynching in the United States, 1898–1918* (New York: NAACP National Office, April 1919), 29.

11. Booker T. Washington, ed., *Tuskegee and Its People: Their Ideals and Achievements* (New York: D. Appleton, 1916), viii.

12. State Board of Agriculture Minutes, Michigan Agricultural College, November 19, 1919, UAHC; Widder, *Michigan Agricultural College*, 91.

13. Washington, *Tuskegee and Its People*, 22; Kevin K. Gaines, "Racial Uplift Ideology in the Era of 'the Negro Problem,'" Freedom's Story, TeacherServe, National Humanities Center, accessed February 2014, http://nationalhumanitiescenter.org/tserve/freedom/1865-1917/essays/racialuplift.htm. Also see Gaines, *Uplifting the Race: Black Leadership, Politics and Culture during the Twentieth Century* (Chapel Hill: University of North Carolina Press, 1996).

14. *M.A.C. Record* 11, no. 32 (May 1, 1906): 2.

15. Leach, "Black MSU Grad Found in 1904 Class"; Phillip Lewis, "Tuskegee Airman Who Chartered a Chapter of Alpha Phi Alpha in the 1940s Shares His Story," Watch the Yard: Black Greekdom's Digital Yardshow, 2014, https://www.watchtheyard.com/alphas/alpha-phi-alpha-william-thompson/.

16. Widder, *Michigan Agricultural College*, 346.

17. "Birth Announcements," *LSJ*, March 15, 1919. William Jr. was born in Sparrow Hospital on March 12, 1919.

18. "Feeling Heightened by Seeing 'Birth of a Nation' Barber and Negro Clash in 'Near Riot,'" *LSJ*, February 10, 1916.

19. "Colored People to Meet in Detroit," *LSJ*, June 25, 1921.

20. "In the Churches," *LSJ*, February 13, 1926; "Colored People's Ass'n Re-Elects President," *LSJ*, November 16, 1926; "NAACP Open Session in City," *LSJ*, October 6, 1945; Virginia Redfern, "50 Years in Own Home: 'Long Way' for Seatons," *LSJ*, January 19, 1979.

21. *M.A.C. Record* 28, no. 19 (February 19, 1923): 12. Thompson died on February 7, 1923, about two months after his father, Savannah. He and his father may have succumbed to the same flu-induced illness. Seven years after Savannah's death, Violet Thompson died on December 19, 1929.

CHAPTER 8. OF THE HIGHEST QUALITIES OF CHARACTER

1. See the cover of the *Grapevine Journal*, September 18, 1973. This issue included W. Kim Heron's feature article, "Black Students at MSU," one of the first published essays of its kind.

2. Cindi Steinway, "Mrytle Mowbray, '07: MSU's First Black Graduate, Remembers M.A.C.," *MSU Alumni Magazine*, November 1972, 15.

3. Darlene Clark Hine, "Rape and the Inner Lives of Black Women in the Middle West," *Signs* 14 (Summer 1989): 912, 915.

4. "Death Elsewhere," *Battle Creek Enquirer*, November 19, 1974.

5. Rose M. Nolen, "Black Residents Were Key in City's Growth," *Sedalia Democrat*, February 4, 2010.

6. See National Association for the Advancement of Colored People, *Thirty Years of Lynching in the United States, 1889–1918* (New York: NAACP National Office, April 1919), 41, 81.

7. Jacqueline Jones, *Labor of Love, Labor of Sorrow: Black Women, Work, and the Family, from Slavery to the Present* (New York: Basic Books, 2010), 105, 110, 111.

8. Jones, *Labor of Love, Labor of Sorrow*, 113, 115.

9. Stephanie J. Shaw, *What a Woman Ought to Be and Do: Black Professional Women Workers during the Jim Crow Era* (Chapel Hill: University of North Carolina Press, 1996), 5.

10. Keith R. Widder, *Michigan Agricultural College: The Evolution of a Land-Grant Philosophy, 1855–1925* (East Lansing: Michigan State University Press, 2005), 149, 151.

11. Steinway, "Myrtle Mowbray, '07," 15.

12. Widder, *Michigan Agricultural College*, 347.

13. W. C. Bennett, "The Anglo Saxon Society Woman," *M.A.C. Record* 8, no. 27 (March 24, 1903): 4; "Tic Minstrel," *M.A.C. Record* 11, no. 23 (February 27, 1906): 1; *Belding Banner*, March 22, 1906; "College Minstrels," *M.A.C. Record* 11, no. 28 (April 3, 1906): 1.

14. *Catalogue of Officers and Students of the Michigan Agricultural College for the Year 1903–1904* (Agricultural College, 1904).

15. *New York Age*, July 1, 1909.

16. *Columbia University in the City of New York, Directory of Summer Session Students 1912*; *New York Age*, June 10, 1915; *New York Age*, March 9, 1916; *New York Age*, June 15, 1918; *New York Age*, June 22, 1918; "Bleeks Dressmaking School," *New York Age*, September 1, 1923. In a 1918 Columbia University annual, a "Miss Emma C. Baker" was appointed by the president to "make recommendations in regard to the University Commons."

17. *M.S.C. Record* 31, no. 14 (January 11, 1926): 227, 228.

18. Heron, "Black Students at MSU"; State Board of Agriculture Minutes, Michigan Agricultural College, November 19, 1919, UAHC.

19. Snyder to Washington, April 12, 1907, Jonathan L. Snyder Papers, UA 2.1.7, box 813, folder 117, UAHC.

20. Washington to Snyder, February 3, 1908; Snyder to Washington, February 8, 1908; Mrs. Booker T. Washington to Snyder, February 28, 1908, Snyder Papers, UA 2.1.7, box 813, folder 117, UAHC.

21. W. E. Burghardt Du Bois, *The College-Bred Negro* (Atlanta: The Atlanta University Press, 1910), 5, 15, 45, 48, 51;

"Western University Notes," *The Rising Son* (Kansas City, MO), October 19, 1907.

22. *M.A.C. Record* 13, no. 11 (December 3, 1907): 1.

23. *M.A.C. Record* 16, no. 18 (January 24, 1911): 1.

24. *M.A.C. Record* 17, no. 10 (November 28, 1911): 2.

25. "Eaton Rapids," *LSJ*, July 12, 1912.

26. Steinway, "Myrtle Mowbray, '07," 15.

CHAPTER 9. SPARTAN SUPERHERO

1. Robert Bao, "The Masterpiece of 1913," *MSU Alumni Magazine*, Fall 2013, 70–71. Smith was named the American Football Coaches Association's recipient of the 2014 Trailblazer award.

2. Steve Grinczel, "Celebrating the Legacy of Gideon Smith," Michigan State Spartan Athletics, October 15, 2013, https://msuspartans.com/news/2013/10/15/Celebrating_the_Legacy_of_Gideon_Smith.aspx.

3. Grinczel, "Celebrating the Legacy of Gideon Smith."

4. *LSJ*, October 18, 1953; "Smith to Rejoin 1913 Teammates at Spartans' Fete," *Daily Press* (Newport News, VA), October 15, 1953. For general coverage of the event, see "State's 1913 Undefeated Team to Be Honored," *LSJ*, October 16, 1953.

5. "Smith to Rejoin 1913 Teammates at Spartans' Fete"; "Reunion for Old Aggies," *Jet* 5, no. 1 (November 12, 1953): 56.

6. "1915 Gridders Return," *LSJ*, October 31, 1965.

7. In 1935, the Michigan State College's stadium was officially named Macklin Field in honor of John F. Macklin. Macklin was invited back to campus and insisted his former players be invited. *Detroit Free Press* wrote that Smith, the "giant Negro lineman, who gloried in ripping touted lines to shreds . . . is expected back to meet his old coach." Smith did not attend. He was busy coaching at Hampton. See "State Dedication Honors Macklin," *Detroit Free Press*, November 9, 1935; "Camera Catches Thrilling Plays, Impressive Ceremonies at Dedication Game," *LSJ*, November 11, 1935.

8. "Classes Rally for Alumni Day," *M.S.C. Record* 51, no. 3 (July 1946): 5–6.

9. Jim Ward, "The Sports Parade," *Escanaba (MI) Daily Press*, April 13, 1947; George S. Alderton, "Thirty Years Ago," *LSJ*, April 11, 1947. Emphasis added.

10. Grinczel, "Celebrating the Legacy of Gideon Smith."

11. Alderton, "Thirty Years Ago."

12. Earl T. Trangman, "Even Police Retain Their Smiles While Aggies Celebrate," *LSJ*, October 26, 1915.

13. "Tuskegee Institute Wants Gideon Smith for Coach," LSJ, February 19, 1916. Months later, the *Lansing State Journal* reported that Smith was doing some assistant coaching at Tuskegee. See "Former Aggie Players Hold Coaching Jobs," *Detroit Free Press*, October 1, 1916.

14. "Cosmopolitan Club Elections," *Holcad*, January 17, 1916.

15. "Chappie' Finds Loyalty Lacking," *M.A.C. Record* 28, no. 10 (November 27, 1922): 12.

16. "Smith Will Be Banqueted at African M. E. Church," *LSJ*, December 5, 1913.

17. Phil Waters, "A Football Wizard," *New York Age*, December 23, 1915.

18. Jaime Schultz, *Moments of Impact: Racialized Memory, Injury, and Reconciliation in College Football* (Lincoln: University of Nebraska Press, 2016), 20.

CHAPTER 10. FROM NORFOLK TO EAST LANSING

1. *West Virginia*, Registration County: *Kanawha*, Roll: *1992561*, Draft Board: *2. U.S., World War I Draft Registration Cards, 1917–1918*, United States, Selective Service System; *Selective Service Registration Cards, World War II: Fourth Registration*, Records of the Selective Service System, Record Group Number 147, Washington, D.C., National Archives and Records Administration, *U.S., World War II Draft Registration Cards, 1942*.

2. Earl Lewis, *Race, Class, and Power in Twentieth-Century Norfolk, Virginia* (Berkeley: University of California Press, 1991), 10, 19, 22, 23.

3. United States of America, Bureau of the Census, *Twelfth Census of the United States, 1900*, Census Place: *Pleasant Grove, Norfolk, Virginia*.

4. Paul Lawrence Dunbar, *Major and Minors: Poems* (Toledo: Hadley & Hadley, 1895), 21.

5. United States of America, Bureau of the Census, *Thirteenth Census of the United States, 1910*, Census Place: *Pleasant Grove, Norfolk, Virginia*.

6. "Legendary HI Coach Headed for CIAA Hall," *Daily News*, May 20, 1981; "CIAA Hall of Fame Inducts Gideon Smith," *New Pittsburgh Courier*, June 6, 1981.

7. James D. Anderson, *The Education of Blacks in the South, 1860–1935* (Chapel Hill: University of North Carolina Press, 1988), 74, 77.

8. Anne Hogenson, "Pilgrim, Hughes Uncover Forgotten History of Campus Diversity, Identify Prominent African-American Attendees in Early 20th Century," *Ferris Magazine Online*, April 3, 2015, http://www.ferrismagazine.com/hidden-stories/.

9. "Oliviet Won the Final," *Detroit Free Press*, November 29, 1091; "Olivet Winds," *M.A.C. Record* 7, no. 12 (December 3, 1901): 1; Cheryl Roland, "100 Years Later, WMU's famed 'Black Ghost' Remembered," *WMU News*, July 26, 2017, https://wmich.edu/news/2017/07/41428; "Western State Blanks Albion," *Detroit Free Press*, October 7, 1916; "Coach Works Normal Hard for Ag Game," *LSJ*, November 3, 1916; "All-Fresh Snowed Under by Kazoo," Holcad, November 7, 1916; *True Northerner*, October 17, 1919; "Kalamazoo Normal Puts Over First Defeat," *M.A.C. Record* 25, no. 4 (October 17, 1919), 5.

10. "M.A.C. Closes Season: Visitors Outclassed at Every Point," *M.A.C. Record* 16, no. 10 (November 22, 1910); *Holcad*, November 21, 1910; "M.A.C. Closes Season: Victors Outclassed at Every Point," *M.A.C. Record* 16, no. 10 (November 22, 1910): 1.

11. "M.A.C.'s Minstrels," *M.A.C. Record* 13, no. 28 (April 14, 1908): 1; "The Minstrels a Great Success," *M.A.C. Record* 13, no. 29 (April 21, 1908): 1; "Ero Alphian Ten O-Clock," *Holcad*, May 12, 1909; "Alabama," *Holcad*, February 13, 1911; *Holcad*, February 20, 1911; "General Exodus for College Last Thursday Night," *Holcad*, March 20, 1911; "Watermelon Jubilee Quartette," *Holcad*, January 11, 1915; "'J' Hop to Be a Cotton Party," *Holcad*, February 22, 1915; "The Delightful Junior Hop of the Class of 1916," *Holcad*, March 1, 1915. In March

1915, students put on a play, *The Captain of Plymouth*. The American Indians in the cast were played by White students in brownface and appeared on the paper's front page. See "Comic Opera a Grand Success," *Holcad*, March 22, 1915. Also see "'Three Hats' to be Presented," *Holcad*, January 31, 1916. The Dramatic Club put on this play whose cast included an "unwilling slave."

12. "Hai-Cut?," *Holcad*, February 10, 1910.

13. For derogatory cartoons of African Americans in the *Holcad*, see, for instance, "Hints for Hopper," February 9, 1914; cartoon of shoeshiner, October 26, 1914; "Down at the Barbecue," November 1, 1914.

CHAPTER 11. MERIT COUNTS

1. See, for instance, "Negro Is Lynched," *LSJ*, August 5, 1912; "Pursuers Still Follow Trail," *LSJ*, August 27, 1912; "Negro Shot to Death by Mob," *LSJ*, November 30, 1912.

2. "Asks Negroes to Support G. O. P.: J. M. Vance, Colored Orator Addresses Republican Rally at Masonic Temple," *LSJ*, October 22, 1912.

3. See Harvey T. Woodruff, "Coach Macklin, Whose Eleven Proved Surprise of 1913 Football Season," *Chicago Tribune*, November 30, 1913.

4. Steve Grinczel, "Celebrating the Legacy of Gideon Smith," Michigan State Spartan Athletics, October 15, 2013, https://msuspartans.com/news/2013/10/15/Celebrating_the_Legacy_of_Gideon_Smith.aspx.

5. Dewey R. Jones, "Michigan Learns the Power of Race All Over Again," *Chicago Defender*, October 13, 1934.

6. "Showed Nerve When His Nose Was Broken: Colored Lad on Freshman Team Injured in Normal Game," *LSJ*, October 22, 1912.

7. "Foot Ball for 1912: A Brief Review of the Season's Work," *M.A.C. Record* 18, no. 14 (December 24, 1912), 2; "Varsity 19; Scrubs 17," *Holcad*, November 25, 1912.

8. "Past Season on the Football Field," *Holcad*, June 16, 1913; "Aggies Humble Alma, 77–12," *Holcad*, October 11, 1915.

9. Edward J. Bernstein to Jonathan L. Snyder, November 14, 1912, and Snyder to Bernstein, November 23, 1912, Jonathan L. Snyder Papers, UA 2.1.7, box 818, folder 31, UAHC.

10. "Excellent Early Showing Pleases Coach J. F. Macklin," *M.A.C. Record* 19, no. 2 (October 7, 1913): 4.

11. "Aggies Defeat Olivet Saturday 26 to 0 in First Game of Season," *LSJ*, October 6, 1913.

12. "M.A.C. Beats Crimson in First Game of New Season," *M.A.C. Record* 19, no. 2 (October 7, 1913): 1.

13. "Announcement," *M.A.C. Record* 19, no. 1 (September 30, 1913): 1.

14. "Some of the Veterans," *Holcad*, September 27, 1915; "These Boys Battle at Columbus for the Football Honor of M.A.C.," *LSJ*, November 28, 1912; "M.A.C. Football Squad, 1913," *M.A.C. Record* 19, no. 7 (November 11, 1913): 2.

15. George S. Alderton, "Thirty Years Ago," *LSJ*, April 11, 1947; Grinczel, "Celebrating the Legacy of Gideon Smith."

16. "Detroit Association to Banquet Team," *M.A.C. Record* 19, no. 9 (November 25, 1913): 1.

17. See "M.A.C. Humbles Michigan," *M.A.C. Record* 19, no. 4 (October 21, 1913): 1–2; "Monster Celebration after

Great Victory," *M.A.C. Record* 19, no. 5 (October 28, 1913): 2.

18. "Letter Sent to Colored Tackle by Gov. Ferris," *LSJ*, October 31, 1913; Phil Waters, "Smith, the Negro Tackle," *New York Age*, February 12, 1914, 6.

19. Wendell Smith, "Sports Beat," *Pittsburgh Courier*, November 1, 1958.

20. "Race Problem in the South: University Student Speaker on the 'White Man's Burden' Sunday," *LSJ*, January 15, 1912.

21. "Dusky Sprinter Is Not Welcomed," *LSJ*, February 21, 1912. This case was also covered in the *Crisis*: see "Along the Color Line," *Crisis* 1, no. 6 (April 1911): 9–10.

22. "Two Plays in M.A.C.–Buchtel Game at College Field Saturday," *LSJ*, November 3, 1913.

23. "'Carp' Julian to Lead M.A.C. Next Season," *M.A.C. Record* 19, no. 8 (November 18, 1913): 13.

24. "Smith Will Be Banqueted at African M. E. Church," *LSJ*, December 5, 1913.

25. "Colored Folk Enjoy Banquet," *LSJ*, May 22, 1914.

26. "City in Brief," *LSJ*, April 25, 1916.

27. "Aggies Turn Out Better Than a Point a Minute against University of Akron," *M.A.C. Record* 20, no. 6 (November 3, 1914): 6.

28. Phil Waters, "A Foot Ball Wizard," *New York Age*, December 23, 1915.

29. Waters, "Smith, the Negro Tackle."

30. "Gideon E. Smith, the Wizard of the Western Gridiron," *Freeman* (Indianapolis), January 1, 1916.

31. "This Is Gideon Smith—M.A.C.'s Great Left Tackle: How Would You Like to Face Him on the Gridiron?," *LSJ*, September 26, 1914.

32. "Aggies Have a Taste of Real Scrimmage," *Detroit Free Press*, September 14, 1915; "Local Man Makes Good Showing at Aggie Camp," *South Bend (IN) Tribune*, September 15, 1915; "Several Laid on the Shelf at Lansing," *Detroit Free Press*, September 18, 1915; "Aggies in Training Two Weeks—Look Good, Says Macklin," *M.A.C. Record* 21, no. 1 (September 21, 1915): 8.

33. "Aggie Eleven that Opens against Carroll College This Afternoon Dopesters Think Will a Start in Big Battle at Ann Arbor Next Saturday," *LSJ*, October 15, 1915.

34. "Coffee Colored Phantom Returns," *Detroit News Tribune*, September 19, 1915.

35. "Olivet Downed in the Opener," *M.A.C. Record* 21, no. 3 (October 5, 1915): 6; "Aggies Total 77 Points While Alma Garners 12 Losers Play Good Ball," *M.A.C. Record* 21, no. 4 (October 12, 1915): 6; "Aggies Take 56 to 0 Victory from Carroll," *M.A.C. Record* 21, no. 5 (October 19, 1915): 7.

36. "M.A.C. Smothers Michigan, 24 to 0," *M.A.C. Record* 21, no. 6 (October 26, 1915): 1; "Macklin's One Ambition Accomplished," *Holcad*, October 25, 1915.

37. "Fumbling Mars Win of Aggies," *Detroit Free Press*, October 17, 1915.

38. "Carroll College Is Victim, 56-0" *Holcad*, October 18, 1915.

39. "Jerry DaPrato Obliges with a Few Yards Straight through the Michigan Line," *Detroit Free Press*, October 24, 1915. Gideon appears to be in the background. Waters, "A Football Wizard."

40. "Aggies Outplay the Pride of Michigan," *Adrian Daily Telegram and Times*, October 25, 1915.

41. "Smith Stars against Wolverines," *Chicago Defender*, October 30, 1915.

42. Earl T. Trangman, "Even Police Retain Their Smiles While Aggies Celebrate," *LSJ*, October 26, 1915.

43. *LSJ*, May 26, 1915. In 1912, a White woman, Miss Doyle, performed in blackface "as a darky" at the Bijou in a skit called *The Vampire*. See "The Bijou," *LSJ*, January 26, 1912.

44. "Big Celebration for the Victorious Team," LSJ, November 14, 1914.

45. "Injuries May Handicap Aggies against Marquette Saturday," *Detroit Free Press*, November 2, 1915. Sportswriters for the *Detroit Free Press* mentioned Gideon's injuries on several other occasions. See, for instance, "Aggies Are Working on Pass Plays," *Detroit Free Press*, October 28, 1915; "Three M.A.C. Regulars Are on Side Lines," *Detroit Free Press*, November 3, 1915.

46. "This Is Gideon Smith—M.A.C.'s Great Left Tackle," 8.

47. "Marquette No Match for Aggies," *Detroit Free Press*, November 7, 1915.

48. "5 East Lansing Starts Are Closing Gridiron Careers," *LSJ*, November 6, 1915; "Farmers Lose Star Quintet by Graduation," *Daily Times News* (Ann Arbor), November 12, 1915.

49. "Gideon Smith to Be Given a Gold Watch," *Times Herald*, November 10, 1915; "Aggies' Negro Star Handed Gold Watch," *Detroit News Tribune*, November 21, 1915.

50. "Ags to Decorate Negro Grid Star," *Detroit Times*, October 29, 1915.

51. Waters, "A Football Wizard."

52. "Macklin Can't Place 'Mauly,'" *Detroit News*, December 11, 1915.

53. Grinczel, "Celebrating the Legacy of Gideon Smith."

54. Michigan Agricultural College, *The Wolverine* (East Lansing, MI: 1916), 165.

CHAPTER 12. OF FOOTBALL FAME

1. "'Chappie' Finds Loyalty Lacking," *M.A.C. Record* 28, no. 10 (November 27, 1922): 12.

2. "Tip is Out," *Pittsburgh Courier*, April 26, 1930.

3. Charles K. Ross, *Outside the Lines: African Americans and the Integration of the National Football League* (New York: New York University, 1999), 18.

4. George S. Alderton, "Thirty Years Ago," *LSJ*, April 11, 1947.

5. "Board of Regents Appoints Teachers for Institute and Bluefield," *McDowell Times*, July 7, 1916.

6. Byrd Prillerman, ed., "The New Additions to the Faculty," *The Institute Monthly* 9, no. 1 (October 1916): 5–6.

7. "Graduate and Ex-Students," in *The Southern Workman* (Hampton, VA: The Press of the Hampton Normal and Agricultural Institute, 1920), 577.

8. "Eyes Focused on N. Y. Meeting of Hampton, Union," *Washington Tribune*, November 22, 1935.

9. Dale Stafford, "To Whom It May Concern," *Detroit Free Press*, July 3, 1941.

10. "Hampton Institute to Honor Ex-Star Gideon E. Smith," *Daily Press* (Newport News, VA), May 15, 1955.

11. "Hampton to Fete Charles Williams, Gideon Smith," *Norfolk (VA) Journal and Guide*, October 18, 1958.

12. "Gideon E. Smith, Hampton's Football Coach, Makes Out Strong Case for Reinstatement of Ivory W. Richmond," *Norfolk (VA) Journal and Guide*, December 24, 1932.

13. "Coach Gid Smith to Speak at Norfolk USO Tuesday Night," *Norfolk (VA) Journal and Guide*, October 16, 1943.

14. See "The Brains Behind Hampton's Offensive," *New York Amsterdam News*, October 16, 1929.

15. "H. N. I. Alumni Issues First Number Journal," *Daily Press* (Newport News, VA), July 4, 1924.

16. Gideon Smith and George Lyle, "Hampton Has Won Half of CIAA Championships: Seasiders Have Established Enviable Record in Organized Athletics in 20 Years of Competition in C. I. A. A.," *Washington Tribune*, February 19, 1932.

17. "Transition at Hampton," *New York Age*, January 25, 1941.

18. "Athletes Report Sports Great Aid in Preparation for Life," *Daily News*, December 13, 1941.

19. Tony Anthony, "Retrospect: Dr. Hill Keeps Himself Busy," *Daily News*, September 27, 1984.

20. "Ex-HI Coach to Get Honor from Ferris," *Daily News*, June 11, 1961; "Ferris State Honors Former Hampton Coach," *Norfolk (VA) Journal and Guide*, June 17, 1961.

21. "Retired Hampton Coach: Rites for Gideon Smith, Football Great, Friday," *Norfolk (VA) Journal and Guide*, May 11, 1968; "Rites for Gideon Smith, One of Football Greats," *Norfolk (VA) Journal and Guide*, May 18, 1968; "Gideon E. Smith," *Daily News*, May 9, 1968.

22. "Legendary HI Coach Headed for CIAA Hall," *Daily News*, May 20, 1981.

23. Dewey R. Jones, "Michigan Learns the Power of Race All Over Again," *Chicago Defender*, October 13, 1934.

24. Grinczel, "Celebrating the Legacy of Gideon Smith"; "Alumni Notes," *M.A.C. Record* 23, no. 25 (March 15, 1918): 16; "Alumni Notes," *M.A.C. Record* 25, no. 3 (October 10, 1919): 11; "Class Notes," *M.A.C. Record* 25, no. 22 (March 5, 1920): 9; "Alumni Affairs," *M.S.C. Record* 40, no. 3 (November 1934): 13.

CHAPTER 13. BETWEEN THE WARS PATHFINDERS

1. This list includes the African Americans I've been able to locate who graduated between 1916 and the end of the Great Depression in approximately 1939. There was a small group of African Americans who attended Michigan State College without graduating. An interesting case during the mid-1920s is a young man referred to as "Ben Jones," "Benjamin Jones," and "B. D. Jones," a talented clarinet player who for one year roomed with Chester Smith in 17A Wells Hall. In the mid-1920s he performed in a musical group called the Burnt Corkers. There are other examples as well. Born in Adrian, Michigan, in 1896, Harold A. Lett attended Michigan State for a period of time. He worked for the Michigan Department of Labor and later became a well-known "leader in race relations in New Jersey." It has also been recounted that assistant prosecutor in the U.S. District Court for the Eastern District of Michigan John K. Graham, who died at age forty-three in 1947 while arguing a case, attended Michigan State before earning his law degree at Wayne State University. See "Urban League Gets Lett as Secretary," *New York Amsterdam News*, March 10, 1934; "New Federal Judge Admits Three Lawyers to U.S. Court," *Pittsburgh Courier*, March 28, 1936; "Harold Lett 78, Rights Aide, Dies," *New York Times*, July 30, 1974. Michigan State was far beyond several other similar predominantly White institutions in terms of Black enrollment. For instance, during the 1932–1933 academic year when MSC had about a half dozen Black

students, Ohio State University had 250, University of Illinois 141, U of M had 71, and University of Minnesota had 34. See "2,548 Finished Our Colleges in Year 1933," *Afro-American*, August 12, 1933.

2. Keith R. Widder, *Michigan Agricultural College: The Evolution of a Land-Grant Philosophy, 1855–1925* (East Lansing: Michigan State University Press, 2005), 405.

3. For overviews of the presidents between Kedzie and the beginning of Hannah's term, see Madison Kuhn, *Michigan State: The First Hundred Years* (East Lansing: Michigan State University Press, 1955), 260–399; David A. Thomas, *Michigan State College: John A. Hannah and the Creation of a World University, 1926–1969* (East Lansing: Michigan State University Press, 2008), 1–8.

4. Kuhn, *Michigan State*, 305.

5. Kuhn, *Michigan State*, 288.

6. Kuhn, *Michigan State*, 273.

7. For changes in curriculum during the 1920s, see Widder, *Michigan Agricultural College*, 167–176.

8. Widder, *Michigan Agricultural College*, 232.

9. See David A. Thomas, *Michigan State College: John Hannah and the Creation of a World University, 1926–1969* (East Lansing: Michigan State University Press, 2008), 1–86.

10. Thomas, *Michigan State College*, 26–27. For an account of new structures built on campus during the interwar period, see Linda O. Stafford and C. Kurt Dewhurst, *MSU Campus—Buildings, Places, Spaces: Architecture and the Campus Park of Michigan State University* (East Lansing: Michigan State University Press, 2002).

11. Thomas, *Michigan State College*, 56.

12. "Negro with Red Mask Causes 'Riot Call,'" *LSJ*, November 4, 1921.

13. "Much Property Held by Negroes, Said," *LSJ*, January 19, 1920.

14. Douglas Kermit Meyer, "The Changing Negro Residential Patterns in Lansing, Michigan, 1850–1969" (PhD diss., Michigan State University, 1970).

15. "And Again–," *M.S.C. Record* 34, no. 3 (November 1928): 9. The author intimates that Allen, "an old colored gentleman," contributed money to the construction of the "Union Memorial Building." Allen was not elderly. According to the 1930 U.S. census, Robert Allen was born in about 1900 in Georgia and was working as a "Truck Diver" at Michigan State. The "old colored gentleman" might have been Allen's father who was also named Robert.

16. "Biggest Meeting in College's History Set 7:30 Saturday," *Holcad*, November 12, 1920; "Elks' Minstrels Ready for Show," *LSJ*, January 10, 1950; "Minstrel Show Is Planned Here: Will Raise Funds for Catholic Schools," *LSJ*, February 22, 1960.

17. "Colonial Picture Is 'Birth of a Nation,'" *LSJ*, October 22, 1924; "'Birth of a Nation' at the Plaza Tues.," *LSJ*, January 5, 1925.

18. "'Close Beside the Winding Cedar,'" *M.S.C. Record* 40, no. 6 (February 1935): 11; "Fine Concert Series to Be Offered Here," *LSJ*, March 28, 1937; "They Will Appear on College Course," *LSJ*, April 4, 1937; "Two 'Name' Bands Will Play at Hop," *LSJ*, January 9, 1959; Ruth Martens, "J-Hop Holds Limelight on Campus," *LSJ*, February 11, 1962.

19. "Celebrations of Yesterday," *M.S.C. Record* 37, nos. 10–11 (June–July 1932): 4; "Flint Club," *M.S.C. Record* 35,

no. 9 (May 1930): 15.

20. "Memories of a College Student at Michigan State College, East Lansing, Michigan, 1931–1935," Jon L. Young Papers, UA 3.3116, January 18, 1935, UA 12.7.3, box 2641, folder 4, UAHC.

21. Carissa Harris, "A History of the Wench: How a Medieval Word Meaning 'Servant' or 'Child' Evolved to Become a Racist Slur," *Electric Literature*, June 3, 2019, https://electricliterature.com/a-history-of-the-wench/.

22. "Wilberforce Wins Debate from Michigan College," *New York Age*, May 12, 1923; "Debaters Make Successful Trip," *M.A.C. Record* 28, no. 30 (May 21, 1923): 8. During the modern Civil Rights Movement, a small group of White students became involved in the Black Freedom Struggle, joining the campus NAACP and protesting housing discrimination in East Lansing. One of the first major antiracist White student organizations was the Students for White Community Action, founded in mid-April 1968. See "White Community Action: New Campus Racial Group Formed to Destroy Apathy," *State News*, May 24, 1968.

23. Craig Fox, *Everyday Klansfolk: White Protestant Life and the KKK in 1920s Michigan* (East Lansing: Michigan State University Press, 2011), xv–xviii.

24. "Klan Vanguard Arriving Here," *LSJ*, August 30, 1924; "Estimate Near 50,000 at Mammoth Klan Meet Here," *LSJ*, September 2, 1924; "Klan Commends Chief," *LSJ*, September 4, 1924.

25. *The Wolverine* (1927), 372. The reference to the KKK in East Lansing is intriguing. There were members of this group living in East Lansing during the 1920s, and some were clandestine in their affiliation. Fox argues that business establishments often adopted "the triple-K moniker." During the mid-1920s when the Klan was at its peak in Michigan, at 225 E. Grand River Ave. there was a store called "Kollege Kandy Kitchen."

26. Bruceray Walker, "Hooded Trio Protests Discrimination," *State News*, February 18, 1976; "Opinion: KKK Story Proper," *State News*, February 23, 1976; "Conflicts—Case Studies—MSU Black Students/Ku Klux Klan, February 1976," RSH Papers, UA 17.269, box 2359, folder 52, UAHC. Cartoons of the Klan would reappear in student publications. For instance, on May 9, 1969, in the *State News*, adjacent to an "Editorial" from the papers' editors, appears a cartoon depicting "Greek Week" with a man dressed in a Klan robe with the caption: "I don't care if it IS a toga—you're giving us a bad name."

27. Katie Matvias, "'Trailblazer' Smith Dies in Lansing at 88," *LSJ*, March 27, 2001.

28. On more than a few occasions, the Black press mentioned Black women who attended Michigan State, implying that they did not graduate. This was the case with Black women like Leona Mills and Gertrude Mae Barber. See "Lansing, Mich," *Pittsburgh Courier*, March 7, 1931.

29. Evelyn Brooks Higginbotham, *Righteous Discontent: The Women's Movement in the Black Baptist Church, 1880–1920* (Cambridge, MA: Harvard University Press, 1993), 186–188.

30. Deborah Gray White, *Ar'n't I a Woman? Female Slaves in the Plantation South* (New York: W. W. Norton, 1985), 119–141.

CHAPTER 14. IT IS MORE BLESSED TO GIVE THAN RECEIVE

1. Keith R. Widder, *Michigan Agricultural College: The Evolution of a Land-Grant Philosophy, 1855–1925* (East Lansing: Michigan State University Press, 2005), 349; Kalyn Womack, "Michigan State's First Black Drum

Major Still Missing after 49 Years," *The Root*, May 31, 2022, https://www.theroot.com/michigan-state-s-first-black-drum-major-still-missing-a-1848997718. For a tribute to Baltimore after his disappearance, see John McAleenan, "Henry's Gone, but Not Forgotten," *LSJ*, November 3, 1973.

2. Widder, *Michigan Agricultural College*, 349.

3. *The Wolverine* (1912), "The Band."

4. "The Sherwin-Hyde Parents Association," *School Journal: A Weekly Journal of Education* 75, no. 20 (November 30, 1907): 492.

5. *The Wolverine* (1912), "The Band."

6. "Band Gives First Sacred Concert," *Holcad*, February 14, 1916; "See a Thousand Men on Dress Parade at M.A.C. Tomorrow," *LSJ*, May 24, 1916.

7. "M.A.C. Band Is Better Than Ever," *Holcad*, October 4, 1915.

8. "Faculty Celebration of Wisconsin Victory," *Holcad*, November 3, 1913.

9. *LSJ*, May 16, 1914; "City in Brief," *LSJ*, April 25, 1916.

10. *Massachusetts*; Registration County: *Suffolk*; Roll: *1685005*; Draft Board: *13*; United States, Selective Service System, *World War I Selective Service System Draft Registration Cards, 1917–1918*, Washington, D.C., National Archives and Records Administration, M1509, 4,582 rolls.

11. United States of America, Bureau of the Census, *Thirteenth Census of the United States, 1910*, Census Place: *Detroit Ward 3, Wayne, Michigan*; Roll: *T624_681*, Page: *11A*, Enumeration District: *0040*, FHL microfilm: *1374694: 1910 United States Federal Census*.

12. Herman W. Erde, "History of the Class of 1915," *The Wolverine* (1911), 95–96.

13. *Illinois*; Registration County: *Cook*; Roll: *1452472*; Draft Board: *05*; United States, Selective Service System, *World War I Selective Service System Draft Registration Cards, 1917–1918*, Washington, D.C., National Archives and Records Administration, M1509, 4,582 rolls.

14. For discussions of Claudius A. Reid's various activities, see "Coleridge-Taylor Club," *Chicago Defender*, November 7, 1914; "Clubs and Societies: The Clover Leaf Club," *Chicago Defender*, May 22, 1915; "Singing Club Elects Officers," *Chicago Defender*, October 9, 1915; "Hon. Richard T. Greener to Appear at Institutional," *Chicago Defender*, October 9, 1915; "Negro Welfare Association Forms Branch Club," *Chicago Defender*, October 26, 1940; "Commonwealth League Plans Brooks Rally," *Chicago Daily Tribune*, October 11, 1942; "Anti-Lynching Legislation to Be Meeting Subject," *Chicago Tribune*, October 25, 1942; "Political Advice: Demands for Race Listed by Randolph," *Pittsburgh Courier*, July 8, 1944. Reid died in 1954.

15. "Rites Saturday for Educator Everett Yates," *Boston Globe*, February 2, 1967.

16. "Everett," *Boston Globe*, May 22, 1937; "Asks Senators Aid Anti-Lynching Bill: Association Telegraphs Walsh and Lodge," *Boston Globe*, February 25, 1938, 2; *Boston Globe*, February 11, 1939.

17. "Ex-Rice School Students Saying Goodbye Mr. Yates," *Boston Globe*, June 15, 1960; "Rites Saturday for Educator Everett Yates."

18. "Commencement at Institute," *Advocate* (Charleston, West VA), June 10, 1909.

19. "Birthday of Morrill Observed at Institute," *Charleston Daily Mail*, April 16, 1915.

20. Widder, *Michigan Agricultural College*, 350.

21. Byrd Prillerman, "Responsibility of the Educated Negro," *McDowell Times*, May 8, 1914.

22. "National Body of Educators," *Denver Star*, March 25, 1916.

23. "Bryd Prillerman," *Chillicothe Gazette*, May 16, 1979.

24. Clifton R. Wharton Jr., *Privilege and Prejudice: The Life of a Black Pioneer* (East Lansing: Michigan State University Press, 2015), 219.

25. "Only Half of Freshman Are in Churches," *LSJ*, October 2, 1916.

26. "The Higher Training of Negroes," *Crisis* 22, no. 3 (July 1921): 107.

27. Brian Williams, "Stuck to Choice: First Negro Engineer at Ford Retiring," *Detroit Free Press*, October 27, 1958.

28. "Death Summons Aged Resident of East Lansing," *LSJ*, June 19, 1914; "Let This Home Buy Itself for You," *LSJ*, December 7, 1916; "Let This Home Buy Itself for You," *LSJ*, December 9, 1916; *LSJ*, June 30, 1917.

29. Williams, "Stuck to Choice."

30. "Residents Unite to Guard Area," *Detroit Free Press*, March 31, 1953; "Clement C. Johnson Sr. Obituary," *Detroit Free Press*, September 2, 1966.

31. "Class of 126 to Graduate June 13 from High School," *LSJ*, May 19, 1916; "Lansing and East Lansing Contribute 60 members of Class Entering This Year," *LSJ*, October 2, 1916.

32. For coverage of Tate and her mother in the *LSJ* from 1911 until 1919, see *LSJ*, March 31, 1911; June 19, 1911; February 21, 1912; "Students of Kalamazoo St. School Will Give an Entertainment Friday and Saturday Evenings," April 12, 1912; June 14, 1912; "Hillsdale Baptist Church," March 22, 1913; May 15, 1914; "Annual Junior Ex.," April 9, 1915; "Concert in Honor of Pastor by Colleagues," April 6, 1916; June 22, 1916; October 9, 1916; "Committees Are Announced and Team Captains Named for Campaign," March 23, 1918; June 8, 1918; August 14, 1919.

33. "500 M.A.C. Students Join in Big Historical-Patriotic Play," *LSJ*, June 9, 1920.

34. "First 'Co-Ed Prom,'" *M.A.C. Record* 25, no. 17 (January 30, 1920): 7.

35. "Baseball Team Adds Two Victories," *M.S.C. Record* 31, no. 33 (June 7, 1926): 534.

36. "Class Notes," *M.A.C. Record* 29, no. 18 (February 11, 1924): 12.

37. "Class Notes," *M.S.C. Record* 31, no. 32 (May 31, 1926): 520.

38. "V.N. & I.I. Will Give Vocational Training: Disabled Veterans Will Be Permitted to Purpose Courses in Trades Department at U.S. Expense," *Norfolk (VA) Journal and Guide*, September 2, 1922.

39. *M.S.C. Record* 34, no. 6 (February 1929): 17; "Negro Shriners Will Meet Here: Jubilee Day to Be Observed at George R. Collins Church Sunday," *LSJ*, June 29, 1929; "'Collegiate Night' to Be Marked by Church: M.S.C. to Present Program for A.M.E. Congregation Sunday; Music, Talks Included," *LSJ*, July 27, 1929; "Church Societies," *LSJ*, September 6, 1930.

40. "City in Brief," *LSJ*, November 12, 1943; "Speaker Discusses 'Women of Africa,'" *LSJ*, February 24, 1944; "Ex-Lansing Woman Addresses Club," *LSJ*, February 28, 1944; *LSJ*, March 23, 1944; *LSJ*, May 10, 1944; "Health Institute Held for Negroes," *LSJ*, September 14, 1944; "Negroes Here Form Citizens' League," *LSJ*, September 17, 1944.

41. "Group Plans Four Events: Lincoln Center to Mark Brotherhood Week with Program," *LSJ*, February 12, 1953; "Esther Tate Holley," *Philadelphia Inquirer*, March 22, 1977.

42. "Herbert McFadden Dies," *Detroit Free Press*, January 21, 1981.

43. "Herbert McFadden Dies."

44. On his World War I registration card, Green listed his birthday as September 12, 1894. On paperwork for the University of Michigan, Green listed several different dates of birth. His certificate of death indicates he was born in about 1898.

45. "The Mass Meeting," *M.A.C. Record* 24, no. 33 (June 20, 1919): 5–6.

46. Dorsey is listed in the Lansing city directory in 1888 as being a cook for Rall & McIver.

47. "Grand Rapids, Mich.," *Pittsburgh Courier*, May 31, 1924.

48. "179 Pass Examination," *Detroit Free Press*, September 25, 1924.

49. Oliver M. Green, "Unemployed Masses Indifferent to 'Isms,'" *Detroit Free Press*, December 20, 1931.

50. Oliver M. Green, "Asserts Poor Men Pay for Rich Men's Wars," *Detroit Free Press*, February 19, 1932.

51. "Oliver M. Green Killed in Crash," *Pontiac Daily*, March 21, 1932; "Arrest of Flint Man in Accident Forecast," *Detroit Free Press*, March 28, 1932.

CHAPTER 15. CHIEF

1. "Aggie Training Season Starts Monday," *LSJ*, September 15, 1917; *Holcad*, November 6, 1917; "Good Material on New Aggie Eleven," *LSJ*, September 28, 1918.

2. "Aggie Gridders Work for Albion," *LSJ*, September 26, 1918; "Spring Football Has Big Squad at M.A.C.," *LSJ*, April 6, 1918; "Graves, 185 Pounds," *LSJ*, September 28, 1918; "11 M.A.C. Men Given Letters," *LSJ*, December 14, 1918.

3. Bill Gibson, "Hear Me Talkin' to Ya," *Afro-American* (Baltimore), December 12, 1931; "'Force Coach Graves, Once Jinx to the Immortal Rockne, Scored Over the Mighty George Gipp," *Pittsburgh Courier*, November 19, 1932; "Graves Leaves Glorious Record at 'Force," *Pittsburgh Courier*, May 19, 1934.

4. "Graves Will Attend M.A.C.," *LSJ*, September 8, 1921; "Farmers Grid Outfit Starts Practice at Clear Lake Camp," *LSJ*, September 13, 1921.

5. Lyman L. Frimodig to George "Potsy" Clark, August 25, 1920, Clarence L. Munn Papers, UA 17.75, box 769, folder, 38–39, UAHC.

6. Fred Stanley, "'Frim: A Man and His Legend," *MSU Alumni Magazine*, July 1972, 26–27.

7. *Holcad*, October 18, 1921.

8. "Graves Will Attend M.A.C.: Negro Fullback Is in Great Shape," *LSJ*, September 8, 1921.

9. "The Outlook on the Gridiron," *M.A.C. Record* 27, no. 1 (September 30, 1921): 10; "Graves Will Attend M.A.C."; "Farmers Grid Outfit Starts Practice at Clear Lake Camp;" Walter Eckersall, "Big 10 Payers Given 9 Places on All-Western," *Chicago Tribune*, December 7, 1919. It's interesting to know that Eckersall placed Iowa's African American right tackle who played from 1918 until 1921, Duke Slater, on his All-Western first team.

10. "Aggies Put Up Stiff Fight in Annual Michigan Contest," *LSJ*, October 17, 1921; "Varsity Loses Hard-Fought Game to Michigan," *M.A.C. Record* 27, no. 4 (October 21, 1921): 8.

11. "Graves Hurried into Game to Win for Aggies, 17—14," *LSJ*, October 24, 1921.

12. "Varsity Comes from Behind to Trim W.S.N.," *M.A.C. Record* 27, no. 5 (October 28, 1921): 10.

13. "Victory Staged for Homecomers," *M.A.C. Record* 27, no. 7 (November 11, 1921): 9.

14. *Wolverine* (1922), 152, 157.

15. "Albion Fights Aggies to Tie Score," *M.A.C. Record* 28, no. 3 (October 9, 1922): 8; *Detroit Free Press*, September 23, 1922; "Aggie 1st and 2nd Teams Stage Third Tilt," *LSJ*, September 25, 1922; "Seniors Honored," *LSJ*, March 2, 1923; "Alumni Movies Will Show Football Team," *M.A.C. Record* 29, no. 3 (October 8, 1923): 10.

16. "Large Football Squad Starts Training at Va. Normal under New Coach," *New York Age*, October 6, 1923.

17. "Departs with Best Hopes for Ohio Team," *Pittsburgh Courier*, June 3, 1933.

18. Ruth A. Gray, ed., *Bibliography of Research Studies in Education, 1932–1933* (Washington, D.C.: Government Printing Office, 1934), 112.

19. Edgar G. Brown, "29 Negro Advisors in Civilian Conservation Corps, 65,000 Negro Youth in Camp," *New York Age*, December 22, 1934.

20. "Graves Reported as Howard Coach," *Evening Star* (Washington, D.C.), May 10, 1934; *Pittsburgh Courier*, June 2, 1934; "Mrs. Harry Graves Visits Force," *Pittsburgh Courier*, January 26, 1935; "Assistant Is New Football Mentor There," *Xenia Daily Gazette* (Xenia, Ohio), June 29, 1935; "Harry Graves, Ex-Coach of Wilberforce, Here," *New York Amsterdam News*, August 3, 1940; "Washington Lions Open Grid Season Sept. 27," *Chicago Defender*, September 19, 1942; *Washington Tribune*, March 25, 1944; Dan Burley, "Negro Changed World of Sports," *New York Age*, July 22, 1950; "Prowess of Athletes Beats Bias," *New York Age*, August 23, 1952; "Only Four of 1925–1930 'Heroes' Survive Depleted Coaching Ranks," *Pittsburgh Courier*, February 20, 1965.

CHAPTER 16. GRIDIRON AND DAIRY FARM

1. "Aggie Grid Candidates Put through Snappy Scrimmage," *LSJ*, September 18, 1922.

2. "Freshmen Look Good," *M.A.C. Record* 27, no. 1 (September 30, 1921): 11; "All Fresh Continue Better," *M.A.C. Record* 27, no. 6 (November 4, 1921); 13; "Aggie Fresh Squad Takes Game from Notre Dame Team," *Holcad*, November 22, 1921; "M.A.C. Fresh Show Class in Win from Notre Dame," *M.A.C. Record* 27, no. 9 (November 25, 1921); 9–10.

3. "Lake Forest Opens New Stadium," *M.A.C. Record* 29, no. 3 (October 8, 1923): 8.

4. "Lake Forest Opens New Stadium," 8–9; "Aggies Initiate New Stadium with Win Over Lake Forest," *LSJ*, October 8, 1923; "Aggies Given Needed Rest," *Detroit Free Press*, October 25, 1923; "Varsity Surprise Michigan Eleven," *M.A.C. Record* 29, no. 6 (October 29, 1923): 9; "Football Awards," *Holcad*, November 23, 1923.

5. "7 Ames Gridmen Finish Football Play This Week," *Courier* (Waterloo, IA), November 14, 1927. In 2012, the Iowa State football program chronicled Smith's legacy. Smith appears in Iowa State yearbooks, and in 1926 and 1927, he received coverage in Iowa newspapers. See, for instance, "Ames Grid Men Prepare for Homecoming Battle with Drake Saturday," *Des Moines Tribune,* November 11, 1926; "Lutjens May Be a Regular on Ames Team," *Des Moines Tribune*, April 12, 1927; "Ames to Lose Seven Gridders by Graduation," *Des Moines Register*, November 14, 1927; "Ames Looks for Good Boxing Team This Year," *Sioux City Journal*, November 28, 1926;

"Ames' 1927 Grid Hopes Bright, to Lose Four Vets," *Sioux City Journal*, December 3, 1926; "Iowa State Football Bakers Expect Classiest Eleven in Years This Fall," *Sioux City Journal*, September 2, 1927. In the 1940s, he worked with the National Youth Administration and moved to California. He died in January 1970 in Reno, Nevada.

6. John Mathew Smith, "Black Power in Green and White: Integration and Black Protest in Michigan State University Football, 1947–1972" (MA thesis, Western Michigan University, 2006), 26, 27.

7. H. A. Lett, "Michigan State Has Negro Star," *Pittsburgh Courier*, November 8, 1924; "Instructor," *Pittsburgh Courier*, March 7, 1931; "Kappas Turn Southland for Conclave," *Chicago Defender*, December 23, 1939; "Vice Polemarch," *Pittsburgh Courier*, January 28, 1939; "Chess Tourney to W. Va. State," *Chicago Defender*, May 25, 1940; "CIAA Delegates Hold 30th Meeting at St. Augustine," *Afro-American* (Baltimore), December 19, 1942; "The Defender Newsreel," *Chicago Defender*, September 6, 1947; "West Virginia Legion Vice-Commander Dead," *Shawnee American*, February 20, 1948; "Obituary," *Charleston Gazette*, January 13, 1948.

8. According to Henry Lockert's death certificate he died at age fifty-one in Clarksville, TN, on August 7, 1914, and was "widowed." Aeolian's mother, Julia Sallie Lockert, died sometime before 1914.

9. "Many Men Called for Army Service," *Nashville Banner*, August 29, 1918; "150 Are Graduated at A. & I. State Normal," *The Tennessean*, May 20, 1923.

10. "TSU Grads Recall School Life in '24," *The Tennessean*, August 24, 1974.

11. Keith R. Widder, *Michigan Agricultural College: The Evolution of a Land-Grant Philosophy, 1855–1925* (East Lansing: Michigan State University Press, 2005), 352.

12. "A. & I. State Normal," *The Tennessean*, September 12, 1926.

13. Sheila T. Gregory, ed., *A Legacy of Dreams: The Life and Contributions of Dr. William Venoid Banks* (Lanham, MD: University Press of America, 1999), 1–42.

14. "Mrs. Clara Banks: Mother of the Week," *Michigan Chronicle*, April 4, 1959; The information pertaining to Banks's early years is from Gregory, *A Legacy of Dreams*, 44–70.

15. "Mrs. Clara Banks"; Widder, *Michigan Agricultural College*, 352, 127.

16. "Bordentown Industrial School Urges Youth towards Farm Life," *Pittsburgh Courier*, August 4, 1928.

17. "Bordentown Institute Has Large Enrollment," *Pittsburgh Courier*, September 25, 1926; "Exercises for Opening Are Closed," *Pittsburgh Courier*, March 21, 1925; "Bordentown Industrial School Urges Youth towards Farm Life."

18. "Honors for Bordentown," *Opportunity: A Journal of Negro Life* 14, no. 8 (August 1936): 228–229; Floyd J. Calvin, "Bordentown Takes Lead in Pure Breeding of Cows, Hogs, Horses," *New York Amsterdam News*, February 20, 1937.

19. "Cow State Champion at Training School," *Chicago Defender*, August 23, 1941.

CHAPTER 17. IN MYRTLE'S FOOTSTEPS

1. H. A. Scott, "Goode Makes Good on Michigan Aggies," *Afro-American* (Baltimore), October 24, 1924.

2. See Keith R. Widder, *Michigan Agricultural College: The Evolution of a Land-Grant Philosophy, 1855–1925* (East Lansing: Michigan State University Press, 2005), 145. In a photo, "M.A.C. Girls, 1909," there is an African

American woman seated in the third row. There is also another young woman who appears to be Black.

3. Necia Brown, "Negro Coeds View the Future," *State News*, March 4, 1964. Brown interviewed several Black women from Detroit, and this article was part of a series of pieces on the Black experience.

4. See "Henderson, Margaret Collins," *LSJ*, September 21, 1994.

5. John M. Green, ed., *Negroes in Michigan History* (Detroit: John M. Green, 1985), 7, 136, 137.

6. Widder, *Michigan Agricultural College*, 351.

7. *Crisis* 78, no. 2 (March 1971); "Death Notices," *Chicago Tribune*, June 16, 1993.

8. Widder, *Michigan Agricultural College*, 350–351.

9. "Michigan," *Chicago Defender*, June 23, 1917.

10. "'V' Notes," *LSJ*, April 6, 1918.

11. Scott, "Goode Makes Good on Michigan Aggies"; "Michigan State College Honors Senior Student," *Chicago Defender*, November 13, 1926; "Elected to Tau Sigma," *Pittsburgh Courier*, November 20, 1926.

12. "38 State College Co-eds Given Athletic Awards at Annual Dinner," *LSJ*, December 6, 1926.

13. "Elected to Tau Sigma."

14. "Principal W. R. Banks Makes Plain Talk," *Prairie View Standard* 9, no. 21 (October 15, 1927): 1.

15. "Principal Letter to Colleagues," *Prairie View Standard* 17, no. 12 (May 1931): 8.

16. "Among the Alumni," *M.S.C. Record* 34, no. 1 (September 1, 1928): 15; "Alumni Affairs," *M.S.C. Record* 35, no. 11 (July 1930): 15.

17. Mabel Lucas to Frank S. Kedzie, January 9, 1930; Kedzie to Lucas, February 5, 1930; Lucas to Kedzie, May 8, 1930; Kedzie to Lucas, May 15, 1930; Lucas to Kedzie, October 4, 1930; Kedzie to Lucas, October 7, 1930; Frank S. Kedzie Papers, UA 2.18, box 894, folder 26, UAHC. See "Alumni Write Tributes to 'Uncle' Frank S. Kedzie," *M.S.C. Record* 40, no. 6 (February 1935): 6–9.

18. "City in Brief," *LSJ*, May 17, 1930.

19. "The Mayor's C. R. A.," *Chicago Daily Tribune*, August 31, 1933; "Miss Mable Jewel Lucas," *LSJ*, September 17, 1941; "News About These Alumni," *M.S.C. Record* 47, no. 1 (October 1941): 15.

20. For the information about Clarice's birth and her parents' lives, see Virginia Department of Health, *Virginia, Death Records, 1912–2014* (Richmond, VA); United States of America, Bureau of the Census, *Thirteenth Census of the United States, 1910*, Census Place: *Newport, Isle of Wight, Virginia*; "Kenneth Wesley Pretlow," *U.S. World War I Draft Registration Cards, 1917–1918*, Registration State: *Virginia*, Registration County: Isle of Wight County.

21. *Polk's Princeton (Mercer County, N.J.) City Directory, 1955–56* (R. L. Polk & Co., Publishers: Pittsburgh, 1956), 211; Widder, *Michigan Agricultural College*, 352.

22. "Lansing, Mich.," *Pittsburgh Courier*, March 6, 1926.

23. "'Collegiate Night' to Be Marked by Church: M.S.C. to Present Program for A.M.E. Congregation Sunday; Music, Talks Included," *LSJ*, July 27, 1929.

24. United States of America, Bureau of the Census, *Sixteenth Census of the United States, 1940*, Census Place: *Newport, Isle of Wight, Virginia*; "Area Deaths and Funerals," *Daily News*, August 12, 1976.

25. "Va. Farmers Make What Makes Smithfield Ham," *Pittsburgh Courier*, October 22, 1949.

26. "Many Virginia Farmers Grow Hogs for Smithfield Ham," *Alabama Tribune*, October 21, 1949.

27. According to the 1955 city directory for Princeton, New Jersey, Pretlow was living in the city on Boudinot Street working for Clinton Farms, reformatory for women.

28. "Area Death and Funerals," *Daily Press* (Newport News, VA), August 12, 1976, 8.

29. Sylvia Penn, "Glimpses in Detroit's Mirror," *Tribune Independent* (*Detroit Tribune*), April 6, 1935. There are several ways that Frances's maiden last name is spelled in historical documents, including Llewellyn, Lewellyn, and Lewellen. For a brief biography, see her great-niece's website, "Who Is Great Aunt Francis?," Karen Lewellen, http://karenlewellen.com/owens.htm.

30. In the 1933 yearbook for Cass Technical High School, there is a picture of a "Francis Langford" who appears to be Frances L. Langford.

31. "Race Girl Wins First Place in Music Contest," *Michigan Chronicle*, April 1, 1939; "Sister of Local Musician Wins Marian's Praise," *Pittsburgh Courier*, June 24, 1939.

32. "Appointed," *Detroit Free Press*, January 4, 1942; Vivienne Cooper, "Pleased Palate a Joy to YMCA Food Expert," *Michigan Chronicle*, May 3, 1947; Penn, "Glimpses in Detroit's Mirror."

33. "Who Is Great Aunt Francis?"

CHAPTER 18. DEMANDING EQUAL OPPORTUNITY, SERVING OTHERS

1. "Art Bowman Endorsed by Committee," *Michigan Chronicle*, October 31, 1942; Chester Smith, "As I Recall: My Greatest Sports Thrill," *Detroit Tribune*, April 3, 1954.

2. Smith's name didn't appear in MSC commencement programs. He may have graduated during the summer of 1930 or 1931. A memoriam published in 1986 indicated he received a bachelor's degree from Michigan State and became a member of Omega Psi Phi fraternity, the National Bar Association, the National Lawyers Guild, the Detroit Chamber of Commerce, the Wolverine Bar Association, and the MSU Alumni Association. See Zachare Ball, "Stylish Detroit Lawyer Chester Smith," *Detroit Free Press*, March 1, 1986.

3. *LSJ*, February 3, 1933, 19.

4. "Michigan Athlete Enters Five Events," *Harrisburg Telegraph*, April 11, 1934.

5. Clark Bullett Jr., "Gary, Ind.," *Chicago Defender*, August 4, 1934; "Pros to Resume March for Title on Local Court," *Oshkosh Northwestern*, December 31, 1936; "Old Tymers Will Have Amateur Basketball Team," *Chicago Defender*, December 28, 1940. Jackson was born on December 19, 1910, in Oklahoma City, Oklahoma. He grew up in Gary, Indiana, and attended Froebel High School. In the late 1930s, he settled down in Gary, Indiana, and became a police officer. A veteran of World War II, he retired in the late 1950s and was murdered on March 14, 1975. See "File Charges of Assault and Battery," *Chicago Defender*, March 12, 1938; "Teens Kill Ex-Gary Policeman," *Times* (Munster, Indiana), March 14, 1975; "Businessman Slain, 2 Held," *Chicago Defender*, March 17, 1975.

6. John Mathew Smith, "Black Power in Green and White: Integration and Black Protest in Michigan State University Football, 1947–1972" (MA thesis, Western Michigan University, 2006), 32.

7. "Engineer Smith Retiring," *LSJ*, February 11, 1977; Katie Matvias, "'Trailblazer' Smith Dies in Lansing at 88,"

LSJ, March 27, 2001.

8. Malcolm B. Fulcher, "Team to Hotel; Two Mich. State Stars Sent to Y," *Afro-American* (Baltimore), November 3, 1934. Fulcher reported that the manager of the hotel claimed that Manhattan College requested McCrary and Baker be denied accommodations.

9. Smith, "Black Power in Green and White," 36, 37.

10. "Announce Leaders for Negro Camp," *LSJ*, July 21, 1934.

11. "Order 'Equal Opportunity' at Michigan State: Remove Bar from Practice Teaching," *Pittsburgh Courier*, June 29, 1935.

12. "Oscar Baker, Lawyer, Buried," *New York Age*, January 3, 1953.

13. See "Well Known Negro Lawyer Dies at 73," *Battle Creek Enquirer*, December 18, 1952; Jeanne May, "Family of Lawyers Roasts Patriarch," *Detroit Free Press*, September 17, 1985; Ben Schmitt, "Oscar Baker Jr.: Lawyer Joined Fight for Civil Rights," *Detroit Free Press*, March 23, 2000.

14. Russell J. Cowans, "Civic Leader Points Out False Theory under Religion," *Chicago Defender*, April 25, 1935; William Pickens, "Pickens Says North Denies Negro Equal Educational Changes, Cites Facts," *Atlanta Daily World*, November 28, 1935; "Order 'Equal Opportunity' at Michigan State."

15. State Board of Agriculture Minutes, Michigan Agricultural College, June 10, 1935, UAHC.

16. "Morris Brown Stakes All in Clash with Wilberfoce," *Chicago Defender*, December 28, 1940; "Typovision," *Chicago Defender*, November 7, 1942; "Carter Joins Green Wave Coaching Staff," *Atlanta Daily World*, July 19, 1949. Baker registered for World War II in 1940 and was a corporal in the U.S. Marine Corps. He died on March 26, 1992.

17. George S. Alderton, "Along Lansing Sports Sidelines," *LSJ*, October 11, 1934.

18. See, for instance, "Spartans Reaching National Football Spotlight," *M.S.C. Record* 39, no. 3 (November 1933): 9.

19. "Spartan Fullback Tricky Runner and All Opponents Respect Him," *LSJ*, October 5, 1934.

20. "McCrary through for Entire Season," *LSJ*, November 12, 1934; "Titans to Find M.S.C. at Peak," *Detroit Free Press*, November 13, 1934.

21. "Along the Spartans' Trail," *LSJ*, November 23, 1934.

22. "Stale Spartans Get Rest Cure," *LSJ*, November 22, 1934.

23. "Ward, McCrary, Salters, and Other Michigan College Stars to Be Classic Guests," *Pittsburgh Courier*, November 24, 1934. Other references to McCrary in the *Pittsburgh Courier* include "Sez 'Ches,'" November 18, 1933; "Grid Phantoms Who Streaked to Fame in Major Colleges," December 8, 1934.

24. George S. Alderton, "Sport Antic-Dope!," *LSJ*, February 1, 1934.

25. "Camp for Colored Youths Announced," *LSJ*, July 12, 1934.

26. Frank H. Saunders, "Former Grid Star James McCrary Rites Saturday," *Michigan Chronicle*, November 8, 1975.

27. "James McCrary Honored; Gives All to Community," *Michigan Chronicle*, June 15, 1957.

28. Russ J. Cowans, " The Sports Mirror," *Detroit Tribune*, June 1, 1940.

29. Julia Grant, *The Boy Problem: Educating Boys in Urban America, 1870–1970* (Baltimore: Johns Hopkins University Press, 2014), 111–112.

30. "James McCrary, Ex-MSU Football Player, Is Dead," *Detroit Free Press*, October 31, 1975; "Rites Held for

McCrary, 'S' Star of Bachman Era," *LSJ*, November 1, 1975; "Ex-MSU Star Fullback Dies at Health Center," *Livingston County Daily Press and Argus*, November 5, 1975.

31. "Kentucky's Favorite Son . . . ," *The Sphinx* 63, no. 2 (Spring 1977): 14–15; David Holt, "Ground Broken for 20-Story Senior-Citizens House," *Courier-Journal*, October 19, 1970; "Stenson Broaddus, Leader in Black Community, Dies," *Courier-Journal*, April 18, 1977.

32. The J. O. Blanton House for Senior Citizens was opened in 1970. It was a major project, costing $3.3 million to construct. See "Blanton House Groundbreaking Set," *Courier-Journal* (Louisville, KY), October 15, 1970.

33. "Gets Post," *Michigan Chronicle*, January 6, 1940; Jeanne May, "Judge Arthur Bowman Gave His Services to Poor," *Detroit Free Press*, August 15, 1988.

34. The *Detroit Tribune* covered Bowman's political career. See Ben Clark, "Boosters Club for Richard Reading Makes Progress," July 3, 1937; "Politics," June 18, 1938; "Lively Rivalry Seen in G. O. P.," July 27, 1938; "Elect Arthur M. Bowman State Senator," August 6, 1938; "Mayor Endorses A. Bowman," August 13, 1938; "Progressive Ministers Support Arthur M. Bowman for State Senator," September 3, 1938; "Elect Arthur Bowman GOP Candidate for Michigan House," October 17, 1942; "Vote for McLeod and Bowman— Republican," October 31, 1942; "Bowman's Candidacy Chance to Get Negro in State Legislature," October 21, 1942.

35. May, "Judge Arthur Bowman Gave His Services to Poor."

36. *Lansing and East Lansing City Directory, 1940* (Lansing, MI: Hallenbeck Printing Company, 1940), 271; United States of America, Bureau of the Census, *1920 United State Federal Census*, Census Place: *Lansing Ward 4, Ingham, Michigan*, Enumeration District: *98*; United States of America, Bureau of the Census, *1930 United States Federal Census*, Census Place: *Lansing Ward 4, Ingham, Michigan*, Enumeration District: *0027*; Michigan Department of Community Health, Division of Vital Records and Health Statistics, *Michigan, Marriage Records, 1867–1952* (Lansing, MI); "Delegates Named to Training Camp," *LSJ*, June 9, 1928; "Holt Churches Join in Union Service," *LSJ*, November 16, 1929; "High Schools Will Graduate 151 at Mid-Winter Commencement," *LSJ*, January 14, 1930.

37. W. Kim Heron, "Black Students at MSU," *Grapevine Journal*, September 18, 1973.

38. Shirley Reed, "Black Educator Achieves Many Goals in Long, Devoted Career," *LSJ*, July 30, 1992.

39. Reed, "Black Educator Archives Many Goals in Long, Devoted Career."

40. "With the 4 H Clubs," *Semo News* (Lilbourn, MO), April 22, 1948; "Farm, Home Meet to Open," *Journal-Every Evening* (Wilmington, DE), March 23, 1945.

41. "Local Negroes Have Prominent Part in Program at Pilgrim Church," *LSJ*, January 27, 1934; "Contributions of Various Nations and Races to American to Be Discussed," *LSJ*, January 13, 1934; "Announce Leaders for Negro Camp," *LSJ*, July 21, 1934; "Colored Boys Going to Y. M. C. A. Camp," *LSJ*, August 8, 1935; "Negroes Enjoying Community Center," *LSJ*, October 27, 1936; "Lincoln School Community Center Fills Long-Felt Need in District It Serves," *LSJ*, May 18, 1937; "N. A. A. C. P. Group Elects Officers," *LSJ*, April 6, 1941.

42. "Special Services Planned by Church," *LSJ*, January 13, 1934; "Announce Program of Special Service," *LSJ*, January 27, 1934; "Announce Leaders for Negro Camp," *LSJ*, July 21, 1934; "Financial Worries Beset Lansing Y. M. C. A.," *LSJ*, January 1, 1935; "Colored Boys Going to Y. M. C. A. Camp," *LSJ*, August 8, 1935; "Negroes

Enjoying Community Center," *LSJ*, October 27, 1936; "Lincoln School Community Center Fills Long-Felt Need in District It Serves," *LSJ*, May 18, 1937; Rose Toomer Brunson, "A Study of the Migrant Negro Population in Lansing, Michigan, during and since World War II" (MA thesis, Michigan State University, 1955), 34, 38–41, 52–53, 56.

43. "Playground Staff Is Appointed Here," *LSJ*, June 16, 1938; "Lincoln Community Center Reveals Beehive of Activity," *LSJ*, May 17, 1938; "Lincoln Center's Work Is Portrayed," *LSJ*, May 21, 1938; "Lincoln Center Is Outstanding," *LSJ*, January 1, 1940; "Beulah Irons Sponsors Special A. M. E. Service," *LSJ*, April 19, 1941; "N. A. A. C. P. Group Elects Officers," *LSJ*, April 6, 1941; "Events Planned to Mark Negro History Week," *LSJ*, February 8, 1941.

44. "Lansing Man Promoted at Southern University," *LSJ*, August 12, 1947; "About These Alumni," *M.S.C. Record* 52, no. 1 (January 20, 1947): 18.

45. Dennis Knockerbocker, "Once Shunned, Irons Now Has Key Teachers' Role," *LSJ*, September 14, 1977.

46. "Instructor Is Awarded Grant to Pursue Ph.D.," *New Journal and Guide* (Norfolk, VA), May 28, 1955; Reed, "Black Educator Archives Many Goals in Long, Devoted Career."

CHAPTER 19. AND TO HAPPEN, OF ALL PLACES, IN OUR OWN STATE SCHOOL

1. See "Dr. Franklyn Verlett Duffy," *Blade* (Toledo, OH), April 22, 2010, https://www.legacy.com/obituaries/toledoblade/obituary.aspx?n=franklyn-verlett-duffy&pid=142084652.

2. "New Building Named Mason Hall," *M.S.C. Record* 43, no. 2 (February 1938): 9.

3. Fred T. Mitchell to Hazel Marshall, July 23, 1940, Robert S. Shaw Papers, UA 2.1.11, box 840, folder 68, UAHC.

4. G. R. Heath to Franklyn V. Duffy, August 16, 1940, Shaw Papers, UA 2.1.11, box 840, folder 68, UAHC.

5. Ken Coleman, "Charles Diggs Sr.: Black Bottom and Paradise Valley Business Mogul," *Michigan Chronicle*, February 8, 2017, https://michiganchronicle.com/2017/02/08/charles-diggs-sr-black-bottom-and-paradise-valley-business-mogul/; Charles C. Diggs to Robert S. Shaw, September 4, 1940, Shaw Papers, UA 2.1.11, box 840, folder 68, UAHC.

6. "Diggs Demands Removal of Dean at College," *Detroit Tribune*, September 7, 1940.

7. "Mitchell Is Named to Presidency of History Alma Mater," *M.S.C. Record* 50, no. 4 (September 1945): 6.

8. David A. Thomas, *Michigan State College: John Hannah and the Creation of a World University, 1926–1969* (East Lansing: Michigan State University Press, 2008), 52, 53.

9. John A. Hannah to Charles C. Diggs, September 6, 1940, Shaw Papers, UA 2.1.11, box 840, folder 68, UAHC.

10. Hannah to Diggs, September 6, 1940, Shaw Papers, UA 2.1.11, box 840, folder 68, UAHC.

11. Fred T. Mitchell to Franklyn V. Duffy, September 6, 1940; Hannah to Shaw, September 11, 1940, Shaw Papers, UA 2.1.11, box 840, folder 68, UAHC. "The other day when the delegation from Detroit interested in Mr. Duffy was in," Hannah pointed out in this memo to Shaw, "it was understood that after you had checked into the possibility of providing housing for him in Mason or Abbot Hall that Dr. James J. McClendon whose card is attached would be informed of what we can do if anything." This memo suggests Hannah looked into the possibility of locating arrangements for Duffy in Mason or Abbot Hall.

12. Shaw to James J. McClendon, September 13, 1940, Shaw Papers, UA 2.1.11, box 840, folder 68, UAHC.

13. Shaw to Diggs, September 16, 1940, Shaw Papers, UA 2.1.11, box 840, folder 68, UAHC.

14. J. J. McClendon to Shaw, September 16, 1940, Shaw Papers, UA 2.1.11, box 840, folder 68, UAHC.

15. Shaw to James J. McClendon, September 19, 1940, Shaw Papers, UA 2.1.11, box 840, folder 68, UAHC.

16. Duffy to Secretary Hannah, September 16, 1940, Shaw Papers, UA 2.1.11, box 840, folder 68, UAHC.

17. Shaw to Duffy, September 16, 1940, Shaw Papers, UA 2.1.11, box 840, folder 68, UAHC.

18. "Race Students Admitted to Michigan State Dorms," *Pittsburgh Courier*, September 21, 1940.

19. "State News Editorial of 1951 Issue Pays Tribute to Hannah," *State News*, September 25, 1961; "Hannah Serves Many Roles," *State News*, September 25, 1961; Thomas, *Michigan State College*, xiv.

20. Betsy Miner, "Hannah Revered Land-Grant Philosophy," *LSJ*, February 25, 1991.

CHAPTER 20. MAKING OF A CIVIL RIGHTS ICON

1. William Burke, "Exponent of Civil Rights: Dr. Hannah Foe of Segregation," *LSJ*, November 10, 1957.

2. John T. McQuiston, "John Hannah, Who Headed Michigan State and Rights Panel," *New York Times*, February 25, 1991.

3. Johnathan L. Snyder to S. L. Maddox, April 13, 1905, Jonathan L. Snyder Papers, UA 2.1.7, box 809, folder 17, UAHC.

4. "Suspend 4 On Campus: MSU Officials Act after Alcohol Is Found, Negro Bumped," *LSJ*, November 9, 1957.

5. David Bailey, "MSU Leadership Helped to Advance Civil Rights," MSU Alumni, January 1, 2014, https://alumni.msu.edu/stay-informed/alumni-stories/feature-msu-leadership-helped-to-advance-civil-rights; David A. Thomas, *Michigan State College: John Hannah and the Creation of a World University, 1926–1969* (East Lansing: Michigan State University Press, 2008), 397.

6. John A. Hannah, *A Memoir* (East Lansing: Michigan State University Press, 1980), 14, 24.

7. Randal Maurice Jelks, *African Americans in the Furniture City: The Struggle for Civil Rights in Grand Rapids* (Urbana: University of Illinois Press, 2006).

8. Hannah, *A Memoir*, 42; Betsy Miner, "MSU Shares Last Farewell to John Hannah," *LSJ*, February 27, 1991.

9. "Rights Unit to Spur Probe of Shocking 'Injustices,'" *Chicago Defender*, December 8, 1959.

10. "'Rights the Top Issue'–Dr. Hannah: US Commission Head Sees Bigotry as Nation's Worst Foe," *Norfolk (VA) Journal and Guide*, November 5, 1960.

11. "Commission on Civil Rights Sets Hearings in Mississippi," *New York Amsterdam News*, January 16, 1965.

12. Alice A. Dunnigan, "'Rights' Probers Face Alabama Resistance," *Pittsburgh Courier*, December 13, 1958.

13. "Wilson Honors Hannah, Leaving Pentagon Post," *Evening Star* (Washington, D.C.), July 29, 1954.

14. "Two Years to Kill Jim Crow," *Chicago Defender*, September 26, 1953.

15. Enoc P. Waters Jr., "Wilkins Steals Probe Spotlight," *Chicago Defender*, December 11, 1958; "Senate Group Okays Rights Commissioners," *Chicago Defender*, March 15, 1958.

16. "Rights Unit to Spur Probe of Shocking 'Injustices'"; "A Close-Up of Rights Chairman," *Chicago Defender*, January 4, 1958; "Our Opinions: The Commission on Civil Rights," *Chicago Defender*, January 18, 1958; "In

the Guide Spotlight: New Rights Commission Head Optimistic about Job," *Norfolk (VA) Journal and Guide*, January 4, 1958.

17. Albert J. Dunmore and Luther Webb, "Civil Rights Commission Warns: Detroit Must Face Racial Problems," *Pittsburgh Courier*, December 24, 1960.

18. Burke, "Exponent of Civil Rights."

19. "Race, Nationality Survey Conducted at Registration," *State News*, December 1, 1967; "Radical Identification Form Warning Flyer from Black Students' Alliance," n. d. (ca. 1968), Barry D. Amis Papers, UA 10.3.500, box 6539, folder 1, UAHC.

20. Thomas, *Michigan State College*, 55.

21. John Mathew Smith, "Black Power in Green and White: Integration and Black Protest in Michigan State University Football, 1947–1972" (MA thesis, Western Michigan University, 2006), 36; for a discussion of the challenges faced by McCrary, Baker, and Smith and their predecessors, see 15–58.

22. Horace White, "The Facts in Our News: Calling Gov. Kim Sigler," *Michigan Chronicle*, October 11, 1947.

23. "Wake Up MSC," *Michigan Chronicle*, October 18, 1947. For other coverage of the discrimination Horace Smith faced in the *Michigan Chronicle*, see, for instance, Bill Matney, "Horace Smith Kept on Bench to Please MS," October 11, 1947; Matney, "UAW-CIO Joins Fight Against MSC Race Bias," October 18, 1947; Matney, "MSC 'Appeasement' Policy Hit by Alumnus as KY Game Nears," October 25, 1947; "Chronicle Cracks Bias on MSC Football," November 1, 1947.

24. John Matthew Smith, "'Breaking the Plane': Integration and Black Protest in Michigan State Football during the 1960s," *Michigan Historical Review* 33 (Fall 2007): 104.

25. Mike Pryson, "Former Jackson Great Dies," *Evening Citizen-Patriot* (Grand Rapids, MI), October 17, 2006, https://groups.google.com/forum/#!topic/alt.obituaries/KzlK14NmStg.

26. "Chronicle Cracks Bias on MSC Football"; "MSC Loses Star, Game," *Detroit Free Press*, October 26, 1947.

27. Katie Koener and Ben Phelgar, "Willie Thrower: Breaking Barriers," Michigan State Spartan Athletics, February 24, 2010, https://msuspartans.com/news/2010/2/24/Willie_Thrower_Breaking_Barriers.aspx; "Spartan Soph Can Pitch!," *LSJ*, April 18, 1950; "Comparing Hands," *LSJ*, May 16, 1950; "State Loses Soph Passer," *LSJ*, September 26, 1950; "Jail Grid Player as Reckless Driver," January 22, 1951; "Wille (The Thrower) Connects," *LSJ*, November 16, 1952; "Wille Thrower Makes Grade after 4 Years at Michigan State," *Pittsburgh Post-Gazette*, November 17, 1952; Will Robinson, "M. S. Loaded with Negro Grid Talent," *Pittsburgh Courier*, November 7, 1953.

28. Smith, "'Breaking the Plane,'" 110–114.

29. Maya Washington, *Through the Banks of the Red Cedar: My Father and the Team that Changed the Game* (New York: Little A, 2022), 100; Smith, "'Breaking the Plane,'" 110–114.

30. Smith, "'Breaking the Plane,'" 101, 102, 119–121. Other starting Black quarterbacks to follow in Thrower's and Raye's footsteps included William Tripplett, Charles Baggett, Bobby McAllister, Tony Banks, and Damon Dowdell.

31. Smith, "'Breaking the Plane,'" 102, 128, 129.

32. Dave Hanson, "Raye's Doing OK: Ex-Spartan Grid Star Discusses Future Goals," *LSJ*, May 28, 1969.

33. Ernie Boone, "MSU's Jim Bibbs Is a Whole Lot of Man," *Michigan Chronicle*, September 27, 1975; Terry Cabell, "Former MSU Track Coach Enjoying Retirement," *Michigan Chronicle*, October 1, 2003; "Long Run Ends for Track Coach: Michigan State's Bibbs Retires after 27 Years," *LSJ*, June 30, 1995.

34. Richard W. Ouderluys, "Hannah Tops GOP Senate Possibles," *Detroit News*, March 9, 1964; "Polls Pick Hannah as GOP Favorite," *LSJ*, March 10, 1964; John Green, "Picket Protest Action on Fair Housing," *LSJ*, June 3, 1964, emphasis added.

35. "Grad Student in USIA Film: Little Rock Negroes Studied," *State News*, March 4, 1964.

36. Burke, "Exponent of Civil Rights"; "MSU Head, Ike to Talk: Hannah Awaits Briefing in Washington as Civil Rights Chief," *LSJ*, December 24, 1957.

37. "President Reviews Career at MSU," *State News*, February 10, 1969. This special section of the *State News* included an interview between Hannah and the paper's editor-in-chief Edward Brill. Other relevant articles included in this special issue include Mitch Miller, "'U' Surges During Hannah Era," and Linda Gortmaker, "Hannah—A Portrait of Service."

38. "Civil Rights Policy Urged at Michigan State," *Afro-American* (Baltimore), March 6, 1948. For a professor's story of how Hannah supposedly integrated the barbershop in the Union Building, see David Thomas, "John A. Hannah: 'Only People Are Important,'" *Michigan State Law Review* 3 (2014): 397.

39. Bailey, "MSU Leadership Helped to Advance Civil Rights."

CHAPTER 21. FORGOTTEN FIRSTS FROM THE FORTIES

1. "Scholarships Available Now for College Students," *Detroit Tribune*, January 10, 1948. This announcement appeared in newspapers throughout the nation in January 1948.

2. David A. Thomas, *Michigan State College: John Hannah and the Creation of a World University, 1926–1969* (East Lansing: Michigan State University Press, 2008), 56.

3. Sandy McClure, "Retired City Bus Driver Made Work His 'Hobby,'" *Detroit Free Press*, December 23, 1985.

4. F. M. Leonard, "Coast Guard Officer Offers Unlimited Opportunities for Negro Youth," *Michigan Chronicle*, August 21, 1943; "More Michigan Men Train as Pilots at TAF," *Michigan Chronicle*, June 24, 1944; "Ecorse Soldier Promoted to S-Sgt.," *Michigan Chronicle*, November 24, 1945; *LSJ*, February 7, 1949. The eight-room home was for sale to "colored buyers" for $7,500.

5. "New York Athlete St. Frosh Captain," *LSJ*, December 6, 1935.

6. Mark E. Havitz and Eric D. Zemper, "'Worked Out in Infinite Detail': Michigan State College's Lauren P. Brown and the Origins of NCAA Cross Country Championships," *Michigan Historical Review* 39 (Spring 2013): 16.

7. Jack Warner, "Putting Fun on a Business Basis," *LSJ*, April 4, 1937.

8. "Veterinary Surgeon," *Michigan Chronicle*, August 16, 1947; "Other People's Business," *Michigan Chronicle*, August 20, 1947; "Ezell Veterinary Hospital," *Detroit Tribune*, January 17, 24, 31, and February 7, 1948; "In Poultry Business," *Michigan Chronicle*, September 29, 1945; "Services Set for Frederick Smith Jr.," *Tennessean*,

August 29, 1991. Smith was hailed the first African American to earn a DVM from Michigan State. See "First of Race to Get Veterinary License in North Carolina," *New Journal and Guide* (Norfolk, VA), July 1, 1950.

9. Douglas Kermit Meyer, "The Changing Negro Residential Patterns in Lansing, Michigan, 1850–1969" (PhD diss., Michigan State University, 1970), 99, 100.

10. "Lincoln Community Center Enlarges Progress in 1940," *LSJ*, January 1, 1941; "Race Relations Group Being Formed in City," *LSJ*, November 28, 1943.

11. Ula Y. Taylor, *The Veiled Garvey: The Life and Times of Amy Jacques Garvey* (Chapel Hill, University of North Carolina Press, 2002).

12. Melissa Anders, "Local Woman Honored for Tuskegee Service," *LSJ*, November 27, 2011.

13. For an overview of the 1939 team, see Larry Lage, "Central Untouchable: Unbeaten 1939 Team Captured State Crown," *LSJ*, July 7, 1997.

14. "Dwight Rich Cager Rewrites Record Books," *LSJ*, March 10, 1974; Ed Senyczko, "Earvin Johnson's Other Side," *LSJ*, March 14, 1976.

15. Tom O'Brien, "Hugh Davis, Sub Halfback, Is Here of Titular Game," *LSJ*, November 13, 1937; "Central's Squad Stages Practice," *LSJ*, September 2, 1938; "Big Reds Display Power in Contest . . . Hugh Davis Is Star," *LSJ*, October 8, 1939; Tom O'Brien, "Highlights," *LSJ*, November 5, 1939; Tom O'Brien, "Hugh Davis Scampers for Three Touchdowns," *LSJ*, November 11, 1939.

16. "Central Grid Star to the Banqueted," *LSJ*, November 20, 1939; "West Side Honoring Hugh Davis Tonight," *LSJ*, November 21, 1939; "Semi-Annual Awards Presented to Central High School Seniors," *LSJ*, January 17, 1940; "Hugh Davis Honored," *LSJ*, February 3, 1940.

17. "Bachman Asks 49 to Report," LSJ, August 24, 1941; "Forget Their High School Rivalries," *LSJ*, September 11, 1941; George S. Alderton, "Hugh Davis Impressive," *LSJ*, October 19, 1941; "The First Tome," *LSJ*, May 18, 1941; "Casanega Tosses Perfectly to Beals on Tricky Delivery," *San Francisco Examiner*, October 19, 1941.

18. Bill Ellis, "Why Is a Rabbit's Foot Lucky? Body Parts as Fetishes," *Journal of Folklore Research* 39, no. 1 (January–April 2002): 51–84.

19. Tom O'Brien, "The Tom-Tom," *LSJ*, November 23, 1941.

20. George S. Alderton, "Purdue Track Team Coming," *LSJ*, April 16, 1943; "Hugh Davis Is Army Private," *Chicago Defender*, February 19, 1944; "Even Hughie Can't Save Lincoln '5,'" *LSJ*, January 5, 1944; "HBC vs. All Stars," *New York Age*, April 9, 1949; "Boxing Notes," *New York Age*, May 7, 1949; "Hugh Davis Is OK," *New York Age*, March 12, 1949; "Dope Charge Holds Physical Director," *New York Age*, September 22, 1951; "Harlem Violence Laid to Drug Use," *New Journal and Guide* (Norfolk, VA), September 29, 1951; "Gridiron Ace Nabbed as Dope Addict Here," *New York Amsterdam News*, September 29, 1951; "Talladega Defeats Fisk and Alabama," *Chicago Defender*, March 8, 1958; "Southeastern Cage Tourney Opens Feb. 24," *Chicago Defender*, February 18, 1961.

21. "Ex-Football Star Dies," *LSJ*, April 2, 1963.

22. "Negro Grabs Honors," *LSJ*, February 19, 1939; "Track," *M.S.C. Record* 44, no. 3 (May 1939); "Best Jumper in State's History," *LSJ*, May 9, 1939; George S. Alderton, "The Sports Grist," *LSJ*, February 14, 1940; George S. Alderton, "Sports Review," *M.S.C. Record* 45, no. 3 (April 1940): 10.

23. "Cloteele Rosemond, Former Band Vocalist, Hopes to Be 'Visiting Teacher in the City,'" *Detroit Tribune*,

August 24, 1940.

24. "Forrest Hainline in Speech Finals at Augie Tonight," *Daily Times* (Davenport, IA), April 26, 1940; "Colored Girl Winner of Oratorical Event," *Dispatch* (Moline, IL), April 26, 1940; "Sophomore Wins State, Then National Meet," *State News*, April 27, 1940; "Close Beside the Winding Cedar—Two Firsts," *M.S.C. Record* 45, no. 4 (July 1940): 8; "Cloteele Rosemond, Former Band Vocalist," *Detroit Tribune*, August 24, 1940; "Thunder on the Social Front," *Detroit Tribune*, April 25, 1942; "Students Give Many Talks for College Bureau," *LSJ*, January 1, 1942.

25. "In the Churches," *LSJ*, April 16, 1927; "Colored Lads in New Scout Troop," *LSJ*, May 31, 1929; "Scout Installation Is Set for Sunday," *LSJ*, June 1, 1929; "Colored Group Hears Urban League Speaker," *LSJ*, May 15, 1930; "Unique Graduate in Central Class," *LSJ*, June 12, 1935.

26. "Health Worker," *LSJ*, January 28, 1943; "Negroes to Report on Seal Sale Drive," *LSJ*, December 12, 1943; Charlie Hass, "Crusader for Education," *LSJ*, July 10, 1970. For other intriguing coverage of Williams's interesting life story, see "Lansing Birthdays: Today We Honor," *LSJ*, October 2, 1957; "Local Man Is Elevated," *LSJ*, August 27, 1960; "State OES Banquet Fetes Lansing Man," *LSJ*, August 13, 1967; "He's Retired," *LSJ*, August 28, 1972; Virginia Redfern, "Proud of Age, Full of Love: 'Mr. and Mrs. Senior,'" *LSJ*, March 4, 1977.

27. "In the Service," *Napa Valley Register* (Napa, CA), July 25, 1956; "Stockton State Doctor Takes Michigan Post," *Sacramento Bee*, August 20, 1964; "Dr. Peal Named Assistant Chief," *LSJ*, September 10, 1964; "9 Named to Four Groups," *LSJ*, August 16, 1966; "State Aide to Quit for California," LSJ, February 9, 1967; Gene Grigg, "New Mental Health Director Diagnoses County Situation," *Fresno (CA) Bee*, March 12, 1967.

28. Dr. James Peal, "Letter to the Press," *Escanaba (MI) Daily Press*, January 14, 1965.

29. "Dr. and Mrs. Peal Feted at Buffet Supper," *LSJ*, March 1, 1967; "Board Names New Mental Health Chief," *Fresno (CA) Bee*, February 7, 1967; "Appointment Set for June 5," *LSJ*, May 29, 1967; "Welcome Additions to the New York Scene," *New York Age*, March 26, 1949; "Jury Weighs Verdict in Bomb Threat Case," *Sacramento Bee*, January 16, 1975.

30. "In the Service of U.S.A.," *M.S.C. Record* 50, no. 3 (July 1945); Register Staff, "Longtime Music Teacher to Be Honored Sunday," *New Haven Register*, December 16, 2004, https://www.nhregister.com/news/article/Longtime-music-teacher-to-be-honored-Sunday-11672839.php.

31. "2 Playground Supervisors Named for Dover Program," *Morning News* (Wilmington, DE), June 17, 1949; "W. W. Bowie Named Bethel Choir Leader," *News Journal* (Wilmington, DE), November 5, 1954; "2 Honored for Work in Civil Rights," *Morning News* (Wilmington, DE), February 10, 1964; "Caution Urged in Relocation," *News Journal* (Wilmington, DE), June 2, 1965; "Two Real Estate Offices Picketed," *News Journal* (Wilmington, DE), August 25, 1965; Registered Staff, "Longtime Music Teacher to Be Honored Sunday."

32. Other Blacks who earned master's degrees during the 1940s include Madison Broadax (agriculture), E. S. Burke (agriculture), and Arthur Totten (poultry).

33. "Blazes a Trail," *New Journal and Guide* (Norfolk, VA), November 14, 1936.

34. Henry Lewis, "A Study of the Fragmentation of Some Tertiary Carbinols of Aluminum Chloride" (PhD diss., Michigan State College, 1944), "Acknowledgement"; "Dr. Huston Rites Slated," *LSJ*, May 18, 1954; "Division Offers Degrees in Mathematics, Science," *Montgomery (AL) Advertiser*, February 23, 1964.

35. "Receives Doctorate in Chemistry," *New Journal and Guide* (Norfolk, VA), February 24, 1945; "Receives Ph.D.," *Chicago Defender*, March 3, 1945; "Michigan Cites Retired Alabama State Educator," *Montgomery (AL) Advertiser*, August 31, 1968; Dave Hanson, "Mayor Forwards 10 Appointees for Model Cities Task to Council," *LSJ*, February 24, 1969.

36. "Helped Bring Hampton Boxing Crown," *New Journal and Guide* (Norfolk, VA), March 28, 1942; Burleigh Carlyle Webb, "Relationships Between Easily Available Carbohydrates, Nitrogen Recovery, and Growth of Sugar Beets Fertilized with Several Green Manures" (PhD diss., Michigan State College, 1952); E. F. Corbett, "A & T Agricultural Grads Find More, Better Jobs," *News and Observer* (Raleigh, NC), June 20, 1966; Pat Borden, "Challenges, Firsts Don't Frighten Her," *Charlotte (NC) Observer*, December 24, 1971; "Dr. Burleigh C. Webb," *News and Observer* (Raleigh, NC), June 22, 1997.

37. "Committee of 16: Graduate School Seeks Negroes," *State News*, May 28, 1968; Graduate Department of Human Resources, Michigan State University, *Affirmative Action at Michigan State University, 1974–75: Annual Report to the Department of Health, Education and Welfare* (East Lansing: Michigan State University, 1974–1975), 63.

CHAPTER 22. VIRTUALLY SEGREGATED, STRENGTH IN (SMALL) NUMBERS

1. Nelis J. Saunders, "Honor Student to Executive: Michigan Grad Is Telephone Trainee," *Michigan Chronicle*, February 18, 1956.

2. Jemelle Hill, "Underwood Take Charge, Spartanly," *Detroit Free Press*, April 17, 1999; Jack Ebling, "Underwood Set to Dive in as AD," *LSJ*, April 17, 1999.

3. Clarence Underwood and Larry Paladino, *Greener Pastures: A Pioneer Athletics Administrator Climbs from Spartan Beginnings to the Top at Michigan State* (self-pub., 2005), 23, 38.

4. Underwood and Paladino, *Greener Pastures*, 64–65; "Rep. R. G. Clark to Represent Holmes, Yazoo," *Clarion-Ledger* (Jackson, MS), August 1, 1968.

5. "Integration Leader Due," *LSJ*, February 2, 1957; "Soft-Spoken Negro Leader Race's Pillar of Strength," *LSJ*, February 17, 1957; Fred Olds, "Rev. King Speaks to 3,000 in City," *LSJ*, February 18, 1957.

6. Underwood and Paladino, *Greener Pastures*, 69–70.

7. Underwood and Paladino, *Greener Pastures*, 72.

8. Allen B. Ballard, *The Education of Black Folk: The Afro-American Struggle for Knowledge in White America* (New York: First Harper, 1974), 1–8, 52.

9. Kenneth B. Clark and Lawrence Plotkin, *The Negro Student at Integrated Colleges* (Washington, D.C.: U.S. Department of Health, Education, & Welfare, Office of Education, 1963), 7–52.

10. See Phillip Lewis, "Tuskegee Airman Who Chartered a Chapter of Alpha Phi Alpha in the 1940s Shares His Story," Watch the Yard: Black Greekdom's Digital Yardshow, 2014, https://www.watchtheyard.com/alphas/alpha-phi-alpha-william-thompson/.

11. "Negro Fraternity Formed at College," *LSJ*, May 2, 1948.

12. Bill Haithco, *From the Farm to the Pharmacist and Beyond* (New York: iUniverse, Inc., 2007), xv, 2–4, 27–32, 83–85.

13. "Ex-GI Seen as Strong Olympic Prospect," *New Journal and Guide* (Norfolk, VA), June 14, 1947.

14. "Mich. State Frosh Star Steals Show," *Afro-American* (Baltimore), June 7, 1947; George Alderton, "Irish Prove Only Black 'S' in Path," *LSJ*, March 7, 1948; "Wind Nullifies Horace Smith's World Performance in Low Hurdles," *Michigan Chronicle*, May 21, 1949; "Johnson Best in CCC Meet," *Chicago Defender*, June 11, 1949; "Fred Johnson Stars Again," *Michigan Chronicle*, June 11, 1949; "Fred Johnson Stars for MSC at Purdue," *Michigan Chronicle*, April 1, 1950; Charles Johnson, "Marshall Dill Quits MSU; Headed for His Choice, USC," *State News*, November 15, 1972.

15. "Fred Johnson's College Track Career Ends: M. S. C. Ace Forced to Hang Up Spikes," *LSJ*, April 2, 1950; "Thomas Rewrites Records at MSC," *Michigan Chronicle*, June 2, 1951; "Open House Set at Lincoln Center," *LSJ*, November 8, 1949; "Lincoln Center Aids Youth," *LSJ*, May 13, 1950; "Lincoln Center Programs Starting," *LSJ*, September 19, 1950; "Lincoln Center Becoming Crowded," *LSJ*, May 13, 1950.

16. "MSC Leaders Ask Reports on Bias," *LSJ*, January 25, 1951.

17. Jeanne Saddler, "Black Fraternity Leaves IFC," *State News*, October 10, 1969. Kappa Alpha Psi didn't join members of Alpha Phi Alpha in withdrawing from the IFC. See Irene Pickens, "Vote to Stay: Blacks Back IFC," *State News*, October 24, 1969.

18. "Alphas First to Buy Frat House at Michigan State," *Detroit Tribune*, September 11, 1954.

19. "Negro Fraternity Finds New Home," *LSJ*, June 20, 1954. In the summer of 1957, the realtor advertised the home as being "excellent for sorority, fraternity or regular student income." See, for instance, *LSJ*, August 15, 1957. "Fraternity Fetes Housemother," *LSJ*, February 24, 1955.

20. "Basketball Game Here to Aid March of Dimes," *LSJ*, January 28, 1949; "Local Student to Edit Magazine," *LSJ*, December 12, 1949.

21. "MSC Frat Wins the 'Little 500,'" *LSJ*, May 18, 1952; "Alpha Phi Alpha Car Wins in M.S.C. Pushcart Classic," *LSJ*, May 17, 1953; "New Record Established in MSU's Pushcar Derby," *LSJ*, May 20, 1956; "New Record Set in MSU Junior 500," *LSJ*, May 26, 1957.

22. Underwood and Paladino, *Greener Pastures*, 69.

23. "From Romulus: First Negro Wins GM Scholarship," *Michigan Chronicle*, July 30, 1955. In 1956, MSU student Amy Davis was Detroit's popular "Miss Panorama of Progress." See "She's Panorama Queen," *Chicago Defender*, June 20, 1956.

24. "A Queen at MSU," *Michigan Chronicle*, April 18, 1964; "She's a Standout," *Michigan Chronicle*, May 9, 1964. It's possible that the photo of the young Black woman on the cover of the *State News* in 1964 was selected by George Junne, the African American chief photographer of the student newspaper.

25. Barbara Bullitt, "Scribe Escapes Typewriter Jungle to Visit College Campus Cuties," *Michigan Chronicle*, October 24, 1953; Barbara Bullitt, "Barbara Gives Dope on the Younger Set," *Michigan Chronicle*, December 18, 1954; Barbara Bullitt, "Youth Speaks at Forum," *Michigan Chronicle*, April 3, 1954; Barbara Bullitt, "Scribe Gets Bird's Eye View of Campus Life," *Michigan Chronicle*, May 22, 1954.

26. Photos of the members of Alpha Kappa Alpha Sorority, Inc. were included in Michigan State yearbooks

beginning in the mid-1950s. For a description of the variety show, see "Alpha Kappa Alpha Sorority Plans Variety Show Saturday," *LSJ*, April 29, 1955.

27. "Alpha Kappa Alpha Sorority to Have Chapter at M.S.C.," *LSJ*, January 29, 1954; Mary Lou Folger, "Inter-Racial Sorority Activated," *LSJ*, February 14, 1954; Dorothy Wilson, "'Not a Negro Society,'" *LSJ*, May 27, 1956.

28. "Hate Should Die in U.S., Forum Speaker Declares," *LSJ*, February 22, 1954; "Members Growing Out of Clubhouse," *LSJ*, March 21, 1954; Bob Miller, "Spartan Gridders Push Coed to Derby Record," *LSJ*, May 21, 1961.

29. "MSC Six Triumphs on Lord's 2 Goals," *Detroit Free Press*, December 6, 1952; "Wolves Post 6-0 Hockey Victory Over Spartans," *Escanaba (MI) Daily Press*, January 8, 1953; "U–M Sextet Drubs Spartans," *Traverse City (MI) Record-Eagle*, January 8, 1953; Will Robinson, "Dick Lord an Oddity Among Tan Athletes," *Pittsburgh Courier*, January 17, 1953; Tim McRoberts, "Remembering a Spartan: Dick Lord," Archives @ MSU, February 27, 2020, https://msuarchives.wordpress.com/2020/02/27/remembering-a-spartan-dick-lord/.

CHAPTER 23. BELATED WELCOME

1. "NAACP Seeks to Combat Prejudice," *State News*, Welcome Week edition, September, 1964.

2. Theresa Brown, "AKA's Most Active at Michigan State Univ.," *Michigan Chronicle*, December 19, 1964.

3. "Omega Psi Phi," *State News*, Welcome Week edition, September, 1964.

4. "Minutes of the Meeting of the Finance Committee," Michigan State University Board of Trustees, March 17, 1960, https://projects.kora.matrix.msu.edu/files/157-544-383/MARCH171960.pdf.

5. "Park Bans Pickets," *LSJ*, May 31, 1963.

6. Curt Hanes, "Hymns, Chants, Silence—200 March for Rights," *LSJ*, August 20, 1963.

7. "Industry Blamed for Race Crisis," *State News*, September 30, 1963.

8. "'East Lansing Has Race Problem' Negro Tells National Conference," *LSJ*, November 22, 1963.

9. Campus NAACP, "Human Rights Rules," *State News*, January 28, 1964.

10. "Lesson from a Governor," *State News*, February 19, 1964; "Wallace Doesn't Fit 'Devil' Image," *State News*, February 19, 1964. In his inauguration speech on January 14, 1963, Wallace made his infamous remarks about segregation remaining embedded in the South.

11. Necia Brown, "View Complexities of Racial Prejudice," *State News*, March 3, 1964.

12. Sue Jacoby, "Pickets Protest Wallace Profile: Area NAACP Expresses 'Shock,'" *State News*, February 20, 1964.

13. Necia Brown, "Two Give Reactions to Racial Prejudice," *State News*, March 5, 1964.

14. "Dick Gregory to Appear in Special Program Today," *State News*, April 27, 1964.

15. John Green, "Negro Mad, Unafraid, Gregory Says at MSU," *LSJ*, April 28, 1964; Linda Miller, "Negro Comedian Quips Charm Students," *State News*, April 28, 1964.

16. "Roy Wilkins to Address Symposium," *LSJ*, May 8, 1964; John Green, "NAACP Chief Praises LBJ's Atlanta Speech," *LSJ*, May 9, 1964; Austin Snyder, "Racial Crisis Greatest Since Civil War," *State News*, May 11, 1964.

17. Necia Brown, "Negro Coeds View the Future," *State News*, March 4, 1964.

CHAPTER 24. EARLY BLACK STUDENT MOVEMENT

1. "NAACP Seeks to Combat Prejudice," *State News*, Welcome Week edition, September, 1964; Jacqueline Trescott, "Just Who is Bunny Mitchell?," *Washington Post*, July 20, 1977.

2. See Ibram H. Rogers [Ibram X. Kendi], *The Black Campus Movement: Black Students and the Racial Reconstruction of Higher Education, 1965–1972* (New York: Palgrave Macmillan, 2012), 1–3, 97–98.

3. Don E. Coleman, "The Status of the Black Student Aide Program and the Black Student Movement at Michigan State University" (PhD dissertation, Michigan State University, 1971).

4. "NAACP Schedules Meeting for Forming Campus Group," *State News*, January 13, 1958; "NAACP Plans in Progress for Campus," *State News*, January 15, 1958.

5. For reporting on MSU students' 1957 application for membership in the NAACP, see "College Chapters Win Recognition," *Michigan Chronicle*, December 21, 1957. "MSU Student Heads NAACP Youth Group," *Michigan Chronicle*, February 20, 1965. Williams was killed in a car accident in 1973. From the late 1960s until his death, he promoted Black cultural nationalist activities, neighborhood revitalization efforts, and Black politics, serving as a delegate to the National Black Caucus. See "Crash Kills Black Community Leader," *South Bend (IN) Tribune*, May 19, 1973.

6. For the History Makers' video oral history interview with Ernest Green see "Ernest Green," The History Makers, January 22, 2003, https://www.thehistorymakers.org/biography/ernest-green-39.

7. "NAACP Chapter at MSU Proposed," *LSJ*, January 14, 1958; "Negro Grad Is Admitted: Alumnus of Little Rock's High School Formally Accepted at MSU," *LSJ*, June 19, 1958; "No Sports, But Study for Green," *LSJ*, September 11, 1958; George Weeks, "Little Rock Grad Has White Roommate at MSU," *Chicago Defender*, September 23, 1958; "Little Rock Youth Gives Campus Talk," *LSJ*, October 10, 1958; "New Officers to Be Installed," *LSJ*, January 31, 1959.

8. "Local NAACP Stages Picket at Chain Store," *State News*, March 8, 1960.

9. "Inviting Trouble," *State News*, March 7, 1960; Don Pemmer, "Local NAACP Stages Picket at Chain Store," *State News*, March 8, 1960; "NAACP, 'Little' 10 Editorials Sir Up Criticism," *State News*, March 9, 1960; MSU Chapter of NAACP, "Human Rights," *State News*, March 9, 1960.

10. "Negroes to Picket," *LSJ*, March 4, 1960; "Negro from Little Rock to Head East Lansing Demonstration," *LSJ*, March 5, 1960; "Picketing Quiet Here," *LSJ*, March 6, 1960; "Meet Set on Campus by NAACP," *LSJ*, April 11, 1960; "Negro Aid Drive Set," *LSJ*, May 31, 1960.

11. Mary Basing, "Civil Liberties: Do Students Have Any?," *State News*, May 25, 1961.

12. "MSU Unit of NAACP Plans Play," *LSJ*, February 7, 1961.

13. "Little Rock Hero Makes Good Up North: Ernest Green Heads NAACP Chapter at MSU," *Ebony* 16, no. 7 (May 1961): 74–78.

14. "NAACP Reviews Progress; McKee States Further Goals," *State News*, May 24, 1961; Samuel E. Harris, "Plans Research: Information Aim of Local NAACP," *State News*, January 27, 1961.

15. Marion Nowak, "Historical Outline of Radicalism at MSU," *State News*, April 22, 1969.

16. "$2,000 Sought: Campus Community to Aid Freedom Rider," *State News*, February 13, 1962; "Raise Funds for

Student," *Holland Evening Sentinel*, February 28, 1962; "Would Aid Bus Rider: Raise $1250 to Help Woollcott Smith," *LSJ*, March 1, 1962; "Freedom Rider from MSU Guilty," *LSJ*, March 29, 1962.

17. Ivanhoe Donaldson, interview by Rachel Reinhard, September 20, 2003, Center for Oral History and Cultural Heritage, University of Southern Mississippi.

18. Ivanhoe Donaldson, "Week Tells Story of Negro History," *State News*, February 13, 1961; Ivanhoe Donaldson, "Negroes Demand Complete Equality," *State News*, February 15, 1961; "Chauvinism?," *State News*, February 20, 1961.

19. See Lloyd J. Moles, "Muslims Are Opposed to Race Integration," *LSJ*, May 30, 1961. Moles describes a talk Malcolm delivered in Lansing on the afternoon of May 29, 1961, indicating he was also scheduled to speak on campus later that evening.

20. Donaldson, interview.

21. "Free 2 Students Who Took Food to Miss. Needy," *Chicago Defender*, January 28, 1963. For the detailed account, see Anne Braden, "The Power of Protest—Even in the Deep South," *Gazette and Daily* (York, PA), February 9, 1963.

22. "Festival Date Set," *LSJ*, April 29, 1961; Neil Hunter, "MSU Campus Busy with Weekend," *LSJ*, May 13, 1961; Joseph S. Syfax, "The New Twist Is Old Stuff," *Detroit Free Press*, November 10, 1961, "Sgt. Joseph Syfax, Detroit Policeman," *Detroit Free Press*, December 25, 1975; "Campus NAACP to Test Race Bias," *State News*, December 4, 1961.

23. "Campus NAACP to Test Race Bias," *State News*, December 4, 1961; "MSU Bias Is Denied," *LSJ*, December 7, 1961.

24. Linda Miller, "Hannah Hits Biased Housing," *State News*, January 31, 1964.

25. "MSU President Greets Students," *State News*, Welcome Week edition, September, 1963; "Campus NAACP to Test Race Bias," Jerry Chiapetta, "Race Bias Hit Here," *LSJ*, December 6, 1961; "MSU Bias Is Denied."

CHAPTER 25. FAIR HOUSING IS A MUST

1. Bill Castanier, a writer for the *Lansing City Pulse*, wrote an excellent essay on the challenges of integrating East Lansing in the 1960s: "EL Rewind: Historic East Lansing Battles Over Racist Housing Discrimination," Eli Archives: News from 2013–2020, May 3, 2015, https://archive.eastlansinginfo.org/content/el-rewind-historic-east-lansing-battles-over-racist-housing-discrimination.html.

2. For a brief overview of Brookover's life, see "Deaths and Funerals Brookover, Wilbur Bone," *LSJ*, April 9, 2003.

3. "Legal Notices," *LSJ*, June 28, 1963.

4. "Legal Notice," *LSJ*, September 27, 1963.

5. The following discussion of the activities of the East Lansing Human Relations Commission from its founding until the June 2 protests are from the following accounts in the *LSJ*: "Ordinance Key Rules Listed," April 2, 1964; "Local Realtors Oppose Open Occupancy Laws," "Fair Housing Recommendation Made to Council," "Human Relations Body Favors Fair Housing Ordinance," and "Ask Fair Housing in East Lansing," May 7, 1964.

6. Enora Brown, "Phillips Hall," RSH Papers, UA 17.269, box 2359, folder 44, UAHC.

7. Kimberly Popiolek, "The Trailblazing Life of MSU's First Black Faculty Member," Michigan State University, College of Arts and Letters, February 16, 2021, https://cal.msu.edu/news/the-trailblazing-life-of-msus-first-black-faculty-member/.

8. Alice Dreger, "As Friday's Dedications Near, We're Learning More about East Lansing's History of Racial Integration," *East Lansing Info*, September 22, 2021.

9. Clarence Underwood and Paladino, *Greener Pastures: A Pioneer Athletics Administrator Climbs from Spartan Beginnings to the Top at Michigan State* (self-pub., 2005), 78–80.

10. Barbara Stanton, "MSU Gives Zoom Treatment to 23," *Detroit Free Press*, March 9, 1964.

11. "Students File Bias Complaint," *State News*, April 3, 1964.

12. "NAACP to Start Demonstration to Fight Housing Discrimination," *State News*, April 13, 1964; "MSU NAACP Girds for Direct Action," *Michigan Chronicle*, April 25, 1964.

13. John Green, "Ask Fair Housing in East Lansing," *LSJ*, May 7, 1964.

14. Green, "Ask Fair Housing in East Lansing."

15. At the time of the June 2 protests, what is now known as Robert S. Linton Hall served as the Administration Building. Completed in 1881 as the Library-Museum, Linton Hall "is the second oldest extant building on campus." Until 1927, when the library's holdings were moved into what is now the MSU Museum, the building served as the college's library-museum, administration building, and president's office. The administration offices for the college and university remained in Linton Hall, "Old Administration," until 1969 when the administrative offices of MSU as well as the Office of the President were moved to the John A. Hannah Administration Building. Except for a handful of years between 1881 and 1969, the Office of the President was located in Linton Hall. See Linda O. Stafford and C. Kurt Dewhurst, *MSU Campus—Buildings, Places, Spaces: Architecture and the Campus Park of Michigan State University* (East Lansing: Michigan State University Press, 2002).

16. John Green, "Pickets Protest Action on Fair Housing Law," *LSJ*, June 3, 1964.

17. "Student Pickets Protest Vote Defeating Open Occupancy," *State News*, June 3, 1964.

18. "Group To Rewrite Housing Law," *State News*, June 3, 1964; "Student Pickets Protest Vote Defeating Open Occupancy"; "Against Open Housing Stand: Single Out 3 Members of Council," *State News*, June 8, 1964.

19. The descriptions of the events that took place on June 2, 1964, come from the following accounts: by John Green, "Pickets Protest Action on Fair Housing" and "Councilmen Explain Position after Voting 'No' on Housing," *LSJ*, June 3, 1964; and by Necia Brown, "City Council Opposes Open Housing Plan," "Group to Rewrite Housing Law," and "Student Pickets Protest Vote Defeating Open Occupancy," *State News*, June 3, 1963.

20. Oyars Balcers, "Discussions, Decisions in 'Year That Was,'" *State News*, June 8, 1964.

21. Examples of the *State News* editors' belittling of the campus NAACP include "Where Are the Backers?," May 16, 1964; "Faculty Committee Cancels Talk On Off-Campus Bias," May 27, 1964; "NAACP Off Target," June 5, 1964.

22. "Point of View: Defends Right to Hate," *State News*, May 20, 1964.

23. Susan J. Filson, "Spartans Aid Miss. Negroes," *State News*, June 30, 1964.

24. The following are all from the *State News*: "Here and There," January 27, 1965; "Letters to the Editor," January 27, 1965; "Malcolm X. Killed in New York Hall: Ex-Muslim Once Lived in Lansing," February 22, 1965; "Equality," February 24, 1965; Charles T. O. King III, "Negro Revolt Includes Malcolms," February 25, 1965; "The Man Called Nigger," February 26, 1965.

25. "Students Picket East Lansing Home," *State News*, April 30, 1965.

26. "Committee for Student Rights: For Immediate Release," April 29, 1965, Civil Rights Protests, 1965, UA 7.0, box 105H, folder 10, UAHC; Donald Karl, "Co-ed Denied Room, Students Protest," *Michigan Chronicle*, May 8, 1965.

27. "March on City Hall for Open Housing flyer, 1965," May 18, 1965, On the Banks of the Red Cedar, UAHC; "Editorial: Pictures at an Exhibition," *State News*, May 20, 1965.

28. Jim Sterba, "MSU Offers 'Mutual Problems' Talks," *State News*, May 19, 1965.

29. "Students Vow Sit-In Renewal," *LSJ*, May 20, 1965; John Green, "Halt Demonstration," *LSJ*, May 21, 1965; John Green, "Demonstrators Taken to Court," *LSJ*, May 26, 1965; "Demonstrators Arraigned after Night in County Jail," *State News*, May 27, 1965.

30. Norris Ingells, "Group Defers Bid for 'Open Housing,'" *LSJ*, March 3, 1966; John Green, "Local Rights Law Rejected," *LSJ*, June 7, 1966; "Rights Post Removal of Hannah Requested," *LSJ*, June 13, 1966.

31. "Conciliation Effort Said Successful," *LSJ*, April 26, 1967; "City of Lansing Notice of the Passage of an Ordinance, Number 139 (Open-Housing)," *LSJ*, October 14, 1967; "Council Backs Fair Housing," *LSJ*, November 7, 1967.

32. Brian Vallee, "Council Gets Tougher Discrimination Ordinance," *LSJ*, April 9, 1968.

33. Brian Vallee, "East Lansing Makes Discrimination Unlawful," *LSJ*, April 16, 1968; Robert Stuart, "Governor Romney Signs 'Historic' Fair Housing Bill," *LSJ*, June 11, 1968.

34. Jeanne Saddler, "Blacks File Housing Complaint," *State News*, October 3, 1969.

CHAPTER 26. APEX OF THE STRUGGLE

1. Brian Vallee and Helen Clegg, "Convocation at MSU Honors Martin Luther King," *LSJ*, April 5, 1968.

2. Michael Eric Dyson, *April 4, 1968: Martin Luther King Jr.'s Death and How It Changed America* (New York: Civitas Books, 2008); Vallee and Clegg, "Convocation at MSU Honors Martin Luther King."

3. David A. Thomas, *Michigan State College: John Hannah and the Creation of a World University, 1926–1969* (East Lansing: Michigan State University Press, 2008), 456.

4. Jim Sylvester, "1,244 So Far: Black Recruiting Expands," *State News*, May 2, 1969; Jeanne Saddler, "Admissions Policy Challenged," *State News*, October 28, 1969.

5. Walter R. Allen, Joseph O. Jewell, Kimberly A. Griffin and De'Sha S. Wolf, "Historically Black Colleges and Universities: Honoring the Past, Engaging the Present, Touching the Future," *Journal of Negro Education* 76 (Summer 2007): 263–280; Joy Ann Williamson, "In Defense of Themselves: The Black Student Struggle for

Success and Recognition at Predominantly White Colleges and Universities," *Journal of Negro Education* 68 (Winter 1999): 94–95.

6. Martha Biondi, *The Black Revolution on Campus* (Berkeley: University of California Press, 2012), 2–3.

7. Ibram H. Rogers [Ibram X. Kendi], *The Black Campus Movement: Black Students and the Racial Reconstruction of Higher Education, 1965–1972* (New York: Palgrave Macmillan, 2012). See, for instance, Richard P. McCormick, *The Black Student Protest Movement at Rutgers* (New Brunswick: Rutgers University Press, 1990); Donald Alexander Downs, *Cornell '69: Liberalism and the Crisis of the American University* (Ithaca: Cornell University Press, 1999); Wayne Glasker, *Black Students in the Ivory Tower: African American Student Activism at the University of Pennsylvania, 1967–1990* (Amherst: University of Massachusetts Press, 2002); Joy Ann Williamson, *Black Power on Campus: The University of Illinois, 1965–75* (Urbana: University of Illinois Press, 2003); Fabio Rojas, *From Black Power to Black Studies: How a Radical Social Movement Became an Academic Discipline* (Baltimore: Johns Hopkins University Press, 2007); Stefan M. Bradley, *Harlem vs. Columbia University: Black Student Power in the Late 1960s* (Urbana: University of Illinois Press, 2009); Stefan M. Bradley, *Upending the Ivory Tower* (New York: New York University Press, 2018); Brian Jones, *The Tuskegee Student Uprising: A History* (New York: New York University Press, 2022).

8. While Martha Biondi, *Black Revolution on Campus*, focuses on Black student activism at a group of colleges and universities, Rogers, *The Black Campus Movement*, touches upon incidents at countless institutions. In passing, he mentions the *Grapevine Journal*, the MSU BSA, and the 1968 Black athlete boycott.

9. Barney Young, "Blacks Seek Legislative Aid," *State News*, May 20, 1970.

10. Reginald Thomas, "'Black Power' Fades, Groups in Turmoil: Activism of the Late 1960s Wanes—Can It Rise Again," *State News*, Welcome Week edition, September 1978.

11. George White, "3 Incidents in '72 Trigger Black Activism," *State News*, Welcome Week edition, September 1972. In their founding documents, BSA's spokespersons identified the organization as the *Black Students' Alliance*, signaling that the group was an alliance possessed by Black students. After their founding, they referred to themselves, and were identified as others, as being the *Black Student Alliance*. I prioritize *Black Students' Alliance* as the organizations' founders used it in most of their statements.

12. "Students Can Lose Financial Aid," *Grapevine Journal*, September 18, 1973; Cassandra Spratling, "Aid Cut for Low-Income Students," *Grapevine Journal*, March 4, 1975.

13. Kim Shanahan, "'Closet Racism' Plagues Black Faculty, but the Real Battles May Yet to Be Fought," *State News*, Welcome Week Edition, September 1978.

14. "Negro Economist Is Named Head of Michigan State U.; Clifton Wharton, Aide on Development Council, to Succeed Hannah," *New York Times*, October 18, 1969.

15. Shanahan, "'Closet Racism' Plagues Black Faculty."

16. Shanahan, "'Closet Racism' Plagues Black Faculty."

CHAPTER 27. RADICAL DEPARTURES

1. "Editorials," *State News*, February 26, 1965; "BSA Statement: Why We Honor Brother Malcolm," *State News*, February 20, 1969; Karen Fitzgerald, "Malcolm X Day Observed," *State News*, February 20, 1970; Jeff Elliott, "Spotlight Still on Ex-Champ," *State News*, March 2, 1970.

2. Malcolm Askia, "Lessons of Malcolm Still Important," *Grapevine Journal*, March 4, 1975.

3. Samuel E. Harris, "Information Aim of Local NAACP," *State News*, January 27, 1961; "NAACP Seeks to Combat Prejudice," *State News*, Welcome Week edition, September, 1964.

4. Ibram H. Rogers [Ibram X. Kendi], *The Black Campus Movement: Black Students and the Racial Reconstruction of Higher Education, 1965–1972* (New York: Palgrave Macmillan, 2012), 3.

5. "Lumumba? Dead?," *State News*, January 20, 1961.

6. Katherine Elizabeth White, "Student Activism at Michigan State University during the Decade of the 1960's" (PhD diss., Michigan State University, 1970); Jeanne Saddler, "Few Black Students 'Integrate' Strike," *Westside News* (Lansing, MI), May 9, 1970.

7. "A Report from the President," May 11, 1970; "STRIKE NOW," May 6, 1970; "Strike Demand Fact Sheet," n.d.; "Black Faculty and Student Teach-In: A Position Paper," n.d.; and *MSU Faculty News* 1, no. 27 (May 12, 1970) in RSH Papers, UA 17.269, box 2359, folder 4, UAHC. Ron Johnson and Gerald Evelyn, "Blacks Boycott Classes," *State News*, May 26, 1970; Estella Chambers, "Involvement of Blacks Stressed," *State News*, May 29, 1970.

8. Barry D. Amis, "MSU, the Do Nothing 'U,'" *State News*, June 26, 1968.

9. For discussions of the "Long Civil Rights Movement," see Jacquelyn Dowd Hall, "The Long Civil Rights Movement and the Political Uses of the Past," *Journal of American History* 91 (March 2005): 1233–1263; Sundiata Keita Cha-Jua and Clarence Lang, "The 'Long Movement' as Vampire: Temporal and Spatial Fallacies in Recent Black Freedom Studies," *Journal of African American History* 92 (Spring 2007): 265–288. Many scholars have challenged the nonviolent direct action orthodoxy of the modern Civil Rights Movement by examining the history of armed self-defense during the movement, including Christopher B. Strain, Akinyele Omowale Umoja, Timothy Tyson, Charles E. Cobb Jr., Lance Hill, and Nicholas Johnson.

10. Jill Witherspoon, "White 'Mainstream' Not Enough," *Collage: The State News Bi-Weekly Magazine*, April 4, 1968; Stokely Carmichael and Charles V. Hamilton, *Black Power: The Politics of Liberation* (New York: Random House, 1967).

11. Peniel E. Joseph, "Reinterpreting the Black Power Movement," *OAH Magazine of History* 22 (July 2008): 4.

12. Amis, "MSU, the Do Nothing 'U.'"

13. "Little Rock Hero Makes Good Up North: Ernest Green Heads NAACP Chapter at MSU," *Ebony* 16, no. 7 (May 1961): 78; "Joe Wright, "Negroes Ignore NAACP Meet," State News, May 15, 1964.

14. "Michigan State Chief: Clifton Reginald Wharton Jr.," *New York Times*, October 18, 1969.

15. Don E. Coleman, "The Status of the Black Student Aide Program and the Black Student Movement at Michigan State University" (PhD diss., Michigan State University, 1971), 38.

16. Robert L. Green, "The Admission of Minority Students: A Framework of Action," October 22, 1970, Robert

L. Green Papers, UA 17.20, drawer F.D., folder 3, UAHC; Coleman, "The Status of the Black Student Aide Program," 29.

17. Green, "The Admission of Minority Students"; William Grant, "MSU Chief Backs Universal Education," *Detroit Free Press*, March 31, 1970; Helen Clegg, "Wharton Explains Commission Purpose," *LSJ*, April 1, 1970; "MSU Minority Enrollment Up," *LSJ*, January 27, 1972; "MSU Minority Employment Gains Nearly 71 Per Cent in 5 Years, Report Discloses," *LSJ*, May 13, 1971.

18. Denise A. Outram, "Increase Expected in Black Enrollment," *Grapevine Journal*, May 9, 1972.

19. The university did not begin collecting data on the number of Black faculty until 1970 and 1971 in the annual *Affirmative Action at Michigan State University: Annual Report to the Department of Health, Education and Welfare*. In 1969, a writer for the *Lansing State Journal* reported that there were twenty-one Black faculty and the *New York Times* announced that there were thirty-two. In 1969, there were most likely approximately twenty to twenty-six Black faculty of various designations at the university. Early on, they called themselves the Black Faculty Association, the Black Faculty Caucus, and the Black Faculty Association.

20. "A Note to Black Faculty from the Black Students' Alliance," February 24, 1969, RSH Papers, UA 17.269, box 2359, folder 64, UAHC.

21. Deborah Fitch, "Fall Curriculums Expanded," *State News*, Welcome Week, September 1968.

22. Clarissa Brown, "Honors, ATL Omits Blacks," *State News*, February 10, 1970.

23. Karen Fitzgerald, "Blacks Criticize Irrelevance of 'U' Courses," *State News*, March 13, 1970; Abduhl Jamal, "Philosophy 294 Unique to American University," *Grapevine Journal*, September 20, 1971.

24. Michael Fox, "Rise in Campus Race Tension Seen," *State News*, March 2, 1972.

CHAPTER 28. BLACK POWER ARRIVES IN EAST LANSING

1. Steven V. Roberts, "Student Group Endorses Militant Black Power Resolution," *Times Record* (Brunswick, ME), August 22, 1967.

2. Stokely Carmichael and Charles V. Hamilton, *Black Power: The Politics of Liberation* (New York: Random House, 1967), xvi.

3. Helen Clegg, "Negro Leader Outlines Goals," *LSJ*, October 31, 1967; Dan Brandon, "Parallel Society for Blacks Sought by CORE Leader," *State News*, October 31, 1967; "Green to Teach, Consult This Fall," *State News*, Welcome Week, September 1966.

4. Clegg, "Negro Leader Outlines Goals."

5. Clegg, "Negro Leader Outlines Goals"; Brandon, "Parallel Society for Blacks Sought by CORE Leader."

6. "Variety of Speakers Find MSU Platform," *State News*, Welcome Week edition, September 1964; "Carmichael Sees Ghettos as Black Power Bloc in '72," *State News*, February 10, 1967.

7. "Carmichael Sees Ghettos as Black Power Bloc in '72."

8. Kate Fitzgerald, "Blacks Hesitant on Moratorium," *State News*, October 15, 1969.

9. Leigh Montville, *Sting Like a Bee: Muhammad Ali vs. the United States of America, 1966–1971* (New York:

Anchor Books, 2017), 145; "Kimath [*sic*] and the Draft," *Grapevine Journal*, September 20, 1971.

10. Mitch Miller, "Dorm Holds Slave Auction," *State News*, February 14, 1967. Under the header "Two Fine White Slaves with Rhythm," there is also a photo of a grinning Black man handling two jovial White students on the auction block.

11. Robert L. Green, "The Admission of Minority Students: A Framework of Action," October 22, 1970, Robert L. Green Papers, UA 17.20, drawer F.D., folder 3, UAHC.

12. Abramson and Schwartz, "Admission of High Risk Students at Michigan State University," Faculty Senate, Michigan State University, November 20, 1968, https://files.eric.ed.gov/fulltext/ED028730.pdf; Barbara Stanton, "'Operation Ethyl': MSU Gives Zoom Treatment to 23," *Detroit Free Press*, March 9, 1964.

13. William T. Trent, "College Compensatory Programs for Disadvantaged Students," Report 3 (Washington, D.C.: ERIC Clearinghouse on Higher Education, George Washington University, September 1970), 14.

14. Abramson and Schwartz, "Admission of High Risk Students at Michigan State University."

15. Green, "The Admission of Minority Students."

16. Laurel Pratt, "Detroit Project: 'U' Gives Deprived Youths a Better Chance at College," *State News*, July 31, 1967; Linda Gortmaker, "Detroit Project Freshman Here for Orientation," *State News*, August 15, 1967.

17. "Negro Youth to Visit White Homes in Area," *State News*, July 27, 1967; Alana D. Smith, "Now It's Whitey's Turn," *State News*, July 31, 1967; Barry D. Amis, "MSU, the Do Nothing 'U,'" *State News*, June 26, 1968.

18. Marilyn Patterson, "Admissions Head Sees Increase of Blacks," *State News*, April 10, 1970.

19. W. Kim Heron, "Black Students at MSU," *Grapevine Journal*, September 18, 1973; "Handwritten Notes—Black Student Alliance Roster," "Black Fact Sheet about Black Student Alliance Meeting," "Black Fact Sheet No. 2, Meeting Announcement," Barry D. Amis Papers, UA 10.3.500, box 6539, folder 1, UAHC; "Interview: Toni Eubanks," RSH Papers, UA 17.269, box 2359, folder 40, UAHC.

CHAPTER 29. MCKISSICK'S AND KING'S PROGENY

1. "The Many Shades of Student Power," *State News*, November 27, 1967; Stan Morgan, "'U' Embarks on Era of Student Involvement," *State News*, Welcome Week edition, September 1968.

2. Marion Nowak, "Historical Outline of Radicalism at MSU," *State News*, April 22, 1969.

3. Kimberly Popiolek, "Alumnus Reflects on Legacy as a Student Activist and a Black Student Alliance Founder," College of Arts and Letters, Michigan State University, February 1, 2022, https://cal.msu.edu/news/alumnus-reflects-on-legacy-as-a-student-activist-and-a-black-student-alliance-founder/.

4. Barry D. Amis, "Educational Tokenism at MSU," *State News*, January 9, 1968.

5. Amis, "Educational Tokenism at MSU."

6. "Negro Students Unite to Combat 'Bias' at 'U,'" *State News*, January 18, 1968.

7. Barry D. Amis, "MSU, the Do Nothing 'U,'" *State News*, June 26, 1968.

8. Jill Witherspoon, "White 'Mainstream' Not Enough," *Collage: The State News Bi-Weekly Magazine*, April 4, 1968; Barry Amis, "The Kerner Commission Report," *Collage: The State News Bi-Weekly Magazine*, April 4, 1968.

9. Don E. Coleman, "The Status of the Black Student Aide Program and the Black Student Movement at Michigan State University" (PhD diss., Michigan State University, 1971), 27, 30, 42; Eric Von Winston, "Black Student Activism at MSU: September, 1967 to June 30, 1972" (PhD diss., Michigan State University, 1973), "Abstract," 76–77.

10. James Spaniolo, "Alliance Delivers Grievances to University Administration"; Trinka Cline, "1,500 in Memorial March for King"; Linda Gortmaker, "Students Stunned as News of King's Death Circulates," *State News*, April 8, 1968.

11. Coleman, "The Status of the Black Student Aide Program," 26, 29, 30; Spaniolo, "Alliance Delivers Grievances to University Administration."

12. Leo Zaine, "King Eulogy: Hannah Gives Priority to Blacks' Grievances," *State News*, April 10, 1968.

13. Letter from John A. Hannah to Barry D. Amis, April 8, 1968, Barry D. Amis Papers, UA 10.3.500, box 6539, folder 3, UAHC.

14. "An Open Letter to Black Students," UA 7.0, box 1950, folder 11, UAHC.

15. Barry D. Amis, "Fate of a Nation in Black and White," *State News*, April 24, 1968.

16. "Athlete Boycott," ca. 1971 or 1972, RSH Papers, UA 17.269, box 2359, folder 26, UAHC.

17. John Matthew Smith, "'Breaking the Plane': Integration and Black Protest in Michigan State Football during the 1960s," *Michigan Historical Review* 33 (Fall 2007); Joe Mitch, "Negro Athletes Call Boycott; Make Demands of University," *State News*, April 26, 1968.

18. "Cheerleader Conflict," RSH Papers, UA 17.269, box 2359, folder 33, UAHC.

19. See Beth J. Shapiro, "Intercollegiate Athletics and Big-Time Sport at Michigan State University: Or 'The Difference Between Good and Great Is a Little Extra Effort'" (PhD diss., Michigan State University, 1982), 150.

20. Mitch, "Negro Athletes Call Boycott."

21. Pete Axthelm, "The Angry Black Athlete," *Newsweek*, July 15, 1968, 58; Smith, "Breaking the Plane," 126; Hugh "Duffy" Daugherty with Davis Diles, *Duffy: An Autobiography* (New York: Doubleday, 1974), 128–129.

22. "MSU Students Stage Rally," *State News*, April 27, 1968; Tom Brown, "Black Athletes Settle against 'U,'" *State News*, April 29, 1968.

23. Brown, "Black Athletes Settle against 'U,'"; Joe Mitch, "Clarification Statement Issued by Black Athletes," *State News*, May 1, 1968; "Black Athletes Cite Distortion, Misquotation," *State News*, May 1, 1968.

24. Coleman, "The Status of the Black Student Aide Program," 35, 55.

25. Amis, "MSU, the Do Nothing 'U'"; "SDS, BSA Representatives Warn of Student Needs," *State News*, June 21, 1968.

26. "Prepared Statement of Ronald Bailey, Treasurer, Black Students' Alliance, Michigan State University, East Lansing, Michigan," "Series of Three Articles from the Michigan State News, by Ronald W. Bailey," and "Functional Implications of Black History," in *Commission on Negro History and Culture: Hearing Before the Special Subcommittee on Arts and Humanities of the Committee on Labor and Public Welfare, United States Senate, Ninetieth Congress, Second Session on S. 2979, July 23, 1968* (Washington, D.C.: U.S. Government Printing Office, 1968), 83–85, 87, 90–92. Bailey was a gifted young scholar. In 1969, while serving as a teaching assistant for economics, he was awarded the prestigious Danforth Graduate Fellowship. See "3 Win Danforth

Fellowships," *LSJ*, April 2, 1969.

27. Barry D. Amis, "Racism in the Social Structure," *State News*, July 2, 1968.

28. "BSA: Movement in Society, World," *State News*, Welcome Week edition, September 1968.

29. "Tinkertoy Fan Lists MSU Organizations," *State News*, Welcome Week edition, September 1968.

30. Trinka Cline, "New Black Era Foreseen," *State News*, Welcome Week edition, September 1969; "Wilson Hall Controversy Remains Significant," *State News*, Welcome Week edition, September 1969.

31. "Black Students' Alliance Statement," *State News*, October 23, 1968; "BSA Hints of Protests at N.D. Game," *State News*, October 24, 1968; Pat Anstett, "BSA, Officials Propose New 'U' Committee," *State News*, October 25, 1968.

32. Coleman, "The Status of the Black Student Aide Program," 40.

33. "A Note to Black Faculty from the Black Students' Alliance," February 24, 1969, RSH Papers, UA 17.269, box 2359, folder 64, UAHC; Coleman, "The Status of the Black Student Aide Program," 41.

34. Ronald Lee, "Black Week Should Stress Future, Not History," *State News*, February 12, 1969.

35. Helen Clegg, "MSU's Lee Expects New Job by May 5," *LSJ*, April 24, 1969; Coleman, "The Status of the Black Student Aide Program," 225–229.

36. Coleman, "The Status of the Black Student Aide Program," 221–224.

37. Coleman, "The Status of the Black Student Aide Program," 220, 222–223; Black Students' Alliance, "Editorial" and "King . . . Remembering," *State News*, April 4, 1969.

38. Steve Waterbury, "'U' Trustees Approves Proposals to Aid Disadvantaged Students," *State News*, April 21, 1969.

39. Jeanne Saddler, "BSA Raps Sabine, Urges Larger Role for Urban Center," *State News*, April 24, 1969.

40. Chris Mead, "11 Days Later: Tension Lingers at Wilson," *State News*, May 9, 1969; "Wilson Hall Controversy Remains Significant"; Emerson E. Williams, "Point of View/Black Activism," *Grapevine Journal*, October 24, 1972.

CHAPTER 30. TAKEOVER

1. Julie Morris, "MSU Black Students Sit-In," *Detroit Free Press*, April 30, 1969. Emphasis added.

2. The numerous documents in "Demonstrations—Wilson Hall Black Protest—1969," Media Communications, UA 8.1.1, box 1477, folder 11, UAHC are extremely useful to reconstructing why Black students occupied the Wilson Hall cafeteria and what happened during and after the sit-in.

3. Trinka Cline, "State Journal Hit for Biased Wilson Reporting," *State News*, May 26, 1969; "Will the State Journal Support Honest Reporting," *State News*, May 27, 1969.

4. Don E. Coleman, "Wilson Hall Protest, 1969," UA 7.0, box 1050H, folder 43, UAHC. This document, along with announcement cited from BSA, is also located in "Demonstrations—Wilson Hall Black Protest—1969," Media Communications, UA 8.1.1, box 1477, folder 11, UAHC. Charles A. Dillard authored an investigative report on the Wilson Hall takeover for which he conducted interviews with key participants and supporters, including Don Coleman and Sam Riddle. See Dillard, "Report on the Wilson Hall Incident," RSH Papers, UA 17.269, box 2359, folder 50, UAHC.

5. For the testimonies of Hatcher, Shane, and Triplett, see Coleman, "Wilson Hall Protest, 1969"; "Demonstrations—Wilson Hall Black Protest—1969," Media Communications, UA 8.1.1, box 1477, folder 11, UAHC.

6. Pat Murphy, "Wilson Hall Prompts Look at Grievance Procedures," *LSJ*, June 8, 1969.

7. Chris Mead, "Tension Lingers at Wilson," *State News*, May 9, 1969.

8. "Next President's Task: Race Issue Takes Priority," *State News*, May 21, 1969.

9. Jerry Pankhurst, "Reaction to Sit-in Handling Echoes Through 'U,' Capital," *State News*, May 9, 1969.

10. Jim Sylvester and Denise Fortner, "BSA Holds Wilson Cafeteria; Claims Harassment of Blacks," *State News*, April 29, 1969; Jeanne Saddler, "Wilson Hearing Airs Charges; BSA Stays; Decision Pending," *State News*, April 30, 1969.

11. Sylvester and Fortner, "BSA Holds Wilson Cafeteria; Saddler, "Wilson Hearing Airs Charges"; "Wilson Hall Controversy Remains Significant," *State News*, Welcome Week edition, September 1969.

12. Sylvester and Fortner, "BSA Holds Wilson Cafeteria. "

13. "Opening Statement of the Black Students' Alliance on Behalf of Black Employees," Media Communications, UA 8.1.1, box 1477, folder 11, UAHC; Jim Sylvester, "BSA Leaves Wilson Cafeteria; Committee Suggests 9 Changes," *State News*, May 1, 1969; Helen Clegg, "Blacks Win Concessions, End Sit-in," *LSJ*, May 1, 1969.

14. Clegg, "Blacks Win Concessions, End Sit-in"; "Demonstrations—Wilson Hall Black Protes—1969," Media Communications, UA 8.1.1, box 1477, folder 11, UAHC.

15. Barb Parness, "Action Defended," *State News*, Welcome Week edition, September 1969; Walter Adams, *The Test* (New York: Macmillan, 1970), 57–92; "Adams Explains Settlement," *LSJ*, May 3, 1969.

16. Robert Stuart, "MSU Furor May Lead to Legal Action," *LSJ*, May 1, 1969; Steve Waterbury, "Adams Draws Varied Comment for Handling of Wilson Conflict," *State News*, May 2, 1969; "Recommendations Sadly Necessary," *State News*, May 2, 1969; Helen Clegg, "Real Story at MSU Slow to Emerge," *LSJ*, May 3, 1969; "Wilson Trial: Rape of Due Process," *State News*, May 6, 1969.

17. "Open Letter to Adams," *State News*, May 2, 1969.

18. Helen Clegg, "Petitions Delivered at MSU," *State News*, May 10, 1969.

19. Larry Lee, "Wilson Workers to File Lawsuits for Defamation," *State News*, May 2, 1969; Helen Clegg, "Trantham Assails One-Sided 'Trial,'" *LSJ*, May 2, 1969; Whit Sibley, "Businessmen March, Protest Wilson Sit-In," *State News*, May 5, 1969; Steve Waterbury, "Letters, Calls Bombard Adams after 'Wilson,'" *State News*, May 7, 1969.

20. "Hate Mail to Barry Amis," May 3, 1969" and "Hate Mail," n.d., Barry D. Amis Papers, UA 10.3.500, box 6539, folder 6, UAHC.

21. Clegg, "Blacks Win Concessions, End Sit-In."

22. Dave Hanson, "MSU's Adams Praised: NAACP Supports Student Sit-In," *LSJ*, May 5, 1969; "NAACP Gives Unanimous Support," *Inner City Times* (Lansing, MI), May 7, 1969; Pat Anstett and Jim Sylvester, "Hearing Procedures Disputed," *State News*, May 9, 1969; Ralph R. Barnett Jr., "'The Wilson Hall Incident,'" *Inner City Times* (Lansing, MI), May 7, 1969.

23. Jackie Vaughn III to Black Students' Alliance, May 2, 1969, in Don E. Coleman, "The Status of the Black

Student Aide Program and the Black Student Movement at Michigan State University" (PhD diss., Michigan State University, 1971), 235; Jeanne Saddler, "Black Legislators Ask End to Campus Discrimination," *State News*, May 15, 1969.

24. Dhirendra Sharma, "White Majority Distorts Justice for Black Minority," *State News*, May 14, 1969.

25. Sylvester and Fortner, "BSA Holds Wilson Cafeteria"; Saddler, "Wilson Hearing Airs Charges." For a discussion of Coleman, see Pat Anstett and Jim Sylvester, "Hearing Procedures Disputed," *State News*, May 9, 1969.

26. Sylvester and Fortner, "BSA Holds Wilson Cafeteria."

27. The Black Faculty Committee, "Black Faculty Statement Regarding Wilson Hall," *State News*, May 7, 1969.

28. "Rehearing Out, Says Hall Aide," *LSJ*, August 3, 1969. In early August, Mishler declined a second hearing. Trantham indicated he wanted a second hearing, but it doesn't appear it took place.

29. Helen Clegg, "Trantham Assails One-Sided 'Trial,'" *LSJ*, May 2, 1969.

30. Chris Mead, "11 Days Later: Tension Still Lingers at Wilson," *State News*, May 9, 1969; "Open Letter," *Westside News*, May 17, 1969.

31. Coleman, "The Status of the Black Student Aide Program," 48.

32. Eric Von Winston, "Black Student Activism at MSU: September, 1967 to June 30, 1972," (PhD diss., Michigan State University, 1973), "Abstract," 76–77.

33. Jeanne Saddler, "Wilson Hall Court of 'Black Indignation,'" *Westside News*, May 17, 1969.

34. "MSU Ends Intensive Black Students' Search," *Michigan Chronicle*, May 24, 1969.

35. Parness, "Action Defended"; Richard W. Thomas, "Rap-Time: The University and the Politics of Its Relationship to the Black Movement," *Grapevine Journal*, June 3, 1971.

CHAPTER 31. GOLDEN AGE OF ORGANIZING

1. Jeanne Saddler, "Blacks: Prepare for Revolution," *State News*, Welcome Week edition, September 1970; Elaine Brown, *Seize the Time*, Vault Records, Los Angeles, SLP-131 (LP), 1969.

2. Kat Brown, "Black Groups Reflect Rising Self-Interest," *State News*, Welcome Week edition, September 1977.

3. The organizations included many Black student caucuses. See "Black Student Orientation Program— Participants," *Grapevine Journal* Collection, UA 12.73, box 2638, folder 45, UAHC; "Registered Black Student Organizations, School Year 1972–73," *Grapevine Journal* Collection, UA 12.73, box 2638, folder 10, UAHC.

4. "Black Affairs (Office of), 1970, 1973," RSH Papers, UA 17.269, box 2359, folder 56, UAHC; "Office of Black Affairs, 1976–1978," RSH Papers, UA 17.269, box 2539, folder 72, UAHC; Interview with Rodney Watts, RSH Papers, UA 17.269, box 2359, folder 40, UAHC.

5. Don E. Coleman, "The Status of the Black Student Aide Program and the Black Student Movement at Michigan State University," (PhD diss., Michigan State University, 1971), 64.

6. Roxy Sheffield, "OBA Lends Support," *Grapevine Journal*, September 18–22, 1972.

7. Angela Martin, "Black Freshman Orientation," *Grapevine Journal*, September 25, 1973.

8. For coverage from the *State News*, see James Barfield, "Blacks Oust Whites from Talk; 'U' Official Plans

Investigation," November 15, 1972; "Incident in Conrad Shows Racial Views," November 16, 1972; "Racial Incident Probed," November 17, 1972; "Talk Issue Distorted in News: OBA," November 20, 1972; "OBA Ignores Need to Explain Conrad," November 20, 1972; Teri Albrecht, "ASMSU, OBA Plan Discussion," November 21, 1972; Teri Albrecht, "ASMSU Delays Talk on Conrad Incident," November 27, 1972. Also see Conrad Hall Incident 1972, 1973, RSH Papers UA 17.269, box 2359, folder 35, UAHC.

9. Jane Seaberry, "Conrad Becomes History," *State News*, November 11, 1972; Teri Albrecht, "Judiciary Rules in Favor of OBA in Conrad Case," *State News*, February 19, 1973; "A Retrospective on Conrad," *Grapevine Journal*, March 6, 1973.

10. It is unclear exactly when BSA was reestablished at MSU. By the late 1980s and early 1990s, BSA was one of the leading Black student organizations on campus. Following a second golden age of Black student organizations in the 1990s, BSA became the leading Black student organization of the twenty-first century.

11. Coleman, "The Status of the Black Student Aide Program," 55.

12. Mike Hudson, "Nightmarish Trance of the Black Experience"; Trinka Cline, "New Black Era Foreseen"; "Wilson Hall Controversy Remains Significant"; and Barb Parness, "At Wilson Sit-In: Action Defended," *State News*, Welcome Week edition, September 1969.

13. Jeanne Saddler, "More Than a Slogan: BSA Changes Emphasis," *State News*, September 25, 1969.

14. Saddler, "More Than a Slogan."

15. Coleman, "The Status of the Black Student Aide Program," 54–55, 60–61, 260–262.

16. Coleman, "The Status of the Black Student Aide Program," 55–58; "BLFI Memo to Aides Relating to Meetings," in Coleman, "The Status of the Black Student Aide Program," 252; J. Ballard, "Bro. Don Coleman Speaks about the Black Aide Program," *Grapevine Journal*, June 3, 1971; Wanda Herden, "Do Black Aids Actually Assist Students?," *Grapevine Journal*, September 20, 1971.

17. Coleman, "The Status of the Black Student Aide Program," 55–58; Herden, "Do Black Aids Actually Assist Students?"; Jane Seaberry, "Project Aids Black Kids," *State News*, March 7, 1972; George White, "Only One in the Nation: Aide Program Helps Minorities," *State News*, Welcome Week edition, September 1972; Angela Martin, "The Role of the Black Aide Questioned," *Grapevine Journal*, February 13, 1973.

18. From the *Westside News* (Lansing, MI), see "BLF Reaffirms Pledge to Lansing's Blacks," October 11, 1969; Jeanne Saddler, "BLFI Demands Control of MSU' African Studies Center," October 17, 1969; James Kenyon, "BLFI Reorganizes, Holds Elections," May 2, 1970; Kenyon, "BLF Elects Members to Executive Council," May 16, 1970.

19. Committee for Change, 1970, RSH Papers, UA 17.269, box 2359, folder 6.

20. From the *LSJ*, see Judith Brown, "Some 100 Youths Protest Incident at High School," October 6, 1969; "Two Fact-Finding Committees Start Incident Investigation," October 7, 1969; "Condition Said Normal at Eastern," October 8, 1969; Brown, "School's Principal's Actions Upheld by Lansing Board," October 10, 1969; Brown, "Black Delegation Presents Claims," October 17, 1969.

21. Jeanne Saddler, "BLF Protests at African Center," *State News*, October 17, 1969.

22. "BLFI and PASOA Manifesto," in Coleman, "The Status of the Black Student Aide Program," 253–260; "Africanization History of African Studies Center at Michigan State University, Issued Jointly by

BLFI–PASOA–BUF," November 12, 1970, in Coleman "The Status of the Black Student Aide Program," 313–319; Jeanne Saddler, "African Groups Backs BLF in Studies Center Takeover," *State News*, October 20, 1969; Helen Clegg, "Bigger Role in Program," *LSJ*, October 30, 1969; Pan African Students Organization of the Americas, 1970–1971, RSH Papers, UA 17.269, box 2359, folder 73.

23. Coleman, "The Status of the Black Student Aide Program," 65–69; "Black Students Force Cafeteria Shutdown," *State News*, October 22, 1969; Sharon Templeton and Larry Lee, "Holden Takeover Elicits Racist Tag from Senator," *State News*, October 24, 1969; Holden Hall Incident, no date, RSH Papers, box 2359, folder 38.

24. Coleman, "The Status of the Black Student Aide Program," 67.

25. James Barfield, "Culture Room Need Cited," *State News*, March 12, 1971; Angela Martin, "Black Dorm Organizations Mobilizing, Building Unity," *Grapevine Journal*, November 7, 1972; Patra Brown, "Holden Hall Discriminating," *State News*, April 2, 1979.

26. Estella Chambers, "Redecoration in Fee: Blacks Plan Remodeling of Grill," *State News*, February 20, 1970; Ray Anderson, "Students' Study Guide Offers Help to Minorities," *State News*, Welcome Week Edition, September 1972.

27. Denise McCourt, "Room Aids Racial Empathy," *State News*, February 24, 1970.

28. "BLFI and PASOA Manifesto"; Jeanne Saddler, "Two Groups Blast African Center," *State News*, October 30, 1969; Helen Clegg, "Committee Checks Black Proposals," *LSJ*, November 13, 1969; "Blacks Form Picket Line on Campus," *LSJ*, November 22, 1969.

29. Jeanne Saddler, "African Demands: Center Studies New Manifesto," *State News*, January 13, 1970.

30. Norman Sinclair, "Blacks Disrupt Showing of Film," *LSJ*, February 28, 1970; Barney C. Young, "BLF, PASOA Stop Show," *State News*, March 2, 1970; Coleman, "The Status of the Black Student Aide Program," 76–77, 91–92; The "Africa Addio" Incident, 1970, RSH Papers, UA 17.269. box 2359, folder 19, UAHC; Charles A. Dillard, "The Africa Addio Incident," RSH Papers, UA 17.269. box 2359, folder 20, UAHC.

31. W. Kim Heron, "Black Students at MSU," *Grapevine Journal*, September 18, 1973; "MSU News Bureau Immediate Release," May 18, 1970, RSH Papers, UA 17.269, box 2359, folder 3; Helen Clegg, "Black Culture Center Asked by Wharton," *LSJ*, May 19, 1970; "President Wharton Promises a Black Cultural Center," *BUF Newsletter*, June 4, 1970, RSH Papers, UA 17.269, box 2359, folder 67.

32. Coleman, "The Status of the Black Student Aide Program," 87–101, 117–121, 128–131, 291–293; Curt Hanes, "West Side Children Benefit: Black Students to Serve Meals," *LSJ*, August 13, 1970; Ahmed Karega, "BUF— Bringing Out the Power in the People," *Grapevine Journal*, June 3, 1971; "BUF Welcomes Black Students," *Grapevine Journal*, September 20, 1971; "BUF Vows to Continue Breakfast Program," *Grapevine Journal*, March 7, 1972; Daphne Wells, "Director Sees Dim Future for Breakfast Program," *Grapevine Journal*, May 9, 1972; Judith Hand, "BUF Breakfast Program Returns," *Grapevine Journal*, October 10, 1972; Roxy Sheffield, "'Teach a Brother' to Continue," *Grapevine Journal*, October 10, 1972.

33. Jeanne Saddler, "Huey Newton to Talk at Black Moratorium," *State News*, November 16, 1970; Jeanne Saddler, "Huey Newton Talk: 'Free the People' Called Panthers' Battle Slogan," *State News*, November 18, 1970; BUF— Black United Front, 1970–1971, RSH Papers, UA 17.269, box 22359, folder, 66; BUF (Black United Front) Newsletter, 1970, RSH Papers, UA 17.269, box 22359, folder, 67.

34. "BUF Basketball," *Grapevine Journal*, November 7, 1972; Madelyn Bridget, "BUF Basketball League Threatened by Low Funds," and Harriet Wilkes, "BUF Basketball Promotes Unity," *Grapevine Journal*, September 25, 1973.

CHAPTER 32. I HEARD IT THROUGH THE *GRAPEVINE*

1. "What Is Project Grapevine: Rationale and Objective," *Grapevine Journal* Collection, UA 12.7.3, box 2639, folder 12, UAHC.

2. James Ballard to Brian Raymond, July 31, 1975, *Grapevine Journal* Collection UA 12.7.3, box 2638, folder 32, UAHC.

3. "Student Units Get Offices," *LSJ*, January 29, 1971; "Michigan State University Application for Agency Account—Student Organization," June 3, 1970, *Grapevine Journal* Collection, UA 12.7.3, box 2639, folder 9, UAHC; "What Is Project Grapevine."

4. James Ballard, "Summer Project: Grapevine Journal," n.d., *Grapevine Journal* Collection, UA 12.7.3, box 2639, folder 106, UAHC; "Script for Slide Show," 1974, *Grapevine Journal* Collection, UA 12.7.3, box 2641, folder 14, UAHC; James E. Ballard, "Save the 'Grapevine,'" April 7, 1970, *Grapevine Journal* Collection UA 12.7.3, box 2638, folder 41, UAHC.

5. Linda Medina, "'Grapevine' Not an All Black Paper," *Grapevine Journal*, June 3, 1971.

6. "The Grapevine Journal Is Dying," *Grapevine Journal*, March 7, 1972; Ibram H. Rogers [Ibram X. Kendi], *The Black Campus Movement: Black Students and the Racial Reconstruction of Higher Education* (New York: Palgrave Macmillan, 2012), 85.

7. "Negro Editor Charges Poor Press Coverage," *State News*, October 20, 1967; "Journal Expands Faces Closing," *Grapevine Journal*, September 18, 1973.

8. Ernie Boone, "Why the Westside News," *Westside News*, May 17, 1969.

9. See, for instance, Richard Thomas, "Resurrection City: Meaning Out of Futility," *State News*, July 1, 1968; Thomas, "U.S. Social Revolution Becoming a Reality," *State News*, July 3, 1968. These two articles also included accompanying photos of Thomas.

10. "Point of View: SN Controlled by White Liberals," *State News*, February 18, 1972.

11. "Crate Names Miss Saddler to Editor Post," *State News*, January 21, 1970; Jeanne Saddler, "Editorial Dissent: Wharton Criticism Unfair," *State News*, January 23, 1970; "Jeanne Saddler Honors Grad at Mich. State," *Michigan Chronicle*, July 15, 1972.

12. Office Files, Memos, n.d., *Grapevine Journal* Collection, UA 12.7.3, box 2638, folder 41, UAHC; Memo from George White, July 7, 1972, *Grapevine Journal* Collection, UA 12.7.3, box 2638, folder 42, UAHC; "Script for Slide Show"; "Project Grapevine: Charter and By-Laws," *Grapevine Journal* Collection, UA 12.7.3, box 2637, folder 65, UAHC.

13. Joyce Conway, "Grapevine Journal Serving MSU," *Grapevine Journal*, May 29, 1973.

14. "Editors' Comments," *Grapevine Journal*, June 3, 1971.

15. Linda Medina, "'Grapevine' Not an All Black Paper"; PFC Ronald L. Blevins (Cherokee-Shoshoni), "Letter of

Interest"; and Ying Li, "The 'Ah So!' Syndrome," Editors' Comments," *Grapevine Journal*, June 3, 1971.

16. "Proposal: Alternative Voices," *Grapevine Journal* Collection, UA 12.7.3, box 2639, folder 13, UAHC; "Job-Task Descriptions," *Grapevine Journal* Collection, UA 12.7.3, box 2638, folder 10, UAHC.

17. "The Grapevine Journal Is Dying"; Ron Johnson, "The Struggle of the Black Athlete," *Grapevine Journal*, May 9, 1972.

18. The citations and information here comes from "Narrative on the Grapevine Journal," *Grapevine Journal* Collection, UA 12.7.3, box 2641, folder 4; "Successes on a Rough Road," *Grapevine Journal* Collection, UA 12.7.3, box 2638, folder 4, UAHC.

19. George White, "Journal Needs Support," *State News*, Welcome Week edition, September 1972.

20. Mike Wagoner, "'Grapevine' Flourishes: Paper for Minorities Eyes Highest Awards," *LSJ*, January 14, 1973.

21. Joyce Conway, "*Grapevine Journal* Serving MSU," *Grapevine Journal*, May 29, 1973.

22. Carol Morello, "Tax Charge 'Cheap Shot,'" *LSJ*, May 14, 1973; "Black Leaders to Speak at MSU Friday," *LSJ*, May 17, 1973; Jan Gugliotti, "Grapevine Journal Asks for Aid," *LSJ*, May 26, 1973; Angela Martin, "A Message to Black Students," *Grapevine Journal*, May 29, 1973; W. Kim Heron to President Wharton and the Board of Trustees, July 19, 1973, *Grapevine Journal* Collection, UA 12.7.3, box 2637, folder 51, UAHC; Wharton to Heron, July 26, 1973, *Grapevine Journal* Collection, UA 12.7.3, box 2638, folder 15, UAHC.

23. "Successes on a Rough Road"; Jan Gugliotti, "Grapevine Journal Asks for Aid," *LSJ*, May 26, 1973.

24. Jan Gugliotti, "MSU Black Publication Broke," *LSJ*, October 12, 1973; "Narrative on the Grapevine Journal," *Grapevine Journal* Collection, UA 12.7.3, box 2641, folder 4, UAHC.

25. George Logan to Clifton R. Wharton Jr., June 5, 1973, *Grapevine Journal* Collection, UA 12.7.3, box 2637, folder 51, UAHC.

26. John Conyers to W. Kim Heron, June 28, 1973; Charles C. Diggs, Jr. to Heron, July 24, 1973, *Grapevine Journal* Collection, UA 12.7.3, box 2638, folder 15, UAHC.

27. Heron to President Wharton and the Board of Trustees.

28. "Journal Expands Faces Closing," *Grapevine Journal*, September 18, 1973.

29. George White to "the Editor," n.d. [circa January 1974], *Grapevine Journal* Collection, UA 12.7.3, box 2638, folder 15, UAHC.

30. Gail Russell, "State News Sponsors Workshop," *Grapevine Journal*, May 29, 1973.

31. Summer Workshop, July 1973, *Grapevine Journal* Collection, UA 12.7.3, box 2641, folder 15, UAHC; "Schedule of Activities, Summer Journalism Workshop, July 8–21, 1973," and "Students Participating in the Journalism Summer Workshop, July 8–21, 1973, *Grapevine Journal* Collection, UA 12.7.3, box 2639, folder 13, UAHC; "MSU Journalism Workshop," *Flint Spokesman*, August 4, 1973.

32. *Otabala: New Arts Magazine*, 1973–1974, *Grapevine Journal* Collection, UA 12.7.3, box 2638, folder 70; Personal File, box 2639, folder 21, UAHC.

33. "Students to Vote on Publication Tax," *LSJ*, January 19, 1974; Office Files, n.d. (ca. 1974), *Grapevine Journal* Collection, UA 12.7.3, box 2638, folder 4, UAHC; Letter from George White, February 12, 1975, *Grapevine Journal* Collection, UA 12.7.3, box 2638, folder 32, UAHC.

34. White to Warren Huff, May 23, 1975, *Grapevine Journal* Collection, UA 12.7.3, box 2638, folder 32, UAHC;

Ballard to Raymond, July 31, 1975, *Grapevine Journal* Collection.

35. James Ballard, "Personal Note to Editorial Staff of Grapevine Journal," October 9, 1972, *Grapevine Journal* Collection, UA 12.7.3, box 2638, folder 42, UAHC.

36. "Successes on a Rough Road"; Office Files, n.d. (ca. 1974), *Grapevine Journal* Collection, UA 12.7.3, box 2638, folder 4, UAHC; "Tentative Itinerary—Robert E. Johnson, Executive Editor, Jet Magazine," *Grapevine Journal* Collection, UA 12.7.3, box 2638, folder 11, UAHC.

37. Media Achievement Grants, 1974–1975, "Media Grant Established," and "For Immediate Release," *Grapevine Journal* Collection, UA 12.7.3, box 2638, folder 38, UAHC; "Report on Media Achievement Grant Award Dinner," October 24, 1974, *Grapevine Journal* Collection, UA 12.7.3, box 2638, folder 39, UAHC.

38. Bro. Larry X. Davis to W. Kim Heron, October 12, 1973; George Leon Thomas to Heron, September 3, 1973, *Grapevine Journal* Collection, UA 12.7.3, box 2638, folder 15, UAHC.

39. Omari M. Asifa, "Black Prisoners Library Fund," *Grapevine Journal*, September 20, 1971; Angela Martin, "Women in Prison Work," *Grapevine Journal*, April 24, 1973.

40. Wagoner, "'Grapevine' Flourishes"; Bill Wallis to the Editors, n.d. [circa early 1970s], *Grapevine Journal* Collection, UA 12.7.3, box 2638, folder 15, UAHC.

41. "Journal Expands Faces Closing," *Grapevine Journal*, September 18, 1973; People's Choice Magazine 1977, *People's Choice* Publication, UA 12.7.41, drawer f.d., folder 1, UAHC.

42. "Grapevine Provides," *Grapevine Journal*, May 29, 1973.

43. "Telephone Survey," *Grapevine Journal* Collection, UA 12.7.3, box 2639, folder 4, UAHC.

44. Untitled document written by George White, n.d. [circa 1974], *Grapevine Journal* Collection, UA 12.7.3, box 2638, folder 4, UAHC.

CHAPTER 33. RISE AND FALL

1. Sue Belniak, "Jones Calls Nationalism 'Animosity of the Times,'" *State News*, May 6, 1969; "Black Poet Jones Sees Nationalism as 'Key to Change,'" *LSJ*, May 6, 1969.

2. "Getting Down Is the Bomb! But It Won't Get You Over: Get Involved with the Minority Student Organization of Your Choice," *State News*, Welcome Week edition, September 1972; Richard W. Thomas, "The University and the Politics of Its Relationship to the Black Movement," *Grapevine Journal*, June 3, 1971.

3. Angela Martin, "Black Dorm Organizations Mobilizing, Building Unity," *Grapevine Journal*, November 7, 1972.

4. "Black Brothers of Shaw (BBS)," RSH Papers, UA 17.269, box 2359, folder 58, UAHC; James Kenyon, "Black Brothers of Shaw Are Moving Up," *Westside News* (Lansing, MI), May 9, 1970; "Interview: Toni Eubanks," RSH Papers, UA 17.269, box 2359, folder 40, UAHC.

5. Crispin Campbell, "King's Daughter Examines Campus," *State News*, April 5, 1972.

6. "Black Orpheus Gospel Choir," *Grapevine Journal*, September 25, 1973.

7. Maryam Aziz, "They Punched Black: Martial Arts, Black Arts, and Sports in the Urban North and West, 1968–1979," *Journal of African American History* 106, no. 2 (Spring 2021): 304–327.

8. George White, "Third World Karate Teaches Unity," *Grapevine Journal*, May 9, 1972; Gail Russell, "Karate Club Teaches Martial Arts, *Grapevine Journal*, September 18, 1973.

9. The descriptions of the student groups in this section come from Elizabeth Driscoll, "Black Groups Provide Academic, Social Life Aid," *State News*, Welcome Week Edition, September 1972; "Getting Down Is the Bomb! But It Won't Get You Over"; Angela Martin, "Black Students Enjoy Singing in MSU's Talented Gospel Choir," *State News*, Welcome Week Edition, September 1974; Bob Ourlian, "A Guide to Campus Living: Something for Everyone," *State News*, Welcome Week Edition, September 1974. Gayle Harden, "Music and Information Pour from WKAR Radio into Black Community," *LSJ*, February 3, 1975.

10. "1973-Summer-Fall-Winter-Spring Program Proposal," n.d. [circa May 1973], *Grapevine Journal* Collection, UA 12.7.3, box 2639, folder 51, UAHC. The descriptions of this proposed program and the activities of the three organizations that worked with OBA are cited from this document.

11. "1973-Summer-Fall-Winter-Spring Program Proposal."

12. "1973-Summer-Fall-Winter-Spring Program Proposal"; Floresta Jones, "Motivation, Black Pre-Med's Aim," *Grapevine Journal*, May 15, 1973; Peggy Gossett, "Students Charge Nursing School with Discrimination Against Blacks," *State News*, February 3, 1975; "Rise Against Racism" and "Viewpoint: Nursing: Alleged Racial Bias Discounted," *State News*, February 5, 1975; Delilah Nichols, "Black Nursing Students Feel many Frustrations," *Grapevine Journal*, March 4, 1975.

13. "1973-Summer-Fall-Winter-Spring Program Proposal."

14. Denise Outram, "Black Engineering Students Unite," *Grapevine Journal*, May 15, 1973.

15. Jeanne Saddler, "Black Fraternity Leaves IFC," *State News*, October 10, 1969; Irene Pickens, "Blacks Back IFC," *State News*, October 24, 1969.

16. F. Lewis, "Black Greeks on Campus" and "Relevancy Thru Brotherhood," *Grapevine Journal*, June 3, 1971; "Getting Down Is the Bomb! But It Won't Get You Over"; Reginald Thomas, "'Black Power' Fades, Groups in Turmoil," *State News*, Welcome Week edition, September 1978.

17. Ron Johnson, "CUA Director Supports Black Athletes," *Grapevine Journal*, February 15, 1972; Bob Hoerner, "Black Athletes at MSU Present Seven 'Demands,'" *LSJ*, February 22, 1972; Rick Gosselin, "Black Athletes Want Aid," *State News*, February 23, 1972; Ron Johnson, "The Struggle of the Black Athlete," *Grapevine Journal*, May 9, 1972.

18. Gosselin, "Black Athletes Want Aid"; Steven Stein, "Coleman–Webster: That Special Honor," *Grapevine Journal*, April 24, 1973.

19. Bob Hoerner, "Protest by Black Students Delays Start of MSU Game," *LSJ*, February 27, 1972; Crispin Y. Campbell, "Blacks Reveal Demands before MSU-Iowa Game," *State News*, February 28, 1972; Stan Morgan, "Sam Riddle Fights Society's Contradictions," *State News*, March 27, 1972.

20. Mike Wagoner, "Blacks Hit 'Racism' in Big Ten," *LSJ*, February 10, 1972; Wagoner, "3 MSU Trustees Support Reforms Sought in Big Ten Conference," *LSJ*, February 15, 1972; Beckie Brenneman, "Conflict Brewing," *LSJ*, March 3, 1972; Randy Garton, "Wharton Criticizes Blacks' Tactics," *State News*, March 3, 1972.

21. Garton, "Wharton Criticizes Blacks' Tactics"; "No Delay Expected at U-M, MSU Game" and "Dr. Wharton Issues Get Tough Policy," *LSJ*, March 3, 1972; Crispin Y. Campbell, "Black Protest at Game," *State News*,

March 6, 1972. In November 1972, Nigel Goodison staged a protest on the court for nearly an hour in the MSU Green–White game. See Charles Johnson, "Demonstration Cancels Green–White Contest," *State News*, November 20, 1972.

22. Morgan, "Sam Riddle Fights Society's Contradictions"; Barbara Parness, "Black Plans Charge Against MSU Police," *State News*, April 10, 1972.

23. "Plea of Not Guilty Entered by Riddle," *State News*, April 12, 1972; Bob Novosad, "Riddle to Urge Public Safety Changes," *State News*, April 14, 1972; Carol Thomas, "District Court Hearing Open in Prosecution of Sam Riddle," *State News*, May 3, 1972; Carol Thomas, "Riddle Found Not Guilty," *State News*, May 4, 1972; Kristen Kelch, "Riddle Charges Refuted," *State News*, May 5, 1972. It seems that Riddle's leadership abilities were recognized by the White student community. On June 26, 1972, a student journalist penned an article in the *State News*, "Sam's Riddle Leads Crowds," dubbing him "one of the most influential black men on campus."

24. Cassandra Spratling, "Commitment: It's Up to Us," *State News*, Welcome Week edition, September 1975.

25. Omari M. Asifa, "Black Political Prisoners Libarary [*sic*] Fund," *Grapevine Journal*, September 20, 1971.

26. "Point of View," *Grapevine Journal*, November 18, 1971.

27. Denise A. Outram, "Black Apathy," *Grapevine Journal*, May 9, 1972.

28. W. Kim Heron, "Black Students at MSU," "Call for New Actions," and "Students Evaluate Progress of 60's," *Grapevine Journal*, September 18, 1973; Jane Seaberry, "Black Progress: Has It Died?," *Counterpoint: A Bi-Weekly Supplement to the State News*, February 19, 1974.

29. Kat Brown, "Black Groups Reflect Rising Self-Interest," *State News*, Welcome Week edition, September 1977; Reginald Thomas, "'Black Power' Fades, Groups in Turmoil," *State News*, Welcome Week Edition, September 1978.

CHAPTER 34. BLACK AND GREEN AND WHITE

1. "Race Bias Charged in Hiring at MSU," *LSJ*, March 15, 1968.

2. Helen Clegg, "Qualified Negroes Studied," *LSJ*, July 24, 1968.

3. Around the time MSU was publicly called out for "racial discrimination in some hiring practices," President Hannah created the Committee of Sixteen that in mid-May 1968 submitted a report to the Board of Trustees that urged the university to engage in efforts to recruit more Blacks students and faculty and to establish a Center for Race and Urban Affairs.

4. See Department of Human Relations, Michigan State University, *Affirmative Action at Michigan State University: Annual Report to the Department of Health, Education and Welfare* (September 1973).

5. John Green, "Picket Protest Action on Fair Housing," *LSJ*, June 3, 1964. Emphasis added.

6. See "U of M Editor's Letter to Hannah"; "Reprint from *National Review*"; "Hannah's Reply to Kirk," *State News*, September 27, 1962. Accompanying this full-page coverage of Kirk's op-ed is a cartoon of Hannah sitting at his desk shooing away flies identified as Kirk and the *National Review*.

7. Russell Kirk, "The Mind and the Head at MSU," *National Review*, August 28, 1962.

8. William Burke, "Dr. Hannah Foe of Segregation: Accomplished Racial Integration at M.S.C.," *LSJ*, November 10, 1957; "No Time for Bias: John Alfred Hannah," *New York Times*, December 24, 1957.

9. "Hannah Answers Plaints of Ex-Faculty Member," *LSJ*, September 28, 1962. Emphasis added.

10. Austin C. Wehrwein, "Chicago Appoints Negro Professor: Dr. Franklin, Historians, Will Join Faculty This Fall," *New York Times*, April 14, 1963; "11 of 17 Major Universities Have Negro Faculty Members," *Chicago Defender*, April 20, 1963; "University of Texas Hires First Negro as Faculty Member," *New York Times*, May 12, 1964; "Add 6 Negroes to U. of Ill. Urbana Faculty," *Chicago Defender*, October 5, 1964.

11. Duane De Loach, "Negro Scientist Aiding Wound Studies at Wayne," *Detroit Free Press*, December 3, 1943.

12. O. S. Dukes, "Breakthrough in Education," *Michigan Chronicle*, April 22, 1961.

13. "Historical Summary of Faculty and Academic Staff—Headcount," n.d. (ca. 1999/2000); Eric Von Arthur Winston, "Black Student Activism at MSU: September, 1967 to June 30, 1972" (PhD diss., Michigan State University, 1973), 89.

14. Department of Human Relations, Michigan State University, *Affirmative Action at Michigan State University: Annual Report to the Department of Health, Education and Welfare* (East Lansing: Michigan State University, September 1973), table 26.

15. For more about Brimmer's life, see Matt Schudel, "Ex-Federal Reserve Governor," *Miami Herald*, October 12, 2012; Stephanie Strom, "Andrew Brimmer, 86, First Black on Fed," *New York Times*, October 12, 2012.

16. "Negro Added to Economics Staff at MSU," *Michigan Chronicle*, October 5, 1957; "Civil Rights Discussed," *LSJ*, November 23, 1959; "NAACP to Hear Dr. Alvin Loving," *LSJ*, June 4, 1960; "Officers Are Named," *LSJ*, December 5, 1960; Personality of the Week: Andrew Brimmer 'Man in the Middle,'" *Afro-American* (Baltimore), March 12, 1966.

17. "Southern Farm Families Seen Facing Bleak Days," *Afro-American* (Baltimore), December 28, 1963.

18. "Alfred Edwards Obituary," *Grand Rapids Press* Obituaries, January 30, 2007, https://obits.mlive.com/us/obituaries/annarbor/name/alfred-edwards-obituary?id=13632833.

19. "To Dedicate Nigeria U: Three M.S.U. Officials for Fly to African Nation Oct. 9," *LSJ*, September 27, 1960. In September 1960, Johnson was "named a professor in the college of education but he was primarily appointed to be acting principal of the University of Nigeria and director of the 10-member M.S.U. team in Nigeria."

20. George M. Johnson is not included here because, unlike Dickson, Pipes, Thornton, and Chavis, he was not actively teaching on campus at the time. His appointment as professor in the College of Education was largely symbolic and directly related to his administrative appointment.

21. Effective September 2, 1969, Cofer became a full professor as well as the first African American to be named "special assistant to the president for special projects."

22. Gary Walkowicz, "Coleman to Make Decision Friday," *State News*, April 11, 1968; "Ex-Spartan Returns to Alma Mater," *LSJ*, April 13, 1968; "Coleman May Join Spartan Grid Staff," *LSJ*, April 17, 1968; "Board Approves Coleman Hiring," *LSJ*, April 18, 1968; Jim Nichols, "Gene Washington: MSU Job Aide," *LSJ*, July 19, 1968; "Coleman Vacates MSU Grid Post," *LSJ*, January 16, 1969; Bob Hoerner, "Washington Busy Viking," *LSJ*, February 2, 1970.

23. For discussions of Fuller, see the following articles from the *LSJ*: "Fuller, Curzi First to Share Brewer Award,"

June 3, 1966; "Kenney Named Aide to Munn; Fuller to Coach," June 19, 1970; Robert Berg, "Faculty, Athletes Claim Big Ten Segregated," February 11, 1972; Fred Stabley Jr., "Tiff Follows Change of MSU Soccer Coach," May 23, 1974; Neil Hunter, "Ex-MSU Coach Fights Firing," October 20, 1974; Jack Walkden, "Unity Keys Spartan Soccer Team Success," October 27, 1974; Lynn Henning, "I'm Bitter Inside—Burt Smith," October 29, 1975; "Spartifacts," June 3, 2015.

24. Marcia Van Ness, "Prof Heads Equality Drive," *LSJ*, May 17, 1968; Jim Schaefer, "Negro Educator to Head 'U' Panel on Race Relations," *State News*, May 17, 1968.

25. "Democrats Sweep Education Posts," *LSJ*, November 6, 1968; Marcia Van Ness, "Board Candidate Martin Oks Sliding Scale at MSU," *LSJ*, October 31, 1968; Dave Hanson, "NAACP Convention Lashes at Wallace's Candidacy," *LSJ*, September 29, 1968; Marcia Van Ness, "MSU OK's Funds for Negro Aid," *LSJ*, April 19, 1969.

26. Barbara Parness, "Black Woman Weighs Bid for Trustee Position," *State News*, April 7, 1972.

27. "Position Paper and Affirmative Action Program for Increasing Black Faculty, Michigan State University," n.d. (ca. 1976), Clifton R. Wharton Papers, UA 2.1.14, box 419, folder 53, UAHC; "Black Faculty Statement Regarding Wilson Hall," *State News*, May 7, 1969.

28. "Negroes on MSU Staff Like Adams," *News-Palladium*, September 30, 1969, 23; Helen Clegg, "MSU Black Faculty Backs Adams as 'Prime Candidate,'" *LSJ*, September 29, 1969, 3.

29. For early Black faculty lists, see "Black Faculty and Administrators, 1968–1979," Ruth Simms Hamilton Papers, UA 17.269, box 2360, folder 3, UAHC.

30. "U. S. Report Gives MSU Poor Grades," *LSJ*, May 2, 1979.

31. James Spaniola, "Alliance Delivers Grievances to University Administration," *State News*, April 8, 1968; "Black Students' List," *State News*, April 8, 1968; Joe Mitch, "Negro Athletes Call Boycott; Make Demands of University, *State News*, April 26, 1968.

32. Jim Schaefer, "Group Urges Involvement of 'U' with Negro Students," *State News*, April 26, 1968.

33. Robert Bruce Slater, "The First Black Faculty Members at the Nation's Highest-Ranked Universities," *Journal of Blacks in Higher Education*, no. 22 (Winter 1998–1999): 97–106.

34. Colleen Flaherty, "The Souls of Black Professors," Inside Higher Ed, October 21, 2020, https://www.insidehighered.com/news/2020/10/21/scholars-talk-about-being-black-campus-2020.

35. There were a handful of early Black scholars who were hired to teach at PWIs. In 1849, Charles L. Reason was named professor at New York Central College. During Reconstruction, Patrick Healy taught at Georgetown, George F. Grant taught at Harvard's Dental School, and Richard Greener taught at the University of South Carolina. During the Progressive era, W. E. B. Du Bois was appointed "assistant in sociology" at the University of Pennsylvania.

36. Elijah Anderson, "Introduction to the 1996 Edition," in W. E. B. Du Bois, *The Philadelphia Negro: A Social Study* (Philadelphia: University of Pennsylvania Press, 1996), xv.

37. For the numbers of Blacks teaching at PWIs during the 1940s and 1950s, see James Allen Moss, "Negro Teachers in Predominantly White Colleges," *Journal of Negro Education* 27 (Autumn 1958): 451–462. Carlton Inde reported that approximately one hundred Black scholars taught at northern PWIs. See Inde, "Lauds Gains by Negro Americans," *Akron Beacon Journal*, February 24, 1955.

38. Francis A. Kornegay, "After Thoughts," *Detroit Tribune*, September 22, 1945; Albert Anderson, "50 Negro Professors Teach at White Colleges," *Chicago Defender*, February 8, 1947; Arthur P. Davis, "With a Grain of Salt," *Norfolk (VA) Journal and Guide*, December 11, 1948; "Cornell Faculty Not Averse to Race Professors," *Norfolk (VA) Journal and Guide*, January 24, 1948.

39. In 1947, Francis M. Hammond (PhD, University of Laval, Quebec, Canada) was named chair of Seton Hall College's Department of Philosophy. Three years later, C. H. Parrish broke new ground when he was appointed chair of the University of Louisville's Sociology Department.

40. There were more than a dozen African American tenure-system faculty hired between the late 1960s and early 1970s. The point here is that they were not hired at the country's most highly ranked research universities. The number of Black tenure-system faculty in tenure-system appointments during this period was microscopic and their hiring made news.

41. "Will Continue Art Exhibit at College," *LSJ*, January 13, 1944; "Around the Town . . . City in Brief," *LSJ*, January 16, 1944.

CHAPTER 35. TRAILBLAZING EDUCATORS

1. Dickson was hired as an instructor in 1948 with the understanding that when he completed the requirements for the PhD from Harvard University, he would be appointed assistant professor. I don't profile Black faculty who were hired after 1971 in this volume. Beginning in 1972, the number of Black faculty significantly increased. The growth was quick. Between 1969 and 1971, the number of Black tenure-system faculty members doubled. These scholars were concentrated in the Provost's Office and five other colleges. I highlight the lives and careers of those who appear to have made some of the most important impacts on campus and the broader MSU community.

2. See Ryan Stanton, "The Story of Albert Wheeler, Ann Arbor's First and Only Black Mayor," MLive, February 28, 2021, https://www.mlive.com/news/ann-arbor/2021/02/the-story-of-albert-wheeler-ann-arbors-first-and-only-black-mayor.html.

3. See Stanton, "The Story of Albert Wheeler, Ann Arbor's first and only Black Mayor."

4. David W. D. Dickson, "The Book Shelf," *LSJ*, March 19, 1961; Dickson, "The Book Shelf," *LSJ*, May 21, 1961; W. E. Burghardt Du Bois, *The Souls of Black Folk: Essays and Sketches* (Chicago: A. C. McClurg & Co., 1903), 9–16.

5. "Senior Recognition Day: Blacks Honored," *LSJ*, May 4, 1975. Redd was hired in September 1970 to run "things at the groove station of WKAR." See Linda Delgado, "Sweet 'Sounds' with Larry Redd," *Grapevine Journal*, June 3, 1971; Jeanne Saddler, "'TCB Offers Black Emphasis," *State News*, October 5, 1970.

6. Wolfgang Saxon, "David W. D. Dickson, 84, Scholar and College Leader," *New York Times*, December 22, 2003; David A. Thomas, *Michigan State College: John Hannah and the Creation of a World University, 1926–1969* (East Lansing: Michigan State University Press, 2008), 391–392.

7. "Dickson Bros.' Record Unique at Bowdoin," *Pittsburgh Courier*, July 31, 1943; Saxon, "David W. D. Dixon."

8. Kimberly Popiolek, "The Trailblazing Life of MSU's First African American Faculty Member," MSU College of Arts & Letters, February 16, 2021, https://cal.msu.edu/news/the-trailblazing-life-of-msus-first-african-american-faculty-member/.

9. "It wasn't until MSU President John Hannah intervened that the Dicksons were able to purchase the home of the outgoing Dean of Women, a short distance from campus." See Popiolek, "The Trailblazing Life of MSU's First African American Faculty Member."

10. "M.S.C. English Professor Receives Teacher Award," *LSJ*, April 25, 1952; "Dr. Dickson Receives High Teaching Honor," *M.S.C. Record* 57, no. 4 (June 1952): 5; "Gets First Michigan State Alumni Teaching Award," *Norfolk (VA) Journal and Guide*, May 10, 1952; "Negro Teacher Voted Best at Michigan State," *Plaindealer* (Kansas City, MO), May 16, 1952.

11. Popiolek, "The Trailblazing Life of MSU's First African American Faculty Member."

12. Popiolek, "The Trailblazing Life of MSU's First African American Faculty Member."

13. "U.S. Motto Application Is Favored," *LSJ*, October 25, 1957.

14. "Dickson Links Festival, Love," *LSJ*, November 22, 1962.

15. For Dickson's activities with the NAACP, see the following from the *LSJ*: "Dickson to Talk at Lincoln Center," September 11, 1959; "'Careers Unlimited' to Study Vocations," October 9, 1960; "M. S. U. Man to Lecture on Careers," October 16, 1960; "200 Attend Jobs Fair," October 17, 1960; "Conference Here Told: 3 Goals Remain in Integration," January 9, 1961.

16. "Dr. Dickson Is Elected," *LSJ*, February 15, 1962, 2; Virginia Redfern, "Society Notebook," *LSJ*, May 5, 1963.

17. "Mrs. Jacquelyn Williams," *Atlanta Daily World*, January 7, 1956; "Appointed Instructor at M. S. U.," *Chicago Defender*, January 21, 1956; "Pat Taylor, Dancer, Weds MSU Instructor," *Afro-American* (Baltimore), April 7, 1956. Howard University history professor Merze Tate is listed in the *Detroit Tribune* (July 16, 1955) as teaching at MSC (most likely in reference to Western Michigan College) during a summer session in 1955.

18. William Pipes, *Death of an "Uncle Tom"* (New York: Carlton Press, 1967), 83–84.

19. Pipes, *Death of an "Uncle Tom"*, 49; "Best," *Pittsburgh Courier*, June 22, 1929; "Cadets Will Seek Prizes at Tuskegee," *Chicago Defender*, May 24, 1930; "Police Guard DePriest: Institute's Campus Upset by 'Joke' Book," *Afro-American* (Baltimore), October 20, 1934.

20. William Pipes, "Sources of Booker T. Washington's Effectiveness as a Public Speaker" (MA thesis, Atlanta University, 1937).

21. Pipes, *Death of an "Uncle Tom"*, 50–51.

22. "Firing Charges at Alcorn Denied," *Pittsburgh Courier*, June 5, 1948; "High Price for Progress," *Afro-American* (Baltimore), July 23, 1949; Pipes, *Death of an "Uncle Tom"*, 40–54.

23. Pipes, *Death of an "Uncle Tom"*, 104, 108.

24. Robert Bickford, "Chronicle of MSU Racism," *State News*, May 1, 1968; Pipes, *Death of an "Uncle Tom"*, 71, 116.

25. Pipes is often celebrated as being the first African American to reach the rank of full professor at MSU. George M. Johnson was appointed professor in the College of Education in 1960. Pipes was the first African American to be hired as an assistant professor to reach the rank of professor.

26. Cornel West, "Introduction," in William H. Pipes, *Say Amen, Brother! Old-Time Negro Preaching; A Study in*

American Frustration (Detroit: Wayne State University Press, 1992), xi, xii, xiii; William H. Pipes, *Say Amen, Brother!: Old-Time Negro Preaching; A Study in American Frustration* (New York: The Frederick Press, 1951), 159–160.

27. A year before *Death of an "Uncle Tom"*, Pipes published *Is God Dead?* (1966).

28. "Preface," in Pipes, *Death of an "Uncle Tom"*.

29. "Preface," in Pipes, *Death of an "Uncle Tom"*, 9.

30. Robert Bao, "Feature: MSU's Iconic Professors," MSU Alumni, April 1, 2003, https://alumni.msu.edu/stay-informed/alumni-stories/feature-msus-iconic-professors.

CHAPTER 36. ANYTHING BUT SILENT GENERATIONERS

1. Gail Russell, "Black Biologist on Campus," *Grapevine Journal*, April 3, 1973.

2. "Michigan Cancer Society to Honor Eagle Woman," *LSJ*, October 24, 1966; Virginia Redfern, "Cancer Research Expands at MSU," *LSJ*, April 23, 1967; Jeanne Saddler, "Cheer Director Accused of Racism," *State News*, February 4, 1970. There is little available on Pollard's time at MSU. His obituary is brief. See "Dr. Clifford Pollard," *Tyler Morning Telegraph*, May 29, 2002; "Homecoming Highlights 2019," Residential College in the Arts and Humanities, MSU, https://rcah.msu.edu/alumni-friends/homecoming/homecoming-2019.html.

3. "In and Around Lansing: Former Dean Celebrates 39 Years at MSU," *LSJ*, September 3, 1998.

4. "MSU Launches Own Recruiting Probe," *LSJ*, April 22, 1975; Fred Stabley Jr., "A Man for All Crises," *LSJ*, April 24, 1975; Neil Hunter, "NCAA Sets MSU Hearing for Oct. 13," *LSJ*, September 26, 1975.

5. Rich Barrs, "MSU 'Actively' Seeking Minorities for Faculty," *LSJ*, January 22, 1977.

6. Chris Andrews, "MSU Budget Ax Enters Phase Two," *LSJ*, April 6, 1981.

7. "Thousands See Exhibit: 2,400 Weekend Visitors Tour MSU Kresge Art Center on Campus," *LSJ*, May 11, 1959.

8. Jeanne Whittaker, "Bob Weil, a New MSU Legend," *Detroit Free Press*, August 1, 1971.

9. "Students of the Week," *Detroit Tribune*, January 22, 1949; W. Kim Heron, "Three Artists: Styles and Ideas," *Grapevine Journal*, March 6, 1973.

10. Alma Forrest Parks, "A City Survey: The Arts in Detroit," *Negro Digest*, November 1962.

11. "2 Detroiters Get Whitney Fellowships," *Detroit Free Press*, June 15, 1961. Weil was one of the forty-nine college students throughout the nation selected for this fellowship.

12. "Dr. and Mrs. Clifton R. Wharton Jr: His Appointive Earnings Donated for Art," *Detroit Free Press*, August 29, 1974; Jeff Charnley, "Interview with Delores Wharton," Michigan State University Sesquicentennial Oral History Project (UA 3), June 1, 2001, https://d.lib.msu.edu/otb-sohp/291, UAHC; Virginia Redfern, "'Arts in Residence' Film Shown," *LSJ*, June 2, 1971.

13. "Street-Corner Philosopher Is An Artist," *LSJ*, August 11, 1974.

14. Whittaker, "Bob Weil, a New MSU Legend."

15. Helen Clegg, "From Scrap Pile . . . to Works of Art," *LSJ*, September 15, 1969.

16. Gail Morris, "Robert Weil: Reclaiming Human Resources," *MSU Faculty News* 6, no. 6 (November 4, 1969): 2; "Art Festival Featured in Observance of Week," *LSJ*, February 9, 1969; "Socially Speaking," *LSJ*, February 24, 1972; "Black Artists' Paintings Go on Display at Gallery," *LSJ*, February 27, 1969; Heron, "Three Artists."

17. Morris, "Robert Weil: Reclaiming Human Resources"; Heron, "Three Artists."

18. "Street-Corner Philosopher Is an Artist."

19. Mark Nixon, "'Gas Station Garden': Art Instructor Thinking Big," *LSJ*, November 12, 1974.

20. Mike Hughes, "Boettcher Clears Alley Hurdle," *LSJ*, July 17, 1974; "Street-Corner Philosopher"; Nixon, "Gas Station Garden"; Tim Kenny, "Quest for Art: Sculptures to Deck East Lansing," *LSJ*, November 17, 1975; Julie Lehr, "12 Sculptures to Adorn East Lansing Streets," *LSJ*, March 7, 1976; "Shiawassee Bridge Project," *LSJ*, July 5, 1976; "Observers Blow Hot 'n' Cold on Sculptures," *LSJ*, July 30, 1976.

21. David Thomas, "Artists Try Again to Create Haven," *LSJ*, October 25, 1989.

22. On September 1, 1967, King delivered the invited distinguished lecture at the American Psychological Association conference in Atlanta, GA. Martin Luther King Jr., "The Role of the Behavioral Scientist in the Civil Rights Movement," *Journal of Social Issues* 34, no. 1 (January 1968): 1–12.

23. Ron Karle, "The Greening of M.S.U. and Maybe Some Other Places, Too," *MSU Alumni Magazine* (May 1972): 11, 13, 34; Jan Brydon, "Dean Robert Green: A Scholar-Activist," *MSU Alumni Magazine* (March/April, 1978): 10–11.

24. Chester A. Higgins Sr., "For Black History Month," *Crisis* 89, no. 2 (February 1982): 70.

25. Vickki Dozier, "A Memoir of MLK, MSU and Discrimination in East Lansing," *LSJ*, February 18, 2016.

26. "Human Relations Commission Member Resigns," *LSJ*, January 7, 1965.

27. David A. Thomas, *Michigan State College: John Hannah and the Creation of a World University, 1926–1969* (East Lansing: Michigan State University Press, 2008), 209.

28. "R. L. Green New UDC President," *LSJ*, July 20, 1983.

29. "R. L. Green New UDC President."

30. Higgins, "For Black History Month," 70.

31. Alison Muscatine, "Robert Green and Turmoil," *Washington Post*, August 20, 1985.

32. Wilbur B. Brookover, "Education in Prince Edward County, Virginia, 1953–1993," *Journal of Negro Education* 62 (Spring 1993): 150, 151. For the PEC officials' refusal to obey the Supreme Court's 1954 decision, see Kristen Green, *Something Must Be Done about Prince Edward County: A Family, a Virginia Town, a Civil Rights Battle* (New York: HarperCollins, 2015).

33. "From the Midwinter SPSSI Council Meeting—The Civil Rights Committee and the Association for Black Psychologists," *SPSSI Newsletter*, 3; Robert L. Williams, "A 40-Year History of the Association of Black Psychologists (ABPsi)," *Journal of Black Psychology* 34 (August 2008): 249–260.

34. "SCLC's Director Deplores South's Educational System," *Afro-American* (Baltimore), March 5, 1966.

35. Robert L. Green, *At the Crossroads of Fear and Freedom: The Fight for Social and Educational Justice* (East Lansing: Michigan State University Press, 2015), 63. For Green's discussion of his activities during the March Against Fear and in Greenwood, MS, see *At the Crossroads of Fear and Freedom*, 31–65.

36. Dozier, "A Memoir of MLK, MSU and Discrimination in East Lansing."

37. "MSU Prof Raps Sen. Bayh: Senate Critic of Stokely Hit," *LSJ*, December 13, 1967.

38. Mike Wagoner, "MSU Urban Affairs Role Up in the Air," *LSJ*, May 8, 1972.

39. "Green Confirmed as Dean of MSU's Urban College," *LSJ*, October 27, 1973; Susan Ager, "Green OKd as College Dean," *State News*, October 29, 1973.

40. James B. Hamilton, *What a Time to Live: The Autobiography of James B. Hamilton* (East Lansing: Michigan State University Press, 1995), 48–49; Chuck Stone, "Michigan, MSU Get High Marks," *LSJ*, February 22, 1974; Green, *At the Crossroads of Fear and Freedom*, xviii–xix.

41. "'Upward Bound' Fights Roadblocks to High Education," *LSJ*, July 21, 1966; "Lesson in Living Given to Tutors," *LSJ*, August 11, 1966.

42. "Lesson in Living Given to Tutors"; "69 Poverty Students on Campus," *LSJ*, July 10, 1967; Helen Clegg, "Project Points Way to College," *LSJ*, July 13, 1967; "'Upward Bound' Plan Confidence Builder," *LSJ*, July 25, 1968; Alex Cade, "Black Man, Black Man, Find the Individual," *State News*, February 13, 1969; "Volunteers For Project Sought," *LSJ*, April 30, 1969; Helen Clegg, "62 Prep for Campus Life," *LSJ*, July 29, 1970; "Dr. Cade to Address Churchmen," *LSJ*, June 5, 1971; "Education Post to Member Here," *LSJ*, October 24, 1971. For a brief biography of Cade, see his obituary in the *LSJ*, August 11, 2013.

43. Dave Hanson, "'Agency Ignores Economically Deprived,'" *LSJ*, November 21, 1968; Beverly Hall, "E. Lansing Human Relations Group Adopts Action Plan," *LSJ*, October 8, 1970.

44. Helen Clegg, "Accord Reached on Minority Students," *LSJ*, November 5, 1970; "Exhibit Features Black Pioneers," *LSJ*, July 9, 1969.

45. "Gifts, Grants Accepted," *LSJ*, July 18, 1969; Charlie Bass, "One Time Being Kicked Out Was Acceptable," *LSJ*, September 2, 1970; "Crisis Intervention," *LSJ*, February 15, 1971; "Crisis Intervention Center to Be Opened," *LSJ*, May 16, 1971.

46. During the 1990s, I was among those who benefited from his counsel and generosity. While I had two children, and one on the way, and no secure employment, he provided me with a research fellowship. This act of generosity changed my life at the time.

CHAPTER 37. EXCELLENCE IN MATHEMATICS, HISTORY, AND COUNSELING

1. Johnny Houston, "The Founding of the National Association of Mathematicians, Inc. (NAM)," in Omayra Ortega, Emile D. Lawrence, and Edray Herber Goins, *Golden Anniversary Celebration of the National Association of Mathematicians* (Providence, RI: American Mathematical Society, 2020), 1–20.

2. Scott W. Williams, "A Modern History of Blacks in Mathematics," The Mathematics Department of the State University of New York at Buffalo, 2008, http://www.math.buffalo.edu/mad/madhist.html.

3. Patricia Clark Kenschaft, "Black Men and Women in Mathematical Research," *Journal of Black Studies* 18 (December 1987): 189.

4. "The Most Highly Cited Black Mathematicians," *Journal of Blacks in Higher Education*, 2005, https://www.jbhe.com/news_views/49_mostcited_blackmathematicians.html.

5. Amy Harmon, "For a Black Mathematician, What It's Like to Be the 'Only One,'" *New York Times*, February 18, 2019.

6. "MSU Math Project Aiding Inner City," *LSJ*, April 22, 1971.

7. The description of the MSUIC-MP is based upon Irvin E. Vance, "MSUIC-MP [Michigan State University Inner City Mathematics Project]," Document Resume, ED 038 325 SE 008 364, U.S. Department of Education & Welfare, Office of Education (1970).

8. "MSU Math Project Aiding Inner City"; "Ethnic Studies Director Named at University," *Las Cruces Sun-News*, August 18, 1971; "Ethnic Program Director Named," *Albuquerque Journal*, August 19, 1971; "Irvin Vance on Faculty at New Mexico," *New Mexico Ledger*, September 7, 1971.

9. Catherine Lazorko, "On King's Birthday, NMSU Professor Calls for Hiring More Black Instructors," *El Paso Times*, January 17, 1989.

10. Jessi De La Cruz, "Kids Study Math, Science MSU," *LSJ*, July 25, 1994; Rosene Cobbs, "Minority Students Experience Hands-on Activities at MSU," *LSJ*, July 27, 1995; Vickki Dozier, "People News," *LSJ*, February 1, 2006.

11. For the remembrances of Vance, see "Dr. Irvin Elmer Vance," Legacy.com, 2018, https://www.legacy.com/obituaries/name/irvin-vance-obituary?pid=187722299.

12. Mark Stryker, "Bassist on the Brink," *Detroit Free Press*, May 12, 1996.

13. John F. Bratzel, "Leslie B. Rout, Jr. (1935–1987)," *Hispanic American Historical Review* 68 (1988): 101–102; "'U' Student Tootles Sax at White House," *Star Tribune*, November 22, 1962.

14. Nancy Crawley, "New MSU Aide Seeks the 'Practical,'" *LSJ*, October 8, 1970.

15. Leslie B. Rout, "Jazz's Debt to the Negro," *Collage: The State News Bi-Weekly Magazine*, April 4, 1968, 5, 7, 11.

16. Dick Stoimenoff, "Students Ask ATL Teach Negro Role," *State News*, February 21, 1968; "What Is the Price, Negro History?," *State News*, February 23, 1968; "History of Negro Demanded at MSU," *LSJ*, February 23, 1968.

17. Shirley Brunner, "Black Class Poses Problems," *State News*, May 8, 1969; Pat Murphy, "MSU May Expand Black History Courses," *LSJ*, July 17, 1969; "BUF Accuses a Negro Professor—The Case of Dr. Leslie B. Rout Jr," *BUF Newsletter*, October 14, 1970, RSH Papers, UA 17.269, box 2359, folder 67, UAHC.

18. Shirley Brunner, "Black Class Poses Problems," *State News*, May 8, 1969; Pat Murphy, "Culture Classes Popular: MSU May Expand Black History Courses," *LSJ*, July 17, 1969; Dudley K. Pierson, "Prof Wants 'Fine Tuning' on Black History Month," *LSJ*, February 20, 1983.

19. "20 Appointed to MSU Anti-Bias Committees," *LSJ*, May 17, 1970; Nancy Crawley, "He'll Bolster MSU Minorities," *LSJ*, August 23, 1979; Crawley, "Mackey Picks Two New VPs," *LSJ*, September 19, 1979; "Counseling Official Will Head MSU Provost Jobs," *LSJ*, August 29, 1979; "June to Study MSU Minorities Problems," *LSJ*, April 26, 1982; "MSU Minorities Aided on Computers," *LSJ*, September 19, 1979; "MSU Professor Leslie Rout Dies," *LSJ*, April 3, 1987.

20. Matthew Miller, "Gunnings a Champion for Minorities," *LSJ*, August 25, 2010.

21. Sonya Gunnings-Moton, "Dr. Thomas Sylvester Gunnings" (in author's possession, no date).

22. Helen Clegg, "Black Counselor Gunnings Busy," *LSJ*, February 18, 1970; Clegg, "Nonwhite Students

Counseled," *LSJ*, March 25, 1970.

23. Norris McDowell, "Speakers Emphasize Needs: 'Equality before Ecology,'" *LSJ*, June 30, 1970; Helen Clegg, "Black Culture Center Asked by Wharton," *LSJ*, May 19, 1970; Clegg, "Student Protest Seeks Funds for Detroit Project," *LSJ*, October 13, 1970; "Black Retirees to Be Honored," *LSJ*, June 8, 1972; "Minority Counselors Told 'Treat System,'" *LSJ*, May 20, 1971.

24. Mike Wagoner, "Blacks Hit 'Racism' in Big Ten," *LSJ*, February 10, 1972; Wagoner, "3 MSU Trustees Support Reforms Sought in Big Ten Conference," *LSJ*, February 15, 1972; Beckie Brenneman, "Conflict Brewing," *LSJ*, March 3, 1972.

25. "Counselors' Session Set," *LSJ*, January 2, 1975; Gayle Harden, "Minorities Counseling Meeting Set," *LSJ*, October 6, 1975; "Black Youth Is Topic," *LSJ*, May 9, 1979.

26. Carol Haskin, "Social, Economic Factors Keep Them at Home," *LSJ*, February 24, 1980; Chris Andrews, "Psychologists Helps," *LSJ*, April 28, 1981.

27. Patrick J. Fitzgerald, "Radcliffe Says His Candidacy Points to a Changing GOP," *LSJ*, April 7, 1980; "MSU Prof Named to Bush Committee," *LSJ*, October 29, 1990.

28. Miller, "Gunnings a Champion for Minorities."

CHAPTER 38. A CENTURY OF COMBINED SERVICE

1. The information in this chapter pertaining to the lives and experiences of Drs. Lee June and Joe Darden is based upon interviews the author conducted with June and Darden in June of 2021.

2. For a discussion of the extended Civil Rights Movement in South Carolina which includes Manning, see Winfred B. Moore Jr. and Orville Vernon Burton, eds., *Toward the Meeting of the Waters: Currents in the Civil Rights Movement of South Carolina during the Twentieth Century* (Columbia: University of South Carolina Press, 2008).

3. Brian Jones, *The Tuskegee Student Uprising* (New York: New York University Press, 2022), 101. For Jones's discussion about the broader impact of Younge's death, see *The Tuskegee Student Uprising*, 98–102.

4. "Nomination Splits MSU Groups," *LSJ*, October 27, 1978.

5. "Profs Attend Science Meet," *Clarion-Ledger* (Jackson, MS), May 15, 1963.

6. Donald R. Deskins Jr., Saul B. Cohen, and Linda J. Speil, "Geography and Afro-America: The Anatomy of a Graduate Training and Curriculum Development Project, *Journal of Geography* 70 (1971): 465–471.

7. Harold M. Rose, "The Geography of Despair," *Annals of the Association of American Geographers* 68 (December 1978): 453–464.

8. Malcolm Johnson (Associated Press), "Study Says Blacks' Progress Static since '67 Detroit Riots," *LSJ*, July 17, 1987.

9. I was in attendance at the AAAS meeting in 2017, and this is my recollection of the meeting. I have paraphrased what Darden expressed at the meeting.

CHAPTER 39. SHATTERING THE GLASS CEILING

1. Black Women Employees Association of Michigan State University (BWEA), "Presentation to the Board of Trustees, Michigan State University, East Lansing, Michigan, Pertaining to Employment of Black Women at Michigan State University," February 25, 1972, in author's possession.

2. "Appointed Instructor at M. S. U.," *Chicago Defender*, January 21, 1956; BWEA, "Presentation to the Board of Trustees."

3. Smith and Brunson are the first Black women who earned doctorates at MSU who I have been able to identify. There may have been others before them. In the early 1960s, there were other Black women who earned and were working on doctorates from MSU, including Barbara Beth Battle and Sylvia Taylor. In the 1970s, there were also standout Black women PhD holders like Annamarie Hayes, the 1971 Michigan State "Woman of the Year," and Sandra Leola Leavell, who earned a doctorate of medicine from the MSU Medical School in 1974. In 1975, Coretta Scott King was awarded an honorary doctor of laws degree from MSU. See "Gadabouting U. S. A. with Lulu Jones Garrett," *Afro-American* (Baltimore), July 27, 1963; "FEPC Examiner Admits Former Teacher Victim of Race Bias," *Chicago Defender*, January 12, 1963; "Dr. Hayes in German," *Michigan Chronicle*, March 4, 1972; "Gets Doctorate," *Chicago Defender*, December 14, 1974; "Doctorate for Coretta King," *New York Amsterdam News*, December 3, 1975.

4. "Dr. Mildred Smith Holds Unique Post," *Michigan Chronicle*, February 10, 1962; "Senate Confirms Dr. M. B. Smith," *Michigan Chronicle*, April 20, 1963; "Dr. Rose Brunson Will Be the Archives Speaker in Lansing," *Michigan Chronicle*, April 25, 1964; Mildred B. Smith, "Education Begins at Home," *Michigan Chronicle*, October 17, 1970; "Eastern Regent HEW Appointee," *Michigan Chronicle*, July 8, 1972; "Flint Education Is Cited at Denver Sorority Meet," *Michigan Chronicle*, September 2, 1972; Theresa A. Glab, "Intellectual Started in Pasture," *Courier-Post* (Cherry Hill, NJ), January 26, 1977.

5. Virginia Baird, "Helping People Is Her Way of Life," *LSJ*, June 10, 1962; William J. Duchane, "City's Poor Parallels Appalachia, Study Shows," *LSJ*, May 26, 1965.

6. *Chicago Defender*, July 22, 1933; Josie Craig Berry, "Over My Shoulder," *Black Dispatch*, February 11, 1939; Angela Martin, "Black Migrant Study Adds to City's Lore," *LSJ*, September 2, 1974.

7. "Drive Launched to Raise $3,000," *LSJ*, October 12, 1947.

8. "Association of Women's Clubs Buys Clubhouse," *LSJ*, January 1, 1948; "Mother Feted," *LSJ*, May 9, 1949.

9. "Urbandale Residents Told How to Better Community," *LSJ*, March 7, 1960.

10. Baird, "Helping People Is Her Way of Life."

11. Marshanda Ann Latrice Smith, "A History of Black Women Faculty at Michigan State University, 1968–2009" (PhD diss., Michigan State University, 2012), 217; Department of Human Relations, Michigan State University, *Affirmative Action at Michigan State University: Annual Report to the Department of Health, Education and Welfare* (East Lansing: Michigan State University, September 1973), 2; Department of Human Relations, Michigan State University, *Affirmative Action at Michigan State University, 1977–78: Annual Report to the Department of Health, Education and Welfare* (East Lansing: Michigan State University, 1977–1978), 44.

12. Department of Human Relations, *Affirmative Action at Michigan State University* (September 1973), 7, 19, table 17.

13. Department of Human Relations, *Affirmative Action at Michigan State University* (September 1973), table 26; Roxanne Brown, "Three Strikes for Affirmative Action," *Grapevine Journal*, March 4, 1975.

14. Department of Human Relations, *Affirmative Action at Michigan State University, 1977–78*, 44–45, 53, 90; "Historical Summary of Faculty and Academic Staff," n.d. (ca. 1999/2000), in author's possession; "Historical Summary of Faculty and Academic Staff—Headcount," n.d. (ca. 2014/2015), in author's possession.

15. Christine Rook, "Slain Professor Remembered as Visionary," *LSJ*, November 14, 2003.

16. "TIAA Ruth Simms Hamilton Graduate Merit Fellowship," The Graduate School, Michigan State University, https://grad.msu.edu/fellowships/tiaacref.

17. James B. Hamilton, *What A Time to Live: The Autobiography of James B. Hamilton* (East Lansing: Michigan State University Press, 1995), 41.

18. "James Hamilton, Teacher, Advocate," *LSJ*, May 19, 1994; "Hamilton, Dr. James B.," *LSJ*, May 20, 1994; Helen Clegg, "Trustees Debate Staff Changes," *LSJ*, June 19, 1971; Mike Wagoner, "Changes on Campus," *LSJ*, September 27, 1972.

19. "Committee to Evaluate MSU Veep Candidates," *LSJ*, February 29, 1972; Chris Andrews, "Trustees to Hear Layoff Pros, Cons," *LSJ*, December 23, 1980; "Faculty Group Gets Heat," *LSJ*, March 8, 1981; "MSU Commencement to Be Saturday," *LSJ*, March 10, 1987; "Your Guide to Candidates," *LSJ*, April 8, 1993.

20. "MSU's Ruth Simms Hamilton Elected," *LSJ*, February 4, 1981; "MSU Looks at Migration of Blacks," *LSJ*, October 24, 1979; Kelly Donahue, "Policy on Apartheid Topic of Conference," *Journal Times*, March 17, 1983; Millicent Lane, "15 Women Honored at Diana Awards," *LSJ*, May 6, 1982.

21. Rita Wieber, "It's Never Too Late to Start," *LSJ*, July 15, 1997.

22. Millicent Lane, "Med School Staff to Add Negro Woman Physician," *LSJ*, August 21, 1969.

23. Millicent Lane, "Dedicated to Dad: Booklet Shows Poetic Bent of Three Johnson Sisters," *LSJ*, May 9, 1970. Ray Walsh, "Local Author Takes Path to 'Freedom,'" *LSJ*, February 11, 1990.

24. The ensuing discussion of Johnson's case comes from *Johnson v. Michigan State University*, 547 F. Supp. 420 (W. D. 1982).

25. For reference to Johnson's book project, see Ray Walsh, "Area Authors Create 2 Diverse Murder Stories," *LSJ*, August 22, 1993.

26. Beverly Hall, "Teachers, Bailey Parents Split on 'Brown Bag' Plan," *LSJ*, January 12, 1971.

27. Candace Hollar, "New East Lansing Program to Help Newcomers Adjust," *LSJ*, June 5, 1974; "Non White Death Rates Improve at Middle Age," *Herald-Palladium* (Benton Harbor, MI), March 17, 1977.

28. "Blacks Who Live to Middle Age May Out Last Whites," *Jet* 52, no. 2 (March 31, 1977): 45.

29. "13-Person Panel Named in Search," *LSJ*, June 9, 1984; Karen Douglas, "People, Etc.," *LSJ*, October 6, 1989.

30. Verna Hildebrand, "Racial Discrimination, Sexism Rife at MSU," *LSJ*, October 30, 1991.

31. Joyce Conway, "Faculty Focus," *Grapevine Journal*, September 25, 1973.

32. "Woman Named," *LSJ*, June 3, 1971.

33. Diane St. John, "Happy to Serve, If . . . ," *LSJ*, June 8, 1971; St. John, "Women's Commission, Past and Present . . . ," *LSJ*, November 30, 1971; St. John, "Equal Rights Amendment Queried," *LSJ*, May 2, 1972; "Group to Study Equal Rites Law," *LSJ*, November 13, 1972.

34. Floresta Jones, "Effect of Women's Liberation Deep in Lives of Black Females," *LSJ*, March 26, 1974.

35. Hugh Leach, "Equality Worker Rejects 'Thanks,'" *LSJ*, November 17, 1977.

36. Elisha McDowell, "The Minorities: Losing Ground in Our Schools," *LSJ*, February 25, 1979. The following represents the number of Blacks enrolled in doctorate programs at MSU: 151 in 1976, 151 in 1977, 98 in 1978, 111 in 1979, and 97 in 1980. In 1979, the provost directed college deans to develop affirmative action plans for graduate and graduate professional programs. See "Excerpts from the May 22, 1981 Presentation to the Board of Trustees on the Affirmative Action Plan for Graduate and Graduate Professional Students," in Department of Human Relations, Michigan State University, *Annual Report on Affirmative Action Prepared for Michigan State University Board of Trustees* (East Lansing: Michigan State University, January 21, 1982).

37. "Black Woman to Lead College: Her Appointment Is a First for SUNY," *Democrat and Chronicle* (Rochester, NY), June 19, 1986; George Basler, "Make Way for Minorities, Black SUNY President Says," *Press and Sun-Bulletin* (Binghampton, NY), December 6, 1986; L. Eudora Pettigrew, "Look Past Race to the Press," *News Journal* (Wilmington, DE), February 18, 2001.

38. Trudy Westfall, "Eleven Achievers Take Home 'Diana,'" *LSJ*, September 29, 1977.

39. For a description of the award and Evans and Warr, see Gayle Harden, "Diana Award Pendant," *LSJ*, October 29, 1975; Harden, "YW Hails 11 'Dianas,'" *LSJ*, October 30, 1975.

40. "Women's Choral Society Will Appear in Newark High School," *Newark Advocate* (Newark, OH), February 6, 1957; "Valley in Brief," *Journal Herald* (Dayton, OH), March 25, 1958; "Graduation Recital Set," *Dayton Daily News* (Dayton, OH), May 20, 1959.

41. Gloria Smith, "Counseling for a Lifetime," *Second National Conference on Counseling Minorities Proceedings, October 27–30, 1974*, 47–48, personal papers of Gloria Smith in author's possession.

42. Gloria Smith, interview by author, East Lansing, MI, 2021; John McFadden and Wanda D. Lipscomb, "History of the Association for Non-White Concerns," *Journal of Counseling and Development* 63 (March 1985): 444–447.

43. Personal papers of Gloria Smith in author's possession; Wanda Lipscomb, interview by author, East Lansing, MI, 2021.

44. Wanda E. Dean, "Training Minorities in Psychology," *Journal of Non-White Concerns in Personnel and Guidance* 5, no. 3 (July 1977): 119–125; Lipscomb, interview by author. For an example of Smith's impact on Lipscomb's approach, see John McFadden and Wanda Dean Lipscomb, "Multicultural Approaches," *Elementary School Education and Counseling* 17, no. 1 (October 1982): 72–75. For a brief biography of Lipscomb, see "Wanda Lipscomb, PhD," College of Human Medicine, Michigan State University, https://humanmedicine.msu.edu/directory/lipscomb-wanda.html.

45. Personal papers of Gloria Smith in author's possession.

46. BWEA, "Presentation to the Board of Trustees"; "Minutes of the Meeting of the Board of Trustees," Michigan State University, November 19, 1971, https://projects.kora.matrix.msu.edu/files/157-544-775/NOVEMBER191971.pdf.

47. "Black Women Employes [*sic*]: MSU Officers Elected," *LSJ*, February 10, 1972.

48. Diane St. John, "MSU Black Women Refuse Token Status," *LSJ*, September 27, 1972; "'Human Liberation' Is

Coordinator's Goal," *MSU News Bulletin*, August 10, 1972.

49. BWEA, "Presentation to the Board of Trustees."

50. BWEA, "Presentation to the Board of Trustees."

51. St. John, "MSU Black Women Refuse Token Status."

52. See Smith, "A History of Black Women Faculty at Michigan State University, 1968–2009," 65–103, 217. The data for the number of Black women faculty from 1980 until the 2000s is from "Historical Summary of Faculty and Academic Staff" (1980–1999), in author's possession.

CHAPTER 40. A HISTORIC PRESIDENCY

1. Willard Baird, "Negro Successor to Hannah Urged," *LSJ*, February 7, 1969; "Negro Asks Black Head for MSU," *Detroit Free Press*, February 8, 1969.

2. Larry Lee, "'U' Needs Man of Courage," *State News*, May 21, 1969; "Next President's Task: Race Issues Take Priority," *State News*, May 21, 1969.

3. Clifton Wharton Jr., *Privilege and Prejudice: The Life of a Black Pioneer* (East Lansing: Michigan State University Press, 2015), 206.

4. William Grant, "Wharton: Son of Diplomat," *Detroit Free Press*, October 18, 1969.

5. "Clifton R. Wharton, Sr.: Ambassador," National Museum of American Diplomacy, https://diplomacy.state.gov/encyclopedia/clifton-r-wharton-sr-ambassador/.

6. Wharton, *Privilege and Prejudice*, 8, 23, 34.

7. Wharton, *Privilege and Prejudice*, 69, 76.

8. Wharton, *Privilege and Prejudice*, 194.

9. Jacqueline Korona, "New MSU Chief Man of World: Black Educator Advocates 'Positive Militancy,'" *Herald-Press* (Saint Joseph, MI), October 17, 1969; Helen Clegg, "Wharton Pledges 'Assistance to All' at MSU," *LSJ*, October 24, 1969; "Extra Pressure? Wharton Says He Expects It as MSU President," *LSJ*, October 25, 1969.

10. Korona, "New MSU Chief Man of World"; Wharton, *Privilege and Prejudice*, 217, 218.

11. Wharton, *Privilege and Prejudice*, 219, 275, 276, 279, 227.

12. Helen Clegg, "Wharton Will Head MSU," *LSJ*, October 17, 1969; Marilyn Patterson, "Hartman Charges Trustees Rigged Wharton Election," *State News*, October 19, 1969.

13. Wharton, *Privilege and Prejudice*, 217.

14. "Achievement Not Judged by 'Badge of Color,'" *State News*, October 20, 1969.

15. "Clifton R. Wharton, Jr. Elected 14th President," *Michigan State University Alumni Association Magazine*, November–December 1969, 3–6.

16. Louis Martin, "Choice of Wharton as MSU President Stirs New Hopes," *Chicago Defender*, October 25, 1969.

17. "Michigan Picks Wharton," *Afro-American* (Baltimore), November 1, 1969.

18. "1st Black Named President of Michigan State U.," *Jet* 37, no. 4 (October 30, 1969): 22.

19. Valerie Jo Bradley, "Black President Runs Michigan State University," *Jet* 38, no. 7 (May 21, 1970): 16, 17, 18.

20. Bradley, "Black President Runs Michigan State University," 20, 21.

21. "A New Boss Takes Over at Michigan State: Dr. Clifton R. Wharton Jr. Is President of Nation's 11th Largest University," *Ebony* 25, no. 9 (July 1970): 60, 61, 62, 68, 70.

22. "A Talk with Wharton: MSU's Black President," *Chicago Defender*, July 6, 1970.

23. Helen Clegg, "Dr. Wharton Tells Belief in Individual," *LSJ*, January 21, 1970; William Grant, "MSU Chief Backs Universal Education," *Detroit Free Press*, March 31, 1970; Clegg, "Speechmaking Important Part of MSU President's Duties," *LSJ*, July 6, 1970.

24. Helen Clegg, "Trustees Balk at Antidiscrimination Policy," *LSJ*, February 21, 1970.

25. Helen Clegg, "Wharton Explains Commission Purpose," *LSJ*, April 1, 1970.

26. Helen Clegg, "Equal Opportunity Staff Acts as 'Bias' Watchdog," *LSJ*, October 9, 1970; Michael Wagoner, "Wharton Asks New Law, Urban Colleges," *LSJ*, February 15, 1972; Clifton R. Wharton Jr., "Point of View: Arts Center to Be for All," *LSJ*, April 13, 1975; Wharton, "MSU Goal: Improving Quality," *LSJ*, February 4, 1973; Clegg, "Black Culture Center Asked by Wharton," *LSJ*, May 19, 1970; Clegg, "Urban Center Dedicated," *LSJ*, June 11, 1970.

27. Department of Human Resources, Michigan State University, *Affirmative Action at Michigan State University: Annual Report to the Department of Health, Education and Welfare* (East Lansing: Michigan State University, 1976–1977), 91; "Historical Summary of Faculty and Academic Staff," n.d. (ca. 1999/2000), in author's possession. During Wharton's presidency, the Black student enrolled was as follows: 1,954 in 1970; 2,509 in 1971; 2,678 in 1972; 2,573 in 1973; 2,567 in 1974; 2,587 in 1975; 2,451 in 1976; 2,436 in 1977; and 2,252 in 1978. See "Michigan State University Number of Black Students Enrolled by Year," in *Annual Report on Affirmative Action Prepared for Michigan State University Board of Trustees*, Department of Human Resources, Michigan State University (East Lansing: Michigan State University, January 21, 1982).

28. "Clifton Wharton to Head Largest U.S. University," *Associated Press*, October 26, 1977.

29. Robert L. Green, *At the Crossroads of Fear and Freedom: The Fight for Social and Educational Justice* (East Lansing: Michigan State University Press, 2016), 100.

30. "NMA Celebrates 75th Anniversary," *Afro-American* (Baltimore), November 14, 1970.

CHAPTER 41. 1989, THE NUMBER

1. Beth LeBlanc, "MSU Freshman Class One of Largest in School's History," *LSJ*, August 27, 2017; Jack Roskopp, "Michigan State University Has Largest African American Freshman Class of Any Big Ten School," *Detroit Metro Times*, August 24, 2017; "MSU to Welcome Largest, Most Diverse Freshman Class," *MSUToday*, May 9, 2018, https://msutoday.msu.edu/news/2018/msu-to-welcome-largest-most-diverse-freshman-class/; Sarah Rahal, "MSU to Welcome Largest, Most Diverse Freshman Class," *Detroit News*, May 9, 2018; Henry Mochida, "Office for Inclusion and Intercultural Initiatives Releases Diversity at MSU Report," Institutional Diversity and Inclusion, July 7, 2021, https://inclusion.msu.edu/news/Office%20for%20Inclusion%20and%20Intercultural%20Initiatives%20releases%20Diversity%20at%20MSU%20Report.html; Dan Olsen, "It's Official: MSU Fall Enrollment Totals 51,316," MSUToday, September 29, 2023, https://msutoday.msu.edu/news/2023/total-fall-enrollment.

2. Chris Andrews and James A. Mallory, "After a Blazing Start, MSU Fades in Recruiting Blacks," *LSJ*, February 22, 1982.

3. Andrews and Mallory, "After a Blazing Start."

4. Angela Martin and Delilah Nichols, "MSU Still Committed to Blacks," *Grapevine Journal*, April 1975.

5. Chris Andrews, "Professors: We Must Recruit More Black Scholars," *LSJ*, May 21, 1989.

6. Tim Martin, "MSU Black Faculty Members Pray for Progress," *LSJ*, January 24, 1997.

7. Jim Rasmussen, "Some Find It's Life as Usual," *LSJ*, May 12, 1989.

8. Sue Nichols, "70 Students Stage Sit-in," *LSJ*, May 10, 1989.

9. "200 MSU Protesters: We'll Stay," *Battle Creek Enquirer*, May 12, 1989.

10. Phyllis-Lynne Burns, "MSU Campus Is Hit by Rash of Racial Incidents," *Michigan Chronicle*, March 4, 1989.

11. James A. Harris, "Theta Chi Cited for 'Racial Slur' Ad," *LSJ*, May 25, 1982; James A. Mallory, "Mackey Meets with 300 Protesters," *LSJ*, June 5, 1982; Mallory, "MSU Fraternity on Probation," *LSJ*, June 16, 1982; Mallory, "State News Board Apologizes for Ad," *LSJ*, June 17, 1982.

12. Dudley K. Pierson, "Trustees Told Minorities Handling Race Slurs Better," *LSJ*, February 3, 1984.

13. Lee Mitgang, "Colleges Admit Rise in Bigotry," *LSJ*, March 16, 1987.

14. John DiBiaggio, "Slurs Have No Place at MSU," *State News*, March 2, 1989.

15. "Fight Racism," *LSJ*, May 8, 1989.

16. Colleen Gehoski, "Parents, MSU Tackle Racism," *LSJ*, February 28, 1989.

17. Loyce D. Lester to John DiBiaggio, March 2, 1989, John A. DiBiaggio Papers, UA 2.1.17, box 5405, folder 10, UAHC.

18. "Parents' Group Voices Racial Concerns," *MSU News-Bulletin* 20, no. 19 (March 2, 1989).

19. Lester to DiBiaggio, March 2, 1989, DiBiaggio Papers.

20. Lester to Governor James Blanchard, March 2, 1989, DiBiaggio Papers, UA 2.1.17, box 5405, folder 10, UAHC.

21. DiBiaggio to Black Parents, March 13, 1989, DiBiaggio Papers, UA 2.1.17, box 5405, folder 10, UAHC.

22. Chris Graves, "Blacks Confront DiBiaggio at Budget Meeting," *LSJ*, March 8, 1989.

23. "Statement by John A. DiBiaggio before the Michigan State House Subcommittee on Higher Education," March 7, 1989, DiBiaggio Papers, UA 2.1.17, box 5405, folder 10, UAHC.

24. James Tobin, "Detroit Minister in Spotlight with MSU Racism Issue," *LSJ*, March 25, 1989.

25. Chris Graves, "Apology Not Enough for Everyone at MSU," *LSJ*, April 8, 1989.

26. Terry Denbow to DiBiaggio, April 5, 1989, DiBiaggio Papers, UA 2.1.17, box 3062, folder 9, UAHC.

27. Karen A. Davis, "MSU Talks Stall as Sit-in Swells," *LSJ*, May 11, 1989.

28. Jim Rasmussen, "MSU, Students Disagree about Sit-in Outcome," *LSJ*, May 18, 1989. For a concise assessment of the MSU IDEA, "MSU's 50-Point Plan," *LSJ*, May 12, 1989.

29. DiBiaggio to "Students Protesting in the Hannah Administration Building," May 16, 1989, DiBiaggio Papers, UA 2.1.17, box 5405, folder 7, UAHC.

30. Elizabeth Atkins, "Joyful Students Troop Out," *LSJ*, May 17, 1989.

31. "Chronology," *LSJ*, May 17, 1989.

32. Flodean S. Riggs, "College Students Continue Protest," *Michigan Citizen*, October 21, 1989.

33. Josh Mansour, "BSA Holds Heated Meeting with MSU Administrators," *State News*, October 28, 2011.

34. Riley Murdock, "BSA Storms Administration Building in 1989," *State News*, October 18, 2016.

AFTERWORD

1. Various flyers in author's possession.

2. Michigan State University Black History Committee documents, in author's possession.

3. Edward Hallett Carr, *What Is History?* (London: Penguin, 1967).

Select Bibliography

MICHIGAN STATE UNIVERSITY ARCHIVES AND HISTORICAL COLLECTIONS

Manuscripts

Associate Provost Records, UA 3.4

Barry D. Amis Papers, UA 10.3.500

Center for Urban Affairs Records, UA 3.23

Center of Urban Development Records, UA 15.20

Clarence L. Munn Papers, UA 17.75

Clifton R. Wharton Jr. Papers, UA 2.1.14

Don Stevens Papers, UA 1.1.2

Eric V. A. Winston Papers, UA 10.3.396

Frank Stewart Kedzie Papers, UA 2.1.8

Grapevine Journal Records, UA 12.7.3

John A. DiBiaggio Papers, UA 2.1.17

John A. Hannah Papers, UA 2.1.12

Jonathan LeMoyne Snyder Papers, UA 2.1.7

Lana Dart Papers, UA 17.263

Lewis Griffin Gorton Papers, UA 2.1.6

Media Communications Records, UA 8.1.1

Office for Inclusion and Intercultural Initiatives Records, UA 8.2

Oscar Clute Papers, UA 2.1.5

People's Choice Publication, UA 12.7.41

Red Cedar Log yearbooks

Robert L. Green Papers, UA 17.20

Robert S. Shaw Papers, UA 2.1.11

Ruth Simms Hamilton Papers, UA 17.269

Sports Information Records, UA 8.1.3

Student Organizations and Publications Records, UA 12

Vice President for Student Affairs Student Protest Files, UA 7.0

Wolverine yearbooks

Women's Resource Center Records. UA 8.2.2

On The Banks of the Red Cedar

https://onthebanks.msu.edu

Civil Rights, Holden Hall, 1969

Civil Rights, Wilson Hall, 1969–1970

Civil Rights Protests, 1965, 1968, 1969, 1970

College Speculum

Commencement Programs, 1860–1979

Faculty and Student Directories, 1903–1936

Faculty Handbooks, 1930–1959

Jon L. Young Reminiscences, 1931–1935

M. A. C. Calendars, 1900–1925

M.A.C. Record, 1896–1925

M.S.C. Record, 1926–1955

Malcolm X Speaks at Michigan State University, 1963

Martin Luther King Jr. Speaks at Michigan State University, 1965

Meeting Minutes of the Board of Trustees

MSU News Bulletin

MSU Yearbooks, 1877–1919

Student Handbooks

Transcript with Blanche Martin on March 31, 2000

Wilson Hall Protest, 1969

MICHIGAN STATE UNIVERSITY LIBRARIES

Special Collections

Holcad, vols. 1–17, 1909–1925

NEWSPAPERS AND PERIODICALS

Adrian Daily Telegram and Times (Adrian, MI)

Advocate (Baton Rouge, LA)

Akron Beacon Journal (Akron, OH)

Alabama Tribune (Montgomery, AL)

Albuquerque Journal (Albuquerque, NM)

Associated Press (New York, NY)

Atlanta Daily World (Atlanta, GA)

Baltimore Afro-American (Baltimore, MD)

Battle Creek Enquirer (Battle Creek, MI)

Black Dispatch (Oklahoma City, OK)

Blade (Toledo, OH)

Boston Globe (Boston, MA)

Charleston Daily Mail (Charleston, WV)

Charleston Gazette (Charleston, WV)

Chicago Daily Tribune (Chicago, IL)

Chicago Defender (Chicago, IL)

Chicago Tribune (Chicago, IL)

Chillicothe Gazette (Chillicothe, OH)

Colored American (Washington, D.C.)

Courier-Journal (Louisville, KY)

Crisis (New York, NY)

Daily Press (Newport News, VA)

Daily Times News (Detroit, MI)

Denver Star (Denver, CO)

Des Moines Tribune (Des Moines, IA)

Detroit Free Press (Detroit, MI)

Detroit Metro Times (Detroit, MI)

Detroit News (Detroit, MI)

Detroit News Tribune (Detroit, MI)

Detroit Times (Detroit, MI)

Diamond Drill (Crystal Falls, MI)

Ebony (Chicago, IL)

Eli Archives (East Lansing, MI)

El Paso Times (El Paso, TX)

Escanaba Daily Press (Escanaba, MI)

Evening Citizen-Patriot (Grand Rapids, MI)

Flint Spokesman (Flint, MI)

Freeman (Indianapolis, IN)

Good Times Magazine (East Lansing, MI)

Grapevine Journal (East Lansing, MI)

Harrisburg Telegraph (Harrisburg, PA)

Hartford Courant (Hartford, CT)

Herald-Palladium (St. Joseph, MI)

Herald-Press (Harvey, ND)

Holland Evening Sentinel (Holland, MI)

Jet: The Weekly Negro News Magazine (Chicago, IL)

Journal and Guide (Norfolk, VA)

Journal of Blacks in Higher Education (Bartonsville, PA)

Journal Times (Racine, WI)

Lansing City Pulse (Lansing, MI)

Lansing Post (Lansing, MI)

Lansing State Journal (Lansing, MI)

Las Cruces Sun-News (Las Cruces, NM)

Livingston County Daily Press and Argus (Howell, MI)

McDowell Times (Keystone, WV)

Mexico Ledger (Mexico, MO)

Miami Herald (Miami, FL)

Michigan Chronicle (Detroit, MI)

Michigan Citizen (Detroit, MI)

Michigan History Magazine (Lansing, MI)

Michigan State University Alumni Magazine (East Lansing, MI)

Morning Call (Wilmington, NC)

MSU Faculty News (East Lansing, MI)

Nashville Banner (Nashville, TN)

National Review (New York, NY)

Negro Digest (Chicago, IL)

New Pittsburgh Courier (Pittsburgh, PA)

New York Age (New York, NY)

New York Amsterdam News (New York, NY)

New York Daily Record (Rochester, NY)

New York Times (New York, NY)

News-Palladium (St. Joseph, MI)

Norfolk Journal and Guide (Norfolk, VA)

Opportunity: A Journal of Negro Life (New York, NY)

Oshkosh Northwestern (Oshkosh, WI)

Outlook (New York, NY)

Owosso Times (Owosso, MI)

Philadelphia Enquirer (Philadelphia, PA)

Pittsburgh Courier (Pittsburgh, PA)

Plaindealer (Kansas City, MO)

Pontiac Daily (Pontiac, MI)

Prairie View Standard (Prairie View, TX)

Shawnee American (Shawnee, OK)

Sioux City Journal (Sioux City, IA)

South Bend Tribune (South Bend, IN)

Star Tribune (Minneapolis, MN)

State News (East Lansing, MI)

Tennessean (Nashville, TN)

Times Herald (Port Huron, MI)

True Northerner (Paw Paw, MI)

Tuskegee Student (Tuskegee, AL)

Tyler Morning Telegraph (Tyler, TX)

Washington Bee (Washington, D.C.)

Washington Tribune (Washington, D.C.)

Weekly Palladium (Benton Harbor, MI)

Westside News (Lansing, MI)

SELECT PRINTED WORKS

Alkalimat, Abdul. *The History of Black Studies*. London: Pluto Press, 2021.

Allen, Walter R., Joseph O. Jewell, Kimberly A. Griffin, and De'Sha S. Wolf. "Historically Black Colleges and Universities: Honoring the Past, Engaging the Present, Touching the Future." *Journal of Negro Education* 76, no. 3 (2007): 263–280.

Alridge, Derrick P., Cornelius L. Bynum, and James B. Stewart, eds. *The Black Intellectual Tradition: African American Thought in the Twentieth Century*. Urbana: University of Illinois Press, 2021.

Alumni Catalogue Number: Michigan State College Bulletin: List of Graduates, Officers and Professors of the Faculties

1857–1930. East Lansing: Michigan State College, 1930.

Anderson, Elijah. "Introduction to the 1996 Edition." In *The Philadelphia Negro: A Social Study*, by W. E. B. Du Bois, ix–xxxvi. Philadelphia: University of Pennsylvania Press, 1996.

Anderson, James D. *The Education of Blacks in the South, 1860–1935*. Chapel Hill: University of North Carolina Press, 1988.

Bailey, David. "MSU Leadership Helped to Advance Civil Rights." MSU Alumni, February 3, 2014. https://alumni.msu.edu/stay-informed/alumni-stories/feature-msu-leadership-helped-to-advance-civil-rights.

Ballard, Allen B. *The Education of Black Folk: The Afro-American Struggle for Knowledge in White America*. New York: HarperCollins, 1973.

Bao, Robert. "The Masterpiece of 1913." *MSU Alumni Magazine*, Fall 2013, 70–71.

Beal, W. J. *History of Michigan Agricultural College and Biographical Sketches of Trustees and Professors*. East Lansing, MI: Agricultural College, 1915.

Biondi, Martha. *The Black Revolution on Campus*. Berkeley: University of California Press, 2012.

Black Women Employees Association of Michigan State University. "Presentation to the Board of Trustees, Michigan State University, East Lansing, Michigan, Pertaining to Employment of Black Women at Michigan State University." Unpublished manuscript, February 25, 1972.

Blair, Lyle, and Madison Kuhn. *A Short History of Michigan State*. East Lansing: Michigan State College Press, 1955.

Blaisdell, Thomas C., ed. *Semi-Centennial Celebration of Michigan State Agricultural College*. Chicago: University of Chicago Press, 1908.

Bradley, Stefan. *Harlem vs. Columbia University: Black Student Power in the Late 1960s*. Urbana: University of Illinois Press, 2009.

———. *Upending the Ivory Tower: Civil Rights, Black Power, and the Ivy League*. New York: New York University Press, 2018.

Brookover, Wilbur B. "Education in Prince Edward County, Virginia, 1953–1993." *Journal of Negro Education* 62, no. 2 (1993): 149–161.

Brunson, Rose Toomer. "Socialization Experiences and Socio-Economic Characteristics of Urban Negroes as Related to Use of Selected Southern Foods and Medical Remedies." PhD diss., Michigan State University, 1962.

———. "A Study of the Migrant Negro Population in Lansing, Michigan, during and since World War II." MA thesis, Michigan State University, 1955.

Carr, Edward Hallett. *What Is History?* London: Penguin, 1967.

Carver, George Washington. "Some Ceresporae of Macon Co., Alabama." *Bulletin No. 4, 1901*. Tuskegee, AL: Tuskegee Institute Steam Print, 1901.

Castanier, Bill. "EL Rewind: Historic East Lansing Battles Over Racist Housing Discrimination." ELi Archives: News from 2013–2020, May 3, 2015. https://eastlansinginfo.org/archive/content/el-rewind-historic-east-lansing-battles-over-racist-housing-discrimination.html.

Catalogue of Officers and Graduates, 1857–1911. East Lansing, MI, 1911.

Catalogue of Officers and Students of the Michigan Agricultural College for the Year 1903–1904. Michigan Agricultural College, 1904.

Catalogue of the Officers and Students of the State Agricultural College. Lansing, MI: John A. Kerr & Co., Book and Job Printers, 1861.

Cha-Jua, Sundiata Keita, and Clarence Lang. "The 'Long Movement' as Vampire: Temporal and Spatial Fallacies in Recent Black Freedom Studies." *Journal of African American History* 92, no. 2 (2007): 265–288.

Clark, Kenneth B., and Lawrence Plotkin. *The Negro Student at Integrated Colleges*. New York: National Scholarship and Fund for Negro Students, 1963.

Cole, Eddie. *The Campus Color Line: College Presidents and the Struggle for Black Freedom*. Princeton, NJ: Princeton University Press, 2020.

Coleman, Don E. "The Status of the Black Student Aide Program and the Black Student Movement at Michigan State University." PhD diss., Michigan State University, 1971.

Cone, James H. *Martin & Malcolm & America: A Dream or a Nightmare*. Maryknoll, NY: Orbis Books, 1992.

Cullen, Maurice Raymond, Jr. "The Presidency of Jonathan LeMoyne Snyder at Michigan Agricultural College, 1896–1915." PhD diss., Michigan State University, 1965.

Dagbovie, Pero Gaglo. "Reflections on Conventional Portrayals of the African American Experience during the Progressive Era or 'the Nadir.'" *Journal of the Gilded Age and Progressive Era* 13 (January 2014): 4–27.

Darden, Joe T., and Richard W. Thomas. *Detroit: Race Riots, Racial Conflicts, and Efforts to Bridge the Racial Divide*. East Lansing: Michigan State University Press, 2013.

Daugherty, Duffy, with Davis Diles. *Duffy: An Autobiography*. New York: Doubleday, 1974.

Department of Human Relations, Michigan State University. *Affirmative Action at Michigan State University: Annual Report to the Department of Health, Education and Welfare*. East Lansing: Michigan State University, 1973–1982.

Dennis, Benjamin Gumbu. "The Level of Formal and Informal Integration of Negroes in the External Community of Lansing, Michigan." PhD diss., Michigan State University, 1965.

Deskins, Donald R., Jr., Saul B. Cohen, and Linda J. Speil. "Geography and Afro-America: The Anatomy of a Graduate Training and Curriculum Development Project." *Journal of Geography* 70, no. 8 (1971): 465–471.

Dreger, Alice. "As Friday's Dedications Near, We're Learning More about East Lansing's History of Racial Integration." East Lansing Info, September 22, 2021. https://eastlansinginfo.news/as-fridays-dedications-near-were-learning-more-about-east-lansings-history-of-racial-integration/.

Dressel, Paul L. *College to University: The Hannah Years at Michigan State, 1935–1969*. East Lansing: Michigan State University Publications, 1987.

Du Bois, W. E. B. *The Souls of Black Folk: Essays and Sketches*. Chicago: A. C. McClurg & Co., 1903.

Du Bois, W. E. Burghardt, and Augustus Granville Dill, eds. *The College-Bred Negro*. Atlanta: Atlanta University Press, 1910.

Dunbar, Paul Laurence. *Major and Minors: Poems*. Toledo: Hadley & Hadley, 1895.

Dyson, Michael Eric. *The Black Presidency: Barack Obama and the Politics of Race in America*. Boston: Houghton Mifflin Harcourt, 2016.

Finkelman, Paul, and Martin J. Hershock, eds. *The History of Michigan Law*. Athens: Ohio University Press, 2006.

Foner, Eric. *Forever Free: The Story of Emancipation and Reconstruction*. New York: Vintage Books, 2005.

Fox, Craig. *Everyday Klansfolk: White Protestant Life and the KKK in 1920s Michigan*. East Lansing: Michigan State University Press, 2011.

Frye, Dorothy. "The African American Presence at MSU: Pioneers, Groundbreakers, and Leaders." In *Tales from the Archives: Volume One: Campus and Traditions*, edited by Ed Busch, Hillary Gatlin, Megan Badgley Malone, Susan O'Brien, and Jennie Russell. East Lansing: Michigan State University, 2017.

Gaines, Kevin K. *Uplifting the Race: Black Leadership, Politics and Culture during the Twentieth Century*. Chapel Hill: University of North Carolina Press, 1996.

Green, John M., ed. *Negroes in Michigan History*. Detroit, MI: John M. Green, 1985.

Green, Kristen. *Something Must Be Done about Prince Edward County: A Family, a Virginia Town, a Civil Rights Battle*. New York: HarperCollins, 2015.

Green, Robert L. *At the Crossroads of Fear and Freedom: The Fight for Social and Educational Justice*. East Lansing: Michigan State University Press, 2015.

Greene, Harry Washington. *Holders of Doctorates among American Negroes: An Educational and Social Study of Negroes Who Have Earned Doctoral Degrees in Course, 1876–1943*. Boston: Meador Publishing Company, 1943.

Greene, Robert, II, and Tyler D. Parry, eds. *Invisible No More: The African American Experience at the University of South Carolina*. Columbia: University of South Carolina Press, 2021.

Gregory, Sheila T., ed. *A Legacy of Dreams: The Life and Contributions of Dr. William Venoid Banks*. Lanham, MD: University Press of America, 1999.

Grinczel, Steve. "Celebrating the Legacy of Gideon Smith." Michigan State Spartan Athletics, October 15, 2013. https://msuspartans.com/news/2013/10/15/celebrating_the_legacy_of_gideon_smith.aspx.

———. *Michigan State Football: They Are Spartans*. Charleston, SC: Arcadia, 2004.

Haithcho, Bill. *From the Farm to the Pharmacist and Beyond*. New York: iUniverse, Inc., 2007.

Haley, Sarah. *No Mercy Here: Gender, Punishment, and the Making of Jim Crow Modernity*. Chapel Hill: University of North Carolina Press, 2016.

Hall, Jacquelyn Dowd. "The Long Civil Rights Movement and the Political Uses of the Past." *Journal of American History* 91, no. 4 (2005): 1233–1263.

Hamilton, James B. *What a Time to Live: The Autobiography of James B. Hamilton*. East Lansing: Michigan State University Press, 1995.

Hannah, John A. *A Memoir*. East Lansing: Michigan State University Press, 1980.

Harlan, Louis R. *Booker T. Washington: The Making of a Black Leader, 1856–1901*. New York: Oxford University Press, 1972.

Harlan, Louis R., and Raymond W. Smock, eds. *The Booker T. Washington Papers*. Volume 5, *1899–1900*. Urbana: University of Illinois Press, 1974.

———. *The Booker T. Washington Papers*. Volume 9, *1906–8*. Urbana: University of Illinois Press, 1980.

Havitz, Mark E., and Eric D. Zemper. "'Worked Out in Infinite Detail': Michigan State College's Lauren P. Brown and the Origins of NCAA Cross Country Championships." *Michigan Historical Review* 39, no. 1 (2013): 1–39.

Hill, Lena M., and Michael D. Hill. *Invisible Hawkeyes: African Americans at the University of Iowa during the Long Civil Rights Era*. Iowa City: University of Iowa Press, 2016.

Hine, Darlene Clark. "Rape and the Inner Lives of Black Women in the Middle West." *Signs* 14, no. 4 (1989): 912–920.

Hines, Linda O. "George Washington Carver and the Agricultural Experiment Station." *Agricultural History* 53, no. 1 (1979): 71–83.

Houston, Johnny. "The Founding of the National Association of Mathematicians, Inc. (NAM)." In *Golden Anniversary Celebration of the National Association of Mathematicians*, edited by Omayra Ortega, Emile D. Lawrence, and Edray Herber Goins, 1–20. Providence, RI: American Mathematical Society, 2020.

Hunt, Lynn. *History: Why It Matters.* Cambridge, UK: Polity Press, 2018.

Jarvis, Joseph. *Golden Jubilee: African American Methodist Episcopal Church, Lansing, Michigan, 1867–1917.* N.p., 1917.

Jelks, Randal Maurice. *African Americans in the Furniture City: The Struggle for Civil Rights in Grand Rapids.* Urbana: University of Illinois Press, 2006.

Johnson, Rossiter, ed. *The Twentieth Century Biographical Dictionary of Notable Americans.* Boston: The Biographical Society, 1904.

Jones, Brian. *The Tuskegee Student Uprising: A History.* New York: New York University Press, 2022.

Jones, Jacqueline. *Labor of Love, Labor of Sorrow: Black Women, Work, and the Family, from Slavery to the Present.* New York: Basic Books, 2010.

Joseph, Peniel E. "Reinterpreting the Black Power Movement." *OAH Magazine of History*, July 2008, 4–6.

———. *The Sword and the Shield: The Revolutionary Lives of Malcolm X and Martin Luther King Jr.* New York: Basic Books, 2020.

Kapur, Getta N. *To Drink from the Well: The Struggle for Racial Equality at the Nation's Oldest Public University.* Durham, NC: Blair, 2021.

Kenschaft, Patricia Clark. "Black Men and Women in Mathematical Research." *Journal of Black Studies* 18, no. 2 (1987): 170–190.

Kestenbaum, Justin L. *Out of a Wilderness: An Illustrated History of Greater Lansing.* Woodland Hills, CA: Windsor Publications, 1981.

Kinsey, Morris. "Financial Assistance as a Significant Factor in the Educational Survival of Selected Black Students at Michigan State University." PhD diss., Michigan State University, 1972.

Kuhn, Madison. *Michigan State: The First Hundred Years.* East Lansing: Michigan State University Press, 1955.

Lansing Alumna Chapter, Alpha Kappa Alpha Sorority, Inc. *Hallmarks in Black Achievement.* Ingham County Bicentennial Committee, 1975.

Lewis, Earl. *Race, Class, and Power in Twentieth-Century Norfolk, Virginia.* Berkeley: University of California Press, 1991.

Lewis, Phillip. "Tuskegee Airman Who Chartered a Chapter of Alpha Phi Alpha in the 1940s Shares His Story." Watch the Yard: Black Greekdom's Digital Yardshow, 2014. https://www.watchtheyard.com/alphas/alpha-phi-alpha-william-thompson/.

Logan, Rayford W. *The Betrayal of the Negro from Rutherford B. Hayes to Woodrow Wilson.* New York: Collier Books, 1965.

Malcolm X. "'Message to the Grass Roots,' November 10, 1963, Detroit." In *Malcolm X Speaks*, edited by George Breitman, 3–17. New York: Grove Press, 1965.

Malone, Megan Badgley. "MSU's First Black Women Cheerleaders." *Archives@MSU* (blog), February 28, 2020. https://msuarchives.wordpress.com/?s=cheerleaders.

Maza, Sarah. *Thinking about History*. Chicago: University of Chicago Press, 2017.

McAdoo, Harriette Pipes, ed. *Black Families*. Thousand Oaks, CA: Sage Publications, 1997.

McCormick, Richard P. *The Black Student Protest at Rutgers*. New Brunswick: Rutgers University Press, 1990.

McFadden, Johan, and Wanda D. Lipscomb. "History of the Association for Non-White Concerns." *Journal of Counseling and Development* 63, no. 7 (1985): 444–447.

McRoberts, Tim. "Remembering a Spartan: Dick Lord." *Archives@MSU* (blog), February 27, 2020. https://msuarchives.wordpress.com/2020/02/27/remembering-a-spartan-dick-lord/.

Meyer, Douglas Kermit. "The Changing Negro Residential Patterns in Lansing, Michigan, 1850–1969." PhD diss., Michigan State University, 1970.

Michigan State Agricultural College General Catalogue of Officers and Students, 1857–1900. Michigan State Agricultural College, 1900.

Michigan State University, Department of Human Relations and Michigan State University, Affirmative Action Plan. *Affirmative Action at Michigan State University*. East Lansing: Michigan State University, 1972/1973–1977/1978.

Miles, Tiya. *The Dawn of Detroit: A Chronicle of Slavery and Freedom in the City of the Straits*. New York: New Press, 2017.

———. "'Shall Woman's Voice Be Hushed?': Laura Smith Haviland in Abolitionist Women's History." *Michigan Historical Review* 39, no. 2 (2013): 1–20.

Miller, Whitney. *East Lansing: Collegeville Revisited*. Charleston, SC: Arcadia Publishing, 2002.

Moore, Louis, and Derrick E. White. "Introduction." In "New Directions in African American Sports History." Special issue, *Journal of African American History* 106, no. 2 (2021): 177–181.

Moss, James Allen. "Negro Teachers in Predominantly White Colleges." *Journal of Negro Education* 27, no. 4 (1958): 451–462.

Myers, Joshua M. *We Are Worth Fighting For: A History of the Howard University Student Protest of 1989*. New York: New York University Press, 2019.

National Association for the Advancement of Colored People. *Thirty Years of Lynching in the United States, 1889–1918*. New York: NAACP, 1919.

Niehoff, Richard O. *John A. Hannah: Versatile Administrator and Distinguished Public Servant*. Lanham, MD: University of America Press, 1989.

Norrell, Robert J. *Up from History: The Life of Booker T. Washington*. Cambridge, MA: Belknap Press of Harvard University Press, 2009.

Noverr, Douglas A. *Michigan State University: The Rise of a Research University and the New Millennium, 1970–2005*. East Lansing: Michigan State University Press, 2015.

Palmer, David Allen. "Student Perceptions of Residence Hall Environment at Michigan State University." PhD diss.,

Michigan State University, 1976.

Payne, Les, and Tamara Payne. *The Dead Are Rising: The Life of Malcolm X.* New York: Liveright, 2021.

Pipes, William H. *Death of an "Uncle Tom."* New York: Carlton Press, 1967.

Pipes, William H. *Say Amen, Brother! Old-Time Negro Preaching; A Study in American Frustration.* Detroit: Wayne State University Press, 1992.

Pipkin, J. J. *The Negro in Revelation, in History, and in Citizenship.* St Louis: N. D. Thompson Publishing Company, 1902.

Prillerman, Byrd, ed. "The New Additions to the Faculty." *Institute Monthly* 9, no. 1 (October 1916): 5–6.

Rampersad, Arnold. "Design and Truth in Biography." *South Central Review* 9, no. 2 (1992): 1–18.

Rankin, Jennie. "African Americans at MSU: A Guide to Resources in the Michigan State University Archives." East Lansing: Michigan State University Archives & Historical Collections, February 2022 (updated 2023).

———. "A Force to Be Reckoned With." *Archives@MSU* (blog), March 21, 2023. https://msuarchives.wordpress.com/2023/03/21/a-force-to-be-reckoned-with/.

Robinson, Marc Arsell. *Washington State Rising: Black Power on Campus in the Pacific Northwest.* New York: New York University Press, 2023.

Rogers, Ibram H. [Ibram X. Kendi]. *The Black Campus Movement: Black Students and the Racial Reconstruction of Higher Education, 1965–1972.* New York: Palgrave Macmillan, 2012.

Rojas, Fabio. *From Black Power to Black Studies: How a Radical Social Movement Became an Academic Discipline.* Baltimore, MD: Johns Hopkins University Press, 2007.

Rose, Harold M. "The Geography of Despair." *Annals of the Association of American Geographers* 68, no. 4 (1978): 453–464.

Rosentreter, Roger. "Pomp and Presidents: TR and Bill Clinton Visit MSU." *Michigan History Magazine*, September/October 1995, 31.

Ross, Charles K. *Outside the Lines: African Americans and the Integration of the National Football League.* New York: New York University, 1999.

Sanders, Crystal R. "'We Very Much Prefer to Have a Colored Man in Charge': Booker T. Washington and Tuskegee's All-Black Faculty." *Alabama Review* 74, no. 2 (2021): 99–128.

Schultz, Jaime. *Moments of Impact: Racialized Memory, Injury, and Reconciliation in College Football.* Lincoln: University of Nebraska Press, 2016.

Segal, Theodore D. *Point of Reckoning: The Fight for Racial Justice at Duke University.* Durham, NC: Duke University Press, 2021.

Shanahan, Tom. *Jimmy Raye, Duffy Daugherty, the Integration of College Football, and the 1965–66 Michigan State Spartans.* St. Louis Park, MN: August Publications, 2014.

Shapiro, Beth J. "The Black Athlete at Michigan State University." MA thesis, Michigan State University, 1970.

Shaw, Stephanie J. *What a Woman Ought To Be and Do: Black Professional Women Workers during the Jim Crow Era.* Chapel Hill: University of North Carolina Press, 1996.

Slater, Robert Bruce. "The Blacks Who First Entered the World of White Higher Education." *Journal of Blacks in Higher Education* 4 (Summer 1994): 47–56.

———. "The First Black Faculty Members at the Nation's Highest-Ranked Universities." *Journal of Blacks in Higher Education* 22 (Winter 1998–1999): 97–106.

———. "The First Black Graduates of the Nation's 50 Flagship State Universities." *Journal of Blacks in Higher Education* 13 (Autumn 1996): 72–85.

Smith, John Matthew. "Black Power in Green and White: Integration and Black Protest in Michigan State University Football, 1947–1972." Master's thesis, Western Michigan University, 2006.

———. "'Breaking the Plane': Integration and Black Protest in Michigan State Football during the 1960s." *Michigan Historical Review* 33, no. 2 (2007): 101–129.

Smith, Marshanda Ann Latrice. "A History of Black Women Faculty at Michigan State University, 1968–2009." PhD diss., Michigan State University, 2012.

Stabley, Fred W. *The Spartans: A Story of Michigan State Football*. Huntsville, AL: Strode Publishers, Inc. 1975.

Stafford, Linda O., and C. Kurt Dewhurst. *MSU Campus—Buildings, Places Spaces: Architecture and the Campus Park of Michigan State University*. East Lansing: Michigan State University Press, 2002.

Stanton, Barbara, and William T. Trent. "College Compensatory Programs for Disadvantaged Students." Report 3. Washington, D.C.: ERIC Clearinghouse on Higher Education, George Washington University, September 1970.

Steinway, Cindi. "Myrtle Mowbray, '07: MSU's First Black Graduate, Remembers M.A.C." *Michigan State University Alumni Magazine*, November 1972, 15.

The Agricultural College of the State of Michigan. Lansing, MI: Hosmer & Fitch, 1857.

Thelin, John R. *A History of American Higher Education*. 3rd ed. Baltimore, MD: Johns Hopkins University Press, 2019.

Thomas, David A. *Michigan State College: John Hannah and the Creation of a World University, 1926–1969*. East Lansing: Michigan State University Press, 2008.

Thornbrough, Emma Lou. *The Negro in Indiana Before 1900: A Study of a Minority*. Indianapolis: Indiana Historical Bureau, 1957.

"The Trailblazing Life of MSU's First African American Faculty Member." Michigan State University College of Arts and Letters, February 16, 2021. https://cal.msu.edu/news/the-trailblazing-life-of-msus-first-african-american-faculty-member/.

Underwood, Clarence, and Larry Paladino. *Greener Pastures: A Pioneer Athletics Administrator Climbs from Spartan Beginnings to the Top at Michigan State*. self-pub., 2005.

Van Deburg, William L. *New Day in Babylon: The Black Power Movement and American Culture, 1965–1975*. Chicago: University of Chicago Press, 1992.

Vance, Irvin E. "MSUIC-MP [Michigan State University Inner City Mathematics Project]." Document Resume, ED 038 325 SE 008 364, U.S. Department of Education & Welfare, Office of Education (1970).

Walker, Lewis, Benjamin C. Wilson, and Linwood Cousins. *African Americans in Michigan*. East Lansing: Michigan State University Press, 2001.

Warren, Francis H. *Michigan Manual of Freedmen's Progress*. Authorized By Act 47, Public Acts 1915. Detroit, 1915.

Washington, Booker T. *My Larger Education: Being Chapters from My Experience*. Garden City, NY: Doubleday,

Page & Company, 1911.

———. "Solving the Negro Problem in the Black Belt of the South." In *Thirty-Ninth Annual Report of the Secretary of the State Board of Agriculture and the Thirteenth Annual Report of the Experiment Station from July 1, 1899 to June 30, 1900.* Lansing, MI: Wynkoop Hallenbeck Crawford Co. of Lansing, Mich. State Printers, 1900.

———. *Tuskegee and Its People: Their Ideals and Achievements.* New York: D. Appleton and Company, 1916.

———. *Up from Slavery: An Autobiography.* Garden City, NY: Doubleday & Company, Inc., 1900, 1901.

Washington, Maya. *Through the Banks of the Red Cedar: My Father and the Team That Changed the Game.* New York: Little A., 2021.

Wharton, Clifton, Jr. *Privilege and Prejudice: The Life of a Black Pioneer.* East Lansing: Michigan State University Press, 2015.

Wharton, Delores. *A Multicultured Life: From the Little Red School House to Halls of Academe and Corporate Board Rooms.* Doeclif Publishing, 2019.

White, Deborah Gray. *Ar'n't I a Woman? Female Slaves in the Plantation South.* New York: W. W. Norton & Company, 1985.

White, Derrick E. *Blood, Sweat, and Tears: Jake Gaither, Florida A&M, and the History of Black College Football.* Chapel Hill: University of North Carolina Press, 2019.

White, Katherine Elizabeth. "Student Activism at Michigan State University during the Decade of the 1960's." PhD diss., Michigan State University, 1972.

Widder, Keith R. *Michigan Agricultural College: The Evolution of a Land-Grant Philosophy, 1855–1925.* East Lansing: Michigan State University Press, 2005.

———. "White Privilege at Michigan Agricultural College, 1855–1925." Unpublished manuscript, 2005.

Williams, Clarence G. *Technology and the Dream: Reflections on the Black Experience at MIT, 1941–1999.* Cambridge, MA: MIT Press, 2001.

Williams, G. Bernell. *Look Not upon Me Because I Am Black.* New York: Carlton Press, 1970.

Williams, Robert L. "A 40-Year History of the Association of Black Psychologists (ABPsi)." *Journal of Black Psychology* 34, no. 3 (2008): 249–260.

Williamson, Joy Ann. *Black Power on Campus: The University of Illinois, 1965–75.* Urbana: University of Illinois Press, 2003.

———. "In Defense of Themselves: The Black Student Struggle for Success and Recognition at Predominantly White Colleges and Universities." *Journal of Negro Education* 68, no. 1 (1999): 92–105.

Winston, Eric Von Arthur. "Black Student Activism at MSU: September, 1967 to June 30, 1972." PhD diss., Michigan State University, 1973.

Woodson, Carter G. "Negro Life and History in Our Schools." *Journal of Negro History* 4, no. 3 (1919): 273–280.

Wycliff, Don, and David Krashna. *Black Domers: African-American Students at Notre Dame in Their Own Words.* South Bend, IN: University of Notre Dame Press, 2017.

Index

Note: Page numbers in *italics* refer to illustrative matter.